AGS

World History

by
Wayne King and
Marcel Lewinski

AGS®
American Guidance Service, Inc.
Circle Pines, Minnesota 55014-1796
800-328-2560

About the Authors

Wayne E. King is currently the Academic Dean at the Baltimore School for the Arts. He earned his Bachelor of Science and Master of Science degrees from The Johns Hopkins University. He has taught history and social studies at all educational levels. With extensive experience as a curriculum writer, he has served as a consultant to schools, museums, and federal agencies. He has lectured at numerous national and international conferences on the teaching of history and cultural studies.

Marcel Lewinski is currently Associate Professor of History Education at Illinois State University. Previously, he was an award winning high school social studies teacher. He has taught a wide range of subjects, including world history, United States history, geography, political science, economics, sociology, and contemporary problems. Lewinski is professionally active in many organizations and has given presentations at many state, regional, and national conferences. He has conducted numerous workshops for social studies teachers and has traveled all over the world. As author of several books in social studies, Mr. Lewinski acts as a consultant to school systems and has served as a frequent contributor to educational publications.

Content Reviewer:

Lois Barnes
Assistant Superintendent of Curriculum and Instruction
Woodford County Board of Education
Versailles, KY

Printed in the United States of America

ISBN 0-7854-2212-9

Product Number 93100

19 20 21 22 V051 14 13 12 11 10

Contents

Unit 3   Classical Traditions, Major Religions: 2000 B.C. to A.D. 476 140

Jupiter

Mars

Mercurius

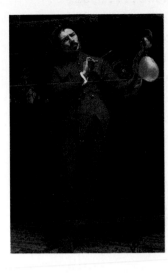

Biographies

History in Your Life

Source Readings

Spotlight Stories

Communication in History

Skills Lessons

Then and Now

Writing About History

Maps

Maps continued

How to Use This Book: A Study Guide

Welcome to a study of world history. You may be asking yourself, "Why do I need to know about people, places, and events that happened a long time before I was even born?" When we study the past, we can have a better understanding of why some things happened the way they did. We can learn from the mistakes and the successes of the past.

This book is a story of the world. As you read the units, chapters, and sections of this book, you will learn about the important people and events that shaped our world.

How to Study

- Plan a regular time to study.

- Choose a quiet desk or table where you will not be distracted. Find a spot that has good lighting.

- Gather all the books, pencils, and paper you need to complete your assignments.

- Decide on a goal. For example: "I will finish reading and taking notes on Chapter 1, Section 1, by 8:00."

- Take a five- to ten-minute break every hour to keep alert.

- If you start to feel sleepy, take a short break and get some fresh air.

Before Beginning Each Unit

> "Lo, the god knows me well,
> Amun, Lord of Thrones of the Two Lands;
> He made me rule Black Land and Red Land as reward,
> No one rebels against me in all lands.
> All foreign lands are my subjects,
> He placed my border at the limits of heaven. . . .
> I am his daughter in very truth. . . ."
> —Hatshepsut, pharaoh of Egypt, the "Speech of the Queen" it was inscribed
> on a granite shaft in the temple she built to the god Amun at Karnak.

Early Civilizations

6000 B.C. to 30 B.C.

The most important development of prehistoric times was farming. Small farm communities grew into cities. As more people gathered in one place, they made rules and government began. Then they developed record keeping. Writing followed. Civilizations had begun!

The first civilizations began along river valleys because people could more easily grow food there. The Sumerians built the first great civilization about 7,000 years ago along the shores of the Tigris and Euphrates rivers. About 1,000 years later, people built cities in India's Indus River Valley. Nearly 1,000 years after that, Chinese villages grew into cities around the Yellow River. Later, the Egyptian civilization developed along the shores of the Nile River. In Unit 2, you will learn about the gifts each of these ancient civilizations has given us.

Chapter 2: Early Civilizations in the East
6000 B.C. to 206 B.C.

Chapter 3: Civilization Develops in the Middle East
5000 B.C. to 600 B.C.

Chapter 4: Middle-Eastern Empires
800 B.C. to 330 B.C.

Chapter 5: Egypt—The Gift of the Nile
3100 B.C. to 30 B.C.

Each unit covers a period of time in world history.

■ Read the title and the dates the unit covers.

■ Read the opening paragraph.

■ Study the picture. Do you recognize anything in the picture?

■ Read the quotation. Try to connect the ideas to the picture.

■ Read the titles of the chapters in the unit.

■ Look at the headings of the sections. They will help you locate main ideas.

■ Read the chapter and unit summaries to help you identify the key ideas.

Before Beginning Each Chapter

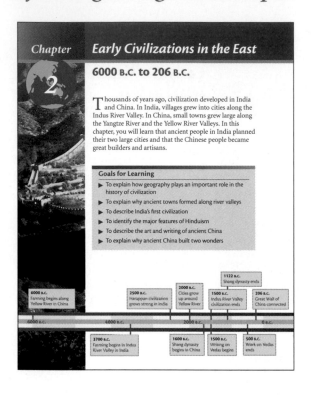

- Read the chapter title and the dates.

- Study the goals for learning. The chapter review and tests will ask questions related to these goals.

- Study the timeline.

Using the Timelines

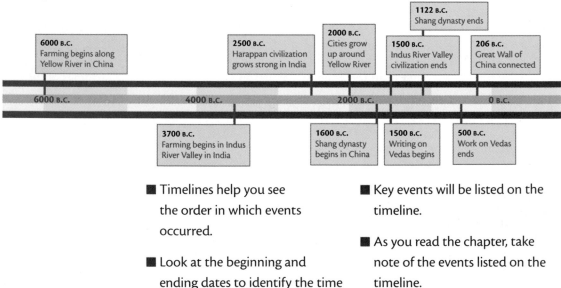

- Timelines help you see the order in which events occurred.

- Look at the beginning and ending dates to identify the time period.

- Key events will be listed on the timeline.

- As you read the chapter, take note of the events listed on the timeline.

Before Beginning Each Section

Read the section title and rephrase it in the form of a question. For example:

Section	1	The Meaning of History

Write: **What is the meaning of history?**

Look over the entire section, noting . . .

- pictures
- graphs
- maps
- boldface words
- text organization
- timelines

Early River Valley Civilizations

MAP STUDY

This map shows four early river valley civilizations. Which one was farthest west? farthest east? Were any of them in Europe? Name two rivers where civilization began.

Stonehenge is a puzzling prehistoric monument near Salisbury, England. Today, experts can only guess what this ancient mass of huge stones was used for long ago.

LOUIS LEAKEY: 1903–1972
MARY LEAKEY: 1913–1996

Louis and Mary Leakey made exciting discoveries about early humans. Louis Leakey believed that humankind had developed in Africa. The two British scientists worked in East Africa for about 40 years. They collected stone tools and pieces of bone, skulls, and teeth. These were clues to what early people were like. One major site was Olduvai Gorge, Tanzania. Mary Leakey found a large piece of skull there. Tests showed it was 1.75 million years old. That was much older than other human-type fossils. Later she found footprints more than 3 million years old. These showed that hominids (almost-humans) were walking upright that long ago.

As You Read the Section

■ Read the major headings. Each subhead is in the form of a question.

■ Read the paragraphs that follow to answer the question.

■ Before moving on to the next heading, see if you can answer the question.

■ If you cannot, reread the section to look for the answers. If you are still unsure, ask for help.

■ Answering the questions in the section will help you see if you know the key ideas in the section.

bold type
Words seen for the first time will appear in bold type

glossary
Words listed in this column are also found in the glossary

◆ red diamonds
Words that are key to studying history and may appear on a test

Using Vocabulary

Knowing the meaning of all the boxed words will help you understand what you are reading.

These words will appear in **bold type** the first time they appear in your text and will usually be defined in the paragraph.

our **culture**, or our customs, languages, and values

Remember, all of the words in the side column are also defined for you in the **glossary**.

Humanity — The human race (p. 34)

The words with the **red diamonds** (◆) identify important words. These words are key to studying history. They may also appear on a test.

What to Do With a Word You Do Not Know

When you come to a word you do not know, ask yourself these questions:

- Is the word a compound word?
  Can you find two words within the word? This could help you understand the meaning. For example: *courtyard*.

- Does the word have a prefix at the beginning?
  For example: *independent*. The prefix *in-* means 'not,' so this word refers to something or someone not dependent on another thing or person.

- Does the word have a suffix at the end?
  For example: *laborer, -er*. This means one who labors or works.

- Can you identify the root word? Can you sound it out in parts? For example: *in vade*.

- Are there any clues in the sentence that will help you understand the word?

Look for the word in the margin box, glossary, or dictionary.

If you are still having trouble with a word, ask for help.

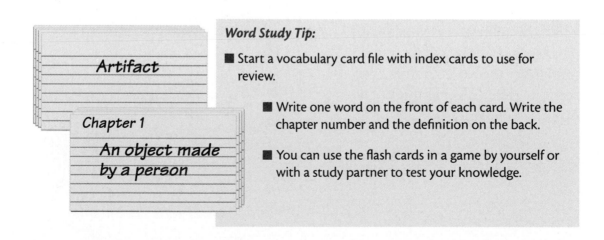

Word Study Tip:

- Start a vocabulary card file with index cards to use for review.

  - Write one word on the front of each card. Write the chapter number and the definition on the back.

  - You can use the flash cards in a game by yourself or with a study partner to test your knowledge.

Artifact

Chapter 1

An object made by a person

Taking Notes in Class

As you read, you will be learning many new facts and ideas. Writing these key ideas down will help you remember. Your notes will be useful when preparing for class discussions and studying for tests.

There are many ways to take notes. You may want to try several methods to decide which one works best for you.

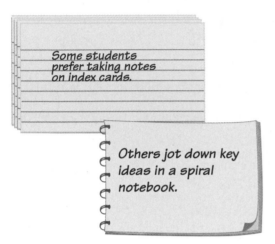

Some students prefer taking notes on index cards.

Others jot down key ideas in a spiral notebook.

■ Always write the main ideas and supporting details.

■ Using an outline format will help save you time.

■ Keep your notes brief. You may want to set up some abbreviations to speed up your note-taking. For example: *with=w/ and=+ dollars=$*

■ Use the same method all the time. Then when you study for a test, you will know where to go to find the information you need to review.

Using an Outline

You may want to outline the section using the subheads as your main points. An outline will help you remember the major points of the section. Here's an example of an outline for Chapter 1, Section 1.

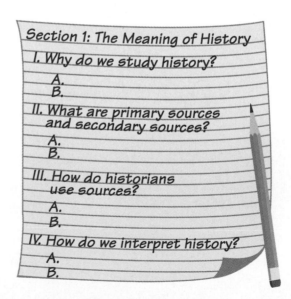

Section 1: The Meaning of History

I. Why do we study history?
   A.
   B.

II. What are primary sources and secondary sources?
   A.
   B.

III. How do historians use sources?
   A.
   B.

IV. How do we interpret history?
   A.
   B.

Listening in Class

■ Plan to listen to remember.

■ Concentrate on the topic. Do not allow your mind to wander.

■ If you do not understand, raise your hand and ask a question.

■ Listen for these key phrases: this is important..., do not forget..., the first reason..., because of this..., in conclusion..., you need to know this... .

Tips for Taking Notes During Class Discussion:

■ Use your own words.

■ Do not try to write everything the teacher says.

■ Write down important information only.

■ Do not be concerned about writing in complete sentences. Use phrases.

■ Be brief.

■ Rewrite your notes to fill in possible gaps as soon as you can after class.

Getting Ready to Take a Test

The Summaries and Reviews will help you get ready to take tests. Getting information about the test ahead of time and having a study plan will help you do well on the test.

■ Ask what type of test it will be. For example: true/false, multiple choice, short answer, matching, essay.

■ Keep current on your reading assignments. Do not put off reading the chapter until the night before the test.

■ A couple of days before the test, gather all of your notes, vocabulary lists, corrected worksheets, answers to questions in the book, and your textbook.

Use the Summaries

■ Read the summaries from your text to make sure you understand the main ideas that you will be reviewing.

■ Make up a sample test of items you think may be on the test. You may want to do this with a classmate and share your questions.

■ Review your notes and test yourself on vocabulary words and key ideas.

■ Practice writing about some of the main events from the chapter.

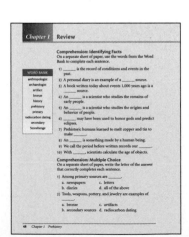

Use the Reviews

■ Answer the questions under Identifying Facts.

■ Answer the questions under Multiple Choice.

■ Answer the questions under Understanding Main Ideas.

■ Write what you think about the questions under Write Your Opinion.

Use the Test-Taking Tips

■ Read Test-Taking Tips with each Chapter Review and Unit Review from your text.

Test-Taking Tip	Avoid waiting until the night before a test to study. Plan your study time so that you can get a good night's sleep the night before a test.

When Taking a Test

■ Arrive well rested and alert.

■ Look over the entire test before you start.

■ Plan so you will have time to complete each section.

■ If you have trouble with a question, mark it and come back to it later. This will save you time.

■ Proofread your essay answers for errors. Double-check to see that you answered the question that was asked.

■ If time allows, read over all of your answers. Make sure your writing is readable.

Remember to save your corrected test when it is returned. Use it to study for future tests. Identify the type of errors you made. For example: Were most of your errors in a certain section? Perhaps you could study ways to improve in that area.

This introduction has been included as a study tool that you can refer to later. You are now ready to begin your journey into world history.

"We archaeologists shine scientific flashlights into the past, throwing narrow beams of light hundreds, thousands, even millions of years back into remotest prehistory. Each site, each find, reflects backward from ancient times like . . . a brilliant diamond . . ."

—Brian Fagan, professor of anthropology at U.C. Santa Barbara in his introduction to *Time Detectives* (Simon & Schuster, 1995)

The Beginnings of Human History

The Time Before Written Records

What was life like long, long ago, when human beings first walked on earth? What did they eat? Where did they live? What was important to them? Were they hunters? artists? farmers? builders? fire-makers? tool-makers? dreamers?

The people of the Stone Age lived before the time of written records. So we cannot find newspapers or letters to tell us about them. We must depend on other things they left behind. In this unit, you will learn what life may have been like for these prehistoric humans.

Chapter 1: Prehistory
    The Time Before Written Records

The Time Before Written Records

Long years ago human beings roamed the land in search of food. Then they learned to grow it. That changed everything! This chapter explains some of the things we have learned about these Stone-Age people. You will also learn more about what changed their life.

Goals for Learning

▶ To define history

▶ To describe the difference between primary and secondary sources of information

▶ To explain why people interpret history differently

▶ To describe how historians use artifacts to learn about the past

▶ To describe some important events in the Stone Age

▶ To explain the difference between the Stone Age and the Bronze Age

▶ To discover the importance of farming to the history of humanity

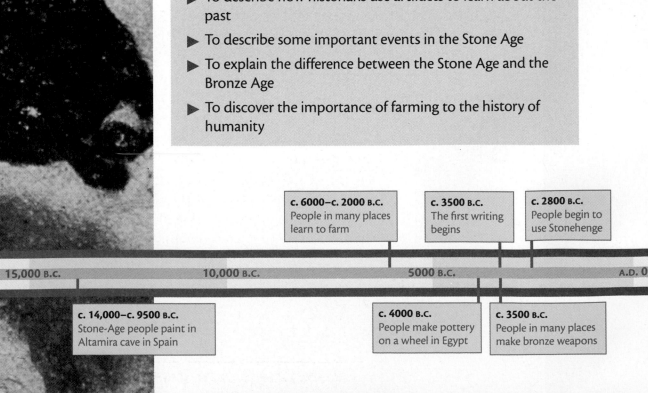

c. 6000–c. 2000 B.C.
People in many places learn to farm

c. 3500 B.C.
The first writing begins

c. 2800 B.C.
People begin to use Stonehenge

15,000 B.C.   10,000 B.C.   5000 B.C.   A.D. 0

c. 14,000–c. 9500 B.C.
Stone-Age people paint in Altamira cave in Spain

c. 4000 B.C.
People make pottery on a wheel in Egypt

c. 3500 B.C.
People in many places make bronze weapons

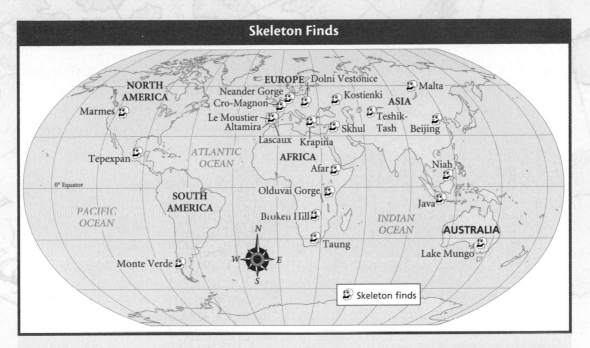

Skeleton Finds

NORTH AMERICA · EUROPE · Dolni Vestonice · Neander Gorge · Cro-Magnon · Kostienki · Malta · ASIA · Marmes · Le Moustier · Altamira · Teshik-Tash · Skhul · Beijing · Lascaux · Krapina · ATLANTIC OCEAN · AFRICA · Tepexpan · Afar · Niah · 0° Equator · SOUTH AMERICA · Olduvai Gorge · Java · PACIFIC OCEAN · Broken Hill · INDIAN OCEAN · AUSTRALIA · Taung · Lake Mungo · Monte Verde · N · W E · S · Skeleton finds

Geography Skills

We can use a map that shows direction to find where things are. When you face the direction of the North Pole, you face north. If you face the South Pole, you face south. When you face north, east is to your right; west is to your left.

Most maps use a symbol to show where north is. From this information, you can figure out the three other directions. Note the direction symbol on this map. We call this symbol a compass rose.

The map on this page contains another symbol—a skull. It shows where archaeologists have found clues about early humans.

Study the map, then answer the following questions:

1) Which of the six pictured continents contains the skeleton find known as Marmes?

2) Which of the six pictured continents contains the skeleton find known as Krapina?

3) In what direction would you be traveling if you went from Monte Verde to Lake Mungo?

4) What skeleton finds are south of the imaginary line called the equator?

5) What skeleton finds are located farthest west on the map?

The Time Before Written Records

◆**Culture**
The values, attitudes, and customs of a group

Diary
A daily record of what happens to a person

◆**Historian**
One who is an expert of history

◆**History**
The record of past events and the story of what happened to people in the past

Humanity
The human race

◆**Primary source**
A first-hand account of a historical event

◆**Secondary source**
A second-hand account of a historical event; an account written by a person who was not there

History is the record of past events. It is the story of people and what happened to them. Each group of people has its own history. In this book, you will learn about the combined history of all peoples—the history of **humanity.**

Why Do We Study History?

The people who lived before you learned many lessons they could share with you. Imagine knowing nothing about those people. You would have to learn all their lessons for yourself. If this happened, history would be dead. But happily, history is alive and well! It lives in our **culture,** or our customs, language, and values. So it can teach us its lessons.

What Are Primary Sources and Secondary Sources?

When writing history, **historians** ask themselves five W's: What happened? When and where did it happen? Who was involved? Why did it happen? To find answers, they look for **primary sources.** These sources are first-hand, or eyewitness, accounts of the event. They also seek out **secondary sources,** or second-hand records of what happened.

Imagine an argument in the school cafeteria. It will show you the difference between these two sources. You see the argument, so you are an eyewitness. That makes you a primary source. You tell someone about the argument. That person is not an eyewitness. So that person becomes a secondary source.

How Do Historians Use Sources?

A historian writing about the American Revolution would read what people living at the time wrote. These primary sources would include newspapers; **diaries,** or daily personal records; and letters.

The same historian would also read what recent historians have written about the war. Their books are secondary sources because these historians were not eyewitnesses.

IN CONGRESS, July 4, 1776.

The unanimous Declaration of the thirteen united States of America,

The American Declaration of Independence is a primary source.

You have used secondary sources ever since you started school. This textbook is a secondary source. But you are a primary source for what you actually see and hear each day.

How Do We Interpret History?

Interpret
To explain something

Interpretation
An explanation of the meaning of something

Individual people, like yourself, record history. Because people differ, what they record differs. You **interpret,** or explain, the cafeteria argument one way. Another eyewitness interprets it another way. So your two **interpretations,** or explanations, differ. Secondary sources differ in their interpretations too.

This section of your history book is a secondary source. After reading it, each of your classmates will interpret it differently. Check out your various views.

SECTION 1 REVIEW On a separate sheet of paper, write *True* if the statement is true or *False* if the statement is not truc. Makc cach false statement true by changing the underlined word.

1) History is the record of <u>future</u> events.

2) Historians ask <u>four</u> questions that begin with *W*.

3) <u>Secondary</u> sources are first-hand, or eyewitness, accounts of what happened.

4) <u>Primary</u> sources might include what an eyewitness wrote in newspapers, diaries, and letters.

5) Historians interpret, or explain, events in <u>different</u> ways.

What do you think ?

Why do history books differ?

Global
Having to do with the whole world

History helps us remember our past. It also helps us understand how we got to the present. This knowledge helps us figure out what to do tomorrow.

What Does History Teach Us About People?

History tells us the story of all the people in every country of the world. We discover their new ideas. We realize that they did great things.

History helps us understand their problems. Remember that cafeteria argument? To really understand what caused it, we need to question each person involved. Then we discover all the things that caused the argument. The same is true with history.

How Does History Connect Us to the Past?

History connects us to all the people who have ever lived. Much happened before our lives began. Much will happen after our lives end. But the past gives us roots.

Roots anchor, or hold, a tree in the ground. A family tree helps you understand who you are. The family tree, or history, of the world helps you understand the human race. You are a part of the **global** community. It stretches back through time to the beginning of humanity.

WORD BANK

future	present
history	roots
people	

SECTION 2 REVIEW On a separate sheet of paper, write the word from the Word Bank that completes each sentence.

1) We study _____ to help us understand how we got where we are today.

2) History helps us understand how we got to the _____.

3) The past gives us _____. These anchor, or hold, us to those people who have gone before us.

4) History gives us a sense of being connected with the _____ of the past.

5) By knowing the past, we may be able to decide what to do in the _____.

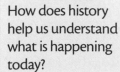

What do you think

How does history help us understand what is happening today?

◆**Anthropologist**
A person who studies the beginnings and the behavior of people

◆**Archaeologist**
A person who finds and studies the things humans left behind in the past

◆**Artifact**
An object made by a person

Historians write about history. To do this, they study written sources that earlier people left behind. But early people did not write books, newspapers, or letters. So what tells us about them?

How Do Scientists Explore the Past?

Archaeologists are scientists who find and study things people left behind. We call these things **artifacts.** They include tools, weapons, pottery, and jewelry.

Anthropologists are scientists who study the beginnings and the behavior of people. For example, they may study the garbage Americans throw out! The garbage tells them about the eating habits of Americans. It also tells them what Americans do for fun, what they read, and much more.

Why Are Dates Important?

Most students think that history is nothing but dates: 2186 B.C. and A.D. 1096. But dates help us measure time. Dates tell us when things happened. For example, a great earthquake shook India in 1897. By dating it, we know that this event happened over 100 years ago. Another earthquake rocked Nicaragua in 1972, so it happened not too long ago.

Why Do We Have Different Calendars?

Calendars help us keep track of time. Throughout the world, people use different calendars. Each is based on a different event.

Archaelogists study things that are left behind from the past—even human remains.

The calendar used in many parts of the world is based on the birth of Jesus, who Christians believe is the "Christ." This kind of calendar lists some historical events as B.C., or "Before Christ." It lists other events as A.D. The letters A.D. stand for the Latin words *anno Domini.* This means "in the year of our Lord." So, A.D. 1776 is "in the year of our Lord 1776." People in America, Europe, and many other parts of the world use this calendar system.

The Jewish calendar begins with the year in which the Jews believe God created the world. Many Muslims use a calendar based on the date of the founding of their religion.

What Is Radiocarbon Dating?

Scientists use **radiocarbon dating** to determine the age of an artifact. All living things contain carbon. A small number of carbon atoms in living things are radioactive. Some of these atoms stay in animals and plants for thousands of years after they die. Archaeologists carefully measure the amount of radioactivity left in an artifact. By doing this, they can date it.

Ancient artifacts such as these help scientists learn about the past.

Calculate
To figure something out

◆**Radiocarbon dating**
A way of measuring the radioactivity of historic artifacts to determine how old they are

How Else Do Archaeologists Date Artifacts?

Sometimes, archaeologists must guess the age of an object. They do this by studying where they found the object. For example, they might find one object near another one made of plastic. This material is a fairly new invention. So both objects are probably fairly new. In the same way, an archaeologist might find an object near ancient bones. Because the bones are old, the object probably is too.

Archaeologists must **calculate,** or figure out, how ancient people lived. To do this, they become detectives who use artifacts as clues. For example, an artifact is made of a

What Can You Learn From a Bone?

A trained scientist would say you can learn a lot from a bone. Scientists carefully study the bones and teeth of early humans. Bones are clues to diet, health, and lifestyles. The prehistoric man known as "the Iceman" was a Bronze-Age hiker. His 4,000-year-old frozen body was found in the Alps in 1991. The Iceman's worn-down teeth showed that he ate tough, raw foods. Scientists also analyze the chemicals in bones. Some experiments showed when early Americans stopped eating wild plants and began to eat corn. That meant they had become farmers.

Science
History in Your Life

Bones and teeth give other clues. They can show whether a person had a good diet or certain diseases. A fractured skull may mean that someone died violently. The long thigh bone is a good clue to a person's height. Measuring that bone can tell how tall or short people were in the past.

LOUIS LEAKEY: 1903–1972
MARY LEAKEY: 1913–1996

Louis and Mary Leakey made exciting discoveries about early humans. Louis Leakey believed that humankind had developed in Africa. The two British scientists worked in East Africa for about 40 years. They collected stone tools and pieces of bone, skulls, and teeth. These were clues to what early people were like. One major site was Olduvai Gorge, Tanzania. Mary Leakey found a large piece of skull there. Tests showed it was 1.75 million years old. That was much older than other human-type fossils. Later she found footprints more than 3 million years old. These showed that hominids (almost-humans) were walking upright that long ago.

certain material. We find this material in only a few areas of the world. So the archaeologists can calculate where the object may have been made. Or, they can figure out where the people who used it came from.

How Is the Past Like a Jigsaw Puzzle?

For some periods of history, historians have few artifacts. So learning about people from the past is hard. It is like a 1,000-piece jigsaw puzzle with no picture and few pieces. They can only guess what the finished puzzle of the past might look like.

But their guess can change. Sometimes, archaeologists discover new artifacts. They gather more missing pieces. Then their guess about the finished puzzle changes.

SECTION 3 REVIEW On a separate sheet of paper, write answers to these questions:

1) What does an archaeologist do?

2) What does an anthropologist do?

3) What is an artifact?

4) Why are dates necessary to historians?

5) What does B.C. tell you about a date?

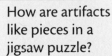
What do you think ?

How are artifacts like pieces in a jigsaw puzzle?

Decay
To rot away or spoil

Embers
The glowing remains of a fire

◆**Nomad**
A person who moves from place to place

Obsidian
A volcanic glass

◆**Prehistory**
The time before humans left written records

We know little about the earliest people who lived on earth. Why? Because they left no written records. We have written records for only about the last 5,500 years. The long, long time before humans left written records is our **prehistory.**

What Is the Stone Age?

We call the earliest period of human prehistory the "Stone Age." During that time, people made weapons and tools from stone. They shaped **obsidian,** a volcanic glass, into weapons as sharp as a modern knife. They used these stone weapons to hunt, chop, and cut. Later, they developed hand axes and spears.

We learn about these prehistoric humans from garbage, broken tools, and trash. They left these behind wherever they camped. Other materials, besides stone, were probably part of their garbage. However, these other materials **decayed,** or rotted away. So only stone objects were left.

How Did Fire Help Early Humans?

The discovery of fire is one of the most important events in human history. Stone-Age humans knew that lightning caused fire. At some point, they learned that fire creates heat. With fire, they could warm themselves.

Much later, these early people learned how to move a fire inside a cave. They learned how to keep the **embers,** or glowing remains of the fire, burning. With these embers, they could start a new fire. Finally, they learned to cook with fire.

How Did Farming Help Early Humans?

Another important event in the history of humanity is farming. As **nomads,** the earliest humans moved from place to place to hunt and gather food. They probably had to travel far and wide to find enough to eat. An important source of food was wild plants.

Humans Learn to Say "Hello"

What did early humans sound like? What language did they speak? No one can be sure. Anthropologists think that humans developed language over millions of years. Very early humans probably used a "call system." They made sounds with a certain meaning, like those that some animals use. Calls showed feelings. "Look out! There's a lion!" "I'm scared." "This plant tastes good."

Then life changed for early humans. For one thing, they began to walk upright on two feet. This freed their hands to make tools. People also began to live in larger groups. They worked together to find wild plants. Groups of hunters tracked animals. Now people needed a better way to share ideas. Hunters had to plan for the next day's hunt. A skillful potter needed to teach younger workers the craft. Humans also changed physically. Their brains developed. So did the voice box, which animals don't have. By about 100,000 years ago, some early humans were ready for complex human speech.

Gradually they learned to plant seeds from these wild plants. Then they began to grow their own food. They no longer needed to depend on hunting for food. Now they could control their food supply. They could live in one place and grow crops each year.

How Did Pottery Help Early Humans?

Growing food created a new problem for these Stone-Age humans. They harvested crops once or twice a year. But how could they store the grains for later use?

Prehistoric humans solved their problem by making pottery. They made pottery jars out of clay from riverbeds. These pottery jars protected food from insects, mice, and dampness. Today, the broken parts of this pottery are like puzzle pieces. They help scholars calculate the dates a certain people lived.

What Art Did Early Humans Create?

Prehistoric humans left no written records. However, they did leave us some important artwork. In 1859, a young girl and her father explored a cave in northern Spain. They discovered beautiful pictures on the cave walls. The drawings pictured animals—deer, wild **boar,** horses, and **bison.**

Today, most **scholars** believe that Stone-Age artists painted these pictures. They probably used twigs or bits of moss for brushes. To make the paint, they mixed meat grease with colored clay and vegetable colorings.

What Other Art Did Prehistoric Humans Create?

Stonehenge is a famous prehistoric **monument.** It is a type of building that stands near the city of Salisbury in England. It consists of a series of great stone circles. Over 30 huge stones make up the circles. Each stone weighs over 35 tons.

Scientists have discovered that the stones at Stonehenge came from as far away as 135 miles. About 250 workers would have had to move each stone that long distance. How could early humans do this before the invention of the wheel?

The piled-up bank of earth around Stonehenge had a ridge nearly six feet high. A six-foot-deep ditch lay outside it. Prehistoric people worked with primitive tools. How many people worked to build this bank and this ditch? And for how long did they work? We do not know.

Stonehenge is a puzzling prehistoric monument near Salisbury, England. Today, experts can only guess what this ancient mass of huge stones was used for long ago.

A Human's Best Friend

You may have something in common with early humans—a dog. Dogs have lived with humans for about 9,000 years. At first, an orphan wolf cub may have found food near a human campsite. Because wolves are used to living in a pack, the cub stayed nearby. Gradually the wolf became tamer. It guarded the camp against other animals. Then it began to help the humans hunt.

Dogs soon became very different from their wolf ancestors. People bred different breeds for certain qualities. Dogs with a keen sense of smell made good hunting dogs. Some dogs were bred for strength, to pull heavy sleds. Today some dogs are trained for police work. Others act as guides for the blind. About 300 different breeds of dogs exist. They live everywhere in the world with their best friends—humans.

Bronze
A hard metal made of a blend of copper and tin

Eclipse
The hiding of the sun by the moon

How Did Early Humans Use Stonehenge?

Stonehenge was in use for more than 1,700 years. Most scholars think prehistoric people honored their gods there. Or Stonehenge might have helped people guess when an **eclipse,** such as the moon hiding the sun, would happen. Scholars know none of this for sure because the monument has fallen into ruin.

What Turned the Stone Age Into the Bronze Age?

Stone tools broke easily. So prehistoric humans looked for other materials for their tools. First, they used the metal copper. Later they discovered how to melt copper and tin, another metal, together to make **bronze.** Bronze is harder than copper and holds a sharper cutting edge.

From about 3500 B.C., prehistoric people made their tools from bronze. They used it for the next 2,000 years. We call this time period the "Bronze Age."

How Did Bronze Change Life?

Bronze does not break easily. With it, ancient people invented many new tools. These made their lives easier. Bronze-Age people also invented a sled to carry things on land. They hollowed out logs and made canoes to carry things on water.

To What Does Prehistory Lead?

Prehistory is an exciting period of humanity's story. At first, humans were nomads. They moved from place to place to hunt and gather food. Then they learned to grow crops. So they settled close to their fields and formed small groups.

Now prehistoric humans had a sure supply of food. Because of this, their population grew more quickly. This began a chain of fast changes. These changes brought about the first **civilizations** in which people built cities and set up governments.

◆**Civilization**
A people who have cities and government; a large group of people with a high level of development as a group

SECTION 4 REVIEW Choose the letter of the answer that correctly completes each sentence. Write your answers on a separate sheet of paper.

1) The _____ Age came first in the history of early people.

   a. Modern   c. Bronze

   b. Stone   d. American

2) The discovery of _____ helped ancient people cook food and stay warm.

   a. fire   c. painting

   b. pottery   d. monuments

3) Drawings in _____ tell us something about the life of prehistoric people.

   a. riverbeds   c. caves

   b. bronze   d. tools

4) Because they began to _____ , early people stopped being nomads.

   a. make drawings   c. farm

   b. make bronze   d. make pottery

5) Bronze is a mixture of copper and _____ .

   a. obsidian   c. tin

   b. clay   d. stone

What do you think ?

What do cave drawings and Stonehenge tell you about prehistoric people?

"In the Beginning..."

The Bible is the holy book for both Jews and Christians. Its parts, or books, were written in different places over about 1,500 years. The Jewish Bible is made up of the books that Christians call the Old Testament. The first five books trace Hebrew history to the death of Moses. Later books tell the words of the prophets and the history of Israel. The Christian Bible has two parts. One is the Old Testament. The other is the New Testament. It tells about the life and teachings of Jesus. It also includes writings about the early Christian Church.

The Bible was written in Hebrew, Aramaic, and Greek. It has been translated into many languages. The following reading is from the first book, Genesis. The word genesis means "beginning." In a poetic way, Genesis describes the creation of the world. Read the excerpt below. Then answer the questions that follow.

In the beginning God created the heavens and the earth. The earth was without form and void.... And God said, "Let there be light...." God called the light Day and the darkness He called Night....

And God said, "Let the waters under the heavens be gathered together into one place, and let the dry land appear." And it was so. God called the dry land Earth and the waters ... he called Seas....

And God said, "Let the earth put forth vegetation ... and fruit trees...." And it was so.... "Let there be lights ... to separate the day from the night; and let them be for signs and for seasons and for days and years...." And it was so.

And God said, "Let the waters bring forth swarms of living creatures, and let birds fly above the earth...." So God created ... every living thing that moves, with which the waters swarm ... and every winged bird.

[On the sixth day] God said, "Let the earth bring forth living creatures according to their kinds...." And the Lord God formed man of the dust of the ground, and breathed into his nostrils the breath of life. And the man became a living soul. Then the Lord God planted a garden eastward in Eden, and there he put the man whom he had formed.... Thus the heavens and the earth were finished.... And on the seventh day God ended his work ... and he rested ... from all the work which he had done.

Source Reading Wrap-Up

1) What two religions consider the Bible a holy book?

2) What names did God give the waters and the dry land?

3) What do you think were the "lights" that separated day from night?

4) Where did the first man live?

5) According to Genesis, what happened on the seventh day?

The Search for the Truth

The ancient Greeks had two ways of thinking about the truth. They called them by different terms: *logos* and *mythos*. Logos meant the kind of truth that can be found through argument and demonstrations. You can see the word *logos* in the ending of words like *archaeology* and *anthropology*. These refer to careful study. Scientists in these fields study evidence and make experiments. They try to find the truth about human origins.

Mythos meant a different kind of truth. These were stories that everyone accepted as true. They were not questioned. Today, we use the word *myth* for made-up stories. That is the opposite of what the Greeks meant. For them, a myth was a special story that spoke the truth.

Like the Greeks, other people in history have asked basic questions about themselves and their world. When did the world begin? Where did human beings come from?

Scientists look for answers to these questions. They collect and study evidence. They develop theories to explain what they have found. Most scientists accept certain answers to basic questions. They accept evidence showing that the earth is about 4.5 billion years old. They also agree with the evidence that life on earth began about 1.5 billion years later, with simple organisms. More complex forms of life developed gradually over time.

Much like the Greeks and their myths, many cultures explain how the world began in non-scientific ways. One creation story comes from

Zeus, the father of the Greek gods, was a key part of Greek mythology—stories that spoke the truth for ancient Greeks.

the Navaho of the American Southwest. It says there were once smaller worlds inside the earth. The first man and woman made so many mistakes that those worlds were destroyed. The story tells how people escaped to the earth's surface by climbing up a reed.

The Chinese have another story. It begins with a great void, or emptiness. Yin and yang were opposing forces in the void. Yin is the force of stillness. Yang is the force of action. Yin and yang combined and created the world.

The Bible gives another explanation of how the world began. The book of Genesis describes how God created the world and all life in six days. Because of this account, some Christians reject scientific explanations for human origins. Other Christians accept both scientific evidence and the biblical story.

Other peoples in other places have other explanations. Humans still seek the truth about themselves. In different ways, they will go on looking for answers to important questions.

Spotlight Story Wrap-Up

1) What methods did the ancient Greeks use to find the truth of "logos?"

2) How was "mythos" different from "logos?"

3) What methods do scientists use to determine the truth?

4) What were the two forces in Chinese myth?

5) What book of the Bible describes the creation?

➥ Human history is a record of events that have happened to people everywhere.

➥ Historians ask five questions about an event: What happened? When and where did it happen? Who was involved? Why did it happen?

➥ Primary sources, such as letters and newspapers, give a first-hand account of events. Secondary sources report events as they were seen by others. Both kinds of sources depend on how individuals interpret events.

➥ Studying history helps connect us to people of the past. It helps us understand what caused events. It helps us see how we got where we are today. It helps us make decisions about the future.

➥ Archaeologists are scientists who study tools and other things people have made. These objects are called artifacts.

➥ Anthropologists are scientists who study people's customs and behavior.

➥ Using dates is a way to measure time. Americans and Europeans commonly use a calendar based on what is believed to be the birth of Jesus. The abbreviations B.C. and A.D. refer to years before and after that date. Other people may use other calendar systems.

➥ Scientists use radiocarbon dating to find the age of once-living things. This method measures the amount of radioactive atoms left in an artifact. Scientists may also guess the age of an object by the age of nearby objects. Other clues help them tell when and where something was made.

➥ The time before humans left written records is called prehistory. The earliest period of human prehistory is the Stone Age. Tools and weapons left from that time were made of stone.

➥ Learning to use fire was a major step forward in human history.

➥ The earliest humans were nomads. They hunted and gathered wild food. When humans began to farm and grow crops, they settled in one place. To store food, they learned to make pottery.

➥ Early humans created art. They made cave paintings and built large monuments such as Stonehenge.

➥ By about 3000 B.C. prehistoric people learned to work metals. They made tools and other objects from copper or bronze (a mix of tin and copper). The next time period is called the Bronze Age. It lasted about 2,000 years.

➥ Farming gave prehistoric people a sure supply of food. As the number of people increased, they built cities and set up governments. This marked the beginning of civilization.

Comprehension: Identifying Facts

On a separate sheet of paper, use the words from the Word Bank to complete each sentence.

WORD BANK

anthropologist
archaeologist
artifact
bronze
history
prehistory
primary
radiocarbon dating
secondary
Stonehenge

1) _____ is the record of conditions and events in the past.

2) A personal diary is an example of a _____ source.

3) A book written today about events 1,000 years ago is a _____ source.

4) An _____ is a scientist who studies the remains of early people.

5) An _____ is a scientist who studies the origins and behavior of people.

6) _____ may have been used to honor gods and predict eclipses.

7) Prehistoric humans learned to melt copper and tin to make _____.

8) An _____ is something made by a human being.

9) We call the period before written records our _____.

10) With _____, scientists calculate the age of objects.

Comprehension: Multiple Choice

On a separate sheet of paper, write the letter of the answer that correctly completes each sentence.

1) Among primary sources are _____.

   a. newspapers   c. letters
   b. diaries   d. all of the above

2) Tools, weapons, pottery, and jewelry are examples of _____.

   a. bronze   c. artifacts
   b. secondary sources d. radiocarbon dating

3) For archaeologists, the past is like a _____.

    a. cave   c. bronze pot

    b. jigsaw puzzle   d. matchstick

4) Prehistoric people werc nomads who moved from place to place searching for _____.

    a. food   c. primary sources

    b. artifacts   d. bronze

5) The making of _____ helped prehistoric people store food.

    a. fire   c. pottery

    b. bronze   d. Stonehenge

Comprehension: Understanding Main Ideas

On a separate sheet of paper, write the answer to each question. Use complete sentences, or statements.

1) Why was the discovery of fire important?

2) Why were bronzc tools and weapons better than those made of stone?

Critical Thinking: Write Your Opinion

1) Why are historians lucky that early humans left trash behind?

2) Stone-Age people were very different from modern people. Do you agree or disagree? Explain your answer.

3) Why do you think schools often make history a required subject?

| Test-Taking Tip | Avoid waiting until the night before a test to study. Plan your study time so that you can get a good night's sleep the night before a test. |

Timelines show dates and events on a line, or scale. They may span thousands of years or only a few months. A timeline may show key events in a region. It may list events in one person's lifetime. It may show events of a certain kind, such as scientific discoveries. In reading a timeline, always look at the beginning and ending dates.

Timelines show the time relationships between events. They help you think about events in the order they occurred. You see when an event happened. Then you can see what happened before and after it.

Each chapter in this book begins with a timeline. Those timelines will help you focus on key events and ideas in the chapter. As you read a chapter, create your own timeline of events. That will help you study those events.

This timeline gives the dates of some important events in the first half of the twentieth century. Study it. Then answer the questions.

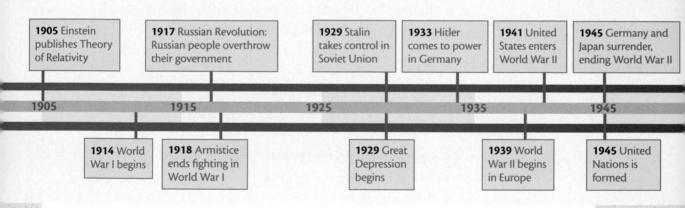

1905 Einstein publishes Theory of Relativity

1917 Russian Revolution: Russian people overthrow their government

1929 Stalin takes control in Soviet Union

1933 Hitler comes to power in Germany

1941 United States enters World War II

1945 Germany and Japan surrender, ending World War II

1905   1915   1925   1935   1945

1914 World War I begins

1918 Armistice ends fighting in World War I

1929 Great Depression begins

1939 World War II begins in Europe

1945 United Nations is formed

1) What are the beginning and ending dates on this timeline?

2) Did Einstein publish the Theory of Relativity before or after World War I?

3) In what year did World War I begin?

4) What event on this timeline happened during World War I?

5) What two events on this timeline happened in 1929?

6) Who came to power first—Hitler or Stalin?

7) How many years after Hitler came to power did World War II begin?

8) How long did World War II go on before the United States entered the war?

9) When was the United Nations formed?

10) Create a timeline showing key events in your life during the last school year.

➡ History records events that have happened to people throughout the world. Historians try to answer the questions *who, what, when, where,* and *why* about an event.

➡ Historians draw on two types of sources. Primary sources give an eyewitness account. Secondary sources record what others have seen and heard.

➡ We study history to understand people and events in the past. Knowing history can help us decide what to do in the future.

➡ Several kinds of scientists study early humans. Archaeologists study artifacts such as tools and pottery. Anthropologists study people's customs and culture.

➡ Dates and a calendar system are needed to measure time. Scientists use different methods to find the age of an object. They may use radiocarbon dating. Or they may compare it with nearby objects.

➡ Prehistory is the long period of time before humans made written records.

➡ The earliest period of human history is the Stone Age. People made stone tools and weapons. They were nomads who hunted and gathered wild food.

➡ Humans gradually learned new skills. They learned to use fire. They began to live in one place and plant crops. They made pottery and created art.

➡ In about 3000 B.C., some early people learned to work with metals. That began the Bronze Age. Better tools and weapons made life easier. Populations grew. People built cities and the first civilizations began.

Comprehension: Identifying Facts

On a separate sheet of paper, use the words from the Word Bank to complete each sentence.

WORD BANK
A.D.
B.C.
bison
bronze
culture
humanity
nomads
pottery
stone
Stone Age

1) The earliest people were _____ who traveled from place to place.

2) These first people used _____ tools, which did not decay, or rot.

3) We call the period in which these people lived the _____.

4) Later, these people mixed copper and tin and made ____.

5) They also developed _____ in which they could store their food.

6) In their cave paintings, we find pictures of the _____, or buffalo, which they hunted.

7) Many people use a calendar based on the birth of Jesus Christ. They call the time before his birth _____.

8) These people refer to the time after the birth of Jesus Christ as _____.

9) The ancient people had a _____, for they had customs, language, and values.

10) Sometimes we study the history of _____, or the whole human race.

Comprehension: Multiple Choice

On a separate sheet of paper, write the letter of the answer that correctly completes each sentence.

1) A newspaper written in 1864 would be a _____ source if we were studying the Civil War of the United States. This war took place between 1861 and 1865.

   a. primary   b. secondary   c. B.C.   d. A.D.

2) A newspaper article written today about the Civil War would be a _____ source.

   a. primary   b. secondary   c. B.C.   d. A.D.

3) A scientist who studies the remains of early people is an
_____.

    a. artifact   c. archaeologist

    b. anthropologist   d. aviator

4) Tools and weapons are examples of _____, which
human beings make.

    a. history   c. bronze

    b. artifacts   d. stone

5) Prehistory is the period in which people did not produce
_____ records.

    a. cave   c. written

    b. stone   d. painted

Comprehension: Understanding Main Ideas

On a separate sheet of paper, write the answer to each
question. Use complete sentences, or statements.

1) What is a primary source of information?

2) Why do historians interpret, or explain, history
differently?

3) How does the study of history help us to better
understand the present?

Critical Thinking: Write Your Opinion

1) Some people think that farming was the beginning of
civilization. Do you agree or disagree? Explain your
answer.

2) What would your life be like as a Stone-Age human
being? How would you live? What would you eat? What
tools would you have?

Test-Taking Tip When studying for a test, write facts and definitions on
index cards. Use them as flash cards with a partner to
practice remembering the items.

"Lo, the god knows me well,
Amun, Lord of Thrones of the Two Lands;
He made me rule Black Land and Red Land as reward,
No one rebels against me in all lands.
All foreign lands are my subjects,
He placed my border at the limits of heaven. . . .
I am his daughter in very truth. . . ."

—Hatshepsut, pharaoh of Egypt, the "Speech of the Queen." It was inscribed
on a granite shaft in the temple she built to the god Amun at Karnak.

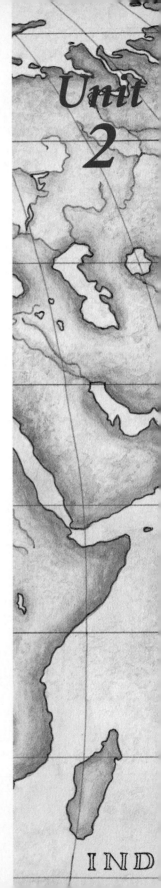

Early Civilizations

6000 B.C. to 30 B.C.

The most important development of prehistoric times was farming. Small farm communities grew into cities. As more people gathered in one place, they made rules and government began. Then they developed record keeping. Writing followed. Civilizations had begun!

The first civilizations began along river valleys because people could more easily grow food there. The Sumerians built the first great civilization about 7,000 years ago along the shores of the Tigris and Euphrates rivers. About 1,000 years later, people built cities in India's Indus River Valley. Nearly 1,000 years after that, Chinese villages grew into cities around the Yellow River. Later, the Egyptian civilization developed along the shores of the Nile River. In Unit 2, you will learn about the gifts each of these ancient civilizations has given us.

IND

Chapter

Early Civilizations in the East

2

6000 B.C. to 206 B.C.

Thousands of years ago, civilization developed in India and China. In India, villages grew into cities along the Indus River Valley. In China, small towns grew large along the Yangtze River and the Yellow River Valleys. In this chapter, you will learn that ancient people in India planned their two large cities and that the Chinese people became great builders and artisans.

Goals for Learning

▶ To explain how geography plays an important role in the history of civilization

▶ To explain why ancient towns formed along river valleys

▶ To describe India's first civilization

▶ To identify the major features of Hinduism

▶ To describe the art and writing of ancient China

▶ To explain why ancient China built two wonders

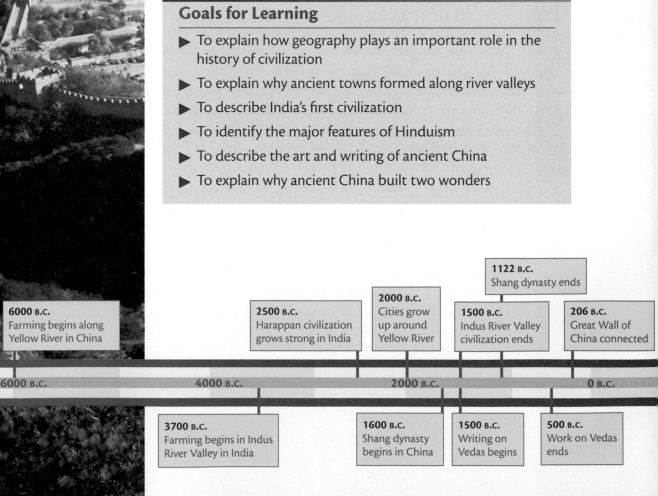

6000 B.C.
Farming begins along Yellow River in China

2500 B.C.
Harappan civilization grows strong in India

2000 B.C.
Cities grow up around Yellow River

1122 B.C.
Shang dynasty ends

1500 B.C.
Indus River Valley civilization ends

206 B.C.
Great Wall of China connected

6000 B.C.   4000 B.C.   2000 B.C.   0 B.C.

3700 B.C.
Farming begins in Indus River Valley in India

1600 B.C.
Shang dynasty begins in China

1500 B.C.
Writing on Vedas begins

500 B.C.
Work on Vedas ends

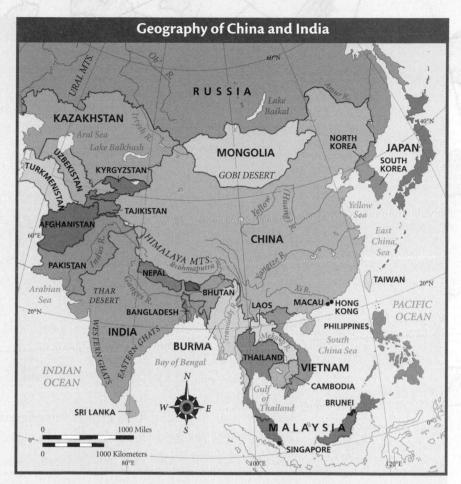

Geography of China and India

Civilization began thousands of years ago along the river valleys of Asia. Geography, or the land and the weather, was important in the history of India and China. Both countries are large. Mountains cut them off from other countries. The people get water from the rivers and use them for travel.

Geography Skills

Study the map and answer the following questions:

1) Name the large desert in Mongolia.

2) Name two rivers in China.

3) Name one river in India.

4) What country is directly south of Mongolia?

5) Mountains separate China from the West. How do you think this has changed China's history?

Fertile
Able to grow crops

◆**Geography**
The science that deals with land, weather, bodies of water, and plant and animal life

◆**Monsoon**
Seasonal winds

◆**Pass**
An open place in a mountain

◆**Peninsula**
Land surrounded by water on three sides

◆**Subcontinent**
A large piece of land that is somewhat smaller than a continent

The civilization of India is one of the oldest in the world. People have lived along its river valleys for about 4,500 years. These valleys helped to shape India's history. Of course, **geography**—land, weather, bodies of water, plant and animal life—shapes all civilizations.

How Large Is India?

From north to south, India extends about 2,000 miles. It is a **peninsula** surrounded on three sides by water. The world's highest mountains—the Himalayas and the Hindu Kush—stand at its northern edge. These two mountain ranges and the Bay of Bengal separate India from the rest of Asia.

We often call India a **subcontinent** because it is so large. Like a continent, it is a big piece of land. However, it is smaller than the seven continents.

What Has Geography Done for India?

Most of the time, geography has protected India. However, many armies marched into India over the past 4,000 years. These armies reached India through low points, or **passes,** in the mountains. The best known passage, or opening, into India is the Khyber Pass.

The people who came through these passes changed India's history. Each group brought new ideas. The newcomers sometimes married the people who had come before. Indian culture became a blend of many different groups.

What Rivers Help Indians Grow Crops?

The land of northern India is **fertile,** for it grows good crops. But the land needs water; it is dry. Life in India depends on water from two great rivers—the Ganges and the Indus. India's first great civilization began in the Indus River Valley. The Ganges is so important to the Indians that they call it "Mother Ganges."

Why Is the Monsoon Important?

Life in India depends on winds called **monsoons.** In the summer, wind blows over the warm waters of the Indian

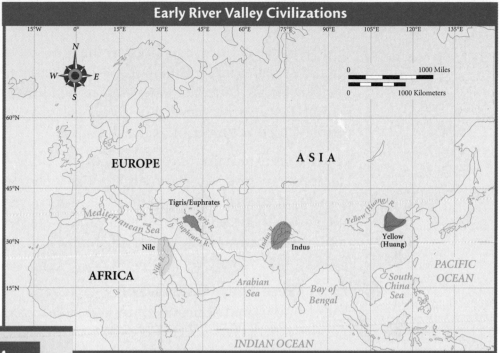

Early River Valley Civilizations

MAP
STUDY

This map shows four early river valley civilizations. Which one was farthest west? farthest east? Were any of them in Europe? Name two rivers where civilization began.

Ocean. When this air reaches land, rain falls. Sometimes rain pours down for weeks. In fact, 90 percent of India's yearly rain comes from the summer monsoon. But sometimes the monsoon is late or little rain falls. Then crops fail, and many people go hungry.

India is hot most of the year. The temperature usually stays above freezing. Its two seasons depend on the rain. Summer is the rainy season; winter is the dry season.

SECTION 1 REVIEW On a separate sheet of paper, write *True* if the statement is true or *False* if the statement is not true. Make each false statement true by changing the underlined word.

1) We sometimes call India a <u>continent.</u>
2) The two most important rivers in India are the Ganges and the <u>Indus.</u>
3) A <u>pass</u> is a seasonal wind that brings rain to India.
4) Armies marched into India through the <u>Khyber Pass.</u>
5) <u>Social Studies</u> is the study of how land, bodies of water, weather, plants, and animals change people's lives.

What do you think ?

In what ways has its geography helped or hurt the people of India?

Alabaster
A stone through which light can shine

District
A certain area of a place

Patio
An inner room open to the sky

Silt
A rich layer of soil left behind after a flood

Transport
To move from one place to another

India's first civilization developed in the Indus River Valley. This river begins in the Himalayas. When the snow melts, the river floods. Later, the water retreats and leaves **silt** behind. Because this rich dirt helps people grow crops, people settled along the Indus River Valley.

The first Indian civilization began with two cities—Harappa and Mohenjo-Daro. About 30,000 people lived in each city. The river connected the cities, which were 400 miles apart. Between these two large cities were smaller ones. Boats **transported,** or carried, people and supplies between the two cities.

What Were These Cities Like?

Both Harappa and Mohenjo-Daro looked like modern, planned cities. Their streets were wide and straight. The people built with clay bricks. Each brick was exactly the same size. A brick fort looked down on each city.

City planners divided their city into different **districts,** or areas. The business district had shops and buildings in which to store food. The living district was in another part of each city.

What Were the Homes Like?

People's homes were sometimes two stories high. Most had a **patio,** or inner room open to the sky. Stairs led up to the roof. The people built **alabaster** windows. This marble-like stone allowed light to shine through. Some homes had indoor bathrooms and toilets. Dirty water drained away through clay pipes.

Why Were the Cities Walled?

A great wall surrounded each city and protected it. Built into the wall were towers. From these, the people could see any enemy. In the center of the city was another walled area. Behind this wall stood a fort, a place to store food, and a large bath. The people probably used it as a place to honor their gods.

It is not known what these pictograms mean. No one can read the writing of the Indus Valley civilization.

Irrigate
To bring water to fields and crops

◆**Pictogram**
A picture symbol, or figure; a type of early writing

Tablet
A flat writing pad

What Do These Cities Tell Us?

The people who lived along the Indus River Valley must have known mathematics. Why? Because each city is laid out so exactly. Also, they must have had a strong government because everything is so alike. For example: All the bricks were exactly the same. Most buildings were the same.

How Did These People Live?

The people of the Indus River Valley raised grains and vegetables in their rich soil. They learned how to **irrigate,** or bring water to, their fields during the dry season.

The farmers grew enough food to feed everyone. Because of this, the city people could make pottery, cloth, jewelry, and metal tools. How do we know? Because archaeologists have dug up beautifully painted pottery, stone carvings, and gold and silver jewelry. We also know that Indians made the first cotton cloth.

Archaeologists have also found things from faraway in the ruins of ancient India. This early civilization traded goods with other civilizations.

Did These People Have a Written Language?

Archaeologists have discovered many clay **tablets,** or flat writing pads, in the Indus River Valley. On them are **pictograms**—figures that tell a story. They have also found hundreds of small carved markers. Did business people use these to stamp the things they sold? We do not know because at this time no one can read the Harappan language.

What Caused This Ancient Civilization to End?

About 1500 B.C. this civilization suddenly ended. Perhaps the coastline changed so trading became harder. Maybe the monsoon failed. Or maybe disease, an earthquake, or a flood struck. Maybe farmers could no longer grow enough food. Or maybe armies from central Asia invaded.

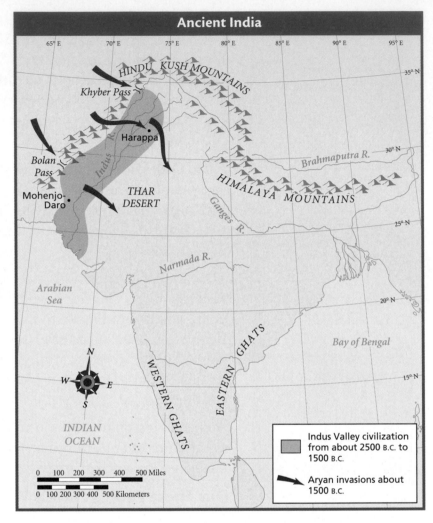

Ancient India

HINDU KUSH MOUNTAINS

Khyber Pass

Harappa

Bolan Pass

Mohenjo-Daro

Indus

THAR DESERT

Brahmaputra R.

HIMALAYA MOUNTAINS

Ganges R.

Narmada R.

Arabian Sea

Bay of Bengal

WESTERN GHATS

EASTERN GHATS

INDIAN OCEAN

0 100 200 300 400 500 Miles

0 100 200 300 400 500 Kilometers

Indus Valley civilization from about 2500 B.C. to 1500 B.C.

Aryan invasions about 1500 B.C.

MAP STUDY

This map shows the Indus River Valley civilization. What time period does it cover? Name the mountain passes through which armies marched into India. What mountain range are these passes in? What mountain range lies to the east of the Indus River Valley civilization?

WORD BANK

alabaster
Harappa
Indus
pictograms
silt

What do you think ?

Why do you think we call Harappa and Mohenjo-Daro "planned cities"?

SECTION 2 REVIEW On a separate sheet of paper, write the word from the Word Bank that completes each sentence.

1) The first civilization in India grew up along the _____ River Valley.

2) This happened because of the rich _____ that the spring floods left behind in the valley.

3) The two great cities of this civilization were _____ and Mohenjo-Daro.

4) The people in these cities built _____ windows to let in light.

5) In this valley, archaeologists have discovered clay pads with _____, or pictures, on them.

Development
Growth of something

◆Hinduism
The main religion of India that stresses the belief in the Vedas

Religious
Having to do with a belief in a higher being

For the next 500 years, people fought wars in the Indus River Valley. Many wandering soldiers poured into India. They fought with each other and with the people who came before them.

Over hundreds of years, these peoples married one another. They developed a set of beliefs and practices called **Hinduism.** The **development,** or growth, of Hinduism took place over a period of more than a thousand years.

What Is the Vedas?

The earliest written records about life in India is the Vedas. This word means "books of knowledge." The Vedas contains the legends and **religious** beliefs of the ancient Indians. Many people in India believe the Vedas are holy writings.

There are many religious temples in India. This is the Vimal Vasahi Temple at Mount Abu, India. It is from the Jainist religion, which uses parts of Hinduism.

For over a thousand years, writers added to the Vedas. These writings ended about 500 B.C. The Rig-Veda, the oldest of the Vedas, has 1028 **hymns,** or songs, to different gods. It is the world's oldest religious writing still being used today.

What Is the Hindu Name or God?

The Hindus, or the people who practice Hinduism, believe that everything is God, or Brahman. Their many gods are just different faces of Brahman. Their holy writings explain that "Brahman is One, and yet expresses itself as many."

Hindus especially honor Brahma, Vishnu, and Shiva, as different faces of God. Brahma **creates,** or makes life. Vishnu preserves. Shiva destroys. These three faces show us the main powers of God.

What Is Rebirth?

Hindus believe that all living things have souls. These souls are part of Brahman. To Hindus, all things—weeds, water, insects, animals, people—are different forms of the One.

Hindus believe in **reincarnation,** or the rebirth of the soul into a new body. After people die, their souls find a new home. This home is in the body of another person or animal. Each animal has a human soul and is part of Brahman. Hindus do not kill animals. They believe that cows are especially holy.

This **cycle** of birth, death, and rebirth keeps happening until a soul becomes perfect. Then the cycle ends, and the soul becomes one with Brahman.

What Is a Caste?

Hinduism teaches that people are born into **castes,** or classes. Hindus have four main castes:

1. the Brahmin caste made up of religious leaders
2. the ruler and warrior caste
3. the shopkeeper, landowner, and skilled-worker caste
4. the farmer, unskilled worker, servant, and slave caste

The Brahmin caste is the highest; the fourth caste listed is the lowest.

Expel
To throw out of something

Over thousands of years, the Hindus have divided their four main castes into smaller and smaller groups. They divide according to work, money, skin color, and religious beliefs.

Why Were Castes Important?

The members of each caste remained in the caste for life and followed its rules. For example, a person could marry only within the same caste. Another rule was that all the people in a caste did the same kind of work. When people broke these rules, they were thrown out, or **expelled,** from the caste. People called them "outcasts," because they had been cast out.

What Is Sanskrit?

The Hindus wrote their holy writings in Sanskrit. It is one of the earliest written languages. Later, they developed spoken Sanskrit. Many English words come from Sanskrit. For example, the Sanskrit word for mother is *mata*.

Sanskrit is the base language for all Indo-European languages. These include Latin, English, German, Spanish, Greek, and Persian, as well as many other languages.

SECTION 3 REVIEW On a separate sheet of paper, write answers to these questions.

1) What is the Vedas?

2) What does the saying "Brahman is One, and yet expresses itself as many" mean?

3) Why do some Hindus not kill animals?

4) What is an Indian caste?

5) What does Sanskrit have to do with the English language?

What do you think ?

What can the Hindu religion teach us?

Isolate
To keep apart or away from others

Plateau
A flat area that rises above the land close by

People have lived in China for thousands of years. In fact, farming began there more than 8,000 years ago. These farm villages grew into cities. The first Chinese cities began near the Yellow River about 2000 B.C.

What Is China's Geography?

China is huge. In ancient times, its geography **isolated** or kept it away from other peoples. The enormous Gobi Desert lies to the north. The Tibetan mountain **plateau**— a flat area that rises above the land close by—stretches toward the west. The mighty Himalayas rise in the southwest. Boundless seas guard the east and south.

What Keeps the Yangtze From Flooding?

The Yangtze is the longest and most important river in China. Because it is deep and runs swiftly, it hardly ever floods. In fact, it is the world's deepest river. Large ships travel inland on it as far as 600 miles. The Yangtze flows through southern China. It has been one of China's main trade routes since ancient times.

Why Does the Yellow River Flood?

The Yellow River, which the Chinese call the Huang Ho, flows 3,000 miles across northern China. Because the river is shallow, it often floods. Throughout the years, it has destroyed both cities and farms. Hunger, disease, and death follow. For this reason, we sometimes call the Yellow River "China's Sorrow."

The Yellow River in China is about 3,000 miles long. The first Chinese civilization began near the Yellow River in about 2000 B.C.

Canal
A waterway made by humans

Invade
To attack or march into another country

Why Did the Chinese Build a Grand Canal?

A great wonder of the ancient world was the Grand Canal. No river flows from south to north in China. The Chinese rulers built a 1,100-mile **canal,** or waterway. It joined the Yellow and the Yangtze Rivers.

The Chinese transported supplies on the canal. Grain grown in the fertile south came to the north. The ruling family and its army lived there.

Who Built the Canal?

The Chinese rulers began the canal about 2,400 years ago. More than 5 million people worked on it. In some areas, the rulers forced all men between the ages of 15 and 50 to work on the canal. An army of 50,000 guards beat and sometimes beheaded those who refused to work.

One person in every five families had to supply and prepare food for the workers and guards. During the building of the canal, 2 million workers died, became ill, or ran away.

Why Did the Chinese Build a Great Wall?

In ancient times, nomads **invaded,** or attacked, China on its northern and western frontier. Rulers built walls to keep them out. Two rulers joined all the walls together and created the Great Wall of China. It is another wonder of the ancient world.

How Big Was the Great Wall?

Builders started work on the wall over 2,000 years ago. It stretched nearly 1,400 miles from the Yellow Sea westward. In some places, it stood 40 to 50 feet high. Its base was 15 to 30 feet thick. The workers built towers along the wall. From these, guards looked far to the north and to the west. They watched for signs of invaders.

An ancient Chinese historian says 300,000 workers built the Great Wall of China. Others believe that 1 million people worked on it and that 400,000 of them died while building the wall.

The Yellow River, Sweet and Sour

Many popular Chinese dishes mix sweet and sour flavors. China's Huang Ho, the Yellow River, has "sweet and sour" traits too. This river flows out of the western mountains across the flat North China Plain. For farmers, the river can be "sweet." It waters the fields. It also brings *loess*, a rich yellow soil, from the mountains. The yellow mud gives the river its name. It also makes the soil the most fertile in China.

Sometimes, though, the river turns "sour." It overflows its banks and floods the plains. Then it becomes deadly. More than 1,500 floods have been recorded in the past 3,000 years. One terrible flood in 1887 killed almost a million people. The Chinese people have built dikes and dams to control the river. Even today, the floodwaters of the Huang Ho can be a "sour" threat.

Geography

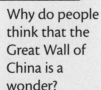

History in Your Life

SECTION 4 REVIEW Choose the letter of the answer that correctly completes each sentence. Write your answers on a separate sheet of paper.

1) For nearly 1,000 years China was nearly cut off from the rest of the world because of _____.

   a. the Gobi Desert   c. the Himalayan Mountains

   b. the Tibetan   d. all of the above
      mountain plateau

2) The _____ River is the deepest river in China and in the world.

   a. Yangtze   b. Yellow   c. Ganges   d. Indus

3) The _____ joins together the Yangtze and the Yellow Rivers.

   a. Great Wall of China   c. Gobi Desert

   b. Grand Canal   d. Tibetan mountain plateau

4) The Great Wall protected the Chinese from invaders from the north and the _____.

   a. east   b. west   c. south   d. all of the above

5) "China's Sorrow" is another name for the _____.

   a. Great Wall of China   c. Yellow River

   b. Grand Canal   d. Yangtze River

What do you think ?

Why do people think that the Great Wall of China is a wonder?

In ancient times in the Yellow River Valley, many rulers fought one another. Around 1600 B.C., one powerful ruling family took over the whole Yellow River plain. This family ruled for many years. A family that rules a country for a long period of time is called a **dynasty.** We call China's first dynasty the Shang.

What Was a Shang City Like?

Like the people of ancient India, the ancient Chinese built cities. The people of the Indus River Valley in India built brick homes. However, the people of the Yellow River Valley in China built wooden ones.

Archaeologists have discovered over 130 Shang villages and cities. Among the most important was Anyang. The Chinese carved it out of a forest. A palace and a temple stood in its center.

Near these important buildings, the **nobles**—people of high birth—lived. Their homes were large and rectangular in shape. Like Mohenjo-Daro in the Indus River Valley, Anyang had a business area. Shops, places for storing food, and government buildings stood in this area.

What Did Shang Farmers Grow?

Most of the common people in China were farmers. They lived outside the city. Their chief crop was **millet**—a type of grain. But they also raised rice, barley, wheat, and vegetables. They also raised cattle, sheep, pigs, and chickens. Because plows had not been invented yet, the farmers worked with stone tools.

What Were Some Shang Crafts?

Chinese **artisans** made beautiful objects for everyday use. Shang artisans created beautiful jewelry out of wood and **ivory**—the tusks, or teeth, of elephants and walrus. They carved marble and **jade,** a precious stone that is usually green, into many different objects.

Artisan
A person who makes useful, and often beautiful, objects for everyday use

◆**Dynasty**
A family that rules a country over a long period of time

Ivory
The name for the tusks, or teeth, of animals like the elephant and the walrus

Jade
A precious stone that is usually green

Millet
A type of grain

◆**Noble**
A person of high birth

When people remember the Shang dynasty, they think of its beautiful bronze works. The Chinese used some of these in religious practices. Others became everyday objects the people used around their homes.

The Shang made beautiful things out of bronze, such as this kettle with human faces on all four sides.

What Is a Chinese Character?

During the Shang dynasty, the Chinese developed writing. At first, they wrote pictograms. Later they included **symbols.** These figures stood for ideas. It was a difficult language with over 3,000 symbols or **characters.**

Each Chinese character includes two parts. One gives the meaning of the character. The other tells how to pronounce it. The language of modern China still uses the same characters the Shang dynasty used.

Character
In language, a symbol that means something

Scribe
In ancient times, a person who could read and write

Symbol
Something that stands for something else

Who Were the Scribes?

The written language of the Shang dynasty was difficult. Only a few people could read and write. We call these people **scribes.** Shang scribes wrote on bamboo strips and rolled them into bundles. These strips were long and narrow. The scribe wrote the characters up and down the strip rather than across.

The Secret of Silk

Ancient China had an important secret—silk. Long ago, no one else knew how to make this soft cloth. Silk thread is spun from the cocoons of silkworms. These caterpillars live on mulberry trees. One cocoon can produce a thread 1,000 yards long. Chinese legend says that the secret of silk was discovered about 2700 B.C. by Xilingshi. She was the wife of Emperor Huangdi.

Silk was a valuable export during the Han dynasty (202 B.C.–A.D. 220). Persian traders bought silk and other luxuries. Then camels carried these purchases across the deserts of Central Asia to the Middle East. This route was called the Silk Road. China is still the world's leading silk producer. Other countries that make silk are Japan, Brazil, and India.

Confucius was China's greatest teacher. (In Chinese, he was called "Master Kung.") Confucius did not teach religion, but he advised local rulers. His students later wrote down his sayings.

China was in great disorder when Confucius was alive. He hoped his ideas would bring back order. Confucius thought each person had a place in society. People owed respect to superiors, such as a ruler or a father. They should obey him. In turn, that person should set a good example. Confucius also taught his students to be loyal and honest. Culture and polite behavior were important too.

Collapse
To fall apart

Society
A group of people whose members live together for the good of all

Writing About History

Geography influenced ancient India and China. What is the land like where you live? In your notebook, write an essay. Tell how rivers, mountains, or other features have affected the way people live in your area.

What Is Ancestor Worship?

The Shang people believed that the gods controlled all things, such as business, floods, and sickness. They believed that the spirits of nature gave their rulers power. Among these spirits were the spirits of dead ancestors.

The Shang respected their ancestors' spirits. By doing this, they hoped to gain a reward. When bad things happened, families thought that dead ancestors were not pleased with them. So ancestor worship was an important part of Shang religion.

Why Did the Shang Decline?

The Shang dynasty lasted over 500 years. Then in 1122 B.C., the Zhou people captured the city of Anyang. What brought about the fall of this Shang city? Perhaps the Shang **society** was sharply divided into rich and poor people.

The rich nobles lived in large houses in the cities. They owned bronze weapons. They were proud of their beautiful silk clothes and jade jewelry. But the poor lived in small huts or in caves. They owned no land. They could only work the land the nobles owned. This work was long and hard. When invaders came, the poor may have welcomed them. Perhaps because of this, the Shang dynasty **collapsed,** or fell apart.

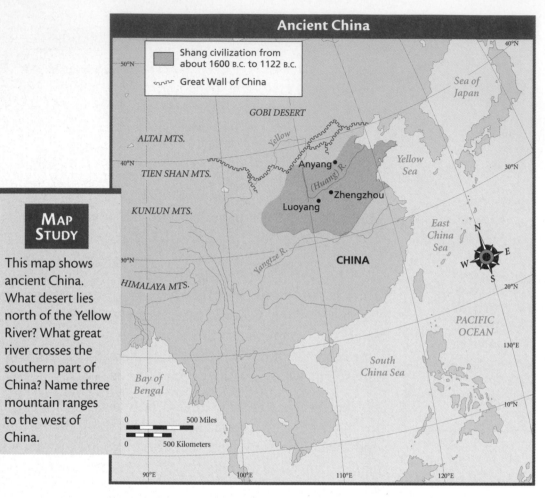

Ancient China

Shang civilization from about 1600 B.C. to 1122 B.C.

∿∿∿ Great Wall of China

GOBI DESERT

ALTAI MTS.

TIEN SHAN MTS.

KUNLUN MTS.

HIMALAYA MTS.

Yellow (Huang) R.

Anyang

Zhengzhou

Luoyang

CHINA

Yangtze R.

Sea of Japan

Yellow Sea

East China Sea

PACIFIC OCEAN

South China Sea

Bay of Bengal

0   500 Miles

0   500 Kilometers

50°N, 40°N, 30°N

40°N, 30°N, 20°N, 10°N

130°E

90°E, 100°E, 110°E, 120°E

N E S W

SECTION 5 REVIEW On a separate sheet of paper, write *True* if the statement is true or *False* if the statement is not true. Make each false statement true by changing the underlined word.

1) A <u>character</u> is a family that rules a country over a long period of time.

2) The houses in the Shang cities were built of <u>bricks.</u>

3) Five crops that Chinese farmers grew were millet, barley, rice, <u>wheat,</u> and vegetables.

4) Shang artisans made objects of the <u>metal</u> jade.

5) In their writing, the Chinese use <u>characters.</u>

The Bhagavad Gita

Hinduism is the major religion of India. Over 80 percent of India's 986 million people follow it. Hinduism is one of the oldest of the great world religions. It is different from the others in several ways. Hinduism is not based on the teachings of one person. It grew slowly over hundreds of years. It also does not have one holy book, such as the Bible or the Koran. Instead, there are many religious hymns and poems.

In Hinduism, there are many hymns and poems in the Vedas. This drawing shows Vishnu, one of the three main faces of Brahman.

This excerpt is from the Bhagavad Gita. The name means "Song of the Lord." This poem was probably written about A.D. 100. It is part of an older epic, or long poem. In it, the god Krishna teaches lessons about life and death.

What is work? What is beyond work? Even some seers [wise men] see this [incorrectly]. I will teach thee the truth of pure work, and this truth shall make thee free.

He whose undertakings are free from anxious desire and fanciful thought, whose work is made pure in the fire of wisdom: he is called wise by those who see. In whatever work he does such a man in truth has peace: he expects nothing, he relies on nothing, and ever has fullness of joy.

He has no vain hopes, he is the master of his soul, he surrenders all he has, only his body works: he is free from sin. He is glad with whatever God [the eternal spirit] gives him, and he has risen beyond the two contraries here below; he is without jealousy, and in success or in failure he is one: his works bind him not.

He has attained liberation: he is free from all bonds, his mind has found peace in wisdom, and his work is a holy sacrifice. The work of such a man is pure.

Greater is thine own work, even if this be humble, than the work of another, even if this be great. When a man does the work God gives him, no sin can touch this man.

And a man should not abandon his work, even if he cannot achieve it in full perfection; because in all work there may be imperfection, even as in all fire there is smoke.

Source Reading Wrap-Up

1) What does the speaker want to teach?
2) Who is a wise man?
3) Why should a person do his or her own work?
4) Should a person give up a job if he or she is not good at it? Why or why not?
5) How does the advice in this reading relate to the caste system?

Family Ties—
The Ties That Bind

The family has always been the backbone of Chinese society. In ancient China, people thought that the dead were still part of the family. Living family members honored those who had died. People offered them food and drink. They took care of family graves. These ancestors were seen as powerful spirits. Families hoped their ancestors could help them gain the gods' approval. That would bring good luck.

During the Shang dynasty, ancestors had a special role. People asked their help before making decisions. Even rulers asked their advice. People would go to a priest and ask him a question. To answer, priests used animal bones or tortoise shells. These were called oracle bones. The priest scratched a question on a bone. Next, he touched it with a red-hot bronze rod. The heat made cracks in the bone. These lines were the ancestors' answer. The priest studied the shape of the cracks. Then he explained what they meant.

Traditional Chinese families were very close. The family made sure every member was taken care of. It provided work, especially in farming areas. In turn, people were loyal to their families. A person's actions affected his or her whole family. If one member did wrong, it would shame them all.

The Chinese had great respect for old age. Children were expected to care for aging parents and grandparents. Older members of the family

Family is still very important in Chinese society.

also had the most power. The teachings of Confucius made such relationships very important. A father had authority over his children and wife. Men were seen as better than women.

In the past, families arranged marriages for their children. Often the groom and bride met for the first time at their wedding!

Chinese society has changed a lot in recent times. In general, families are smaller. The government makes some decisions that families used to make. But even in modern times, Chinese family ties remain strong.

Spotlight Story Wrap-Up

1) What is the backbone of Chinese society?

2) How did the ancient Chinese people show respect for their ancestors?

3) When and for what were oracle bones used?

4) In general, what did the Chinese think of older family members?

5) How did Confucius affect beliefs about the family?

CHAPTER SUMMARY

➡ India is a large peninsula in south Asia. The world's highest mountains are in the north.

➡ India gets water from the Ganges and Indus rivers. Annual storms called monsoons also bring rain.

➡ The first Indian civilization began in the Indus River Valley. The largest cities were Harappa and Mohenjo-Daro.

➡ Harappa and Mohenjo-Daro were walled cities. The careful planning of these cities shows their people knew mathematics. They had a strong government.

➡ People in the Indus River Valley irrigated crops. They made pottery and cotton cloth. They traded with other peoples and wrote pictograms on clay tablets. The civilization ended suddenly about 1500 B.C.

➡ A set of religious beliefs and practices called Hinduism developed. The Vedas contains its legends and religious beliefs.

➡ Hindus developed a spoken and written language called Sanskrit. Most European languages are based on it.

➡ The Hindu name for God is Brahman. Hindus believe in a cycle of birth, death, and rebirth (reincarnation).

➡ Hinduism is based on castes, or classes. Everyone is born into a caste. A person's job and way of life depend on his or her caste.

➡ China is a huge region. A desert, mountains, and oceans kept it isolated. Chinese rulers built the Great Wall to keep out invaders.

➡ The Yangtze, in southern China, is its longest river. It was an important trade route. The Yellow River (Huang Ho), in northern China, often floods. Farming began there about 8,000 years ago. The first cities were built along this river about 2000 B.C. The Grand Canal connected the Yangtze and Yellow Rivers.

➡ The Shang was China's first dynasty. It began about 1600 B.C. Its center was in the Yellow River Valley.

➡ Shang society was sharply divided between rich and poor. Most Chinese were farmers. They grew millet and other crops. Shang artisans are famous for their bronze work.

➡ The Shang developed a written language. It had many characters. It is still used today. Only scribes could read and write.

➡ Ancestor worship was an important part of the Shang religion.

Comprehension: Identifying Facts

On a separate sheet of paper, write the words from the Word Bank to complete each sentence.

WORD BANK

bronze

Grand Canal

Harappa

Hinduism

monsoon

planned

Sanskrit

Shang

Vedas

Yangtze

1) The ancient language of India is _____.

2) _____ was one of the two big cities of the Indus River Valley civilization.

3) Farming in India depends on the _____, or the seasonal winds.

4) Mohenjo-Daro in the Indus River Valley is a _____ city.

5) One religion practiced in India is _____

6) The earliest written record in India comes from the _____, or "books of knowledge."

7) The two most important rivers in China are the Yellow and the _____.

8) The two great wonders of ancient China are its Great Wall and its _____.

9) The first dynasty, or ruling family, in China was the _____.

10) Ancient artisans in China made beautiful _____ works.

Comprehension: Multiple Choice

On a separate sheet of paper, write the letter of the answer that correctly completes each sentence.

1) Along the northern part of India stand the _____.
   a. Yellow and Yangtze Rivers   c. Gobi and Sahara Deserts
   b. Himalayan Mountains   d. all of the above

2) Rivers are important for the birth of towns because _____.
   a. people can travel on them to other places
   b. people can send objects and food on them to other places
   c. they connect the villages and cities of the country
   d. all of the above

3) When rivers flood and the water retreats, it leaves behind rich dirt called _____.

    a. bronze   c. jade

    b. silt   d. monsoon

4) The first villages in India and China grew up around ____.

    a. deserts   c. oceans

    b. river valleys   d. mountains

5) The Hindus believe that they are born or reborn into one of _____ castes.

    a. two   c. four

    b. three   d. five

Comprehension: Understanding Main Ideas

On a separate sheet of paper, write the answer to each question. Use complete sentences, or statements.

1) Why did ancient civilizations all start in river valleys?

2) Why is geography important to history? (Hint: Use the geography of China and India to explain your answer.)

3) What are three facts about Hinduism?

Critical Thinking: Write Your Opinion

On a separate sheet of paper, write the answer to each question. Use complete sentences, or statements.

1) What does the saying "the monsoon means life or death to the Indian people" mean?

2) What was the same about life in ancient India and life in ancient China? What was different? (Hint: You might think about where the cities grew up, city life, and religion.)

| Test-Taking Tip | When you review your notes to prepare for an exam, use a marker to highlight key words and sample questions. |

Chapter 3

Civilization Develops in the Middle East

5000 B.C. to 600 B.C.

As early as 7,000 years ago, civilization began to develop in the Middle East. Many people settled along the Tigris and the Euphrates Rivers there. We call this area Mesopotamia, a word that means "land between the rivers." Mesopotamia and the land to its east form the "Fertile Crescent." In this chapter, you will learn about the people who lived along the Fertile Crescent. You will also discover the gifts they gave to us.

Goals for Learning

▶ To learn that people have lived in Mesopotamia for thousands of years

▶ To describe life in Sumer

▶ To identify four things the Sumerians added to world civilization

▶ To describe how the Akkadian and Babylonian civilizations became powerful in Mesopotamia

▶ To analyze why Hammurabi was an outstanding king

▶ To evaluate the role of the Phoenicians and the Hebrews in world civilization

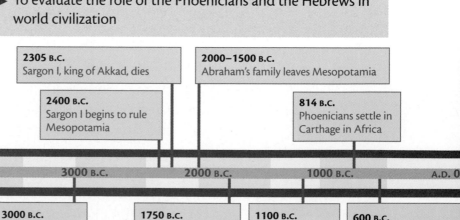

2305 B.C.
Sargon I, king of Akkad, dies

2000–1500 B.C.
Abraham's family leaves Mesopotamia

5000 B.C.
Sumerians begin to farm in Mesopotamia

2400 B.C.
Sargon I begins to rule Mesopotamia

814 B.C.
Phoenicians settle in Carthage in Africa

5000 B.C.	4000 B.C.	3000 B.C.	2000 B.C.	1000 B.C.	A.D. 0

3000 B.C.
Rise of Sumerian civilization

1750 B.C.
Hammurabi, king of Babylonia, dies

1100 B.C.
Phoenicians build city-states

600 B.C.
Phoenician sailors may have sailed around the tip of Africa

Geography Skills

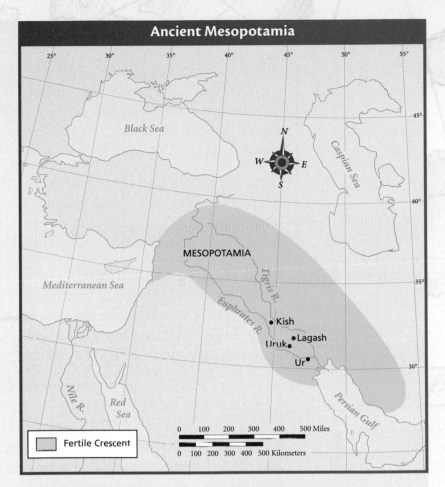

Ancient Mesopotamia

Fertile Crescent

We have given Mesopotamia, the "land between the rivers," many names. Since the first great civilizations developed there, we called it "the cradle of civilization." We also called it the "Fertile Crescent." Why? Because Mesopotamia and the land to its west is shaped like a crescent, or quarter, moon.

Because of the oil in this area, the Fertile Crescent is important to the whole world today.

Study the map and answer the following questions:

1) What are the names of the five seas shown on the map?

2) What four cities appear on the map?

3) What two great rivers flow in Mesopotamia?

4) About how many miles long is the Fertile Crescent?

5) In what direction is Mesopotamia from the Mediterranean Sea?

City-state
A city surrounded by villages on the surrounding land

Dike
A bank of earth that keeps out water

Legal
Lawful; based on the law of the government

Military
Having to do with the army or other people who fight wars

About 7,000 years ago, several groups of people settled between the Tigris and the Euphrates Rivers. The rivers helped them raise crops and care for their goats, cows, and sheep. We call where they settled Mesopotamia. This word means "the land between the rivers."

Every spring the rivers flooded their banks and made the land fertile. But few trees grew there. Also, the land had little stone for building. Yet in this place, an unusual people—the Sumerians—began to build a great civilization.

Who Were the Sumerians?

The Sumerians were one of many different tribes that lived in this area. They shared a common language and religion. In the beginning, they lived in the hills northeast of Mesopotamia. But gradually they moved into the river valleys.

There they built several large **city-states,** or cities surrounded by smaller villages. More than 20,000 people lived in the largest cities. The Sumerians built strong, protective walls around these cities. They also built canals and **dikes**—banks of earth that keep out water. Then they drained the nearby water-soaked land and irrigated the farmlands.

Each city had its own government. In the beginning, the people chose their leader. But then the city-states began to fight with each other. **Military,** or army, leaders became the rulers.

What Was Life Like in Sumer?

Sumerians lived far better than prehistoric humans had. Even the poorest citizens owned their own farm or house. Women had many **legal,** or lawful, rights. They could own property and run a business. Sumerian slaves could set up a business, borrow money, and buy their freedom.

Children had to obey. If they disobeyed, their parents could sell them into slavery! In school, teachers could beat children who made mistakes. The children's parents chose whom they would marry.

What Was a Sumerian Home Like?

The Sumerians learned to make bricks by putting clay in molds. Then they baked the bricks in the hot sun. They used these clay bricks to build one-story houses. Each had several rooms surrounding an open patio.

People with more money built larger, two-story houses. They coated the walls with a mixture of water, sand, and perhaps other materials. Then they painted the inside and the outside of their house white.

What Were Ziggurats?

The main building in each Sumerian city was its **temple.** There, the people **worshiped,** or honored, their gods. Each temple was in a **ziggurat,** or pyramid, shape with four sides. A temple ziggurat was up to six or seven stories high.

Inside the temple, the Sumerians built rooms for their **priests,** or religious leaders. The priests made sure that the workers built the ziggurat correctly. But building was expensive. So the priests asked for and received a part of each farmer's crop.

What Were the Sumerian Gods Like?

Like most people at that time, the Sumerians believed in gods who had human feelings. They believed that when the gods became angry, they punished the Sumerians. They made rivers flood and crops fail.

The ziggurat was the main part of every Sumerian city. It was a temple with rooms inside for priests and worship. Ziggurats were many stories high and had long stairways (see above top). Some ziggurats are still standing today (see above bottom).

To keep their many gods happy, the Sumerians built ziggurats in which to worship them. They kept statues of the gods in these temples. They also **sacrificed** daily to their gods by killing or burning an animal.

What Is the Most Important Sumerian Invention?

The Sumerians invented writing. We call their writing **cuneiform**. Writing probably began when the priests started to keep records. Later, the Sumerians made cuneiform more simple by creating a different symbol for each sound or word. They created 550 characters, or symbols.

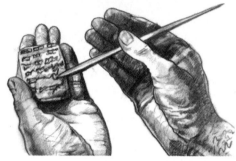

Sumerians used styluses like this one to write on clay tablets.

The Sumerians had no paper. They wrote on soft clay tablets with a sharp, pointed tool called a **stylus.** Then they baked the tablets to make them hard.

Archaeologists have found many of these tablets. Most of them are legal and business records. About 5,000 of them, however, contain our oldest known writings—hymns, stories, and poems. Some tablets list the names of cities, trees, insects, and many other

The Story of Gilgamesh

The story of Gilgamesh is the world's oldest known written literature. It is a long poem, or epic, that tells Sumerian myths. It is on clay tablets written about 4,000 years ago. The story itself is even older. Gilgamesh was a real person. He probably ruled Uruk, a city in Mesopotamia, before 2500 B.C. The myth makes him a hero king. He is part god and part human. The poem centers on his hunt for a way to live forever. There are battles with spirits and divine animals. Enkidu is another character. He lived in the forest with animals. Gilgamesh beat him in a fight. Then Enkidu became his friend and companion.

Literature
History in Your Life

Some stories in the Gilgamesh epic are similar to those in the Bible. One story tells about a great flood in Mesopotamia. A man tells Gilgamesh how he built a boat and lived through the flood. This is similar to the story of Noah and the Great Flood from the Bible.

Arch
A curved opening that supports something

Ramp
A smooth stairway

things. This means the Sumerians were the first people to write down history.

What Other Gifts Did the Sumerians Give Us?

The Sumerians may have been the first people to use a plow and a sailboat. They were the first to put wheels on carts. They also invented the potter's wheel. On this wheel, they could make more useful pottery shapes.

Sumerians created **arches** and **ramps.** These curved openings and smooth stairways helped them build taller and stronger buildings. To do this, they needed to know arithmetic. They based their arithmetic on the number 60. Even today, we use this number to measure time. For example, we have a 60-second minute and a 60-minute hour.

SECTION 1 REVIEW On a separate sheet of paper, write *True* if the statement is true or *False* if the statement is not true. Make each false statement true by changing the underlined word.

1) The <u>Chinese</u> were one of many different tribes that lived in the Middle East.

2) The largest Sumerian cities had more than <u>50,000</u> people.

3) A ziggurat is the name for a Sumerian <u>temple.</u>

4) The Sumerians built with <u>wood.</u>

5) The <u>Sumerians</u> invented writing.

What do you think

What do you think was the most important invention of the Sumerians? Why do you think this?

System
A way of doing something; a plan for doing something

Translate
To change the words of one language into those of another

Years after the Sumerians built their city-states in Mesopotamia, Sargon I united them. He ruled a kingdom north of the Sumerians called Akkad. Because his Akkadian army used bronze weapons, they were stronger than other armies.

In time, Sargon's kingdom spread from the shores of the Mediterranean Sea eastward. It covered all of the Tigris and Euphrates River Valleys to the Persian Gulf. For the first time in history, one person ruled all this land. He ruled for about 35 years, from around 2340 B.C. to 2305 B.C.

What Did Sargon I Borrow From the Sumerians?

Sargon borrowed many ideas from the Sumerians. The most important was their **system,** or way, of writing. The Akkadians had their own language, but they used the Sumerian cuneiform to make written records.

This memorial made of marble shows the Babylonian king (left) and the Lord Mayor of Babylon (right). Above them are cuneiform symbols of different gods.

Scribes **translated** many Sumerian writings. That is, they changed the Sumerian words into their own Akkadian ones. In this way, the Akkadians discovered many of Sumer's ideas about religion and government.

Sargon I was a strong leader. He repaired dikes and made the irrigation systems longer. His army protected important trade routes. However, soon after he died in 2305 B.C., Akkad collapsed and lost its power.

Who Were the Babylonians?

Around 1800 B.C., a new city-state called Babylon arose. People feared its powerful army. Hammurabi, the king of Babylon, fought both the Akkadians and the Sumerians and won. His kingdom stretched from the Persian Gulf northward through Mesopotamia.

Hammurabi built a giant ziggurat to honor the god Marduk. He also built a wall around

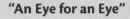

Code
A group of laws

Merchant
One who buys and sells; one who trades

Reign
To rule; the period of time a king or queen rules

Babylon to protect it. The wall was 11 miles long and nearly 80 feet wide. He improved roads and helped develop trade. **Merchants,** or traders, from as far away as India and China came to Babylon to do business.

Why Do We Remember Hammurabi?

People today remember Hammurabi because he created the first system of laws. We call these laws "Hammurabi's Code." He looked at the laws of all the lands he ruled. Then he collected what he thought were the best ones. Hammurabi put these into a **code,** or group of laws. He expected everyone in his kingdom to obey them. He also expected his government to carry out these laws.

Writing About History

Think about ancient laws, such as Hammurabi's Code and the Ten Commandments. Then write a code of laws for your school. In your notebook, list ten laws to govern people's behavior.

Hammurabi ruled, or **reigned,** for almost 40 years. He was proud of all he had done during that time. Near the end of his reign, he ordered a scribe to carve his record on a large block of stone. In this way everyone knew his laws. The scribe carved nearly 300 laws on the stone! Archaeologists found it buried in the sands of Iran in 1902.

We call Hammurabi's reign the Golden Age of Babylon. After his death in 1750 B.C., the Babylonians lost their power. Then Mesopotamia was again divided into small city-states.

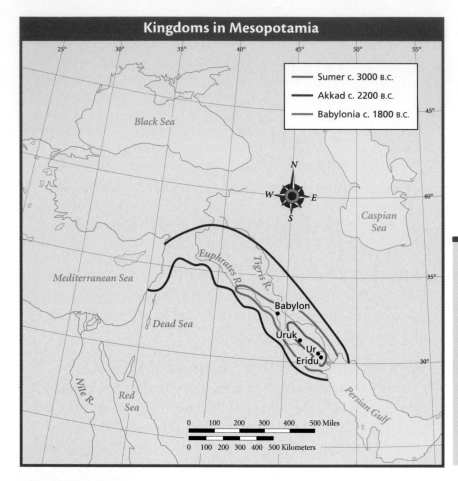

Kingdoms in Mesopotamia

Sumer c. 3000 B.C.
Akkad c. 2200 B.C.
Babylonia c. 1800 B.C.

Black Sea

Caspian Sea

Mediterranean Sea

Euphrates R.

Tigris R.

Babylon

Dead Sea

Uruk

Ur

Eridu

Nile R.

Red Sea

Persian Gulf

0 100 200 300 400 500 Miles

0 100 200 300 400 500 Kilometers

MAP STUDY

This map shows the kingdoms of ancient Mesopotamia. What three kingdoms does it show? Which is the oldest? Which is the smallest?

WORD BANK
Akkadians
Babylon
code
Hammurabi
Sargon I

SECTION 2 REVIEW On a separate sheet of paper, write the word from the Word Bank that completes each sentence.

1) The first ruler to unite the city-states of Mesopotamia was _____.

2) He was the leader of the _____.

3) Around 1800 B.C. a new city-state called _____ came to power.

4) One of its great leaders was _____.

5) He collected laws from many groups of people and put them into a _____.

What do you think

What made Sargon I and Hammurabi great leaders?

◆Fertile Crescent
An area of land in the Middle East shaped like a quarter moon

Navigate
To steer or sail a boat or ship

Sometimes we call the Middle East the **Fertile Crescent** because it is shaped like a quarter moon. We call its western tip Canaan and its eastern end Mesopotamia.

Why Did the Phoenicians Become Sailors?

Around 1100 B.C., a people we call the Phoenicians built a number of city-states in Canaan. Phoenicia was a narrow civilization squeezed between the mountains and the Mediterranean Sea. It had little land for farming.

The Phoenicians did, however, live in an area with many tall cedar trees. The Phoenicians used these to build ships. Soon they became sea traders. The merchants and traders became rich and built the great cities of Tyre and Sidon.

These traders sold cloth, glass, wood, and beautiful metal objects to people in other lands. Phoenician sailors carried this cargo in their ships. Then they sailed back home with ivory, metals, weapons, slaves, and wine.

Where Did the Phoenician Sailors Travel?

Phoenician sailors traveled to places no one else had been. They sailed to England in search of tin and copper. They traveled to Africa to trade for ivory. During their travels, they founded colonies in places such as France and Spain.

About 814 B.C., some Phoenicians settled in Carthage in northern Africa. Around 600 B.C., Phoenician sailors may have sailed around the tip of Africa. Some historians believe they even sailed across the ocean to America!

Phoenicians sailed in ships with a single sail. Many sailors pushed and pulled the oars that moved the ship forward. Phoenician sailors could sail far and wide because they mapped sea routes. They also used the North Star to **navigate,** or steer, their boats. They were the first sailors to do this.

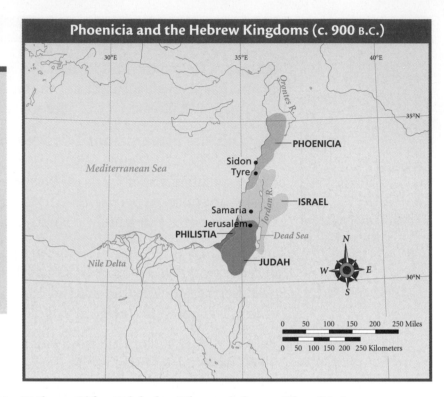

Phoenicia and the Hebrew Kingdoms (c. 900 B.C.)

MAP STUDY

This map shows Phoenicia, Philistia, and the Hebrew kingdoms. Which kingdom is farthest south? What river is important to these kingdoms? In what direction is Israel from Judah?

◆Bible
Hebrew and Christian book that is thought to be holy

What Gifts Did the Phoenicians Give Us?

We remember the Phoenicians for two important reasons: First, they developed a simple alphabet of 22 letters. These few letters took the place of the 550 letters of the cuneiform alphabet. The Greeks and Romans used this alphabet to build their own. The English and Spanish languages also use it. Second, the Phoenicians spread the culture and the products of the Middle East to many places. They did this through their trade and their colonies. Because of this, important ideas spread around the world.

What Is the Holy Book of the Hebrews?

The Hebrews are another Middle Eastern people. For many centuries, Hebrew scribes wrote books to tell their story. These books have been collected into one large book that we call the **Bible.** We find the story of the Hebrew people in the first part of today's Bible.

Where Did the Hebrews Come From?

Abraham was the first leader of the Hebrew people. The Hebrew part of the Bible says that God called Abraham's

Commandment
A rule, or way to act

Covenant
An agreement

Famine
A time when crops do not grow and there is no food

◆Judaism
The religion developed by the Hebrews that Jews practice today

family out of Mesopotamia. With his family and relatives, he was to go to a new country. Historians think that this happened sometime between 2000 and 1500 B.C.

For many years, they wandered the deserts as nomads. During a **famine**—a time when crops do not grow and there is no food—they traveled to Egypt. Years passed, and the Hebrews grew large in number. The Egyptian rulers made them slaves.

Who Led the Hebrew People Out of Slavery?

A Hebrew leader named Moses led his people out of Egypt sometime between 1300 and 1200 B.C. According to the Bible, the people wandered in the desert to the east of Egypt. There Moses climbed Mount Sinai to pray.

And there, the Hebrew god—Yahwch—gave Moses ten **commandments.** These rules told thc Hcbrews what to do to live peacefully with God, themselves, and other people. The commandments became the roots of the religion of the Hebrews. Today, we call this religion **Judaism.** We now call the Hebrew people Jews.

What Covenant Did the Hebrews Make?

The Hebrew people believed that their god had made a **covenant,** or agreement, with them. They promised to honor Yahweh's commandments and worship him alone. In return, God promised to protect the Jews. The land of Canaan would belong to them forever.

SOLOMON: Ruled c. Mid–900s B.C.

Solomon was the son of King David and the greatest king of ancient Israel. According to the Bible, he ruled for 40 years. Solomon became a famous ruler.

To keep the throne, Solomon had his enemies killed. Then he made Israel a rich empire. His ships traded with other countries for gold and silver. The king had new cities built in the lands he ruled. His most famous building was the magnificent temple in Jerusalem. Thousands of workers cut cedar wood for it. They brought huge blocks of stones. The temple was richly carved and covered with gold.

Morality
The right way of behaving toward others

After many years of wandering, the Hebrews came to Canaan. There they fought the people who lived in Philistia, along the coast of the Mediterranean Sea. In time, the Hebrews settled two kingdoms in Canaan—Judah and Israel. Later, invading armies destroyed both kingdoms. Today, we call this land Palestine. A large part of Palestine is the Jewish state of Israel.

What Gifts Did the Hebrews Give Us?

The Hebrews were the first people to believe in one all-powerful god. They set a high standard of **morality,** or the right way to behave toward others. Their commandments and their morality stood out in the ancient world.

SECTION 3 REVIEW Choose the letter of the answer that correctly completes each sentence. Write your answers on a separate sheet of paper.

1) The Phoenicians lived in _____.
   a. Egypt   b. Sumer   c. Babylon d. Canaan
2) The Phoenicians became famous as _____.
   a. sailors   b. soldiers c. painters d. lawyers
3) The Phoenicians were the first people to use the _____ to help them navigate.
   a. North Star b. compass c. astrolabe d. Orion
4) The holy book of the Hebrew people is called the _____.
   a. Vegas   b. Bible   c. Ziggurat d. Cedar
5) The Hebrews differed from other ancient people because they believed in one _____.
   a. commandment b. Marduk c. god   d. Sanskrit

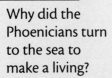

What do you think **?**

Why did the Phoenicians turn to the sea to make a living?

Hammurabi's Code

Hammurabi was very concerned about justice. Having a written code of laws was fairer to his people. The laws applied to everyone. They dealt with all parts of daily life. Some laws set rules for business and trade. Others listed punishments for crimes. Still others protected women's rights. Hammurabi's Code was an important step forward in government. Many systems of laws that came later were based on Hammurabi's Code.

1. If a man destroys the age of another man, they shall destroy his age.

2. If he breaks a man's bone, they shall break his bone.

3. If he destroys the age of a common man or breaks a bone of a common man, he shall pay one mina of silver.

4. If a man knocks out a tooth of a man of his own rank, they shall knock out his tooth.

5. If he knocks out a tooth of a common man, he shall pay one-third mina of silver.

6. If a house falls in and kills the owner's son, the son of the builder shall be put to death.

7. If a man strikes his father, they shall cut off his hand.

8. If a man is robbed and the robber is not caught, the governor of the city shall give the victim the value of the stolen goods.

9. If a man has stolen goods from a temple or house, he shall be put to death.

10. If a man has broken into a house, he shall be killed in front of the place where he broke through and buried there.

11. If a man wishes to divorce his wife who did not bear him children, he shall return to her the dowry [the property a woman brings to the husband at marriage] which she brought from her father's house and then he may divorce her.

This stone shows Hammurabi receiving laws from the sun god. He had his code of laws carved on this stone.

Source Reading Wrap-Up

1) Compare the third law with the first and second. How were laws different for harm done to ordinary people and people of high rank?

2) Think about the saying "an eye for an eye, a tooth for a tooth." How do these laws fit with Hammurabi's Code?

3) What did Babylonians seem to value more—human life or personal property? Explain.

4) How was a careless builder punished? Do you think this punishment fits the crime?

5) How was a childless woman protected in a divorce?

Technology Moves Ahead

Clever, curious people have always made inventions and discoveries. Very early in history, people learned to control floods. They built impressive buildings. Before 1500 B.C., technology was moving ahead in the ancient Middle East.

One giant step was learning to work with iron. Much earlier, people had mixed copper and tin to make bronze. Iron, however, was stronger than bronze. It made better knives and tools. Iron swords had a sharper edge. But it was harder to work with, too. It took a very hot fire to melt, or smelt, iron out of the rock. Then a worker called a smith hammered it into shape while it was red-hot.

We know little about the Hittites. Their craftsmen, however, were the first in the Middle East to work with iron. Hittites probably came from central Europe to what is now Turkey. Iron swords and horse-drawn war chariots helped them conquer their neighbors. The Hittite empire fell about 1200 B.C. After that, the secret of working iron spread to others. Iron could then be used for new purposes. In Israel, farmers had iron-tipped plows. They used iron sickles to harvest grain. This equipment made farming easier. Carpenters had sharper iron tools.

Trade also encouraged the development of new technology for better transportation. For example, iron ore and tin were scarce. People had to travel long distances to find them. Trading ships of the time had both a sail and oars. Most of the time, human crews rowed the ship. Large crews, however, were not practical for long trips. Then the Phoenicians turned a problem into an advantage. They did not have much good

This carving shows what a phoenician ship looked like.

farmland. They did have tall cedar trees. Phoenicians used them to make sturdy wooden ships. Instead of rowers, their ships had a single, large, square sail. The Phoenicians had developed the technology to sail long distances.

In the 1300s B.C., traders sailed all over the eastern Mediterranean Sea. Usually they stayed within sight of land. The stars were their only navigation tools. Traders from different cultures carried goods to and from many places. Caravans brought goods to the coast from far inland. Hardwoods and gold came from Africa. Amber came from the Baltic Sea. Traders might bring a new ship into a region. Then others would copy it. Even in ancient times, coastal cities were busy places.

Spotlight Story Wrap-Up

1) Why was iron more useful than bronze?
2) Describe how iron tools were made.
3) What people in the Middle East were the first to work with iron?
4) How did Phoenicians change the way ships were made? Why?
5) Describe how trade and technology worked together.

➥ Civilization developed in Mesopotamia about 7,000 years ago. People settled the land between two rivers—the Tigris and the Euphrates. Floods made the land good for farming. People built canals and dikes to control the water.

➥ The Sumerians were a tribe in Mesopotamia. They built walled city-states. Most people in Sumer could own property. Women and slaves had legal rights. Sumerians built houses out of baked clay bricks.

➥ Sumerians feared their gods. A ziggurat, or temple, was the most important building in a city. Their buildings had ramps and arches.

➥ Sumerian inventions included a writing system called cuneiform. They used a stylus to make symbols on clay tablets. They were the first to use the wheel on carts. Their counting system was based on the number 60.

➥ Sargon I was the ruler of Akkad in about 2340 B.C. He made the Sumerian city-states part of his lands. The Akkadians learned cuneiform.

➥ Hammurabi ruled the city-state of Babylon about 1800 B.C. His army conquered the Sumerians and Akkadians. Hammurabi organized his laws into a system, or code. They applied everywhere in the kingdom.

This time is called the Golden Age of Babylon. It ended with Hammurabi's death in 1750 B.C.

➥ The term "Fertile Crescent" refers to the Middle East. It is a curved area of land from Mesopotamia to the Mediterranean Sea.

➥ The Phoenicians built city-states in Canaan. They became ship-builders and sea traders. Their main cities were Sidon and Tyre. Phoenicians also built the city of Carthage in North Africa. They made maps of the seas. They used the North Star for navigation.

➥ The Phoenicians developed a 22-letter alphabet. It is the ancestor of the alphabet we use today. They took ideas from the Middle East to many places.

➥ The first books of the Bible tell the history of the Hebrews. Their first great leader was Abraham. He led them out of Mesopotamia, probably between 2000 and 1500 B.C.

➥ The Hebrews were desert nomads for many years. Then they became slaves in Egypt. A leader named Moses led them out of Egypt.

➥ The Hebrews settled in Canaan. They believed God had promised them this land. They divided it into the kingdoms of Judah and Israel.

Chapter 3 Review

Comprehension: Identifying Facts

On a separate sheet of paper, use the words from the Word Bank to complete each sentence.

WORD BANK
Hammurabi
Hebrews
Marduk
Mesopotamia
Phoenicians
Sargon I
Sumerians
wheels
Yahweh
ziggurats

1) The Sumerians built _____, which were pyramid-shaped buildings.

2) We call the region between the Tigris and the Euphrates rivers _____.

3) _____, the king of Akkad, united the city-states of the Middle East.

4) _____ developed the first code of law.

5) The _____ were the first great sailors and traders.

6) The _____ were the first people to believe in one all-powerful god.

7) The _____ invented writing.

8) The name of the chief Babylonian god was _____.

9) The name of the Hebrew god was _____.

10) The Sumerians were the first people to put _____ on carts.

Comprehension: Multiple Choice

On a separate sheet of paper, write the letter of the answer that correctly completes each sentence.

1) The Sumerians built _____.
   a. city-states   c. the Bible
   b. boats   d. a code

2) The Akkadians _____ Sumerian writings into their own language.
   a. translated   c. stylus
   b. cuneiform   d. painted

3) The Babylonian king Hammurabi collected laws into a
_____.

    a. Bible   c. ziggurat

    b. Vedas   d. code

4) The Phoenicians built boats of _____.

    a. jade   c. clay

    b. marble   d. cedar

5) The Hebrews became slaves in _____.

    a. Egypt   c. Phoenicia

    b. Canaan   d. Palestine

Comprehension: Understanding Main Ideas

On a separate sheet of paper, write the answer to each
question. Use complete sentences, or statements.

1) What gifts did the Sumerians give us?

2) Why do we remember Hammurabi?

3) In what way did the Hebrew people differ from other
ancient people?

Critical Thinking: Write Your Opinion

On a separate sheet of paper, write the answer to each
question. Use complete sentences, or statements.

1) Which country or group of people in the ancient Middle
East gave us the greatest gifts? Explain your opinion.

2) Why is the invention of writing an important step in
world civilization?

Test-Taking Tip   To prepare for a test, study in short sessions rather than
one long session. In the week before the test, spend time
each evening reviewing your notes.

800 B.C. to 330 B.C.

The Middle East was home to many city-states and kingdoms. For hundreds of years, they made war against each other. Finally, one group—the Assyrians—controlled most of the area. In fact, they controlled so much land that they became an empire. This chapter introduces you to the Assyrian Empire and to the Chaldean and Persian Empires that followed it. One by one, these empires controlled the Fertile Crescent.

Goals for Learning

▶ To describe the Assyrian army and government

▶ To compare the way the Assyrians, the Chaldeans, and the Persians treated conquered peoples

▶ To compare the size of the Assyrian, Chaldean, and Persian Empires

▶ To explain the ways the Persians unified their great empire

▶ To describe the religion known as Zoroastrianism

800 B.C.
Assyrian Empire expands in Mesopotamia

612 B.C.
Nineveh, the capital of Assyria, is destroyed

570 B.C.
Zoroaster preaches a new religion in Persia

538 B.C.
Cyrus defeats the Chaldeans

800 B.C.　　　　　600 B.C.　　　　　400 B.C.

650 B.C.
King Assurbanipal builds Nineveh

586 B.C.
Nebuchadnezzar, king of the Chaldeans, captures Jerusalem

562 B.C.
Nebuchadnezzar dies

530–330 B.C.
Persian Empire dominates Middle East

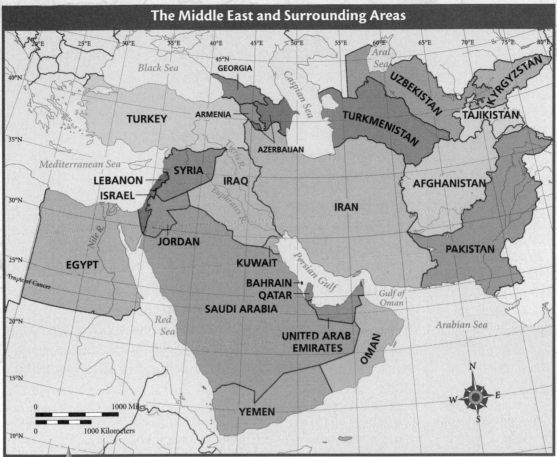

The Middle East and Surrounding Areas

Many seas touch the shores of the Middle East. Many rivers flow through it. Deserts stretch for miles, and mountains stand tall. This geography has helped to shape the cultural and political history of the region.

Study the map and answer the following questions:

1) What Egyptian river empties into the Mediterranean Sea?

2) What are the names of three countries that border the Mediterranean Sea?

3) What body of water separates Iran from Saudi Arabia?

4) Which country is farther south—Yemen or Egypt?

5) Which country is farther east—Iraq or Iran?

Geography Skills

Archer
A soldier who fights with a bow and arrows

Artisan
A person who works with his or her hands to create something

Cavalry
Soldiers on horseback

Chariot
A two-wheeled, horse-drawn carriage

Dominate
To control

◆**Empire**
A nation that rules a large area of land

Smelt
To quickly cool hot iron that has been hammered to remove any unwanted materials

Between 900 B.C. and 700 B.C., the Assyrian **Empire,** or nation, began to develop in Mesopotamia. It developed on the eastern side of the Fertile Crescent in the Tigris River Valley. The Assyrians were a fierce tribe of warriors. Their enemies hated and feared them. For several hundred years, they **dominated,** or controlled, the cities and trading routes of Mesopotamia.

Why Did People Fear the Assyrians?

Assyrian soldiers had iron weapons. The Assyrians had learned to **smelt** iron from the people known as the Hittites. The smelting process required three steps. First, the **artisan,** or worker, heated the iron until it was red hot. Second, the artisan hammered the iron to remove unwanted materials. Third, the artisan quickly cooled the iron. Then the iron was shaped into weapons. These were harder and stronger than the copper and bronze weapons other armies used.

The Assyrian army divided itself into groups. Some became charioteers who drove **chariots**—two-wheeled, horse-drawn carriages. The army also had a **cavalry.** These soldiers on horseback were the first of their kind. But the most feared soldiers were the **archers** who fought with bows and arrows.

How Did the Assyrian Army Attack?

With its iron weapons, the Assyrian army became a fighting machine. On the field of battle, the soldiers marched forward shoulder to shoulder. Then they let fly a shower of iron-tipped arrows. These killed and wounded the enemy.

Next, the cavalry and the charioteers attacked. They wore iron helmets and breast plates; they carried iron spears and swords. Their weapons and their skill forced the enemy to run back into the city and hide behind its walls.

But walls did not stop the Assyrians! They battered down the gates with a thick iron-tipped tree trunk! Sometimes they tunneled under the walls or climbed over them on ladders.

What Did the Assyrians Do When They Won?

After beating their enemies, the Assyrians burned some alive or cut their heads off. Others they made into slaves. Then they forced them to move to lands far from home. Next, the Assyrians **looted** the city. That is, they took away everything they wanted. Finally, they burned the captured city to the ground.

Where Was the Assyrian Capital?

Everyone in Mesopotamia feared the Assyrians. Who could win against them? Some paid **tribute** rather than fight. That is, they gave offerings or gifts to the kings of Assyria. This tribute, the loot won in war, and taxes made the

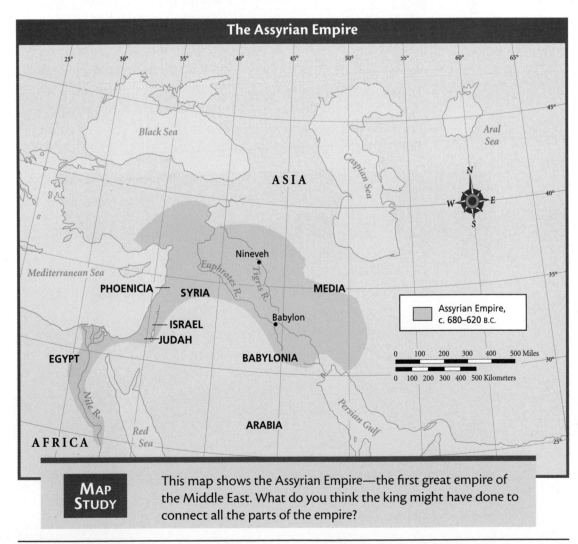

The Assyrian Empire

Assyrian Empire, c. 680–620 B.C.

MAP STUDY

This map shows the Assyrian Empire—the first great empire of the Middle East. What do you think the king might have done to connect all the parts of the empire?

◆Capital
*The city from
which a ruler, or
emperor, rules*

Assyrian kings rich. One of these kings used this money to build a mighty **capital.** There he ruled his empire.

Nineveh, on the Tigris River, was the largest city of its day. In 650 B.C., King Assurbanipal made it the showplace of the ancient world. Assurbanipal was one of the most powerful kings on earth. He boasted "I am Assurbanipal, the Great King, the Mighty King . . . King of Kings." He had a scribe carve these words on stone.

How Did King Assurbanipal Help Historians?

At his palace in Nineveh, Assurbanipal set up a library. There he collected and saved the ancient writings from the old Mesopotamian kingdoms of Sumer and Akkad. Hundreds of years later, in A.D. 1852, an archaeologist uncovered what was left of this library. He found 22,000 clay tablets!

These tablets contained dictionaries, which gave the same words in different languages. Some listed names of kings and important events in the ancient world. Still others contained songs and stories about the past. These tablets helped historians learn about life in the ancient Middle East.

Assurbanipal (shooting the bow) was the last great Assyrian king. Assyrians were mighty fighters and were the first to use cavalry.

King Sennacherib sits on his thrown in this Assyrian carving.

How Did the King Govern the Empire?

The Assyrian Empire included all of Mesopotamia, the Fertile Crescent, and Egypt. To help rule all this land, the Assyrian king divided it into **provinces,** or areas. Then he chose a **governor** for each province. This governor collected taxes and made sure that everyone obeyed the king's laws.

The king needed to control his empire and keep it connected. The Assyrians built a road system. They made all the roads level so that chariots traveled easily on them. Because of these roads, merchants and soldiers moved quickly from Nineveh to the provinces.

Why Did the Assyrian Empire Fall?

The Assyrian Empire became too large to **govern,** or rule. The people who had lost wars against the Assyrians began to **rebel,** or disobey, them. Fighting began. Soon the Chaldeans from Babylon and the Medes from Persia made an **alliance.** They agreed to help one another fight the Assyrians.

In 612 B.C., the Babylonians, Medes, and other armies captured the city of Nineveh and destroyed it. People throughout the empire celebrated!

SECTION 1 REVIEW On a separate sheet of paper, write *True* if the statement is true or *False* if the statement is not true. Make each false statement true by changing the underlined word.

1) The Assyrians learned to smelt iron from the <u>Medes.</u>

2) Soldiers who fight on horses are called the <u>cavalry.</u>

3) The capital of Assyria was <u>Nineveh.</u>

4) The Assyrians built a system of <u>dikes</u> to connect their empire.

5) The Medes and the <u>Chaldeans</u> won the war with the Assyrians.

◆Alliance
An agreement to work together to help one another

◆Govern
To rule

Rebel
To disobey or fight against

◆Governor
A ruler of a province or state

◆Province
An area, such as a state, that is part of a larger country

What do you think ?

Why is the library of Assurbanipal important to historians?

Expand
To grow; to stretch

Like the Assyrians, the Chaldeans defeated many different peoples. After destroying Nineveh, they became the leading Middle-Eastern empire. We often call their society Neo-Babylonia or the new Babylonia. Their ancestors were the people Hammurabi ruled hundreds of years before.

Who Did King Nebuchadnezzar Defeat?

One of the greatest Chaldean kings was Nebuchadnezzar. Under his rule, the Chaldean empire **expanded,** or stretched, as far west as Syria and Canaan.

Nebuchadnezzar defeated the army of Egypt when it tried to take over Syria and Phoenicia. He ruled the Hebrew, or Jewish, people too. After years of warfare, his armies defeated the Jews in 586 B.C. The soldiers destroyed Jerusalem and its temple. They marched 15,000 Jews to Babylon as slaves.

What Made Babylon Beautiful?

Nebuchadnezzar made the city of Babylon the most beautiful city in the ancient Middle East. In A.D. 1899, a German archaeologist found ancient Babylon. He discovered that a long wall—300 feet high and 80 feet wide—surrounded the city! The wall was so wide that a chariot with four horses could turn around on top of it! From its 250 towers, soldiers watched for the enemy. People and chariots entered the city through several bronze gates.

Bulls and dragons decorate the Ischtar gate in Babylon, the city Nebuchadnezzar made beautiful.

Glaze
A coat of shiny polish

Sculpture
A carving from stone or other hard material

A broad street ran down the center of Babylon. At one end stood a beautiful gate of bricks coated with a blue **glaze,** or shiny polish. Animal **sculptures,** or carvings, decorated the gate. Red-brick sidewalks ran down both sides of this long street. Carved into each brick was the message "I am Nebuchadnezzar, king of Babylon, who made this."

What Were the Hanging Gardens?

Nebuchadnezzar's palace had walls covered with brightly colored tiles. The most famous part of the palace was the Hanging Gardens. Some say that Nebuchadnezzar built the gardens for a queen who had lived in a mountainous country.

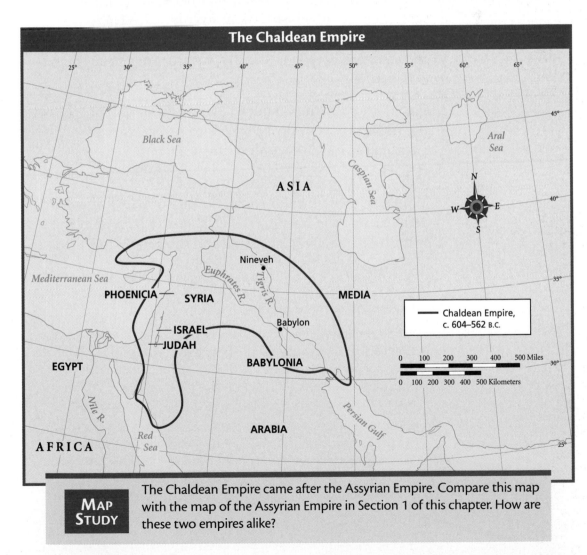

The Chaldean Empire

Chaldean Empire, c. 604–562 B.C.

0   100   200   300   400   500 Miles
0 100 200 300 400 500 Kilometers

MAP STUDY

The Chaldean Empire came after the Assyrian Empire. Compare this map with the map of the Assyrian Empire in Section 1 of this chapter. How are these two empires alike?

The king built **terraced,** or stepped, gardens, which rose upward like a mountain. In them, he planted the flowers and bushes of the queen's homeland. He had well water pumped up to the terraces to water the plants.

How Did Priests Use the Ziggurat of Babylon?

The highest building in Babylon was a 300-foot-high ziggurat. From the top of this great temple, the Chaldean priests studied the night sky. These early **astronomers** mapped the heavens and tracked the sun, the planets, and the stars.

Some groups of stars brought pictures to the astronomers' minds. They called these star pictures **constellations**. In fact, they saw 12 constellations evenly spaced across the sky. These became the **zodiac**. The astronomers believed that the stars **predicted**, or told, the future. They thought that stars had power over a person's life.

For many years the Chaldean priests **observed**, or viewed, the night sky. They broke time into seven-day weeks. They also figured out the length of the year.

Why Did the Chaldean Empire Fall?

While Nebuchadnezzar ruled, the city of Babylon was a great trading and learning center. But after he died in 562 B.C., war broke out. The Chaldeans and the people they had

Reading Signs in the Stars

People today read their horoscopes for clues to the future. This idea goes back to ancient Babylonia. There, priests were also astronomers. They studied the movements of the sun, moon, and stars. During a year, the sun seemed to circle through 12 constellations. The priests named these star patterns mostly after animals, such as the goat.

Using the sun and stars, priests predicted natural events. They also set the times for holidays. About the 6th century B.C., Chaldean priests began to make horoscopes. They told the future for rulers and nobles. A horoscope was based on the time of birth and the sun's position. Later the Greeks conquered Babylon. They gave the 12 star signs the names we use today. They named this circle of constellations the "zodiac."

Then and Now

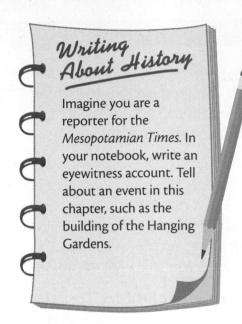

Writing About History

Imagine you are a reporter for the *Mesopotamian Times*. In your notebook, write an eyewitness account. Tell about an event in this chapter, such as the building of the Hanging Gardens.

Conquer
To defeat

conquered, or defeated, did not like the kings who followed Nebuchadnezzar.

The Book of Daniel in the Hebrew Bible describes how Babylon was destroyed. In 538 B.C., King Belshazzar held a great feast. Suddenly, a strange hand appeared and wrote mysterious words on the wall. No one except Daniel, a young Hebrew, could interpret the writing. Daniel told the king what the words meant: His days were coming to an end, and the Persian army would defeat his empire.

That night the Persians killed Belshazzar. Cyrus the Great, king of Persia, captured Babylon. The Chaldean Empire then became part of the great Persian Empire.

SECTION 2 REVIEW On a separate sheet of paper, write the word from the Word Bank that completes each sentence.

WORD BANK
astronomers
Babylon
Chaldean Empire
Hanging Gardens
Nebuchadnezzar

1) The Middle-Eastern empire that Nebuchadnezzar ruled was the _____.

2) The capital of his empire was _____.

3) One of the wonders of this capital was its _____.

4) _____ died in 562 B.C.

5) The Chaldean priests became _____, for they mapped the night skies.

What do you think

Why did Nebuchadnezzar carve his name on the red bricks of Babylon's sidewalks?

Barter
To trade by exchanging things without using money

Inspector
Someone who looks at how things are being done

Relay
To pass along from one to another

Unify
To connect; to bring together as one

In 538 B.C., Cyrus the Great, king of Persia, defeated the Chaldeans. In a few years, he conquered all his neighbors. Under later kings, the Persian Empire stretched more than 3,000 miles—from the Nile River of Egypt to the Indus River of India.

Because the Persian Empire was large, Darius I, another king, divided it into 20 provinces. A governor ruled each province. To keep an eye on his governors, he hired government **inspectors.** They became "the eyes and ears of the king." Traveling around the empire, they reported back to the king.

How Did the Persians Keep Their Empire Together?
To hold their empire together, the Persians built a great system of roads. One road stretched for more than 1,600 miles! It took merchants three months to go from one end to the other. But messages from the king went faster than this.

Horseback riders carried these messages across the empire. They could stop at 100 different places to change horses. The Persians could **relay,** or pass along, messages in one week, not three months! Another way to **unify,** or connect, the empire was to use the same weights and measures throughout the land. Because of this, doing business was easier.

How Did Coins Help Traders?
From a people called the Lydians, the Persians got the idea of using metal coins. Then two people no longer had to **barter,** or trade things. The problem with bartering is that both people must want to trade something of equal worth. Money took care of this problem.

How Did the Persians Treat Others?
The Persians treated other people fairly. They did not destroy a city when they conquered it. They also did not loot from the people they defeated. They let conquered people keep their own language and religion. They even allowed some groups to follow their own laws. The Persians did ask everyone to pay taxes. But the taxes were small.

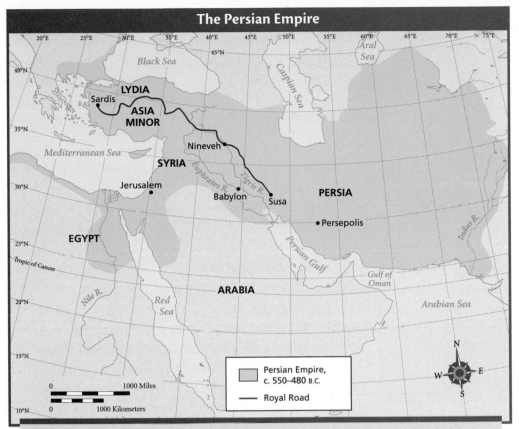

The Persian Empire

MAP STUDY

The Persian Empire came after the Assyrian Empire and the Chaldean Empire. Compare this map with the maps of the Assyrian Empire and the Chaldean Empire in Sections 1 and 2 of this chapter. Which empire is the largest? What might have happened to make the difference?

What Was Life Like for the Persians?

Litter
A stretcher for carrying people

The art of Persia tells us how people lived. It shows rich men on horseback. Slaves carry others on **litters,** or stretchers. The men often had long beards and wore makeup on their faces and eyelids.

Women were not allowed much freedom. They lived apart from the men. Girls were taught to be good wives and mothers. Boys were taught to ride horses, use the bow and arrow, and speak the truth.

The Persians protected merchants, but they refused to become traders. Why? Because they thought that buying or selling made people selfish. It made them lie and cheat other people. So Persians became soldiers, farmers, or shepherds.

ZOROASTER: c. 628–551 B.C.

Zoroaster grew up in the Persian countryside, where people were herders. This religious teacher was probably a priest. He taught that the world was a fight between good and evil. The highest god was Ahura Mazda, the Wise Lord. He stood for light and truth. The evil spirit of darkness was Ahriman. Zoroaster taught that good would win in the end. His followers called him a great prophet. Others saw him as a healer and magician. Zoroaster's teachings became the official religion of Persia.

Influence
An effect; to affect someone or something

Preach
To talk about the gods or how to live

Who Was Zoroaster?

The Persians worshipped many gods. Then, in about 570 B.C., a religious leader called Zoroaster began to **preach.** He told people that there were two forces in the world. One force was goodness and light; the other, evil and dark. Zoroastrianism had a strong **influence** on other religions, especially Judaism and Christianity. Both religions share the idea of life after death and a final reward or punishment.

SECTION 3 REVIEW Choose the letter of the answer that correctly completes each sentence. Write your answer on a separate sheet of paper.

1) One great king of the Persian Empire was _____.
   a. Hammurabi   c. Daniel
   b. Nebuchadnezzar   d. Cyrus the Great

2) The Persian Empire stretched from Egypt to _____.
   a. China   b. England   c. India   d. Phoenicia

3) The Persian Empire had _____ provinces.
   a. 20   b. 100   c. 1,600   d. 3,000

4) The Persians built a system of _____.
   a. dikes   b. litters   c. canals   d. roads

5) To trade things without using money is to _____.
   a. barter   b. govern   c. litter   d. tribute

What do you think ?

How would a system of weights and measures help to unify a country?

A Few Words From the "Great King"

Two Persian kings (Cyrus and Darius) are known as "the Great." Starting in about 550 B.C., Cyrus the Great built the Persian Empire. It became the largest empire ever known in the region. Cyrus died in battle about 529 B.C. His son became king, but others fought for the throne. Darius, a general, became king in 522 B.C. He was an outstanding leader. The empire grew. Darius was also a good organizer. He found ways to run the huge empire efficiently. Darius wanted to make sure he was remembered as "the Great." He planned a great tomb for himself. Then he wrote what he wanted carved on it. The excerpt below is part of what he wrote.

Darius I and an attendant are pictured in this carving.

A great god is Ahura Mazda, who created this earth, who created yonder sky, who created man, who created happiness for man, who made Darius king, one king of many, one lord of many.

I am Darius the great King, king of kings, king of countries containing all kinds of men, king in this great earth far and wide. . . .

Saith Darius the King: By The Favor of Ahura Mazda these are the countries which I seized outside Persia, I ruled over them; they bore tribute to me; what was said to them by me, that they did; my law—that held them firm: Media, Elam, Parthia, Aria, Bactria, Sogdiana, Chorasmia, Drangiana, Arachosia, Sattagydia, Gandara, Amyrgian, Sind, Scythians with pointed caps, Babylonia, Assyria, Arabia, Egypt, Armenia, Cappadocia, Sardis, Ionia, Scythians who are across the sea, Skudra, petasos-wearing Ionians, Libyans, Ethiopians, men of Maka, Carians.

Saith Darius the King: Much which was ill-done, that I made good. Provinces were in commotion; one man was smiting another. The following I brought about by the favor of Ahura Mazda, that the one does not smite the other at all, each one has his place. My law—of that they feel fear, so that the stronger does not smite nor destroy the weak.

Saith Darius the King: By the favor of Ahura Mazda, much handiwork which previously had been put out of its place, that I put in its place. . . .

Saith Darius the King: May Ahura Mazda, together with the gods protect me and my royal house, and what has been inscribed by me.

Source Reading Wrap-Up

1) Who is Ahura Mazda?

2) According to Darius, who gave him the right to rule as king?

3) What titles does Darius give himself?

4) What did Darius require people in conquered countries to do?

5) List at least two things that Darius is proud of.

The Babylonian Captivity

The Bible tells us a lot about Middle Eastern history. Several books are about the history of the Jews. They tell about the Jewish kingdoms. The Bible also talks about neighboring rulers. In the 6th century B.C., the Chaldeans of Babylonia conquered the Jewish kingdom. But the Jews rebelled against their rule. The Bible tells how the king of Babylon put down the rebels. Nebuchadnezzar's soldiers attacked Jerusalem. His soldiers captured the Jewish king and his family. They were taken to Babylon as prisoners. So were thousands of skilled craftsworkers. Strong men were taken for the army. These Jews were kept in Babylon for many years. This period is known as the Babylonian Captivity.

Meanwhile, the Jews rebelled again a few years later in 586 B.C. Again the Babylonians attacked Jerusalem. They burned the Great Temple. They destroyed the city. They took away most of the city's people. Only poor people and farmers were left in the country. The Babylonians also took gold and silver from the temple.

The Jews suffered greatly in Babylon. Psalm 137 tells how sad they were. "By the rivers of Babylon, . . . we wept, when we remembered our Zion. . . ." The Babylonian Captivity was an important time in Jewish history. It tested the strength of the Jews' faith. They were in a strange place with different customs. There was pressure to change their religion and culture. Through many years away from home, they never lost their faith. Their leaders set up houses of worship, or

Jewish houses of worship are called synagogues. This ancient synagogue is at Capernaum.

synagogues. People observed the Sabbath and religious holidays. Their communities stayed strong.

At the same time, the Jewish people learned new skills in Babylon. They learned to be traders. They learned about banking. They slowly gave up farming in favor of business.

In 538 B.C., Persian armies led by Cyrus the Great conquered Babylon. The next year, Cyrus sent the Jews home to Jerusalem. In the Bible, Cyrus is praised for his actions. He gave the Jews money to rebuild the temple. He also gave back the silver and gold vases that the Babylonians had stolen.

Spotlight Reading Wrap-Up

1) Why did Nebuchadnezzar attack Jerusalem?

2) What was the Babylonian Captivity?

3) What did the Jews do to keep their religion in Babylon?

4) What did the Jews learn from the Babylonians?

5) What events ended the Babylonian Captivity?

➡ The Assyrians were a warrior tribe in Mesopotamia. They built an empire between 900 and 700 B.C. People feared the Assyrian armies. They had iron weapons. Other armies only had bronze weapons. The Assyrian army also had archers, war chariots, and cavalry. The Assyrians were cruel to defeated peoples.

➡ Nineveh was capital of Assyria. Assurbanipal was king in 650 B.C. He built a huge library. It included writings from earlier kingdoms in Mesopotamia.

➡ Assyrian kings divided their empire into provinces. They built roads to link its parts. But the empire got too large to rule. Conquered peoples banded together against Assyria. They captured Nineveh in 612 B.C.

➡ The Chaldeans were next. Their capital was Babylon. Nebuchadnezzar made it beautiful. One feature was its Hanging Gardens.

➡ Nebuchadnezzar expanded the Chaldean empire. He defeated Egypt and the Jews. He brought the Jews to Babylon as slaves.

➡ Chaldean priests were astronomers. They studied the stars. They named the constellations of the zodiac. They set up a seven-day week.

➡ Nebuchadnezzar died in 562 B.C. Then wars broke out. In 538 B.C., the Persians captured Babylon.

➡ Cyrus the Great was king of Persia. He conquered the peoples around him. At its largest, the Persian empire stretched from Egypt to India. King Darius divided it into 20 provinces. His inspectors kept track of governors. Good roads connected all parts of the empire. Relays of messengers on horseback carried news quickly.

➡ Persian rulers treated other people well. They could keep their own language and religion.

➡ The Persians were not merchants. They did, however, encourage trade. Metal coins were used throughout the empire. Everyone used the same weights and measures for trade.

➡ Men and women lived separately in Persian society. Men had more freedom.

➡ Zoroaster brought a new religion to Persia. He saw life as a fight between good and evil. His teachings influenced Judaism and Christianity.

Comprehension: Identifying Facts

On a separate sheet of paper, use the words from the Word Bank to complete each sentence.

WORD BANK

alliance
astronomers
barter
cavalry
chariots
iron
litters
provinces
terraced
zodiac

1) Everyone feared the Assyrian army because it had weapons made of _____.

2) The Assyrian army was the first to use a _____ with its soldiers riding war horses.

3) Some Assyrian soldiers drove horse-drawn _____.

4) Both the Assyrians and the Persian kings divided their kingdoms into _____, or smaller areas.

5) The Chaldeans and the Medes formed an _____ and agreed to help one another defeat the Assyrians.

6) Nebuchadnezzar, the king of the Chaldeans, built a _____, or stepped, garden for his queen.

7) The Chaldean priests became the first _____, for they mapped the night sky.

8) These priests saw 12 constellations, or star pictures, which would later become the _____.

9) People in the Persian Empire had coins, so they no longer needed to _____, or trade things without money.

10) From Persian art, we learn that slaves sometimes carried Persian men on _____, or stretchers.

Comprehension: Multiple Choice

On a separate sheet of paper, write the letter of the answer that correctly completes each sentence.

1) The first great empire of the Middle East was the _____.

   a. Assyrian   c. Persian
   b. Chaldean   d. Hebrew

2) The largest city of the Assyrian Empire was _____.
- a. Babylon
- c. Nineveh
- b. Jerusalem
- d. Canaan

3) One powerful king of Assyria was _____.
- a. Hammurabi
- c. Nebuchadnezzar
- b. Assurbanipal
- d. Cyrus the Great

4) One powerful king of the Chaldeans was _____.
- a. Nebuchadnezzar
- c. Cyrus
- b. Daniel
- d. Darius

5) One powerful king of the Persians was _____.
- a. Daniel
- c. Moses
- b. Cyrus
- d. Zoroaster

Comprehension: Understanding Main Ideas

On a separate sheet of paper, write the answer to each question. Use complete sentences, or statements.

1) What helped the Assyrians become a war machine?

2) What was the difference between the way the Assyrians treated defeated people and the way the Persians did?

Critical Thinking: Write Your Opinion

1) Why do you think so many people in the Assyrian Empire were happy when the Chaldeans captured and destroyed Nineveh?

2) Think about the Persian religion of Zoroastrianism. What influence might it have had on the way Persians treated the people they conquered?

3) Which of the Middle Eastern peoples described in this chapter have influenced the course of world history the most? Explain your opinion.

Test-Taking Tip
Sometimes it is easier to learn new vocabulary words if you make them a part of your speaking and writing in other discussions and subject areas.

Egypt—The Gift of the Nile

5

3100 B.C. to 30 B.C.

In the last two chapters, you read about some of the people of the ancient Middle East. These people lived in an area known as the Fertile Crescent. Their city-states did not last long. However, the Egyptian civilization, which grew along the Nile River, lasted for more than 3,000 years! In this chapter, you will learn about the three kingdoms of the Egyptians.

Goals for Learning

▶ To explain why Egypt is "the gift of the Nile"

▶ To describe how Egypt was united in the Old Kingdom

▶ To explain how and why the pyramids were built

▶ To identify differences between the Old and the Middle Kingdoms

▶ To compare the New Kingdom with earlier periods of Egyptian history

▶ To list key contributions Egypt has made to world civilization

3400 B.C.
Upper Egypt is unified

3000 B.C.
Egyptians make paper from papyrus

2100 B.C.
The Old Kingdom ends

1630 B.C.
Hyksos invade Egypt

1570 B.C.
Egyptians drive out the Hyksos

332 B.C.
Alexander the Great conquers Egypt

3000 B.C.   **2000 B.C.**   **1000 B.C.**   **A.D. 0**

3100 B.C.
Upper and Lower Egypt unite; Old Kingdom begins

2686 B.C.
Egyptians build great pyramids

2040 B.C.
Middle Kingdom begins

1600 B.C.
New Kingdom begins

1372 B.C.
Ikhnaton becomes pharaoh

30 B.C.
Cleopatra dies

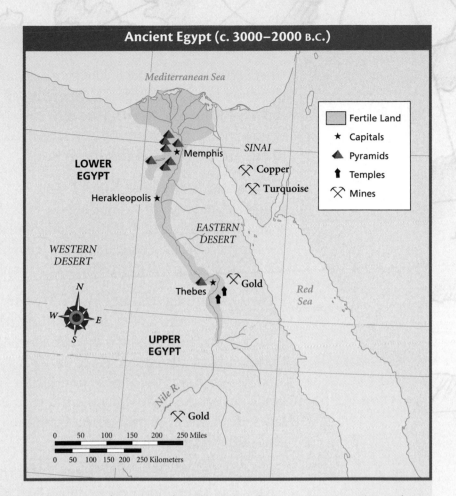

Ancient Egypt (c. 3000–2000 B.C.)

Mediterranean Sea

LOWER EGYPT

★ Memphis

SINAI

⚒ Copper

⚒ Turquoise

Herakleopolis ★

EASTERN DESERT

WESTERN DESERT

Thebes ★ ⚒ Gold

Red Sea

UPPER EGYPT

Nile R.

⚒ Gold

Legend

- Fertile Land
- ★ Capitals
- ▲ Pyramids
- ⬘ Temples
- ⚒ Mines

0   50   100   150   200   250 Miles

0   50 100 150 200   250 Kilometers

Geography Skills

The Nile River dominates the geography of Egypt. In ancient times, the river provided water for irrigation. It also served as a highway that unified Upper and Lower Egypt. The Egyptians built their main cities and temples in the Nile Valley.

Study the map carefully and answer the following questions:

1) Upper Egypt is in what direction from Lower Egypt?

2) What two deserts protected Egypt from invaders?

3) What are the names of the three Egyptian capitals shown on the map?

4) What is the distance from Thebes to Memphis?

5) What sea lies to the north of Lower Egypt?

◆**Delta**
An area of fertile land at the mouth of a river

Disaster
Something that causes harm or problems

The Egyptian civilization, like those of earlier civilizations, developed in a river valley. Historians call Egypt "the gift of the Nile." The Nile River is the longest in the world. It begins in the mountains of central Africa. Then it flows northward to the Mediterranean Sea.

How Long Is the Nile River?

For most of its 4,000 miles, the Nile cuts through desert. It seldom branches out, but this changes just before it reaches the Mediterranean. There, it forms a triangular-shaped area of fertile land. We call such an area at the mouth of a river a **delta**.

How Did the Egyptians Use Floods?

Every spring, snow melts in the mountains of eastern Africa. Rain falls. Then the Nile floods. Most people think that floods are **disasters,** which cause harm. However, the ancient Egyptians used these floodwaters to irrigate their fields. When the floodwater went down, it left behind a rich layer of silt. Because of this, the Egyptians harvested two, and sometimes three, crops a year.

Along the banks of the Nile, Egyptian farmers grew wheat, barley, and many other crops. They had more than enough food for themselves. They traded their extra food for the things they did not have.

The Nile River is the longest in the world. Egypt is often called "the gift of the Nile."

How Did the Nile Unify Egypt?

The Nile became an excellent "highway" for trade. Going north on it was easy because the Nile flows north. To go south, the Egyptians put large sails on their boats. These sails caught the

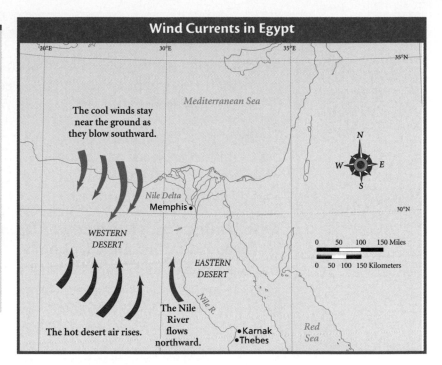

Wind Currents in Egypt

The cool winds stay near the ground as they blow southward.

Mediterranean Sea

Nile Delta
Memphis

WESTERN DESERT

EASTERN DESERT

The hot desert air rises.

The Nile River flows northward.

Karnak
Thebes

Red Sea

Nile R.

0   50   100   150 Miles
0   50   100   150 Kilometers

winds that blew from north to south. Egyptian traders, government workers, and the rulers easily traveled up and down the river.

What Gods Did the Egyptians Worship?

Ancient Egyptians worshiped the forces of nature and believed in many gods. Their two most important gods were Ra, the sun-god, and Hapi, the river god. For the Egyptians, the east, where the sun rose, was a symbol of birth. The west, where the sun set, was a sign of death.

SECTION 1 REVIEW On a separate sheet of paper, write *True* if the statement is true or *False* if the statement is not true. Make each false statement true by changing the underlined word or words.

1) Like other ancient people, the Egyptians settled in <u>desert</u> valleys.
2) The Nile River is <u>2,537</u> miles long.
3) Each year the Nile River floods and this <u>helps</u> the farmers.
4) For traveling up the Nile, the Egyptians put <u>sails</u> on their boats.
5) <u>Ra</u> was the name of the Egyptian river god.

What do you think **?**

Why do you think historians call Egypt "the gift of the Nile"?

Caravan
A group of traders traveling together, often through deserts

Project
A plan of work; a series of jobs

Unite
To bring together as one

At first, the ancient Egyptians lived in small villages. The people of the north, or Lower Egypt, lived near the Nile delta. Swampy, marshland cut them off from one another.

The Egyptians living in the south, or Upper Egypt, began big irrigation **projects**, or work plans. To finish these projects, they needed to work together. Upper Egypt was already unified around 3400 B.C.

Who United Upper and Lower Egypt?

We do not know who **united,** or brought together, Upper and Lower Egypt. One story says that a god-king named Menes conquered Lower Egypt around 3100 B.C. He built his capital where Upper Egypt and Lower Egypt meet and called it Memphis. It is near Egypt's present capital—Cairo.

Menes wanted to show that Egypt was now united. He put the red crown of Lower Egypt and the white crown of Upper Egypt together into one crown. Pictures often show the later rulers of Egypt wearing this double crown.

We do not know if Menes was a real person. But Menes and the kings who followed him made up the first dynasty of Egypt. During the following 2,500 years, Egypt had 30 different dynasties!

What Was Life Like in the Old Kingdom?

Historians call the time from 3100 B.C. to 2186 B.C. the Old Kingdom. During this time, Egyptian cities became centers of business. Groups of traders, called **caravans,** traveled together to Sumer to trade things. They also traveled to parts of Africa and the Mediterranean to trade.

Some Egyptians were traders, but most were farmers. They lived in mud-brick houses in small villages. They built their homes on the highest land. This protected them from the yearly floods. Because of the heat, people often slept on the roof.

One of the most well-known monuments of the Old Kingdom is the stone Sphinx at Giza, Egypt. It was built about 2500 B.C.

How Powerful Were Egyptian Pharaohs?

We call the Egyptian rulers **pharaohs.** They were both kings and priests. In Mesopotamia, the kings spoke for the gods. But in Egypt, the people thought the kings were gods!

The pharaoh of the Old Kingdom controlled the lives of his people. He owned all the land and water. The Egyptians believed that he even made the waters of the Nile rise and fall. Because life depended on the Nile, who would turn against this god-king? No one.

Why Did the Egyptians Build Pyramids?

The Egyptians believed that pharaohs continued to rule even after they died. So they built great **tombs,** or places to bury the dead ruler. To make these tombs last forever, the Egyptians built with stone. About 75 pyramids still stand in the Egyptian desert. The three most famous are in an area called Giza, outside modern Cairo.

Building the pyramids was hard work. The builders had no iron tools to cut the stone. They had no wheels or work animals to carry the huge stone blocks, which weighed about 5,000 pounds each.

Building a pyramid took years. The farmers worked when they could be away from their fields. But the Egyptians needed even more workers, so they hired workers and used slaves.

What Was the Afterlife?

The ancient Egyptians believed that life after death was much like life on earth. If people had led good lives before they died, they lived happily forever. If they had lived bad lives, a monster ate them!

As god-kings, the pharaohs would live happily forever. But the Egyptians wanted their dead rulers to be comfortable in the afterlife. So they filled their tombs with treasure: food, clothing, jewelry, furniture, and beautiful art.

The Egyptians painted pictures of the king's friends and servants on the walls. They thought that the pharaoh would want these people with him in the afterlife. They believed everything pictured on the walls would magically come alive!

The towering pyramids at Giza are amazing examples of Egyptian architecture.

How to Build a Pyramid

- Work 20,000 men for 20 years; feed them.
- Have 10,000 workers make about 26 million mud bricks for the inside of the pyramid.
- Have the other 10,000 workers cut huge stone blocks.
- Transport these blocks—about 12,600 of them—up the river to the building site.
- Dig a canal to connect the site to the river.
- Find a rock base, clear it of sand, and make it level.
- Make the sides of the stone blocks smooth; polish them.
- Build ramps upon which to haul the stone blocks higher and higher.
- Remove the building ramps as you work back downward.
- Build a funeral temple, the surrounding walls, a valley temple, and smaller pyramids for family members.

◆Civil war
Fighting between people within their own country

◆Economy
The system of making and trading things

Powerful
Having great power

How Did the Egyptians Protect Pharaohs?

The Egyptians buried the dead pharaoh in rooms deep within a pyramid. Then they sealed the rooms with huge stone blocks. However, robbers broke into the tombs and stole the treasures there. Even though the treasures are gone, archaeologists can still learn from a pyramid. Its wall paintings tell us much of what we know about ancient Egypt.

Why Did the Old Kingdom Fall?

Around the year 2100 B.C., the Old Kingdom ended. The pharaohs had lost power and government officials had become more **powerful.** The city leaders began to fight each other. Then **civil war** broke out as the people within Egypt began to fight each other.

Some historians believe that natural disasters may have caused the troubles in Egypt. Perhaps little rain fell for many years. Perhaps the people then began to doubt that the pharaoh controlled the rain. Egypt's **economy,** or system of making and trading things, collapsed.

The Rosetta Stone

Scribes in ancient Egypt wrote with picture symbols. This writing system is called hieroglyphics. The term comes from the Greek for "sacred carving." As time passed, though, people could no longer read them. Centuries later, the key to hieroglyphics was found. It was a stone tablet we now call the Rosetta Stone.

In 1799 Napoleon's army was in Egypt. French engineers were working near the Nile River. They dug up a tablet carved with three kinds of writing. One was Greek. One was a newer form of Egyptian writing. The third was hieroglyphics.

Jean François Champollion, a French scholar, knew many languages. He found that the inscriptions in Greek and the new Egyptian writing were the same. Then he compared the hieroglyphics with the Greek. After a long time, Champollion could read many of the symbols. The Rosetta Stone opened the door to learning about ancient Egypt.

SECTION 2 REVIEW On a separate sheet of paper, write the word from the Word Bank that completes each sentence.

WORD BANK

afterlife

Lower Egypt

Menes

pyramids

Upper Egypt

1) _____ was the northern part of Egypt.

2) _____ was the southern part of Egypt.

3) According to an old story, _____ united Upper and Lower Egypt.

4) The Egyptians believed in an _____ that was like the life they lived on earth.

5) The Egyptians built wonderful tombs, or _____, for their pharaohs.

What do you think

How does the building of pyramids show that the pharaohs had money and power?

Basin
A bowl-like area for storing water

Drain
To draw off water from a swampy or wet place

Around 2040 B.C., a new dynasty of powerful pharaohs reunited Egypt. This was the beginning of the Middle Kingdom. Its capital was Thebes.

Once again, traders sold artifacts and other products in faraway places. To help trade, the Egyptians dug a long canal. It joined the Nile River with business centers near the Red Sea.

They also emptied out, or **drained,** many swampy marshes and then dug a 300-foot-wide canal. The water they drew from these swamps flowed through this canal to a large natural **basin.** In this bowl-like place, they kept the water from the swamp. During dry months, farmers used it for irrigation. Once again, the Egyptians had more than enough food for everyone.

How Did the Two Kingdoms Differ?

The Old Kingdom and the Middle Kingdom differed in three ways. First, the Old Kingdom Egyptians thought their pharaohs were gods. People of the Middle Kingdom still thought this, but their pharaohs no longer had complete power. They had to share their power with other officials.

Farming Along the Nile

Egypt's success depended on thousands of peasants. But raising good crops depended on the Nile flooding every year. These floodwaters covered the land along its banks, making a strip of rich farmland. The rich soil came from farther up the river. The Nile also provided water for irrigation. The rest of Egypt was desert.

Men and women worked in the fields during the day. They grew grains such as wheat and barley. The flour from these grains was mixed with honey to make sweet bread. Farmers grew grapevines and picked dates too. Other peasants tended herds of sheep, goats, or cattle. They also hunted deer and water birds.

Besides food crops, Egyptian farmers grew cotton and flax, a plant that was used for its fibers. They spun the fibers to make cotton and linen cloth. Most farmwork was done by hand. Tomb paintings show farmers using metal tools to cut grain. Oxen were used for heavy work, such as turning water wheels.

Careers

History in Your Life

Second, the people of the Old Kingdom thought that only the pharaoh would live forever. However, the Middle Kingdom Egyptians thought that all people would live forever. So they **mummified** everyone after death. They wrapped the dead body in strips of cloth to keep it from decaying.

Third, the Egyptians buried the Old Kingdom pharaohs in pyramids. However, they buried later pharaohs in tombs cut into cliffs near Thebes.

Who Invaded Egypt?

About 1630 B.C., nomads from Asia known as the Hyksos invaded Egypt. The Egyptians knew medicine and arithmetic. But the Hyksos knew war. They had horse-drawn chariots, bronze and iron weapons, and **armor.** This strong covering of metal protected their bodies. Because of all this, the Hyksos easily defeated the Egyptians. For the first time in Egypt's history, **foreigners,** or people from somewhere else, ruled.

How Long Did the Hyksos Rule?

The Hyksos were mean rulers. They buried some Egyptian cities and destroyed temples. Meanwhile, the Egyptians **adopted,** or began to use, the weapons, chariots, and armor of the Hyksos. In 1570 B.C., the Egyptians drove out the foreign invaders.

SECTION 3 REVIEW On a separate sheet of paper, write answers to these questions.

1) What is one thing of which Middle Kingdom pharaohs could be proud?

2) How did Middle Kingdom pharaohs help traders?

3) What are three differences between the Old Kingdom and the Middle Kingdom?

4) Why were the Hyksos able to conquer Egypt?

5) What did the Egyptians learn from the Hyksos?

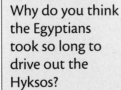

What do you think

Why do you think the Egyptians took so long to drive out the Hyksos?

About 1600 B.C., the New Kingdom began. During that time, strong pharaohs ruled Egypt. Like the pharaohs of the Old Kingdom, they controlled the people of Egypt.

Who Was the First Woman Pharaoh?

With its strong army, Egypt began to expand. It **annexed,** or took over, lands next to the upper Nile and along the eastern Mediterranean. Hatshepsut—the first woman pharaoh—spread the influence of Egypt down into the heart of Africa. From there, traders got products such as beautiful wood, animal skins, and feathers.

What Pharaoh Was a Great Conqueror?

When Hatshepsut died, Thutmose III became pharaoh. He spread Egypt's influence all the way to the Euphrates River. Almost every year for 20 years, his soldiers won victories in Asia. As they did so, he built army bases in all the lands he controlled. He also **organized,** or set up, a navy to conquer the cities along the eastern Mediterranean.

Under Thutmose, Egypt's empire stretched far and wide. For this reason, historians sometimes call the period of the New Kingdom the "empire age." The many people the Egyptians conquered paid tribute, or taxes, to the pharaohs. The rulers and the nobles became **wealthy,** or rich.

◆**Annex**
To take over; to add a piece of land to one's country

Organize
To set up; to get a series or number of things in order

Wealthy
Rich; having wealth

HATSHEPSUT: Reigned c. 1490–1469 B.C.

Most people think of Egypt's pharaohs as men. Most were. The most famous woman pharaoh was Hatshepsut. She was a pharaoh's daughter. As was the custom, she married her half-brother, Thutmose II. He died suddenly about 1490 B.C. For a while, Hatshepsut ruled in the name of her young stepson. Then she had herself crowned pharaoh, calling herself a daughter of the god Amon. Statues show her with a false beard, a sign of power. Hatshepsut ruled for about 20 years. During that time, Egypt had a long period of peace. She had many great temples and monuments built.

What Did the New Kingdom Pharaohs Build?

The rulers and nobles of the New Kingdom used their money to build temples, palaces, and statues. Hatshepsut built a beautiful temple near Thebes, the capital of the New Kingdom. Artists painted and carved the story of Egypt's victories on the temple's walls.

Thutmose III used slaves to build great palaces and to rebuild temples. Tall, pointed stone pillars called **obelisks** were also built. Artists carved **hieroglyphics,** or picture writing, on the sides of these pillars.

The Egyptians honored their pharaohs by building giant statues, which stood many stories high. With its beautiful palaces and temples, Thebes became the most wonderful city in the ancient world.

Obelisks are tall pillars carved from a single stone. This one is from the ancient Egyptian village of Karnak.

Where Did Egyptian Children Go to School?

The Egyptians built great temples to honor their gods. These were both religious centers and schools. In them, the children of Egyptian nobles and those from conquered lands learned what Egyptians believed. The pharaohs hoped that these schools would make the children **loyal,** or faithful, to Egypt when they got older. The schools trained boys as young as five years old to be scribes. These scribes kept important records and wrote down religious laws.

How Did Ikhnaton Change the Egyptian Religion?

The people of Thebes worshiped many gods. Sometimes they **combined** gods. For instance, they combined Amon, the god of the

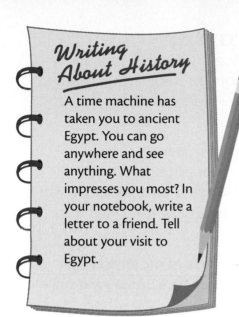
wind, with Ra, the sun god. The two became one. In fact, Amon-Ra became the most powerful god of all. He had power over both the sun and the air.

Around 1372 B.C., Ikhnaton became pharaoh. He believed that the sun god, now called Aton, was the only god. The new pharaoh closed the temples of the other gods. He took power away from the priests.

Ikhnaton built new temples that were completely open to the light and air. Often, Egyptian art shows this pharaoh and his wife, Nefertiti, making **offerings,** or giving gifts, to Aton. The rays of the sun god beam down on them.

How Did Egypt Lose Its Power?

Offering
A gift made to a god

Many Egyptians did not like the new religion with its one god. The priests became angry and jealous because they had lost power. Soon they began to fight with the pharaoh. When that happened, he could not pay as much attention to the empire. The conquered people in many parts of the empire began to rebel against Egypt.

A later pharaoh, Ramses III, rebuilt the empire, but Egypt never became as powerful as it had once been. He built many obelisks, giant statues, and beautiful temples. He was the last great ruler of Egypt.

The First Solar Calendar

Ancient Egyptians carefully watched the regular rise and fall of the Nile River. It stood for the cycle of birth and death. It also gave people a way to measure time. Egyptians discovered that the time between floods averaged about 365 days. So, nearly 5,000 years ago, they developed a calendar. It had 12 months, each 30 days long. An extra five days were added at the end of the year. Egyptians used the extra days as holidays. This calendar was almost perfectly in tune with the *solar year*. That's the time it takes the earth to circle the sun—$365\frac{1}{4}$ days. Today's calendar is a solar calendar, too. It has 12 months and 365 days, except in leap year.

Who Conquered Egypt in 332 B.C.?

Egypt could no longer defend itself. Over the years, many people invaded the land—Ethiopians from farther south in Africa; Babylonians; Assyrians; and Persians from the Fertile Crescent.

The Persians ruled Egypt until Alexander the Great defeated them in 332 B.C. Many years later, in 30 B.C., Queen Cleopatra killed herself to avoid surrendering Egypt to the Romans. The wonder of ancient Egypt ended with her death.

SECTION 4 REVIEW Choose the letter of the answer that correctly completes each sentence. Write your answer on a separate sheet of paper.

1) The first woman pharaoh was _____.

    a. Cleopatra   c. Ramses III

    b. Hatshepsut   d. Ikhnaton

2) The capital of the New Kingdom was _____.

    a. Memphis   c. Thebes

    b. Cairo   d. Persia

3) Thutmose III organized a _____ to help him conquer other lands.

    a. caravan   c. navy

    b. obelisk   d. religion

4) The name of the one god worshiped by Ikhnaton was

    _____.

    a. Aton   c. Amon

    b. Ra   d. Amon-Ra

5) The glory of ancient Egypt ended in _____ B.C.

    a. 1600   c. 332

    b. 1372   d. 30

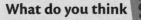

What do you think ?

Why do you think Ikhnaton's new religion was unpopular?

Fever
A high body temperature

Papyrus
A reed from the Nile River used to make paper

Scroll
A roll of papyrus

Egyptian civilization has given many gifts to the modern world. As early as 3000 B.C., the Egyptians learned how to use **papyrus,** a reed from the Nile River, to make paper. (The English word *paper* comes from the word *papyrus.*) Their paper was so well made that even today we can still read the writing on it!

This invention was important because writing on paper is much easier than writing on stone. Of course, in order to write on paper, they also had to invent ink.

What Did the Egyptians Know About Medicine?

The Egyptians made papyrus **scrolls**, or rolls. Archaeologists have discovered some of these in Egyptian tombs. One of the most famous papyrus scrolls shows the Egyptians' interest in medicine. The scroll describes how to set broken bones, how to check for a heartbeat, and how to deal with **fevers**—high body temperatures—and accidents. People who lived at later times learned much of their medicine from these ancient Egyptians.

What Were Egyptian Temples Like?

The Egyptians were skilled builders. Some of their statues, temples, and pyramids stood several stories high! People from all over the world still come to see their size and beauty. However, most of the great temples that the Egyptians built are in ruins today.

What Artwork Did Egyptian Artists Produce?

Egyptian artists carved huge statues from stone. Many had heads about twelve feet high, with ears three feet long! They made small figures of people and animals from wood, bronze, or copper.

Egyptian figures such as this one of the goddess, Isis, and her child, Horus, show that Egyptians were talented artisans.

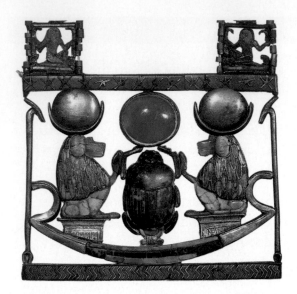

Egyptian pectoral jewelry, such as this "Sacred Animals of Thot" pectoral, was worn on the wearer's chest.

These same artists decorated temples with many drawings. We can still see much of their beautifully colored artwork today. Archaeologists have also found beautiful jewelry, pottery, and furniture in the pharaohs' tombs.

How Much Arithmetic Did the Egyptians Know?

The Egyptians invented a system of counting based on ten. This helped them add and subtract. They used this system to collect taxes. They also invented a system for measurement and weights. They measured things in **cubits**—the length of an arm from the end of the middle finger to the elbow. They used geometry to **survey,** or measure, land.

◆Cubit
A measurement that is the length of an arm from the end of the middle finger to the elbow

Survey
To measure land

SECTION 5 REVIEW On a separate sheet of paper, write *True* if the statement is true or *False* if the statement is not true. Make each false statement true by changing the underlined word.

1) The Egyptians made paper from a <u>tree</u> called papyrus.

2) The Egyptians built tall <u>statues,</u> temples, and pyramids.

3) The Egyptians knew how to set broken <u>bones.</u>

4) The Egyptians decorated their temples with <u>drawings.</u>

5) The Egyptians used <u>algebra</u> to survey their land.

What do you think

What is good and what is bad about measuring something in cubits?

Opening King Tut's Tomb

Tutankhamen was eight when he became pharaoh of Egypt. He ruled for about 11 years. Then he died suddenly about 1352 B.C. For thousands of years, his tomb was lost. Another tomb was built over it. Grave robbers broke in, but never reached the main room. As a result, this tomb kept almost all its original contents. It is the only pharaoh's tomb ever found in this condition.

The gold mask of Tutankhamen.

"King Tut" was not a powerful ruler, but he is famous today. The reason is the discovery of his tomb in 1922 by British archaeologist Howard Carter. This is Carter's retelling of the event.

The day following (November 26th) was the day of days, the most wonderful that I have ever lived through. . . . Throughout the morning the work of clearing continued. Then, in the middle of the afternoon, 30 feet down from the outer door, we came upon a second sealed doorway. . . .

With trembling hands I made a tiny breach in the upper left-hand corner. Darkness and blank space . . . showed that whatever lay beyond was empty. . . . Widening the hole a little, I inserted the candle and peered in. . . . At first I could see nothing, but presently, as my eyes grew accustomed to the light, details of the room within emerged slowly from the mist, strange animals, statues, and gold—everywhere the glint of gold.

For the moment . . . I was struck dumb with amazement. When Lord Carnarvon, unable to stand the suspense any longer, inquired anxiously, "Can you see anything?" it was all I could do to get out the words, "Yes, wonderful things!"

Gradually the scene grew clearer, and we could pick out individual objects. First, right opposite to us . . . were three great gilt couches, their sides carved in the form of monstrous animals. . . . Next, on the right, two statues caught and held our attention: two life-sized figures of a king in black, facing each other like sentinels. . . .

These were the dominant objects that caught the eye at first. Between them, around them, piled on top of them, there were countless others— exquisitely painted and inlaid caskets; alabaster vases, some beautifully carved . . . ; beds; chairs beautifully carved; a golden inlaid throne; . . . on the left a confused pile of overturned chariots, glistening with gold and inlay; and peeping from behind them another portrait of a king.

Source Reading Wrap-Up

1) Why was the discovery of this tomb important to historians?

2) Is this reading a primary source or a secondary source? Why?

3) What did Carter see all around after he got used to the darkness?

4) How did Carter answer Lord Carnarvon?

5) List three things found in the tomb.

Burying the Dead

The people of ancient Egypt saw their pharaohs as god-kings. They believed that each pharaoh was the human form of a god. Egyptians also believed in an afterlife. It was much like life on earth. After death, a pharaoh would continue to rule in the next life.

The Egyptians believed that a dead person's body must not decay. Otherwise a person could not enjoy the afterlife. To protect the body, Egyptians used a process called embalming.

Embalming took time. First, the embalmers removed all the internal organs. The heart and other important organs were put in small jars. These are called canopic jars. Then the body was put in a pine box. It was covered with a salty liquid called natron. The natron removed most of the water in the body, making it shrink. That took about 70 days. Then the body was wrapped with bandages of wax-covered cloth. The wrapped body was now a mummy. It was placed in a decorated coffin and put in a tomb.

The tombs of the pharaohs were meant to last forever. They were decorated like a palace. The tombs were filled with things the dead might need in the next life. That would include food, furniture, jewels, and cosmetics. A ruler needed servants, too. Early in Egypt's history, servants were buried with the ruler. They were probably smothered or given poison. The pharaoh Djer ruled Egypt around 2900 B.C. When he died, about 580 members of the court may have been buried with him. Later, small pottery figures were buried in tombs to act as servants instead of killing actual servants.

Mummies were prepared with great care. This one is an Egyptian priestess from about 100 B.C., with the original wood coffin.

Ancient embalmers were very skillful. Thousands of years later, many mummies are well preserved. You can see some in museums. Today scientists are also interested in mummies. They examine their bones, hair, and other parts. Research on mummies can discover much about the lives and health of ancient Egyptians.

Spotlight Story Wrap-Up

1) Who did the ancient Egyptians see their pharaoh as?

2) What did the Egyptians believe happened after death?

3) Why did the Egyptians not want the body to decay?

4) Why were things like food and furniture placed in a tomb?

5) What can scientists learn from mummies?

➡ Egyptian civilization developed in the valley of the Nile River. The river runs north from central Africa. There is a delta where it enters the Mediterranean Sea. The Nile's yearly floods made the soil rich. Farmers could grow many crops in a year. The river was also a good route for trade.

➡ Egyptians had many gods. Ra was the sun-god. Hapi was the river god.

➡ Upper Egypt, in the south, was unified by about 3400 B.C. Stories say that Menes, a god-king, conquered Lower Egypt about 3100 B.C. He unified Upper and Lower Egypt. The symbol for this new Egypt was the double crown. Its capital was Memphis. His rule began Egypt's first dynasty.

➡ The Old Kingdom in Egypt began about 3100 B.C. The rulers were called pharaohs. They were all-powerful. People believed they were gods. Trade became important.

➡ Egyptians believed in an afterlife that was much like life on earth. Pharaohs built pyramids for tombs. People filled them with things the ruler would need in the afterlife.

➡ The pharaohs lost power. Then civil war broke out. The economy collapsed. As a result, the Old Kingdom ended about 2100 B.C.

➡ Egypt was reunited about 2040 B.C. The Middle Kingdom began. Its capital was at Thebes. The pharaohs had less power than in the Old Kingdom.

➡ Beliefs about the afterlife changed in the Middle Kingdom. Pharaohs were buried in tombs cut into cliffs. Ordinary people could share the afterlife.

➡ The Hyksos from Asia ended the Middle Kingdom about 1630 B.C. They had iron weapons and metal armor. They ruled until 1570 B.C.

➡ The New Kingdom began about 1600 B.C. Egypt took over more land. Hatshepsut, the first woman pharaoh, encouraged trade. Thutmose III made the empire much larger.

➡ The pharaoh Ikhnaton tried to change Egypt's religion. He believed in only one god. The fight over religion that followed made Egypt weak. Other peoples invaded it. Persia ruled Egypt until 332 B.C.

➡ The ancient Egyptians made paper from the papyrus reed.

➡ Egyptian doctors were skillful.

➡ Egyptian artists carved huge statues. They created jewelry, pottery, and artwork. They invented a counting system based on ten. They used geometry.

Comprehension: Identifying Facts

On a separate sheet of paper, use the words from the Word Bank to complete each sentence.

WORD BANK
Hatshepsut
hieroglyphics
Ikhnaton
Menes
mummy
papyrus
pharaoh
Ra
Ramses III
Thutmose III

1) The reed from which the Egyptians made paper is _____.

2) The Egyptians made a _____ by wrapping a dead body in cloth strips to keep it from decaying.

3) The Egyptians used _____, which is a kind of picture writing.

4) The Egyptians called their king or ruler a _____.

5) _____ was the god-king who unified Upper and Lower Egypt and began the Old Kingdom.

6) _____ was the Egyptian sun-god.

7) _____ was the first woman pharaoh.

8) _____ was the pharaoh who enlarged the Egyptian empire to its greatest size.

9) _____ was the last great ruler of Egypt.

10) The Egyptian pharaoh _____ believed in only one god.

Comprehension: Multiple Choice

On a separate sheet of paper, write the letter of the answer that correctly completes each sentence.

1) Upper Egypt was the _____ part of Egypt.
   a. northern
   b. eastern
   c. southern
   d. western

2) Lower Egypt was the _____ part of Egypt.
   a. northern
   b. eastern
   c. southern
   d. western

3) The Egyptians thought their rulers were _____.

   a. children   c. wind

   b. gods   d. sun

4) Building a pyramid took about _____ years.

   a. 3   c. 13

   b. 7   d. 20

5) The _____ invaded Egypt in 1630 B.C.

   a. Persians   c. Assyrians

   b. Babylonians   d. Hyksos

Comprehension: Understanding Main Ideas

On a separate sheet of paper, write the answer to each question. Use complete sentences, or statements.

1) Why was the Nile River so important to the Egyptians?

2) How did the three kingdoms of Egypt differ?

3) Why were the Hyksos and later invaders able to defeat the Egyptians?

Critical Thinking: Write Your Opinion

1) The Egyptians buried treasures with pharaohs when they died. We learn about the Egyptian society from this treasure. Think of things that would tell other people about our society. What five things from our society would you choose to put in your tomb? Explain your choices.

2) What gift from the ancient Egyptians do you think is best? Why do you think so?

Test-Taking Tip | Look over a test before you begin answering questions. See how many parts there are. See what you are being asked to do on each part.

To read a map, you need to understand its symbols. Most maps have a key, or legend, that explains the symbols.

Some maps are drawn exactly to scale. You can use the scale to find the actual distances on a map.

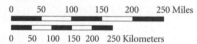

Most maps show direction. A compass rose shows at least the four major directions: north, east, south, and west. Some compass roses also include northeast, southeast, northwest, and southwest. To show north, some maps just use an arrow and the letter *N*.

Many maps show lines of longitude and latitude. Vertical (up and down) lines are longitude. Horizontal (across) lines are latitude. The line for zero degrees (0°) longitude goes through Greenwich, England. Zero degrees latitude is at the equator—the widest part of the globe.

There are many different kinds of maps. Each kind of map provides different information. Here are some examples:

Physical map—Shows the roughness of Earth's surface, including mountains, rivers, and plains

Elevation map—Shows different heights of land above sea level

Political map—Shows borders between countries

Climate map—Shows different kinds of climates, including, hot, dry, cold, and wet

Natural resources map—Shows location of natural resources such as minerals, oil, and natural gas

Choose the kind of map you would use to answer each question.

1) What parts of Asia have land above 10,000 feet?

2) What present-day country is west of Egypt?

3) Where are the Tigris and Euphrates located?

4) Which nations in the Middle East have oil resources?

5) In what part of China does the most rain fall?

➡ Indian civilization began in the Indus River Valley. The people of this area invented a system of writing called Sanskrit. Their beliefs developed into the Hindu religion.

➡ The first Chinese cities were built about 2000 B.C. along the Yellow River. Early Chinese rulers built the Grand Canal and the Great Wall. The Shang was China's first dynasty.

➡ Mesopotamia is the land between the Tigris and Euphrates Rivers. Sumerian civilization began there about 3000 B.C. They invented cuneiform, a writing system, and a counting system.

➡ Sargon I ruled Akkad. He united the Sumerian city-states.

➡ Hammurabi ruled Babylon in about 1800 B.C. He organized laws into a written code.

➡ The Phoenicians were sea traders. They invented a 22-letter alphabet.

➡ The Bible tells the history of the Hebrew people. Their first leader was Abraham. Another leader, Moses, led them from Egypt to Canaan where they established kingdoms. The Hebrews believed in one, all-powerful god, Yahweh. He gave Moses ten commandments. They were the basis of Judaism.

➡ Assyrian armies began building an empire in Mesopotamia about 900 B.C. The capital, Nineveh, had a very large library. Nineveh fell in 612 B.C.

➡ The capital of the Chaldean empire was Babylon. Nebuchadnezzar made it a beautiful city and he made the empire larger.

➡ Cyrus the Great of Persia captured Babylon in 538 B.C. Persian rulers built a huge empire. To rule it better, Darius divided it into provinces. Good roads linked the empire.

➡ Zoroaster introduced a new religion in Persia. It was based on a struggle between good and evil.

➡ Egyptian civilization began along the Nile River. In about 3100 B.C., Menes united Upper and Lower Egypt. The Old Kingdom began. Egyptians believed in an afterlife. They built pyramids as tombs for the pharaohs.

➡ The Middle Kingdom began about 2040 B.C. Egypt was united again. In this period, kings were buried in rock tombs. The Hyksos invaded Egypt about 1630 B.C.

➡ The New Kingdom began about 1600 B.C. Egypt grew into a powerful empire. Egyptians invented paper and produced great artwork. The Persian Empire conquered Egypt and ruled it until 332 B.C.

Comprehension: Identifying Facts

On a separate sheet of paper, use the words from the Word Bank to complete each sentence.

WORD BANK

Assyrian
Brahman
China
Harappa
Mesopotamia
Moses
Nebuchadnezzar
Phoenicians
Ra
Shang

1) The first Indian civilization was centered in the city of _____ .

2) For the Hindus of India, everything is God, or _____ .

3) The Great Wall of _____ is a wonder of the ancient world.

4) The first dynasty, or family of rulers, of China was the _____ .

5) The Sumerians built city-states in the land between two rivers known as _____ .

6) The ancient _____ became famous sailors.

7) _____ led the Hebrew people out of slavery in Egypt.

8) The _____ army had iron weapons and could easily defeat other people.

9) _____ made Babylon the most beautiful city in the ancient Middle East.

10) _____ was the name of the sun-god of Egypt.

Comprehension: Multiple Choice

On a separate sheet of paper, write the letter of the answer that correctly completes each sentence.

1) Egypt was the gift of the _____ River.
   a. Nile   c. Indus
   b. Ganges   d. Yangtze

2) On rivers, civilizations can transport _____ .
   a. traders   c. kings
   b. soldiers   d. all of the above

3) A _____ is a seasonal wind.

a. monsoon   c. pictogram

b. bronze   d. hieroglyphic

4) The sacred book of the Jewish people is the _____ .

a. Vedas   c. Papyrus

b. Bible   d. Sanskrit

5) One of the earliest written languages was _____ .

a. English   c. Sanskrit

b. Latin   d. Spanish

Comprehension: Understanding Main Ideas

On a separate sheet of paper, write the answer to each question. Use complete sentences, or statements.

1) Why did ancient civilizations all start in river valleys?

2) What did the Hebrew religion have in common with the religion of the Egyptian pharaoh Ikhnaton?

3) What is the difference between a country and an empire?

Critical Thinking: Write Your Opinion

1) Does the Middle East deserve the name "the cradle of civilization"? Explain your answer.

2) In this unit you have studied the ancient Indians, Chinese, Sumerians, Akkadians, Babylonians, Phoenicians, Hebrews, Assyrians, Chaldeans, Persians, and Egyptians. Which of these have given the greatest gift to the modern world? Explain your answer.

| Test-Taking Tip | Before you begin an exam, skim through the whole test to find out what is expected of you. |

"Here are set forth the researches of Herodotus of Halicarnassus, that men's actions may not in time be forgotten nor things great and wonderful, accomplished whether by Greeks or barbarians, go without report, nor, especially, the cause of the wars between one and the other."

—Herodotus, Greek historian, introducing his *History*, about 450 B.C.

Classical Traditions, Major Religions

2000 B.C. to A.D. 476

Think of yourself living in ancient Greece or Rome. Would you be an Athenian citizen? a Spartan soldier? an aristocrat? a tyrant? a helot? a patrician? a plebeian? a senator? a dictator? an emperor? After reading this next unit, you will know what each of these people did. Then you can decide!

In this unit you will learn why ancient Greece became a model for democratic government, art, literature, and philosophy. You will see how Rome organized a huge empire under one legal system and built fine roads that connected its empire. Today, thousands of years later, we can still see and feel the influence of ancient Greece and Rome.

Greek Civilization

2000 B.C. to 323 B.C.

The civilizations of India, China, and the Middle East developed in river valleys. However, the Greek civilization developed on a rocky peninsula. This geography greatly influenced the Greek people. In this chapter, you will learn about the city-states that developed because of this geography. You will also discover the many gifts the Greeks have contributed to our life.

Goals for Learning

▶ To explain how the geography of Greece influenced Greek civilization

▶ To describe the Mycenaean civilization

▶ To explain why the Greek city-states developed

▶ To identify the differences between Athens and Sparta

▶ To define direct democracy

▶ To explain why democracy came to an end in Greece

▶ To list the contributions the ancient Greeks made to world civilization

▶ To explain the importance of Alexander the Great

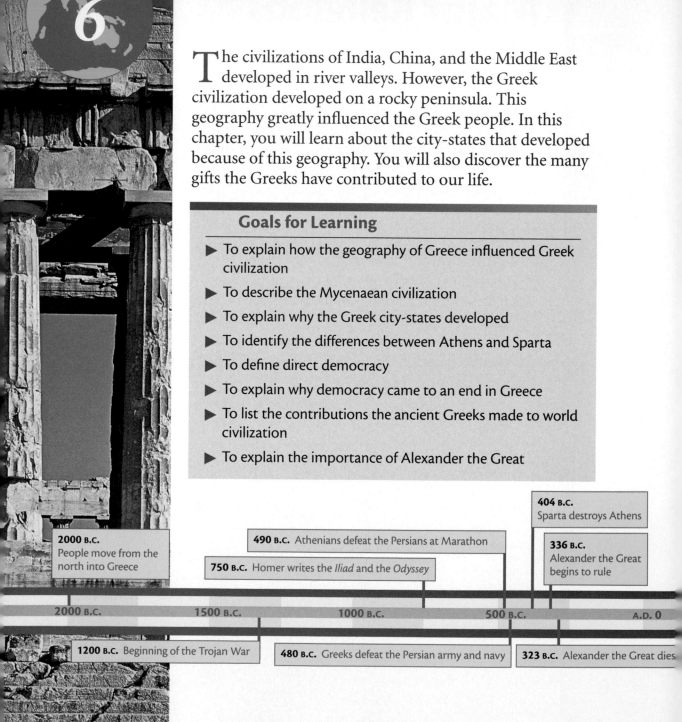

404 B.C. Sparta destroys Athens

2000 B.C. People move from the north into Greece

490 B.C. Athenians defeat the Persians at Marathon

750 B.C. Homer writes the *Iliad* and the *Odyssey*

336 B.C. Alexander the Great begins to rule

| 2000 B.C. | 1500 B.C. | 1000 B.C. | 500 B.C. | A.D. 0 |

1200 B.C. Beginning of the Trojan War

480 B.C. Greeks defeat the Persian army and navy

323 B.C. Alexander the Great dies

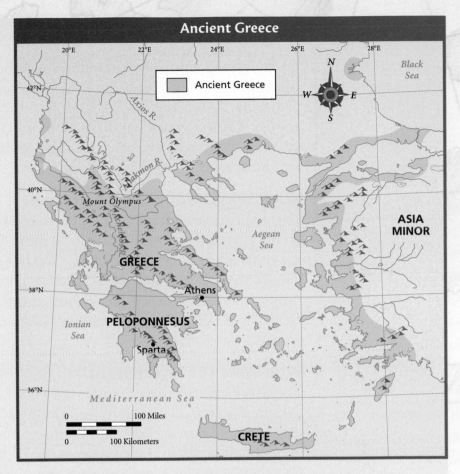

Ancient Greece

Ancient Greece

20°E   22°E   24°E   26°E   28°E

Black Sea

N

W   E

S

42°N

Axios R.

Haliakmon R.

40°N

Mount Olympus

ASIA MINOR

Aegean Sea

GREECE

38°N

Athens

Ionian Sea

PELOPONNESUS

Sparta

36°N

Mediterranean Sea

0   100 Miles

0   100 Kilometers

CRETE

Geography Skills

The geography of Greece has had an effect on its growth and its history. Its mountains made traveling by land hard. The Greeks took to the seas, which surrounded them on three sides, and became sailors. The geography of Greece helps us understand how its city-states developed their own cultures.

Study the map and answer the following questions:

1) What Greek city-state is located closest to the Aegean Sea?

2) Many islands surround Greece. What is the name of the largest island that lies near Greece?

3) What three seas surround Greece?

4) What tall mountain stands in the north of Greece?

5) What city-state is located in Peloponnesus?

◆Century
A period of a hundred years

Heroic
Brave and bold

Raid
To attack suddenly; a surprise attack

Unlike Mesopotamia, Egypt, India, and China, the Greek civilization did not develop around river valleys. Greece is a peninsula. Its mainland reaches out into the Mediterranean Sea like the fingers of a hand. One ancient Greek teacher said that the Greeks lived on the shores of the sea "like frogs around a pond."

What Was the Minoan Civilization?

The first people to develop a civilization in this area lived on the island of Crete. In 1900, Sir Arthur Evans discovered the ruins of this island civilization. One town he dug up was Knossos. It probably had a population of 100,000 people in ancient times. Evans named this island civilization Minoan because a legend said that a king named Minos once ruled it.

Who Were the Mycenaeans?

The Greek civilization came after the Minoan. About 2000 B.C., people from the north moved southward into the peninsula of Greece. Historians call these people the Achaeans. They built walled cities in the southern part of Greece. Warrior kings ruled these cities. Their most important city was Mycenae. Because of this city, historians call the Achaeans by a second name—the Mycenaeans.

These warlike people sailed to other cities around the Aegean Sea and **raided,** or attacked, them. Their most famous attack was on the city of Troy around 1200 B.C. Hundreds of years, or **centuries,** later, Greeks saw this time in their history as an age of heroes. The Trojan War became a symbol of **heroic,** or brave and bold, actions.

How Do We Know About the Trojan War?

We remember the Trojan War because of two long poems—the *Iliad* and the *Odyssey*. A blind poet named Homer probably wrote them about 500 years after the war ended. He spoke or sung the stories. For centuries, the Greeks continued to sing these poems. In this way, they

The Lion's Gate at Mycenae and similar ruins show what Mycenaean buildings were like.

remembered the story of the war. Then, many years after Homer died, someone wrote them down.

Why Did the Mycenaeans Fight the War?

According to Homer, the Mycenaeans fought the Trojans because of a beautiful woman named Helen. She was the wife of an Achaean king. Paris, a son of the king of Troy, took her back to Troy. The Achaeans fought the Trojan War to win Helen back.

How Did the Mycenaeans Win the War?

After ten years of war, the Mycenaeans destroyed Troy with a clever trick. They pretended to sail away from Troy. But they left behind a giant wooden horse. The Trojans thought that they had won the war and that the Mycenaeans had left behind a victory gift. So they opened their gates and brought the wooden horse within the city's thick, protective walls. Then they closed their gates. They thought they had locked the enemy out. But instead, they had locked the enemy in! Mycenaean warriors hid inside the wooden horse! During the night, these warriors silently left the horse and opened the gates of Troy. The rest of the Mycenaean army poured into the city and destroyed it.

SECTION 1 REVIEW On a separate sheet of paper, write *True* if the statement is true or *False* if the statement is not true. Make each false statement true by changing the underlined word.

1) The Minoan civilization came <u>after</u> the Mycenaean civilization.

2) The Minoan civilization was located on the island of <u>Crete.</u>

3) The Mycenaeans fought a <u>20</u>-year war with Troy.

4) They fought the war because Paris, a son of the king of <u>Troy,</u> had stolen the beautiful Helen.

5) We can read the story of the Trojan War in the *Iliad* and the <u>Bible.</u>

What do you think

Do you think the Mycenaeans won the Trojan War fairly?

♦Acropolis
A hill on which the people in a Greek city built their main temple

♦Aristocrat
A member of the powerful ruling class

Independent
Self governing, separate, free

♦Polis
The Greek name for a city-state

Theater
A place where people present plays

Greece is rocky and mountainous. In ancient times, the mountains kept the people isolated from one another. So the Greeks had many small settlements or city-states. They called each city-state a "**polis.**" Each polis was **independent,** or self-governing. A Greek was a citizen of the polis, or city-state.

The Greeks built their polis around a hill called an **acropolis.** On this high ground stood their main temple. Below the acropolis, they built homes and a marketplace. They also built **theaters** where they enjoyed plays and meeting places for the government.

What Kinds of Government Did the Greeks Try?

Over a period of time, the Greek city-states tried several different forms of government. In 800 B.C., kings ruled and passed their power to their sons. By 700 B.C., a small group of families with large amounts of land had taken over. We call these powerful families **aristocrats.** They also passed the right to rule from father to son.

The acropolis was a hill overlooking the city where temples were built. This photo shows the acropolis at Athens—the most magnificent of all in the Greek city-states.

◆Democracy
Rule by the people

◆Tyrant
A leader who rules by force and not by law

In about 600 B.C., strong leaders began to use force to take over the government of several city-states. We call such a person a **tyrant.** At first, tyrants kept the peace and passed fair laws. They also helped trade grow. But then some tyrants became cruel and unjust. Today, the word *tyrant* means anyone who uses power in a cruel and unfair way.

What Is the Greatest Contribution of the Greeks?

A leader named Solon helped create **democracy,** or rule by the people, in Athens. In 594 B.C., the Athenian leaders were fighting among themselves. Solon set out to improve the government. Because of his improvements, the average citizens of Athens had political power for the first time. Democracy has become the most important contribution the ancient Greeks made to civilization.

SECTION 2 REVIEW On a separate sheet of paper, write the word from the Word Bank that completes each sentence.

WORD BANK

acropolis

Athenians

democracy

polis

Solon

1) A _____ is a Greek city-state.

2) On the _____ in each city-state, the people built their main temple.

3) The form of government known as _____ is the most important contribution the ancient Greeks made to civilization.

4) The _____ were the first Greeks to develop a democratic government.

5) A leader named _____ helped to create the democratic form of government.

What do you think

Why do you think the Greek people built their main temple on a hill in each city-state?

Athenian democracy meant rule by only some people, not all. Only 40,000 of the 300,000 Athenians had the right to **vote,** or choose leaders and pass laws. Only citizens had this right, and only Athenian men could be citizens. Women, the more than 100,000 slaves, and Greeks from other city-states could not be citizens.

An Athenian leader expected three things of each citizen. He had to be loyal to Athens. He had to take part in the government. And he had to defend the city when necessary.

Why Did the Athenians Change Their Direct Democracy?

At first, each Athenian citizen voted on every law. We call this a **direct democracy.** Soon, however, the number of citizens at the city **assembly,** or meeting, became too large. So the government created a council of 500 citizens.

The government chose the members of this council by **lottery.** That is, they picked names from a container. In that way, each citizen had an equal chance of being chosen. The council members served for one year. During that time, they carried out the day-by-day **public,** or governmental, business of Athens.

A Greek legend says that the goddess, Athena, named Athens after herself. This is the "Contemplating Athena" sculpture.

How Large Was an Athenian Jury?

Athenian courts did not use judges, but they did use large **juries**. A jury listens to a case in court and decides the outcome. Each year, the Athenians chose 6,000 citizens by lottery to serve on juries.

Between 201 and 501 people made up each jury. (In the United States, juries usually have 12 members.) When a court case was serious, 1,000 citizens might serve on the jury. Why so many? Because Athenians believed that no one could **bribe,** or pay, a large jury to make a certain decision.

Why Did People Come to Athens?

Athens was near a seaport. Its sea trade helped this city-state grow in wealth and power. Because the citizens had money to pay artists, writers, and teachers, many of them came to Athens. They created beautiful art and built beautiful buildings. They started schools that lasted for centuries.

SECTION 3 REVIEW On a separate sheet of paper, write answers to these questions.

1) How many slaves lived in ancient Athens?

2) Which people were not allowed to vote in Athens?

3) What is a direct democracy?

4) Why did the Athenian citizens begin to use a lottery for their government meetings?

5) How did Athenian juries differ from American juries?

What do you think

Do you think large juries are better than small ones? Why or why not?

Enslave
To force people to become slaves

◆**Helot**
A slave in Sparta

Migrate
To move from one place to another

Sparta, another city-state, was located on a peninsula in southern Greece called the Peloponnesus. Around 1100 B.C., **migrating,** or moving, people settled in the area. They built the city of Sparta and became known as Spartans. They **enslaved** the farmers who already lived there and called these new slaves **helots.** The helots farmed the land surrounding the city.

What Was Sparta's "Wall of Men"?

For every Spartan, there were five helots. This many slaves was a danger to the Spartans. What if the helots rebelled? Yet, the leaders built no protective wall around their city. They thought that their military skills would protect them. According to one leader, they had a wall of men instead of bricks.

About 600 B.C., the helots did rebel. The Spartans defeated them, but the event frightened them. So they sent people to spy on the helots. They also killed any helot who started to make trouble.

What Was Life Like for a Spartan Man?

In Sparta, government officials examined each baby. They left a sick child on a hill to die. When a boy was seven, the government took him from his parents. It kept him hungry and expected him to steal food. And if he got caught, the leaders punished him severely. At the age of 20, he became a citizen. At 30, he married. Until age 60, he lived in a military camp with all the other soldiers.

Spartan women were to be supportive of their husbands when the men went to war.

**Writing
About History**

Imagine that you are an Athenian visiting Sparta or a Spartan visiting Athens. In your notebook, write a letter home. Describe what you have seen. Tell what you think of this city-state.

Architecture
The art of building

◆Patriotic
Loyal toward one's country; love for one's country

What do you think ?

Why do you think the Spartans wanted boys to steal and then punished them if they got caught?

What Did Spartan Women Say to the Men?

Spartan women were independent and **patriotic,** or loyal, to their city-state. When a husband went off to war, his wife told him two things: Come home as a victor carrying your shield, or come home dead, being carried on your shield. He was to do one or the other, nothing else.

What Price Did the Spartans Pay for Being Warriors?

Art or **architecture,** which is the art of building, did not interest the Spartans. They did not trade with others, and they feared new ideas. Yet, many people thought that they were the best soldiers in Greece and maybe in the whole world!

SECTION 4 REVIEW Choose the letter of the answer that correctly completes each sentence. Write your answer on a separate sheet of paper.

1) Sparta was located on the _____ peninsula.
   a. Athenian   c. Sinai
   b. Indian   d. Peloponnesus

2) The helots were Spartan _____.
   a. citizens   c. traders
   b. slaves   d. officials

3) For every Spartan citizen there were _____ helots.
   a. 5   b. 10   c. 20   d. 100

4) Spartan boys began training to be soldiers at the age of _____.
   a. 7   b. 20   c. 30   d. 60

5) A Spartan woman wanted her warrior husband to come home carrying his _____ or to be carried home on it.
   a. horse   c. spear
   b. shield   d. chariot

◆Fleet
A group of ships

Outnumber
To have more soldiers, ships, or war machines than someone else has

Between 500 and 400 B.C., the Greeks fought several wars. They fought the first two against the huge and powerful Persian Empire. It lay to the east of Greece. These wars united the city-states and made the Greeks proud. In the next war, the city-states of Athens and Sparta battled. We call this the Peloponnesian War. It lasted for 27 years.

Why Did the Persians Invade Greece?

In 519 B.C., the Persians conquered a group of people called the Ionian Greeks who lived in Asia Minor. Twenty years later, in 499 B.C., they asked the mainland Greeks to help them rebel. Athens sent warships, but the Ionian Greeks could not win their freedom. All this made King Darius of Persia angry.

In 490 B.C., Darius sent 600 ships and thousands of soldiers to invade Greece. According to legend, Athens sent the runner Pheidippides to ask the Spartans for help. He ran 150 miles in two days. But the Spartans were celebrating a religious feast and refused to help until the next full moon.

Who Won the Battle of Marathon?

The Persian **fleet,** or group of ships, landed at the Bay of Marathon. (Marathon was about 25 miles northeast of Athens.) The Persian army was much bigger than the Athenian army, and the **outnumbered** Athenians had no one to help them.

After a few days, the Persians decided to attack Athens by sea. While they were loading their ships, the Athenians attacked and defeated them. A Greek legend says that Pheidippides ran 25 miles from Marathon to Athens to announce the victory. When he arrived, he yelled, "Nike!" or victory. Then he fell dead, worn out by his run. Today, we remember what Pheidippides did in the modern-day 26-mile marathon run.

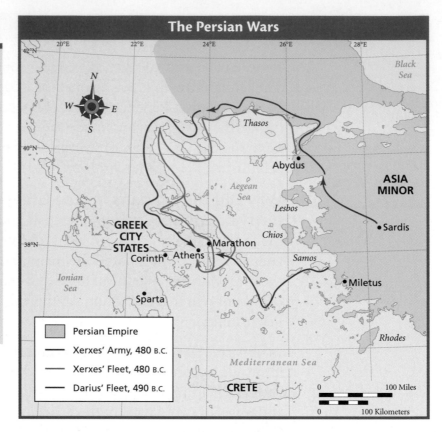

The Persian Wars

This map shows
Greece and the
Persian Empire
between 490 B.C.
and 480 B.C. In
what direction did
Darius and his fleet
sail to get to
Athens? In what
direction would a
runner run from
Marathon to
Athens?

Persian Empire
Xerxes' Army, 480 B.C.
Xerxes' Fleet, 480 B.C.
Darius' Fleet, 490 B.C.

What Happened at Thermopylae?

Ten years later in 480 B.C., Xerxes, the son of Darius, sent 200,000 soldiers and nearly 1,000 ships against the Greeks. This time, 20 Greek city-states joined together to meet the Persian invaders. The Spartans took charge of the army; Athens supplied the navy.

The great Persian army had little trouble as it moved through northern Greece. Then it came to a narrow mountain pass called Thermopylae. There, 7,000 Spartans waited for the Persians. For several days, they stopped the Persian army from moving forward.

Then someone led the Persians behind the Greek army. The Spartan soldiers began to retreat to their ships. As the Persians marched forward, 300 Spartan warriors faced them. To protect the retreat of the others, they gave up their lives.

Who Won at Salamis?

The Persians marched almost 100 miles south and destroyed Athens. But the Athenians had already moved to Salamis, a small island nearby. More than 800 Persian ships attacked the Athenian navy near this island. Yet the Athenians defeated the powerful empire. How? The large Persian ships could not **maneuver,** or move easily, in the water. The smaller Greek ships destroyed them. Historians call this one of history's great sea battles. Defeated, King Xerxes returned to Persia. The Greeks had won the battle with a wooden wall of Athenian ships.

What Caused the Peloponnesian War?

In 477 B.C., more than 100 Greek city-states formed a military alliance. Each city-state agreed to give money or ships to be used to defend all of them. Athens led the alliance. During the next 30 years, the Athenians used the alliance money to rebuild Athens. This made Sparta and the other city-states angry.

In 431 B.C., war broke out between Athens and Sparta. We call it the Peloponnesian War because Sparta was located on the Peloponnesian peninsula. The war lasted 27 years and ended in 404 B.C. Sparta destroyed Athens. The war divided and weakened the other Greek city-states. They were unable to form a new alliance. Sparta tried to rule all of them.

In 371 B.C., the city-state of Thebes defeated Sparta. In 338 B.C., King Philip II of Macedon led his army from the north and conquered Greece. The Greeks lost their **independence,** or freedom. They no longer governed themselves. However, their ideas continued to influence the world.

Spartan soldiers were trained to be fighters from a very early age.

HERODOTUS: c. 480–430 B.C.

The Greek writer Herodotus was born in Asia Minor. He had enough money to travel widely, so he toured Egypt and the Middle East. He is known as "the father of history" because he wrote the first history of the ancient world. Herodotus wrote about events he saw. He also included stories and legends.

His book *History* has two main parts. The first describes the people of the huge Persian Empire. It is a travel guide to customs and geography. The other part tells about the wars between Persia and Greece. Most of what we know about this period comes from his books.

SECTION 5 REVIEW On a separate sheet of paper, write *True* if the statement is true or *False* if the statement is not true. Make each false statement true by changing the underlined word.

1) <u>Sparta</u> helped the Ionian Greeks rebel against Persia.

2) The <u>Athenians</u> defeated the army of King Darius at the Bay of Marathon in 490 B.C.

3) In 480 B.C., <u>Pheidippides,</u> the son of Darius, tried to defeat the Greeks.

4) The brave <u>Athenian</u> warriors lost the battle at Thermopylae.

5) In the Peloponnesian War, Sparta defeated <u>Persia.</u>

What do you think ?

Why do you think the Spartans won the Peloponnesian War?

Column
*A tall, solid
structure used to
support a building;
a pillar*

◆Goddess
A woman god

On the Athenian acropolis stand the ruins of a temple to Athena—a woman god, or **goddess.** We call the temple the Parthenon. Many people think it is one of the most beautiful buildings ever built. The Athenians built it after the Persian Wars ended. We call this period of time the "Golden Age of Athens."

Their love of beauty led the Greeks to create beautiful works of art. Besides making beautiful things with their hands, they used their minds. They asked questions about nature, society, and themselves. Their art and their search for truth are two of Greece's greatest contributions to civilization.

How Did Greek Architecture Please the Eye?

The Athenians built many beautiful public buildings and decorated them with fine works of art. Their Parthenon, with its 46 **columns,** or pillars, is 237 feet long and 110 feet wide. The builders knew that columns seem to bend when seen from a distance. So they made each column curve a little. Because of this, the columns seem to be perfectly straight when someone sees them from a distance.

The Parthenon, built in the 400s B.C. in Athens, is considered by many to be the most perfect building ever made. Several modern banks, government buildings, libraries, and schools were built using the Parthenon's design.

Why Did the Statue of Athena Shine?

A 39-foot-high statue of Athena stood inside the Parthenon. The great sculptor Phidias carved her face from ivory and gave the goddess a helmet of gold. In early morning, the rays of the rising sun made Athena shine! Greek sculptors also created beautiful figures of the human body. Their statues showed the human body as perfect, without any flaws.

What Are the Two Kinds of Greek Plays?

The Greeks invented the performing of plays in outdoor theaters. A group of actors, called the **chorus,** stood on stage and talked about what was happening in the play. Only men could act in a Greek play.

Greek playwriters wrote **tragedies** and **comedies.** In a tragedy, the gods defeat the hero. The hero is always smart and he always has courage. But he also has too much pride. He tries to achieve more than the gods want him to. After seeing a tragedy, the Greeks felt both sad and happy. They were sad because the hero met defeat. They were happy because the hero had shown courage and strength.

A Gift From the Muses

Ancient Greeks believed music was a gift from the gods. Their word for music meant "arts of the Muses." The Muses were nine goddesses. They looked after music (songs and dances), poetry, history, drama, and astronomy. Musical instruments also came from the gods. The lyre and the pipes were two popular instruments. A lyre is a small stringed instrument.

Some special humans also had the gift of music. The most famous was Orpheus. It was believed that even wild animals stopped to hear him play and sing.

Fine Arts

History in Your Life

Early Greek poets sang or chanted their verses. They played along on the lyre. Music was part of most special occasions. Some poets wrote lyrics for a chorus to sing. These songs often honored winners of athletic games. Music and dancing went with them. Greek drama used music, too. A chorus danced and sang between scenes in a play.

Some Greek theaters are still standing today. Greek plays were performed outdoors.

Philosopher
A person who seeks answers to what is true and what is good

Greek comedies made fun of important people or ideas. A writer named Aristophanes wrote many famous comedies. In his play *The Clouds,* he made fun of Socrates, a famous **philosopher,** who tried to find truth by asking questions.

What Do Philosophers Want to Prove?

In Greek, the word *philosopher* means "a lover of wisdom." Most philosophers ask questions to lead them to wisdom. They want to find truth. In fact, they want proof of the truth. They do not stop asking questions until they have this proof. Greece produced three of the greatest philosophers in history: Socrates, Plato, and Aristotle.

Why Did the Athenians Want to Get Rid of Socrates?

By asking questions, the philosopher Socrates forced people to examine what they believed. This great teacher always said, "Know thyself." He meant that people need to know why and what they believe. They need to look at why they think something is true, beautiful, just, or good.

Socrates questioned everything, even Athenian democracy. Many Athenians did not trust him. They had just lost the Peloponnesian War, and they thought that anyone who asked questions was unpatriotic.

In 399 B.C., when Socrates was 70 years old, the Athenian citizens spoke out against him. They said that his teachings hurt the young people of Athens. More than half of the 501 members of the jury voted against him. They said that he must kill himself by drinking poison. His friends and pupils arranged for his escape from Athens, but Socrates refused. He chose to obey the Athenian law, and was put to death.

What Was Plato's Republic?

Plato, a pupil of Socrates, was 28 years old when his teacher died. What the Athenians had done upset Plato. He wrote a book called *The Republic* about a made-up society. It was perfect, orderly, and just. In this society, three classes of people lived: workers, soldiers, and philosophers.

Plato's make-believe society was not a democracy. He thought that only the wisest men and women—philosophers—should rule. Why? Because they would decide things with their brains, not with their feelings. A fine teacher, Plato began a school in Greece that lasted for 900 years. We still study his ideas today.

What Kind of Things Did Aristotle Write About?

Plato's most famous pupil was Aristotle. He wrote important works on **astronomy** (the study of the stars); **biology** (the study of living things); **ethics** (the study of what is good and bad); **logic** (the study of how to think); **physics** (the study of matter); and **politics** (the study of government).

Today, we can only imagine what the death of Socrates looked like. This is one artist's version.

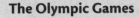

The Olympic Games

Today's Olympic Games come from ancient Greece. The Greeks loved sports. At that time, sporting contests were part of religious festivals. The Olympic Games began about 776 B.C. They were held at Olympia, sacred to the god Zeus.

Ancient Olympic athletes hoped to win glory for themselves and their city. Contests included foot races, boxing, the broad jump, and the discus throw. Unlike now, women could not compete. Nor were there any team sports.

The first modern Olympics took place in 1896 in Athens, Greece. They were the idea of a Frenchman, Pierre de Coubertin. Today, there are Olympic Games every two years. The winter games alternate with the summer games. They take place in different countries. The games include many new sports.

In his book *Politics*, Aristotle wrote about different kinds of governments. He said that no government was perfect. Just as we still study Plato's writings today, so we study what Aristotle had to say about government.

SECTION 6 REVIEW On a separate sheet of paper, write the word from the Word Bank that completes each sentence.

WORD BANK
Aristophanes
Aristotle
Phidias
Plato
Socrates

1) One Athenian writer of comedies was _____.

2) _____ created a statue of Athena for the Parthenon.

3) The philosopher _____ had to drink poison because the Athenians thought he was unpatriotic.

4) The philosopher _____ wrote a book about a government ruled by philosophers.

5) The philosopher _____ thought that no government was perfect.

What do you think

Do you think philosophers would make the best leaders of a country? Why or why not?

Aristotle's most famous pupil was Alexander, the son of Philip II of Macedon. After Philip II conquered the Greeks in 338 B.C., he planned to conquer Persia too. But he died before he could make that happen. So his son set out to conquer the world. Soon people would call him Alexander the Great.

What Did Alexander Conquer?

When Philip II died in 336 B.C., Alexander was 20. Two years later, Alexander marched eastward with 35,000 soldiers. They quickly conquered Asia Minor. At the eastern end of the Mediterranean, they defeated the armies of Darius III, the Persian king. Swinging south, Alexander freed Egypt from Persian rule. At the mouth of the Nile River, he built the city of Alexandria.

How Far Did Alexander's Army March?

Next, Alexander moved east again and conquered Babylon. He continued to move eastward, deeper into the Persian Empire. By 330 B.C., Alexander had defeated all the Persian armies. He was now king of Persia and dreamed of uniting the known world under one government.

For four more years, Alexander's tired army moved eastward. They went as far as the Indus River. For the Greeks, this was the end of the known world. Alexander wanted to push on, but his men begged him to turn back.

In 323 B.C., Alexander developed a fever in Babylon. Within a few days, the 32-year-old leader was dead. For 13 years, Alexander ruled. During that time he had changed the world.

Alexander the Great conquered many lands at a very young age.

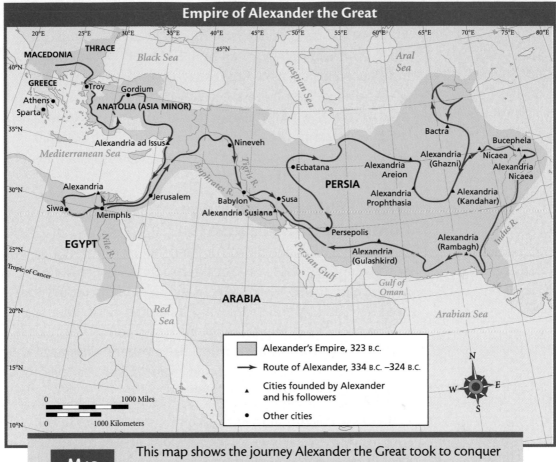

Empire of Alexander the Great

Legend:
- Alexander's Empire, 323 B.C.
- → Route of Alexander, 334 B.C.–324 B.C.
- ▲ Cities founded by Alexander and his followers
- • Other cities

MAP STUDY

This map shows the journey Alexander the Great took to conquer the known world. What do many of the cities he founded, or built, have in common? Which sea did his army pass by northern Persia? What body of land lies directly south of the Black Sea? In what direction is Persepolis from Athens?

What Is the Hellenistic Culture?

◆Hellenism
The blend of western and eastern cultures made possible by Alexander the Great

Alexander's huge empire fell apart after his death. His three generals divided the empire into three kingdoms—Macedon, Egypt, and Syria. These three kingdoms often fought each other. But one thing held them together—their Greek culture.

Throughout the Middle East, people adopted Greek customs. They spoke Greek, they built their buildings as the Greeks did, and they gave themselves Greek names. As Greek culture spread eastward, it blended with other cultures. We call this blend of eastern and western cultures **Hellenism.** The word comes from the Greek word "Hellas," which means "their own land."

Geometry
The study of the measurement of flat and round things

◆Hellenistic Age
The time between 323 B.C. and 31 B.C. when Greek culture influenced the world

Pulley
A wheel for a rope to pass over

What Made Alexandria Famous?

The people of the **Hellenistic Age** (323–31 B.C.) built great cities. Antioch, in Syria, had lighted streets, which the builders paved to make them smooth and level. However, Alexandria in Egypt was the greatest city in the Hellenistic Age. In fact, the lighthouse in its harbor was one of the seven wonders of the ancient world. More than 500,000 people lived in this center of learning. Its library had nearly 500,000 works for them to read.

What Did the Hellenistic Age Contribute to Civilization?

During this time, Euclid of Alexandria put together everything people knew about **geometry**—the study of measurements. Some schools in the twentieth century still used his book. Archimedes was Euclid's student. He used mathematics to explain how to lift heavy things with levers and **pulleys.** (A pulley is a wheel for a rope to pass over.) Archimedes said, "Give me a place to stand, and a lever long enough, and I will move the Earth."

Hellenistic culture shaped the Mediterranean world for nearly 300 years. However, Alexander's dream did not come true during this time. He hoped to create an empire ruled by one government. The Greeks did not do this, but the Romans did. Their homeland lay to the northwest of Greece.

SECTION 7 REVIEW On a separate sheet of paper, write answers to these questions.

1) How far eastward did the empire of Alexander the Great go?

2) What city did Alexander build in Egypt?

3) For how many years did Alexander rule the known world?

4) What word describes the blend of eastern and western cultures after Alexander's death?

5) What mathematical information did Euclid organize?

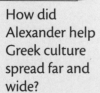

What do you think?

How did Alexander help Greek culture spread far and wide?

Pericles Praises Athens

Pericles was a great leader of Athens. In about 431 B.C., he made a famous speech. It honored Athenians who had died in the war with Sparta. It is known as "Pericles' Funeral Oration." In the speech, Pericles explains why Athens is great. He tells what Athenians care about.

Thucydides was the greatest Athenian historian. This speech is in his History of the Peloponnesian War. Thucydides probably heard it. This is the way Thucydides remembered the speech. These are probably not Pericles' exact words.

Our form of government does not enter into rivalry with the institutions of others. We do not copy our neighbors, but are an example to them. It is true that we are called a democracy, for government is in the hands of the many and not of the few. But while the law secures equal justice to all alike in their private disputes, the claim of excellence is also recognized; and when a citizen is in any way distinguished, he is elected to the public service, not as a matter of privilege, but as the reward of merit. Neither is poverty a bar, but a man may benefit his country whatever may be the obscurity of his condition.

And we have not forgotten to provide for our weary spirits many relaxations from toil; we have regular games and sacrifices throughout the year; at home the style of our life is refined; and the delight which we daily feel in all these things helps to banish melancholy. Because of the greatness of

Pericles: c. 495–425 B.C.

our city, the fruits of the whole earth flow in upon us, so that we enjoy the goods of other countries as freely as of our own.

And in the matter of education, whereas the Spartans from early youth are always undergoing laborious exercises which are to make them brave, we live at ease, and yet are equally ready to face the perils which they face.

. . . For we are lovers of the beautiful, yet simple in our tastes, and we cultivate the mind without loss of manliness. . . . An Athenian citizen does not neglect the state because he takes care of his own household; and even those of us who are engaged in business have a very fair idea of politics. We alone regard a man who takes no interest in public affairs, not as a harmless, but as a useless character. . . .

Source Reading Wrap-Up

1) According to Pericles, why is Athens a democracy?

2) Why is a person elected to public service?

3) How do Athenians relax?

4) According to Pericles, how are the Athenians different from the Spartans?

5) How important are public affairs to Athenians? How can you tell this from the speech you just read?

Greek Mythology

Have you ever admired the strength of Hercules? He is a famous person in Greek mythology. Myths are stories that try to answer questions about natural events. Why does the sun move across the sky? Why do the seasons change? What causes thunder and lightning?

The Greeks believed in many gods. The chief family included twelve gods and goddesses. They lived on Mount Olympus. These gods were powerful, but not perfect. They acted like the Greeks themselves. They had quarrels. They got angry. Often they took part in people's lives. Many Greek poems and plays retold myths about the gods.

Zeus was the father of the gods. He was lord of the sky. When he was angry, he threw lightning bolts. His brother, Poseidon, ruled the sea. His other brother, Hades, ruled the underworld. One of his sons was Apollo, god of the sun. The Greeks believed that every morning he drove his fiery chariot across the sky. Apollo was also the god of music and medicine. Artemis was his twin sister. She was the goddess of the moon. Artemis protected the young, wild animals, and women. Zeus's favorite child was Athena. She protected city life, especially Athens.

Myths also tell about giants and heroes. Atlas was a giant. He and other giants went to war against the Olympians. They lost. Zeus punished Atlas harshly. He would have to hold the world on his shoulders forever. A book of maps, an atlas, gets its name from this giant.

Some Greek heroes were part god. Others were human beings with special gifts. The greatest hero was Hercules. He was brave and strong. He also had a quick temper. One story tells how he had to perform 12 difficult tasks. Then he would be forgiven for a terrible crime.

The story of the Trojan War has many heroes. Achilles was the greatest Greek warrior. When he was a child, his mother dipped him in a magic river. Its water would always protect him. She did not notice that the heel she held stayed dry. His "Achilles' heel" was the one place where he could be hurt. At Troy an arrow struck his heel, and he died.

The hero Odysseus was both brave and clever. He thought of the idea for the Trojan Horse. That trick helped the Greeks capture Troy. After the war, it took him many years to get home. Homer's *Odyssey* tells of his adventures on the way.

Spotlight Story Wrap-Up

1) What is a myth?

2) Where did the main Greek gods live?

3) Who was the father of the gods?

4) What was Atlas's punishment?

5) Who are two heroes of the Trojan War?

➡ Greece is on a hilly peninsula in the Mediterranean Sea. The Minoan civilization started on the island of Crete. About 2000 B.C., the Achaeans built walled cities in southern Greece. Their main city was Mycenae.

➡ The Mycenaeans fought a 20-year war with Troy. Two long poems by Homer, the *Iliad* and the *Odyssey*, tell about heroes of the Trojan War.

➡ The Greeks lived in small city-states. Each was a *polis*. At the center was a hill, or *acropolis*, and temple.

➡ The city-state of Athens began the first democracy. Its citizens ran the government. Only Athenian men were citizens. Women, slaves, and foreign residents were not citizens.

➡ Sparta was a city-state on a peninsula called the Peloponnesus. Slaves called helots farmed the land.

➡ Spartan men were soldiers all their lives. Spartan women expected them to fight heroically. Unlike Athenians, Spartans did not care about trade or the arts.

➡ The Greek city-states united to fight the Persian Empire twice. In 490 B.C., King Darius of Persia tried to invade Greece. The Greeks defeated the Persians at Marathon.

➡ Persians under Xerxes invaded Greece again in 480 B.C. Spartan soldiers held off the Persians at Thermopylae. The Athenian navy defeated them at Salamis.

➡ In 431 B.C., Athens and Sparta went to war against each other. This was the Peloponnesian War. Sparta won. The war weakened all the city-states. In 338 B.C., Philip of Macedon conquered Greece.

➡ Athens's "Golden Age" followed the Persian Wars. Greek writers invented two kinds of drama—tragedy and comedy. Socrates, Plato, and Aristotle were Greek philosophers who explored ideas.

➡ Alexander the Great was the son of Philip II of Macedon. Alexander had studied with Aristotle. He became ruler of Greece in 336 B.C. Alexander's army conquered the Persian Empire.

➡ Alexander died in 323 B.C. His conquests helped spread Greek culture. A new culture, Hellenism, began. Alexandria, Egypt, was a center of Hellenistic culture.

Comprehension: Identifying Facts

On a separate sheet of paper, use the words from the Word Bank to complete each sentence.

<table>
<tr><td>

WORD BANK

Alexander

Aristophanes

Aristotle

Homer

Minos

Parthenon

Philip II

Plato

Socrates

Xerxes
</td></tr>
</table>

1) The Minoan civilization is named after King _____.

2) _____ was a blind poet who wrote the *Iliad*.

3) In 480 B.C., the Greeks defeated the Persian Army of King _____.

4) _____ wrote a play called *The Clouds,* which made fun of the philosopher Socrates.

5) The name of the temple of Athena in Athens is the _____.

6) In 399 B.C., the Athenians found the philosopher _____ guilty of teaching things that hurt the young people of Athens.

7) The philosopher _____ wrote *The Republic* about a perfect society.

8) The philosopher _____ wrote a book about the different kinds of governments.

9) Alexander the Great was the son of _____ of Macedon.

10) The conquering army of _____ spread Greek culture into Asia.

Comprehension: Multiple Choice

On a separate sheet of paper, write the letter of the answer that correctly completes each sentence.

1) The Greek city-state that trained all its citizens to be soldiers was _____.

   a. Persia   c. Sparta

   b. Athens   d. Alexandria

2) The philosopher Aristotle wrote books on _____.

   a. ethics   c. astronomy

   b. biology   d. all of the above

3) The Athenians defeated the Persian fleet at the battle of _____ in 480 B.C.

   a. Marathon   c. Thermopylae

   b. Salamis   d. Babylon

4) Alexander the Great's army fought against the _____ Empire.

   a. Persian   c. Mycenaean

   b. Roman   d. Minoan

5) The _____ civilization developed on the island of Crete.

   a. Mycenaean   c. Minoan

   b. Persian   d. Greek

Comprehension: Understanding Main Ideas

On a separate sheet of paper, write the answer to each question. Use complete sentences, or statements.

1) Greece is on a peninsula and has many rocky mountains. What effect did this geography have on its history?

2) Why did the Greeks want to defeat the Persian Empire?

3) What are three contributions the Greek civilization made to the world? Give three details of each contribution.

Critical Thinking: Write Your Opinion

1) Which ancient Greek city-state would you want to live in—Athens or Sparta? Give three reasons why.

2) Does Alexander deserve to be called "the Great"? Why or why not?

| Test-Taking Tip | Before you begin a test, look it over quickly. Try to set aside enough time to complete each section. |

Chapter 7

The Roman Republic

753 B.C. to 27 B.C.

The ancient Romans had a legend that Romulus and Remus founded Rome in 753 B.C. Cruel leaders ruled the Romans until 509 B.C. In that year, they rebelled and created a republic. In this chapter, you will learn about the patricians who ruled this republic. You will also learn about the plebeians who fought as citizen-soldiers for the republic. Finally, you will learn what happened to bring the Roman Republic to an end.

Goals for Learning

▶ To describe the early history of the Roman peninsula

▶ To tell the story of the legend of how Rome was founded

▶ To define the term *republic*

▶ To explain the organization of the Roman republican form of government

▶ To compare the Roman plebeian and patrician classes

▶ To explain how Rome lost its republican form of government

▶ To identify Julius Caesar and Octavian and explain their importance to Roman history

753 B.C.
Legendary founding of the city of Rome

509 B.C.
The Roman Republic begins

264 B.C.
The First Punic War begins

149 B.C.
The Third Punic War begins

44 B.C.
Julius Caesar is assassinated

27 B.C.
The Roman Republic ends

600 B.C.	400 B.C.	200 B.C.	A.D. 0

494 B.C.
Plebeians are given some political rights

218 B.C.
The Second Punic War begins

60 B.C.
The First Triumvirate begins

45 B.C.
Julius Caesar is made dictator for life

Italy

Italy is a boot-shaped peninsula in southern Europe. It has two mountain ranges. One of these—the Alps—forms the northern border of Italy. This is an important natural barrier, or wall, between Italy and other nations. Three important rivers flow through Italy. Its capital city sits next to one of them—the Tiber.

Study the map and answer the following questions:

Geography Skills

1) What is the name of the mountain range that lies northeast of the city of Rome?

2) What are the names of three rivers in Italy?

3) What is the name of the large island that lies near the southern tip of Italy?

4) What is the name of the sea along Italy's east coast?

5) What European country lies to the far northwest of Italy?

◆**Advanced**
Beyond the beginning stage

◆**Founded**
To have begun a country or city; to have built a city

◆**Patrician**
In Rome, a person who owned land and helped a ruler govern

◆**Senate**
A governing body

Rome sits on the western side of the boot-shaped peninsula of Italy. It is 20 miles inland on the Tiber River.

No one really knows how or when Rome began. An ancient legend says that the twin brothers Romulus and Remus **founded,** or began, it in 753 B.C. According to this legend, the baby twins were left to die on the banks of the Tiber River. A she-wolf found them and cared for them. Then a shepherd killed the wolf and raised the twins as his sons. As men, Romulus and Remus built a city. But they fought over who should rule. Romulus killed his brother, became king, and named the city Rome.

Who Were the Latins and the Etruscans?

A group of people called Latins lived on a plain called Latium. This plain lay south of the Tiber River. This tribe spoke Latin. But because they could not write, they have left us no written records. However, they did build small villages on hills near the Tiber. Rome grew from these settlements.

People from Greece built several city-states on the southern coast of the Italian peninsula. They brought their Greek culture with them. The Latin people learned many things from their Greek neighbors.

The Etruscans were a tribe of people who lived north of the Tiber. Like the Greeks, they were **advanced.** They had a written language and made pottery and fine clothing. They were also expert sailors and traded throughout the Mediterranean. By 600 B.C., the Etruscans had conquered Rome and the plain of Latium. They drained the marshes around Rome to create more living space.

Etruscan kings ruled the Romans for more than a century. The king appointed men to a **senate.** This governing body helped him make decisions. The senate members controlled large amounts of land. The Romans called them **patricians,** which is the Latin word for father. They were thought to be the "fathers of the state."

This map shows the people who lived in ancient Italy. Besides the Etruscans and the Greeks, what other people lived in Italy at this time? In Chapter 3, you learned about the Phoenicians. According to this map, where did they settle?

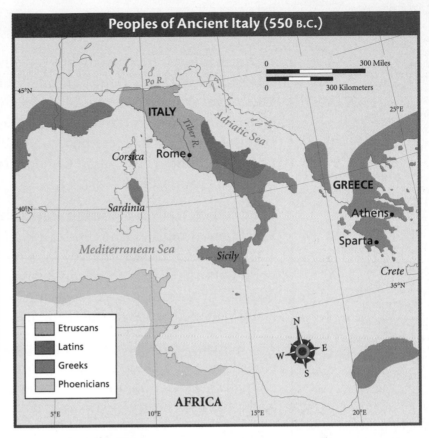

Peoples of Ancient Italy (550 B.C.)

SECTION 1 REVIEW On a separate sheet of paper, write answers to these questions.

1) According to Roman legend, who founded Rome?

2) What was the name of the tribe that lived to the south of the Tiber River and built settlements on the surrounding hills?

3) What people ruled the Romans for a century?

4) What does the word *patrician* mean in Latin?

5) Why did the Romans call wealthy landowners patricians?

What do you think

Do you think the legend about Romulus and Remus is at all true? Why or why not?

◆Consul
A Roman leader who served a one-year term

◆Dictator
A person who rules a country with force and makes all the laws

◆Representative
A person who speaks and governs for others

◆Republic
A type of government with no king in which a few people represent, or speak for, the many

◆Term
A period of time a person serves in a government office

◆Veto
To say no to a ruling or law

Etruscan kings were cruel. In 509 B.C., the patricians rebelled. They defeated the king and set up a different kind of government—a **republic.** In a republic, citizens vote to elect **representatives,** or people who will speak and govern for them. (In a republic, rule does not pass from parent to child.) This Roman Republic lasted from 509 B.C. to 27 B.C.—almost 500 years.

Who Governed the Roman Republic?

The Romans replaced the Etruscan king with two **consuls.** They managed the government for a one-year **term,** or period of time. Each consul could **veto,** or say no to, a decision by the other consul. Serving only one year and being vetoed kept the consuls from becoming too powerful.

The Roman senate, made up of 300 patricians, helped the consuls rule. It had the power to pass laws. In times of war, it could choose a **dictator** for six months. This kind of leader has full control of laws, and rules with force.

What Class Ruled Rome?

The Roman Republic was not a democracy because it allowed only patricians to vote. They were from the oldest

The Roman senate was made up of 300 patricians.

and the richest families in Rome. This wealthy patrician class made up only 10 percent of the **population,** or all the people in Rome. Yet, patricians ran the government. They thought of themselves as the ruling class.

Who Were the Plebeians?

Most Romans were not wealthy. They were small farmers, merchants, and **laborers**—people who did hard work with their hands. Yet they were citizens of Rome. The Romans called them **plebeians,** which means "from the common people." The plebeians were thought to be related to the Latin people.

As citizens, the plebeians paid taxes and served in the army. But they had little power. They could not marry out of their class. Also, the patricians could sell plebeians into slavery if they did not pay their debts.

How Did the Plebeians Gain Political Rights?

The plebeians had one important power. They were citizen-soldiers. The patricians needed them to defend Rome against its enemies. In 494 B.C., the Roman Republic gave the plebeians the right to **elect,** or choose by voting, two **tribunes.** These two representatives protected the rights of the plebeian class.

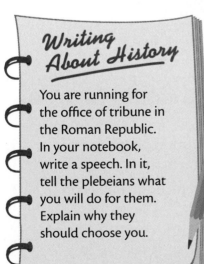

Writing About History

You are running for the office of tribune in the Roman Republic. In your notebook, write a speech. In it, tell the plebeians what you will do for them. Explain why they should choose you.

As time passed, the number of tribunes increased from two to ten. They sat outside the door of the senate and shouted "Veto!" when they did not like a law that a patrician wanted. By 350 B.C., the senate could pass only those laws to which the tribunes said yes.

What Is the "Law of the Twelve Tables"?

In the beginning of the republic, the senate did not write down the laws it passed. The plebeians were not sure what the laws were. As a result, patrician judges were unfair to plebeians. Soon, they demanded that the senate write the laws down. Around 450 B.C., the senate wrote their laws on 12 bronze tablets. Then they put them in the marketplace. Every school child had to learn these laws.

◆Political
Having to do with governing

When Did the Republic Become More Democratic?

By 280 B.C., Rome had become more democratic. Plebeians could hold **political,** or governing, offices. They could also serve in the senate. In fact, one consul could come from the plebeian class. Still, problems continued between the patricians and the plebeians. The struggle between these two classes became an important part of Roman history for several centuries.

SECTION 2 REVIEW On a separate sheet of paper, write the word from the Word Bank that completes each sentence.

WORD BANK
Etruscan
patricians
plebeians
republic
tribune

1) In 509 B.C. some Romans rebelled against the _____ king.

2) After defeating him, they set up a _____, or representative form of government.

3) In the beginning, only _____ sat in the senate and made laws.

4) As time passed, the _____, or common people, got some power in the Roman government.

5) A _____ was a person who represented the plebeians in the Roman Republic.

What do you think

What can happen when laws are not written down?

Barrier
Something that blocks the way; a wall

Mighty
Powerful

Plank
A long, wide, flat piece of wood

During the years of the republic, Rome was often at war with its neighbors. First, the Romans defeated the Etruscans to the north. By 275 B.C., they had conquered the Greeks in southern Italy.

What Caused the Punic Wars?

To the south of Rome, on the northern coast of Africa, lay Carthage. The Phoenicians had settled Carthage, and it had a powerful navy. It controlled northern Africa, Spain, and several islands close to Italy. Then in 264 B.C., Carthage tried to take control of all of Sicily, an island at the southern tip of Italy. This led to war. In fact, Rome and Carthage fought three wars that lasted over 100 years. The Romans called them the Punic Wars, because *Punici* is the Latin word for *Phoenician.*

How Did the Romans Win the First Punic War?

The First Punic War lasted 23 years—from 264 B.C. to 241 B.C. Carthage had a **mighty,** or powerful, navy. Also, its population of 250,000 was three times the size of Rome. Rome had a fine army, but no navy. So how could Rome defeat Carthage?

Hannibal's bold attack on Rome surprised the Romans.

The Romans added a **plank,** or long, wide, flat piece of wood, to their ships. When they got close enough to a Carthaginian ship, the plank hooked it and linked the two ships together. Then Roman soldiers ran across the plank and jumped down into their enemy's ship. In this clever way, the Roman army defeated the Carthaginian navy. In 241 B.C., Carthage asked for peace. Rome took control of Sicily and the other islands off its coast.

What Did Hannibal Do in the Second Punic War?

In 218 B.C., Hannibal, a great Carthaginian soldier, planned a bold attack on Rome. His army of 60,000 soldiers, 38 elephants, and many horses marched across Spain, over the Pyrenees, to the foot of the Alps. The Romans thought that these mountains were a natural **barrier,** or wall.

For two weeks, his soldiers, elephants, and horses moved through narrow, snow-covered mountain paths. They faced cruel snowstorms and bitter cold. Half of his men and most of the elephants died.

Finally, Hannibal's army came down onto the northern plain of Italy. He attacked and defeated the surprised Romans. In less than two years, he defeated three more Roman armies. Filled with fear, the Romans retreated behind the strong walls of Rome. Even Hannibal could not knock them down.

For 15 years, Hannibal's army moved up and down the Italian peninsula. He destroyed towns and farmland. Then, in a surprise move, the Romans crossed the Mediterranean and attacked Carthage in North Africa. Hannibal had to rush home to defend the city.

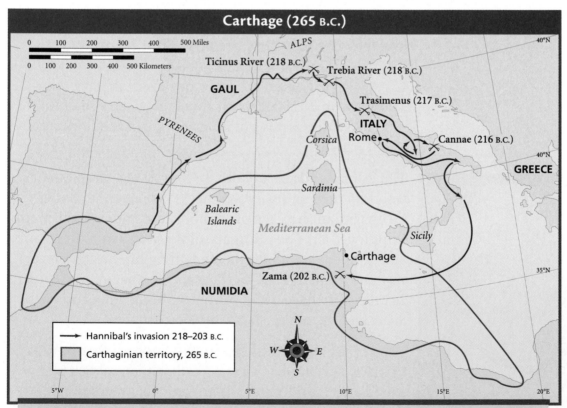

Carthage (265 B.C.)

MAP STUDY

This map shows Carthaginian territory in 265 B.C. and the route of Hannibal's invasion of Rome in 218 B.C. What two mountain ranges did he cross to get to Italy? Name one battle fought in Italy. How far is Carthage from Rome?

Our Legacy From Latin

Is Latin a "dead language"? Has anyone used it since the ancient Romans? In fact, Latin lives on. For many years, educated people in Europe learned it. Scientists still use Latin for plant and animal names. The French, Spanish, and Romanian languages are partly based on Latin.

The English language has two main sources. One is German. The other is Latin. In fact, the word *language* comes from the Latin word *lingua. School, library, table*—all of these words have Latin roots.

Latin came into English in two ways. At first, many people in England spoke the language of the Angles, Saxons, and Jutes. These were Germanic languages. Then, in 1066, Normans from France conquered England. They added many French words to the language. Other Latin words came from scholars and scientists. For a while, ordinary people used Saxon words. People of higher rank used Latin-based words. Over time, the two blended to form our modern English language.

◆Ally
A friend; a country or person who helps another

In 202 B.C., the Roman general Scipio defeated Hannibal's army at Zama. This ended the Second Punic War. Rome forced Carthage to destroy most of its navy and took control of Spain.

What Happened in the Third Punic War?

The Third Punic War began in 149 B.C. Carthage attacked an **ally,** or friend, of Rome. Rome then invaded Carthage. When the Romans cut off food supplies to the city, many Carthaginians starved to death. The Romans burned Carthage to the ground and sold its people into slavery. A legend says that the Romans covered the farmland outside the city with salt so that nothing would grow. Carthage was no more.

SECTION 3 REVIEW On a separate sheet of paper, write *True* if the statement is true or *False* if the statement is not true. Make each false statement true by changing the underlined word.

What do you think ❓

Do you think Hannibal was a great general? Why or why not?

1) The Punic Wars were fought between Rome and <u>Greece.</u>

2) The <u>Greeks</u> won the First Punic War.

3) Hannibal fought against the Romans in the <u>Third</u> Punic War.

4) Hannibal lost the war at the battle of <u>Zama.</u>

5) The Romans destroyed <u>Athens</u> around 150 B.C. and won the Third Punic War.

By 133 B.C., Rome controlled the Greek city-states and Asia Minor. It was the most powerful state in the Mediterranean area. The Romans even called this sea *Mare Nostrum,* which means "Our Sea."

Why Did the Roman Poor Grow Poorer?

The early Roman Republic depended on its soldiers, who were free citizens. These citizen-soldiers worked as farmers, laborers, and merchants when they were not fighting a war. Before Rome expanded, its citizen-soldiers fought only in Italy. When a battle ended, they returned home.

But Rome had gained more **territory,** or land, to defend. Soldiers traveled overseas for long periods of time to fight. Many returned home to nothing, because the government had sold their farms for unpaid **taxes.** Tax is money that citizens pay to support the government.

Having no land, the farmers moved to the city. Jobs were hard to find because slaves were doing most of them. With no land and no jobs, many plebeians lost hope. To get a little money, they sold their votes to people running for political office. In this way, the rich became richer; the poor became poorer.

What Happened to Those Who Helped the Poor?

In 134 B.C., a tribune named Tiberius Gracchus tried to give public land to the poor. He said that soldiers fought to protect the wealthy, but they got nothing in return. The plebeians liked Gracchus, but the patrician **senators,** or members of the senate, feared him. They started a **riot,** in which Gracchus and his followers were killed.

When Tiberius's brother Gaius was elected tribune in 123 B.C., he too helped the poor plebeians. He was able to lower the price of grain for the poor. He also helped more people in Italy become citizens. But once again, the patrician senators stopped the **reform** movement. They did not want change that would make things better for the plebeians. Gaius Gracchus and several thousand of his followers were killed.

Reform
To make something better through change

◆**Riot**
A noisy and sometimes deadly uprising

◆**Senator**
A person who is a member of a senate

◆**Tax**
Money that people pay to support the government

◆**Territory**
A large area of land

One third of the Roman population were slaves.

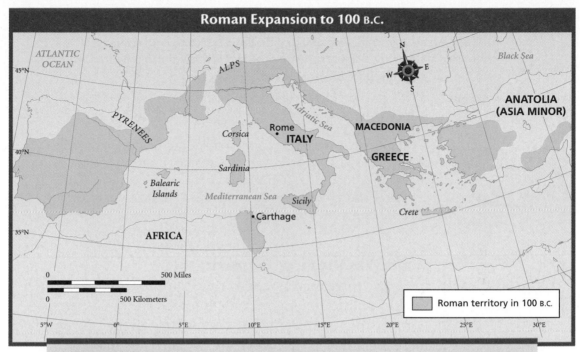

Roman Expansion to 100 B.C.

Roman territory in 100 B.C.

MAP STUDY

This map shows the territories of Rome in 100 B.C. How much of the Italian peninsula does Rome control? What peninsula to the east does Rome control? Who controls Carthage?

Challenge
To question if something is right or wrong; to invite someone to fight

How Did Military Leaders Gain Power?

The plebeians and the tribunes wanted reform. The patrician senators hated it. What happened? Military generals took power. In 110 B.C., Marius, a popular army general, formed an army from the poor who had no land. He promised them a share of the money made from conquering other people. His army won victories in North Africa and Gaul. Then his soldiers became more loyal to him than to the republic.

In 88 B.C., Lucius Sulla, another powerful general, **challenged** the power of Marius. A civil war started. Thousands of people died before Sulla defeated Marius and made himself dictator. By law, dictators had power for only six months. But Sulla threw out this law so he could rule longer. Military generals continued to rule Rome until 27 B.C.

◆Politician
A government leader; someone who runs for office

◆Triumvirate
Rule by three people

What Was the First Triumvirate?

In 60 B.C., three men agreed to rule Rome together: Crassus, a wealthy **politician,** or government leader, and two generals—Pompey the Great and Julius Caesar. We call the rule by these men the First **Triumvirate.** It lasted less than ten years.

SECTION 4 REVIEW Choose the letter of the answer that correctly completes each sentence. Write your answer on a separate sheet of paper.

1) The Roman Republic depended on its _____.
   a. navy   c. citizen-soldiers
   b. dictators   d. enemies

2) A tribune named _____ tried to give land to the poor.
   a. Pompey the Great   c. Tiberius Gracchus
   b. Julius Caesar   d. Crassus

3) The citizen-soldiers became loyal to _____.
   a. senators   c. laws
   b. Carthaginians   d. generals

What do you think ❓

Imagine that you are a citizen of a republic. Why would selling your vote to someone hurt the republic?

4) _____, a military general, threw out the Roman law that allowed a dictator for only six months.
   a. Tiberius Gracchus   c. Marius
   b. Gaius Gracchus   d. Lucius Sulla

5) We call the rule of three Romans in 60 B.C. the _____.
   a. Mare Nostrum   c. senate
   b. tax   d. First Triumvirate

Pompey feared Julius Caesar. He got the senate to limit Caesar's power. In 49 B.C., the senate ordered Caesar to return to Rome without his army. He challenged their power by marching his army to the Rubicon River between Gaul and Italy, crossing it, and marching on to Rome. He had broken Roman law, but he had won power.

How Did Caesar Use His Power?

Now Caesar had more power than the senate. He gave jobs to the poor. He told the rich to stop wearing pearls and other signs of their wealth. He passed tougher laws against crime. He also forgave his old enemies and made them government officials. He also made the Roman calendar more **accurate,** or correct. People in Europe used his calendar for the next 1,500 years.

Who Assassinated Julius Caesar?

In 44 B.C., the senate made Caesar a dictator for life. Many artists carved statues of him, and people could see these everywhere in Rome. The government even stamped his face on Roman coins. Because of all this, some senators feared that he wanted to become a king. Then the republic would end. Some senators **assassinated,** or killed, him on March 15, 44 B.C. These senators, some of them his friends, said that they had killed Caesar to save the republic.

Who Formed the Second Triumvirate?

After Caesar's death, his 19-year-old adopted son, Octavian, and two generals—Mark Antony and Marcus Lepidus—formed the Second Triumvirate. They divided the Roman Empire into three areas. Octavian ruled the West; Antony ruled the East; and Lepidus ruled North Africa. Each shared power over Italy. After Lepidus **retired,** or gave up his job, Octavian and Mark Antony fought for complete power.

Accurate
Correct

◆**Assassinate**
To kill someone who is important or in government

Retire
To give up one's job

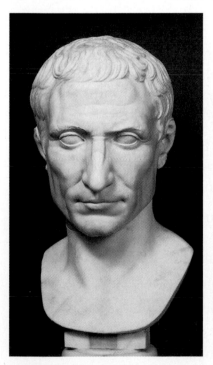

Julius Caesar ruled for a short time before he was assassinated.

CLEOPATRA: 69–30 B.C.

Cleopatra is famous for her charm. She was also brave and ambitious. She became queen of Egypt at age 17. Her family was Greek. They had ruled Egypt for almost 300 years.

Cleopatra and her brother were at war. Julius Caesar helped her win. After his death, she turned to Mark Antony, a Roman general. He helped her keep Egypt independent. They married and had three children.

Then Rome declared war on Antony and Cleopatra. Octavian's fleet defeated them, so Antony killed himself. Cleopatra could not bear to be Octavian's prisoner, so she also killed herself. She and Antony were buried together.

◆**Emperor**
A person who rules an empire; a king

How Did Octavian Become Rome's First Emperor?

Mark Antony formed an alliance with Cleopatra, the queen of Egypt. This upset Octavian, because he feared that Antony and Cleopatra would create their own empire. Octavian asked the senate to take away Antony's power. Then Octavian declared war on Antony and Cleopatra. Upon finding out Octavian's plans to attack Egypt, Antony and Cleopatra killed themselves. In 31 B.C., at the battle of Actium, the Romans defeated the Egyptians.

Four years later, in 27 B.C., the Roman Republic ended. The senate made Octavian the **emperor,** or king. For the next 500 years, emperors ruled Rome.

SECTION 5 REVIEW On a separate sheet of paper, write *True* if the statement is true or *False* if the statement is not true. Make each false statement true by changing the underlined word or words.

What do you think ?

Do you think the senators who assassinated Julius Caesar did so for the good of the republic? Why or why not?

1) Pompey the Great feared the power of <u>Mark Antony.</u>

2) Julius Caesar disobeyed the senate, crossed the <u>Rubicon River,</u> and marched on Rome.

3) The Roman Senate made Julius Caesar a <u>dictator</u> for life.

4) The Second Triumvirate was made up of <u>five</u> men.

5) <u>Marcus Lepidus</u> became the first emperor of Rome.

How to Get Elected in Rome

Ancient Rome was a republic. It did not have a king, and it was not a democracy. Only men who belonged to a small group actually held office. For many years, ordinary people tried to get some voice in government. They won some rights, but power stayed with just a few.

Roman officials did, however, need the people's support. Like modern politicians, they tried different ways to get it. This reading is from a letter written in 63 B.C. In it, Quintus Cicero tells his brother how to get elected.

Whoever gives any sign of liking you, or regularly visits your house, you must put down in the category of friends. . . . You must take great pains that these men should love you and desire your highest honor as, for example, your tribesmen, neighbors, clients, and finally your freedmen, yes even your slaves; for nearly all the gossip that forms public opinion emanates from your own servants' quarters.

In a word, you must secure friends of every class, magistrates, consuls and their tribunes to win you the vote of the centuries (that elect the consuls): men of wide popular influence. . . .

So you see that you will have the votes of all the centuries secured for you by the number and variety of your friends. . . . After that, review

the entire city, all guilds, districts, neighborhoods. If you can attach yourself to the leading men in these, you will by their means easily keep a hold upon the multitude.

And you should be strenuous in seeing as many people as possible every day of every possible class and order, for from the mere numbers of these who greet you, you can make a guess of the amount of support you will get on the balloting. It often happens that people, when they visit a number of Candidates, and observe the one that pays special heed to their attentions, leave off visiting the others, and little by little become real supporters of the man.

Source Reading Wrap-Up

1) Whom does Cicero say a candidate should consider as friends?

2) Why should a candidate make sure that his servants think highly of him?

3) How can a candidate get support throughout Rome?

4) Why do people often vote for a candidate?

5) Would Cicero's advice be useful to someone running for political office today? Why or why not?

Life in Rome

Rome was the largest city in the Roman Empire. By about A.D. 100, it had nearly one million people. The city was busy and crowded. At the heart of Rome was the Forum. It had great temples, theaters, and markets. The public baths were also important buildings. They were popular meeting places.

Romans also loved games and races. The city had several huge public arenas. People watched chariot races in the huge Circus Maximus. Gladiators and wild animals fought in the Colosseum. (You can still see the ruins of this stadium in present-day Rome.)

In town, wealthy patricians lived in comfortable townhouses. They had gardens and fountains. These nobles also owned large country homes called *villas*. Most ordinary Romans rented small apartments in an *insula*. These apartment buildings usually had four or five floors. Small shops took up the first floor. These wooden buildings were dark and crowded. Fire was a constant danger.

Crime was also a problem in Rome. Wealthy people avoided certain parts of the city. They might walk there only with armed slaves.

The family was the center of Roman life. In early Rome, the father had total control over his household. Later, fathers became less strict. They still made major family decisions. They held religious ceremonies to honor household gods. The goddess Vesta was the spirit of the hearth. The god Janus guarded the doorway. Each family also had its own spirits to protect it.

A Roman father took charge of his sons' education. Tutors were often Greek slaves. Young boys learned to read, write, and do arithmetic. Later they studied Greek and Latin literature. Public speaking was also important. Girls were taught cooking and sewing at home. Young women in patrician families got more education. They learned literature, music, and dance. Poorer women often worked in a shop or laundry.

Like people today, Romans cared about their looks. They wore jewelry. Women had elaborate hairstyles. Men wore a simple short-sleeved garment that fell to the knees. Women wore a similar, but longer, tunic. Their robes were wool, linen, or silk. Men who were Roman citizens could wear a toga. This was a long piece of cloth that was wrapped around the body. Different styles of togas had special meaning. Senators, for example, wore white togas with a purple border. It was hard to move while wearing a toga. Workers and soldiers usually wore just the tunic.

Spotlight Story Wrap-Up

1) What kinds of buildings would you see in ancient Rome?

2) What did Romans do for amusement?

3) Where did most ordinary Romans live?

4) What was the father's role in the Roman family?

5) What was Roman clothing like?

➡ Legends say that Romulus and Remus founded Rome in 753 B.C.

➡ The Latins lived on the plains south of the Tiber River. Greek settlers lived in city-states nearby. The Latins learned from the Greeks.

➡ The Etruscans lived north of the Tiber River. They were more advanced than the Latins. By about 600 B.C., they conquered Rome. Etruscan kings ruled Rome. Wealthy landowners, called patricians, ran the government.

➡ In 509 B.C., the Romans overthrew the Etruscan kings. They set up a republic. Two officials called consuls ran the republic. A senate of patricians made laws.

➡ Most ordinary Romans were plebeians. They paid taxes and served as soldiers. The plebeians wanted political power. Two officials—tribunes—were named to represent them. Tribunes and consuls could veto laws.

➡ In about 450 B.C., Roman laws were written down on 12 bronze tablets. Plebeians gradually got more power.

➡ The Roman Republic fought its neighbors. Rome's land and power grew. Three wars were fought with Carthage, a powerful Phoenician city.

The First Punic War lasted 23 years, from 264 to 241 B.C. Rome won. In the Second Punic War, Hannibal crossed the Alps. He invaded Rome itself. A Roman general then defeated him at Zama in 202 B.C. Rome won the Third Punic War as well. The Romans destroyed Carthage about 149 B.C.

➡ By 133 B.C., Rome ruled the Mediterranean. But the plebeians were getting poorer. Two brothers named Gracchus tried to help. Both were killed along with many followers.

➡ Military leaders took power in Rome. Two popular generals were Marius and Sulla. In 60 B.C., three leaders agreed to rule together as the First Triumvirate. Two were generals—Pompey and Julius Caesar. The other was a wealthy politician, Crassus.

➡ The senate made Caesar dictator for life. Some senators thought that would end the Republic, so they killed Caesar in 44 B.C.

➡ The Second Triumvirate formed. It included Caesar's adopted son, Octavian, and another general, Mark Antony. A third man, Lepidus, dropped out. Antony made an alliance with Cleopatra, queen of Egypt. Octavian declared war on them and defeated them. The Senate named him emperor.

Comprehension: Identifying Facts

On a separate sheet of paper, use the words from the Word Bank to complete each sentence.

WORD BANK
Cleopatra
Gaius Gracchus
Hannibal
Julius Caesar
Lucius Sulla
Mark Antony
Octavian
Pompey the Great
Scipio
Tiberius Gracchus

1) _____ defeated Hannibal at Carthage.

2) _____ got rid of the law about dictators governing only six months.

3) _____, a great general from Carthage, won many victories against the Romans.

4) As a tribune, _____ gave land to poor plebeians.

5) Along with Crassus and Julius Caesar, _____ was a member of the First Triumvirate.

6) _____ took power by disobeying the Roman senate and marching his army across the Rubicon River.

7) As queen of Egypt, _____ formed an alliance against Rome with Mark Antony.

8) Along with Octavian and Marcus Lepidus, _____ was a member of the Second Triumvirate.

9) _____, the adopted son of Julius Caesar, became the first emperor of Rome.

10) As a tribune, _____ was able to lower the price of grain so that the poor could buy it.

Comprehension: Multiple Choice

On a separate sheet of paper, write the letter of the answer that correctly completes each sentence.

1) The word _____ comes from the Latin word for father.
   - a. plebeian
   - b. senate
   - c. patrician
   - d. republic

2) A _____ is a form of government in which citizens elect representatives to govern them.
   - a. dictatorship
   - b. senate
   - c. patrician
   - d. republic

3) To _____ something is to say no to it.

   a. veto   c. term

   b. accurate   d. elect

4) In times of war, the Romans would appoint a _____ to rule for six months.

   a. senate   c. dictator

   b. senator   d. emperor

5) _____ means "from the common people."

   a. Plebeian   c. Senate

   b. Patrician   d. Triumvirate

Comprehension: Understanding Main Ideas

On a separate sheet of paper, write the answer to each question. Use complete sentences, or statements.

1) Explain how each of the following was important for the Roman Republic: two consuls; the senate; the veto; the tribunes; the Law of the Twelve Tables.

2) What was one difference between the patricians and the plebeians?

3) Why did the Roman patricians need the Roman plebeians?

Critical Thinking: Write Your Opinion

1) The Roman Republic lasted 500 years. Why do you think it lasted so long?

2) Why do you think the Roman Republic finally ended?

Test-Taking Tip

When you read test directions, try to restate them in your own words. Tell yourself what you are expected to do. That way, you can make sure your answer will be complete and correct.

Chapter 8

The Roman Empire

27 B.C. to A.D. 476

In 27 B.C., Rome began the second great period of its history. It became an empire that lasted for 500 years. People of different races, customs, and religions lived in the Roman Empire. In this chapter, you will learn about the Pax Romana, which Octavian began. You will also learn about the new religion of Christianity and about the fall of the Roman Empire in A.D. 476.

Goals for Learning

▶ To describe the reign of Octavian, who was known as Augustus Caesar

▶ To distinguish between Rome's good and bad emperors

▶ To explain how the Roman Empire treated the Jewish people

▶ To describe the rise of Christianity

▶ To identify the major conflict between Rome and Christians

▶ To list at least three reasons for the decline of the Roman Empire

▶ To recognize the practical gifts of the Romans to world civilization

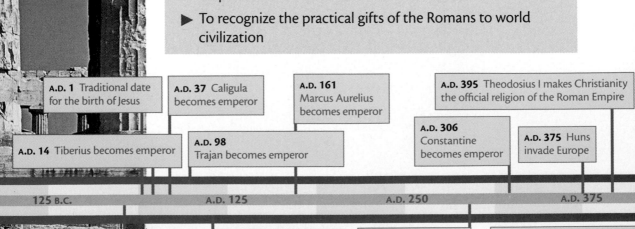

A.D. 1 Traditional date for the birth of Jesus

A.D. 37 Caligula becomes emperor

A.D. 161 Marcus Aurelius becomes emperor

A.D. 395 Theodosius I makes Christianity the official religion of the Roman Empire

A.D. 306 Constantine becomes emperor

A.D. 375 Huns invade Europe

A.D. 14 Tiberius becomes emperor

A.D. 98 Trajan becomes emperor

| 125 B.C. | A.D. 125 | A.D. 250 | A.D. 375 |

27 B.C. Augustus Caesar becomes first emperor of Rome

A.D. 117 Hadrian becomes emperor

A.D. 284 Diocletian divides the Roman Empire into two parts

A.D. 476 The German Odoacer takes control of Rome; fall of Rome in the West

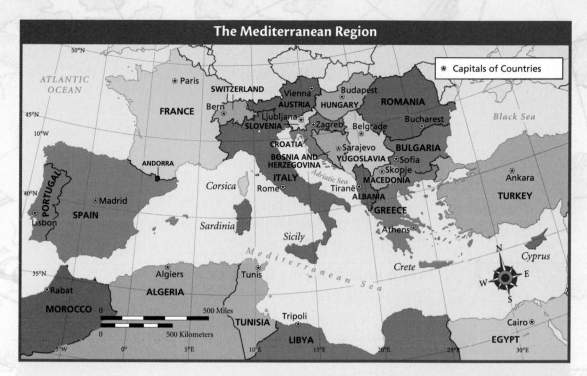

The Mediterranean Region

⊛ Capitals of Countries

By 27 B.C., Rome controlled most of the known world. The Roman Empire was very large. Much of the empire included what we now call the Mediterranean Region. The Romans called the Mediterranean Sea *Mare Nostrum*. This means "Our Sea." They thought the sea belonged to them!

Study the map and answer the following questions:

1) What is the capital of Greece?

2) Which country lies directly west of Italy and what is its capital?

3) What countries in northern Africa lie to the south of Italy?

4) What sea touches the coastline of Italy on its east?

5) How many miles does the Mediterranean Sea stretch from east to west?

Geography Skills

Aqueduct
A bridge that carries flowing water

Eternal
Lasting forever

In 27 B.C., Octavian, now known as Augustus Caesar, began the second great period of Roman history. Rome was no longer a republic; it had become an empire. This empire lasted for five hundred years—from 27 B.C. to A.D. 476.

The empire stretched north to Britain and the Rhine and Danube Rivers. It controlled the Mediterranean Sea, much of North Africa, and Egypt. It reached the Euphrates River in the East and the Atlantic Ocean in the West. Nearly 100 million people lived under its rule.

Who Ruled During Rome's Golden Age?

We call Augustus Caesar's 41-year reign the "Golden Age of Rome." He wanted to bring back the old customs of the republic. He slept on a plain bed and wore the same clothes that common people wore. But Augustus brought new things to the empire, too.

Augustus Caesar

Augustus built new temples, theaters, public buildings, roads, and a large **aqueduct**—a bridge that carried water to Rome. He said, "I found Rome a city of brick and left it a city of marble." The Romans were proud of their beautiful city, which was hundreds of years old. They thought it would last forever; it was the "**eternal** city."

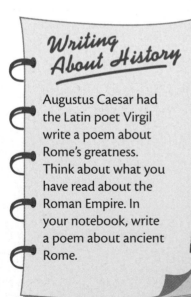

Writing About History

Augustus Caesar had the Latin poet Virgil write a poem about Rome's greatness. Think about what you have read about the Roman Empire. In your notebook, write a poem about ancient Rome.

What Kept Government Officials Honest?

The Romans called the lands outside of Italy the provinces. The people in these provinces paid heavy taxes. But some officials were not honest. Much of this money never reached Rome. What could Augustus do to change this?

He divided the provinces into two groups. The senate controlled the older provinces. The emperor controlled the newer provinces on the frontier. Two government officials took care of the business of each province. One official took

Over 50,000 people could attend sporting events in the Roman Colosseum. It was completed in A.D. 80.

care of military and governmental things. The other official took care of everything that had to do with money. Each official watched the other. This kept them honest.

What Is the Pax Romana?

With these changes, Augustus brought peace to Rome and order to the empire. This period of peace lasted for 200 years—from 27 B.C. to A.D. 180. We call it the **Pax Romana,** or the Roman peace. During this time, each province could trade with every other province, and the people lived **civilized** lives. That is, the people had good government and the things that make life easier and more beautiful.

◆Civilized
Having more of the things that make life easier

◆Pax Romana
The Roman peace that began during the reign of Augustus Caesar

SECTION 1 REVIEW On a separate sheet of paper, write answers to these questions.

1) What do we call the reign of Augustus Caesar?

2) About how many people lived under the rule of the Roman Empire?

3) How did Augustus change the city of Rome?

4) Why did Romans call their city the "eternal city"?

5) What do we call the period of peace that began during the reign of Augustus?

What do you think

How could having two government officials in each province keep them both honest?

Debate
To talk about something; to have two or more sides talk about something

Insane
To be ill in one's mind

Augustus did good things for the people in his empire. After his death in A.D. 14, however, some emperors did well; others did poorly. Because these emperors served for life, people had to accept them. But sometimes, citizens refused to accept the bad. Then they murdered the emperor. Between A.D. 180 and 284, 4 out of 29 emperors died a natural death; 25 were murdered.

Who Were Some Bad Emperors?

After Augustus's death in A.D. 14, his adopted son, Tiberius, became Rome's second emperor. He knew how to lead, but he was not popular. He thought that everyone wanted to hurt him, but he had no proof of this. One Roman wrote that Tiberius put someone to death every day of his reign!

In A.D. 37, Caligula became emperor. He was **insane,** or ill in his mind. Some say he made his favorite horse a senator and demanded that people call him a god. He also spent all the government's money on foolish things. Because he was such a bad emperor, his own guards killed him. (The job of these soldiers was to protect him!)

How Did Claudius Become Emperor?

After Caligula's death, the senate tried to decide who should be the next emperor. While they **debated,** or talked

CLAUDIUS PTOLEMY: c. A.D. 100–165

Ptolemy was a famous scientist. He lived and worked in Alexandria, Egypt. We know little else about his life.

Ptolemy observed the sun and stars. He studied Greek geometry. His writings on these topics are in 13 books. They are called the *Almagest.* That means "the greatest." Ptolemy said the Earth was the center of the universe. It stood still. The sun and stars moved around it. For about 1,400 years, almost everyone believed this. Ptolemy was also a geographer. In his *Geography,* he corrected the mistakes of earlier geographers. He drew a map of the world that everyone accepted.

Condemn
To say that someone must suffer or die; to say that something is wrong

Entertainment
Plays and other things that amuse people

Lyre
A small musical instrument with strings

over the problem, the guards picked Claudius. (He was the 50-year-old uncle of Caligula.) Most senators thought he was a fool. However, Claudius surprised everyone! He became a fine ruler.

Claudius helped Rome to be orderly and peaceful. Then, in A.D. 54, his wife poisoned him. She wanted Nero, her 16-year-old son from another marriage, to be emperor. Most historians think that Nero was one of Rome's worst emperors.

What Kind of Artist Was Nero?

Nero thought of himself as an artist. He sang and played the **lyre,** which was a small musical instrument with strings. When he played, people were forced to listen. They could not leave the theater. Even the senators and the soldiers thought he played poorly!

In A.D. 64, a fire lasting nine days destroyed half of Rome. Some people said that Nero started the fire. They even said that he played his lyre while Rome burned!

Then, in A.D. 68, some powerful army generals rebelled against Nero. The senate **condemned** him to death. That is, they said that the government must kill him. However, Nero took his own life. His last words were, "What an artist the world is losing!" After his death, army generals once again fought to become emperor. The empire had four emperors in one year.

How Did Trajan Improve the Empire?

For 80 years—from A.D. 98 to 180—three good leaders ruled Rome. Under Trajan, who ruled from A.D. 98 to 117, Rome reached its greatest size. The government gave free grain to the poor and let farmers borrow money at a low cost. It also gave everyone free **entertainment.** That is, people could go to theaters for plays and other amusing things.

What Did Hadrian Do for the Empire?

Hadrian followed Trajan as emperor and ruled from A.D. 117 to 138. He passed laws that protected women, children, and slaves. He also made these laws the same in every part

Marcus Aurelius spent much of his time as emperor in the field with soldiers.

of the empire. He built new buildings, lowered taxes, and built a wall across England. This wall defended Roman territory in the south of England from the enemy in the north. (Parts of Hadrian's Wall are still standing.)

Why Did Emperor Marcus Aurelius Become a Soldier?

Marcus Aurelius became emperor in A.D. 161. He lived a simple life and liked books and ideas. But he soon became a soldier and took direct command of the Roman army. He did this because German tribes from the north attacked the empire's **borders** along the Danube River. These Germanic people wanted to settle within the empire.

◆Border
The dividing line between two countries

Decline
To lose power; to turn downward

◆Treasury
The money collected by the government and used to pay for things

Why Did Marcus Aurelius Let in Invaders?

As the empire grew larger, Rome needed many soldiers to defend and protect it. Of course, the government had to pay them. This cost a lot of money and drained the government's **treasury.**

Aurelius wanted peace. He let the German invaders along the Danube River settle inside the borders of the empire. The empire lasted for another 300 years. But already it had started to **decline,** or lose its power. A Roman historian wrote that Rome had changed "from a kingdom of gold to one of iron and rust."

Why Did the Empire Decline?

The Roman Empire began to decline for several reasons. First, its government never found a simple way to choose a new emperor. Too often when an emperor died, civil war broke out. Often, military generals fought each other for

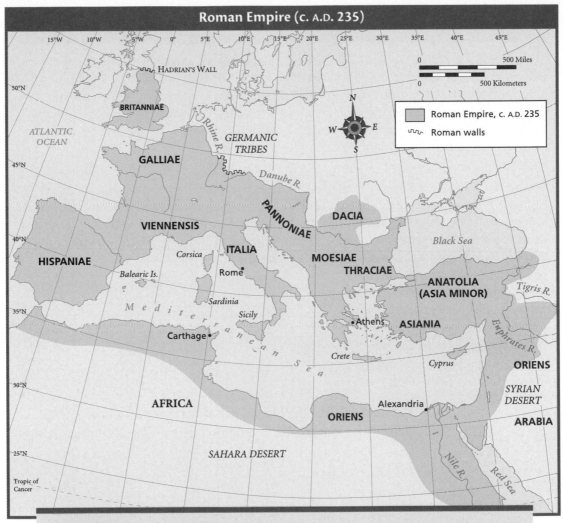

Roman Empire (c. A.D. 235)

Roman Empire, c. A.D. 235
Roman walls

HADRIAN'S WALL

BRITANNIAE

ATLANTIC OCEAN

GERMANIC TRIBES

GALLIAE

Rhine R.

Danube R.

PANNONIAE

DACIA

VIENNENSIS

ITALIA

Corsica

Rome

MOESIAE

THRACIAE

Black Sea

HISPANIAE

Balearic Is.

Sardinia

Sicily

Mediterranean Sea

ANATOLIA (ASIA MINOR)

Tigris R.

ASIANIA

Athens

Euphrates R.

Carthage

Crete

Cyprus

ORIENS

AFRICA

Alexandria

SYRIAN DESERT

ORIENS

ARABIA

SAHARA DESERT

Nile R.

Red Sea

Tropic of Cancer

MAP STUDY

This map shows the borders of the Roman Empire in about A.D. 235. What is the name of the wall at the most northern point of the empire? Near what rivers did the Romans build other protective walls? What direction would someone travel when going from Rome to Alexandria?

◆**Plague**
A disease that spreads from person to person and kills many people

the power to govern Rome. Sometimes, as with Claudius, soldiers chose the new leader. Second, because of its wars, the government had too little money. Third, a **plague**—a disease that spreads from person to person and causes many to die—hit the empire. (It probably killed Marcus Aurelius in A.D. 180.) All this weakened the empire.

THE BURIED CITY OF POMPEII

The year was A.D. 79. The day was August 24, a day just like any other day in the Roman city of Pompeii. Then Mount Vesuvius exploded! Fiery lava, or hot melted rock, lit the sky. Ash and cinders—small pieces of burnt rock—rained down on everyone and everything. They made the sky dark as night for three days.

Thousands of frightened people tried to run from the city. They tied pillows on their heads for protection from the rain of fire. Within days, 30 feet of ash and cinders buried Pompeii. Poison gas killed the people who had not gotten away. Some fell dead in the streets; others died in their homes. One merchant died next to a stack of coins. Pets died with their masters.

Then the rain of fire ended. Only the tops of walls and a few columns stood above the blanket of ash and cinders. The city of Pompeii had disappeared! Over time, it was completely buried and forgotten. Then in 1748, a man hit a wall while digging one day. He had discovered Pompeii after more than 1,600 years!

For many years, archaeologists have been digging up the ruins of Pompeii. They have discovered that mud had covered and hardened on many dead bodies. When the bodies decayed, they left their shape, or mold, behind in the hardened mud.

The archaeologists have also discovered nuts, bread, figs, eggs on dinner tables, furniture, and children's toys that still work! Today, visitors can see the Pompeii of 1,600 years ago. Its ruins stand frozen in time.

SECTION 2 REVIEW On a separate sheet of paper, write *True* if the statement is true or *False* if the statement is not true. Make each false statement true by changing the underlined word.

1) Tiberius was the adopted son of <u>Caligula.</u>

2) Emperor <u>Claudius</u> was insane.

3) Historians think that Nero was one of Rome's <u>worst</u> emperors.

4) <u>Claudius</u> passed new laws to protect women, children, and slaves.

5) Defending the borders of the Roman Empire led to more <u>soldiers.</u>

What do you think

How would a plague weaken a country or an empire?

◆**Christianity**
The religion based on the teachings of Jesus Christ and the Bible

Divine
Having something to do with the gods or with God

Gospel
One of four books of the New Testament part of the Bible; a word that means "good news"

◆**Homeland**
The land that belongs to a people; the country people call their home

Messiah
A king sent by God who will save people from something

Prophet
A person who speaks for God

While Augustus Caesar was emperor, Jesus of Nazareth was born. His home was in the far eastern section of the Roman Empire called Palestine. Jesus preached a new message to the poor. Out of his preaching grew a new religion—**Christianity**. It changed the Roman Empire and became one of the world's great religions.

Why Did the Jewish People Want a Messiah?

Rome allowed the people in its empire to believe in their own gods. However, everyone had to offer religious sacrifice to the emperor. The Romans thought he had **divine,** or godlike, powers. The only people who did not have to do this were the Hebrews or Jews. For hundreds of years, they had believed in one god. Rome respected this belief. The Jews in Palestine had religious freedom.

However, the Jews did not have political freedom. For centuries their **prophets**—people who speak for God—said that the Jews would one day rule their own **homeland.** Palestine was their homeland. They felt it belonged to them, not to Rome. The Jews believed that their god would send a **messiah,** or king, to lead them to political freedom. Some people thought that Jesus of Nazareth was this messiah.

What Did Jesus of Nazareth Teach?

Four books called the **Gospels** tell about Jesus. Gospel means "good news." The Gospels are the first four books of the New Testament of the Bible. Jesus's followers wrote these books after his death.

Jesus grew up as a Jew in the small town of Nazareth. He earned his living as a carpenter. When he was 30, he began to preach a new message—God loved all people equally. Jesus asked his followers to love all people, just as God did. They were to show this love through service. Finally, he asked them to love even their enemies.

Jesus said that God had sent him to preach this good news to the poor. The poor in Palestine liked his message. Large

Betray
To stop being loyal to someone; to do something to hurt someone

Crucify
To hang someone on a cross so that the person dies

Miracle
An amazing or wonderful event that no one can explain

crowds gathered to hear him speak. The Gospels report that he healed the sick, gave sight to the blind, and performed other **miracles.** (A miracle is an amazing or wonderful event that no one can explain.) Because of this, many people began to follow him.

Why Did Some People Fear Jesus of Nazareth?

For three years, Jesus preached God's love. Then some Jewish leaders turned against him. They feared that his followers would rebel against Rome. Then Roman soldiers would kill the Jewish people. Jesus himself said that he did not come to free the bodies of men and women from the rule of Rome. He came, he said, to free their spirits. Still, people feared him.

The Gospels report that one of Jesus's followers—Judas Iscariot—**betrayed** him. That is, he turned Jesus over to his enemies. Roman soldiers arrested Jesus. Pontius Pilate, the Roman governor, charged him with being a rebel. Then soldiers **crucified** Jesus, or hung him on a cross to die.

According to the New Testament, Roman governor Pontius Pilate sentenced Jesus to death.

Why Did His Followers Call Jesus the Christ?

According to the New Testament, Jesus's followers believed that God raised him from the dead. They also believed that he was the son of God and that he had returned to his father in heaven. These followers, or **disciples,** carried on his teachings. They began to call him the Christ, or *Christos,* which is the Greek word for messiah. Those who believed he had risen from the dead became known as Christians, or followers of Christ.

How Did the Gospel Spread?

At first, Jesus's disciples preached their good news only to Jews. But then one of them, Saul, began to preach to **gentiles,** or non-Jews. At first, Saul condemned Christians. Then he had a religious experience. He believed that the risen Jesus had spoken to him.

The disciple Paul preached that God had raised Jesus from the dead and that people should love and serve one another.

Disciple
A follower of someone

Gentile
A non-Jew

Because of this experience, Saul, who now took the Roman name Paul, became a follower of Jesus. For 30 years, he traveled from Palestine to Greece to Italy. In each of these places, he preached two things: God had raised Jesus from the dead and people should love and serve others.

Paul wrote letters to many Christian groups in cities around the Roman Empire. In those letters, he told them how they were to live in the Roman world. He helped Christianity take its first steps in becoming a world religion.

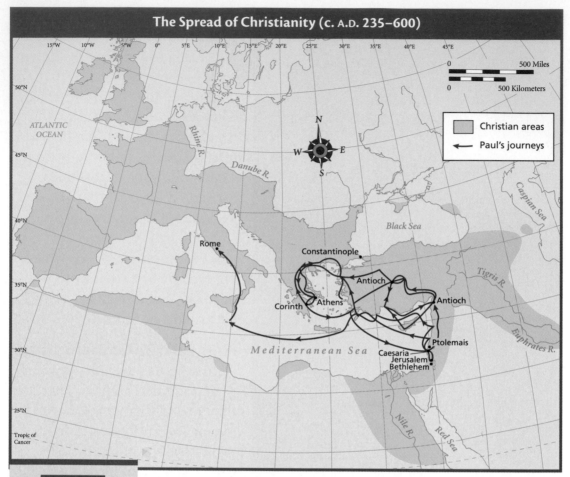

The Spread of Christianity (c. A.D. 235–600)

Christian areas
← **Paul's journeys**

MAP STUDY

This map shows the spread of Christianity. How far had Christianity spread by A.D. 600? Why do you think the Mediterranean Sea was important for the spreading of the Christian message?

Why Did Rome Have Trouble With Christianity?

Roman law said that everyone must honor the emperor as a god. But Christians refused to follow this law. Because of this and because of some other things the Christians believed, the Romans killed many of them. Sometime between A.D. 62 and 67, Nero had Peter, one of the first followers of Jesus, and Paul put to death.

When Did Rome Accept Christianity?

Over the next three centuries, the Roman Empire grew weaker, but Christianity grew stronger. Many people, especially the poor, liked the Christian message. More and more of them saw Christianity as an answer to their problems. Jesus had preached that God loved all people equally. He had promised eternal life to those who believed

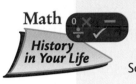
in him. By A.D. 337, Rome had its first Christian emperor—Constantine. In A.D. 395, the emperor Theodosius I made Christianity the official religion of the Roman Empire.

SECTION 3 REVIEW On a separate sheet of paper, write the word from the Word Bank that completes each sentence.

WORD BANK
Constantine
Gospels
Nero
Peter
Saul

1) We learn about Jesus of Nazareth from the four _____ that his followers wrote.

2) One of the first followers of Jesus was _____.

3) Another follower of Jesus was _____, who later became known as Paul.

4) The emperor _____ put Christians to death because of what they believed.

5) The first Christian emperor was _____.

What do you think

Why do you think the Roman Empire feared Christianity and its message?

◆**Coemperor**
A person who rules only part of an empire while another emperor rules another part

In A.D. 284, Diocletian, a general, became the Roman emperor. He thought that the empire was too large for one person to govern, so he divided it into two parts. The dividing line between the two parts lay west of Greece. Diocletian ruled the eastern part. Another person—a **coemperor**—ruled the western part.

Who Moved the Capital to Byzantium?

In A.D. 306, Constantine became emperor. By this time, the western part of the empire—the part in which Rome was located—was weak. Constantine moved the capital to Byzantium. This old Greek city stood on the western edge of Asia Minor. He named his new capital Constantinople after himself.

Who Were the Huns and Visigoths?

For hundreds of years, German tribes had fought the Roman army. In battle, they were skilled warriors. By A.D. 200, many Germans lived within the empire. Some of them even became Roman soldiers.

Around A.D. 375, a non-Germanic tribe called the Huns invaded Eastern Europe. They came from central Asia and were expert horsemen and fierce warriors. Their most famous leader was Attila the Hun.

As king of the Huns, Attila led his warriors on several raids on the Roman Empire.

For many years, the Huns rode across Europe, defeating every tribe they met in battle. One German tribe, the Visigoths, feared them. Rome let the Visigoths move within the Roman Empire. The Visigoths promised not to bring weapons with them. Rome promised to give them land. Neither side kept its promise.

What Year Did the Roman Empire Fall?

The Visigoths began to attack Roman towns. In A.D. 378, Rome sent an army against them. But the Visigoths defeated the Romans at the

Battle of Adrianople. This was one of the most important events in world history. For the first time in hundreds of years, Rome could not defend itself!

In A.D. 410, the Visigoths looted Rome. In A.D. 455, another German tribe, the Vandals, came into Rome and destroyed much of its beauty. (To this day, we call people who destroy property vandals.)

Then in A.D. 476, Odoacer, a German leader, took control of Rome. Roman rule—as a republic and as an empire— had lasted for 1,000 years, but now it was no more. The western part of the empire had collapsed. However, the eastern part **survived,** or continued.

SECTION 4 REVIEW Choose the letter of the answer that correctly completes each sentence. Write your answer on a separate sheet of paper.

1) Emperor _____ divided the Roman Empire into two parts.

   a. Marcus Aurelius   c. Diocletian

   b. Constantine   d. Visigoth

2) Emperor _____ moved the capital of the empire from Rome to Byzantium.

   a. Marcus Aurelius   c. Diocletian

   b. Constantine   d. Attila

3) The name of the new capital was _____.

   a. Adrianople   c. Odoacer

   b. Hun   d. Constantinople

4) The best known leader of the Huns was _____.

   a. Attila   c. Diocletian

   b. Odoacer   d. Visigoth

5) Historians give the date of A.D. _____ for the fall of Rome.

   a. 378   c. 455

   b. 410   d. 476

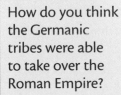

What do you think

How do you think the Germanic tribes were able to take over the Roman Empire?

Basis
The idea or reason behind something

Practical
Useful; having to do with the use of something

Reasonable
Making sense; fair

The fall of Rome did not end its influence. Roman culture influenced the German invaders. Its influence continues to this day, because Rome gave many gifts to world civilization. These gifts were **practical** ones, for the Romans were a practical people. They liked useful things.

Why Is Roman Law a Gift to Civilization?

Roman law is one example of how practical the Romans were. In many ways, these laws made the empire a success for a thousand years. Romans respected the law. They thought that a law should be fair, just, and **reasonable.** (That is, it should make sense to people.) They thought that law should do two things. First, it should protect people's lives and property. Second, it should punish those who do wrong.

A special part of Roman law, called the Law of Nations, applied to non-Romans. Under this, Rome gave them legal protection. Roman law protected people from many different places and cultures.

What Is the Code of Justinian?

In A.D. 527, Justinian, the emperor in the East, feared that Roman law would disappear. He collected and organized all Roman laws into a code. The Code of Justinian became the **basis,** or idea, for the legal system of many European countries.

What Practical Things Did the Romans Build?

The Romans became the greatest road builders before modern times. (People in some countries still use Roman-built roads today!) They also built fine bridges and large aqueducts.

One practical thing the Romans did was build aqueducts like this one. These were used to transport water.

The Romans developed a kind of **concrete** with which to build. (Concrete is a mixture of sand, water, and other materials. It hardens to become rocklike.) To add beauty to their concrete buildings, they covered them with thin, flat, wide pieces of marble. To make the buildings larger, they built high **vaulted** ceilings. A vaulted ceiling has an arch to it and can support a roof that covers a large space.

What Is the Pantheon?

Emperor Hadrian built the Pantheon, which is still standing today. It is a temple for all the Roman gods. With its vaulted ceiling, the Pantheon is 142 feet wide. Some Roman buildings could hold 3,000 people. In fact, the Colosseum, where the Romans went for entertainment, could seat 50,000 people! The practical Romans built their roads and their buildings to last. People still use a few of them today.

How Were Roman Art and Science Practical?

The Romans wanted to find a good use for art and science. This made them different from the Greeks, who wanted perfect beauty and knowledge. For example, Greeks made their statues perfect. Roman artists showed **imperfections,** such as broken noses and wrinkles.

Roman Technology

Roman engineers could build large structures. Two advances helped them. One was the round arch. The arch was not new. The Greeks, for example, had built arched gates. The Romans learned how to use it in new ways, however. The Roman arch was a half circle. Side columns supported it. It could hold up heavy loads. The Romans built arched stone bridges across rivers. They also used round arches to build great aqueducts. They brought freshwater to Roman cities everywhere. The Romans also built arched roofs over large indoor spaces.

The other advance was concrete. Concrete was a Roman invention. It let them build strong walls and arched roofs. Concrete also made Roman roads strong and lasting. Modern builders still use this Roman technology.

Then and Now

Sanitation
The act of making something free from disease, or healthy and clean

Sewer
An underground pipe that carries away dirty water and human waste

Romans also used their knowledge of science in a practical way. They set up the first health-care system. Government doctors cared for the poor. The Romans built **sewers** to improve public **sanitation.** Sewers, which are usually underground pipes, carry away dirty water and human waste. This helps sanitation. That is, it helps keep people clean and free from disease.

Galen, who was a Greek, practiced medicine in Rome around A.D. 180. He wrote a book in which he wrote down everything anyone knew about medicine. We now know that the book has many mistakes. But it influenced medicine for more than a thousand years.

SECTION 5 REVIEW On a separate sheet of paper, write *True* if the statement is true or *False* if the statement is not true. Make each false statement true by changing the underlined word.

1) Romans believed that their laws should be <u>reasonable,</u> fair, and just.

2) The Roman Law of Nations protected people who were <u>non-Romans.</u>

3) The Code of Justinian is a collection of Roman <u>art.</u>

4) The Roman <u>Pantheon</u> could hold 50,000 people.

5) The Romans wanted their art and science to be <u>perfect,</u> or useful.

What do you think

The book of medicine that Galen wrote had mistakes in it. Do you think it still helped people after his time? Why or why not?

Rome's Bloody Sport

Roman rulers tried to keep the people happy. Politicians needed their support. So leaders gave them "bread and circuses." Rulers gave free grain to the poor for food. They built baths and public fountains. They also sponsored free entertainment.

Romans loved chariot races and violent sports. For such events, people went to the huge Colosseum in the center of Rome. There they could watch fighters called gladiators. Sometimes gladiators fought each other. They used spears and swords. At other times, they fought wild animals, such as lions. Fights were often to the death. Once in a while, a fighter was defeated but still alive. Then the crowd could decide what would happen to him. If they pointed thumbs up, he lived. If they showed thumbs down, he died.

Most gladiators were professional fighters. At times, however, untrained slaves or criminals were sent into the arena. One day Seneca went to an event at the Colosseum in A.D. 60. He was a Roman writer and thinker. This reading describes what he saw there.

By chance I attended a mid-day exhibition, expecting some fun, wit, and relaxation, but it was quite the reverse. During the luncheon interval, condemned criminals were often driven into the arena and compelled to fight for the amusement of those spectators who remained throughout the day. The men have no defensive armor. They are exposed to blows at all points, and no one ever strikes in vain. Many persons prefer this program to the usual. Of course they do; there is no helmet or shield to deflect the weapon.

What is the need of defensive armor, or of skill? All these men delaying death. In the morning they throw men to the lions and the bears; at noon, they throw them to the spectators. The spectators demand that the slayer shall face the man who is to slay him in his turn; and they always reserve the latest conqueror for another butchering. The outcome of every fight is death. In the morning they cried, "Kill him!" "Lash him!" "Burn him!" "Why does he strike so feebly?"

Source Reading Wrap-Up

1) What kind of entertainment did Seneca expect at the Colosseum?

2) What kind of fight was held at lunchtime?

3) According to Seneca, why did some spectators prefer this kind of event?

4) How did the spectators act toward the fighters?

5) How does Seneca feel about what he saw at the Colosseum? Explain your answer.

Women in Greek and Roman History

Women led limited lives in ancient Greece and Rome. Few got an education. Still, some women did influence history.

Sappho was a Greek poet. She was born around 630 B.C. She married and had a daughter, Cleis. One of her poems says, "I have a beautiful child who looks like golden flowers." Sappho wrote many poems about feelings and friendship. Only one complete poem exists today. Others have only a few lines.

All Roman emperors were men. But sometimes the real rulers were their wives or mothers. Julia Domna was the wife of the emperor about A.D. 200. She was known as Julia the Philosopher. She invited scholars and artists to court. They discussed art and ideas. Julia's son Caracalla became emperor in A.D. 211. While he went to war, she ruled the empire. A few years later, in A.D. 222, the teenage Alexander Severus became emperor. His mother, Julia Mamaea, ruled the empire for 13 years.

In the early 300s A.D., Constantine became emperor of the eastern part of the Roman Empire. His capital was at Byzantium. He changed its name to Constantinople. In A.D. 395, the empire was divided forever into two parts. Over time, this area became known as the Byzantine Empire.

The most powerful woman in this empire was Empress Theodora (A.D. 497–548). Her family

Empress Theodora and her court.

was poor. Her father worked in a circus. She was an actress. Then she met and married Justinian, the emperor's nephew. Justinian became emperor in A.D. 527. She became empress and coruler.

Theodora was smart and ambitious. She was also brave. In A.D. 532, the rulers faced dangerous riots. Justinian was ready to flee. Theodora changed his mind. She spoke to his advisers. "I'll never see the day," she said, "when I am not hailed as Empress. Caesar [Justinian], if you wish to flee, well and good. You have the money. The ships are ready. The sea is clear. But I shall stay!" Justinian stayed. Then the riots ended.

Spotlight Story Wrap-Up

1) For what was Sappho famous?

2) What did all Roman emperors have in common?

3) How did Julia Domna influence Rome?

4) Where did Justinian and Theodora rule?

5) How did Theodora show she was brave?

➡ Rome became a great empire during the reign of Augustus Caesar. The empire lasted from 27 B.C. to A.D. 476.

➡ Augustus ruled for 41 years. This time is called the Golden Age. He built many new buildings in Rome. He reformed government in the provinces. Roman rule brought peace and order to the empire. Pax Romana, the Roman peace, lasted from 27 B.C. to A.D. 180.

➡ Good and bad emperors followed Augustus. His stepson Tiberius ruled cruelly. The next emperor, Caligula, was insane. The imperial guards killed him. They then picked Claudius to be emperor. He ruled well, but was poisoned by his wife. Her son Nero became emperor. In A.D. 64, while Nero ruled, a fire destroyed much of Rome.

➡ From A.D. 98 to 180, Rome had three good emperors. They were Trajan, Hadrian, and Marcus Aurelius. To avoid war, Aurelius let German tribes settle inside the empire.

➡ The Roman Empire began to decline. Soldiers fought over who would become emperor. Diseases and the cost of wars made the empire weak.

➡ Jesus was born in Palestine during the reign of Augustus. Jews had religious freedom under Roman rule. Jesus preached about God's love. He made enemies among both Jewish leaders and Romans. He was crucified under Roman law. After his death, his followers wrote the Gospels to tell about his life and work.

➡ Followers of Jesus believed he was the son of God. His disciples, called Christians, spread his teachings. Paul helped spread Christianity.

➡ Some Roman rulers harmed Christians. In A.D. 337, however, Emperor Constantine became a Christian. Christianity later become the official religion.

➡ Emperor Diocletian wanted to make the empire easier to rule. He divided it into eastern and western parts.

➡ In A.D. 306, Emperor Constantine moved the capital to Byzantium. He renamed the city Constantinople.

➡ The Huns invaded Eastern Europe in the late 300s. To escape them, the Visigoths moved into the Roman Empire. Then they attacked Roman towns. They beat a Roman army at Adrianople. The Visigoths and the Vandals attacked Rome. The western empire fell in 476. Odoacer, a German, took control.

➡ Roman law was one important Roman contribution. Emperor Justinian brought the laws together in a code. Other gifts were in art, building, and medicine.

Comprehension: Identifying Facts

On a separate sheet of paper, use the words from the Word Bank to complete each sentence.

1) Historians call the reign of _____ the "Golden Age of Rome."

2) When _____ was 30 years old, he began to preach good news to the poor in Palestine.

3) The palace guards picked _____ to be emperor even though most people thought that he was a fool.

4) An old story says that Emperor_____ played his lyre while Rome burned.

5) Emperor _____ had a wall built in what is today called England to protect his soldiers from German tribes.

6) _____ liked to read and think, but he became a soldier to protect the Roman Empire.

7) Emperor _____ divided the Roman Empire into two parts.

8) _____ was the first Christian emperor.

9) _____ made Christianity the official religion of the Roman Empire.

10) A German leader, _____, took control of Rome in A.D. 476 and ended the Roman Empire.

Comprehension: Multiple Choice

On a separate sheet of paper, write the letter of the answer that correctly completes each sentence.

1) Augustus Caesar brought a period of peace to Rome that lasted for _____years.

   a. 41   c. 200

   b. 100   d. 1,000

2) _____ was an unpopular emperor because he thought everyone wanted to hurt him, but he had no proof.

   a. Augustus Caesar   c. Caligula

   b. Tiberius   d. Claudius

3) The Romans gave Jewish people _____ freedom.

   a. religious   c. worldwide

   b. political   d. none of the above

4) The Roman Empire declined because of _____.

   a. a plague   c. no system to pick an emperor

   b. lack of money   d. all of the above

5) The _____ and the Vandals invaded Rome in A.D. 410 and 455.

   a. Visigoths   c. Carthaginians

   b. Huns   d. Greeks

Comprehension: Understanding Main Ideas

On a separate sheet of paper, write the answers to the following questions using complete sentences.

1) In what ways were the Romans a practical people?

2) Why did the Roman Empire decline and then fall?

Critical Thinking: Write Your Opinion

1) Rome never found a good way to pick a new emperor. What happened because of this?

2) Which Roman gift do you think was the most important and why?

3) Who do you think was Rome's greatest emperor? Why?

Test-Taking Tip   If you don't understand the directions to a section of a test, read over the questions to see if you can figure out what you are supposed to do. If you still can't figure it out, ask the person giving the test, if possible.

SKILLS LESSON

Unit 3 *Graphs and Charts*

A graph is a figure that shows relationships between numbers. Types of graphs are bar, line, and circle graphs. **Use a graph to compare numbers and percentages.**

Here are examples of a simple bar graph and a simple circle graph. Each shows the estimated population groups in Athens at the time of Pericles. Population was divided between male citizens, women, slaves, and resident foreigners.

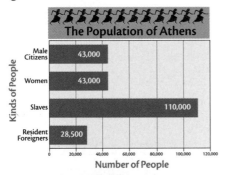

A chart is a way to put information together so it is clear. The information can be put in rows (across) and columns (up and down). **Use a chart to organize information.**

The chart in the next column organizes facts about some Greek and Roman writers.

The first column of the chart names the writer and tells when he or she lived. The second column tells the kind of literature the writer is

Important Greek and Roman Writers

Name of Writer	Type of Writing	Greek	Roman
Homer 700s B.C.	epic poetry	X	
Sappho 600s B.C.	lyric poetry	X	
Sophocles 496–406 B.C.	drama/tragedy	X	
Herodotus c. 480–430 B.C.	history	X	
Aristophanes c. 450–388 B.C.	drama/comedy	X	
Virgil 70–19 B.C.	epic poetry		X
Horace 65–8 B.C.	poetry		X
Livy 59 B.C.–A.D. 17	history		X

known for. The Xs in the last two columns tell whether the writer was Greek or Roman. For information about a certain writer, read across the row. Study the chart to answer the questions.

1) Which poet lived during an earlier time, Homer or Virgil?

2) Who wrote during the fifth century (400s) B.C.?

3) Which writers were historians? Were they Greek or Roman?

4) Which writer wrote comedies? Was he Greek or Roman?

5) Read the information below. Use it to make a bar graph comparing the size of three ancient cities. The vertical (up and down) axis of the graph shows the number of people.

- At its greatest, Rome had almost a million people.
- The second largest city in the Roman Empire was Alexandria. It had 750,000 people.
- Athens at its height had about 225,000 people.

➨ Greek civilization began on a peninsula and islands. Greeks from Mycenae fought the Trojan War. The *Iliad* and the *Odyssey* tell about it.

➨ Athens and Sparta were leading Greek city-states. The Athenians developed an early form of democracy. They admired education and the arts. Sparta had a military government. Greek writers invented tragedy and comedy. Socrates, Plato, and Aristotle were philosophers.

➨ The Persian Empire tried to conquer the Greek city-states in 490 and 480 B.C. The Greeks beat them at Marathon and Salamis.

➨ Athens and Sparta fought the Peloponnesian War against each other. War weakened the city-states. Philip of Macedon conquered them in 338 B.C.

➨ Philip's son Alexander conquered a huge empire by 323 B.C. His conquests spread Greek culture. The center of Hellenistic culture was Alexandria, Egypt.

➨ The Latins were a tribe in central Italy. They learned from the Greeks and Etruscans. Etruscan kings ruled Rome in the 500s B.C.

➨ The Romans overthrew their kings in 509 B.C. They set up a republic. A senate of wealthy patricians made laws. Ordinary Romans—the plebeians—gradually got political power.

➨ The Roman Republic fought and won three wars with the Phoenician city of Carthage. By 133 B.C., Rome dominated the Mediterranean.

➨ Reformers like the Gracchus brothers tried to help Rome's poor people. Then military leaders like Marius and Sulla got power. A popular general, Julius Caesar, won power about 49 B.C. Some senators killed him.

➨ Civil war broke out after Caesar died. Mark Antony was allied with Cleopatra, queen of Egypt. Caesar's heir Octavian defeated them. Octavian, who changed his name to Augustus Caesar, became emperor, and his long reign was a Golden Age.

➨ Roman law brought peace—the Pax Romana. Both good and bad emperors followed Augustus.

➨ The Roman Empire began to decline. Diocletian divided it into east and west. Constantine moved the capital to the east in 306 A.D. German tribes moved into the empire. Visigoths and Vandals attacked Rome. The western empire collapsed in 476. A German, Odoacer, began to rule.

➨ In about A.D. 30, Jesus began to preach in Palestine. He seemed a threat to Jewish leaders. He was crucified under Roman law. His followers believed he was the son of God. His disciples, called Christians, spread his teachings.

Comprehension: Identifying Facts

On a separate sheet of paper, use the words from the Word Bank to complete each sentence.

WORD BANK
citizens
dictator
helots
jury
patricians
plebeians
republic
senate
tyrants
veto

1) About 600 B.C., _____ began to take over the government of Greek city-states by force.

2) Only 40,000 of the 300,000 Athenians were _____.

3) An Athenian _____ could have as many as 1,000 members.

4) The _____ were Spartan farmers who were forced into slavery.

5) The _____ was the governing body in ancient Rome.

6) The Romans who owned land, had money, and helped rule the country were _____.

7) The common people of Rome were the _____.

8) In times of war, the Roman senate in the republic chose a _____ to rule for six months.

9) The republic had two consuls who could _____, or say no to, one another's decisions.

10) The _____ of the Romans lasted for 500 years.

Comprehension: Multiple Choice

On a separate sheet of paper, write the letter of the answer that correctly completes each sentence.

1) The blind poet who wrote the *Iliad* and the *Odyssey* was _____.

   a. Aristophanes   c. Socrates
   b. Plato   d. Homer

2) The soldier who conquered the known world between 334 B.C. and 323 B.C. was _____.

   a. Alexander the Great   c. Julius Caesar
   b. Pompey the Great   d. Augustus Caesar

3) The soldier who crossed the Alps with elephants and invaded Italy was _____.

    a. Julius Caesar   c. Hannibal

    b. Scipio   d. Tiberius Gracchus

4) The Roman senate made _____ dictator for life.

    a. Julius Caesar   c. Xerxes

    b. Aristotle   d. Philip II

5) The first emperor of the Roman Empire was _____.

    a. Minos   c. Augustus Caesar

    b. Mark Antony   d. Claudius

Comprehension: Understanding Main Ideas

On a separate sheet of paper, write the answer to each question. Use complete sentences, or statements.

1) Athens and Rome had different types of government. For a while, Athens had a direct, but limited, democracy. Rome was a republic and then an empire. Explain how these three types of government were different from each other.

2) For over a hundred years, Athens was the greatest city-state. Then the Athenians lost their freedom in 338 B.C. The Roman Empire lasted for 500 years, then it fell. Give at least one reason to explain both events.

Critical Thinking: Write Your Opinion

1) Would you rather be a Spartan helot or a Roman plebeian? Explain your answer.

2) Under which government would you have wanted to live—the Athenian democracy, the Roman Republic, or the Roman Empire? Explain your answer.

3) Of all the people you studied in Unit 3, which was your favorite and why?

| Test-Taking Tip | Be sure you understand what the test question is asking. Reread it if you have to. |

"It is impossible for one person, however intelligent and capable, to be able to make wise decisions by himself. Acting alone, he may be able, if he is fortunate, to make five right decisions out of ten each day. . . . Instead he should delegate authority to the most able and virtuous men he can find and supervise their work from above most diligently."

—Taizong, emperor of China (A.D. 626–649), from "On the Art of Government"

The Middle Ages

A.D. *500 to 1500*

*B*y A.D. 500, the Roman Empire had fallen apart. Historians call the 1,000 years following the fall of Rome the Middle Ages. These years are in the middle between the fall of Rome and the rebirth of learning in Europe in the 1500s.

The Middle Ages were often troubled times in Europe, Africa, Asia, and the Americas. You will find out why in Unit 4. You go on the Crusades, meet Muhammad, journey to Mali, and cross the ocean to visit the Mayas and the Incas. Then you sail back to India to meet Buddha, follow Genghis Khan into China, and travel into Japan.

EQUATO

ATLA

OCE

The Middle Ages in Europe

A.D. 500 to A.D. 1453

During the Middle Ages, the eastern part of the old Roman Empire grew strong. But the western part broke into many parts and fell into decay. In this chapter, you will learn about the Byzantine Empire and its greatest emperor. You will discover the ways this empire influenced the Slavic people of Eastern Europe. You will follow the Germanic tribes as they invade Western Europe. You will sail with the Vikings and find new lands! Finally, you will witness a battle that changed England forever.

Goals for Learning

▶ To compare the Byzantine and the Roman Empires

▶ To describe the influence of the Byzantine Empire on the people of Eastern Europe, especially Russia

▶ To describe some of the Germanic tribal kingdoms that replaced the Roman Empire

▶ To list several reasons why some historians call this period the "Dark Ages"

▶ To explain the importance of Charlemagne to European history

▶ To identify some groups that had success invading Britain and influenced its language and culture

A.D. 527 Justinian becomes Emperor of the Byzantine Empire

A.D. 862 The founding of Russia

A.D. 1240 The Mongols destroy Kiev

A.D. 1066 Normans conquer England

A.D. 1547 Ivan the Terrible becor first czar of Russia

A.D. 500   A.D. 750   A.D. 1000   A.D. 1250   A.D. 1500

A.D. 800 Charlemagne is crowned emperor

A.D. 1016 Canute, a Viking, becomes ruler of England

A.D. 1453 Turks take control of Constantinople and change its name to Istanbul

A.D. 1462 Ivan the Great rules Russia

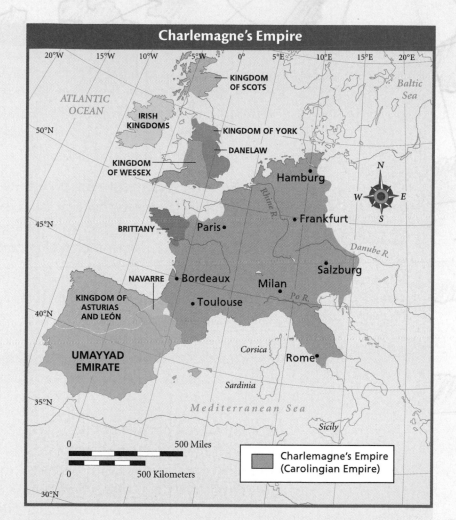

Charlemagne's Empire

KINGDOM OF SCOTS

ATLANTIC OCEAN

IRISH KINGDOMS

KINGDOM OF YORK

DANELAW

KINGDOM OF WESSEX

Baltic Sea

Hamburg

Rhine R.

Frankfurt

BRITTANY

Paris •

Danube R.

Salzburg

NAVARRE • Bordeaux

Milan

Po R.

KINGDOM OF ASTURIAS AND LEÓN

• Toulouse

UMAYYAD EMIRATE

Corsica

Rome •

Sardinia

Mediterranean Sea

Sicily

500 Miles

500 Kilometers

Charlemagne's Empire (Carolingian Empire)

Geography Skills

After the fall of the Roman Empire in A.D. 476, Europe broke into many small kingdoms. Cities disappeared. More than 300 years passed before a strong king united all of Western Europe again. His name was Charlemagne, or Charles the Great. This map shows his empire. It was located where the countries of France, Italy, Spain, Switzerland, Austria, the Czech Republic, and Germany are now located.

Study the map carefully. Then answer the following questions:

1) What are the names of three rivers in Charlemagne's empire?

2) What are the names of five cities in his empire?

3) What sea lies to the south of the empire?

4) How many miles did this empire stretch from east to west at its widest point? from north to south at its widest point?

5) Between what two lines of latitude was much of Charlemagne's empire?

Holy
Following God's ways

Relic
An object from the past that has something to do with God or with a holy person who follows God's ways

Saint
A person who follows God's ways

Remember when Emperor Diocletian divided the Roman Empire into two parts in A.D. 284? The eastern part became the Byzantine Empire. Constantine founded the city of Constantinople there in A.D. 330. He made his new city the capital of the Byzantine Empire.

How Was the Byzantine Empire Like Rome?

Constantine called his capital city the "new Rome." He built as the emperors had in Rome. One building—the Hippodrome—was like Rome's Colosseum. Constantine held chariot races in it.

An army of officials helped the emperor rule. They took charge of building and repairing roads. As in Rome, there was a senate, but the emperor held all the power. He organized the army along Roman lines. In the early years of the empire, all the Byzantine emperors were Roman and spoke Latin.

But Constantinople was not Rome. Most of its people were Greek and spoke the Greek language. Many had come there from other lands. Constantinople was located on one of the most important trade routes between Asia and Europe. Jews, Turks, Persians, Slavs, and Italians lived there.

How Did Rome and Constantinople Differ?

Constantinople was a Christian city. Emperor Constantine built many beautiful Christian churches there. Often, these churches were the most beautiful buildings in the city. He collected **relics** for them. (These relics were **holy** objects from the past. That is, they had something to do with God or with **saints**—people who followed God's ways.) People came from all parts of the empire to pray in these churches.

Who Was the Greatest of the Byzantine Emperors?

In A.D. 527, a man named Justinian became emperor. Most historians call him the greatest of the Byzantine emperors. We remember him for three reasons. First, he tried to win back the Roman lands in the West. Second, he put together a code of laws. Third, he made Constantinople more beautiful.

What Land Did Justinian Win Back?

Justinian tried to win back all the western lands that Rome had lost the century before. One of his armies won back much of Italy and North Africa. Another army threw back the Persians. During this time, several different Germanic tribes took over Rome. Finally, Justinian's armies won control. But the **barbaric** tribes, which were not civilized, had left Rome in ruins.

What Was Good About Justinian's Code of Laws?

Justinian asked a group of Greek and Latin scholars to collect and organize the laws of his empire. They published their code of laws in A.D. 533. Historians call this the greatest thing Justinian did.

The code was a complete record of Roman legal customs. It listed the rights that the empire gave to each person. For 900 years, this code was the basis for Byzantine law. The **principles,** or main ideas, of the code later shaped the legal systems of Europe and the United States.

Justinian (center) is considered to be one of the best emperors of the Byzantine Empire.

How Did Justinian Make Constantinople More Beautiful?

Justinian built a government building in which 20,000 people worked. Across from it, he built one of the world's most beautiful churches—the Hagia Sophia. Its ceiling rises 180 feet from the floor. He used beautifully colored marble for the walls, floors, and pillars. Justinian also built three walls to protect Constantinople. A marketplace on its main street offered **goods,** or trading things, from Africa, Asia, and Europe.

What Caused a Split in the Christian Church?

Icon
A small picture of a saint or Jesus

◆ **Patriarch**
A leader of the church

Justinian's motto was "one empire, one church, one law." He became the head of the church within the lands he controlled. Priests and **patriarchs**, or leaders of the church, became government officials. But some Christians did not want an emperor to control the church. They fought over this.

They also fought over the use of **icons**—small pictures of the saints and Jesus. Several emperors wanted to get rid of them. They thought people were worshipping the icons instead of God.

Soon, riots broke out. Christians in the eastern part of the old Roman Empire and Christians in the western part

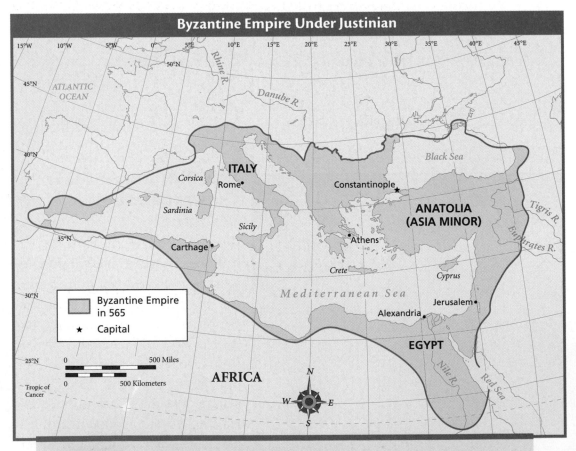

Byzantine Empire Under Justinian

Byzantine Empire in 565

★ Capital

MAP STUDY

This map shows the Byzantine Empire under Emperor Justinian. What was the capital of the Byzantine Empire? How far west did Justinian's empire extend? What lands did Justinian add?

began to think differently. This caused a split in the church. In 1054, the church in the West became known as the Roman Catholic Church. The church in the East became the Eastern Orthodox Church.

Why Did the Byzantine Empire Decline?

The death of Justinian in A.D. 565 marked the beginning of the end for the Byzantine Empire. Garbage filled Constantinople's narrow streets. As it decayed, it spread the plague. Disease-carrying rats roamed the city and spread the plague too.

Civil war broke out. People fought to decide who should become the next emperor. Then the Turks attacked the empire. In 1453, they took control of Constantinople and changed its name to Istanbul. It became the capital of the Ottoman Empire.

SECTION 1 REVIEW On a separate sheet of paper, write *True* if the statement is true or *False* if the statement is not true. Make each false statement true by changing the underlined word.

1) Constantine tried to build his capital like <u>Athens.</u>

2) The <u>Hippodrome</u> was like Rome's Colosseum.

3) Historians think that <u>Justinian</u> was the greatest emperor of the Byzantine Empire.

4) Justinian built the beautiful church known as the <u>Hippodrome.</u>

5) People in the Byzantium Empire began to fight over the use of <u>icons,</u> or small pictures of saints and Jesus.

What do you think

A plague weakened both the western Roman Empire and the eastern Byzantine Empire. Why do you think that the people at that time had such trouble with plagues?

Ceremony
The actions and words of a special event

◆**Cyrillic alphabet**
The alphabet invented by Cyril and Methodius and used to translate the Bible into Slavic languages

Monk
A member of a religious order

Religious order
A group of monks who live and work together

The Byzantine Empire greatly influenced the people of Eastern Europe. We call these people Slavs. They moved from central Asia into the countries we now call Russia, Ukraine, Yugoslavia, Bulgaria, the Czech Republic, Slovenia, Croatia, and Poland.

The Slavs included many groups. Each group had its own culture and language, but they were alike in some ways. The largest group was the Russians.

What Happened When the Slavs Became Christians?

The Slavs admired the Byzantine civilization. Around A.D. 900, two **monks,** or members of a **religious order** or group, began to preach to the Slavs. Cyril and Methodius helped many Slavs give up their old religions and become Christians.

The Slavs had no written language. The monks invented an alphabet for their spoken language. We call this the **Cyrillic alphabet.** Some Slavic countries still use it today. Then the monks translated the church's Bible, songs, and **ceremonies**— actions and words used for special events—into Slavic languages. Because of this, the Slavs could read the Bible and understand the ceremonies and songs.

Byzantine Christianity helped bring the people of Eastern Europe together. However, it caused a problem too. The Slavs accepted the Eastern Orthodox Church. But most of the rest of Europe belonged to the Roman Catholic Church. This difference isolated the Slavs from the rest of Europe. For nearly 300 years, they knew nothing about the discoveries and inventions that were changing civilization in Western Europe.

Two monks named Cyril and Methodius helped Slavs become Christians.

What Ties Did Russia Have With the Byzantine Empire?

In A.D. 989, Eastern Orthodoxy became the official religion of Russia. Now Russians felt closer to the Byzantine Empire. Several things show this. For example, Vladimir, an early Russian king, married the sister of the Byzantine emperor. Also, the empire and Russia traded with one another. Finally, the Russians built their churches to look like the ones in the Byzantine Empire. The beautiful church of Saint Sophia in the city of Kiev is one example of this. By A.D. 1050, Russian civilization was more advanced than any other in Western Europe.

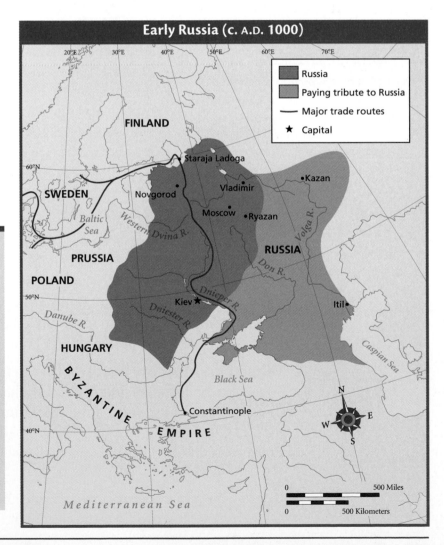

Early Russia (c. A.D. 1000)

Russia
Paying tribute to Russia
— Major trade routes
★ Capital

MAP STUDY

This map shows Russia in about A.D. 1000. Along what river did traders travel north from Constantinople? What city was both a capital and a trade center?

◆Boyar
A Russian noble who owned land

◆Veche
The Russian assembly that represented all free, adult male citizens

What Made Kiev So Important?

Historians give A.D. 862 as the date Russia was founded. In that year, Prince Rurik became ruler. His capital was Kiev. It is located on the Dnieper River—one of the main north-south water trade routes. Whoever controlled Kiev controlled Russia's trade with Constantinople.

Kiev was also at the center of two other trading routes: one between Europe and Asia and one between Scandinavia and the Middle East. By A.D. 1000, Kiev was the biggest city in Europe. It was larger than London or Paris.

At this time, Russia was a group of small territories. The Grand Prince of Kiev ruled these territories. He shared power with other princes and with **boyars**—nobles who owned land. A **Veche,** or assembly, represented all free, adult male citizens. It could accept or remove a prince. It also handled business and government.

Why Did Kiev Fall?

Kievan Russia reached its peak between A.D. 1000 and 1050. Its ruler unified Russia. However, when he died, his sons divided the kingdom among themselves. They fought each other and weakened the kingdom. Trade with Constantinople was cut off. In 1240, fierce Mongol armies from central Asia captured Kiev and completely destroyed it.

When Did Moscow Become Important?

To escape the invaders, many Russians headed north. In that same year, Alexander, a Russian prince, defeated the Swedes at the Neva River. The Swedes had tried to force the Russians to become Catholics. The Russians gave Alexander the title "Nevsky" or "of the Neva."

In 1294, Nevsky's youngest son, Daniel, became ruler of Muscovy, or Moscow. (It is the capital of Russia today.) At that time, Moscow was a small, rich town located on an important trade route. Later, the princes of Moscow took the **title,** or name, of "Grand Prince of All Russia."

Who Was the Founder of Modern Russia?

By the late 1400s, Moscow was the most powerful city in Russia. It became the center of the Russian church. Historians call Ivan III, or Ivan the Great, the founder of modern Russia. He ruled from 1462 to 1505. This great leader freed Russia from foreign rule and set up a government.

Ivan's wife, Sophia, was related to the last Byzantine emperor. She greatly influenced her husband. For example, she got him to adopt the double-headed eagle as his symbol. (It had been the symbol of Byzantine emperors.) Sophia also encouraged Ivan to take complete power of both the church and the government.

What Is the Kremlin?

Ivan the Great rebuilt the **Kremlin.** It became the center of the Russian church and the Russian government. The Kremlin was made up of three great churches and two palaces. Ivan built a thick, 60-foot-high wall around the Kremlin. Today, the Kremlin is still the center of government in Russia.

Who Was Ivan the Terrible?

In 1533, Ivan IV, who was only three years old, became the ruler of Russia. He was the grandson of Ivan the Great. Ivan IV began to govern when he was 14. During his reign, he made his kingdom three times larger by expanding south and eastward. Ivan IV believed that the Roman emperor Augustus Caesar was one of his ancestors. So in 1547, he crowned himself the first **czar** of Russia. This title means the same as the Roman title "caesar."

Ivan IV was a good military leader, but he was also a cruel man. He ordered his government officials to kill thousands of Russians and thousands of enemy soldiers. He beat one of his sons until he died. Because he was so cruel, historians call him Ivan the Terrible.

The Kremlin

For nearly 900 years, the Kremlin in Moscow has been the center of Russian government. But the Kremlin is much, much more. It contains beautiful churches and palaces. They stand inside a walled area more than a mile around. Impressive brick towers guard the entrance gates.

The first Kremlin was a wooden fort on the Moscow River. The Mongols burned it several times. By the late 1400s, however, Moscow was the most powerful city in Russia. Its ruler, Ivan the Great, hired Italian and Russian architects to build a new Kremlin. Inside its thick walls, they built three beautiful cathedrals with gold domes. Rulers were crowned in one church. They married in another. Their funerals were in the third. Later rulers added palaces and other buildings.

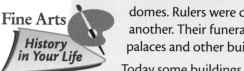

Fine Arts
History in Your Life

Today some buildings in the Kremlin are museums. There you can see the czars' crown jewels and other treasures.

SECTION 2 REVIEW On a separate sheet of paper, write the word from the Word Bank that completes each sentence.

WORD BANK
Cyril
Kremlin
Nevsky
Rurik
Vladimir

1) Methodius and _____, both monks, created an alphabet for the Slavic languages and used it to translate the Bible.

2) _____, an early Russian king, married the sister of the Byzantine emperor.

3) Historians date the founding of Russia to A.D. 862 when Prince _____ became ruler.

4) Prince Alexander became a hero to the Russians, and they called him _____ because of the place where he won a great battle.

5) Ivan the Great rebuilt the _____ as the center for church and government.

What do you think

Would creating an alphabet for a spoken language be hard? Explain your answer.

Literature
Written works that have lasting influence

The fall of Rome brought important changes to Western Europe. Germanic tribes slowly moved south and took over Roman lands. People did not obey Roman laws any longer. Roman soldiers could not keep order.

For 500 years there had been one Roman Empire. Now hundreds of little kingdoms took its place. These kingdoms had no system for collecting taxes. Rulers had no money for a government.

Why Do Historians Call This Period of Time the Dark Ages?

These little kingdoms were always at war with one another. This made doing business almost impossible. Also, along each road, robbers waited to attack travelers. Merchants were afraid to take their goods from city to city. There were no governments to repair roads and bridges. These fell into ruin. Towns and villages did, too.

Clovis united the Franks. He ruled for over 20 years.

As time passed, people lost interest in learning. They lost in war many useful books and artwork. People no longer learned about art, architecture, and **literature,** or written works. The schools closed and the people had only enough time to take care of their day-to-day needs. Civilization lost its knowledge of the past.

Think of what life was like then. All the tribes fought, people were afraid to travel, they had no schools, few could read or write—the world was falling down around them. Because of all of this, historians call this period of history the "Dark Ages."

Who Were the Franks?

The Franks were one of the largest of the German tribes. They began a civilization that later developed into the modern countries of France, Germany, and Italy. In A.D. 481, a warrior named Clovis united the Franks and became their king. He made Paris his capital. He was the first Germanic king to become a Roman Catholic.

Have you ever wondered where the names for the days of the week come from? At one time, they were all named for Roman gods. Then Germanic peoples invaded Western Europe and beat the Romans. This fact may surprise you, but the English language comes from theirs. As a result, most English names for days honor Germanic gods.

Woden was the chief Germanic god. His son Thor's magic hammer made the sound of thunder. Tiw was god of war. Their days are Tuesday (Tiw), Wednesday (Woden), and Thursday (Thor). Friday belongs to Frigg. She was the goddess of love. What about the other days? Sunday and Monday belong to the sun and moon. Saturday is named after the Roman god Saturn.

◆Pope
The head of the Roman Catholic Church

Who United All of Western Europe?

In A.D. 800, one king became strong enough to unite all of Western Europe. His name was Charlemagne, or Charles the Great. First, Charlemagne defeated the other Germanic tribes. Then he united them into one kingdom, with one religion—Roman Catholic. Next, Charlemagne fought against the enemies of the Roman Catholic Church. Leo III, the head of the Roman Catholic Church known as the **pope,** crowned him "Emperor of the Romans."

Charlemagne's rule brought law and order back to Western Europe. But less than 30 years after his death, his empire broke apart. Civil war began. New invaders threatened his kingdom.

How Far Did the Vikings Travel?

One of the invaders that attacked Charlemagne's empire was the Vikings. They came from northern Europe—from the present-day countries of Denmark, Sweden, and Norway. The Vikings were fine sailors who built excellent ships. They could sail them on shallow rivers and in deep oceans. These ships had both sails and long oars. The largest ship held up to 100 men, but as few as 15 men could sail a Viking ship.

Writing About History

Imagine you are a cable news reporter. You have been assigned to report on the Viking voyages. In your notebook, write what you would say in your report.

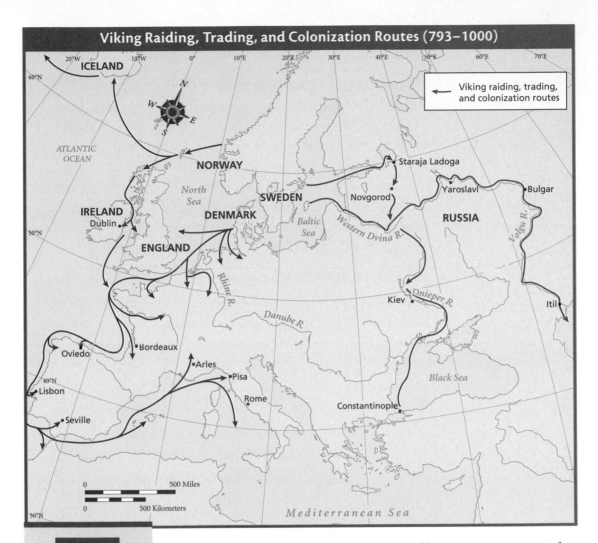

Viking Raiding, Trading, and Colonization Routes (793–1000)

ICELAND

ATLANTIC OCEAN

NORWAY

North Sea

SWEDEN

DENMARK

IRELAND
Dublin

ENGLAND

Baltic Sea

Staraja Ladoga

Novgorod

Yaroslavl

Bulgar

Western Dvina R.

RUSSIA

Volga R.

Rhine R.

Danube R.

Kiev

Dnieper R.

Itil

Oviedo

Bordeaux

Arles

Pisa

Rome

Black Sea

Lisbon

Seville

Constantinople

Mediterranean Sea

Viking raiding, trading, and colonization routes

0 500 Miles

0 500 Kilometers

MAP STUDY

This map shows Viking raiding, trading, and colonization routes. List some places to which the Vikings traveled.

Viking explorers traveled to Russia, all across Europe, and to America. They set up colonies on the islands of Iceland and Greenland. A Viking named Leif Eriksson landed on an island on the northeast coast of North America. He called it Vinland. Today, we call this area Newfoundland. It is part of Canada.

What Viking Became King of England?

After the Romans left Britain in the fifth century, different Germanic tribes invaded the island. Historians know little about the tribes called Angles, Saxons, and Jutes. What they do know is that they destroyed as they invaded. Beginning in A.D. 835 and continuing for over 100 years, the Vikings invaded Britain too. In A.D. 1016, a Viking named Canute became the ruler of England. In A.D. 1042, Edward the Confessor, an Anglo-Saxon, became king.

How Did the Normans Begin to Rule England?

When Edward died, three men claimed they were king. They went to war. After the Battle of Hastings in 1066, William, the Duke of Normandy, became king. (Normandy is a peninsula in present-day France.) The year 1066 is an important date in English history. William's victory meant that the Normans, rather than the Anglo-Saxons, would rule England. This has had a lasting influence on the English language and on the culture of England.

SECTION 3 REVIEW Choose the letter of the answer that correctly completes each sentence. Write your answer on a separate sheet of paper.

1) Historians call the period of time after the fall of Rome the "Dark Ages" because _____.

    a. there were no governments in Western Europe

    b. schools closed

    c. the people lost the learning of the past

    d. all of the above

2) _____ brought the Franks together and made Paris his capital.

    a. Charlemagne   c. Clovis

    b. William of Normandy   d. Leif Eriksson

3) In A.D. 800, Pope Leo III named _____ as the "Emperor of the Romans."

    a. Charlemagne   c. Clovis

    b. William of Normandy   d. Leif Eriksson

4) The Vikings visited _____.

    a. Iceland   c. Newfoundland

    b. Greenland   d. all of the above

5) The Battle of _____ took place in 1066.

    a. Charlemagne   c. Hastings

    b. Normandy   d. Newfoundland

What do you think ?

What would the world be like today if we lost all book and Internet learning from the past?

Life Among the Germans

Tacitus was a Roman historian. He did not like the way that Romans lived during his lifetime—he thought people lived in sin. Tacitus served as an official in several parts of the empire. As a result, he learned about different barbarians—people who were not Romans.

Many Germanic tribes lived on the northern borders of the empire. Tacitus admired their strength and simple life. He thought the Germans stood for an older, simpler way of life. After Rome fell, Germanic tribes conquered much of the empire. They soon controlled Europe.

This reading comes from Tacitus's history of the German tribes. He wrote it in A.D. 98.

They all have blue eyes, reddish hair, and large bodies; they do not submit patiently to work and effort and cannot endure thirst and heat at all, though cold and hunger they are accustomed to because of their climate. . . .

They choose their kings on account of their ancestry, their generals for their bravery. The kings do not have free and unlimited power and the generals lead by example rather than command. . . .

Concerning minor matters the chiefs deliberate, but in important affairs all the people are consulted. . . . When the crowd is sufficient they take their places fully armed. Silence is proclaimed by the priests, who have on these occasions the right to keep order. Then the king or a chief addresses them, each being heard according to his age, noble blood, reputation in warfare and eloquence. . . .

It is well known that none of the German tribes live in cities. They live separated and in various places, as a spring or a meadow or a grove strikes their fancy. . . .

As soon as they awake from sleep, which they prolong till late in the day, they bathe. After the bath they take food, each sitting in a separate seat and having a table to himself. Then they proceed to their business or not less often to feasts, fully armed. It is no disgrace to spend the whole day and night in drinking. Quarreling is frequent enough as is natural among drunken men. . . .

There is no pomp in the celebration of their funerals. The only custom they observe is that the bodies of illustrious men should be burned with certain kinds of wood. In every case a man's weapons burned with him, and sometimes his horse also.

Such are the facts I have obtained in general concerning the origin and customs of the Germans as a whole.

Source Reading Wrap-Up

1) What did Tacitus think were Germanic weaknesses?

2) How did the Germans choose their rulers and generals?

3) How did the Germans govern themselves?

4) Where did Germans live? Why might this seem odd to Romans?

5) Describe a typical day for German men.

How the Russians Became Christians

St. George and the dragon is the oldest religious icon in Russia.

The early Russian state was a mixture of two cultures. It was both Slavic and Viking. Rurik was the first ruler. He was probably a Viking chief and trader from Scandinavia. The people were mostly Slavs. They worshipped the old Slavic gods. In about A.D. 900, some people became Christians. Missionaries from the Byzantine Empire came to Kiev around 950. Olga, the Grand Princess, became a Christian in 957. Her grandson, Vladimir I, made Russia a Christian country.

An old Russian document says that several religions sent groups to Vladimir. He was still a pagan. Each pointed out the advantages of their faith. A group of Muslims came from Bulgaria. Vladimir rejected them because Muslims may not drink wine. "Drink," said Vladimir, "is the joy of the Russians." He also rejected the Jews. He saw that Jews were scattered throughout the world. Vladimir felt that their god had not protected them.

Vladimir still had two choices to consider. There was the Roman Catholic Church, the Christian church in the West. In addition, there was the Byzantine Church, the Christian church in the East.

Vladimir then sent his own men to investigate. They watched people worshipping. From Germany, they wrote, "We beheld no glory there!" German Catholic churches seemed too simple and plain. Another group went to Constantinople. That city was the center of the Byzantine Church. They visited the beautiful cathedral of Hagia Sophia. They were amazed. The church had mosaics of gold. Thousands of candles lit the soaring interior. They wrote, "We knew not whether we were in heaven or on earth. . . . We know only that God dwells there among men."

Two other things about the Byzantine Church appealed to Vladimir. First, the Russians could use their own language in church. He preferred this choice. In contrast, the Western Christian Church insisted that people worship in Latin. Second, the emperor was the head of the Byzantine Church. He had some control over it. The pope in Rome was head of the Western Church. In matters relating to religious faith, the pope could tell rulers what to do. Vladimir kept his independence. He chose the Byzantine Church. He ordered his people to be baptized. It was several hundred years, however, before most Russians accepted this new religion.

Spotlight Story Wrap-Up

1) What religion did most Russians follow before A.D. 900?

2) Who was the first Christian Russian ruler?

3) Why did Vladimir reject the Muslims? the Jews?

4) How did Vladimir's team feel about Hagia Sophia?

5) For what other reasons did Vladimir join the Byzantine Church?

➡ Constantine founded the Byzantine capital Constantinople in A.D. 330. It was a beautiful Christian city with many churches.

➡ Justinian, the greatest Byzantine emperor, began to rule in A.D. 527. He won back Roman lands from the Germans and made a code of laws. He also built the church of Hagia Sophia.

➡ The Byzantine emperor was head of the church. Church leaders ran the government. People disagreed over church rule and the use of icons. In 1054, the Christian church split in two. It became the Eastern Orthodox Church and the Roman Catholic Church.

➡ The Byzantine Empire declined and civil war broke out. In 1453, Turks captured Constantinople and changed its name to Istanbul.

➡ Many people in Eastern Europe were Slavs. The Russians were the largest Slavic group. Byzantine missionaries converted many Slavs to Christianity. To be able to write Slavic languages, two monks invented the Cyrillic alphabet.

➡ The Russian state began about A.D. 862 in Kiev, a trading center. Kiev was ruled by a Grand Prince and nobles, the boyars. Byzantine culture influenced early Russia.

➡ Mongols from Asia destroyed Kiev in 1240. Swedes also invaded Russia, but were held off by Alexander Nevsky. Power then shifted to the princes of Moscow.

➡ Ivan the Great founded modern Russia. He rebuilt the Kremlin, a walled city of palaces and churches. Ivan the Terrible, his grandson, made Russia larger. He became the "czar."

➡ The period after the fall of Rome is called the "Dark Ages." Western Europe split into many kingdoms and wars were frequent. Learning also declined.

➡ The Franks were a Germanic tribe. They lived in what are now France, Germany, and Italy. Clovis became their king in A.D. 481, and he made Paris their capital.

➡ A Frankish king, Charlemagne, united Western Europe in A.D. 800. The Pope crowned him "Emperor of the Romans." However, his empire collapsed after his death.

➡ Vikings attacked various parts of Europe. They also established colonies in Iceland and North America.

➡ Germanic tribes—Angles, Saxons, Jutes—settled in Britain. Vikings also invaded it. In 1066, William of Normandy invaded and conquered Britain, bringing French influence to England.

Comprehension: Identifying Facts

On a separate sheet of paper, use the words from the Word Bank to complete each sentence.

WORD BANK

Charlemagne

Constantine

Franks

Hagia Sophia

Ivan the Great

Justinian

Leo III

Methodius

Rurik

Vikings

1) _____ was Rome's first Christian emperor and built Constantinople.

2) The Byzantine emperor _____ ordered a code of all Roman laws.

3) Cyril and _____, both monks, invented an alphabet so that the Slavic people could read the Bible.

4) Justinian built a great church called the _____.

5) Russia was founded in A.D. 862, which was the year that Prince _____ became ruler.

6) _____ of Russia rebuilt the Kremlin.

7) The _____ were one of the largest of the German tribes.

8) In A.D. 800, _____ united all of Western Europe.

9) Pope _____ crowned Charlemagne "Emperor of the Romans."

10) The _____, who were excellent sailors, came from northern Europe.

Comprehension: Multiple Choice

On a separate sheet of paper, write the letter of the answer that correctly completes each sentence.

1) The name for the leaders of the Russian church is _____.

a. relics

b. icons

c. patriarchs

d. boyars

2) A _____ is a holy object from the past that has something to do with God or the saints.

a. relic

b. patriarch

c. Veche

d. czar

3) The name of the nobles in Russia who owned land is
_____.

    a. icons   c. czars

    b. patriarchs   d. boyars

4) Small religious pictures of saints and Jesus are _____.

    a. relics   c. boyars

    b. icons   d. titles

5) _____ is written works that have a lasting influence.

    a. Literature   c. Principle

    b. Ceremony   d. icons

Comprehension: Understanding Main Ideas

On a separate sheet of paper, write the answer to each question. Use complete sentences, or statements.

1) Why did Constantine call Constantinople the "new Rome"?

2) Why was the development of the Cyrillic alphabet important to the Slavic people?

3) Give three reasons why some historians call the Middle Ages in Europe the "Dark Ages."

Critical Thinking: Write Your Opinion

1) Charlemagne's empire fell apart 30 years after his death. How might world history be different if his empire had stayed together until the present time?

2) Imagine that you are a Viking. Describe the ship you travel on. Name and describe the foreign lands you visit. Describe what you like best about your life.

Test-Taking Tip

If you don't know the answer to a question, put a check beside it and go on. Then when you are finished, go back to any checked questions and try to answer them.

Chapter

Life in the Middle Ages

10

A.D. 1050 to A.D. 1500

After the Roman Empire in the West fell, the Germanic tribes made war on one another for many years. During this time, the monks and nuns of the Roman Catholic Church tried to keep learning alive. Some members of the church also tried to take control of the Holy Land. In this chapter, you will join the Crusades and travel to Palestine. Then you will come home again to your castle and the manor and live the life of a serf, a peasant, a page, a squire, a knight, a vassal, or a lord. While doing this, you will learn about feudalism.

Goals for Learning

▶ To explain the role of the Roman Catholic Church in the Middle Ages in Europe

▶ To recognize the causes and effects of the crusades

▶ To describe European feudalism

▶ To describe life on a manor

▶ To identify changes for the better in education, art, architecture, literature, and law

A.D. 1050
Europe settles down and begins to grow again

A.D. 1170
The windmill is invented in Holland

A.D. 1291
Muslims conquer the last Christian city in the Holy Land; crusades to Holy Land end

A.D. 1000   A.D. 1250   A.D. 1500

A.D. 1095
Pope Urban II calls for the First Crusade

A.D. 1154
Henry II begins to rule in England

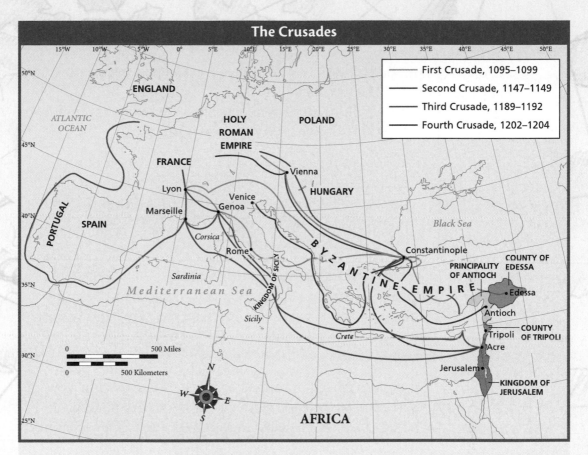

The Crusades

Legend:
- First Crusade, 1095–1099
- Second Crusade, 1147–1149
- Third Crusade, 1189–1192
- Fourth Crusade, 1202–1204

Map labels: ENGLAND, ATLANTIC OCEAN, HOLY ROMAN EMPIRE, POLAND, FRANCE, Lyon, Vienna, HUNGARY, Venice, Genoa, Marseille, PORTUGAL, SPAIN, Corsica, Rome, Black Sea, Constantinople, COUNTY OF EDESSA, PRINCIPALITY OF ANTIOCH, BYZANTINE EMPIRE, Sardinia, Mediterranean Sea, KINGDOM OF SICILY, Edessa, Antioch, Sicily, Crete, COUNTY OF TRIPOLI, Tripoli, Acre, Jerusalem, KINGDOM OF JERUSALEM, AFRICA

Scale: 0 — 500 Miles; 0 — 500 Kilometers

Geography Skills

In A.D. 1095, the Europeans of the western world began a series of military journeys called the crusades. They traveled to Palestine, which they called the Holy Land because Jesus had lived there. But by 1095, people of the Muslim faith lived in Palestine. The Europeans thought that God wanted them to rescue the Holy Land from the Muslims. For almost 200 years, European Christians went on crusades to win back Palestine.

Trace the routes these Christian warriors took and answer the following questions:

1) From what countries did the four biggest crusades begin?

2) On which crusade did Europeans go by land from Constantinople to Jerusalem?

3) Which crusade went to the Holy Land by a water route only?

4) In which crusade did the English take part?

5) Why do you think that each of these four crusades took so long?

Convent
A place where nuns live and work together

Monastery
A place where monks live and work together

Nun
A woman who leaves her home and enters a convent

By the year A.D. 1050, Western Europe had settled down. For years, Germanic tribes had fought wars. But now farming and trade expanded again. We call the period from A.D. 1050 to about 1500 the late Middle Ages.

The Roman Empire fell apart in A.D. 476. Soon Europe broke up into hundreds of small governments. But the Church remained strong. Its officials did things that the Roman government had done before. For example, they set up church courts and collected taxes.

What Did Religious Groups Do?

Some Christian men left the world behind and became monks. Some Christian women did the same and became **nuns.** Both monks and nuns joined together in religious groups to serve God.

The monks lived in **monasteries;** the nuns lived in **convents.** In the early sixth century, a monk named Benedict wrote a rule for monks and nuns. They promised never to marry, never to own property, and never to disobey the head of the monastery or convent.

Mont St. Michel is a famous old monastery in Normandy, France.

The Benedictines spent their lives praying and working. Some took care of the sick and the homeless. Some learned new things about farming and taught the farmers who lived nearby. Some welcomed travelers. (They had no place to stay because there were no hotels at this time.) Religious groups also supplied teachers to the new towns that were springing up.

How Did the Church Keep Learning Alive?

Monks and nuns also copied books from the past to make more copies. They did this by hand because no one in Europe had invented a machine to copy words. They decorated these books with bright colors and pictures. Over time, the largest monasteries and convents became centers of learning. They kept alive the learning from the past.

Where Did Christian Pilgrims Go?

During the Middle Ages, Christians called Palestine the **Holy Land** because Jesus of Nazareth had lived there. Many Christians traveled there to see places that Jesus had visited. We call such a trip a **pilgrimage.** People who go on a pilgrimage are **pilgrims.**

In the seventh century, **Muslims** conquered Palestine. (The Muslims were members of a religion founded by a man named Muhammad.) For nearly 400 years, the Muslims let Christian pilgrims visit the Holy Land. Then another group of Muslims took control of Palestine. According to some reports, this group killed Christians and destroyed churches.

What Were the Crusades?

In 1095, Pope Urban II, the head of the Roman Catholic Church, called for a **crusade,** or war, against the Muslims. He wanted to free Palestine from their control. The pope promised heaven to those who died on the crusade. Historians believe that between 5,000 and 10,000 men on horseback and between 25,000 and 50,000 foot soldiers fought in this First Crusade. A large number of common people also joined the crusade. We call all these people **crusaders.**

Why Did People Volunteer for the Crusades?

Many people became crusaders. Why? Some felt that they were following God's orders. Others wanted adventure. Still others wanted to escape hard work at home. Kings and nobles joined the crusades to get more power. The pope encouraged them to do this by forgiving their debts and by letting them pay fewer taxes.

For almost 200 years—from A.D. 1096 to 1291—European crusaders went to the Holy Land. They fought four big crusades and many small ones. But they did not get control of the Holy Land. In 1291, the Muslims conquered Acre,

This painting shows crusaders storming Jerusalem during the crusades.

the last Christian city. After that, the Muslims controlled Palestine until modern times.

What Were the Results of the Crusades?

The crusades did not win control of the Holy Land for Christians. However, the pope and European kings ended up with more power. Also, because Europe began to trade with the Middle East, Europeans could buy things like sugar, lemons, and **spices.** (We use spices to flavor food.) The crusaders also learned about Arab art, architecture, medicine, and mathematics.

The crusades brought other changes too. During the crusades, Europeans traveled to Palestine, which was far away from their homeland. When they returned home, their small villages in Europe seemed uninteresting. They wanted to see more faraway lands. Many people began to explore Africa, Asia, and America.

A down side of the crusades was that Christians began to kill Jews simply because they were not Christians. During the 200 years of the crusades, Muslims killed thousands of Christians, and Christians killed thousands of Muslims. In fact, some European Christians killed eastern Christians simply because they dressed like the Muslims. This caused a lasting split between the Roman Catholic Church and the Eastern Orthodox Church.

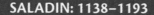

SALADIN: 1138–1193

Saladin was a Muslim leader. He became the ruler of Egypt and Syria. Saladin built schools and mosques there. He was so brave and honorable that even crusaders admired him.

For years, the crusaders held Palestine. Saladin wanted those Muslim lands back. He united Muslims against the crusaders. His forces captured Jerusalem in 1187. Then they took back most of Palestine.

As a result, the Third Crusade began. It ended Saladin's two-year siege of the crusaders at Acre. But they never won back Jerusalem. Finally, Saladin and crusade leader Richard the Lion-hearted met. Their truce let Christian pilgrims visit Jerusalem.

SECTION 1 REVIEW On a separate sheet of paper, write *True* if the statement is true or *False* if the statement is not true. Make each false statement true by changing the underlined word.

1) In the early sixth century, a monk named <u>Francis</u> wrote a rule for monks and nuns.

2) Monks and nuns copied <u>paintings</u> and decorated them with bright colors and pictures.

3) These monks and nuns kept alive the learning of the <u>past.</u>

4) Pope <u>Urban II</u> called for volunteers for the First Crusade.

5) The crusaders fought to gain control of the <u>Russian Empire.</u>

What do you think

Were the crusades good or bad for the people of Europe and the Middle East? Explain your answer.

◆**Feudalism**
A political and military system based on the holding of land

◆**Fief**
Land, and everything on it, which a lord gave to a vassal

◆**Knight**
A soldier who fought for a lord

◆**Lord**
A king or a noble who gave land to someone else

◆**Page**
A young noble who learned certain behaviors to become a knight

◆**Peasant**
A poor farmer or farmworker

◆**Squire**
A young noble who learned how to ride a horse and use weapons so as to become a knight

◆**Vassal**
A person who received land from a king or noble and gave loyalty in return

The Roman Empire had laws to govern people and armies to protect them. But during the Middle Ages, there was no one power in Europe. A new political and military system arose. We call this system **feudalism.** It was based on the holding of land.

How Did Feudalism Work?

Under the feudal system, the king owned all the land. But he needed loyal nobles to serve him. How could he win their loyalty? By giving them land. The nobles could then give land to other people and ask for their loyalty.

What Were the Titles of the Nobles?

We call the kings and nobles who gave land **lords.** We call the nobles who received land **vassals.** When lords gave land, they did so in a special ceremony. The vassal knelt down before the lord and promised loyalty. He would serve the lord and help him in battle.

In return, the lord gave the vassal a **fief,** or piece of land, and the **peasants** who farmed it. To protect his fief, each vassal needed his own soldiers. He had much land, but little money. He offered land to men who agreed to be his vassals. The lords and vassals kept dividing the land into smaller and smaller pieces.

How Many Years Did Someone Train to Become a Knight?

The Middle Ages was a time of thousands of small wars. **Knights** did most of the fighting. Only the son of a noble could become a knight. A young noble started training to be a knight by first becoming a **page.** He learned religion, manners, obedience, and loyalty. When he was about 15 years old, the page became a **squire.** Then he learned to ride a horse and use weapons. At age 21, most squires became knights.

ARMOR OF THE MIDDLE AGES

During the Middle Ages, knights, lords, and even kings rode to their many battles in armor. Armor changed as weapons and ways of fighting changed.

In A.D. 1066, when William the Conqueror invaded England, his knights wore simple cone-shaped helmets and suits of mail. To make this mail, an iron worker heated and then hammered out a small iron bar. When it was long and thin, he wound it around another rod. Next, he cut rings from the thinned iron. Finally, he linked them together so that they overlapped, or partly covered, one another. He spent many months making a complete mail suit. It looked like a mesh suit of iron.

The knights wore padded coats underneath the mail. Because the sun makes metal hot, the knights often wore a loose-fitting cloth coat over their mail suit.

Jousting was popular in the Middle Ages. Knights fought each other for sport on horseback using a long lance.

By the 1200s, knights wore a helmet that covered their face. As time passed, they began to protect their whole body with armor. A breast plate protected their chest; pauldrons protected their shoulders. Gauntlets covered their hands; greaves covered their legs. The knight wore spurs on his armored heels. He used these spiked wheels to make his horse obey.

On his clothes, each knight painted his coat of arms. This was a design in the shape of a shield. Each man wore a different coat of arms. It showed everyone who he was. Some coats of arms were simple. Others contained trees, birds, and animals.

What Did Lords Expect From Their Knights?

A lord **knighted** a squire, or made him a knight, in a special ceremony. The lord commanded the new knight to be brave, polite, and loyal. The knight promised to defend the church, be loyal to the lord, protect the weak, and be polite to women.

Each knight had to be strong. He wore heavy armor and carried a **lance,** or steel-tipped spear; a two-edged sword; a **dagger,** or sharp-pointed knife; and a broad ax called a **battle ax.** His armor and weapons could weigh as much as 100 pounds.

Every knight hoped to become a lord and have a great amount of land to give to vassals some day. But many knights never became lords. They spent their entire lives fighting one war after another.

SECTION 2 REVIEW On a separate sheet of paper, write the word from the Word Bank that completes each sentence.

1) The _____ of the Middle Ages was a political and military system based on the holding of land.

2) A _____ gave land to a vassal and asked for his loyalty.

3) A _____ is the name of the land the vassal received.

4) A _____, or poor farmer, worked the land.

5) A _____ was a soldier who was loyal to a noble and fought for him.

Battle ax
A broad ax used in battle

Dagger
A sharp-pointed knife used for stabbing

◆**Knighted**
To be made a knight

Lance
A steel-tipped spear

WORD BANK

feudalism

fief

knight

lord

peasant

What do you think ?

What would be one good thing and one bad thing about being a knight?

◆**Blacksmith**
A person who works with iron and makes tools and weapons

◆**Manor**
The part of a fief that peasants farm for the lord

Self-sufficient
Being able to take care of one's needs without help

◆**Serf**
A peasant who was bound to the land and whose life was controlled by the lord of the manor

The whole feudal system was based on the control of land. A **manor** was that part of the fief that peasants farmed to support a lord's family.

What Made the Manor Self-Sufficient?

A manor was **self-sufficient** because the people who lived on it grew, raised, or made nearly everything that they needed. They made clothing from the wool of the sheep they raised. They cut wood for building from the manor's forests. They grew or raised all the food that they ate. The **blacksmith** worked with iron to make tools and weapons. The lord of the manor bought only a few things—like salt and iron—from the outside world.

Who Were Serfs?

About 90 percent of the people who lived during the Middle Ages were peasants. A few peasants were free, but most were **serfs.** Serfs were not free, but they were not slaves either. No one could buy or sell them. But they had to stay on the manor on which they had been born.

Women of the Middle Ages spent much of their time spinning wool and weaving cloth.

Serfs worked on the manor farms from early in the morning until late at night. They did the farmwork, cut wood, and built fences. Women serfs worked in the fields, cooked, made clothing, and cared for the house. About 60 percent of what each serf raised went to the lord of the manor and to the church.

What Improved Farming?

During the Middle Ages, farming changed because of five inventions: the three-field system, the horseshoe, a better plow, the waterwheel, and the windmill.

◆Drawbridge
A bridge that can be raised or lowered over a moat

Household
All the people who live and work inside a house

◆Moat
A dug-out area filled with water that circles a castle

Under the three-field system, a lord left one-third of his fields unplanted each year. This allowed the soil to rest. Then the field produced more food when the serfs planted it a year later. Up to this time, people had used the slow-moving ox to do heavy work. But with horseshoes, they could plow with the faster-moving horse.

With a better plow, a tool used to dig up soil before planting seeds, serfs could farm the heavy soil of northern Europe. The newly invented waterwheel used the power of running water to make more power. With this new power, serfs could grind grain, like wheat, into flour. Windmills, invented in Holland around 1170, used wind power for the same purpose.

How Did Better Farming Change the Population?

Because of these new inventions, farmers began to grow their crops in better ways. This meant that they produced more food. More food meant that the population grew. In 300 years—from 1000 to 1300—the number of people living in Western Europe got three times as big. Because they had more food than they needed, some people had time to do other things. This led to a rebirth of learning.

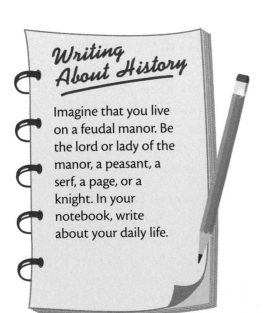

Writing About History

Imagine that you live on a feudal manor. Be the lord or lady of the manor, a peasant, a serf, a page, or a knight. In your notebook, write about your daily life.

Why Did Nobles Build Castles?

Many nobles lived in huge stone castles to protect themselves from their enemies. Most castles had high walls. A **moat,** or dug-out area filled with water, made a circle around the castle. To enter the castle, visitors crossed the moat by using a **drawbridge.** The people inside the castle lowered and raised it over the moat.

The nobles often built their castles on hilltops or by river bends. This made the castle easier to protect and defend. Some castles were big enough to include the noble's house and his **household**—all the people who lived and worked inside the

Castles were designed for protection. This castle is from fifteenth century France.

castle. The fields and the homes of the serfs were outside the castle walls. In times of war, they moved inside the walls for protection.

Inside the castle walls was a large open area called a **courtyard.** In good weather, the lord held his court there. The courtyard also contained many small buildings and sheds: the blacksmith's workshop; the bakery; the kitchen; the stable for the knight's horses; and rooms to store weapons and extra food. An attack against the castle could last many months. The lord of the manor had to store plenty of weapons and food.

◆Courtyard
A yard where a noble could hold court

What Was Life Like in a Castle?

Castles were dark, damp, and dull. Their tiny windows let in little light. Straw covered the floor of the dining area. The straw was usually dirty because the lord and his household threw garbage on the floor for the dogs to eat! The serfs cooked the food in the courtyard. It was often cold by the time the lord and his family ate it.

Chess, the Game of Kings

Have you ever played chess? It was a popular game in the Middle Ages, too. Even then, it was centuries old. Like silk and spices, it came to Europe from the East. It was played in Asia as early as 550 B.C. The Arabs brought it to Spain in the 700s.

Chess pieces changed during the Middle Ages to reflect life at that time. Kings, queens, knights, and bishops moved around the board. There were even foot-soldiers (pawns) and castles (rooks). As in medieval warfare, pawns had the least value. In the language of the game, players "capture" pieces, such as castles. The object of the game is to capture your opponent's king. Playing chess is indeed like looking back into the Middle Ages.

Then and Now

But not everything was dull in a castle. During the long winter nights, the lord and his guests drank and sang. They played board games like chess and backgammon. In better weather, the nobles held **tournaments,** or contests between knights. In these tournaments, two knights in armor would **joust.** They would ride toward each other at full speed. Each would try to knock the other off his horse!

SECTION 3 REVIEW Choose the letter of the answer that correctly completes each sentence. Write your answer on a separate sheet of paper.

1) Most of the peasants were _____.

   a. slaves   c. knights

   b. free   d. serfs

2) Serfs gave _____ percent of what they raised to the lord of the manor and to the church.

   a. 30   c. 90

   b. 60   d. 100

3) Farming improved during the Middle Ages because of the invention of the _____.

   a. three-field system   c. horseshoe

   b. waterwheel   d. all of the above

4) A _____, which was a dug-out area filled with water, made a circle around a castle.

   a. manor   c. moat

   b. fief   d. drawbridge

5) Castles were _____.

   a. dark   c. dull

   b. damp   d. all of the above

What do you think

How does having more food lead to more time to learn?

◆**Bishop**
A priest who is in charge of other priests and a number of churches

Cathedral
The church where the bishop is the main priest

University
A school where students study many subjects of higher learning

When the Roman Empire fell, education stopped. But then monasteries opened schools to prepare boys to become monks or priests. From about A.D. 1000 to 1100, **bishops** set up schools in their **cathedrals.** Bishops are priests who are in charge of other priests and a number of churches. A cathedral is the church where the bishop is the main priest. These cathedral schools were located in towns that later became centers of learning.

What Did Students Study?

Classes at cathedral schools lasted ten hours a day, and the teachers beat lazy students. In addition to religion, they studied seven subjects: Latin; rhetoric—speaking and writing correctly; arithmetic; geometry; astronomy; logic— figuring things out; and music. As years passed, the number of subjects increased. This led to the first **universities,** or schools where students study subjects of higher learning.

What Did Art Teach the People?

Artists and artisans during the Middle Ages built beautiful churches and cathedrals. They made beautiful windows out of colored glass. They carved life-like statues and created

The first schools were set up to prepare boys to become monks or priests.

◆Buttress
A structure that holds up or gives support to something; to hold up

◆Gothic
A style of architecture with thin walls, pointed arches, many windows, and flying buttresses

◆Romanesque
A style of building that was like what the Romans built with thick walls and arches

colorful wall paintings to show the life of Jesus, the saints, and people from the Bible. Most people did not know how to read or write. They learned about Christianity from these windows and statues and paintings.

What Is Gothic Architecture?

Until about 1100, most churches looked like Roman buildings. We call this style of architecture **Romanesque.** The churches had rounded arches. To hold up the heavy roof, the builders built thick walls with narrow openings for windows. Because of this, Romanesque churches were dark and gloomy.

Around 1200, church builders began building in a new style. We call it **Gothic.** Narrow, heavy ribs of stone supported the roof. To keep these thin walls from collapsing, the builders used flying **buttresses.** That is, they built columns outside the walls and then placed a bridge between the church wall and the column. These bridges buttressed, or held up, the thin walls. Finally, they used pointed arches, which drew the eyes upward.

Artists and artisans built hundreds of churches and cathedrals in the Gothic style. Some were so large that

Learning the Latin Language

Why could educated people from different lands understand each other during the early Middle Ages? They spoke Latin. It was the international language of Europe. Knowledge from the past was written in Latin. Any new learning or information, such as a law, would also be in Latin.

But Latin was a foreign language. It was different than what students spoke every day. In English, you say, "I know" but "he knows." The -s is a verb ending. In Latin, there is a different ending for each person—*I, he, we, you, they*. Other kinds of words, such as nouns and adjectives, also have endings. Take, for example, the words *boys, ball, big*, and *hit*. In Latin, endings would tell if the sentence meant:

The big boys hit the ball or *The big ball hit the boys.*

Latin was the key to knowledge. Grammar schools, therefore, became very important.

Language Arts lāng'gwĭj ärts

History in Your Life

This gothic church is Rheims Cathedral in France.

builders worked on them for many years. For example, the beautiful cathedral of Notre Dame in Paris took 150 years to finish. It can hold 9,000 people.

What Was Literature Like in the Middle Ages?

People wrote two kinds of literature in the Middle Ages. Some wrote in Latin. Others wrote in the language of the common people.

The Latin works included important writings on Christianity. Thomas Aquinas wrote a book called *Summa Theologica*. In it, he explained that **faith**—to believe in God—and reason are both gifts from God. He tried to bring the two together. He helped to keep alive much of the learning of the ancient world.

Faith
To believe in God; a religion

Some people wrote stories in the language of the common people. They usually retold an old story. People had passed these stories down in song. Or storytellers had told them long before anyone wrote them down.

One well-known story was the *Song of Roland*. It takes place during the reign of Charlemagne. The *Nibelungenlied* puts together several German legends. The first great work in English is *Beowulf*. Like the two other stories, it tells about the heroic deeds of a warrior.

What Changes Took Place in Law?

Important developments in law took place during the Middle Ages. Henry II, an English king who ruled from 1154 to 1189, introduced the use of the jury in English courts.

The English jury was a group of 12 people who helped the judge. The jury asked questions to discover the truth. Then

Advice
Ideas about how to do something

Evidence
Facts and information

◆**Parliament**
The English council or lawmaking assembly

Trial
A court case in which a jury examines evidence and decides if an accused person has done wrong

it could decide whether a person accused of doing something wrong was guilty or innocent. Today, we call this a grand jury.

If the jury thought that a crime might have been committed, a judge held a **trial** with another jury. This jury examined all the **evidence**—the information and the facts—in court. The jury decided if the person had done wrong. Today, we call this a petit jury.

What Is a Parliament?

During the Middle Ages, kings began to ask nobles for **advice,** or ideas, about government. Soon councils of nobles and church leaders formed in most of Western Europe. The English called their council **Parliament.** The French called their council the Estates General. Nobles organized assemblies in other countries during the Middle Ages, but these rarely lasted.

SECTION 4 REVIEW On a separate sheet of paper, write answers to these questions.

1) What were the seven subjects studied in the cathedral schools of the Middle Ages?

2) How did church buildings help the people of the Middle Ages learn about their faith?

3) What are two differences between Romanesque and Gothic architecture?

4) What is one thing that is the same about the *Song of Roland,* the *Nibelungenlied,* and *Beowulf?*

5) What change did Henry II introduce into English law during the Middle Ages?

What do you think

Would you have liked going to school during the Middle Ages? Explain your answer.

A Crusader's Letter

Thousands of people joined the First Crusade in 1096. Many were princes and nobles. Much of what we know about the crusades comes from letters. This letter is from Stephen, count of Blois in France. His wife, Adele, was the daughter of William the Conqueror.

Count Stephen to Adele, his . . . wife, to his dear children, and to all his vassals of all ranks—his greeting and blessing:

You may be very sure, dearest, that the messenger whom I sent to you left me before Antioch safe and unharmed and, through God's grace, in the greatest prosperity. And already at that time, together with all the chosen army of Christ . . . , we had been continuously advancing for twenty-three weeks toward the home of our Lord Jesus. You may know for certain, my beloved, that of gold, silver, and many other kinds of riches, I now have twice as much as you, my love, supposed me to have when I left you. For all our princes, with the common consent of the whole army, though against my own wishes, have made me, up to the present time, the leader, chief, and director of their whole expedition.

You have . . . heard that after the capture of the city of Nicaea we fought a great battle with the Turks and, by God's aid, conquered them. Next we conquered for the Lord all Romania. . . .

We besieged it [Antioch] and had many conflicts there with the Turks. Seven times we fought with the citizens of Antioch and with the troops coming to their aid; we rushed to meet them and we fought with the fiercest courage under the leadership of Christ; and in all these seven battles, by the aid of the Lord God, we conquered, and most . . . killed . . . [many] of them. In those battles, indeed, and in very many attacks made upon the city, many of our followers were killed, and their souls were borne to the joys of paradise. . . .

I can write to you only a few, dearest, of the many things which we have done. Although I am not able to tell you all that is in my mind, I trust that all is going well with you, and urge you to watch over your possessions and to treat as you ought your children and your vassals. You will certainly see me as soon as I can possibly return to you. Farewell.

Source Reading Wrap-Up

1) What is the "army of Christ"?
2) When Stephen sent the messenger to Adele, how long had he been away?
3) What honor did the other nobles give Stephen?
4) Name two cities where Stephen fought in battles.
5) Reread the advice Stephen gave Adele. What can you tell about her duties at home?

Unlucky King John and the Magna Carta

In all of English history, there has been only one King John. He was so unpopular that no other English king has used the name. John was not just unpopular. He was unlucky, too.

John's older brother was Richard I, the Lion-hearted. Richard was a well-loved hero. While he was on the Third Crusade, John tried to make himself king. When Richard came home in 1199, he banished his brother from England.

After Richard died in 1199, John became king. He was actually able and clever, but things never went right. The French beat him in a war. That defeat cost him money and influence. He lost English lands in France, too. Next, John had a serious disagreement with the pope. The pope cut him off from the Church. John had to agree to be the pope's vassal.

Then the king demanded more services from his vassals. He placed new taxes on the Church. Both the nobles and church leaders got angry at John. Many members from both groups felt that the king had too much power. By the spring of 1215, there was a war going on inside England. Some nobles backed John. Some wanted to get rid of him. A large army marched toward London.

To avoid losing his throne, John gave the rebel leaders new rights. The event took place on June 15, 1215 in a large open field called Runnymede. The leaders and churchmen met King John. They told him the terms that they wanted him to sign, and John agreed to them. Then he put his royal

King John signing the Magna Carta in 1215.

seal on the document that Church leaders had written.

The paper that King John signed is called the Magna Carta, or Great Charter. It gave specific rights to the feudal nobles and to the towns. It also promised church leaders some freedoms. Most importantly, the Magna Carta meant that even the king had to obey the law.

At first, the Magna Carta protected mainly the rights of nobles. Gradually these rights were extended. Finally, every Englishman would claim them. English settlers brought these ideas to America.

Spotlight Story Wrap-Up

1) Why has there only been one King John in English history?

2) What caused John's disagreement with his brother Richard?

3) What actions made leaders angry with John?

4) What is the most important principle in the Magna Carta?

5) How has the importance of Magna Carta changed since 1215?

CHAPTER SUMMARY

➡ After 1050, farming and trade began to grow again in Western Europe.

➡ The Catholic Church was important in the Middle Ages. Monks and nuns were members of religious groups. Some cared for the sick or studied farming methods. Others taught students and supplied places for travelers to stay. The Catholic Church kept learning alive.

➡ Christian pilgrims visited Palestine, or the Holy Land. In about 1095, one group of Muslims stopped pilgrimages. The pope then called for a holy war, or crusade, to regain control of Palestine.

➡ Europeans fought four major crusades between 1096 and 1291. Both nobles and common people were crusaders. In the end, Muslims kept control of Palestine.

➡ The crusades had three results. These included increased trade with the Middle East and curiosity about distant lands. Unfortunately, they were also the beginning of harsh treatment toward Jews and Orthodox Christians.

➡ Feudalism began in Europe in the Middle Ages because there was no central government. It was based on an exchange of a lord's land for a vassal's service.

➡ Knights were medieval soldiers. Knights came from noble families. They trained for knighthood first as pages and then as squires.

➡ Feudal manors were self-sufficient. Most people were peasants; some were serfs who could not leave the land.

➡ Five inventions changed farming. They were the three-field system, the horseshoe, an improved plow, the waterwheel, and the windmill. With better crops and more food, the population of Europe grew larger.

➡ Nobles built strong castles for protection. Sometimes knights practiced their skills in tournaments on castle grounds.

➡ In the Middle Ages, boys began attending school in monasteries and cathedral schools. Classes were conducted in Latin. As a result, educated people knew Latin.

➡ Early medieval churches were Romanesque. They had thick walls with rounded arches. The later Gothic style had pointed arches and tall, thin walls. The stained glass windows taught people religious stories.

➡ There were two kinds of medieval literature. Religious works were written in Latin and traditional stories in local languages.

➡ English law introduced the jury system and Parliament.

Comprehension: Identifying Facts

On a separate sheet of paper, use the words from the Word Bank to complete each sentence.

WORD BANK
convent
fief
knight
lance
lord
manor
moat
page
pilgrim
serf

1) The land given to a vassal by his lord is a _____.

2) A _____ was a young nobleman training to be a knight.

3) A _____ was a peasant bound to the land on which he or she was born.

4) Nuns live in a _____.

5) A _____ visited the Holy Land to see the place where Jesus had lived.

6) A _____ is a steel-tipped spear.

7) A _____ is a dug-out place filled with water that circles a castle.

8) A _____ is a self-sufficient area of land on which the peasants grew or raised almost everything that the lord and they needed.

9) A _____ is a king or noble who gives land to someone else in return for loyalty.

10) A _____ is a soldier who gives loyalty to his lord.

Comprehension: Multiple Choice

On a separate sheet of paper, write the letter of the answer that correctly completes each sentence.

1) The military journeys to the Holy Land that lasted for nearly 200 years are the _____.

    a. Muslims   c. Romanesque

    b. Vassals   d. crusades

2) _____ was a political and military system used in the Middle Ages that was based on the holding of land.

    a. Gothic   c. Feudalism

    b. Monastery   d. Buttress

3) Gothic architecture had _____.

a. pointed arches
c. flying buttresses

b. thin walls
d. all of the above

4) Many castles had _____.

a. courtyards
c. drawbridges

b. moats
d. all of the above

5) The heroic story that takes place in the reign of Charlemagne is the _____.

a. *Beowulf*
c. *Song of Roland*

b. *Nibelungenlied*
d. none of the above

Comprehension: Understanding Main Ideas

On a separate sheet of paper, write the answers to the following questions using complete sentences, or statements.

1) What is one good thing and one bad thing that resulted from the crusades?

2) What was feudalism?

3) What did the church have to do with education, art, and architecture during the Middle Ages?

Critical Thinking: Write Your Opinion

1) Why do you think the people living on manors welcomed travelers, actors, and musicians? Describe how this tells about what life was like living on a manor.

2) If you were a crusader, what reasons would you give for being one? List at least three reasons.

Test-Taking Tip | If you do not know the meaning of a word in a test question, read the question to yourself, leaving out the word. Then see if you can figure out the meaning of the word from its use in the sentence.

Chapter

Africa and the Americas

11

A.D. 300 to A.D. 1590

Things changed in Europe between A.D. 500 and 1500. Things also changed in Africa and the Americas. In Arabia, the prophet Muhammad founded a new religion called Islam. From about 1150 to 1200, the Islamic world was the center of world civilization. In Africa, powerful kingdoms arose during the "Golden Age." About the same time, great civilizations developed in Central and South America. In this chapter, you will travel and trade with the people of Arabia, Ghana, Mali, and Songhai. Then you will cross the ocean and meet the Olmecs, Mayas, Aztecs, and Incas.

Goals for Learning

▶ To recognize that Islam is one of the great religions of the world

▶ To list the five basic duties each Muslim must accept

▶ To identify contributions Arabs have made in science, mathematics, and literature

▶ To compare the West African civilizations of Ghana, Mali, and Songhai

▶ To describe the powerful Mayan, Aztec, and Incan civilizations of Central and South America

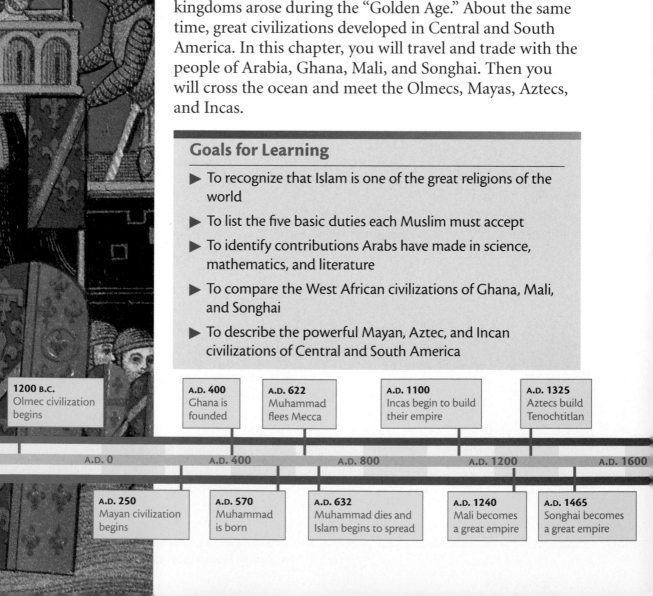

1200 B.C.
Olmec civilization begins

A.D. 400
Ghana is founded

A.D. 622
Muhammad flees Mecca

A.D. 1100
Incas begin to build their empire

A.D. 1325
Aztecs build Tenochtitlan

| A.D. 0 | A.D. 400 | A.D. 800 | A.D. 1200 | A.D. 1600 |

A.D. 250
Mayan civilization begins

A.D. 570
Muhammad is born

A.D. 632
Muhammad dies and Islam begins to spread

A.D. 1240
Mali becomes a great empire

A.D. 1465
Songhai becomes a great empire

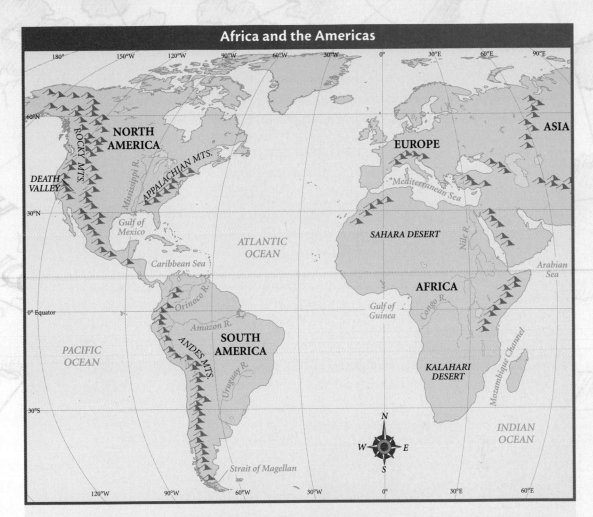

Africa and the Americas

Geography Skills

Look at this map of the world. It shows Africa, the Americas, Europe, and part of Asia. In this chapter, you will study Asia, Africa, and North and South America. You have already learned what was happening in Europe during the Middle Ages. Now you will learn what was happening in these other places.

Study the map carefully and answer the following questions:

1) Which five continents does the map picture?

2) What important American river flows into the Gulf of Mexico?

3) What continent contains the Sahara and the Kalahari Deserts?

4) What is the name of the mountain chain on the western edge of South America?

5) What sea separates Africa from Europe?

Fast
To give up eating food for a while

◆Hegira
Muhammad's flight from danger in Mecca to safety in Medina

Vision
A visit from God or from one of God's angels

In A.D. 570, a man named Muhammad was born in Mecca in Arabia. When he was young, he saw nomads fighting and suffering as they moved from one oasis to another.

Who Visited Muhammad in a Vision?

Once a year, Muhammad went to a desert cave to pray and to **fast,** or give up eating food for a while. One year, the angel Gabriel came to him in this cave. Gabriel said, "O, Muhammad, you are the messenger of Allah." Muhammad was to be God's prophet.

In the beginning, Muhammad told only a few people about his **vision,** or visit from God's angel. Soon, he began to preach, but he had little success. The people of Mecca worshipped hundreds of gods. They did not like the idea of only one god—Allah. Life became dangerous for Muhammad and his followers in Mecca, so they had to flee the city.

Muslims must pray five times a day, no matter where they are. They kneel and face toward Mecca, their holy city.

What Was the Hegira?

In A.D. 622, the people in Yathrib invited Muhammad to come and preach. They accepted his teachings and renamed their city Medina to honor Muhammad. (Medina means "City of the Prophet.") Historians call Muhammad's journey from Mecca to Medina the **Hegira.** This word means a journey, or flight, from danger.

Muhammad's teachings started a new religion—Islam. This Arabic word means to give oneself to God. Those who surrender themselves to Allah are Muslims. The Hegira, or Muhammad's flight, is an important event for Muslims. The year of his journey is the first year of their calendar.

Idol
A statue of a god that people worship

◆**Koran**
The holy book of Islam

Why Did Muhammad Return to Mecca?

Muhammad began to gather around him an army of 10,000 followers. In A.D. 630, he returned to Mecca with his army and took over the city. He went to the center of the city. In a temple there, called the Kaaba, people of Mecca worshipped statues, or **idols,** of their many gods. Muhammad destroyed these idols and told the people, "There is but one God, and Allah is his name."

What Is the Holy Book of Islam?

Do you remember that the Bible contains the holy teachings of the Jews and Christians? The holy book of the Muslims is the **Koran.** It contains the teachings of Islam. That is, it contains the words God spoke to Muhammad through the angel Gabriel.

According to the Koran, God spoke to earlier prophets of the Jews and the Christians. Muslims recognize the teachings of Judaism and Christianity. They believe that Jesus was born of the spirit of God and did many wonderful things.

The Kaaba in Mecca is a small, stone building in the courtyard of the Great Mosque. Thousands of Muslims visit it each day to finish their Hajj—their pilgrimage to Mecca.

The angel Gabriel gave the Koran to the prophet Muhammad in the Arabic language. Because of this, Muslims always study their holy book in Arabic. Translations could be wrong or the reader might not understand them. As Islam spread across the world, so did the Arabic language. Muslims still use Arabic for their religious services, even in non-Arab countries.

What Are the Five Pillars of Islam?

The Koran lists five duties, or pillars, for each Muslim. The first pillar is the **announcement,** or statement, of faith. A person becomes a Muslim by announcing, "There is no God but Allah, and Muhammad is His Prophet."

The second pillar is prayer. Muslims must pray five times a day wherever they are—in a field, at home, or in an office. As they begin to pray, they face Mecca, their holy city. Then they go through the motions of washing their heads, hands, and feet. To show their surrender to God, they kneel, bow, and touch their foreheads to the ground.

The third pillar is the giving of **alms.** That is, Muslims help the poor and needy by giving money to them or by caring for them.

The fourth pillar includes a fast. During the holy month of Ramadan, Muslims fast from sunrise to sunset. At the end of Ramadan, they celebrate with a large meal and then give presents.

The fifth pillar of Islam is the **Hajj.** At least once in their lifetime, all Muslims who are able must visit Mecca. Visiting Mecca, the birthplace of Muhammad, is often the high point of a Muslim's life. All the pilgrims to Mecca wear the same simple clothes. This shows that all people are the same before God. The pilgrims follow special rules about what to do and say. Those who make the trip add the title "hajji" to their name. This means "someone who will go to heaven when he or she dies."

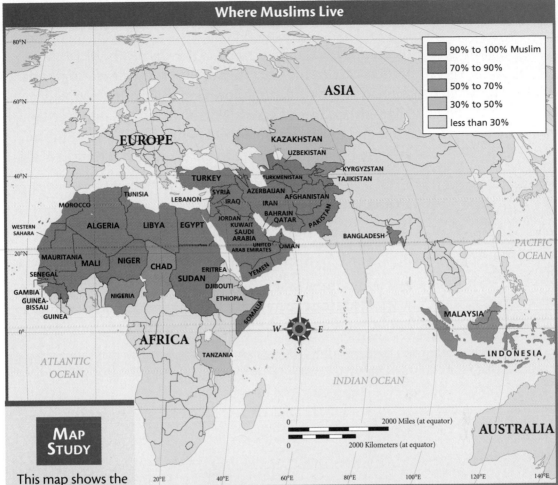

Where Muslims Live

Legend:
- 90% to 100% Muslim
- 70% to 90%
- 50% to 70%
- 30% to 50%
- less than 30%

ASIA

EUROPE

KAZAKHSTAN
UZBEKISTAN
KYRGYZSTAN
TAJIKISTAN
TURKMENISTAN
TURKEY
TUNISIA
SYRIA
LEBANON
IRAQ
AZERBAIJAN
AFGHANISTAN
MOROCCO
IRAN
JORDAN
BAHRAIN
PAKISTAN
KUWAIT
QATAR
WESTERN
SAHARA
ALGERIA
LIBYA
EGYPT
SAUDI
ARABIA
UNITED
ARAB EMIRATES
OMAN
BANGLADESH
MAURITANIA
MALI
NIGER
CHAD
ERITREA
YEMEN
SENEGAL
SUDAN
GAMBIA
DJIBOUTI
GUINEA-
BISSAU
NIGERIA
ETHIOPIA
GUINEA
SOMALIA
MALAYSIA
AFRICA
TANZANIA
INDONESIA
ATLANTIC
OCEAN
PACIFIC
OCEAN
INDIAN OCEAN
AUSTRALIA

2000 Miles (at equator)

2000 Kilometers (at equator)

MAP STUDY

This map shows the percentage of Muslims in Africa and Asia. Which part of Africa, north or south, has the most Muslims? What percentage of Muslims is there in Chad? Name three countries that are 90–100 percent Muslim. Name three that are between 70–90 percent Muslim.

SECTION 1 REVIEW On a separate sheet of paper, write *True* if the statement is true or *False* if the statement is not true. Make each false statement true by changing the underlined word.

1) Muhammad was born in <u>Nazareth</u> in Arabia.

2) We call Muhammad's flight to Medina the <u>Hegira.</u>

3) Muhammad founded the religion of <u>Hinduism.</u>

4) The <u>Koran</u> is the holy book of the Muslims.

5) Muslims must pray <u>seven</u> times a day.

What do you think ?

Why do you think that visiting Mecca is the high point of a Muslim's life?

◆Jihad
A struggle to follow God's will and to spread Islam

Muhammad died in A.D. 632. After his death, Muslim leaders carried his teachings to others by means of **jihads.** A jihad is a struggle to follow God's will and to spread Islam. Islam spread across North Africa and into Europe. West and northward, it spread across the Persian Empire and the Byzantine Empire to parts of India, Southeast Asia, and China.

What Were Islamic Cities Like?

In A.D. 750, the Abbasid dynasty became rulers of the Arabian Empire. The rulers built a new capital— Baghdad—on the banks of the Tigris River. It became, and still is, an important center of trade. Thousands of people worked for four years to build Baghdad. It had many large public buildings, including libraries, hospitals, and gardens.

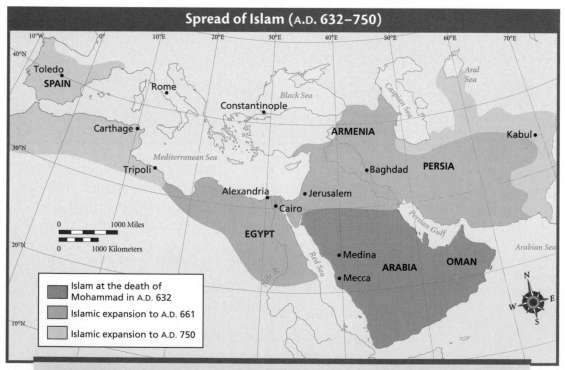

Spread of Islam (A.D. 632–750)

Islam at the death of Mohammad in A.D. 632

Islamic expansion to A.D. 661

Islamic expansion to A.D. 750

MAP STUDY This map shows the three main periods in the spread of Islam from A.D. 632–750. At the time Muhammad died in 632, where was Islam the strongest? What Spanish city did the Muslims control? How far north was Baghdad from Mecca?

How Did Arabs Treat Others?

The Islamic Empire became rich because of its trade, farming, and respect for others. It controlled the most important trade routes in the world. These routes linked together Africa, Europe, and Asia. Islamic traders bought and sold things from all parts of Africa, China, India, and Russia. Arab artisans made many things to sell to people in other places.

The Muslims improved farming. The lands of Mesopotamia and the Nile Valley produced **surplus,** or extra, food. Farmers grew more than enough to feed the people who lived in the many large Arab cities.

Arabs respected the cultures of people they conquered in their holy wars. They allowed Jews and Christians to keep their own religions. Islamic culture blended the cultures of many people with the Arab culture.

What Made Arab Medicine a Science?

The Muslims built hospitals to care for the sick. In these hospitals, doctors studied why people got sick. Muslims became the first people to make a science of medicine. They studied it carefully and they trained their doctors carefully. From their study, they discovered that some sicknesses are **contagious.** That is, a disease can pass from one person to another.

One Arab doctor named Al-Razi wrote books about two diseases—smallpox and measles. He also wrote a set of 25 books about medicine. Students in both the East and the West used these until the 1400s. Al-Razi may have been the first doctor to sew up cuts and to put casts on broken arms and legs.

What Did Muslim Scientists Figure Out About the Earth?

Arab astronomers figured out that the earth is round. They correctly guessed that it was about 25,000 miles around. An Arab geographer was the first to put a map on a ball to show the right shape of the earth.

Other Arab scientists studied light and were the first to learn that it travels in a straight line. They also learned that the curving of a lens makes things appear larger. The greatest Muslim scholar was an Arab named Jabir. His discoveries led to **chemistry.** He may have been the first person to carefully record the results of an experiment. Other Arab scientists invented much of the equipment we use today in chemistry.

What Mathematical Gifts Did the Muslims Give Us?

In mathematics, Muslim scholars expanded on what they learned from other people. From India, they borrowed the nine numbers that we still use today. We call these "Arabic numbers" even though they came from India.

From the Hindus, the Arabs borrowed the decimal system. This is a number system based on the number ten. It includes the idea of zero. This was a good system because it was much easier to use than the Babylonian system based on 60.

Muslim scholars studied medicine, the heavens, chemistry, and mathematics.

What Is Islamic Art Like?

Islamic art never shows people or animals. Artists decorate **mosques,** or Muslim places of worship, with beautiful designs and writing. Islamic art also appears on their world-famous rugs, on leather goods, and on swords.

Many Arab artists wrote poems about the beauty of nature and love. The best known Muslim poet was Omar Khayyam who wrote *The Rubaiyat.* Westerners know another collection of Arab stories called the *Arabian Nights.* In it are the stories *Ali Baba and the Forty Thieves* and *Aladdin and His Lamp.*

Borrowed Words

Have you eaten *sherbet?* Are you studying *algebra?* We borrowed these words from the Arabic language. We got some from the Muslims who lived in Spain. Others were the names of products from the Middle East—*sugar, alcohol,* and *syrup.* Traders also brought the *lime, orange,* and *artichoke* to Europe. *Mohair* and *cotton* are Arabic, too.

Muslim scholars studied chemistry and astronomy. The words *alkali* and *zenith* resulted from their knowledge. They gave us the names for stars, such as Aldebaran. From Arab mathematicians came *tariff* and *zero.* We use Arab words that describe how people live or the world around us. People sit on a *sofa.* A *sultan* and a *sheik* are kinds of rulers. The commander of a fleet is an *admiral.* English is indeed a richer language because of these Arabic words.

SECTION 2 REVIEW On a separate sheet of paper, write the word from the Word Bank that completes each sentence.

WORD BANK
Al-Razi
Baghdad
Jabir
jihads
Khayyam

1) The Arabs spread their religion through _____.

2) The Abbasid dynasty ruled the Islamic Empire in A.D. 750 and built the city of _____.

3) _____ may have been the first doctor to put casts on broken arms and legs.

4) The greatest Arab scholar was _____, whose work led to the science of chemistry.

5) Omar _____ wrote the poem *The Rubaiyat,* which is about love and nature.

What do you think ?

What do you think is the best gift the Arab people of the Middle Ages gave the world? Explain your answer.

The crusaders first set out to capture the Holy Land in A.D. 1095. About that time, a series of empires developed in West Africa. Arab geographers called this grassland area the Sudan. It is very different from the dry Sahara Desert to the north and the wet tropical rain forest to the south.

How Did Ghana Become Powerful?

Ghana was founded about A.D. 400. Within 400 years, it had become an important center of trade. In fact, Ghana controlled all the important trade routes from the Sudan to North Africa.

Early stories about Ghana call it "the land of gold." Ghana never owned any gold fields, but it controlled the trade in gold. With gold came power.

The gold came from a region near the Senegal River. People there had much gold, but no salt, and they needed salt to live. Arab traders on camel caravans carried their goods to the people near the Senegal River in the south. Then they traded salt for gold. Next, the caravan turned north again to trade with their gold. On both trips, they traveled through Kumbi, the largest city in Ghana. The government of Ghana taxed the caravan each way. Both the Arabs from the north and the forest people from the south paid tribute to the king of Ghana.

How Did Ghana's Army Create Peace?

By A.D. 1070, Ghana was one of the most powerful empires in the world. Taxes from trade filled the king's treasury. With all this money, he could keep as many as 200,000 warriors. (At this same time, William the Conqueror could raise an army of only 15,000 soldiers to invade England.)

Ghana's large army gave it great power. With this power, Ghana created peace in West Africa and made trade safe. Ghana could easily have conquered its weaker neighbors, but it did not. Instead, it took tribute from these neighbors.

What Made Ghana Fall?

The kings of Ghana invited Muslim teachers to begin schools in Kumbi and other cities. The rulers of Ghana did not become Muslims, but many of the people of Ghana did. This helped improve the connection between the two areas and brought money to the empire.

In A.D. 1076, Arabs from North Africa, called Almoravids, invaded Ghana. They began a holy war against the **infidels,** or non-Muslims, of Ghana and destroyed Kumbi. During this time, people stopped paying tribute to Ghana. In time, Ghana defeated the Almoravids. However, the country was never again as powerful as it had once been.

How Did Mali Become Powerful?

Mali existed as early as A.D. 1000. When Ghana lost its power, Mali was able to form a new empire. It, too, took control of the trade routes.

The man most responsible for Mali's rise to greatness was Sundiata Keita. He took control of the gold fields. His armies swept across Africa, and his empire included large areas of the Sahara. Keita divided his kingdom into provinces. Then he put one general in charge of each province. Each general was responsible for keeping law and order in his province.

African Metalworking

Learning to work with iron was a big step forward in technology. Iron made stronger farming tools and weapons. Ironworking in Africa probably began at Meroë. It was in the kingdom of Kush along the Nile. Kushite artisans began to work with iron about 500 B.C. Iron ore came from local mines. Forests supplied wood for hot fires. These craftspeople worked with gold, too.

Another tribe, the Nok, lived in West Africa. They worked with iron, gold, and tin. The Bantu people learned these skills. Then the Bantu moved south. They carried this knowledge to others.

Technology
History in Your Life

Africa was rich in many metals, such as copper. This beautiful metal was used for jewelry and pots. People combined copper with other metals to make bronze. The kingdom of Benin was famous for its bronze sculptures. Artists made them by pouring melted bronze into molds.

Timbuktu was a great center of learning and trade in West Africa.

Which Famous Mali King Became a Muslim?

Mansa Musa was king of Mali when it was most powerful. Unlike the rulers of Ghana, Mansa Musa became a Muslim. He brought many Arab scholars to his capital. He set up a great center of Islamic learning in Timbuktu. Scholars came from all over the world to study there.

Mansa Musa ran his kingdom well. Arab visitors wrote about the peace and safety of Mali. The visitors saw how the people of Mali obeyed the Five Pillars of Islam. In fact, one writer said that Mali parents wanted their children to learn the Koran by heart. If the children did not do this, they were put in chains until they memorized the holy book.

WHAT A TRIP!—MANSA MUSA'S PILGRIMAGE

Mansa Musa was famous for building a university, being a Muslim, and visiting the holy city of Mecca. Some historians think that 60,000 people made the pilgrimage with Mansa Musa. (About 12,000 of them were his servants.) They loaded 80 camels with bags of gold dust to pay for the 3,000-mile trip from Mali to Mecca. Imagine all the food and supplies 60,000 people would need!

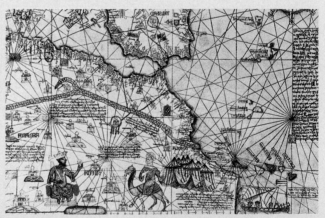

This map shows Mansa Musa holding a gold ball.

The pilgrimage began in A.D. 1324 and took more than a year. Everywhere Mansa Musa went he gave away gold to rulers and government officials. When he reached Mecca, Mansa Musa gave that city gold, too.

Mansa Musa's gifts of gold made news even in Europe. In 1375, someone in Spain drew a map that shows Mansa Musa. He holds a large gold ball in his hand. The artist wrote on the map. The writing says that Mansa Musa has so much gold that "he is the richest and most noble king of all the land."

After Mansa Musa died, civil war broke out in Mali. Within 150 years, the great empire fell. Then the last great empire of this golden age arose—Songhai.

How Did Songhai Become Powerful?

The third and last of the great empires of West Africa was Songhai. Songhai already existed in the 800s. But it did not become powerful until the 1400s. Like Ghana and Mali before it, Songhai grew powerful by controlling the gold and salt trade.

Songhai's greatest king was Sonni Ali. From 1464 until 1492, he never lost a battle. King Sonni Ali made Songhai the largest empire that West Africa ever had. His army captured the university city of Timbuktu. Ali's empire stretched from the Atlantic Ocean eastward nearly 1,800 miles.

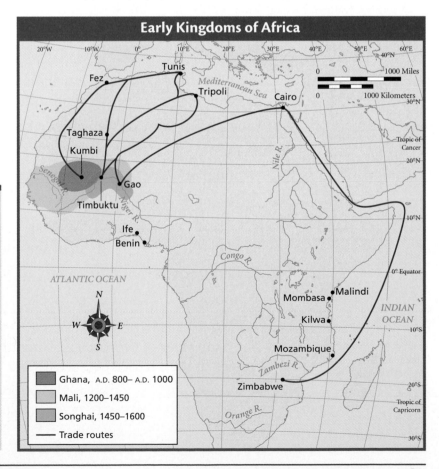

Early Kingdoms of Africa

MAP STUDY

This map shows Ghana, Mali, and Songhai. It also shows trade routes near the kingdoms. Of the three empires, which was the largest? Name two cities that were part of these empires.

King Sonni Ali made Songhai a powerful empire. He took lands from the old Mali empire. It was weak when he became king in 1464. First, he captured Timbuktu in 1468. It was a center of Muslim learning. Later, he captured Jenne. It was a wealthy trade center. Sonni Ali won many victories partly because he used cavalry well.

Sonni Ali was a harsh ruler, however. He had scholars in Timbuktu killed. He executed many people, even close friends. His death in 1492 was a mystery. Some stories said he drowned. Others said he was murdered.

Ali divided Songhai into provinces. Then he chose officials to carry out the laws. He also made sure that all weights and measures were the same in his empire.

Other countries wanted Songhai's riches and attacked it. At first, Songhai's army easily defeated its neighbors. Then, in 1590, the Arab ruler of Morocco in North Africa sent an army to conquer Songhai. The Arab army had only 2,000 soldiers, but it had a new, powerful weapon—the gun. In 1596, Songhai fell. The empire broke apart, and West Africa was never united again.

SECTION 3 REVIEW Choose the letter of the answer that correctly completes each sentence. Write your answer on a separate sheet of paper.

1) The first empire to develop in West Africa was _____.

    a. Ghana   c. Songhai

    b. Mali   d. Timbuktu

2) King Mansa Musa of Mali founded a university at _____.

    a. Kumbi   c. Paris

    b. Songhai   d. Timbuktu

3) _____ controlled trade in West Africa.

    a. Ghana   c. Songhai

    b. Mali   d. all of the above

4) Traders from the north brought _____ to trade for gold.

    a. horses   c. guns

    b. salt   d. fish

5) The Arab ruler of Morocco defeated the last great empire of West Africa because he had _____.

    a. camels   c. gold

    b. guns   d. a large army

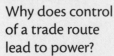

What do you think ?

Why does control of a trade route lead to power?

Maize
A corn-like plant

Slave
A person who someone owns and treats like property

Powerful civilizations also developed in Central and South America. The Olmec civilization was an early one. Archaeologists believe that it began around 1200 B.C. and disappeared about 100 B.C.

What Did the Olmecs Invent?

The Olmecs lived in farm villages and raised **maize.** (This corn-like plant grew wild in the rain forest.) Maize provided a surplus of food, so some people did not have to farm. Instead, they could build large stone cities as religious centers. The priests and government officials lived in these cities. The rest of the people visited them on holidays. The Olmecs invented a kind of hieroglyphic writing. They also developed a calendar and a counting system.

Who Were the Mayas?

From about A.D. 250, the Mayas built a huge civilization in the area that is now Belize and parts of Guatemala, Honduras, El Salvador, and Mexico. First, the Mayas drained swamps. Then they irrigated their fields of corn, beans, and other plants. Next, they built cities. Cities in Europe were falling apart as Mayan cities grew into important religious and trade centers.

What Was a Mayan City Like?

Mayan cities were mostly religious centers. A large, stone temple like a pyramid stood in the middle of each city. The largest Mayan city was Tikal. Its pyramid was 20 stories high! Yet the Mayas had no carts with wheels or horses or oxen to move the heavy stones.

Mayan cities also became centers of trade. The Mayas traded with people in Mexico, over 600 miles away. Traders sold salt, honey, cotton, bird feathers, food, and **slaves.** (A slave is someone who someone else owns and treats like property.) In return, they bought things made of gold and copper.

The Mayas divided themselves into three groups. Rulers belonged in the top group. Warriors and priests belonged

A large, stone temple stood in the center of each Mayan city. This photo shows the temple and surrounding areas of the Mayan city of Chichén Itzá in Yucatán, Mexico.

Abandon
To leave behind; to give up

in the middle group. Artisans, merchants, peasants, and slaves belonged in the bottom group. (People who broke laws became slaves.)

What Did the Mayas Invent?

Mayan priests studied the stars and recorded all that they saw, including eclipses. This helped them invent a calendar that had no mistakes in it. The priests also invented a mathematical system based on the number 20. It included the idea of zero. (Even the ancient Greeks and Romans never came up with the idea of zero.)

The Mayan hieroglyphics used symbols, animal pictures, and faces. But no one today knows how to read them. We do not know why the Mayas **abandoned,** or left, their cities around A.D. 900.

Who Were the Aztecs?

At the same time as the Mayas, the Toltecs built an empire in what is now Mexico. Around 1160, the Aztecs—a fierce, warlike people—destroyed the Toltec capital of Tula. The Aztecs built a new capital called Tenochtitlan on an island in Lake Texcoco.

The Aztecs built their island capital of Tenochtitlan in 1325. As many as 300,000 Aztecs may have lived there. (This made it about five times larger than London, England, at that time.) **Causeways,** or paved roads over water, connected the island to the mainland. Tenochtitlan had temples, pyramids, palaces, gardens, and markets. The Aztec ruler, his family, and thousands of servants and officials lived in the enormous palace. It had both a library and a zoo.

The Aztecs worshipped many gods. Aztec priests believed that the god of the sun—who was also the god of war—needed human sacrifice. They thought the sun would not rise if the priests did not sacrifice a human being. For nearly 200 years, the Aztecs made war with neighboring peoples. Sometimes they did this just to capture people to sacrifice.

This is a sun stone or a calendar from the temple at Tenochtitlan, the Aztec capital city.

Who Were the Incas?

Far to the south, another civilization named the Incas developed. They settled in a valley of the Andes Mountains around 1100. They built their capital—Cuzco—high in the mountains in what is today the country of Peru. To connect their empire, the Incas built roads. One of them was 2,500 miles long.

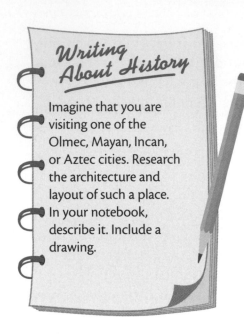

Writing About History

Imagine that you are visiting one of the Olmec, Mayan, Incan, or Aztec cities. Research the architecture and layout of such a place. In your notebook, describe it. Include a drawing.

Because they lived in the mountains, the Incas had no flat land for farming. They built wide step-like areas called terraces. The Incas also built large temples, palaces, and forts. They built these forts with stone blocks that weighed as much as 200 tons, or 400,000 pounds. The Incas cut these blocks so that they fit tightly together. In fact, they fit so tightly that the Incas did not need to use anything to hold them together.

How Do We Know That Incan Rulers Were Rich?

All land belonged to the Incan emperor. But he let other people farm it and pay him taxes. (The Incan Empire included as many as 12 million people.) The emperor lived in a large palace and wore clothes made with gold thread. His bodyguards wore armor made of gold.

HOW ABOUT A GAME OF BASKETBALL?

In the center of Mayan cities near the temples and palaces, lay a large court. Its shape was like today's basketball court. Tall stone walls stood on the two long sides of the court. Artists decorated the two walls. Historians think their drawings may be pictures of different Mayan gods.

High in the middle of each wall was a stone ring, or hoop. Often, it was 30 feet above the ground! The Mayas put the hoop straight up and down instead of parallel to the ground.

The Mayas used the court to play a game with a ball made of solid rubber. The six-inch ball weighed about five pounds. Players were not allowed to use their hands or feet to get the ball through the hoop. They passed the ball back and forth with their hips, knees, and forearms. Players protected themselves with wooden or leather gloves, helmets, knee pads, and belts.

The Mayas probably played this game on religious holidays and before battles. Some people believe that the game represented the battle between life and death. The rubber ball may have been a symbol of the sun.

Crowbar
An iron or steel bar that a person can use as a lever

Most Incan men had to serve some time in the army and on government projects. A young man had to marry. If he did not choose a wife, the government chose one for him. The government also took care of sick, poor, and old people.

The Incas invented the **crowbar,** which is an iron bar that a person uses as a lever. Their doctors could set broken bones and even knew how to perform brain surgery! They also developed medicines from plants. Incan artisans could weave beautiful cloth and make fine pottery. They made beautiful gold and silver jewelry for the priests and nobles.

Why Did the Incan Empire Fall?

The Incan Empire was powerful. However, it had no horses or guns. People in Europe did. In 1533, a small group of people who had sailed from Spain to the Americas conquered the Incas with guns and horses.

MAP STUDY

This map shows four early American empires—the Olmecs, the Mayas, the Aztecs, and the Incas. It also shows the roads in the Incan Empire. Why did the Incan roads run mostly north and south instead of east and west? Which empire seems to have been the biggest? Which was the smallest?

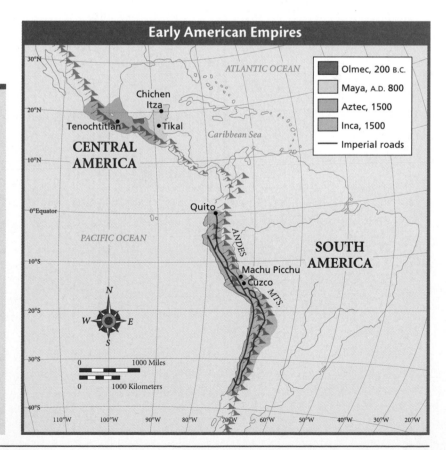

Early American Empires

Olmec, 200 B.C.
Maya, A.D. 800
Aztec, 1500
Inca, 1500
Imperial roads

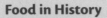

Food in History

What's for dinner? Today, you can choose from many kinds of foods—tacos, pizza, or stir fry. Now imagine it's dinner time in medieval England. Even kings and nobles have a limited choice of foods. They eat lots of meat—pork or chicken or wild deer. Peasants eat home-grown vegetables and fruits. They grow grain for bread.

What is missing? There is no chocolate, corn, tomatoes, or potatoes. They grow in the Americas. These lands haven't been explored yet. People in the Muslim world drink coffee, but it hasn't yet arrived in Europe. There is no pasta. Italian traders have just started bringing it from China. Sugar and spices also come from Asia. Only in modern times do we have access to so many kinds of foods.

SECTION 4 REVIEW On a separate sheet of paper, write answers to these questions.

1) Why were some Olmecs free to build cities?

2) Why do we not know why the Mayas abandoned their cities?

3) Why did the Aztecs use human sacrifices?

4) Why are the forts of the Incas a wonder?

5) Why were the Spaniards able to defeat the Incas?

What do you think

Why do you think the Mayas abandoned their cities around A.D. 900?

Ibn Battuta Visits the Sultan of Mali

Abdallah Ibn Battuta was a great traveler of the Middle Ages. He was born in North Africa and was a Muslim. Ibn Battuta began his travels in 1325. He went across deserts and over mountains. His trips took him through Muslim countries. He traveled deep into Africa, too. He also went to India, central Asia, and China. In total, he traveled about 75,000 miles.

Abdallah Ibn Battuta

Ibn Battuta wrote about his travels. In this reading, he tells how the ruler of Mali meets with his people.

The sultan has a raised cupola [small domed building] which is entered from inside his house. . . . It has on the audience side a chamber with three wooden arches, the woodwork is covered with sheets of beaten silver and beneath these, three more covered with beaten gold. . . . The windows have woolen curtains which are raised on a day when the sultan will be in session. . . . When he sits, a silken cord is put out from the grill of one of the arches with a scarf of Egyptian embroidery tied to it. When the people see the scarf, drums are beaten and bugles sounded. Then from the door of the palace come out about three hundred slaves. Some have bows in their hands and some small spears and shields. . . .

The interpreter Dugha stands at the door of the audience chamber wearing splendid robes of [silk]. On his head is a turban which has fringes. They have a superb way of tying a turban. He is girt with a sword whose sheath is of gold, on his feet are light boots and spurs. And nobody wears boots that day except he. In his hands there are two small spears, one of gold and one of silver with points of iron. The soldiers, the district governors, the pages . . . and others are seated outside the place of audience in a broad street which has trees in it. Each [commander] has his followers before him with their spears, bows, drums and bugles made of elephant tusks. Their instruments of music are made of reeds and calabashes [gourds], and they beat them with sticks and produce a wonderful sound. . . .

Inside the audience chamber under the arches a man is standing: he who wants to speak to the sultan speaks to Dugha, Dugha speaks to the man who is standing, and he speaks to the sultan.

Source Reading Wrap-Up

1) What signs show that the sultan is ready to meet the people?

2) What shows the sultan's wealth?

3) How is the interpreter Dugha dressed? What is he holding?

4) Only Dugha wears boots on that day. What might that show?

5) How does someone get to speak to the sultan?

Farming in Africa and Oceania

Most early societies depended on farming. People ate whatever they could grow. They also fished or hunted. Bringing food from other places was not practical. In Africa south of the Sahara, the economy has always centered on farming. That is also true of the islands in the Pacific Ocean. Both those places have warm climates. They grow some of the same foods. The history of their economies is quite different, though.

Africa is a huge continent. Farming varies greatly from place to place. In the rain forests, people grow small gardens. For thousands of years, yams have been a favorite crop. So has palm oil. Some of its oils are used in cooking. Others make soaps and other products. People also grow several kinds of nuts, including peanuts. Plantains are another popular food.

The grasslands areas of Africa are drier. People here planted fields of grain. These grains can be pounded or ground into flour. Flour is used in porridges, puddings, and flat breads. About 2,000 years ago, people began using iron tools. Iron hoes and knives made farming easier. Farming villages became more stable.

Farming in the Pacific Islands has a different history. In Africa, people have farmed for about 7,000 years. The Pacific Islands were settled only recently. Polynesians reached the islands of Hawaii between about A.D. 300 and 500. By about A.D. 1000, they had settled New Zealand. The first settlers brought yams, taro, and sweet potatoes. They also brought pigs, dogs, and chickens. They grew flax to make cloth. In some places, they built terraces or ponds to grow taro.

People eat the starchy root of this plant. Islanders also planted coconut palms, bananas, and breadfruit trees. These trees grew around fields and gardens.

People used the coconut palm tree in many ways. They ate its meat and drank the liquid inside. The hard shell became a cup or bowl. Palm leaves could be woven into baskets. They were also used for roofs.

Farming is still important in Africa and the Pacific. Some crops have changed, though. Trade brought new foods to Africa. From the Americas came sweet potatoes, chili peppers, and tomatoes. From Asia came taro. Europeans also took new crops to the Pacific Islands when they settled there.

Spotlight Story Wrap-Up

1) How is farming in Africa and the Pacific Islands similar?

2) What kinds of crops did people plant in Africa's grasslands?

3) What major change in technology influenced farming in Africa?

4) Who first settled Hawaii and New Zealand? About when did they arrive?

5) What crops were grown in the Pacific Islands?

➡ Muhammad was born in Arabia in A.D. 570. He preached a new religion, Islam, with one god, Allah. Its followers are called Muslims.

➡ In A.D. 622, Muhammad and his followers fled from Mecca to Medina. This event is called the Hegira.

➡ The holy book of Islam is the Koran, written in the Arabic language. Muslims regard Muhammad as God's prophet. They also recognize Jewish and Christian prophets.

➡ Muslims have five duties, or pillars. They must state their faith, pray five times a day, give alms, and fast. If possible, they make a pilgrimage, or Hajj, to Mecca.

➡ Jihads helped Islam grow. It spread across North Africa, the Middle East, and parts of Asia.

➡ The Abbasid dynasty began in A.D. 750. Its capital was Baghdad. The Islamic Empire excelled in trade and farming. It let Jews and Christians keep their customs.

➡ Muslims made important advances in medicine; science, especially chemistry; and mathematics. Islamic art shows beautiful patterns, not people or animals.

➡ Three rich trading kingdoms grew up in Africa between A.D. 1000 and 1600.

➡ Ghana became rich by taxing the trade in gold and salt. By A.D. 1070, Ghana had built a powerful army to keep peace. Muslim Arabs from North Africa invaded it in A.D. 1076.

➡ Mali followed Ghana as the most powerful empire. Its king, Mansa Musa, became a Muslim. He made Timbuktu a center for Islamic scholars.

➡ The greatest king of Songhai was Sonni Ali. His empire fell to an Arab army armed with guns in 1596.

➡ The Olmec civilization began in Central America about 1200 B.C. They built stone cities and developed a calendar. They also developed systems of writing and counting.

➡ The Mayan civilization grew up in southern Mexico and Central America. Its cities were centers of religion and trade. A pyramid-shaped temple stood in the center of every city. Mayan priests were astronomers, and made an accurate calendar.

➡ The Aztecs gained control of central Mexico around A.D. 1160. Their capital, Tenochtitlan, was on an island in a lake. Aztec religion included human sacrifice.

➡ The Incan empire grew up in the Peruvian Andes Mountains about A.D. 1100. The people farmed on terraces. The empire fell in 1533 to Spaniards with guns and horses.

Comprehension: Identifying Facts

On a separate sheet of paper, use the words from the Word Bank to complete each sentence.

WORD BANK
Allah
Aztec
Ghana
Incan
Islam
Jabir
Mansa Musa
Mayan
Muhammad
Songhai

1) The prophet _____ was born in A.D. 570.

2) He started a religion known as _____.

3) The Muslims call God _____.

4) The greatest Arab scholar was _____.

5) People called _____ "the land of gold."

6) The ruler _____ founded a university in Mali.

7) People from Morocco attacked the empire of _____ with guns.

8) _____ priests invented a calendar with no mistakes in it.

9) The _____ priests sacrificed human beings to their gods.

10) The _____ ruler and his people built forts in the Andes Mountains.

Comprehension: Multiple Choice

On a separate sheet of paper, write the letter of the answer that correctly completes each sentence.

1) Muslims spread Islam through _____ .

   a. mosques   c. causeways

   b. jihads   d. infidels

2) Muslims accept five duties, or _____ , of their religion.

   a. surpluses   c. caravans

   b. visions   d. pillars

3) The holy book of the Muslims is the _____ .

   a. Koran   c. *Rubaiyat*

   b. Arabian Nights d. *Song of Roland*

4) _____ grew powerful because of trade.

    a. Ghana   c. Songhai

    b. Mali   d. all of the above

5) The oldest civilization in the Americas is the _____ .

    a. Olmec   c. Aztec

    b. Mayan   d. Incan

Comprehension: Understanding Main Ideas

On a separate sheet of paper, write the answers to the following questions using complete sentences, or statements.

1) What are the five basic duties each Muslim must accept?

2) What was the key to power for the three empires of West Africa?

3) What shows that the people of the American empires in the Middle Ages were great builders?

Critical Thinking: Write Your Opinion

1) In this chapter, you learned about many important people—Muhammad, Al-Razi, Jabir, Sundiata Keita, Mansa Musa, Sonni Ali, the Aztec emperors, and the Incan rulers. Which one of these people would you like to have met and why?

2) In this chapter, you learned about many wonderful cities—Mecca, Medina, Baghdad, Kumbi, Timbuktu, Tikal, Tenochtitlan, and Cuzco. Which one of these cities would you like to have visited and why?

| Test-Taking Tip | When you read a test question, notice what the question is not asking for, then answer the question. |

Chapter

India, China, and Japan

12

563 B.C. to A.D. 1620

The Middle Ages also came to the continent of Asia. In this chapter, you will learn about India, Buddhism, and the Mongol invaders. Then you will find out about China and its many wonderful inventions. Finally, you will discover the religion called Shintoism that was born in Japan. In all these places, you will meet rulers and scholars, scientists and artists, inventors and warriors.

Goals for Learning

▶ To describe the four noble truths of Buddhism

▶ To compare Buddhism and Hinduism

▶ To identify some inventions that made ancient China the richest and most powerful country in the world

▶ To describe life in China under Mongol rule

▶ To explain how geography has influenced Japan's history

▶ To explain why the Shinto religion is unique

▶ To compare Japanese and European feudalism

▶ To list the reasons why Japan and China turned to isolationism

563 B.C. Buddha is born

A.D. 618 T'ang dynasty begins to rule China

A.D. 1040 Chinese invent printing

A.D. 1279 Kublai Khan rules China

A.D. 1398 Mongols invade India

A.D. 1630 Japan begins 200-year isolation

A.D. 0   A.D. 1000   A.D. 1300   A.D. 1600

A.D. 320 The Golden Age of India begins

A.D. 960 Sung dynasty begins to rule China

A.D. 1206 Genghis Khan, Mongol leader, begins to conquer Asia

A.D. 1368 Mongol dynasty falls in China; a 250-year isolation begins

A.D. 1525 Babur sets up Moghul Empire in India

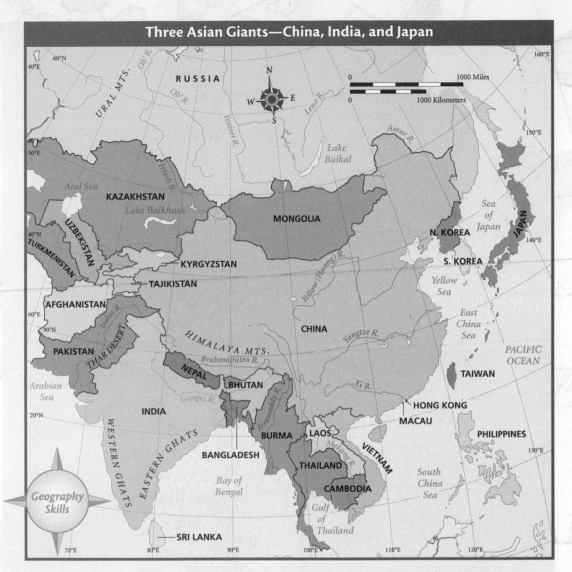

Three Asian Giants—China, India, and Japan

Geography Skills

Asia is the largest of the world's continents. China and India—Asia's two largest countries—have a population of well over two billion people. Out of every five people on the earth, two are either Chinese or Indian. Both in population and in land area, Japan is smaller than China and India. But it has many people for its size.

Study the map and answer the following questions:

1) Which of the three nations—Japan, China, or India—is located farthest south?
2) Which is an island nation?
3) Find the mouth of the Yangtze River at the East China Sea. Then find the mouth of the Indus River at the Arabian Sea. What is the distance—by the most direct route—from one river mouth to the other?
4) What mountains separate India, Nepal, and Bhutan from China?
5) In what direction is Vietnam from China? from India? from Japan?

♦Buddha
A name meaning the "Enlightened One;" the name given to Siddhartha Gautama, the founder of Buddhism

Enlightened
The state of knowing the truth

Around 563 B.C., a prince named Siddhartha Gautama was born in India. As a young man, he had riches, servants, and power. But Gautama felt sorry for the poor people he saw in India. Their religion—Hinduism—taught reincarnation. This means they would be born again into a poor life.

How Did Gautama Become the Buddha?

According to an old story, Gautama left his palace with Channa, his servant. They saw an old man, weak with age. "Such is the way of life, to that we must all come," said Channa. Later they met a man suffering from disease. Again Channa said, "Such is the way of life."

Many statues and sculptures honor Buddha. This one is from the second or third century B.C.

Soon Gautama and Channa saw a group of people getting ready to bury someone who had died. Once more, Channa said, "Such is the way of life." Then and there, Gautama decided to leave his riches. He wanted to find the reason for suffering and unhappiness.

The next day Gautama left his young wife and newborn son. He traded his beautiful silk clothes for a beggar's clothes. For several years, he walked the countryside and studied the Hindu holy books. He nearly starved to death.

One day, Gautama was sitting under a giant tree. He decided not to move from there until he understood the meaning of life. After several hours, truth came to him. From that time on, he was known as the **Buddha,** or the "**Enlightened** One." To be enlightened is to know the truth.

Desire
To wish for something; a wish for something

Nirvana
A condition of complete emptiness in which a person's soul finds perfect peace

Soul
A person's spirit

What Are the Four Noble Truths Buddha Discovered?

For the rest of his life, Buddha taught and preached. He walked from village to village, dressed in a yellow robe. He trusted others to give him the food and shelter he needed.

Buddha preached four "Noble Truths" about the meaning of life:

1. Our life is full of suffering.
2. Our own selfish wishes cause this suffering.
3. We stop suffering when we stop being jealous, greedy, and selfish.
4. We can stop wishing for, or **desiring,** more.

To stop desiring more, Buddha said that people must follow the "Eightfold Path." That is, they must believe, act, think, speak, live, wish, enjoy, and try in the right way. When people follow this Eightfold Path, they enter **nirvana,** for all desire ends. Nirvana is complete emptiness. In this emptiness, a person's **soul,** or spirit, finds perfect peace.

How Are Buddhism and Hinduism Alike and Different?

Gautama was born a Hindu, so many Buddhist beliefs are the same as those of Hinduism. Both religions believe that life is sad and evil. Both believe in reincarnation. Many followers of both religions refuse to kill an animal or eat meat.

The biggest difference between the two religions is that Buddhists do not believe in the caste system. Buddha treated all people alike. He believed that everything depends on a person's own actions. When people follow the Eightfold Path, they reach nirvana in their own lifetime. Buddha also taught people to choose the middle way in all things.

Where Did Buddhism Spread?

Buddha founded several groups of monks. These holy men lived in monasteries that became important centers of learning. Buddhism spread from India into Burma, Thailand, Southeast Asia, China, Korea, and Japan.

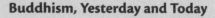

Buddhism, Yesterday and Today

Buddhism spread quickly throughout Asia. Even though Buddhism started in India, it has nearly disappeared there today. Worldwide, there are about 353 million Buddhists.

Buddhism has changed over time. It has split into three main groups: Tibetan Buddhism, Pure Land Buddhism, and Zen Buddhism. The major difference among them has to do with how a person can reach enlightenment.

Buddhism spread to America in the twentieth century. Why? Partly because there were many people from Asia who moved to the United States. Also, Buddhism appealed to some Americans who were looking for a new kind of religious experience and expression.

SECTION 1 REVIEW On a separate sheet of paper, write *True* if the statement is true or *False* if the statement is not true. Make each false statement true by changing the underlined word.

1) Siddhartha Gautama was born a <u>beggar.</u>

2) Gautama preached <u>five</u> "Noble Truths."

3) Because these truths enlightened him, Gautama became known as <u>Buddha.</u>

4) <u>Buddhists</u> follow the "Eightfold Path."

5) When Buddhists give up all desire, they reach <u>nirvana.</u>

What do you think ❓

Why do you think that some Hindus became Buddhists?

◆Stupa
A large building in which a holy monk is buried

Unique
The only one of its kind

The Golden Age of India lasted from A.D. 320 to 535. During this time, India was rich and peaceful. The Gupta dynasty ruled India at this time. Gupta rulers and most of the Indian people were Hindus, not Buddhists. The four major castes of Hinduism had divided into smaller groups. In time, nearly 3,000 castes developed.

How Was Indian Art Unique?

Gupta literature is famous for its fairy tales. People in other countries translated these stories into other languages. Some of these stories influenced European writers like the Brothers Grimm, whose fairy tales you may have read or heard.

Most Indian art during this time had something to do with religion. Indian artists decorated **stupas**—large, rounded buildings in which holy monks were buried. They also decorated temples with carved animals, flowers, and pictures of the Hindu gods.

For centuries, Greek art influenced Indian artists. But during the Golden Age, Indian art became **unique.** That is, it was like no other art anywhere. Wall drawings in the Ajanta caves tell us about ancient India. These colorful paintings show hunting parties, dancing women, and the life of Indian nobles.

Some of the best Indian art can be seen at the Ajanta caves in central India.

What Did Indian Scientists Discover?

During the Golden Age, scientists in India made many discoveries. They figured out the size of the moon. They also understood **gravity,** the force that pulls things to Earth. Indian scientists discovered gravity many years before Europeans did.

Indian mathematicians made important discoveries too. They were the first people to use a system of numbers based on 10. We still use their symbols for 1 to 9. They were also among the first mathematicians to use zero. The Arabs later adopted the Indian decimal and number system.

What Were Indian Doctors Able to Do?

Indian doctors learned to **inoculate** people against disease. That is, they put a small amount of the disease into a person's body to keep the person from getting it. (Europeans first tried inoculations about 1,000 years later.) These doctors performed many different types of **surgery.** The Indians invented hundreds of different medical tools. They set broken bones and made medicine from plants.

What Happened to the Gupta Empire?

The Huns—nomads from central Asia—attacked the Gupta Empire. The empire slowly got smaller until it disappeared during the 600s. From A.D. 600 until 1300, India became a land of small kingdoms. Warriors invaded it again and again. The Indian Muslims and Hindus also fought one another.

Who Were the Mongols?

In 1398, the Mongols invaded India. These fierce warriors had already conquered Persia and Mesopotamia. Their leader's name was Timur the Lame. (Later, he became known as Tamerlane.) Timur and his armies attacked India, killing thousands of Hindus and Muslims. When he marched away from a conquered village, Tamerlane left behind pyramids of human skulls.

How Did Akbar Keep Peace?

In 1525, another conqueror from central Asia named Babur attacked India. Babur **established,** or set up, the Moghul Empire there. (The name Moghul probably comes from the word *Mongol.*) The most famous Moghul ruler was Babur's grandson, Akbar. He ruled the empire from 1556 to 1605. Some of his soldiers rode elephants. Over 12,000 soldiers rode horses. His army helped Akbar add new lands to his empire.

Akbar divided his empire into 12 provinces. He appointed nonmilitary, or **civilian,** officials to run the day-to-day business of each province. This is called **civil service** because civilians run the government. These officials

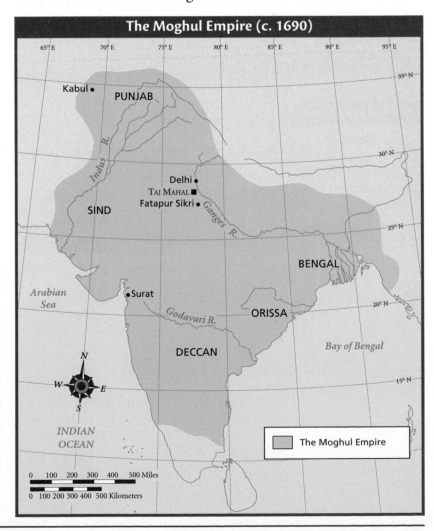

The Moghul Empire (c. 1690)

figured out how much food each province should produce. Then Akbar used their findings to work out fair taxes.

Like all the Moghul rulers, Akbar was a Muslim. To keep peace, he married a Hindu princess and appointed Hindus to important positions in the government. He tried to give everyone religious freedom and to treat them all fairly.

What Did the Moghuls Build?

Akbar and the Moghuls who came after him built beautiful buildings. Shah Jahan built the beautiful Taj Mahal as a tomb for his favorite wife. In addition, Moghul rulers built three royal palaces that contained thousands of jewels from all over Asia. The Red Fort in Agra had ceilings of solid gold. Even today, visitors say that no words can describe the beauty of these buildings.

SECTION 2 REVIEW On a separate sheet of paper, write the word from the Word Bank that completes each sentence.

WORD BANK
Akbar
Hindus
Huns
Mongols
Tamerlane

1) The Gupta rulers during India's Golden Age were _____.

2) Toward the end of this Golden Age, the _____ invaded the Gupta Empire.

3) In 1398, the _____ invaded India.

4) _____, the leader of the Mongols, left behind skull pyramids as he marched through India.

5) _____, who ruled India from 1556 to 1605, was a great ruler.

What do you think ?

Why do you think that Greek ideas influenced Indian artists? (Hint: Remember Chapter 6 and Alexander the Great.)

From A.D. 618 to 907, the T'ang dynasty ruled China. During this period, China became the richest and most powerful country in the world. Civil servants governed T'ang China. They got their jobs after taking hard tests about law, mathematics, and events happening in the world. Any Chinese man could take the test. However, those who passed it always had a good education. China soon had a ruling class of scholars.

With Whom Did T'ang China Trade?

T'ang China welcomed traders from other lands. These traders brought goods into China from Persia, the Middle East, Korea, and Southeast Asia. They carried silk and porcelain out of China to the Middle East and the West. This exchange of goods also led to an exchange of ideas. A large number of foreigners worked side-by-side with the Chinese within the capital city.

What Could Educated People Do in T'ang China?

Every educated person in T'ang China could read, write, and create poems. (During this time, someone said that "whoever was a gentleman was a poet.") Chinese poems were about nature or about the problems ordinary people face in everyday life. During the T'ang dynasty, the artists painted mostly in black and a few other colors. Usually their paintings were about nature.

Why Was the Invention of Printing Important?

Around 1040, the Chinese invented printing. An artisan carved Chinese characters on a block of wood. Then a printer covered the wooden surface with ink and pressed sheets of paper against it. (The Chinese began printing books nearly 400 years before Europeans.)

Before the development of printing, people copied books by hand. Copying took time, so there were few books. But a printer could make more books faster. Since people learn by reading, printing led to the spread of knowledge.

Compass
A tool for finding direction by using a magnet

What Was the Sung Dynasty?

The Sung dynasty ruled China from A.D. 960 to 1279. After 1126, the center of Chinese civilization shifted south, from the Yellow River Valley to the Yangtze River Valley.

Sung China was rich. Its capital city, Hangzhou, was one of the most modern cities of the world. At this time, European cities had dirty, dark, narrow, and crowded streets. Hangzhou had wide streets with streetlights. People cleaned these streets every day. Hangzhou even had a fire department.

What Things Did Sung China Create?

The Chinese invented many things that helped change world history. By the 800s, they had invented gunpowder. At first, they used it only for fireworks. Some think they may have used it later as a weapon.

An Arab trader in China learned how to make gunpowder and introduced it to Europe. Sung rulers were not interested in expanding their borders, so they made little use of gunpowder. However, Europeans developed guns and cannons. This changed the way soldiers fought wars.

Someone in the Sung dynasty also invented the **compass.** This is a tool for finding direction by the use of a magnet. The magnetic needle of this compass always points north-south. The compass allowed Chinese ships to travel far away.

Abacus
A tool that helps people add and do other things with numbers

Detect
To discover or find out

Masterpiece
A piece of art that seems almost perfect

Mood
The feeling of something or someone

The Chinese invented the **abacus.** This tool helps people add and do other things with numbers. They also invented the clock and a machine to **detect,** or discover, earthquakes.

What Did Sung Artisans Create?

The artists of Sung China painted pictures that people today call **masterpieces.** That is, the paintings seem nearly perfect. Sung artists painted on paper or silk scrolls. Most Sung artists tried to show the **mood,** or feeling, of what they saw. Their paintings show people as small and

Nature was often the theme for Sung artists. This scroll painting is by Li Ch'eng, who lived from A.D. 919 to 967. It shows a temple in front of mountain peaks.

Gunpowder

It's the Fourth of July. You watch as brilliant fireworks burst in the sky. Who can you thank for these exciting displays? The chemists of ancient China.

Fireworks are made mainly of gunpowder. Other materials add color. About 1,000 years ago, the Chinese discovered the formula for gunpowder. It was the first explosive. Gunpowder has three ingredients: charcoal, sulfur, and saltpeter. Charcoal is made from burned wood. Sulfur and saltpeter are mined.

In the 1200s, Muslim armies learned the secret of gunpowder from the Chinese. This knowledge reached Europe in the 1300s. Explosives changed warfare and history. Medieval castles could no longer protect the people inside. Bombs and cannons could knock down their walls.

Porcelain
A hard, shiny pottery made from a baked white clay

unimportant. Nature—trees, mountains, and water—are most important.

Artisans of Sung China made beautiful **porcelain.** This is a hard, shiny pottery made from a white clay that the potter bakes. Sung artisans made thin porcelain bowls and vases. When Europeans came to China, they studied the making of porcelain. They used the word *china* to describe the beautiful porcelain.

SECTION 3 REVIEW On a separate sheet of paper, write answers to these questions.

1) Who governed T'ang China?
2) What did trading lead to in T'ang China?
3) Why was the invention of printing important?
4) What was the capital of Sung China like?
5) What are three important inventions of Sung China?

What do you think

Why do you think artisans of the Sung period showed human beings as small and nature as large?

Opera
A play in which people sing all the words

The Mongols rode out of central Asia and conquered Russia, India, and China. Their greatest leader was Genghis Khan. Between A.D. 1206 and 1227, he conquered most of Asia.

What Did Kublai Khan Build?

In 1279, Kublai Khan, a grandson of Genghis Khan, conquered China. He adopted the Chinese name Yuan for his dynasty. Kublai Khan spent almost all his life in China. In time, the Mongol rulers adopted many Chinese ways. Kublai Khan built a new Chinese capital city. (Today we call this city Beijing.) At its center was his palace.

How Did the Mongol Rulers Make Trade Easier?

The Mongol rulers built great highways and protected merchants and travelers. Travel and trade increased. Traders from the Middle East, Russia, and Europe came to China. Some Chinese and Mongols settled in Russia and Europe.

All this was important to world history. The Arabs and the Europeans learned from the Chinese. The Europeans got paper, porcelain, printing, gunpowder, and other inventions from the Chinese. The Chinese got glass, clothes, cotton, silver, carpets, honey, and slaves in return.

Kublai Khan (center), grandson of Genghis Khan, was a Mongol who ruled China under the Yuan dynasty.

How Did Chinese Opera Begin?

Mongol rulers did not allow the Chinese to become high government officials. They gave these jobs to Mongols or to foreigners. Chinese scholars who had been the officials began to write plays and **operas.** The actors, who were all men, acted, sang, and danced while the musicians sat on stage and played music.

WOMEN IN CHINA

The Chinese of the Middle Ages thought that women were unimportant, so they were not allowed to be educated. A woman's family arranged her marriage. Often she met her husband only the day before the wedding. When a wife walked down the street with her husband, she had to walk ten steps behind him.

A wife had little money of her own. She could not own property. If she had no children, her husband could take another wife. Chinese society thought that baby girls were a sign of bad things to come. Sometimes parents let a baby girl die.

During the Sung dynasty, some parents wrapped the feet of their daughters with tight bandages. As the girls grew older, their feet curled under until the toes nearly touched the heels. The parents did this because they thought tiny feet were beautiful. However, this crippled women.

◆Barbarian
*An uncivilized
person*

Why Did China Begin to Isolate Itself?

In 1368, the Mongol dynasty fell. Afterward, the Chinese did not see as many foreigners. The Ming emperors gained power. They thought the people who lived in all countries were **barbarians,** or uncivilized. In the 1500s, these emperors began to isolate China from other countries. They kept foreigners out and the Chinese in.

Isolation kept the Chinese from learning the exciting new things happening elsewhere. For the next 250 years, the Chinese did little trading or traveling, so China changed. It had been ahead of other civilizations, but isolation caused it to fall behind.

SECTION 4 REVIEW On a separate sheet of paper, write *True* if the statement is true or *False* if the statement is not true. Make each false statement true by changing the underlined word.

1) Genghis Khan was a <u>Mongol</u> conqueror.

2) The capital of the <u>Sung</u> dynasty was Beijing.

3) Under Mongol rule, <u>Chinese</u> people could not hold jobs as high officials.

4) Chinese scholars began to write plays and <u>poems.</u>

5) <u>Isolation</u> caused the decline of China.

What do you think ?

Why did the Ming dynasty begin to isolate China?

Japan is a country spread over more than 3,000 islands. The islands stretch for more than 1,200 miles. People have lived on them for thousands of years, perhaps as far back as 30,000 B.C. These Stone-Age people probably came from nearby China and Korea.

How Has Geography Influenced Japan's History?

The waters that surround Japan have protected it from invaders. Unlike China and India, foreign armies never conquered Japan. Yet these same waters brought ideas to Japan from Korea and China. The Japanese **adapted** these ideas to fit their own ideas. This resulted in a unique Japanese culture.

For example, the Japanese adopted the Chinese system of writing. This allowed them to read Chinese books about medicine, mathematics, and science. The Japanese copied Chinese art and literature, wore Chinese clothing, and used the Chinese calendar. For a time, the Japanese adopted the Chinese civil service. Later, they changed this system so that nobles, rather than scholars, ran the government.

What Makes the Shinto Religion Unique?

The religion born in Japan is **Shinto.** Historians do not know who founded it. It has no holy books like the Vedas, the Bible, or the Koran. Shinto followers love nature and worship **kami,** or spirits. They believe that these kami control the forces of nature.

The word *Shinto* means "the way of the gods." The Japanese people worship thousands of gods and spirits. The goddess of the sun is the most important Shinto god. In fact, the Japanese call their country Nippon, which means "source of the sun."

The royal family of Japan traces its ancestors back to Jimmu. The Japanese believe that Jimmu was **related,** or connected, to the sun goddess. Until the end of World War II, they thought that their emperor was a god.

Adapt
To change something to make it fit a different purpose

◆**Kami**
Spirits of the Shinto religion

Related
Connected in some way to another person, idea, or thing; born into the same family

◆**Shinto**
The Japanese religion that involves a love of nature and worship of spirits

This image shows Amaterasu, the Shinto sun goddess.

This map shows Japan. What are the names of Japan's four largest islands? Which bodies of water separate Japan from China and Korea? Which body of water lies east of Japan?

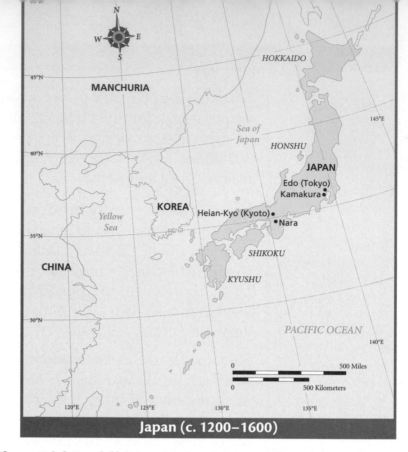

Japan (c. 1200–1600)

Missionary
A person who travels to another country or place to preach a religion

When Did Buddhism Arrive in Japan?

In A.D. 600, a Japanese prince sent a large group of young men to China to study. Many became Buddhists. Later, they returned to Japan. There they tried to get the Japanese to change their religion from Shintoism to Buddhism.

Buddhist **missionaries**—people who go to another country to preach a religion—came to Japan from Korea. Soon, Japanese rulers and warriors accepted many Buddhist ideas. Many artists and writers became Buddhist monks.

SECTION 5 REVIEW On a separate sheet of paper, write answers to these questions.

1) Why did no one invade Japan during its Middle Ages?

2) What did Japan borrow from China?

3) What does the word *Shinto* mean?

4) What is unique about the Shinto religion?

5) From what two countries did Buddhism come to Japan?

What do you think

Why do you think the Japanese call their country Nippon, or the "source of the sun"?

Haiku
A three-line poem with 17 syllables

Shogun
A Japanese word that means "great general;" a military dictator

Tanka
A five-line poem with 31 syllables

Japan had borrowed from the Chinese and Korean cultures. But between A.D. 800 and 1200, it began to develop its own culture. This period of Japanese history is called the Heian era. The life of the Japanese ruling class was different from that of the common people. The common people were mostly farmers and fishermen who lived in small villages. The ruling class was made up of nobles who stayed in the cities.

The nobles played music and games and wrote poetry, especially the **tanka** and the **haiku.** The tanka is a five-line poem with 31 syllables. The three-line haiku has five syllables in its first line, seven in its second, and five in its third. Haiku is often about nature. Both poems usually show a mood or a feeling. The nobles wrote them for special times and put them in letters.

What Was Japanese Feudalism?

During this time, the emperor was the head of the government. But noble families held the real power. Because they refused to pay taxes, they grew rich and bought much land.

To keep their power, these lords gave away some of their land to other people. These people promised to be loyal to the lords. Soon Japan was divided into many pieces of land by different nobles.

In the late 1100s, one noble family grew more powerful than any other. The leader of this family forced the emperor to appoint him **shogun.** This word means "great general." For the next 700 years, powerful shoguns governed Japan. They said that they ruled in the emperor's name. In fact, the shogun was a military dictator who controlled officials, judges, and armies.

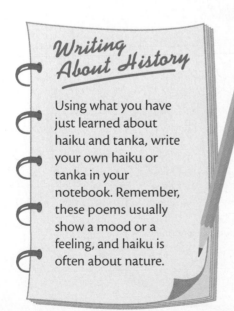

Writing About History

Using what you have just learned about haiku and tanka, write your own haiku or tanka in your notebook. Remember, these poems usually show a mood or a feeling, and haiku is often about nature.

Calligraphy
The art of beautiful handwriting

◆**Daimyo**
A great landowner in feudal Japan

Estate
A large piece of land with a house on it

Martial art
A way of fighting and defending oneself

◆**Samurai**
A Japanese warrior who received land from a lord and fought for him

Who Were Part of Japanese Feudalism?

The highest nobles next to the shogun were the **daimyos.** They controlled large **estates,** or pieces of land. An army of warriors fought for each daimyo. The daimyos gave land to these warriors who were known as **samurai,** which means "one who serves." The samurai were fearless soldiers who carried sharp swords. They believed that to die in battle was an honor.

When the samurai were not fighting, they developed strength through sports. They practiced judo and karate, which are **martial arts.** These are ways of fighting or defending oneself. Sumo wrestling was also popular.

The samurai were also artists. They painted beautiful scroll pictures, wrote poetry, and perfected the Japanese tea ceremony. When they were not using swords, the samurai used brushes to do **calligraphy**—the art of beautiful handwriting.

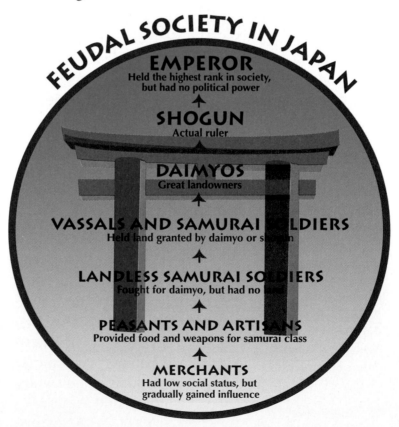

FEUDAL SOCIETY IN JAPAN

EMPEROR
Held the highest rank in society,
but had no political power

SHOGUN
Actual ruler

DAIMYOS
Great landowners

VASSALS AND SAMURAI SOLDIERS
Held land granted by daimyo or shogun

LANDLESS SAMURAI SOLDIERS
Fought for daimyo, but had no land

PEASANTS AND ARTISANS
Provided food and weapons for samurai class

MERCHANTS
Had low social status, but
gradually gained influence

This is what a Samurai warrior looked like.

What Was Bushido?

A samurai had a code of honor called **bushido.** This code demanded that he be brave and loyal to his lord. He had to obey orders and practice **self-discipline,** or control over one's feelings and actions. Honor was the most important thing in his life. If he lost his honor, a samurai committed **hari-kari.** That is, he killed himself with a knife. The nobles believed that hari-kari brought back honor.

How Did Japanese and European Feudalism Differ?

Japanese and European feudalism differed in four ways. First, the connection between the European lord and his vassal was a kind of legal arrangement. However, the Japanese based their connection on morality instead of law. A samurai obeyed because he believed that his daimyo had the right to rule.

Second, when a vassal died in Europe, his property was given to the oldest son. Or it was divided among all his sons. This often led to civil war. In Japan, a man chose the son who could best take care of the land. If a daimyo had no son, he adopted one.

◆Bushido
The warrior code of honor in Japan

◆Hari-kari
To kill oneself with a knife

Self-discipline
The power to control one's feelings and actions

Communication in History

A Romantic Novel From Japan

Literature was important in Heian Japan. Many women at court kept diaries. They described their elegant life. One lady of the court wrote the world's first novel. We know only her court name, Murasaki Shikibu. She came from a noble family. She married and had a daughter. A few years later, her husband died. Lady Murasaki then went to court to serve the empress. Her novel grew out of her diary of court life.

Her novel is called *The Tale of Genji.* Its hero is Prince Genji, the "shining Prince." Genji has many adventures and romances.

The Japanese used many Chinese characters in their writing. There were, however, some Japanese sounds that these characters could not express. As a result, a new way of writing Japanese developed around 1000. It is called kana. *The Tale of Genji* is written in kana.

ANYONE FOR TEA?

The Japanese began to practice tea ceremonies in the 1400s. Since then, they have made rules about how to prepare and serve tea. The ceremony takes place in a small room with a water container, flowers, and a hanging scroll.

To begin the ceremony, the host carefully prepares the tea. Then the host places the tea bowl in front of the most honored guest. The guest takes a sip and praises the tea maker on the flavor of the tea. Next, the guest takes another sip or two and passes the bowl.

This continues until the bowl comes back to the host. The tea maker carefully wipes the rim of the bowl with a special piece of paper.

Four things are important in a tea ceremony: harmony, respect, purity, and peace. Harmony comes from the plain tools the host uses in making the tea, the sounds of the wind and water, and the flowers. The host respects the guests; the guests respect the host. Their minds are pure and clear. When the ceremony is over, the tea maker and the guests are at peace with themselves and nature.

Third, in Europe, lords and vassals thought women were not equal to men, but they still respected women. Japanese warriors expected women to be tough and self-disciplined. They had to accept bad times—even death or hari-kari—without complaining.

Fourth, a European knight did not think that education was important. However, a Japanese samurai took pride in his poetry and calligraphy.

SECTION 6 REVIEW On a separate sheet of paper, write the word from the Word Bank that completes each sentence.

WORD BANK
daimyos
haiku
samurai
shogun
tanka

1) A _____ is a three-line poem with 17 syllables.

2) A _____ is a five-line poem with 31 syllables.

3) The military dictator of Japan was the _____.

4) The great landowners of Japan were the _____.

5) The _____ were Japanese warriors.

What do you think

How did calligraphy and poetry help the samurai win control of his feelings and actions?

Exaggerate
To make better, larger, or more important than in real life

◆Ikebana
The Japanese art of arranging flowers

◆Kabuki
A Japanese play with exaggerated actions

◆Noh drama
A Japanese play with only two actors

In 1603, the Tokugawa family took control of Japan. The shogun forced the daimyos to move to Edo, a small town on the coast. He could keep his eye on them there. (Today, Edo is the city of Tokyo, one of the world's largest cities.) A daimyo could visit his estate only if he left his wife and oldest son in Edo.

Why Did Japan Isolate Itself?

In the 1600s, many foreigners—merchants and missionaries—visited Japan. But the shoguns thought that western influence could hurt their power. Beginning in 1623, they began to isolate Japan. They killed all foreign missionaries or forced them to leave. In 1614, the shogun said that no one could be a Christian. In the next 20 years, thousands of Christian Japanese were killed.

The Japanese could not leave Japan. If they did, they could not return. By 1639, only the city of Nagasaki was open to foreigners. The shogun let some Chinese and Dutch traders live there. For the next 200 years, Japan shut itself off from the world.

The Japanese still have beautiful gardens like they had hundreds of years ago.

What Arts Did Japan Develop?

Japan still developed a rich culture. Among its arts are arranging flowers, writing and acting in plays, painting, and gardening. The Japanese call the art of flower arrangement **ikebana.** This art uses only a few flowers.

Noh dramas began in 1325. A Noh play uses only two actors who wear masks. A storyteller tells the story while musicians play and the two actors act. In 1586, **kabuki** developed. A kabuki play uses song and dance to show strong feelings. Actors tell the story with **exaggerated** movements that are larger than in real life.

Japanese paintings usually show the beauty of Japan. Some samurai painters drew pictures of war. The most famous painter of ancient Japan was Sesshu, a Buddhist monk. In the late 1400s, he painted a beautiful silk scroll that is 52 feet long. It shows the land of Japan as it changes over the four seasons of the year.

In their gardens, the Japanese copy nature in a small way. They carefully choose and place rocks in the garden. They also make hills and ponds that look natural.

SECTION 7 REVIEW Choose the letter of the answer that correctly completes each sentence. Write your answer on a separate sheet of paper.

1) The Tokugawa shogun moved the capital of Japan to
   _____.
   a. Edo   c. Hangzhou
   b. Beijing   d. Nagasaki

2) Noh dramas use only _____ actors.
   a. five   c. three
   b. four   d. two

3) Kabuki plays developed _____ than Noh plays.
   a. earlier   c. at the same time
   b. later   d. 200 years later

4) The Japanese call the art of flower arranging _____.
   a. shogun   c. ikebana
   b. exaggerate   d. hari-kari

5) _____ was the name of the family that began to isolate Japan.
   a. Shogun   c. Samurai
   b. Daimyo   d. Tokugawa

What do you think

What do you like best about the Japanese arts discussed in this section? Explain your answer.

Marco Polo in China

Marco Polo's father and uncle were merchants in Venice, Italy. In 1271, they left Venice for the court of Kublai Khan in China. Marco Polo was 17 years old.

Polo worked as an official for the Khan. He finally went back to Europe in 1295. He then wrote The Travels of Marco Polo. *It told about the wealth and culture of China. This reading from that book describes the Khan's palace.*

Marco Polo wrote a book about China in the late 1200s.

Within the second wall is the Great Khan's palace—the biggest palace ever to be seen. It abuts onto the northern wall, but to the south is a wide open space where barons and soldiers parade. It is built on only one floor, with a very high roof. . . .

The walls inside are covered with silver and gold and there are paintings of horsemen, dragons, and every kind of bird and animal. The vaulted ceiling is also entirely covered with paintings and gold ornamentation. The main reception room can seat more than 6,000 people. There is an overwhelming number of rooms; no architect in the world could have designed the palace better. The roof is beautifully painted in many colors—vermilion, green, blue, yellow, and so forth—so that it shines like a jewel and can be seen from afar. . . .

For three months every year Kublai Khan lives in the capital of Cathay . . . where he has a great palace. It is surrounded by a square wall, each side of which is a mile long. The wall is very thick and ten paces high. . . . At each of the four corners of the square there is a splendid and beautiful palace where the Great Khan's arms are stored. Halfway along each side of the square there is another similar palace, making eight in all. Every palace houses different equipment. For example, in one there is harness for the horses; in another there are bows, ropes, arrows, quivers and all the implements for archery; in a third there are breastplates and armour made of boiled leather; and so it goes on.

There are five gates in the south side of the wall. The central one is only opened for the Great Khan himself. Two small gates on either side of the main gate and two large ones near the corners of the wall are for citizens and other people.

Inside this wall is another one, slightly longer than it is wide. . . .

Source Reading Wrap-Up

1) The Khan's palace was well protected. Describe the area around it.

2) How were the eight palaces on the outer wall used?

3) Why was the central gate special?

4) How were the palace walls and ceilings decorated?

5) How many people could the main reception room hold?

The Taj Mahal— A Monument of Love

The Taj Mahal is one of the most beautiful buildings in the world. It is also a love story in stone.

Shah Jahan was one of the last Moghul emperors. He was the grandson of Akbar. In 1631, Shah Jahan's favorite wife died. They had been close companions for 19 years of marriage. The broken-hearted shah built this tomb to show their great love. The queen's name was Mumtaz Mahal. It means "Chosen One of the Palace." The building's name comes from her name.

Workers brought materials from all over Asia. White marble was brought up the Jumna River to the town of Agra. More than 20,000 workers worked for 22 years to complete it. The building cost millions of rupees.

The Taj Mahal itself is a four-sided marble building. It sits on a raised square platform. Each side has a huge central arch and small domes. Both the inside and outside walls are delicately carved. At each corner stands a slender tower, or *minaret*. Gardens surround the tomb. Nearby are a mosque and other buildings.

Here is one visitor's reaction: "With its minarets rising at each corner, its dome and tapering spire, it creates a sense of airy, almost floating lightness. Looking at it, I decided [that] I had never known what perfect proportions were before."

The Taj Mahal was built for Shah Jahan's favorite wife.

The burial room is eight-sided, with a marble screen around it. The screen is carved so delicately that it looks like lace. At first it was decorated with jewels. A blanket of pearls covered the queen's coffin. Gold and silver decorated the walls. Blue sapphires and red rubies gave color to carved marble flowers. Over time, the pearls and other treasures were stolen.

Shah Jahan planned to build a copy of the Taj Mahal for himself. It would be in black marble. A bridge of silver would join the two tombs. The black tomb, however, was never built. Shah Jahan lost power in 1658. He died in 1666. He was buried next to his beloved queen in the Taj Mahal.

Spotlight Story Wrap-Up

1) Why did Shah Jahan build the Taj Mahal?

2) What material was used for the Taj Mahal?

3) How long did the construction take?

4) How was the inside of the building decorated?

5) What were Shah Jahan's plans for his own burial? What happened?

Chapter Summary

➡ The Indian Siddhartha Gautama became the Buddha. He taught the four "Noble Truths." He said that people should follow the "Eightfold Path" to reach nirvana.

➡ Buddhism shares some beliefs with Hinduism, but not the caste system. Buddhism spread from India into much of Asia.

➡ The Gupta dynasty ruled India during its Golden Age (A.D. 320 to 535). Indian religious artists developed a unique style. Scientists made many discoveries. Mathematicians used zero and the numerals 1 through 9.

➡ In 1398, Mongols led by Tamerlane attacked India. In 1525, another Mongol leader began the Moghul empire. Akbar was its best-known ruler. Moghul architects built beautiful buildings.

➡ China was rich and powerful during the T'ang dynasty (A.D. 618 to 907). Scholars ran the government, and trading brought foreign visitors and new ideas.

➡ In the Sung dynasty (A.D. 960 to 1279), the center of culture shifted south to the Yangtze River Valley. Chinese inventions included gunpowder, the compass, the abacus, the clock, and porcelain.

➡ In the 1200s, Mongols conquered China, India, and Russia. Later, Kublai Khan established the Yuan dynasty. Mongol rulers encouraged trade with the Arabs and Europeans. Scholars wrote and performed in plays and operas.

➡ After the fall of the Mongols in 1368, China began to isolate itself.

➡ The Japanese adapted many ideas from Korea and China. Japan's native religion, Shinto, worships many nature spirits. Many Japanese also became Buddhists.

➡ During the Heian era (A.D. 800 to 1200), Japanese nobles wrote haiku and tanka poetry. Noble families took power from the emperor. The shoguns were the real rulers.

➡ In Japan's feudal system, the daimyos were powerful lords. Samurai were warrior knights. The samurai practiced martial arts and were artists. They followed a code of honor called bushido. Women were also expected to be brave.

➡ Shoguns from the Tokugawa family took control of Japan in 1603. They moved the capital to Edo. They tried to end foreign influence, especially Christianity.

➡ Flower-arranging, plays, painting, and gardening are important arts in Japanese culture. Noh and kabuki are forms of drama.

Comprehension: Identifying Facts

On a separate sheet of paper, use the words from the Word Bank to complete each sentence.

WORD BANK

Buddha

Genghis Khan

Gupta

Mongols

Sesshu

Shinto

Shoguns

Sung

T'ang

Tokugawa

1) In India, Siddhartha Gautama became known as _____.

2) The _____ dynasty ruled India during its Golden Age.

3) The _____ invaded India in 1398.

4) In the _____ dynasty, scholars ruled China.

5) The artists of the _____ dynasty painted masterpieces.

6) The greatest Mongol conqueror was _____.

7) _____ is the religion born in Japan.

8) _____ ruled Japan in the name of the emperor.

9) The _____ shoguns isolated Japan from the rest of the world.

10) _____ was the most famous painter of ancient Japan.

Comprehension: Multiple Choice

On a separate sheet of paper, write the letter of the answer that correctly completes each sentence.

1) Buddha said that the meaning of life can be seen in _____ "Noble Truths."

    a. four   c. eight

    b. six   d. ten

2) Indian doctors learned about _____ 1,000 years before Europeans did.

    a. Shinto   c. inoculation

    b. compass   d. abacus

3) The Chinese invented _____.

    a. gunpowder   c. clocks

    b. compasses   d. all of the above

4) The real ruler of Japan was the _____

    a. shogun   c. samurai

    b. daimyo   d. tanka

5) The Japanese wrote _____.

    a. haiku   c. kabuki

    b. tanka   d. all of the above

Comprehension: Understanding Main Ideas

On a separate sheet of paper, write the answers to the following questions using complete sentences, or statements.

1) What is one gift India has given to world civilization?

2) What is one gift China has given to world civilization?

3) What is one thing that is the same and one thing that is different between Japanese and European feudalism?

Critical Thinking: Write Your Opinion

1) Imagine that you are a European merchant in the Middle Ages. Which country would you choose to visit: India, China, or Japan? Explain why.

2) Chinese and Japanese artists usually paint nature—trees, mountains, and flowers. Western artists often draw people. What does this tell you about the different cultures?

| Test-Taking Tip | Try to answer all test questions as completely as possible. When asked to explain your answer, do so in complete sentences. |

As you study history, you will read many facts. Sometimes people write books about history in which they state their opinions. You need to be able to tell the difference between fact and opinion.

A fact can be proved true or false.

> Mansa Musa ruled Mali in the 1300s.

An opinion is someone's judgment, belief, or way of thinking about something. To identify an opinion, look for words that tell how someone felt. An opinion is more than just a fact.

> Mansa Musa was a rich and noble ruler.
>
> Mansa Musa was generous to everyone.

Read each pair of sentences in items 1–4. Decide which sentence in each pair is fact and which is opinion. Explain your answer.

1) Justinian had Roman laws collected and organized into a code. Justinian was a wise and able ruler.

2) William the Conqueror's victory was a great step in English history. William the Conqueror's victory made him king of England.

3) The pope called for the First Crusade to free Palestine. The crusades were necessary to defend Christianity.

4) The Mayas were the most advanced culture in the Americas. Tikal was the largest Maya city.

5) Write a fact and an opinion about the Middle Ages.

➡ The eastern Roman Empire became the Byzantine Empire. Its greatest ruler, Justinian, organized a code of laws. The empire fell to the Turks, however, in 1453.

➡ In 1054, the Christian Church split into Roman Catholic and Eastern Orthodox.

➡ Russia began in Kiev about A.D. 862. Then power shifted to Moscow. Modern Russia began in the 1400s when Ivan the Great drove out Mongol invaders.

➡ Charlemagne, a Frankish king, united Western Europe in A.D. 800. Later, Vikings attacked parts of Europe. William of Normandy invaded Britain in 1066.

➡ Farming and trade revived in the late Middle Ages. Between 1095 and 1291, Europeans went on crusades to take Palestine from the Muslims.

➡ Under feudalism, a lord granted land to a vassal in exchange for service. Knights fought frequent wars. Peasants and serfs worked the farm on a manor.

➡ Romanesque churches were dark and heavy with rounded arches. Gothic buildings had pointed arches; tall, thin walls; and stained glass windows.

➡ Muhammad started the religion of Islam. Its holy book is the Koran. Muslims made discoveries in medicine, science, and mathematics.

➡ Ghana, Mali, and Songhai were great trading kingdoms in West Africa. Their wealth came from the gold-salt trade.

➡ The Olmec and Mayan civilizations began in Mexico and Central America. The Aztecs gained control of central Mexico in the 1100s. The Incas built an empire in the Andes Mountains.

➡ Buddhism began with the teachings of Siddhartha Gautama in India. It spread throughout Asia.

➡ The Gupta dynasty (A.D. 320 to 535) brought a Golden Age to India. Mathematicians invented zero and the numerals 1 through 9. The Moghul empire in India began in 1525.

➡ China was rich and powerful in the T'ang and Sung dynasties. Trade was important. Chinese inventions included printing, gunpowder, the compass, and porcelain. Mongols led by Genghis Khan conquered China, India, and Russia in the 1200s.

➡ The Heian era (A.D. 800 to 1200) was important in Japanese culture.

➡ In Japan's feudal system, the daimyos were land-owning lords. Samurai, or warrior knights, followed a code that emphasized honor and discipline. Military leaders, called shoguns, ruled Japan instead of the emperor. After 1603, the Tokugawa shoguns ended foreign influence.

Comprehension: Identifying Facts

On a separate sheet of paper, use the words from the Word Bank to complete each sentence.

WORD BANK

boyar
crusader
daimyos
feudalism
gunpowder
icon
jihad
knight
patriarch
samurai

1) A small religious picture of a saint or of Jesus of Nazareth is an _____.

2) A landowning Russian noble in the Middle Ages was a _____.

3) A _____ is a leader of the Russian Catholic Church.

4) A person who went on a military journey to the Holy Land was a _____.

5) Both Japan and Europe had _____, which was based on the holding of land.

6) A European warrior who was loyal to a lord was a _____.

7) A holy war for a Muslim was a _____.

8) The Chinese invented _____.

9) The important landowners of Japan were the _____.

10) A Japanese warrior was a _____.

Comprehension: Multiple Choice

On a separate sheet of paper, write the letter of the answer that correctly completes each sentence.

1) The Byzantine emperor who ordered a code of all Roman laws was _____.

  a. Mansa Musa   c. Justinian

  b. Genghis Khan   d. Sesshu

2) The prophet who founded the Muslim religion in Arabia was _____.

  a. Muhammad   c. Jesus of Nazareth

  b. Buddha   d. Shinto

3) The African ruler who founded a university in Mali was
_____.

a. Aztec   c. Mansa Musa
b. Songhai   d. Islam

4) The founder of the Buddhist religion in India was
_____.

a. Mansa Musa   c. Ivan the Great
b. Tokugawa   d. Siddhartha Gautama

5) The founder of the Shinto religion in Japan was _____.

a. Shogun   c. Mongol
b. T'ang   d. unknown

Comprehension: Understanding Main Ideas

On a separate sheet of paper, write the answers to the following questions using complete sentences, or statements.

1) What is one good thing and one bad thing about feudalism in Europe?

2) What is one good thing and one bad thing about feudalism in Japan?

3) What does trade with other countries do for a society or civilization?

Critical Thinking: Write Your Opinion

1) What was the best invention that you read about in this unit? Explain your answer.

2) If you could talk to a person who is a Muslim, a Buddhist, or a Shintoist about their religion, which would you pick? Why? What questions would you ask? Why?

Test-Taking Tip | If a word on a test looks new to you, separate it into several pieces. Try comparing the parts to words you know.

"I do not know what I may appear to the world, but to myself I seem to have been only like a boy playing on the seashore, and diverting myself in now and then finding a smoother pebble or a prettier shell than ordinary, whilst the great ocean of truth lay all undiscovered before me."

—Sir Isaac Newton, shortly before his death in 1727

The Challenge of New Ideas

1348 to 1750

Historians call the Middle Ages in Europe the Age of Faith. Christian beliefs dominated the culture. At the end of the 1200s, everything and everyone—church, ruler, people—seemed fixed.

But then change began to creep across the land. In this unit, you will settle in Rome to watch great artists create masterpieces. You will be there for the Renaissance, or rebirth of learning. Next, you will travel north to Germany and listen to Luther as his actions send you into the Reformation. Finally, you will journey to many parts of Europe to see how scientists used the new scientific method to question old beliefs.

In Chapter 13, you start with a plague in 1348 that wipes out millions of people in Europe. In Chapter 15, you end with scientific theories that change old ways of looking at the world.

Chapter 13: The Renaissance
        1348 to 1600

Chapter 14: The Reformation
        1415 to 1650

Chapter 15: The New Science
        1540 to 1750

The Renaissance

1348 to 1600

Between the years 1348 and 1600, change came to Europe. During this period, people questioned old beliefs. They also took a new interest in learning, creativity, and independent thinking. Historians call this the Renaissance. It ended the Middle Ages. In this chapter, you will see how the Black Death affected Europe. You will travel to Florence and visit Lorenzo the Magnificent. Then you will journey to England to meet the playwright William Shakespeare. Finally, you will sail back to Italy and watch Leonardo da Vinci, Michelangelo, and Raphael create art masterpieces.

Goals for Learning

▶ To describe the changes the Black Death brought to Europe

▶ To explain why historians use the term *renaissance* for this historical period

▶ To describe the beliefs of humanism

▶ To list the qualities of a Renaissance man and a Renaissance woman

▶ To list the names of Renaissance artists and writers and their works

▶ To explain why the invention of the printing press was important to learning

1348	1381	1469	1508	1605
Black Death comes to Europe	Peasants rebel in England	Lorenzo de Medici comes to power in Florence	Michelangelo begins Sistine Chapel	*Don Quixote de la Mancha* by Cervantes is published

1350	1450	1550	1650

1350	1455	1503	1558	1626
Renaissance begins in northern Italy	Gutenberg prints Bible	Leonardo da Vinci paints the *Mona Lisa*	Queen Elizabeth begins to rule England	Saint Peter's Church is completed

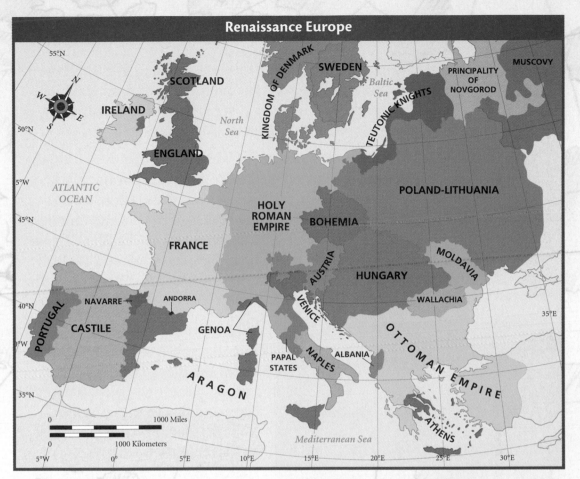

Renaissance Europe

During the Renaissance, many of today's nations began to develop. As you look at the map, you will see names you know, such as England, France, and Sweden. However, two large empires existed during this period that no longer exist now. In addition, the city-states and kingdoms of Italy during the Renaissance took nearly four centuries to unite.

Study the map and answer the following questions:

1) What sea separates England from the Kingdom of Denmark?

2) What sea is northeast of the Holy Roman Empire?

3) What country borders Castile on the west?

4) In what direction are the Papal States from England?

5) What country borders the Holy Roman Empire on the west?

Geography Skills

Clergy
The people who lead a religion

Employer
A person who hires someone else to work for him or her

◆**Rebellion**
A fight by people against a government; a struggle for change

During the 1300s, troubled times came to Western Europe. Workers had little money, and the cost of food was high. Early in the century, when many people had no food, nearly 10 percent of them died.

Then, in 1348, a plague hit Western Europe. It made ugly black spots on people's skin, so they called it the Black Death. People got this disease from fleas. These small, wingless insects live on the bodies of people and animals. In the 1300s, the fleas on sick rats spread the Black Death from one person to the next. Between 1348 and 1400, millions of people died. England alone lost nearly one-third of its population.

The Black Death killed millions of people in Europe. This image shows the burying of plague victims in Tournai, Belgium.

What Did a Smaller Population Mean for Europe?

When the Black Death attacked Europe, people left the towns and cities and fled to the country. Millions died. Fewer people were left alive to pay taxes, so governments had less money. Fewer people were left to work. **Employers** had to pay their workers more money. Also, less food was needed for a smaller population. The price of food dropped, and farmers made less money. Because of this, many serfs wanted to leave the manor farms and work somewhere else.

How Did the Black Death Change Society?

During the Middle Ages, nobles and **clergy**—the people who led the Roman Catholic Church—stood at the top of society. At the bottom stood peasants, or serfs. The law did not let them leave the land on which they worked. But as death marched through Europe, some peasants demanded change.

These peasants began to question old beliefs. In 1381, English peasants started a **rebellion** against King Richard

The Bubonic Plague

The first recorded cases of the Black Death were on the Black Sea in Russia. Starting in 1347, the Black Death, or Bubonic Plague, spread west along trade routes. It attacked seaports, then inland cities, and finally rural areas. At first, people thought poisoned air or water caused the Black Death. They fled from areas where others were sick.

The Black Death spread very easily. It spread by infected fleas on rats, coughing, and sneezing. By fleeing from the disease, people protected themselves somewhat. As of 1352, the plague had killed over 25 million people in Europe. This sickness broke out from time to time in Europe for about 300 years.

The last great outbreak of the Black Death took place in China in 1894. There were two small outbreaks in India in 1994. Modern medicine can control the disease. Today, finding and treating the sickness quickly can save 90–95 percent of its victims.

II. They began to fight for their rights. The king and his nobles stopped it. But the rebellion was a clear warning: change marched with the Black Death!

Why Did People Look Back to Greece and Rome?

Now people wanted to be more independent and **creative.** That is, they wanted to use their imaginations to create things. They looked back to ancient Greece and Rome where people had done this. They studied the art, literature, science, and philosophy of Greece and Rome.

Historians call this new creative period the **Renaissance.** This French word means "rebirth." This period focused on being an individual and expanding on creative thoughts and ideas. With the beginning of the Renaissance, the Middle Ages in Europe ended.

Creative
Able to use one's imagination to create things

◆**Renaissance**
Rebirth; a period in European history that focused on being an individual and expanding on creative thoughts and ideas

SECTION 1 REVIEW On a separate sheet of paper, write *True* if the statement is true or *False* if the statement is not true. Make each false statement true by changing the underlined word.

1) The Black Death came to Western Europe in <u>1348.</u>

2) It killed <u>hundreds</u> of people.

3) Because of the Black Death, fewer people paid <u>taxes,</u> so the government had less money.

4) Peasants started a <u>renaissance.</u>

5) The Black Death led to the Renaissance, which means a <u>rebirth.</u>

What do you think ?

Why did people leave the cities and flee to the country when the Black Death attacked Europe?

◆Humanism
A belief that human actions, ideas, and works are important

◆Humanist
A person who believes in humanism

Ignorant
Having little knowledge or education

The Renaissance dominated Europe for 250 years. It began around 1350 in a few city-states in northern Italy and spread to other countries.

Renaissance people thought that the people of the Middle Ages were **ignorant,** meaning they had little knowledge or education. One Renaissance writer called the Middle Ages the "Dark Ages." He thought that the "light of learning" had gone out in Europe when Rome fell in A.D. 476. Renaissance people believed that progress in art, literature, and science stopped in the Middle Ages.

What Is Humanism?

The Renaissance produced **humanism.** It is the belief that human actions, ideas, and works are important. During the Middle Ages, people wanted to get ready for life after death. That was their reason for living. They believed that happiness came only after death. **Humanists** said that people should be happy while alive.

Humanists discovered that the Greeks and Romans had felt the same way they did. They searched libraries and monasteries for writings from ancient Greece and Rome. Then they studied the Greek and Latin languages to read these writings. All this led to a rebirth, or renaissance, of learning.

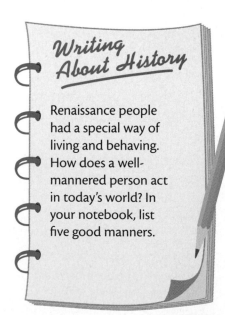

Writing About History

Renaissance people had a special way of living and behaving. How does a well-mannered person act in today's world? In your notebook, list five good manners.

What Could a Renaissance Man Do?

Renaissance thinkers loved learning. They wanted to know many different things. A Renaissance man could read and talk about the writings of ancient Greece and Rome. Art and science interested him, too. However, book learning was not enough. He had to have fine manners and be interesting and funny when he talked. He had to play music, dance, and write poetry.

He had to be strong and good at games. He also had to ride a horse and use a sword well.

What Could a Renaissance Woman Do?

During the Renaissance, many women from wealthy families were also well educated. Teachers, or **tutors,** came to their homes to teach these women. One of the most famous women during the Italian Renaissance was Isabella d'Este. Isabella was born in 1474. When she grew up, she married a wealthy man. Later, however, an enemy captured her husband in a war. Isabella then became the ruler of Mantua, a small territory in Italy.

Isabella d'Este had political power. But she was also a well-educated woman. She studied Greek and Latin, and she collected many books for her home. She also sang beautifully and gave money to artists who created great works. At the time, some called her "the first lady to the world."

Isabella d'Este was a Renaissance woman of many talents and interests.

NICCOLÒ MACHIAVELLI: 1469–1527

Machiavelli was a famous writer and historian. He had a job as secretary to a government council that traveled throughout Italy. During these trips, Machiavelli met many rulers. He wondered how they got and kept power. As a result, he watched how they acted.

Based on what he saw, Machiavelli set up his own ideas about how to rule. He stated them in his book, *The Prince*. He believed that for a ruler, the ends justify the means. He said that the usual rules for behavior do not apply to rulers. He believed they should focus on power and success.

SECTION 2 REVIEW On a separate sheet of paper, write the word from the Word Bank that completes each sentence.

WORD BANK
Greece
Humanism
Italy
Mantua
Renaissance

1) _____ is the belief that studying human actions, ideas, and works is important.

2) The Renaissance began in northern _____.

3) People of the Renaissance studied the writings of ancient Rome and _____.

4) A _____ man was interested in learning to do many things well.

5) Isabella d'Este became the ruler of _____, Italy.

What do you think

Who do you think was right about the way to live life—the people of the Middle Ages or the people of the Renaissance? Explain your answer.

At the beginning of the Renaissance, Italy was made up of more than 200 separate city-states. Many of these city-states had less than 10,000 people. However, as time passed, several cities in northern Italy grew to a population of 100,000. Outside Italy, only Paris had more people.

How Did Italian City-States Become Wealthy?

These city-states grew wealthy and powerful by controlling trade. Most of the trade routes from the East passed through the eastern end of the Mediterranean Sea. Goods then went to the northern Italian city-states of Venice, Milan, Florence, and Genoa.

Because northern Italy was not united, each city-state had its own ruler. At times, these city-states fought each other. In the fourteenth century, Venice defeated Genoa and gained control of Mediterranean trade. Because Venice was by the Adriatic Sea, people called it the "Queen of the Adriatic."

What Type of Government Did Florence Have?

The city-state of Florence showed the creative spirit of the Renaissance. The city became wealthy because it produced wool cloth. As many as 30,000 workers made this cloth.

Florence was an exciting city during the Renaissance. Scholars and artists came to this city from all over Europe.

Florence had a republican form of government. However, several hundred wealthy families controlled the election of government leaders. These leaders were usually bankers and merchants. One of the most important of these ruling families was the Medici. It became the most important ruling family in Florence.

Who Was Lorenzo the Magnificent?

In 1469, the most famous ruler of Florence came to power. His name was Lorenzo de Medici. He used his family's wealth to help artists and scholars. Florence came alive with new ideas, holidays, and beautiful art. **Architects**—people who draw plans for buildings—built wonderful buildings. **Sculptors** carved statues and put them outside so everyone could enjoy them.

Every year on the birthday of the Greek philosopher Plato, Lorenzo held a party. The best scholars in Italy came to it. They ate, drank, listened to music, and talked about new ideas. The ancient Athenians had done this, too. With his yearly party and his support for the arts, Lorenzo made Florence the "Athens of Italy."

Because of all this, people called Lorenzo "the Magnificent." He died in 1492, the year Christopher Columbus sailed west into unknown waters. The king and queen of Spain wanted him to find a new trade route to the East. If Columbus could find this route, the Italian city-states would no longer control trade with the East. Spain would.

Lorenzo de Medici was called Lorenzo "the Magnificent" for his leadership in Florence.

Why Did People Give Up Their Worldly Possessions?

Near the end of Lorenzo's life, the economy of Florence began to decline. People grew poorer. Food was scarce. Then a monk named Savonarola began to preach against the Renaissance. He said

Worldly
Having nothing to do with religion

that the people of Florence thought too much about themselves and not enough about religion.

All over Italy, religious leaders warned people about the dangers of dancing, poetry, and nonreligious music. They asked everyone to throw their nonreligious books, artwork, beautiful clothing, and other goods into a bonfire. All these possessions were **worldly.** That is, they had nothing to do with religion.

How Did Savonarola Gain Power?

In 1494, the French army marched south into Italy to claim the city-state of Naples. On the way, the army attacked Florence. Lorenzo's son, Piero, gave up the city without a fight. This made the citizens of Florence angry. They forced the Medici family out of power.

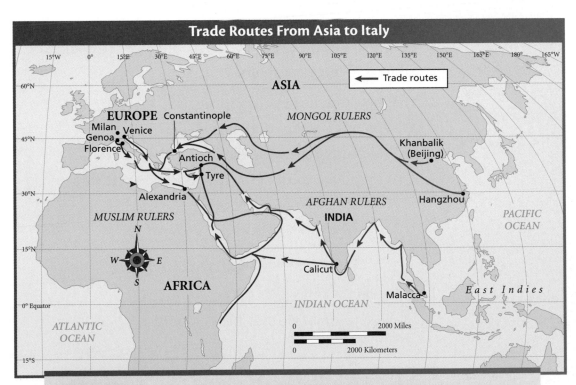

Trade Routes From Asia to Italy

MAP STUDY

This map shows trade routes from parts of Asia to Italy. In what direction did goods go from Beijing to Constantinople? Where was the trading city of Calicut located? What trading city was located on the continent of Africa?

Before this, Savonarola had called Lorenzo Medici a tyrant. When Piero Medici gave up Florence, the people thought that Savonarola had been right. Savonarola became politically powerful.

For four years, he was probably the most powerful man in Florence. During that time, he tried to force the people of Florence to change their lives. He wanted them to give up the worldly happiness that the Renaissance said they had a right to.

What Happened to Savonarola?

Soon the people of Florence became tired of Savonarola and his hard ways. Then he began to **criticize** the pope. That was too much. They arrested him and put him on trial. Then they **executed,** or killed, him in the city square.

Florence continued to decline. However, it remained a powerful symbol of the spirit of the Renaissance.

SECTION 3 REVIEW On a separate sheet of paper, write answers to these questions.

1) Where did the Renaissance begin?

2) Who was Lorenzo the Magnificent?

3) Which city-state was called the "Athens of Italy"?

4) Why did the spirit of the Renaissance upset some religious leaders?

5) What religious leader gained political power in Florence?

What do you think

Why do you think Piero de Medici surrendered Florence to the French army?

Drama
A play to act out on a stage

Genius
A person born with special skills that make him or her different from ordinary people

Sonnet
A 14-line poem about one idea

During the Renaissance, artists wanted to make their paintings and sculptures look real just as Greek artists had. In fact, someone once heard the great Renaissance sculptor Donatello say to one of his sculptures, "Speak then! Why will you not speak!"

But artists also wanted the people in their paintings and sculptures to look even better than they did in real life. By doing this—with paint, bronze, and marble—they created masterpieces. During the Renaissance, people called a gifted artist a **genius.** That is, the artist had been born with special skills and was different from ordinary people. People call several Renaissance writers and artists geniuses.

What Language Did Renaissance Writers Use?

During most of the Middle Ages, people wrote books in Latin—the language of educated people. Then, near the end of the Middle Ages, writers and poets began to write in their own languages. The great Italian poets Petrarch and Dante wrote in Italian. In England, Geoffrey Chaucer wrote stories in English. Even today, people still read the works of these great writers.

Who Was a Great Writer of the Elizabethan Age?

Between 1558 and 1603, Queen Elizabeth I ruled England. She was one of England's greatest rulers. Today, historians call the time of her reign the Elizabethan Age. During these years, England gained new political power and economic wealth.

The Elizabethan Age produced some of the finest writers in English history. William Shakespeare, perhaps one of the greatest writers in the English language, lived during this time. Between 1590 and 1613, he wrote many works, including **dramas,** or plays. He also wrote beautiful **sonnets.** This type of poem is 14 lines about one idea.

Who Was a Great Renaissance Writer From Spain?

Another leading writer of the Renaissance was Miguel de Cervantes, a Spanish writer. He created the wonderful character of Don Quixote. Cervantes published the first part of his novel, *Don Quixote de la Mancha*, in 1605.

Quixote sees himself as a knight who must right the wrongs of the world. With his servant, Sancho Panza, he rides throughout Spain. They have one adventure after another. Don Quixote is a **comic,** or funny, character. People have loved Don Quixote for almost 400 years.

What Was the First Book Printed in Europe?

You already learned that in 1040 the Chinese invented a printing press that used wood blocks. Historians believe that Johann Gutenberg from Germany invented the first printing press that used moveable metal type in the 1400s.

In 1455, Gutenberg printed a Bible. The Gutenberg Bible was one of the first books printed in Europe. Soon printers were printing books in Italy, France, England, and 15 other countries. By the 1500s, they had printed thousands of books. Learning began to spread as books became part of education.

Then and Now

William Shakespeare

William Shakespeare (1564–1616) wrote 39 plays. *Romeo and Juliet* is about two teenagers from warring families who fall in love. In *Macbeth*, the main character is too ambitious. *Hamlet* is the story of a prince who seeks revenge for his father's murder. Although his plays are 400 years old, many are still performed today. Perhaps you have seen one done as a movie.

Many of Shakespeare's plays were first produced in London's Globe Theatre. It has been rebuilt and once again his plays are being performed there. Works by Shakespeare are often seen in major London and New York theaters, too. There are also many Shakespeare festivals. Stratford-upon-Avon, his birthplace, has hosted such an event since 1769.

Newspapers Are Born

When Gutenberg invented movable metal type in the fifteenth century, printing became easier and cheaper. As a result, newspapers were born. Their purpose was to report news and information to people.

Early newspapers were small. They looked like newsletters. Papers usually consisted of one page. They were published weekly, not daily.

The first known newspaper started in Germany in 1609. It told about events in other countries. The first London paper began in 1622. Then in 1665, *The London News Gazette* started. It was published on a regular basis in newspaper format. The *Boston News-Letter* was the first continuously published American newspaper. It began in 1704. Like papers today, it had financial and foreign news. It also recorded births, deaths, and social events.

Gutenberg's printing press allowed people to publish books and newspapers for the first time.

SECTION 4 REVIEW On a separate sheet of paper, write the word from the Word Bank that completes each sentence.

WORD BANK
Chaucer
Dante
Gutenberg
Quixote
Shakespeare

1) The English writer _____ wrote stories in the English language.

2) One of the greatest English writers of plays and sonnets was _____.

3) The Spanish writer Cervantes created a wonderful character named Don _____.

4) The Italian poet _____ wrote in his country's language.

5) The first book _____ printed was the Bible.

What do you think

Why would having books in one's own language lead to more learning?

Dissect
To cut open something that was once alive to study it

◆**Fresco**
A painting done in wet plaster on a wall

◆**Patron**
A person who supports an artist with money

Plaster
A mixture of sand, water, and lime that gives a smooth finish to a wall

Portrait
A drawing of a person

Leonardo da Vinci was a true Renaissance man. Born in the small Italian village of Vinci in 1452, he had many interests and much skill. His curiosity drove him to explore many fields of study. Leonardo was an artist, a scientist, an engineer, and a clever inventor.

What Are Two Famous Paintings by Leonardo?

As an artist, Leonardo left us only a few paintings. He completed his most famous painting in 1503. It is the **portrait,** or drawing, of a 24-year-old woman from Florence. She looks at us with a mysterious smile. The painting, called the *Mona Lisa,* is one of the most famous paintings in the world.

Another important painting of Leonardo's is the *Last Supper.* It shows Jesus of Nazareth eating with his disciples on the night before he died. Leonardo painted it in wet **plaster** on a wall. Plaster is a mixture of sand, water, and lime. It gives a smooth finish to a wall. Leonardo used his own way of doing this **fresco.**

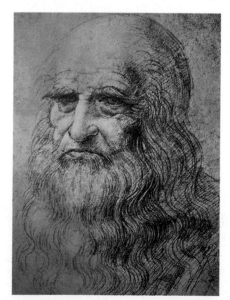
Leonardo da Vinci was a very skilled Renaissance man. This drawing is a self-portrait.

Like all Renaissance artists, Leonardo needed **patrons.** These people supported artists by giving them money. One of Leonardo's patrons was Beatrice d'Este, the wife of the duke of Milan. Another was the king of France, Francis I. Leonardo's work in France helped spread Renaissance ideas to countries beyond Italy.

What Did Leonardo Put in His Notebooks?

As a scientist, Leonardo drew natural objects. In dozens of notebooks, he recorded what he saw. He drew the wings of birds, the bodies of animals, and the tiny lines in a leaf. He **dissected,** or cut open, dead human bodies to study them. He used what he learned to make his paintings look more like real life.

The *Mona Lisa* is one of da Vinci's most famous portraits.

Submarine
A ship that travels beneath the surface of water

What do you think **?**

Why would having a patron be a good thing for an artist? In what way could it be a bad thing?

As an inventor, Leonardo was far ahead of his time. His notebooks of more than 5,000 pages included drawings of a bicycle; a new kind of cannon; a machine gun; a **submarine,** or ship that travels beneath the surface of water; a flying machine; and even a parachute. Long after his death, other people made these things. Leonardo da Vinci, who died in 1519 at the age of 67, was a true Renaissance man.

SECTION 5 REVIEW Choose the letter of the answer that correctly completes each sentence. Write your answer on a separate sheet of paper.

1) Leonardo da Vinci was a true Renaissance man because he was a(n) _____.

   a. painter   c. scientist
   b. inventor   d. all of the above

2) One of his _____, or people who supported him, was Beatrice d'Este.

   a. portraits   c. patrons
   b. plaster   d. frescoes

3) One of Leonardo's greatest portraits is the _____.

   a. *Mona Lisa*   c. *Last Supper*
   b. *Don Quixote*   d. none of the above

4) One of Leonardo's greatest frescoes is the _____.

   a. *Mona Lisa*   c. *Last Supper*
   b. *Don Quixote*   d. none of the above

5) As an inventor, Leonardo drew pictures of _____.

   a. submarines   c. bicycles
   b. parachutes   d. all of the above

Chapel
A small church

Creation
The act of making something; the making of the world

◆Vatican
The home of the pope

During the Renaissance, many artists produced important works of art. However, few of them produced masterpieces like those of Michelangelo and Raphael Santi. For nearly 500 years, people have enjoyed their work.

What Are Two Sculptures of Michelangelo?

Michelangelo was born near Florence in 1475. As a young man, he wanted to be a sculptor, and Lorenzo de Medici helped him in his studies. At the age of 23, Michelangelo became famous for carving the *Pietà*, which means "pity." The sculpture shows Mary, the mother of Jesus, holding his dead body. In 1504, Michelangelo completed a statue of *David*. (In a Bible story, David killed the giant Goliath with a stone thrown from a slingshot.) Michelangelo loved being a sculptor. But he also became famous as a painter.

What Ceiling Did Michelangelo Paint?

In 1508, Pope Julius II asked 33-year-old Michelangelo to come to Rome. The pope wanted him to paint frescoes on the ceiling of the Sistine **Chapel** in the **Vatican.** The chapel was a small church in the Vatican. The Vatican is the home of the pope.

Michelangelo did not want the job. He insisted that he was a sculptor and not a painter. But the pope held firm, and Michelangelo finally accepted.

The pope told Michelangelo that he could paint what he wanted. So on the wet plaster of the ceiling, Michelangelo painted pictures from Bible stories. He started with the **creation,** or the making of the world and ended with the great flood.

For four years, Michelangelo painted the ceiling while lying on his back, 80 feet above the floor. Paint dropped into his eyes. At night he painted by candlelight. He felt tired, gloomy, and anxious. Only his genius and physical strength enabled Michelangelo to complete the ceiling. He painted

Michelangelo was an artistic genius. He thought of himself as a sculptor, but he was also a painter.

Michelangelo painted this fresco in the Sistine Chapel. It is titled *The Last Judgement.*

more than 300 people and pictures on that ceiling! Some were ten feet tall. Most historians think that the ceiling of the Sistine Chapel is one of the greatest masterpieces in the history of art.

On What Church Did Michelangelo Work?

When Michelangelo was in his 70s, he began work on St. Peter's Church in Rome. The Roman Catholic Church was building the cathedral to replace a small church that had stood for 1,200 years. People believed that this old church had been built over the grave of Peter, a disciple of Jesus. St. Peter's Church is the greatest **structure,** or building, built during the Renaissance. It is also the largest Christian church in the world. Michelangelo died in 1564, but the builders did not complete St. Peter's until 1626.

What Is Raphael Remembered For?

Raphael Santi was born in Italy in 1483. He painted mostly religious pictures. People remember him for his paintings of Mary and the baby Jesus. Art historians call these his Madonna paintings. (*Madonna* is Italian for "my lady.") One of Raphael's most famous paintings is the *School of Athens*. At the center of the painting, Raphael placed the Greek philosophers Plato and Aristotle. He surrounded them with other Greek scholars. The painting shows that the learning and culture of ancient Greece influenced the Renaissance.

Raphael Santi painted mostly religious paintings during the Rennaissance.

Pope Julius II liked Raphael and had him paint many frescoes. Pope Leo X used Raphael's skills as an architect to help build St. Peter's. In fact, Leonardo da Vinci, Michelangelo, and Raphael all worked on the design for the huge church at different times. Raphael, another genius of the Renaissance, died in 1520 at the age of 37.

SECTION 6 REVIEW On a separate sheet of paper, write answers to these questions.

1) What powerful leader helped Michelangelo with his study of art?

2) What are two statues Michelangelo carved?

3) Why was working on the Sistine Chapel hard for Michelangelo?

4) What painting of Raphael's showed the Renaissance interest in ancient Greek culture?

5) On which building did Raphael, Michelangelo, and Leonardo da Vinci all work?

What do you think

Why do you think being a sculptor was more important to Michelangelo than being a painter?

The Making of a Renaissance Gentleman

In 1528, Baldassare Castiglione published The Book of the Courtier. *A courtier was a person who visited a royal court. There were special rules for how to behave at court. This book told young gentlemen what the rules were. How important was its advice? Gentlemen followed its rules for several centuries.*

"Besides his noble birth, then I would have the Courtier [show] a certain grace and (as we say) air that shall make him at first sight pleasing and agreeable to all who see him. . . .

[The Courtier should] know how to swim, to leap, to run, to throw stones, for besides the use that may be made of this in war, a man often has occasion to show what he can do in such matters; whence good esteem is to be won, especially with the multitude. . . . Another admirable exercise, and one very befitting at court, is the game of tennis. . . .

I would have him more than passably accomplished in letters, at least in those studies that are called the humanities. . . . Let him be versed in the poets, and not less in the orators and historians, and also proficient in writing verse and prose, especially in [speech] . . . , for besides the enjoyment he will find in it, he will by this means never lack agreeable entertainment with ladies, who are usually fond of such things. . . .

I am not content with the Courtier unless he be also a musician and unless, besides understanding and being able to read notes, he can play . . . instruments. For if we consider rightly, there is to be found no rest from toil or medicine for the troubled spirit more becoming and praiseworthy in time of leisure, than this; and especially in courts, where . . . many things are done to please the ladies, whose tender and gentle spirit is easily penetrated by harmony and filled with sweetness. . . .

When dancing in the presence of many and in a place full of people, it seems to me that he should preserve a certain dignity, . . . and airy grace of movement."

Source Reading Wrap-Up

1) What is a courtier?

2) Why was *The Book of the Courtier* written?

3) What athletic abilities should a courtier have?

4) According to the author, in what two ways may a courtier please the ladies?

5) How may the knowledge of music help a courtier in his personal life?

The Hundred Years' War

The Hundred Years' War extended over the reigns of five English and five French kings. From 1337 to 1453, they fought for control of France. This struggle was actually a series of battles broken by truces and treaties.

The war had several causes. The French kings wanted to control the English province of Gascony in southwest France. Gascony was a valuable wine-producing region. This goal angered the English. The French supported the Scots against the English. These actions angered the English. English and French sailors and fishermen fought over rights in the English Channel. The wool trade in Flanders was also a point of disagreement. In addition, the English king, Edward III, claimed the throne of France in 1337. His uncle, the French king, had died without a male heir. When Edward III landed an army in Normandy, the Hundred Years' War began.

In the fighting that followed, the English won many battles. But the French won the war. The French had three times more resources—soldiers, supplies, and wealth—than the English. Several events also hindered the warfare. The Black Death, the deadliest plague ever known, killed millions of people. There was also a peasant revolt in England.

During the war, new military tactics developed. English archers used the newly developed longbow. With that weapon, they won the war's greatest victory in the Battle of Crecy (1346). The English also won the Battle of Poitiers (1356). Then the Treaty of Bretigny in 1360 began a brief period of peace. Henry V of England renewed the fighting though. He won the Battle of Agincourt (1415). The Treaty of

The Battle of Crecy.

Troyes in 1420 gave him the French crown.

The peace was short-lived, however. Henry V died in 1422 and the French reclaimed the throne. War flared up again. By 1428, the English controlled northern France. They laid siege to Orléans, an important city in central France. Then Joan of Arc, an unknown peasant girl, led a French army to save Orléans. She claimed to have had visions from heaven. In them, saints told her to lead a French army against the English. Joan was victorious in Orléans, Patay, and Reims. Later, the English took her prisoner and burned her as a witch.

The French kept winning battles and the English retreated. At the end of the war in 1453, they only controlled the city of Calais. The French took over this port in 1558.

Spotlight Story Wrap-Up

1) What two countries fought the Hundred Years' War?

2) What were five causes of the war?

3) Why did England's Edward III claim a right to the French throne?

4) What problems inside France and England interrupted the war?

5) Who was a French hero during the war?

➡ A deadly plague, the Black Death, struck Europe in 1348. Millions of people died. As a result, society changed. There were fewer workers, so workers and serfs could demand more rights.

➡ The Renaissance began about 1350, ending the Middle Ages. It was a time of creativity and learning. People studied the classical learning of ancient Greece and Rome.

➡ Men and women of the Renaissance valued education, art, and science. They also valued good manners and skills such as music, dance, and swordplay.

➡ The Renaissance began in the city-states of Italy. City-states such as Venice, Milan, Florence, and Genoa grew rich from trade with the East. Each had its own ruler. In the 1300s, Venice, on the Adriatic Sea, defeated Genoa. It gained control of trade in the Mediterranean.

➡ The Medici were the leaders of Florence, the "Athens of Italy." Lorenzo de Medici encouraged artists and scholars.

➡ Florence began to decline in the late 1400s. The monk Savonarola led a religious movement against the Renaissance. The Medici lost power. Savonarola tried to establish a harsher way of life in Florence. After a few years, people rebelled against him.

➡ Renaissance artists made lifelike paintings and sculptures. Artists depended on wealthy patrons, such as Isabella d'Este and the pope.

➡ Late medieval writers wrote in their native languages, not Latin. Renaissance writers also used local languages. In England, William Shakespeare wrote plays and sonnets. In Spain, Cervantes created the character Don Quixote. In Germany, Gutenberg used moveable metal type to print a Bible in 1455. Printed books spread learning.

➡ Leonardo da Vinci was an artist, scientist, and inventor. His most famous paintings are the *Mona Lisa* and the *Last Supper.* His notebooks include sketches of inventions. When Leonardo worked in France for King Francis I, Renaissance ideas spread.

➡ Michelangelo was a sculptor in Florence. He is famous for statues, such as *David.* He also painted the ceiling of the Sistine Chapel and helped to design St. Peter's Church.

➡ Raphael made many religious paintings. He also worked on St. Peter's Church.

Comprehension: Identifying Facts

On a separate sheet of paper, use the words from the Word Bank to complete each sentence.

WORD BANK

Beatrice d'Este
Cervantes
Gutenberg
Isabella d'Este
Leonardo da Vinci
Lorenzo de Medici
Michelangelo
Raphael
Savonarola
Shakespeare

1) People called _____ "the Magnificent" because he worked to make Florence into a great city.

2) The monk _____ criticized the people of Florence because they liked worldly possessions.

3) _____, the ruler of Mantua, was a true Renaissance woman.

4) People call _____ one of the greatest writers in the English language.

5) _____ wrote a comic novel about a Spaniard who wanted to be a knight so he could right the wrongs of the world.

6) _____ invented the first printing press to use moveable metal type.

7) _____ was an artist, scientist, engineer, and inventor.

8) _____ painted the ceiling of the Sistine Chapel.

9) People remember _____ for his paintings of the Madonna.

10) One of Leonardo da Vinci's patrons was _____.

Comprehension: Multiple Choice

On a separate sheet of paper, write the letter of the answer that correctly completes each sentence.

1) During the Renaissance, many people believed in _____, which said that the actions, ideas, and works of human beings were important.
   a. architect   c. humanism
   b. sculptor   d. philosophy

2) It is the job of _____ to design buildings and other structures.
   a. philosophers   c. humanists
   b. frescoes   d. architects

3) A 14-line poem is a(n) _____.

    a. sonnet   c. tanka

    b. haiku   d. opera

4) A _____ is a person who supports an artist.

    a. portrait   c. sonnet

    b. patron   d. tutor

5) A _____ is a drawing of a person.

    a. portrait   c. plaster

    b. patron   d. sonnet

Comprehension: Understanding Main Ideas

On a separate sheet of paper, write the answers to the following questions using complete sentences.

1) How did the Black Death change Europe?

2) Why was Leonardo da Vinci a Renaissance man?

Critical Thinking: Write Your Opinion

1) Renaissance men and women were skilled and smart. What would a Renaissance person be like today? Write down three people living today whom could be called "renaissance" people.

2) During the Renaissance, some religious leaders asked people to give up their worldly possessions. Imagine that these leaders are alive today. What possessions might they want you to give up?

3) Before the Renaissance, writers wrote in Latin. But few people could read this language. Describe your life if all web sites, books, television shows, and movies were in a language you did not know or understand.

Test-Taking Tip | When taking a matching test, match all of the items that you know go together for sure. Cross these items out. Then try to match the items that are left.

1415 to 1650

In Chapter 13, you read about the Renaissance. Much of this occurred in Italy. This chapter takes you north to Germany. There you will see how a monk named Luther began the religious reform movement. From Germany, you will cross the English Channel and meet Henry VIII, who also led reform. Next, you will travel to Geneva to learn about John Calvin and his beliefs. Finally, you will journey back to Italy. There you will see how the Catholic Church decided to fight the other reformers—the Protestants.

Goals for Learning

▶ To define the term *Reformation*

▶ To explain the importance of Martin Luther in the Reformation

▶ To list the three basic reforms Martin Luther made

▶ To explain how the Anglican Church was founded

▶ To describe the beliefs of Calvinism

▶ To describe the Counter-Reformation of the Catholic Church

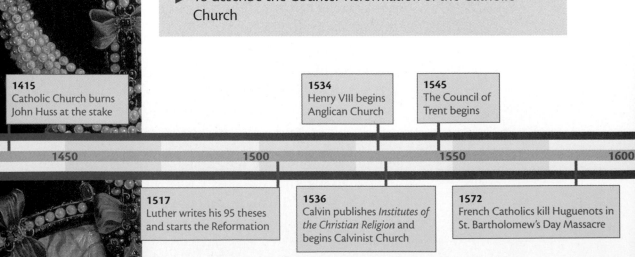

1415
Catholic Church burns John Huss at the stake

1534
Henry VIII begins Anglican Church

1545
The Council of Trent begins

1450   1500   1550   1600

1517
Luther writes his 95 theses and starts the Reformation

1536
Calvin publishes *Institutes of the Christian Religion* and begins Calvinist Church

1572
French Catholics kill Huguenots in St. Bartholomew's Day Massacre

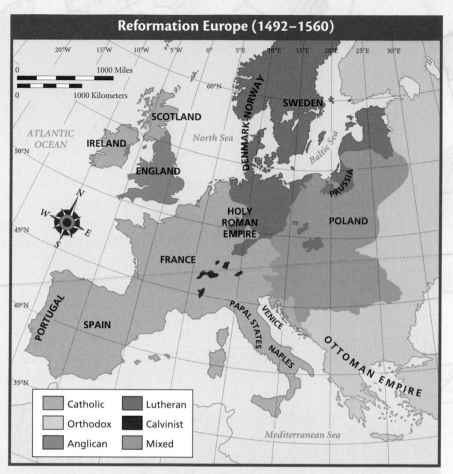

Reformation Europe (1492–1560)

Legend:
- Catholic
- Orthodox
- Anglican
- Lutheran
- Calvinist
- Mixed

Geography Skills

Before the Protestant Reformation, the Catholic Church had great power in Western Europe. However, this changed when people began to challenge this power. New religions began. This map shows where different religions developed between 1492 and 1560.

Study the map and answer the following questions:

1) What religion was practiced in England at this time?

2) What religions were practiced in the Holy Roman Empire?

3) Where was the Catholic religion still practiced?

4) Where did the Calvinist religion develop?

5) What religion dominates Western Europe at this time?

Authority
Power; the right to tell someone what to do

◆**Reformer**
A person who tries to change a system

In Unit 4, you studied the Middles Ages. Historians also call it the Age of Faith. The Catholic Church had great religious and political power. In fact, the pope could command kings. But beginning in the 1300s, some people challenged the **authority,** or power, of the church.

Who Challenged the Church's Political Authority?

In 1294, King Philip IV of France tried to tax church officials. The pope told the French clergy not to pay the tax. In 1303, the king arrested Pope Boniface VIII, an Italian. Six years later, the king helped to elect a French pope, Clement V. The new pope moved from the Vatican in Rome to Avignon in France.

Seventy years passed before a pope lived in Rome again. But problems continued. At different times, more than one person claimed to be pope. Some church leaders suggested that a council should take the place of the pope. All this weakened the church's power.

Who Challenged the Church's Religious Authority?

In the 1500s, some people challenged the religious authority of the church. We call them **reformers** because they believed that the church needed to be reformed, or changed, for the better.

John Wycliffe was an early church reformer.

One early reformer was the Englishman John Wycliffe. He said that the church had too much power and wealth. He also said that the Bible, and not the church, should be the authority for Christians. To allow people to read the Bible, Wycliffe translated the Latin Bible into English.

◆Heretic
A person who teaches a belief that a religious authority thinks is false

People called Wycliffe's followers the "Poor Preachers." They had no interest in money. All they wanted to do was to teach religion to people in their own language instead of Latin.

Why Did John Huss Criticize the Church?

The ideas of John Wycliffe influenced John Huss. He was a well-known scholar at the University of Prague in Bohemia. (Bohemia was part of the Holy Roman Empire. It is now part of the Czech Republic.) Huss thought that the church's clergy were too worldly and that the church should remove them from office.

When Huss and his followers criticized the church, both religious and political leaders feared a rebellion. Church leaders said that Huss was a **heretic.** A heretic teaches a belief that a religious authority thinks is false. In 1415, they arrested Huss and burned him at the stake.

SECTION 1 REVIEW On a separate sheet of paper, write *True* if the statement is true or *False* if the statement is not true. Make each false statement true by changing the underlined word.

1) King Philip IV of <u>Italy</u> challenged the authority of the pope in 1294.

2) In 1309, Pope Clement V moved from the Vatican in Rome to <u>Avignon</u> in France.

3) In <u>Germany,</u> John Wycliffe said that the church had too much money and power.

4) Wycliffe and his followers translated the Latin Bible into <u>English.</u>

5) The church burned John Huss as a <u>heretic.</u>

What do you think

Why did the church not want to lose its political and religious authority?

Guarantee
A promise that something will happen

◆**Reformation**
A mass movement that challenged and changed the Catholic religion in Europe

◆**Salvation**
Eternal happiness for one's soul

Vow
To promise something; a promise

Just over 100 years after Huss was executed, Martin Luther challenged the church's religious authority. What he did began a new period of European history—the **Reformation.** This movement challenged and changed the Catholic religion in Europe.

What Troubled Luther?

Martin Luther was born in Germany in 1483. His father wanted him to become a lawyer. But when Luther studied law, he did not like it. Then, in 1505, Luther was caught in a summer storm and lightning nearly hit him. Fearing for his life, Luther **vowed,** or promised, to become a monk if he lived. In 1507, he kept his vow.

In 1512, Luther began to teach religion at the University of Wittenberg in Saxony. But questions about **salvation,** or eternal happiness for his soul, troubled him. How, he asked, should he act to save his soul? Luther struggled for a long time with this problem. Then, while reading the Bible, he found his answer.

Luther came to believe that he could win salvation by faith alone. He said that fasting, prayer, and religious ceremonies could not **guarantee,** or promise, salvation. But the Catholic Church said that people needed to do these good works to save their souls. Luther said that his discovery made him feel as though he were "born again."

Martin Luther started the Reformation by disagreeing with the Catholic Church.

Indulgence
A church paper that says that a person will not be punished after death for sinning during life

Purgatory
A place of suffering after death

Why Did the Church Begin to Sell Indulgences?

In 1517, Luther and the church leadership began to struggle with one another because Pope Leo X started to sell **indulgences.** These are papers the church gives people that say they will not be punished after death for their sins. People bought indulgences for themselves and for loved ones who were already dead. The church said that doing this was a good deed. The pope sold indulgences because he needed more money to build St. Peter's Church.

In 1517, a monk named John Tetzel began selling indulgences near Luther's university. Tetzel told people to buy an indulgence to free a friend's soul from **purgatory.** This is what is believed to be a place of suffering after death. Tetzel said that the person who bought the indulgence could be sure of salvation. He raised a great deal of money and sent it back to Rome for St. Peter's Church.

What Are Luther's 95 Theses?

Someone asked Luther what he thought about the selling of indulgences. He said that it was wrong because people could not buy forgiveness for sins. On hearing this, Tetzel criticized Luther.

Disks for the Eyes

When were eyeglasses invented? The Chinese claim to have used them before A.D. 300. Marco Polo wrote in 1275 that he saw many Chinese wearing glasses. The scientist Roger Bacon mentioned eyeglasses in his writings in 1268. History, however, has no record of their invention.

We do know that by the 1300s, eyeglasses were popular among Europe's upper classes. People could only use them for seeing at a distance though. What about glasses for seeing objects that were close? It took another hundred years to learn how to make them.

Technology
History in Your Life

Venice became the chief producer of eyeglasses. However, people did not call them glasses. They called them "disks for the eyes."

In the 1500s, the demand for eyeglasses increased. The printing presses were producing more books and more people were reading. Scholars who could no longer read the printed page needed glasses.

Luther began to write a series of 95 **theses,** or statements, against indulgences and other actions of the church. He wanted to argue these theses with church officials. On October 31, 1517, he let other people read his ideas. Printers printed Luther's 95 statements. People sent them to other countries. Because of this, the sale of indulgences went down, and the church lost money. The church decided to take steps to stop Luther's influence in Europe.

SECTION 2 REVIEW Choose the letter of the answer that correctly completes each sentence. Write your answer on a separate sheet of paper.

1) Martin Luther was born in _____.

   a. England   c. Italy

   b. Germany   d. France

2) As a monk and teacher, Luther struggled with the idea of _____.

   a. salvation   c. confrontations

   b. vows   d. translations

3) Luther believed that people could be saved by _____ alone.

   a. the Bible   c. faith

   b. good works   d. indulgences

4) Pope Leo X began to sell _____ to pay for the building of St. Peter's Church.

   a. theses   c. frescoes

   b. portraits   d. indulgences

5) Luther wrote _____ theses, or statements, about church actions that he did not agree with.

   a. 85   c. 105

   b. 95   d. 1500

What do you think

Do you think that Luther had trouble with more than just indulgences? Explain your answer.

◆Excommunicate
To say that someone can no longer be a member of a church

◆Lutheran Church
The church established by Martin Luther

Minister
A person who can lead a religious ceremony in a Protestant church

Ritual
A ceremony

When Luther called for reform, the church ordered him to stop. But Luther said he could not go against his beliefs. He said, "Here I stand. I cannot do otherwise."

What Did the Church Do to Luther?

In 1521, Pope Leo X said that Luther's beliefs were wrong and **excommunicated** him. That is, the pope said that Luther was no longer a member of the Catholic Church. The ruler of the Holy Roman Empire—a Catholic—signed the Edict of Worms. This said that anyone could kill Luther without being punished. But several German princes protected Luther from this.

What Did Luther Want to Change?

Luther called for three reforms. First, he said that only faith in Jesus Christ could save people. Good works alone would not save them. Second, he taught that religious truth came from the Bible. People should read the Bible and decide for themselves what it meant. Third, Luther said that people did not need the clergy to tell them what the Bible means. To help people read the Bible, Luther translated it into German.

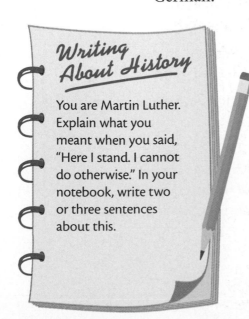

Writing About History

You are Martin Luther. Explain what you meant when you said, "Here I stand. I cannot do otherwise." In your notebook, write two or three sentences about this.

What Church Did Luther Begin?

In the beginning, Martin Luther did not want to break away from the Catholic Church. All he wanted was to debate his 95 theses and reform the church. But in time, he started the **Lutheran Church.** His church had some differences from the Catholic Church. Catholic priests were not allowed to marry, but Lutheran **ministers** could. The job of a minister was to help people find or strengthen their faith in Jesus Christ.

Luther also got rid of most of the **rituals,** or ceremonies, of the Catholic Church.

Luther did, however, keep two rituals—**Baptism,** by which people become Christians, and **Communion,** by which people grow in their faith.

Why Did German Princes Become Lutherans?

Many German princes liked Luther's ideas and began to protest the ways of the Catholic Church. People called them **Protestants.** In the 1530s, war broke out between the armies of the Protestant Lutheran princes and Charles V, a Catholic ruler.

In 1546, Martin Luther died. Nine years after his death, a treaty was signed to stop the fighting. According to this treaty, each German prince could pick his own church. All the people in his area had to follow his religion. Called the Peace of Augsburg, the treaty kept the German princes from fighting for more than 50 years.

SECTION 3 REVIEW On a separate sheet of paper, write answers to these questions.

1) What does the term *excommunication* mean?

2) Why did the Catholic Church excommunicate Martin Luther?

3) According to Luther, where could people find religious truth?

4) What is one difference between a Catholic priest and a Lutheran minister?

5) Why did people call religious reformers Protestants?

What do you think

What might have kept Luther from starting a new church?

Luther's religious reform movement quickly spread beyond Germany. By 1534, it reached England where Henry VIII ruled. Just 13 years before, Henry had attacked Luther's ideas. To thank him, Pope Leo X called the king "Defender of the Faith."

Annul
To announce that a marriage never existed between two people

Divorce
To end a marriage

Why Did Henry VIII Break With the Pope?

A political problem started the Reformation in England. Henry VIII became king there in 1509. He married a Spanish princess, Catherine of Aragon. They had a daughter named Mary. In 1527, Henry VIII tried to end his marriage to Catherine and **divorce** her. He wanted a son, but Catherine could not have more children. However, the Catholic Church did not allow divorce. Henry asked Pope Clement VII to **annul,** or break off, the marriage.

Catherine refused to accept this. She asked her nephew, Charles V, who was the Holy Roman Emperor, to influence the pope's decision. Charles had an army in Italy, so Catherine won the pope's support. He refused to annul the marriage. But by then, Henry had secretly married another woman, Anne Boleyn.

King Henry VIII of England was a powerful ruler who helped start the Anglican Church.

Jacob Amman was a Swiss man who belonged to the Protestant group, the Mennonites. However, he and others disagreed with some of the church's practices. They thought the church rules were not strict enough. Amman led a group away from the church in the 1690s. They became known as the Amish. Following his directions, they shunned, or completely avoided, excommunicated members.

The Amish first came to America in the 1720s. Today they still live in farm communities. They teach separation from the world. Members must not go to war, swear oaths, or hold public office. Their personal life must be simple. They do not use electricity or telephones. They limit education to the eighth grade.

What Was the Name of Henry's New Church?

In order to divorce Catherine, Henry VIII appointed a new **archbishop** of Canterbury. An archbishop is the top religious leader in a church province. This archbishop said that Henry's marriage to Catherine was not legal. In 1534, Parliament made the king the head of the Church of England, or **Anglican Church.** Henry took control of all lands the Catholic Church owned in England.

◆**Anglican Church**
The church established by Henry VIII

◆**Archbishop**
The top religious leader in a church province

What Did Edward Do As King?

Henry and Anne had a daughter they named Elizabeth. But three years after their marriage, Henry said that Anne was not faithful to him and executed her. Then he married Jane Seymour and they had a son named Edward. When Henry died in 1547, his nine-year-old son became King Edward VI. The young king accepted several Protestant reforms. During his reign, Protestant bishops created the *Book of Common Prayer* for Anglican religious services.

Who Tried to Change the Protestant Reforms?

Edward ruled for only six years and died in 1553. Then Mary—Henry's first child—became queen of England. She was a Catholic and used her power to make England a Catholic nation once again. To strengthen her power, she married the Catholic king of Spain, Philip II. But the English Protestants hated Mary and refused to become Catholics again.

What Compromise Did Elizabeth Make?

When Mary died in 1558, her half-sister became Queen Elizabeth I. She tried to join together the Protestants and Catholics into the Anglican Church. The king or queen of England would head the Anglican Church. But Anglican bishops would run the day-to-day church business. Many Anglican rituals became a blend of Catholic and Protestant ceremonies.

Not all Protestants liked this **compromise,** or agreement. Some wanted to rid the Anglican Church of Catholic rituals. Historians call this group the **Puritans** because they wanted to **purify** the church, or make it clean. In the 1600s, some Puritans left England and settled in North America.

WORD BANK

Anglican

Edward VI

Elizabeth I

Henry VIII

Puritans

SECTION 4 REVIEW On a separate sheet of paper, write the word from the Word Bank that completes each sentence.

1) Pope Leo X gave _____ the name "Defender of the Faith."

2) Henry VIII of England began the _____ Church.

3) During the reign of _____, the Anglican clergy produced the *Book of Common Prayer.*

4) _____ tried to work out a compromise between the English Protestants and Catholics.

5) The _____ were English Protestants who did not like the compromise and wanted to purify the church.

What do you think

What do you think Charles V's army might have done if the pope had let Henry divorce Catherine of Aragon?

◆Calvinism
The Protestant religion founded by John Calvin

Elder
An experienced, older person

◆Elect
A Calvinistic term for those whom God has chosen to save

Gamble
To bet money on the outcome of something

Sinful
Going against religious rules

Martin Luther had sparked the religious Reformation in 1517. Almost 20 years later, another man created an organized set of Protestant beliefs. Because his name was John Calvin, we call his religious movement **Calvinism.** He greatly influenced the Protestant Reformation.

What Did Calvin Teach?

John Calvin was born in France in 1509. During his life, his body was weak, but his will was strong. In 1536, he published his most important book—*Institutes of the Christian Religion.* This book contained what he thought each person should believe about religious questions.

First, Calvin taught that people are born **sinful.** That is, people are bad when they are born. Next, he said that few people would be saved from sin. Finally, Calvin told his followers that God had already chosen who would be saved. He called these special people the "**elect.**" Calvin believed that the elect of God had a political mission. They were to rule Christian society.

Why was Calvin's book important? Because for the first time, the Protestant movement had a fully organized set of beliefs. However, not all Protestants accepted Calvin's ideas. The Lutherans in northern Germany accepted none of his ideas. The Anglicans in England accepted some and refused to accept others.

How Big Was Calvin's Religious Community?

John Calvin's teaching quickly spread. In 1541, the city officials of Geneva, Switzerland, asked him to organize their city into a religious community. (Geneva's population was 20,000.) Calvin started a school there to train ministers. Then he set up a council of 12 **elders.** These men were older and experienced.

Next, Calvin gave these elders the power to make laws that said what was right and what was wrong. The elders said that playing cards; **gambling,** or betting money on

John Calvin started his own Protestant religion called Calvinism. This religion was the first Protestant religion with a fully organized set of beliefs. Calvin lived from 1509–1564.

something; drinking alcohol; singing; and dancing were wrong, or sinful.

Finally, Calvin said that citizens had to go to church services several times a week. Members of the council even visited people's homes once a year to make sure that people were leading good lives. The council put people in prison if they did not live the Calvinist way. Sometimes, the council forced people to leave the city. In time, Calvinists began to call Geneva a "city of saints."

What Happened on St. Bartholomew's Day?

Calvinism soon spread to the Catholic country of France. By the year 1560, about 15 percent of the French population was Calvinist. These French Calvinists became known as **Huguenots.** Many Catholics and Huguenots hated one another.

On August 24, 1572, the hate exploded. On that day, the Catholic Church was celebrating St. Bartholomew's Day. At daybreak, in the city of Paris, Catholics began attacking and killing Huguenots. Historians call the attack the St. Bartholomew's Day **Massacre**. A massacre is the act of killing many people who are often defenseless.

◆Huguenot
A French Calvinist

◆Massacre
The act of killing many people who are often defenseless

For a month, in the towns and cities of France, Catholics murdered Protestants. More than 12,000 Huguenots lost their lives. But people still continued to become Calvinists.

SECTION 5 REVIEW On a separate sheet of paper, write *True* if the statement is true or *False* if the statement is not true. Make each false statement true by changing the underlined word.

1) <u>John Calvin</u> was the first Protestant leader to organize a set of Protestant beliefs.

2) Calvinists called <u>Paris</u> the "city of saints."

3) According to Calvin, the <u>elect</u> are those people God has chosen to save.

4) The Huguenots were French <u>Calvinists</u>.

5) St. <u>Peter's</u> Day Massacre led to the death of many Huguenots.

What do you think

Calvin said that people are sinful and that God has already chosen those to be saved. Why do you think so many people accepted these ideas?

Censor
To prevent someone from reading or viewing something

Counter
To speak out or fight back against something or someone

◆**Counter-Reformation**
The Catholic Church's reforms that attempted to fight the Protestant Reformation

◆**Jesuit**
A member of the Catholic religious order known as the Society of Jesus

◆**Roman Inquisition**
A Catholic court that inquired into the beliefs of people to see if they were heretics

In the mid-1500s, the Catholic Church began its own reform—the **Counter-Reformation.** First, it decided to reform itself. Then it decided to **counter,** or fight against, Protestant beliefs.

What Did the Catholic Church Do First?

Pope Paul III tried to fix problems within the church itself. He appointed new church officials who were well educated. He also began to **censor** books by telling people which ones they could read. Finally, he set up a special court—the **Roman Inquisition**. It inquired into people's religious beliefs. The court could execute heretics.

What Did the Council of Trent Do?

In 1545, the Church called for a council of church officials to meet at the Italian city of Trent. This council lasted 18 years. It wrote down the most important beliefs of the Catholic Church and stopped the sale of indulgences. It refused to accept the teachings of Luther and Calvin on salvation. The council said that people found salvation only through the Catholic Church.

The council also said that to be saved people had to go to church and do good deeds. They also had to accept the pope as the only leader of the Christian Church. Finally, Catholics had to agree with the Church's interpretation of the Bible. To counter Protestant translations of the Bible, the council ordered its own new translation.

Who Were the Jesuits?

Ignatius of Loyola played a big part in the Counter-Reformation. He was born in Spain in 1491. Like Luther and Calvin, he asked questions about salvation. But his answers were different from theirs. Ignatius thought that self-discipline and good actions saved people.

Ignatius created a new religious order called the Society of Jesus. Members of this order were called **Jesuits.** They had to be smart, strong, and holy, because they wanted to help

The Council of Trent wrote down the most important beliefs of the Catholic Church.

Catholics stay in the Catholic Church. They also wanted to help Protestants return to it. Over the next 200 years, Jesuit missionaries spread their faith to non-Christians in Africa, Asia, and North and South America.

What Countries Stayed Catholic?

Europe now had two groups of Christian churches—Catholic and Protestant. Many people in northern Germany, Norway, Sweden, the Netherlands, Switzerland, England, and Scotland became Protestants. Most of the people in Italy, France, Spain, and southern Germany stayed Catholic. Soon these different religious beliefs caused wars. Between 1550 to 1650, Europeans fought over their different religious beliefs.

SECTION 6 REVIEW On a separate sheet of paper, write answers to these questions.

1) What did the Counter-Reformation try to do?

2) What was the name of the court that Pope Paul III created to inquire into people's beliefs?

3) What council wrote down the most important beliefs of the Catholic Church?

4) What religious group did Ignatius of Loyola begin?

5) What were the two jobs of Jesuits?

What do you think ?

What kind of books do you think Pope Paul III censored during the Protestant Reformation?

John Calvin's Strict Code of Conduct

John Calvin believed in a very strict moral code of conduct. He published his beliefs in the Institutes of the Christian Religion *in 1536. Later, this code was called puritanical. The English who settled in Plymouth, Massachusetts, in 1620 followed Calvin's rules. They were called Puritans.*

Whoever shall have blasphemed, swearing by the body or by the blood of our lord, or in similar manner, he shall be made to kiss the earth for the first offense; for the second to pay five sous, and for third six sous, and for the last offense be put in the pillory for one hour.

If anyone sings immoral, dissolute, or outrageous songs, or dances the virollet or other dance, he shall be put in prison for three days and then sent to the consistory [church court].

That no one shall take upon interest or profit more than five percent upon penalty of confiscation of the principal and of being condemned to make restitution, as the case may demand.

That no one shall play at any game whatsoever it may be, neither for gold nor silver nor for any excessive stake, upon penalty of five sous and forfeiture of stake played for.

No one who wishes to be thought religious dares simply deny predestination, by which God adopts some to hope of life and sentences others to eternal death.

When we attribute foreknowledge to God, we mean that all things always were, and perpetually remain, under his eyes, so that to his knowledge there is nothing future or past but all things are present. Therefore, as any man has been created to one or the other of these ends, we speak of him as predestined to life or to death.

He has appointed duties for every man in his particular way of life. And that no one may thoughtlessly transgress his limits, he has named these various kinds of living "callings." Therefore each individual has his own kind of living assigned to him by the Lord as a sort of sentry post, so that he may not heedlessly wander about throughout life.

A man of obscure station will lead a private life ungrudgingly so as not to leave the rank in which he has been placed by God. Again, it will be no slight relief from cares, labors, troubles, and other burdens for a man to know that God is his guide in all these things.

Source Reading Wrap-Up

1) What was the punishment for singing outrageous songs?

2) How much profit should a person be allowed to earn?

3) What is Calvin's position on gambling?

4) What does the term predestination mean?

5) In your opinion, what parts of the moral code would help business people be successful?

Spotlight Story

The Harsh Life of the German Peasants

In 1524, German peasants revolted against the princes who ruled them. Peasants were protesting the poor conditions in which they lived. They expected Martin Luther to support their rebellion. Luther had challenged the authority of the Catholic Church. To them, their revolt against the nobles seemed similar to his.

As the revolt spread, however, Luther sided with the German princes. He feared the mob violence that it had caused. Luther condemned the revolt. He wrote, "Let every soul be subject unto the higher powers. Peasants should be obedient." Because of Luther's actions, he lost peasant support.

The Peasants' War, as the revolt is known, was a bloody event. More than 100,000 peasants were killed. Homes and farmlands were destroyed. People starved. Disease spread from one area to another. Children wandered the countryside. They had no parents or means to take care of themselves. Bands of soldiers attacked defenseless villages. Bandits roamed about, attacking the weak and helpless.

Before the revolt, some peasants worked in towns as paid laborers. Some were skilled craftsmen. Serfs, however, could not leave a noble's land. By the 1500s, some peasants were free, but many still worked the nobles' lands. Many were heavily in debt to the landowners.

During the Reformation, the life of a peasant was harsh. Peasants were not allowed to keep or sell all of the crops they raised. The Church, for example, got one-tenth of their crops. This rule also applied to their farm animals. Twice a year, a percentage of their crops went to the lord of the manor. In addition, they had to work for him for two months a year. A landowner could use peasants any way he wished.

Food was often in short supply. Peasants sometimes risked hunting animals, or poaching, in the manor woods. This activity was strictly forbidden. Peasants caught poaching were severely punished.

Peasants could not even get married without permission from their lords. In addition, they had to pay a marriage tax.

Spotlight Story Wrap-Up

1) Why did German peasants revolt in 1524?

2) What did Martin Luther say about this revolt?

3) How did the Peasants' War affect the common people in Germany?

4) What are two examples of the harsh conditions in which German peasants lived?

5) Do you agree or disagree with the position that Luthur took on the revolt? Why?

➡ Beginning in the 1300s, reformers challenged the authority of the Catholic Church. Wycliffe translated the Bible into English, so ordinary people could read it. John Huss in Bohemia criticized the clergy.

➡ Martin Luther, a German monk, questioned Church teachings about salvation. In 1517, he wrote 95 theses, or statements. His actions led to the Reformation.

➡ The pope punished Luther with excommunication. The Holy Roman Emperor agreed that he could be killed. Some German princes protected Luther, however.

➡ Luther taught that people could be saved only by faith. He also translated the Bible into German.

➡ Luther eventually started his own church. The Lutheran Church kept two Catholic rituals—baptism and communion. Unlike priests, Lutheran ministers could marry.

➡ Some German princes agreed with Luther. They were called Protestants. In the 1530s, war broke out between Catholic and Protestant rulers. A peace treaty let each prince decide the religion in his lands.

➡ King Henry VIII of England wanted to divorce Catherine of Aragon. The pope refused to allow a divorce, so Henry broke with the Church and became head of the Anglican Church.

➡ Henry VIII married several more wives. He had three children: Mary, Elizabeth, and Edward VI. In Edward's reign, Anglican bishops wrote the *Book of Common Prayer*.

➡ As queen, Mary tried to make England Catholic again. After her death in 1558, Elizabeth became queen. She compromised with some Catholic beliefs. But strict Protestants, called Puritans, wanted to rid the church of all Catholic rituals.

➡ John Calvin wrote a book organizing Protestant beliefs. He taught that God had already chosen those who would be saved. Angry Catholics killed French Calvinists, or Huguenots, in the St. Bartholomew's Day Massacre of 1572.

➡ The Catholic Church began a Counter-Reformation. The pope reformed the clergy. He began the Inquisition. The Council of Trent restated Catholic beliefs.

➡ Ignatius of Loyola began the Society of Jesus to strengthen the Church.

➡ The Reformation split Europe into Catholic and Protestant areas. Wars of religion went on between 1550 and 1650.

Comprehension: Identifying Facts

On a separate sheet of paper, use the words from the Word Bank to complete each sentence.

WORD BANK
Calvin
Elizabeth I
Henry VIII
Huss
Ignatius of Loyola
Luther
Mary
Pope Leo X
Pope Paul III
Wycliffe

1) The "Poor Preachers" were the religious followers of _____.

2) The Catholic Church burned _____ at the stake in 1415 for his religious beliefs.

3) _____ ordered the Catholic Church to sell indulgences to help build St. Peter's Church.

4) _____ wrote 95 theses to show what he thought about the sale of indulgences.

5) Pope Leo X called _____ the "Defender of the Faith."

6) _____ tried to make England a Catholic nation again.

7) _____ of England tried to talk Catholics and Protestants into a compromise.

8) _____ believed that God had already chosen the people who would be saved.

9) _____ tried to reform the Catholic Church and called a special council to do this.

10) _____ began the Jesuit order to help in the Counter-Reformation.

Comprehension: Multiple Choice

On a separate sheet of paper, write the letter of the answer that correctly completes each sentence.

1) A _____ is a person who teaches a belief that a religious authority thinks is false.

    a. elder   c. thesis

    b. salvation   d. heretic

2) A _____ is a member of the Society of Jesus.

    a. Jesuit   c. Anglican

    b. Calvinist   d. Lutheran

3) _____ were French Calvinists.

   a. Jesuits   c. Huguenots

   b. Archbishops   d. Censors

4) The _____ were Anglicans who wanted to purify their church.

   a. Jesuits   c. Huguenots

   b. Puritans   d. Calvinists

5) The Catholic Church gave _____ that were supposed to take away punishment for sins.

   a. indulgences   c. salvation

   b. heretics   d. theses

Comprehension: Understanding Main Ideas

On a separate sheet of paper, write the answers to the following questions using complete sentences, or statements.

1) What was one cause of the Reformation?

2) How did Calvin's reforms differ from Luther's and King Henry VIII's?

3) What was one thing the Catholic Church did as it tried to counter the Reformation?

Critical Thinking: Write Your Opinion

1) What part do you think the printing press played in the Reformation?

2) Luther, Calvin, and Ignatius of Loyola all asked questions about salvation. Which of their answers do you like best and why?

Test-Taking Tip	When taking a multiple-choice test, read every choice before you answer a question. Put a line through choices you know are wrong. Then choose the best answer from the remaining choices.

Chapter

15

The New Science

1540 to 1750

During the 1500s and 1600s, a new method of learning about the physical world developed. Scientists refused to accept beliefs from the past. Instead, they began to use experiments to find truth for themselves. In this chapter, you will meet many of these scientists and you will learn what they studied.

Goals for Learning

▶ To list the five steps of the scientific method

▶ To describe Copernicus's new theory of the universe

▶ To explain why the Roman Catholic Church condemned the teachings of Galileo

▶ To describe the role Isaac Newton played in the history of science

▶ To list the inventions and contributions of a number of early scientists

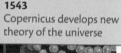

1543
Copernicus develops new theory of the universe

1609
Galileo builds telescope

1628
Harvey publishes work on blood circulation

1687
Newton publishes work on gravity

1550   1600   1650   1750

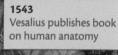

1543
Vesalius publishes book on human anatomy

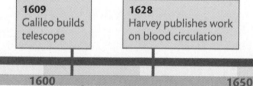

1616
The Roman Catholic Church rules that Copernicus's theory is wrong

1674
Leeuwenhoek makes better microscope

1752
Franklin experiments with electricity

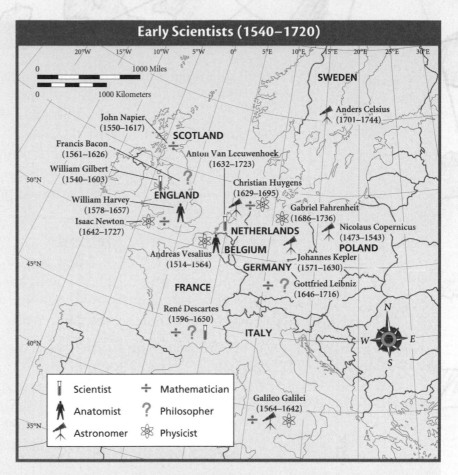

Early Scientists (1540–1720)

John Napier (1550–1617)

SCOTLAND

Francis Bacon (1561–1626)

William Gilbert (1540–1603)

William Harvey (1578–1657)

Isaac Newton (1642–1727)

ENGLAND

Anton Van Leeuwenhoek (1632–1723)

Christian Huygens (1629–1695)

NETHERLANDS

BELGIUM

Andreas Vesalius (1514–1564)

GERMANY

FRANCE

René Descartes (1596–1650)

ITALY

SWEDEN

Anders Celsius (1701–1744)

Gabriel Fahrenheit (1686–1736)

Nicolaus Copernicus (1473–1543)

POLAND

Johannes Kepler (1571–1630)

Gottfried Leibniz (1646–1716)

Galileo Galilei (1564–1642)

Legend:
- Scientist
- Mathematician
- Anatomist
- Philosopher
- Astronomer
- Physicist

Geography Skills

A great number of scientists worked in Europe during the sixteenth, seventeenth, and early eighteenth centuries. Some of them invented new ways to solve mathematical problems. Others looked at the sky above them. Some made discoveries about the physical world. This was an exciting time, but a frightening one as well. These scientists found many things to be incorrect that people had believed right for centuries.

Study the map and answer the following questions:

1) In what country did Galileo work?

2) How long did Francis Bacon live?

3) In what country did Andreas Vesalius do his work?

4) How many great scientists lived in England during this time?

5) What is the name of the French mathematician, scientist, and philosopher from this period?

Conclusion
An answer; a decision reached through step-by-step thinking

◆**Hypothesis**
An educated guess about an answer to a problem

Method
A way of doing something

◆**Scientific method**
A set of steps to follow to reach a true end

Before 1500, most scholars decided what was true or false in two ways: they read the Bible and they read Greek and Roman writers. During the Middle Ages, they believed that the writings of Aristotle were true. Only the Bible was a higher authority than this great Greek philosopher. The word *science* comes from a Latin word that means "to know." As time passed, science became a popular way to find truth.

What Is the Scientific Method?

During the 1500s and 1600s, a new way of learning about the natural world developed. Scientists based their new **method,** or way of doing something, on a few important steps. They called these steps the **scientific method.**

At the heart of the scientific method is the experiment. When scientists experiment, they carefully control a test. The test helps them discover truth for themselves. They no longer depend on authorities who say that something is true or false. Leonardo da Vinci wrote that science should be "born of experiment, the mother of certainty." In the 1500s, this idea was new.

Scientists began to conduct experiments in the 1600s and 1700s. This shows scientists experimenting on the nature of electricity.

What Are the Five Steps of the Scientific Method?

In the 1620s, Francis Bacon, an Englishman, worked out the five steps of the scientific method. First, a scientist picks a problem or question. Second, the scientist makes a guess about the answer. This is an educated guess. That is, the scientist bases the guess on what he or she already knows. We call such a guess a **hypothesis.** Third, the scientist does an experiment and carefully controls it. Fourth, the scientist observes what is happening during the experiment and makes notes. Fifth, the scientist draws a **conclusion,** or answer, from these notes. Then the scientist decides if the hypothesis was right.

The Scientific Method

The scientific method is a well-defined series of steps. Accurate measurement is crucial at each step. Scientists began to use this method in the sixteenth century. However, they did not have today's instruments and techniques.

New technologies have changed what scientists can do. Computers quickly count and compare data. It would take people years to do the same jobs. More powerful microscopes see much smaller objects. Telescopes look further. Unlike in the sixteenth century, scientists can look inside living beings and materials.

Today there is also an increasing number of highly trained scientists. In the sixteenth century, one person might investigate a problem. Today an army of scientists attacks an issue. The growth of science in the past century has been without equal.

Bacon's five steps still influence science today. Scientists still conduct experiments using these ideas.

SECTION 1 REVIEW Choose the letter of the answer that correctly completes each sentence. Write your answer on a separate sheet of paper.

1) Before the 1500s, scholars decided what was true or false by reading _____.

   a. the Bible   c. ancient Roman writers

   b. ancient Greek writers   d. the Vedas

2) The name of the steps that scientists use to discover the truth is the _____.

   a. experiment   c. hypothesis

   b. scientific method   d. conclusion

3) At the heart of the scientific method is the _____.

   a. experiment   c. tool

   b. Bible   d. Aristotle's teaching

4) The _____ is an educated guess in the scientific method.

   a. experiment   c. mathematics

   b. hypothesis   d. note

5) The scientific method has _____ steps.

   a. three   c. five

   b. four   d. six

What do you think

Do you think an experiment can prove that a hypothesis is wrong? Explain your answer.

Revolve
To move around something

◆**Theory**
A statement that explains why or how something happens

Universe
All the planets and stars that exist in space

For thousands of years, humans have looked up at the night sky. They have wondered about the movement of the stars and planets. In the daylight hours, they watched as the sun climbed slowly into the eastern sky, traveled overhead, then disappeared into the west. People could see all of this, but they could not explain it. One question they asked was "Does the sun **revolve,** or move around, a nonmoving Earth?" Most people thought the answer was yes.

What Was Ptolemy's Theory About Earth?

About A.D. 150, Ptolemy, an Egyptian scientist, developed a **theory** about heavenly movement. His theory, or statement that explains something, said that the earth is the center of the **universe.** The universe is all the planets and stars that exist in space. Ptolemy believed that the sun and the five known planets revolved around Earth. This theory lasted for 1,400 years. The Catholic Church and most scholars accepted Ptolemy's theory.

Who Came Up With a New Theory?

A Polish churchman named Nicolaus Copernicus did not accept Ptolemy's theory. In 1543, he published a book that said that the sun was the center

Nicolaus Copernicus was the first to think that the earth traveled around the sun.

Johannes Kepler proved that Copernicus was right—the earth does orbit the sun.

of the universe. The earth, he said, traveled around the sun.

Copernicus did not prove this with an experiment. Instead, he based his ideas on **logical,** or clear, reasonable, step-by-step thinking and the rules of geometry. His theory was a simple explanation for what he saw happening in the skies.

How did he explain the rising and the setting of the sun? Copernicus said that the earth spun like a top. Many people laughed at this idea. Martin Luther said that Copernicus's theory had to be wrong because of a story in the Bible.

The Bible says that a warrior named Joshua commanded the sun to stand still. It said Joshua did not command the earth to stand still, because it was believed that the earth was not moving. For this reason, Luther said that Copernicus was a fool. Other people asked, "If the earth spins, why don't things fly off the earth into space?" (Later, Issac Newton, another scientist, answered that question.)

Who Proved Copernicus's Theory?

Scientific proof of Copernicus's sun-centered theory came early in the 1600s. A German named Johannes Kepler carefully observed the planet Mars and **concluded,** or decided, that Copernicus was right. The earth and the other planets did move around the sun.

Using mathematics, Kepler even showed the shape of a planet's orbit around the sun. He proved that a planet did not orbit in a circle. It orbited in an **ellipse,** which is the shape of an egg. Many years before, Aristotle had written that all movement in the heavens had to be in a circle, because a circle is perfect, and the heavens were a perfect

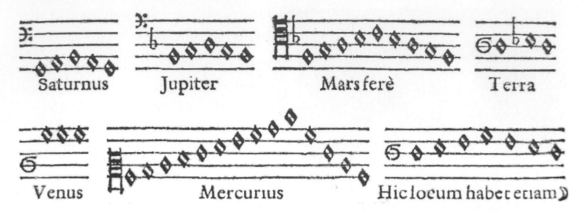

Johannes Kepler thought that the motions of planets around the sun were in harmony like the strings of a musical intrument.

place. For about 1,900 years, people accepted Aristotle's theory. But Kepler proved that Aristotle was wrong.

SECTION 2 REVIEW On a separate sheet of paper, write the word from the Word Bank that completes each sentence.

WORD BANK
Aristotle
Copernicus
Kepler
Luther
Ptolemy

1) In A.D. 150, _____ said that the earth was at the center of the universe.

2) In 1543, _____ said that the sun was at the center of the universe.

3) _____ said that this sun-centered theory was foolish.

4) _____ concluded that the earth's orbit around the sun was in the shape of an ellipse.

5) This orbit theory challenged the theory of _____ that everything in the universe was in the shape of a circle.

What do you think

Why would a person need courage to announce a new scientific theory at this time?

Reject
To refuse to accept something or someone

Galileo Galilei became the most important supporter of Copernicus's theory of a sun-centered universe. He was born in Italy in 1564. Until 1610, he taught mathematics at the University of Padua. At that time, a Dutch lens maker put glass lenses at the ends of a tube to make a telescope. This new tool excited Galileo. In 1609, he built his own telescope and used it to look at the night sky.

What Did Galileo Discover With a Telescope?

When Galileo looked at the moon, he saw its rough surface. Then he looked at the sun. (He did not know that this would hurt his eyes.) On its surface, he saw dark sun spots that changed shape. Through his telescope, Galileo saw that the sun, moon, and planets were imperfect, changing heavenly bodies. (Centuries before, Aristotle had said they were perfect and did not change.)

Next, Galileo discovered that the planet Jupiter had four moons orbiting it. From his observations, Galileo concluded that Copernicus was right. The earth was not the center of the universe; the sun was.

Why Did Galileo's Work Cause Problems?

Many scholars and church officials **rejected,** or refused to accept, Galileo's discoveries. He supported Copernicus's theory, and the Catholic Church said that this theory challenged the Bible. In 1616, the church ruled that Copernicus's theory was wrong and could not be taught. The church censored the work of Copernicus. They said that people could not read his book.

Galileo tried to get around this by publishing a book in 1632. In his book, people debate the strong points and the weak points of the two theories about the universe. However, Galileo made the person who liked Ptolemy's earth-centered theory seem foolish.

The Roman Inquisition found Galileo guilty of heresy. He was then imprisoned in his own home, but he continued his work.

◆Heresy
A teaching or a belief that a religious authority thinks is false

What Did the Catholic Church Do to Galileo?

Church authorities saw Galileo's book as an attack on Catholic teachings. The Roman Inquisition ordered Galileo to appear before it. Galileo went on trial in 1633. He was 69 years old and going blind from studying the sun.

At the end of the trial, the Roman Inquisition forced Galileo to admit that he was wrong. He had to say that Copernicus's theory of a sun-centered universe was **heresy.** That is, it went against the official teaching of the Catholic Church. According to a legend, after he had finished saying that the earth did not move, he whispered, "And yet it does move."

What Other Discovery Did Galileo Make?

The Roman Inquisition ordered Galileo to be imprisoned in his home. But he continued to work. He also wrote about his earlier discoveries. For example, as a younger man, he did careful experiments and measurements with two iron balls. He found that the ten-pound ball fell at the same rate of speed as the one-pound ball. His findings **contradicted,** or went against, the teachings of Aristotle.

Many years before, Aristotle had said that heavier objects fall faster than lighter ones. But, through his experiments, Galileo proved that Aristotle was wrong. Galileo showed that **gravity** makes all objects on Earth fall at the same rate of speed. Today, many scientists call Galileo the father of **experimental science.** That is, he started the science that begins with careful experiments and measurements.

Contradict
To go against; to say the opposite of what has been said

◆**Experimental science**
Science that begins with and depends on careful experiments and measurements

Gravity
The force that pulls objects toward the center of Earth and gives objects weight

SECTION 3 REVIEW On a separate sheet of paper, write answers to these questions.

1) What instrument did Galileo use to prove Copernicus's theory?

2) Why did Galileo's scientific discoveries cause problems for the Roman Catholic Church?

3) How did Galileo try to get around the church's censor of Copernicus?

4) How did the church punish Galileo for his support of Copernicus's theory?

5) What discovery did Galileo make concerning falling objects?

What do you think

What things did Galileo do that show he was a great scientist?

Absorb
To soak up

Attract
To pull something toward oneself

Prism
A three-sided object that can be seen through

Reflect
To bounce off an object or to show an image of something

After Galileo's trial, many Italian scientists stopped their work. They did not want the Catholic Church to censor them. But in 1642—the year Galileo died—Isaac Newton was born in England. He would build on the work of Galileo and others.

What Two Discoveries Did Newton Make?

When Newton was a 23-year-old mathematician at Cambridge University, a plague broke out in London. Newton left Cambridge to protect his health. In the next two years, he made two important discoveries.

First, Newton discovered that white sunlight is a mixture of all colors. Second, Newton discovered why objects appear to be a certain color. He said that a red object appears red because it **reflects** red light and **absorbs** all the other colors in sunlight. When an object reflects a color, the other sunlight colors bounce off the object. When the object absorbs colors, it soaks them up so that they disappear from our sight. Newton proved this with an experiment. He passed light through a **prism,** or a three-sided object that can be seen through.

What Was Newton's Most Important Discovery?

Like the other scientists of his time, Newton knew that the planets orbited the sun. But what force held the planets in their orbits? Galileo had shown how gravity worked on falling objects on Earth. Now Newton began to think of gravity that went as far as the orbit of the moon.

Newton used a falling apple to explain his theory. He said that because of gravity, Earth **attracts** a falling apple. (That is, Earth pulls a falling object toward itself.) Then Newton said that a force exists in the universe. This force causes everything in the universe to attract every other thing. This force is gravity. It increases as objects move closer to each other. Big objects have a greater attractive force than smaller objects. Newton said that the sun's strong gravity kept planets traveling in their orbits.

What Is Newton's Universal Law of Gravitation?

Newton proved that gravity caused different kinds of motion. The motion of the moon followed the same pattern as the motion of a falling apple. He showed that we can predict the pattern for all objects in the universe. We call a predictable pattern in science a **scientific law.** Historians call Newton's discovery of this natural pattern the Universal Law of Gravitation. (Universal means that his law about gravity applies to the whole universe.)

Newton built on the work of Copernicus, Kepler, and Galileo. They showed that the planets orbit the sun. Newton showed that gravity keeps the planets in their orbits. Gravity also holds people and objects to the spinning Earth. Newton's Universal Law of Gravitation proved that the same physical laws apply to both the earth and the heavens.

Isaac Newton used a falling apple to explain gravity.

◆Scientific law
A pattern in nature that someone can predict

In 1687, Newton published a book about his work. His ideas excited scientists. His law showed that the universe was orderly and logical. Scientists began to look for other natural laws. Mathematics, the scientific method, and human reason became powerful tools for unlocking nature's secrets.

How Did Newton Feel About His Genius?

Isaac Newton died in 1727 at the age of 85. People knew he was a genius. One poet wrote, "Nature and nature's law lay hid in night; God said, 'Let Newton be,' and all was light." Newton did not see himself this way. He said of himself, "I seem to have been only like a boy playing on the seashore . . . finding a smoother pebble . . . , whilst the great ocean of truth lay all undiscovered before me."

Tales of Times Past

Isaac Newton's work affected people's lives. So did Charles Perrault's, but in a different way.

Perrault became a lawyer in 1651, but the work bored him. He became a French government official, but that was not satisfying. Then he found work that gave him pleasure. He recorded fairy tales that he was fond of telling to his children.

In 1697, Perrault published a book called *Histories or Tales of Times Passed with Morals*. Its stories were timeless tales that most of us have heard many times. They included "Little Red Riding Hood," "Sleeping Beauty," "Puss in Boots," and "Cinderella." Perrault wrote them in a simple, charming style.

On the front of the book was an engraving of an old woman sitting by a fireplace. A sign on the wall read: "Tales of Mother Goose." For this reason, some people believe Perrault was the original Mother Goose. Others think she was an American named Elizabeth Goose. She published a book of rhymes in 1719.

Literature

History in Your Life

SECTION 4 REVIEW On a separate sheet of paper, write *True* if the statement is true or *False* if the statement is not true. Make each false statement true by changing the underlined word.

1) As a young man, Newton made <u>two</u> important discoveries about light.

2) Newton discovered that <u>light</u> kept the planets in orbit around the sun.

3) Newton used an <u>egg</u> to show the force of gravity.

4) A scientific <u>law</u> is a predictable pattern in science.

5) People thought that Isaac Newton was a <u>genius.</u>

What do you think ?

Do you think Newton was a genius? Explain your answer.

Anatomy
The structure of a human or animal body

Blood vessel
A tube in the body through which blood passes

◆**Community**
A group of people with something in common, such as a topic of study, a belief, or an area in which to live

During this period, scientists developed new ways of doing mathematics. They also invented new scientific tools. By the end of the 1600s, a scientific **community** had developed. This community studied science. Isaac Newton had said that all scientists were friends because they were all seeking truth.

What Did Vesalius Study?

Andreas Vesalius, a Belgian doctor, studied the **anatomy,** or structure, of the human body. Up to his time, people knew little about anatomy. What they did know they had learned from studying animals and from reading Galen, an ancient Greek doctor. Vesalius wanted more than this. He wanted to see for himself.

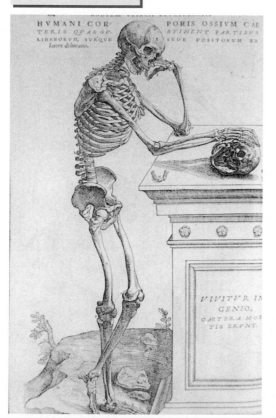

This illustration is from the cover of *Structure of the Human Body,* written by Andreas Vesalius.

The Catholic Church said that dissecting the human body was wrong. But Vesalius went against church law and began to study the anatomy of dead human bodies. In 1543, he published his findings. His book contained thousands of careful drawings of the parts of the human body.

Many of Vesalius's drawings contradicted Galen. (For example, Vesalius discovered that the heart had no bone in it.) Today, historians call Vesalius's work the beginning of the modern study of anatomy.

What Did Harvey Describe?

In the early 1600s, William Harvey, an English doctor, also studied human anatomy. He performed many experiments on the hearts and **blood vessels** of animals. A blood vessel is a tube in the body through which blood passes. He discovered that the heart works as a pump. It **circulates,** or moves, blood through the vessels of the body. (At that time, doctors thought that the blood did not move.) In 1628, Harvey published his findings.

What Did Gilbert Study?

William Gilbert, another Englishman, studied the compass. He wanted to know why a compass needle always points north. After much study, he explained that the earth is a large magnet. A compass needle points to the magnetic **core,** or center, of the earth.

Next, Gilbert explored **amber**—the hard, yellowish remains of a liquid that comes out of trees. Like the ancient Greeks, he wondered why amber attracted other objects when he rubbed it. Gilbert experimented and discovered that glass behaved in the same way. Gilbert called these objects "electric." He got the word from the Greek word *elektron,* which means "amber."

What Did Franklin Prove?

Gilbert's work became the basis for the study of electricity. In 1752, American Benjamin Franklin proved that lightning was a form of **static electricity**. Static electricity builds up in something. When one object rubs up against another, the static electricity escapes. To prove this, Franklin did a dangerous experiment. He tied a metal key to a kite and flew it in a thunderstorm. Lightning struck the kite and traveled down the string. This made the metal key spark. Franklin proved his theory, but he was lucky that he was not harmed from his experiment. His work led to the development of the lightning rod to protect buildings and tall trees from lightning.

What Advances in Mathematics Helped Scientists?

New scientific tools and advances in mathematics helped early scientists make important discoveries about nature. One advance was the use of symbols to represent addition (+), subtraction (−), multiplication (×), division (÷), and equality (=). In Scotland, John Napier discovered a way to make mathematics easier. He turned multiplication and

Early microscopes looked different from those used today. This one is from the 1600s.

division problems into addition and subtraction problems. René Descartes, a great French mathematician, found a way to represent points in space. We call his discovery analytic geometry. Both Isaac Newton in England and Gottfried Leibniz in Germany developed a new way to calculate forces that change all the time. We call their method calculus.

What New Tools Helped Scientists?

Besides the telescope, scientists invented many instruments that helped them observe and measure the natural world. Early in the 1590s, a Dutch maker of eyeglasses invented the microscope. In 1674, Anton van Leeuwenhoek, also from the Netherlands, made a lens that **magnified** an object 270 times. The object looked much bigger than it really was.

Magnify
To make something appear larger than it is

Looking at water, Leeuwenhoek was the first person to see one-celled animals. He proved that fleas and flies hatch from eggs. (At the time, people thought that fleas came from sand and flies from spoiled meat.)

Three scientists who gave us scientific tools to use in our homes were Christian Huygens, Gabriel Fahrenheit, and Anders Celsius. In 1656, Huygens gave us a new kind of clock. Fahrenheit and Celsius gave us the thermometer. It is a tool by which we measure temperature.

In many ways, the modern world began with the investigations of scientists in the sixteenth and seventeenth centuries. The scientific method became the way to search for truth.

MARGARET CAVENDISH: 1623–1674

When you look at Margaret Cavendish's background, she seems like any English noblewoman. She was educated by tutors. She married a noble—William Cavendish, Duke of Newcastle. But Cavendish was an unusual woman. For one thing, she was one of the first females to write a biography. It was about her husband. For another, she was not afraid to speak her mind in the company of men.

Her brother-in-law Charles was a scientist and a member of the Newcastle Circle. She spent many hours in discussion with these scientists and philosophers. She argued in person and in books against using microscopes and telescopes. She thought they were not reliable and did not show the truth.

SECTION 5 REVIEW On a separate sheet of paper, write answers to these questions.

1) What did the scientist Andreas Vesalius study?

2) Which English scientist discovered that the blood circulates through the body?

3) How did William Gilbert answer the question of why a compass needle always points north?

4) Where did the term *electric* come from?

5) What were some advances in mathematics that helped scientists study the natural world?

What do you think ❓

Why would it be exciting to be a scientist during the sixteenth and seventeenth centuries?

True Directions Concerning the Interpretation of Nature

In 1620, Francis Bacon set down the scientific method. It told scientists what they should do to discover how nature worked. Bacon said to ignore all existing ideas on a topic. Scientists should experiment and observe the results. As they worked, scientists should carefully record what they did and saw. New ideas should only come from what they observed. These principles are in

Francis Bacon

his Novum Organum, *or* True Directions Concerning the Interpretation of Nature. *The following is a passage from that writing.*

Those who have taken upon them to lay down the law of nature as a thing already searched out and understood whether they have spoken in simple assurance or professional affectation have therein done philosophy and the sciences great injury. . . . For as they have been successful in inducing belief, so they have been effective in quenching and stopping inquiry; and have done more harm by spoiling and putting an end to other men's efforts than good by their own.

Now my method, though hard to practice, is easy to explain. I propose to establish progressive stages of certainty. . . . I open and lay out a new and certain path for the mind to proceed in, starting directly from the simple . . . perception. . . . Namely, that the entire work of the understanding be commenced afresh, and the mind itself be from the very outset not left to take its own course, but guided at every step; and the business be done as if by machinery.

[First there is] simple experience, which, if taken as it comes is called an accident. If [experience] is sought for, [it is called] an experiment. [A good] experiment [is like] lighting a candle. Then by means of the candle, lights the way [to the truth about nature.]

Let men, therefore, cease to wonder that the course of science is not yet wholly run [its course]. The [scientific] method rightly ordered leads by an unbroken route through the woods of experience to the open ground of [natural laws].

And therefore there are [some] things which [scientists] should be warned [against]. First then, . . . [fancy writing], let it be utterly dismissed. [Next,] all superstitious stories and experiments of ceremonial magic should be altogether rejected.

Source Reading Wrap-Up

1) According to the reading, what was Bacon's main contribution to science?

2) What does Bacon think his system can do?

3) In your opinion, why did Bacon call simple experience an accident?

4) Why does Bacon compare a good experiment to a candle?

5) According to Bacon, what should scientists do with superstitions and magic?

The Importance of the Clock

The work of Newton and other scientists showed that the universe was very orderly. People began to think that there were rules to explain everything in nature. In the 1700s, it seemed that the universe operated like a giant mechanical clock. The idea that the universe was like a machine was very powerful. It lasted until the twentieth century.

Why did people living in the 1700s compare the world to a clock? For them, the clock was a marvelous device. Before its invention, people used many methods to tell time. None of them were very accurate, however.

The ancient Egyptians, Greeks, and Romans used sundials, or "shadow clocks." A sundial was a flat surface with a standing piece of wood or metal. As the sun traveled through the sky, it cast a shadow off this piece. The shadow's length told the time. At night or on cloudy days, water clocks were popular. They had two parts—a large bucket and a pan with measurement lines. Water dripped through a tiny hole in the bucket into the pan. By checking the level of the water in the pan, people could tell the time. Sand glasses were also popular with the Romans. They looked like the egg timers we use today. Sand flowed through a small hole in the top container into the bottom one.

No one knows for sure who invented the first mechanical clock. The first ones were so large they were in towers. How did they work? By allowing gravity to gradually pull heavy weights connected to ropes to the ground. These weights were hooked up to a device that struck the hour.

Then in the early 1500s, there was a new development. A German locksmith built a small

This clock is from the 1660s England.

clock that used a tightened spring. The spring gradually released its energy to turn an hour hand. In 1656, Christian Huygens invented the pendulum clock. It stood upright and had hour and second hands. Falling weights drove the pendulum. In time, this type of clock became the famous grandfather clock.

The mechanical clock changed our concept of time. It became very precise. Now, people could ask the time in the late afternoon. They would get an exact answer, such as "ten minutes after four." The mechanical clock changed people's relationship to each other and to their work. For the first time in history, "being on time" was measured to the minute!

Spotlight Story Wrap-Up

1) What role did Newton play in improving the measurement of time?

2) In the 1700s, what was the universe compared to?

3) What were three early methods of telling time?

4) Who invented the pendulum clock? When?

5) How did the mechanical clock change people's idea of time?

CHAPTER SUMMARY

➡ During the 1500s and 1600s, scholars no longer accepted answers given by the Bible or ancient writers. They used experiments to investigate the natural world.

➡ In the 1620s, Francis Bacon worked out the five steps of the scientific method. It begins with a problem and an educated guess, or hypothesis, about its answer. The next steps are to experiment, to observe, and to make conclusions. Scientists still follow this method.

➡ From ancient times, most people thought Earth was the center of the universe. Ptolemy wrote that the sun and planets revolve around Earth.

➡ In 1543, Copernicus published a new theory. He said that Earth traveled around the sun. Church leaders disagreed. Kepler used mathematics to prove the theory of a sun-centered universe. He showed that planets travel in elliptical, or egg-shaped, orbits, not circles.

➡ Galileo, an Italian scientist, built a telescope to study the sky. He discovered the moons of Jupiter. He concluded that Copernicus was right about a sun-centered universe. The Catholic Church tried to stop Galileo's work. The Inquisition forced him to say that the theory was heresy.

➡ Isaac Newton was an English mathematician of the late 1600s. He studied light and color. He also demonstrated Earth's gravity and how gravity keeps the planets in orbit. He showed that the Universal Law of Gravitation applies throughout the universe.

➡ By the end of the 1600s, a community of scientists was at work in Europe.

➡ Belgian Andreas Vesalius studied human anatomy. His work disproved that of Galen, an ancient Greek doctor. William Harvey, an English doctor, showed how blood circulates.

➡ William Gilbert showed that Earth acts like a magnet. He also discovered electricity. Benjamin Franklin, an American, showed that lightning is a form of electricity.

➡ Mathematics was an important tool of the new science. Napier made multiplication and division easier. Descartes discovered analytic geometry. Newton and Leibniz developed calculus.

➡ New scientific tools included the microscope and the thermometer. Leeuwenhoek used magnifying lenses to observe one-celled animals.

Comprehension: Identifying Facts

On a separate sheet of paper, use the words from the Word Bank to complete each sentence.

WORD BANK
Bacon
Copernicus
Galileo
Gilbert
Harvey
Kepler
Leeuwenhoek
Napier
Newton
Vesalius

1) _____ worked out the basic steps of the scientific method.

2) In 1543, a book by _____ challenged the belief that the sun travels around the earth.

3) Using mathematics, _____ discovered the shape of a planet's orbit around the sun.

4) The Catholic Church put _____ on trial because he said that the earth travels around the sun.

5) _____ discovered the Law of Universal Gravitation.

6) In 1543, _____ wrote a book about human anatomy.

7) After many experiments, _____ discovered that the heart was a pump.

8) _____ used the new word *electric* to describe materials, like amber, that attract feathers and bits of dust.

9) Thanks to _____, multiplying and dividing numbers is easier today.

10) _____ invented a powerful microscope to see one-celled animals for the first time.

Comprehension: Multiple Choice

On a separate sheet of paper, write the letter of the answer that correctly completes each sentence.

1) To _____ something is to make it bigger than it really is.

   a. magnify   c. theory

   b. revolve   d. hypothesis

2) The _____ is a set of steps to follow to reach a true end.

   a. theory   c. scientific method

   b. hypothesis   d. prism

3) A _____ is an educated guess.

    a. theory   c. method

    b. basic   d. hypothesis

4) A _____ is a statement that explains something.

    a. logical   c. universe

    b. theory   d. heresy

5) The tubes in the body through which blood passes are blood _____.

    a. vessels   c. theories

    b. universes   d. prisms

Comprehension: Understanding Main Ideas

On a separate sheet of paper, write the answers to the following questions using complete sentences, or statements.

1) What are the five steps of the scientific method?

2) Before Copernicus, what did most scholars believe about the earth and the heavens?

3) How did Newton build on the work of Copernicus, Kepler, and Galileo?

Critical Thinking: Write Your Opinion

1) Remember what you read in Chapter 13 about the rebirth of learning during the Renaissance. Why do you think the scientists in this chapter went against some of this rebirth?

2) Isaac Newton said, "I seem to have been only like a boy playing on the seashore . . . finding a smoother pebble . . . whilst the great ocean of truth lay all undiscovered before me." In your own words, explain what Newton meant.

Test-Taking Tip	In a matching test, each item should be used just once. Check your answers. If you repeated an item, then another item was left out. Find the best spot for the item you left out.

Looking for causes and effects will help you better understand what you read. An effect is something that happens as a result of a cause. One cause may have several effects. To determine causes and effects, ask these questions:

> Why did the event happen? (cause)
>
> What made the event happen? (cause)
>
> What triggered an event? (cause)
>
> What happened as a result of the event? (effect)
>
> What happened because of that event? (effect)

Here is an example of one cause and effect related to the Hundred Years' War:

Cause: The French wanted control of the English province of Gascony.

Effect: The English fought to keep their control of Gascony.

In the next column are more causes and effects related to the Hundred Years' War. Read each pair of sentences. Decide which statement is the cause and which is the effect. Rewrite each sentence on your paper. Label it with *cause* or *effect*.

1) France's king died without a male heir.

Edward III of England was the French king's nephew. He thought the French throne should go to him.

2) Edward III landed an army in Normandy. It was part of his plan to get the French throne.

Edward III decided to take the French throne by force.

3) The English developed the longbow. The English beat the French in battle.

4) Joan of Arc beat the English at Orléans, Patay, and Reims.

Joan of Arc said that she saw visions from heaven. They told her to lead the French against the English. French soldiers believed what she told them.

5) England had to give up all its land in France except for Calais.

The French won many battles and the Hundred Years' War.

➡ The Black Death in 1348 killed millions of Europeans and changed society.

➡ The Renaissance began about 1350. It was a time of learning and creativity.

➡ The Renaissance began in the city-states of Italy. Wealthy families like the Medici were patrons of artists and scholars.

➡ The monk Savonarola attacked the "worldly" ideas of the Renaissance. After a time, people rejected his ideas.

➡ Renaissance writers used national languages. Shakespeare wrote plays and poetry in English. Cervantes wrote *Don Quixote* in Spanish. In Germany, Gutenberg printed books with moveable metal type. Printed books helped spread learning.

➡ Renaissance painters and sculptors included Leonardo da Vinci, Michelangelo, and Raphael. Leonardo was also an inventor.

➡ Reformers challenged the Roman Catholic Church. Wycliffe translated the Bible into English. John Huss criticized the clergy.

➡ The Protestant Reformation began with Martin Luther, a German monk. He disagreed with the Church about salvation. The Church excommunicated him.

➡ Some German princes followed Luther and became Protestants. In the 1530s, Catholic and Protestant princes went to war. A peace treaty let each prince decide his area's religion.

➡ King Henry VIII of England left the Catholic Church in order to get a divorce. He became head of the Anglican Church. His children were Edward VI, Mary, and Elizabeth. Mary tried to make England Catholic again. Elizabeth kept England Protestant.

➡ John Calvin taught that God had chosen those who would be saved. Calvinist ideas spread through Switzerland and France.

➡ The Church began a Counter-Reformation. The Inquisition looked for heretics. The Jesuits tried to strengthen the Church.

➡ A new science developed in the 1500s and 1600s. Francis Bacon invented the scientific method.

➡ Copernicus said that the sun, not Earth, is the center of the universe. Kepler proved this theory with mathematics. Galileo supported it. Church officials persecuted Galileo for his ideas.

➡ Isaac Newton studied light and color. He also discovered the Universal Law of Gravitation, which works throughout the universe. Other scientists studied human anatomy and electricity.

Comprehension: Identifying Facts

On a separate sheet of paper, use the words from the Word Bank to complete each sentence.

WORD BANK
anatomy
authority
belief
genius
heretic
humanism
hypothesis
patron
reformer
theory

1) A _____ is an idea that a person thinks is true.

2) During the Renaissance, an artist might have a _____ who would support the artist with money.

3) _____ is the belief that human actions, ideas, and works are important.

4) Leonardo da Vinci is an example of a Renaissance _____ because he had special skills that made him different from ordinary people.

5) During the Reformation, some people challenged the _____ of the Roman Catholic Church and said it had no right to tell them what to do.

6) A _____ is a person who teaches a belief that a religious authority thinks is false.

7) A _____ is someone who wants to change things and make them different and better.

8) A _____ is an educated guess about an answer to a problem.

9) A _____ is a statement that explains why or how something happens.

10) _____ is the structure of the human body.

Comprehension: Multiple Choice

On a separate sheet of paper, write the letter of the answer that correctly completes each sentence.

1) People call _____ one of the greatest writers in the English language.
   - a. Cervantes
   - b. Savonarola
   - c. Shakespeare
   - d. Luther

2) _____ painted beautiful pictures during the Renaissance.
   - a. Michelangelo
   - b. Raphael
   - c. Leonardo da Vinci
   - d. all of the above

3) The development of the printing press by _____ brought change to the world.

    a. Luther   c. Raphael

    b. Gutenberg   d. Newton

4) _____ believed that God chose special people to be saved.

    a. Calvin   c. Wycliffe

    b. Galileo   d. Luther

5) _____ believed that the earth traveled around the sun.

    a. Copernicus   c. Newton

    b. Galileo   d. all of the above

Comprehension: Understanding Main Ideas

On a separate sheet of paper, write the answer to the following questions using complete sentences, or statements.

1) How did Leonardo da Vinci show himself to be a true Renaissance man?

2) What caused Martin Luther to begin the Reformation?

3) What did Francis Bacon do to bring about the new age of science?

Critical Thinking: Write Your Opinion

1) In Chapters 13 through 15, you learned about three new ideas: the Renaissance, the Reformation, and the New Science. Which of these ideas do you like best and why?

2) What do you think was the greatest change that took place in the years of this unit—1348 to 1750?

Test-Taking Tip	When you are reading a test question, look for words such as *mainly, most likely, generally, major,* and *best.* Decide which answer choice fits with the meaning of that word.

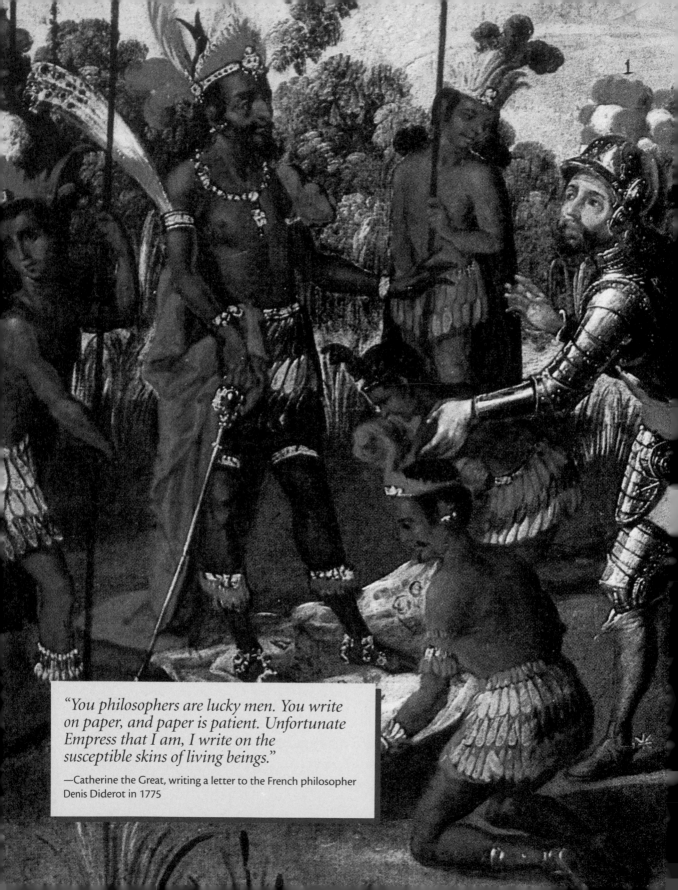

"You philosophers are lucky men. You write on paper, and paper is patient. Unfortunate Empress that I am, I write on the susceptible skins of living beings."

—Catherine the Great, writing a letter to the French philosopher Denis Diderot in 1775

New Worlds

1450 to 1789

Between the years 1450 and 1789, European nations developed and sent out explorers who discovered new worlds. But discovery, exploration, and settlement destroyed whole civilizations of people.

In the next three chapters, you will meet kings and queens, explorers and conquistadors, emperors and warriors, thinkers and musicians. You have maybe heard their names—Louis XIV, Maria Theresa, Columbus, Magellan, Cortés, Pizarro, Montezuma, Atahualpa, Locke, and Bach. Now you will get a chance to learn about them.

In this unit, you will discover three worlds—the world of kings, of exploration, and of reason and enlightenment. Get ready to set sail for Europe to meet the first world; go back across the Atlantic to the Americas to discover the second; and then voyage back to Europe to enjoy the third.

SOUT

AMERI

The Age of Kings

1519 to 1715

In Chapter 10, you read about feudalism. It was the political organization of the Middle Ages. Now you will learn about nationalism. As you watch nations develop, you will study many different kings and queens. Some thought that God gave them the right to rule. Others thought that everything revolved around them.

But you will do more than learn about kings and queens in this chapter. You will sail in an armada, learn about a beautiful capital in St. Petersburg, and see a civil war in England. You will also learn about Prussia and Russia.

Goals for Learning

▶ To compare feudalism and nationalism

▶ To explain how nations developed

▶ To describe the rise and fall of Spain as a powerful nation

▶ To explain rule by "divine right"

▶ To describe England's constitutional monarchy

▶ To explain how Louis XIV help France become powerful

▶ To explain why historians call two Russian monarchs "Great"

▶ To explain how Prussia became powerful

1556
Emperor Charles V retires

1642
Civil war breaks out in England

1649
Puritans put Charles I to death

1688
The Glorious Revolution begins in England

1762
Catherine the Great begins to rule Russia

1500   1600   1700   1800

1588
England defeats Spanish Armada

1643
Louis XIV begins to rule France

1682
Peter the Great becomes ruler of Russia

1740
Frederick the Great of Prussia begins war with Austria

1790
Prussia becomes powerful military force

Spain

10°W   5°W   0°

ATLANTIC OCEAN

45°N

FRANCE

Bay of Biscay

CANTABRIAN MTS.

PYRENEES MTS.

Duero R.

Ebro R.

Barcelona

PORTUGAL

Madrid

40°N

Tagus R.

SPAIN

Balearic Islands

Guadiana R.

Guadalquivir R.

Mediterranean Sea

Seville

Cartagena

35°N

Strait of Gibraltar

AFRICA

N W E S

0   200 Miles
0   200 Kilometers

Geography Skills

Spain became the most powerful nation in Europe during the 1500s. During this time, Spain sent explorers to the Americas. This brought money into the Spanish treasury. Spain used some of this money to build a great navy. Its navy brought Spain more power. Madrid, located in central Spain, was its capital city.

Study the map carefully and answer the following questions:

1) What strait do ships pass through to get from the Mediterranean Sea to the Atlantic Ocean?

2) What mountains separate Spain from France?

3) What bay is directly north of Spain?

4) What river flows through Seville?

5) What are the names of two seaports in Spain?

◆ **Boundary**
The dividing line between one country and another

◆ **Monarch**
A king or a queen

◆ **Nationalism**
Loyalty to one's country or nation

◆ **Tradition**
A custom, idea, or belief handed down from one person to the next

The Renaissance, the Reformation, and new scientific discoveries brought great change to European societies. Each challenged the way people had lived since the Middle Ages. Another challenge came when Europe began to develop into nations.

What Is Nationalism?

Remember reading about feudalism in Chapter 10? It was a political and military system based on the holding of land. In the feudal system, many people might share the same language and customs. But they were loyal to different nobles, because the nobles controlled the land they lived on. People did not think of themselves as English, French, or Spanish. When did they begin to think of themselves that way? When **nationalism** developed.

With feudalism, people were loyal to a noble. With nationalism, people are loyal to their country, or nation. Nationalism began in Europe in the eleventh century when England became a nation. France soon followed. People in these new nations shared the same geographic **boundaries,** or dividing lines.

In these new nations, people shared the same language and history. They also shared the same **traditions,** or customs, ideas, and beliefs that had been handed down from one person to the next. The nation became part of who a person was. When someone asked "Who are you?" a person could answer: "I am English" or "I am French." (Nationalism continues to be an important force today.)

What Is Absolute Power?

All new nations had to answer one question: what form of government shall we have? Different groups wanted power—city governments, the wealthy class, church officials. The English philosopher Thomas Hobbes wrote in the 1600s that a powerful **monarch,** or king or queen, was the best way to unify a nation. Gradually, some monarchs in Europe gained great power.

Louis XIV was a powerful French monarch. This painting shows him unveiling a statue in France.

This power was so great that it had no limits. These monarchs had so much power that historians call them **absolute monarchs.** An absolute monarch had complete power over his or her people. This power was without limit.

But why give all this power to one person? Doing this was one early answer to the question of how to govern a new nation. Historians call this period of absolute monarchs the Age of Kings.

How Absolute Was a Monarch's Power?

How powerful did these monarchs become? Take Philip III for example. Early in the 1600s, Philip III, the king of Spain, fell asleep before a blazing fire. Earlier the king had ordered that only one person could move his chair. But this one person was no longer in the room! Seeing that the fire was going to burn the king, his servants searched the castle. No one found the man who had permission to move the king's chair, so the servants stood there and did nothing! They let the fire burn the king! If they had moved the chair, they would have **disobeyed,** or gone against, a royal order. That is absolute power!

Modern Monarchs

Rulers had absolute, or total, power in the Age of Kings. People often believed this power came from God. Such a monarch ruled by "divine right." During the 1700s and 1800s, some people rebelled against their rulers. World War I ended other monarchies.

Some countries, however, still have a king or queen. They include Great Britain, Spain, Holland, Sweden, and Japan. Present-day monarchs wear rich robes and jeweled crowns for important events. They live in castles and their children inherit the throne. But today's monarchs are only symbols. They stand for a country's tradition and history. In all these countries, a constitution severely limits a monarch's powers. The parliament and prime minister actually make the laws.

SECTION 1 REVIEW Choose the letter of the answer that correctly completes each sentence. Write your answers on a separate sheet of paper.

1) _____ is rule by a king or queen.

    a. Crusades   c. Feudalism

    b. Nationalism   d. Monarchy

2) During the Age of Kings _____, or loyalty to one's country, developed.

    a. nationalism   c. monarchy

    b. feudalism   d. none of the above

3) _____ developed into a nation before France did.

    a. The United States   c. North America

    b. Italy   d. England

4) During this period many monarchs had absolute, or _____, power.

    a. limited   c. little

    b. unlimited   d. some

5) Philip III of _____ was a king with absolute power.

    a. France   c. Spain

    b. England   d. Italy

What do you think

What might happen to someone who questioned a monarch's absolute power?

Both England and France became nations before Spain. But Spain was the first to become truly powerful. During most of the 1500s, its political and economic power was much greater than that of England and France. Spain's story begins with the Moors.

Where Did the Moors Settle?

The Moors were nomads in northern Africa. In the eighth century, they accepted Islam—the religion of Muhammad. Next, they invaded Spain and brought with them their new religion. The Moors pushed through Spain and over the Pyrenees Mountains to Tours. But the Franks defeated them there in A.D. 732. The Moors settled in southern Spain. There, they built a civilization that lasted for almost 800 years.

What Was the City of Córdoba Like?

At that time, civilization was in decline in Europe. But the Moors in Spain built Córdoba. More than a million people lived there. Lamps lit the streets. The library contained thousands of books from all over the world. In fact, the Moors helped to reintroduce ancient Greek and Roman learning into Europe. They studied geometry, astronomy, medicine, and philosophy. Christian scholars came from all over Europe to study in Moorish Spain.

How Did Spain Become a Nation?

Slowly, four Christian kingdoms developed in Spain. Castile and Aragon were the strongest. In 1469, Ferdinand, the king of Aragon, married Isabella of Castile. Their marriage united much of Spain under two strong rulers. They forced Spanish nobles to accept their rule. Ferdinand said that he should make all important decisions because "one head is better than a thousand."

Why Did Isabella Go to War?

Isabella wanted to make all of Spain into a Catholic nation. In 1482, she went to war against Granada—the last

Queen Isabella and her husband, King Ferdinand, united Spain, made the nation Catholic, and paid for Christopher Columbus's voyages to the Americas.

Moorish kingdom in Spain. In 1492, Granada surrendered. Then Isabella said everyone in Spain had to be Catholic. Any Moor or Jew who refused to become a Catholic had to leave Spain. A few months after conquering Granada, the two rulers provided Christopher Columbus with three ships. He sailed west and found great wealth in the Americas. (You will read more about this in Chapter 17.)

What Empire Did Charles V Rule?

King Ferdinand died in 1516. Then his grandson Charles became the second king of Spain. Charles I was also the grandson of the Holy Roman Emperor. When the emperor died in 1519, Charles became Charles V, emperor of the Holy Roman Empire. He was only 19, but he ruled one of the largest empires in history and was the most powerful king in Europe.

What Countries Made Up Charles V's Empire?

Inherit
To receive money, land, or a title from someone who has died

Charles V was a member of the powerful Hapsburg family. It held power for more than 700 years—from the 1200s to 1918. Charles V **inherited** lands in France from his father. To inherit is to receive money, land, or a title from someone who has died. Through his grandfather, he became ruler of Austria. He also ruled half of Italy and all of the Netherlands, Germany, and Belgium. Charles also controlled all the lands that Columbus and other Spanish explorers discovered. The gold and silver from the Americas made Charles's empire rich.

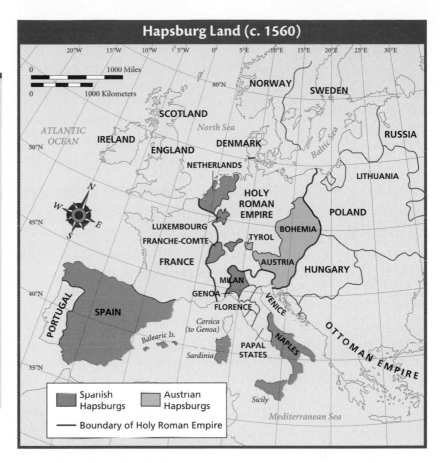

Hapsburg Land (c. 1560)

MAP STUDY

This map shows land that the Spanish and Austrian Hapsburgs owned in about 1560. Which Hapsburgs controlled Bohemia? What was the largest land area controlled by the Spanish Hapsburgs? Which Hapsburgs controlled the Netherlands?

Legend:
- Spanish Hapsburgs
- Austrian Hapsburgs
- Boundary of Holy Roman Empire

Why Did Charles V Retire?

Charles V was one of the most powerful rulers in history. But his large empire kept him busy. He fought religious wars in Germany to stop Lutheranism. He fought against France over lands in Italy. In fact, Charles spent most of his life traveling throughout his empire fighting one thing after another.

Finally, when he was 56, Charles V had had enough. In 1556, he gave up his power. He gave control of the Holy Roman Empire to his brother, Ferdinand I. He gave his lands in Italy, the Netherlands, and the nation of Spain to his son, Philip II. Then Charles went to a monastery and stayed there until he died.

Why Did Philip II Build an Armada?

As a Roman Catholic, Philip II wanted to stop the spread of Protestantism. Elizabeth I of England had made her

Armada
A large fleet of warships

Formation
A shape or pattern

country into a leading Protestant nation. Philip II wanted to defeat Elizabeth I and England. He thought that Europe would then become Catholic again.

Philip II decided to invade England. To do this, he built a naval **armada,** or large fleet of warships. In the spring of 1588, the Spanish Armada of 130 ships sailed for England with 1,100 cannons and 30,000 soldiers.

How Did England Defeat the Armada?

The Spanish fleet sailed north and anchored off the coast of England. Next, the captains put the ships into a protective **formation,** or shape. But then they broke their formation. The English captains sent three burning ships into the Spanish fleet. This scattered all the Spanish ships.

The Spanish Armada ships also had a weakness: they were too big and too slow. The smaller and faster English ships attacked the scattered Spanish ships. One by one, they sank.

The English navy defeated the Spanish Armada in 1588. Only half of the Spanish Armada ships made it back to Spain. The loss put an end to Spain's status as a sea power.

Technology
History in Your Life

Sailing Ships

Explorers in the 1400s used the new full-rigged ships. They had three masts and multiple sails. Such a ship moved under sail power. It did not rely on rowers. The Portuguese developed a full-rigged ship called a caravel to explore the African coast. It was small and very fast. Explorers used it to explore other places, too.

In comparison, galleons were heavier and larger. They were first built in the 1500s. They could carry bulky cargoes or heavy guns. Spanish galleons, for example, brought gold and silver from the Americas to Spain. About one-third of the Spanish Armada in 1588 were galleons. These craft relied on boarding an enemy ship and using soldiers to capture it. English galleons, however, were faster and easier to maneuver. They relied on firepower, which could disable an enemy ship from a distance. This ability defeated the Spanish Armada.

Knowing that the English had defeated them, the Spanish captains tried to sail home. But a sudden storm sank many more of their ships. Only half of them returned to Spain. In 1598, Philip II died. In the next two centuries, England and France became the most powerful nations in Europe.

SECTION 2 REVIEW On a separate sheet of paper, write answers to these questions.

1) From what area of Africa did the Moors come?

2) What important city did the Moors build in Spain?

3) What are the names of the king and queen who first unified Spain?

4) In 1519, who became the most powerful ruler in Europe?

5) What country defeated the Spanish Armada?

What do you think

Where do you think Philip II got the money to build the Spanish Armada?

◆Divine right
The belief that God chooses the ruler of a nation

Elizabeth I was a strong monarch in England. She shared power with the English Parliament. For example, Elizabeth took care of business with other countries. But Parliament made laws and taxed people.

What Is Divine Right?

When Elizabeth died in 1603, King James of Scotland became James I of England and Scotland. He refused to share power with Parliament. Instead, he said that he ruled by **divine right**. That is, James thought that God had chosen him to rule. He thought no one had the right to question him and his decisions.

A simple story shows how divine right worked. In 1603, a man accused of stealing was brought before James. He ordered that the man be hanged without a trial. He believed that as king he was both judge and jury.

What Made Parliament and the People Angry?

James I died in 1625. His son, Charles I, also believed in divine right. But Parliament did not. Soon after becoming king, Charles asked Parliament for money to fight a war with Spain. Parliament said no. Because of this, the king did not have money to pay for a place for his soldiers to stay. Charles forced people to house them in their homes. The people and Parliament did not like this. They had to do something to limit the king's power.

King James I believed that God had given him the right to rule England as he pleased.

When Did Parliament Limit the King's Power?

In 1628, the king asked Parliament for more money. Once again, Parliament refused. Parliament said that it would give money only if the king signed a **document** called the **Petition of Right.** This important paper was a big step in the growth of English democracy. By signing it, the king agreed to three things.

1. Only Parliament can collect taxes.
2. The king can send no one to prison without a trial.
3. No one, not even the king, can force citizens to house soldiers unless these citizens want to.

The next year, Charles asked for more money. This time, Parliament passed a **resolution,** or formal statement, that also said three things.

1. The king cannot change English Protestantism.
2. The king cannot tax the English people unless Parliament says he can.
3. If the king does these things, he commits the crime of **treason.** That is, he turns on his country and its laws.

SECTION 3 REVIEW On a separate sheet of paper, write *True* if the statement is true or *False* if the statement is not true. Make each false statement true by changing the underlined word.

1) The government group in England that makes the laws is <u>Parliament.</u>

2) James I thought that he ruled by <u>divine right.</u>

3) Charles I was the son of <u>Elizabeth I,</u> and he believed that God had chosen him to be king.

4) Parliament made Charles I sign the <u>Petition of Right.</u>

5) The Petition of Right was a big step in the growth of English <u>monarchy.</u>

What do you think

Should Parliament have limited Charles I's power? Explain your answer.

Most of the time Charles I did not pay any attention to the Petition of Right. For the next 11 years, he raised money in many ways. For example, he sold some of the royal jewels. But what would happen when he needed much more money?

What Led to Civil War in England?

In 1639, Charles did need lots of money. The people of Scotland refused to become members of the Anglican Church in England. They threatened to attack England.

Once again Charles asked Parliament for money. And once again, Parliament worked to limit the king's power. Then,

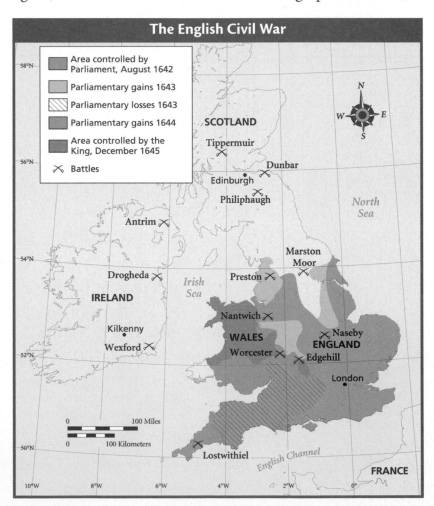

MAP STUDY

This map shows territory gained and lost by the king and Parliament during the English Civil War. Which side controlled London? Which side controlled the land by the English Channel? Name three places where the two sides fought battles.

The English Parliament (above) and the Puritans fought the king and his supporters in the English Civil War.

in 1642, the king tried to arrest the leaders of Parliament. This was too much for the English people. They became so angry that Charles had to leave London! Civil war broke out between two groups: the people who supported the king and the people who supported Parliament.

Who Fought the English Civil War?

The two groups who fought the war were different. They had different religions and they dressed differently. **Cavaliers** fought for the king. They were mostly rich Anglicans or Catholics. They dressed in fancy clothes and wore wigs with long curls.

Puritans fought for Parliament. They were English Protestants who wanted to purify the Anglican Church.

◆Restoration
The period that saw monarchy return to England in 1660

Restore
To bring something back

◆Roundhead
A Puritan who fought for Parliament in the English Civil War

Tolerant
To respect the beliefs of others

The Puritans dressed simply. Because they wore their hair so short, people called them **Roundheads.** Oliver Cromwell led the Roundheads. His army was better than the king's Cavaliers. In 1643, the Roundheads defeated the Cavaliers.

What Did the Puritans Do to Charles I?

The winners of the war put King Charles I on trial. They found him guilty of treason. That is, he had turned against England and its laws. Charles was then beheaded in 1649. Never before had anyone put a king on trial and then put him to death before a crowd of people.

What happened next? In 1653, Cromwell took control of the English government. He became a military dictator. The Puritans began to change English society. They closed the theaters; they said no one could play sports. All this lasted until Cromwell's death in 1658.

Oliver Cromwell led the Roundheads during the English Civil War. He ruled England after defeating the king in the war.

What Is the Restoration?

The English grew tired of Puritan rule. In 1659, Parliament voted to **restore,** or bring back, the monarchy to England. In the spring of 1660, the oldest son of Charles I returned to England. He was crowned Charles II. Historians call his 25-year reign the **Restoration.**

Charles II rejected the idea of the divine right of kings. He tried to avoid religious problems by asking Catholics and Puritans to be **tolerant** toward one another. That is, they should respect one another's beliefs and customs.

The English people liked Charles II. He encouraged the

theater, sports, and other entertainment. He loved to have fun, so people called him the "Merry Monarch."

What New Law Did Parliament Pass?

In 1679, Parliament passed the **Habeas Corpus** Act. This law said that the government has to charge someone with a crime before putting the person in prison. *Habeas corpus* is Latin for "you should have the body." The Habeas Corpus Act is an important protection of a citizen's rights. Now, not even the king could take away this legal right from his people.

What Is the Glorious Revolution?

When Charles II died in 1685, his brother, James, became king. Like Charles, James II was a Catholic. But James wanted the monarchy to have more power.

At the time, two political groups held power in England. The **Tories** supported a strong monarchy; the **Whigs** supported a strong Parliament. But both sides agreed on one thing—they did not want a Catholic king. However, James was old and his two daughters were Protestant. The Tories and the Whigs believed that after the king's death, they would have a Protestant ruler. Then, in 1688, James II's wife gave birth to a son.

This son would have grown up and become a Catholic king. The Tories and the Whigs joined together. They said that Mary, who was James II's older daughter, should become queen. In the fall of 1688, Mary and her husband, William, left the Netherlands and arrived in England with an army.

James II had no support, so he fled to France. Parliament then said that William and Mary were the king and queen of England and Scotland. The English had rebelled against their king without anyone being killed! Historians call this the **Glorious Revolution.**

What Is a Constitutional Monarchy?

Before William and Mary could become monarchs, they had to sign an English Bill of Rights. This document said

◆Glorius Revolution *The period in England that involved the overthrow of James II and the crowning of William and Mary*

◆Habeas Corpus *A law that says that the government has to charge someone with a crime before putting the person in prison*

◆Tory *A person who supported a strong monarchy in England*

◆Whig *A person who supported the English Parliament*

> ◆**Constitutional monarchy**
> *A form of government in which a king and queen rule, but there are laws of a democracy*

that only Parliament can make laws. It also says that the king must obey the laws Parliament passes.

The document also gave the members of Parliament the right to speak freely while in Parliament. Why is that important? Because the king could not arrest them if he did not like what they said!

Within 60 years—1628 to 1688—Parliament passed the Petition of Right, the Habeas Corpus Act, and the English Bill of Rights. These documents showed that England did not want an absolute monarch.

What did England want? Both a democracy and a king. We call this form of government a **constitutional monarchy.** That is, England has a monarchy, plus a body of laws and elected officials to protect the rights of its people.

SECTION 4 REVIEW On a separate sheet of paper, write the word from the Word Bank that completes each sentence.

WORD BANK
Cavalier
Charles I
Cromwell
Roundhead
William

1) _____ was the king of England when civil war broke out.

2) A _____ was a person who supported the king in the civil war.

3) A _____ was a person who supported Parliament in the civil war.

4) _____ was the leader of the group that fought against the king.

5) _____ was the first English king who ruled under a form of government called a constitutional monarchy.

What do you think

Why did the English get tired of Puritan rule?

Adviser
A person who gives advice

◆Cardinal
A high official of the Roman Catholic Church

Oppose
To be against something

Much was happening in England during the seventeenth century. But much was also happening across the English Channel in France. In 1643, Louis XIII of France died. His son, who was only four, then became king. He ruled as Louis XIV.

Who Helped the Young King Rule?

Louis XIII had been a weak king. He had turned over much of his power to a **cardinal,** or high official, in the Catholic Church. From 1624 to 1642, Cardinal Richelieu served as the king's **adviser.** That is, he gave advice to the king. Richelieu **opposed,** or stood against, any form of democratic government.

By the time Louis XIV became king, the French monarchy had a lot of power. For many years, however, Louis XIV was too young to make decisions. Another church official, Cardinal Mazarin, really ruled France. Under the leadership of these two cardinals, France became the strongest nation in Europe.

Louis XIV faced many problems when he decided to rule France alone. He soon became a powerful king, however.

When Cardinal Mazarin died, people wanted to know who would be the king's next advisor. But Louis was now 22. He decided then and there that he alone would rule France.

What Problems Did Louis XIV Face?

Louis wanted to rule France alone. But many problems stood in his way. The nobles often paid little attention to what he wanted. He had a hard time collecting taxes. Each noble had his own army, but he had no national army that he could control. Sometimes the nobles and their armies fought against him.

How Did Louis XIV Centralize France's Government?

All these problems existed because France had no **central,** or main, government that was more powerful than the nobles. Louis wanted to force these nobles to obey his wishes. He thought that he alone should decide what was best for the people of France, so he began to centralize the government.

First, Louis XIV appointed officials to collect taxes. They ruled over different areas of France in the name of the king. Next, Louis reorganized the French army. He gave uniforms to the soldiers to show that they belonged to his army. Then he increased the size of the army from 100,000 to 400,000. This large army made Louis XIV powerful.

What Other Things Did Louis XIV Do As King?

Louis XIV lived in a palace in Paris called the Louvre. But he built a second great palace at Versailles, which was 10 miles away. Versailles took 30 years to complete. More than 30,000 people worked to build this dream palace. His love of beautiful things put a **burden** on the French taxpayers.

Louis XIV built a grand palace at Versailles as a symbol of his power. Some historians estimate that he spent $100 million to build it.

JOAN OF ARC: 1412–1431

By the early 1400s, France and England had been at war for almost a hundred years. A young French peasant Joan of Arc believed she heard heavenly voices. They told her she must defeat the English. So Joan went to Charles VII, France's uncrowned king. She persuaded him to give her an army. Inspired by Joan's leadership, her troops rescued Orléans in 1429 and Charles was crowned king. In a later battle, Joan was captured and given to the English. She was convicted of being a witch and burned at the stake. Today, Joan is a French national heroine.

They had to pay for all of this! They also had to pay for the wars Louis XIV fought. Between 1667 to 1714, he fought many wars to get more land. (After one of these wars, he agreed that the same king would never rule both France and Spain.)

These wars drained the French treasury. At the end of his life, Louis XIV was sorry that he had fought so much. Before he died in 1715, he advised his grandson, the future king, to keep peace. Louis said, "I have been too fond of war."

Louis XIV reigned for 72 years and became the most powerful ruler in Europe. People called him the "Sun King" because all of France seemed to revolve around him like planets around the sun.

SECTION 5 REVIEW On a separate sheet of paper, write answers to these questions.

1) What two cardinals advised Louis XIII and Louis XIV of France?
2) What are five problems Louis XIV faced when he decided to rule alone?
3) What steps did Louis XIV take to improve the army of France?
4) Where did Louis XIV build his second great palace?
5) What advice did Louis XIV give his grandson?

What do you think ?

What could happen to a country like France if an absolute monarch puts too great a burden on the people?

Russia and Prussia also had strong absolute monarchs. In 1613, a young noble was chosen to lead Russia. His name was Mikhail Romanov. His family ruled Russia for the next 300 years until the Russian Revolution of 1917. One of Russia's most powerful leaders was his grandson, Peter the Great. He became king in 1682 and believed in his absolute power.

What Was Peter's "Window on the Sea"?

Peter the Great wanted to make Russia into a modern nation. To improve his nation's culture, he invited scholars and artists to his country. He also wanted to gain warm water seaports. That way, his country could trade with the nations in Western Europe all year.

To do this, Peter fought to gain control of Swedish territory on the Baltic Sea to the north and Turkish territory on the Black Sea to the south. Peter wanted these ports to give his nation a "window on the sea." On the Baltic Sea, Peter built a new, modern capital called St. Petersburg. He said that it was the perfect "window for Russia to look at Europe."

What Did Catherine the Great Do for Russia?

In 1762, Catherine the Great became queen of Russia and ruled strongly. She improved education and allowed more religious freedom in Russia. In 1767, she tried to have a

Catherine the Great of Russia was a strong ruler. She improved education and granted more religious freedom to her people.

constitution written for her nation. A constitution is a body of laws that states the rights of the people and the power of the government. However, this effort failed.

For a time, Catherine favored freedom for Russian serfs. But when the serfs rebelled against the nobles, she abandoned the idea.

When Did Prussia Become a Military State?

Until the 1700s the German states were small and weak. This changed with the rise to power of Prussia—one of the German states. Frederick William I came to power as an absolute ruler in 1713. He increased the size of the Prussian army and made Prussia into a **military state.** A military state is one in which a leader rules by using the military.

How Did Prussia Expand Its Territory?

In 1740, Frederick II became king. He wanted to increase the size and power of Prussia. He invaded the Austrian territory of Silesia, which was south of Prussia.

At that time, Maria Theresa—a strong leader—ruled Austria. She decided to fight the Prussian army. But she had to battle more than one army. Both France and Spain wanted more power, too. They invaded Austria. Then England and Russia entered the war and supported Maria Theresa. The war lasted on and off for many years. It led to fighting even in North America, where there it was called the French and Indian War.

When all the fighting ended, Maria Theresa lost Silesia to Prussia, which doubled its size. Because of his success, the Prussian people called their king Frederick the Great. By the 1790s, Prussia had become a powerful military force in Europe.

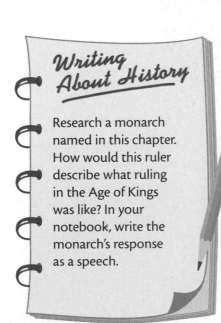

Writing About History

Research a monarch named in this chapter. How would this ruler describe what ruling in the Age of Kings was like? In your notebook, write the monarch's response as a speech.

SECTION 6 REVIEW On a separate sheet of paper, write *True* if the statement is true or *False* if the statement is not true. Make each false statement true by changing the underlined word.

1) Peter the Great built the new Russian capital of <u>Moscow.</u>

2) <u>Peter the Great</u> wanted to have warm water seaports so he could trade with other European nations.

3) For a while, Catherine the Great wanted to free the <u>nobles.</u>

4) <u>Frederick the Great</u> invaded the Austrian territory of Silesia.

5) <u>Maria Theresa</u> fought to save Austria from a Prussian invasion.

What do you think

Why did England and Russia support Maria Theresa in her war with Prussia and Spain?

A Day in the Life of Louis XIV

The term "absolute monarch" could have been invented for Louis XIV. "I am the state," he said. The Duke of Saint-Simon was a noble at Louis's court. His journal of court life covered 1694–1723. This section describes a typical day for the king.

Louis XIV and his court.

At eight o'clock the chief *valet de chambre* on duty, who alone had slept in the royal chamber, and who had dressed himself, awoke the King. The chief physician, the chief surgeon, and the nurse (as long as she lived), entered at the same time. . . .

The King went to mass, where his musicians always sang an anthem. . . . The King amused himself a little upon returning from Mass and asked almost immediately for the council. Then the morning was finished. . . .

The dinner [midday meal] was always *au petit couvert*, that is, the King ate by himself in his chamber upon a square table in front of the middle window. It was more or less abundant, for he ordered in the morning whether it was to be "a little," or "very little" service. But even at this last, there were always many dishes, and three courses without counting the fruit. The dinner being ready, the principal courtiers entered. . . .

Upon leaving the table the King immediately entered his cabinet. That was the time for distinguished people to speak to him. . . .

As he was but little sensitive to heat or cold, or even to rain, the weather was seldom sufficiently bad to prevent his going abroad. He went out for three objects: stag-hunting, once or more each week; shooting in his parks (and no man handled a gun with more grace or skill), once or twice each week; and walking in his gardens for exercise, and to see his workmen. Sometimes he made picnics with ladies, in the forest at Marly or at Fontainebleau. . . .

At ten o'clock his supper was served. The captain of the guard announced this to him. A quarter of an hour after the King came to supper . . . any one spoke to him who wished. This supper was always on a grand scale, the royal household . . . at table, and a large number of courtiers and ladies present, sitting or standing. . . .

The King, wishing to retire, went and fed his dogs; then said goodnight, passed into his chamber . . . to . . . his bed, where he said his prayers, as in the morning, then undressed. . . .

Source Reading Wrap-Up

1) How did Louis XIV spend the morning?

2) Louis met with advisers, courtiers, and important people. When did these meetings usually take place?

3) What did Louis do for fun?

4) How did the king spend his evening?

5) Do you think that being king was a hard job? Explain.

Playing the Fool

Clowns make us laugh. So do other comic actors. They poke fun at people. They get away with pointing out people's faults. Historically, that has been their job.

Playing the fool has a long history. In earlier times, clowns were called fools or jesters. The pharaohs of ancient Egypt had fools, as did the ancient Romans.

Fools were very popular from the Middle Ages to the 1600s. Often they lived at the court of a ruler or wealthy noble. A jester sometimes seemed like a family member. He shared meals and celebrations, played with the children, and heard family secrets.

The jester's costume was a checked coat of many colors. A fool wore bright-colored hose, pointed shoes, and a tight jacket with a pointed hood. Bells jingled on his toes and coat.

Most court jesters acted silly and foolish. They danced and tumbled. They also made up clever songs and verses. They used their wit and sharp tongues to tease.

Jesters held a special place at court. They could say almost anything. Sometimes their purpose was amusement. At other times, they pointed out unwise actions. Fools could have a lot of influence. Richard Tarlton was a famous English comic actor. He was also a jester for Queen Elizabeth I. He was the only person who could criticize her. Louis XIV's court jester was called L'Angely. Nobles were afraid of his sharp wit.

Archie Armstrong was the Fool for King James I of England. He was known as Count Archie. The king sent him to Spain with his ambassadors and he insulted the Spanish. Then Archie wrote the king to say what a good job he had done. Eventually, this jester went too far. He insulted church officials and had to leave the court, but he was already wealthy.

Even the powerful Catholic Church could not avoid foolishness. The Feast of Fools was a popular holiday, especially in France. People chose a mock pope or bishop and made fun of church ceremonies.

Court jesters lost their popularity in the 1700s. Today, clowns are only entertainers, but some comedians still carry on the jester's tradition. They say what no one else dares.

Spotlight Story Wrap-Up

1) How long have there been jesters?

2) How was a jester like a part of a noble family?

3) What did a court jester usually wear?

4) What has been the role of court jesters and fools in history?

5) What used to happen on the Feast of Fools?

➡ As European nations developed, nationalist feelings grew. Absolute monarchs had total power over their subjects.

➡ Moors from North Africa occupied southern Spain in the 700s. They made Córdoba a center for learning.

➡ Christian kingdoms in Spain fought the Moors. Ferdinand of Aragon and Isabella of Castile united Spain. By 1492, they had conquered Granada, the last Moorish kingdom. Jews and Moors had to become Catholic or leave Spain.

➡ In the 1500s, Spain was more powerful than England or France. King Charles I of Spain, a Hapsburg, became the Holy Roman Emperor Charles V. This family ruled large parts of Europe. Charles defended the Catholic faith.

➡ Philip II, the son of Charles V, ruled Spain, part of Italy, and the Netherlands. In 1588, he sent the Spanish Armada against England to make it Catholic again. Philip failed when fast English ships and a storm sank Spanish ships.

➡ King James of Scotland followed Elizabeth I as England's ruler and ruled by divine right. His son Charles I fought with Parliament over money and power. Parliament made Charles sign the Petition of Right.

➡ Civil war broke out in England. The Cavaliers, on the king's side, were mostly Anglican or Catholic. Puritans, or "Roundheads," were Protestant. Their leader was Oliver Cromwell.

➡ The Puritans won the English Civil War in 1643. Charles I was tried for treason and beheaded. Cromwell set up a strict military government. In 1659, Parliament voted to restore the monarchy under King Charles II.

➡ In the Glorious Revolution (1688), Parliament rebelled against James II, a Catholic king. His Protestant daughter Mary and her husband William ruled next. They agreed to a Bill of Rights.

➡ Louis XIV of France became Europe's most powerful ruler. Louis fought many wars and made the central government stronger.

➡ Peter the Great wanted to make Russia more like Europe. He built a new capital at St. Petersburg. Later, Catherine the Great supported education and the idea of a constitution.

➡ Prussia, in Germany, became a military state. Its ruler Frederick II went to war against Maria Theresa, the ruler of Austria. After many years, Prussia defeated Silesia in Austria and became a powerful military force in Europe.

Comprehension: Identifying Facts

On a separate sheet of paper, use the words from the Word Bank to complete each sentence.

WORD BANK
Catherine
Charles I
Charles V
Cromwell
Hobbes
Isabella
James I
Louis XIV
Peter
Philip II

1) _____ was a philosopher who believed that a powerful king should rule a nation.

2) The marriage of Ferdinand and _____ united Spain into one kingdom.

3) _____, a powerful emperor and the king of Spain, gave up his power and went to live in a monastery.

4) _____ sent a powerful Armada to invade England in 1588.

5) The English king from Scotland who believed that he ruled by divine right was _____.

6) During the English Civil War, _____ led the Roundheads.

7) _____ was the first English king to be put to death by his own people.

8) The French called _____ the "Sun King."

9) _____ the Great tried to improve his country's culture by inviting artists and scholars to Russia.

10) _____ the Great tried to have a constitution written for Russia.

Comprehension: Multiple Choice

On a separate sheet of paper, write the letter of the answer that correctly completes each sentence.

1) During the English Civil War, the _____ supported the king.

   a. Cavaliers   c. Parliament

   b. Roundheads   d. Whigs

2) During the Glorious Revolution, the _____ supported a strong Parliament.

   a. Cavaliers   c. Whigs

   b. Roundheads   d. Tories

3) The _____ caused problems for Louis XIV of France.

   a. nobles with armies   c. lack of a national army

   b. collection of taxes   d. all of the above

4) Prussia doubled its territory under the leadership of _____.

   a. Peter the Great   c. Catherine the Great

   b. Frederick the Great   d. Isabella of Castile

5) The queen of Austria when Prussia attacked was _____.

   a. Maria Theresa   c. Isabella of Castile

   b. Catherine the Great   d. Elizabeth I

Comprehension: Understanding Main Ideas

On a separate sheet of paper, write the answers to the following questions using complete sentences, or statements.

1) What is the difference between feudalism and nationalism?

2) What does ruling by "divine right" mean?

3) What is the difference between an absolute monarchy and a constitutional monarchy?

Critical Thinking: Write Your Opinion

1) Do you think that the name "Sun King" was a good description of King Louis XIV? Explain your answer.

2) King Philip II said, "When Spain stirs, the earth trembles." After the defeat of his navy in 1588, what do you think Queen Elizabeth I might have said about his boast?

Test-Taking Tip

Look for specifics in each question that tell you in what form your answer is to be. For example, some questions ask for a paragraph, and others may require only one sentence.

Chapter

Explorers and Explorations

17

1450 to 1650

In the 1400s, European explorers set sail to find a water route to China and India. Portugal began the search, but soon explorers from other countries took to the seas. In this chapter, you will learn about Columbus and other explorers. You will witness how cruel Europeans could be to Native Americans. Then you will study the African slave trade. All of this was part of the settling of the Americas by the Europeans.

Goals for Learning

▶ To explain why some European nations searched for an all-water route to China and India

▶ To list three reasons why Spaniards came to the Americas

▶ To describe what Spanish conquest did to the Native American population

▶ To explain why Portugal introduced African slavery into the New World

▶ To list the plants grown in the Americas that made life different for people around the world

1487
Bartholomeu Dias sails around the tip of Africa

1498
Vasco da Gama sails around Africa to India

1519
Hernando Cortés defeats Aztecs in Mexico

1541
Hernando de Soto reaches the Mississippi

1608
Champlain settles Quebec in Canada

1425   1525   1625

1492
Columbus explores lands in the Americas

1518
Portuguese bring African slaves to the Americas

1532
Francisco Pizarro conquers Incas in Peru

1607
English settle Jamestown in Virginia

1620
Pilgrims settle Plymouth in Massachusett

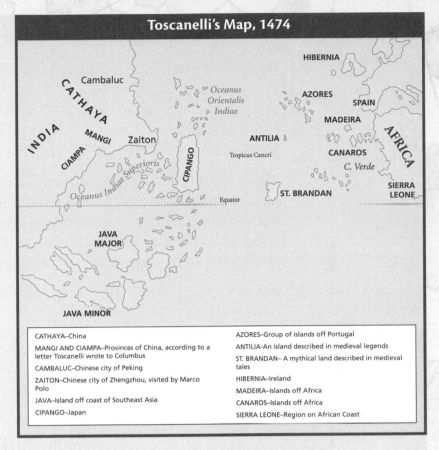

Toscanelli's Map, 1474

CATHAYA–China

MANGI AND CIAMPA–Provinces of China, according to a letter Toscanelli wrote to Columbus

CAMBALUC–Chinese city of Peking

ZAITON–Chinese city of Zhengzhou, visited by Marco Polo

JAVA–Island off coast of Southeast Asia

CIPANGO–Japan

AZORES–Group of islands off Portugal

ANTILIA-An island described in medieval legends

ST. BRANDAN– A mythical land described in medieval tales

HIBERNIA–Ireland

MADEIRA–Islands off Africa

CANAROS–Islands off Africa

SIERRA LEONE–Region on African Coast

Geography Skills

Paolo Toscanelli made a map similar to the above map in 1474. Christopher Columbus used a copy to find a water route to China. As the map shows, a good sailor could do this by sailing west. Clearly, Toscanelli did not know about North or South America!

Study the map and answer the following questions:

1) By what continent are the Madeira Islands?

2) What is the name of a group of islands that lie north of the equator and west of Spain?

3) What was Ireland's name during Columbus's time?

4) On what continent do you find Sierra Leone?

5) Cipango is another name for what country?

◆**Navigation**
The science of planning and directing the route of a ship

During the 1300s and 1400s, Arab merchants bought goods like silks and spices in China and India. Then they carried these goods overland to the eastern end of the Mediterranean Sea. There, they loaded the goods on Italian ships and sold them to the Italian city-states.

The overland journey was slow and hard. But once on the sea, the journey was fast and easy. Soon, the goods arrived in the Italian city-states. Then Italian merchants sold the goods at high prices to other European states. Italian city-states like Venice grew wealthy from this eastern trade.

For many years, these city-states controlled the trade routes to the East. But other countries wanted to become wealthy too. So they began to look for new trade routes. During the 1400s, Portugal began its search for a new route to the East.

How Did Prince Henry Help Portugal?

Prince Henry the Navigator helped the Portuguese prepare for their search. In 1416, he established a school where geographers, astronomers, and mapmakers helped sea captains improve their **navigation.** That is, they learned how to plan and direct a ship's journey.

With this learning, Portuguese captains could sail south to explore the western coast of Africa. There the Portuguese set up trading centers. Merchants in Africa traded gold and ivory for goods from Portugal. Soon,

Prince Henry the Navigator established a school in Portugal to teach sea captains navigation and other skills.

WHY DIDN'T THE CHINESE "DISCOVER" EUROPE?

Between 1405 and 1433, China sent fleets of up to 300 ships out into the seas to explore. These huge ships visited the lands in the Indian Ocean and traveled down the east coast of Africa.

The last Chinese journey lasted two years and ended in 1433. The Chinese emperor called an end to these journeys because they were too expensive. Since the Chinese already had the things they wanted, Chinese explorers gave the people they visited beautiful gifts and treasures to show their wealth. So the more lands the Chinese explorers visited, the more wealth flowed out of the Chinese treasury. If the Chinese had "discovered" Europe, their discovery might have cost them a fortune!

people began calling the western coast of Africa the Gold Coast.

What Did Bartholomeu Dias Do for Portugal?

In 1481, King John II of Portugal had his sea captains begin to look for a water route to India and China. Such a route would make Portugal rich and powerful! So they carefully sailed south along the western coast of Africa. Each captain went a little farther south. Then mapmakers made maps of the coastline.

In 1487, Bartholomeu Dias sailed around the southern tip of Africa. If the Portuguese could do that, they could also sail eastward to India and China. The weather at the tip of Africa was bad. Dias named it the Cape of Storms. But King John II renamed it the Cape of Good Hope. He did not want the other sea captains to be scared off by the name.

SECTION 1 REVIEW On a separate sheet of paper, write *True* if the statement is true or *False* if the statement is not true. Make each false statement true by changing the underlined word.

1) <u>Portugal</u> controlled the trade routes to India and China during the 1300s.

2) Prince Henry the Navigator established a school for sailors in <u>Portugal.</u>

3) Portuguese sailors first explored the <u>eastern</u> coast of Africa.

4) The Portuguese were the first Europeans to sail around the southern tip of <u>Africa.</u>

5) Bartholomeu Dias named the southern tip of Africa the <u>Cape of Storms.</u>

What do you think

Why do you think King John of Portugal did not want sea captains to be scared by the name "Cape of Storms"?

Finance
To provide the money for something

The plan to reach India and China by sailing around Africa had two problems. First, the weather at the southern tip of Africa made the voyage dangerous. Second, reaching the southern tip of Africa took a long time. Sailing on to India would take even longer.

Christopher Columbus thought that he had a better way to reach the East. He would sail west across the Atlantic Ocean. At the time, his idea seemed strange. How could a sailor reach the Indies by sailing west?

What Did Columbus Find When He Sailed West?

For many years, Columbus tried to get an important person interested in his idea. Then, in 1492, he convinced Queen Isabella of Spain to **finance,** or provide the money for, his voyage. On August 3, 1492, Columbus, his officers, and his crew sailed from Spain in three ships.

First, the ships headed south. Then they caught a wind that blew them west into the unknown waters of the Atlantic Ocean. Early on the morning of October 12, 1492, a sailor sighted land! Columbus thought that he had reached the islands of the East Indies, so he called the people he met "Indians." He was sure that China and Japan were nearby.

In 1493, Columbus returned to Spain. Then he made three more voyages across the Atlantic Ocean. In 1506, Columbus died, still believing that he had discovered a new route to Asia.

Columbus convinced Queen Isabella of Spain to pay for his voyage across the Atlantic.

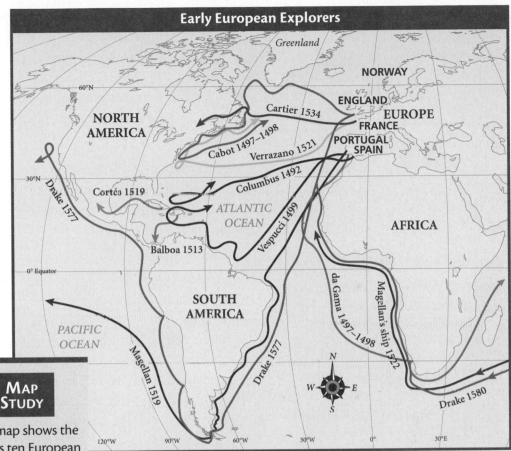

Early European Explorers

Greenland

NORWAY

ENGLAND

EUROPE

FRANCE

PORTUGAL
SPAIN

NORTH
AMERICA

Cartier 1534

60°N

Cabot 1497–1498

Verrazano 1521

30°N

Drake 1577

Cortés 1519

Columbus 1492

ATLANTIC
OCEAN

AFRICA

Vespucci 1499

Balboa 1513

0° Equator

SOUTH
AMERICA

da Gama 1497–1498

Magellan's ship 1522

PACIFIC
OCEAN

Drake 1577

N

W   E

S

Magellan 1519

Drake 1580

120°W   90°W   60°W   30°W   0°   30°E

MAP STUDY

This map shows the routes ten European explorers took during the early years of exploration. In what direction did Drake travel? Who went farther north in the Pacific—Magellan or Drake?

◆Exploration
The act of looking around some unknown place

To Whom Did the Pope Give Land?

As early as the 1450s, the pope gave Portugal control over all African trade and **exploration.** Exploration is the act of looking around some unknown place. Then, 30 years later, the pope gave Portugal the right to explore and trade as far as the East Indies. After the first journey by Columbus, Spain asked the pope what non-Christian areas it might claim.

In 1493, the pope drew a line down a map and divided the world into two parts. He said that Spain could control all new land discovered west of the line. Portugal could control all new land east of the line: Africa and India. But Portugal did not like this decision. So in 1494, officials from Spain and Portugal met to settle the problem. They agreed to move the line farther west. This let Portugal control Brazil in the Americas.

Profit

The amount of money left over after paying for the cost of doing business

What Direction Did Da Gama Sail to Reach India?

Columbus reached land by sailing west. But the Portuguese still wanted to reach India by sailing south and then eastward. In the summer of 1497, Vasco da Gama left Portugal with four ships. Three months later, he rounded the Cape of Good Hope. In May 1498, da Gama reached Calicut, India.

Da Gama and his men returned to Portugal in September 1499. He proved that an all-water route to India existed. Now the Italian city-states would no longer control trade with India and China.

Pass the Pepper, Please

Why did European explorers try so hard to reach the Indies? One answer is in your kitchen—pepper. Ordinary black pepper was not ordinary at all in Europe. Meat was often eaten half-spoiled. Pepper made it taste better. Sailors on long voyages even carried small sacks of peppercorns. But pepper grew only in India and Java.

Italian merchants got rich importing spices, which they sold to the rest of Europe. Then, about 1300, the Turks cut off trade to these eastern lands. So explorers looked for new routes to Asia. Some went south around Africa. Others sailed west . . . and found the Americas.

Europeans did not find the black pepper they were looking for in the Americas. Rather, a new kind of pepper grew there. In 1493, Columbus brought red peppers from Haiti to Spain. Their spicy taste quickly became popular. The use of red pepper then spread to Africa and Asia.

Consumer Science

History in Your Life

Da Gama's ships came back to Portugal loaded with spices like pepper and cinnamon; jewels; and other goods. When they sold this cargo, it brought 60 times the cost of the trip! That was an enormous **profit,** or money left over after the cost of the journey. But of the 170 men who left with da Gama, only 54 were left alive to return to Portugal. He had lost two ships on the journey.

What European Countries Traded With China and Japan?

For most of the 1500s, the Portuguese controlled the spice trade in the East Indies. As the years passed, their ships reached China and Japan, too. But the Chinese and Japanese did not trust Europeans, so the Chinese allowed the Portuguese to trade only in Macau. Soon the Chinese allowed the Dutch and the Spanish to open a trading center in Canton.

Who Was the First to Sail Around the World?

In September 1519, Ferdinand Magellan, a Portuguese captain, set sail from Spain with

Explorer	Explorations Began	Sponsoring Country	Places Explored
Bartholomeu Dias	1487	Portugal	Africa
Christopher Columbus	1492	Spain	West Indies
Vasco da Gama	1497	Portugal	Africa, India
Amerigo Vespucci	1499	Italy	South America
Ferdinand Magellan	1519	Portugal	South America, Pacific Ocean, Philippines, Africa

◆**Expedition**
A long journey of discovery

◆**Native**
Someone born in a particular place

◆**Strait**
A narrow strip of water that connects two bigger bodies of water

five ships and 265 crewmen. King Charles I of Spain asked him to find the western route to India that Columbus had failed to find.

First, Magellan sailed south. Then he turned westward and explored the coast of South America. When some sailors rebelled, Magellan lost one ship. The four remaining ships slowly moved through a **strait** at the tip of South America. A strait is a narrow strip of water that connects two bigger bodies of water. This strait connected the Atlantic Ocean with the Pacific Ocean, but Magellan did not know that. (Geographers now call it the Strait of Magellan.) Soon another ship turned around and returned to Spain.

What Did Magellan Find Beyond the Strait?

After passing through the strait, the three remaining ships reached the calm, open water of the Pacific Ocean. But as they journeyed for three months across this peaceful ocean, things got bad for the crew. They had to eat wormy food, rats, and cooked leather! And their water turned yellow and tasted bad!

Finally the three ships reached the Philippine Islands. Here, in a fight with the **native** people, Magellan was killed. (A native is a person who was born in that place.) Soon, the **expedition**—or long journey of discovery—lost two more ships. All alone, the last ship sailed across the Indian Ocean, down the eastern coast of Africa, around the Cape of Good Hope, and up the western coast of Africa.

In September 1522—three years after leaving Spain—this one ship, with 18 sailors, reached home port. It had sailed around the world and proved three things: First, the world is round. Second, Earth contains much more water than land. Third, the Americas were truly lands that Europeans had not yet seen.

SECTION 2 REVIEW On a separate sheet of paper, write answers to these questions.

1) What was one problem that faced sailors in traveling around the southern tip of Africa?
2) Who thought that he could reach the East by sailing across the Atlantic Ocean?
3) Who was the first European to reach India by sailing around Africa?
4) What are the names of three countries that sent ships to China to trade?
5) Who led the expedition that proved that the world was round?

What do you think

How do you think the Arab and Italian merchants felt when Vasco da Gama's ships sailed into Calcutta? Explain your answer.

◆**Conquistador**
A Spanish conqueror; a person seeking gold and glory

Convert
To change one's religion to another religion or another belief

Some Spaniards liked to explore and discover new places. Others—the **conquistadores,** or conquerors—wanted gold and glory. Jesuit missionaries wanted to **convert** the native population. That is, the missionaries wanted Native Americans to change their religion and become Catholics. These missionaries and the conquistadores came to Central and South America for "God, Gold, and Glory."

What Aztec Legend Helped Cortés?

In 1519 Hernando Cortés sailed with 11 ships to the coast of Mexico. Some 500 soldiers and16 horses sailed with him. Soon, the fleet landed on the Mexican coast in an area that the Aztecs ruled.

Cortés and Montezuma met in peace in 1519. Within months of the meeting, Cortés destroyed Montezuma and the Aztec Empire.

Before this time, the Aztecs had conquered other tribes in the area to create an empire. Montezuma was the Aztec ruler. When he heard that Cortés had landed, the emperor thought of an ancient Aztec legend. According to this legend, the Aztec god Quetzalcoatl had sailed from Mexico toward the East. The legend said that the great feathered god would one day return. According to the legend, Quetzalcoatl was to return that year!

Why Did Montezuma Send Cortés Gifts?

Montezuma had more than 200,000 warriors, but he did not march against the Spanish invaders. Thinking they were gods, he sent golden gifts to them. This was a mistake. The gifts made the Spanish want more gold!

Soon, Cortés met a woman who spoke several native languages. She helped

Cortés speak with the other tribes that the Aztecs had conquered. Many of these tribes hated their Aztec rulers, so they became allies of Cortés.

Negotiate
To talk together, make bargains, and agree on something

How Did the Spanish Treat Montezuma?

Cortés and his 500 men marched to Tenochtitlan, the Aztec city where the emperor lived. When they reached it, Montezuma allowed them to enter. That was his second mistake. For weeks the Aztec emperor and Cortés **negotiated.** That is, they made bargains. Finally, Montezuma agreed to accept the rule of the king of Spain.

But one day, the Spaniards killed Montezuma. Quickly, the Aztecs rebelled and forced the Europeans out of Tenochtitlan. At that point, Cortés asked his Native American allies for help. With the Spaniards, they surrounded the city for three months. Finally, the Aztecs surrendered. Spain had broken the power of the Aztec Empire.

What Did the Conquistadores Do to the Incas?

To the south of Mexico, in the mountains of Peru, the Spanish conquered another empire, the Incas. In 1532, fewer than 200 Spanish conquistadores landed in South America. Francisco Pizarro led them. King Charles V of Spain had told him to conquer South America.

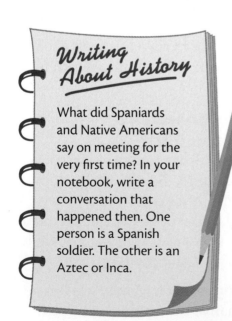

Writing About History

What did Spaniards and Native Americans say on meeting for the very first time? In your notebook, write a conversation that happened then. One person is a Spanish soldier. The other is an Aztec or Inca.

Pizarro and his men marched toward the Inca capital. They came at a time when Atahualpa, the Inca emperor, was fighting a civil war with his brother. Atahualpa heard that the Spanish were coming, so he went out to meet them with many of his people. When they met, Pizarro and his men attacked. The Incas carried no weapons, so the Spanish killed many of them and captured Atahualpa.

The Inca emperor offered to fill a large room with gold if Pizarro would release

Atahualpa was emperor of the Incas in 1532. Pizarro captured and executed him. The Spanish then took control of the Inca Empire.

him. Pizarro agreed. From all parts of the Inca Empire, gold poured into the room until it was full.

How Did Pizarro Treat the Inca Emperor?

The emperor had kept his promise. Now the time had come for Pizarro to keep his. But Pizarro had heard an untrue story that Inca warriors were going to attack. He put Atahualpa on trial and executed him.

The Inca emperor was dead, and his warriors had no guns and no will to fight, so they accepted Spanish rule. By 1535, the Spanish controlled much of the Inca Empire. In time, Pizarro and his men argued over the gold, and they killed him.

Why Did the Empires in the Americas Fall?

In less than 20 years, small groups of Spaniards conquered two large empires in the Americas. How was this possible? Historians give five reasons.

Immunity
A natural protection against a disease

First, they came at the right time. Montezuma believed an Aztec legend was coming true. Pizarro arrived when a civil war was going on. Second, tribes that did not like the Aztecs or Incas joined the Spanish to fight against them. Third, the Spanish had cannons and guns. The Native Americans had never seen weapons like these. Fourth, the Spanish had horses. They were new too. At first, the Native Americans thought that each horse and its rider was a two-headed god. When a rider got off his horse, the god seemed to divide itself into two parts. Fifth, the Spanish brought smallpox and measles to the Americas. But Native Americans had no **immunity,** or natural protection, to these diseases. This killed millions of Native Americans.

Communication in History

The Incan Empire

One problem facing the Incan Empire was that it stretched thousands of miles through the rugged Andes Mountains. At the time, communication was difficult over such a distance. However, to connect its different parts, the Incas built an excellent system of roads. Some ran along the coast. Others crossed the mountains. Woven bridges allowed people to cross rivers and canyons. These roads allowed merchants and officials to travel safely throughout the empire. In addition, they enabled relays of runners to quickly deliver messages.

The Incan Empire faced two other communications problems. Its people spoke several different languages, and there was no system of writing. As a result, the Incas developed an unusual way to keep records—the *quipu*. It was a long cord that had other strings tied to it. The cords were knotted in different ways. Knots and spaces represented different numbers—ones, tens, hundreds. The colors of the cords represented different items. One color meant taxes. Another was used to keep track of food in storehouses.

SECTION 3 REVIEW On a separate sheet of paper, write the word from the Word Bank that completes each sentence.

WORD BANK
Atahualpa
Aztecs
God
Montezuma
Pizarro

1) Many Spaniards came to the Americas in the 1500s for _____, Gold, and Glory.

2) The _____ built a great civilization in present-day Mexico.

3) _____ thought that Cortés was a god.

4) _____ was the leader of the Inca Empire in Peru.

5) _____ put the Inca emperor on trial and executed him.

What do you think

Could the Incas and the Aztecs have defeated the Spaniards? Explain your answer.

◆**Descendant**
A person who comes from a specific group of people

◆**Encomienda**
The Spanish system of forcing Native Americans to do physical work on plantations

◆**Plantation**
A large area of farmland

◆**Viceroy**
An official who governs land for the king or queen

For many years, the Spanish explored the Americas. Hernando de Soto—one of Pizarro's men—went north and explored Florida. Then he turned west. By 1541, he reached the Mississippi River. Another Spaniard, Francisco de Coronado, led an expedition into the southwest of North America. Spain claimed control of this area in 1560 and called it "New Mexico."

Who Ruled New Spain?

Spain also had a name for the land that had once been the Aztec and Inca Empires. These became New Spain. Soon the king of Spain created five provinces in New Spain and sent a **viceroy,** or official, to govern each province. To encourage Spanish settlement, the king gave large areas of land to Spanish conquistadores. Their **descendants,** or family members, formed a class of wealthy landowners.

Why Did the Encomienda Lead to Death?

Spain had a lot of land in the Americas. Spanish landowners wanted to make money on it. To do that, they needed millions of farmworkers. They also needed miners for the silver mines in Mexico. Bringing millions of workers from Spain was not practical. The Spanish forced Native Americans to work for them. The Spanish landowners were cruel to these workers.

Often a Spanish landowner forced a whole village of Native Americans to work on **plantations,** or large areas of farmland. The Spanish called this system of forced labor the **encomienda.** Under this

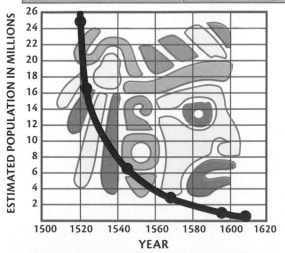

Changes in Native Population of Central America (1519–1605)

ESTIMATED POPULATION IN MILLIONS

YEAR

GRAPH STUDY About how many Native Americans were there in Central America in 1520? in 1560? in 1600?

The Spanish forced Native Americans to work in silver mines. This dangerous work killed many Native Americans.

system, a Spanish landowner had two duties. First, he had to care for the needs of the Native Americans. Second, he had to convert them so that they became Catholics. Most of the time, the landowner paid no attention to the first duty.

Because of the encomienda, thousands of Native Americans suffered and died. At least 20 million Native Americans lived in Latin America when the Spanish first came there. Within 100 years, the Native American population was down to 4 million because of European diseases and hard, dangerous work in the silver mines. But they also died because the Spanish refused to let them practice their customs and traditions. They had to accept new and strange ways of doing things. Because of all this, many Native Americans lost hope.

◆Import
To bring into a country something or someone from another place

How Did Las Casas Try to Help?
A Spanish priest named Bartolomé de las Casas tried to end the sufferings of Native Americans. He wrote to King Charles V and condemned the cruel treatment of the Native Americans by the Spanish. He explained that the Native Americans were dying in great numbers. Something had to be done.

But the plantation owners needed workers, so las Casas suggested that Spain use African workers. Soon Spain began to **import,** or bring, Africans to the Americas. Las

Casas quickly felt sorry that he had ever suggested this. He had solved one problem, but caused another.

SECTION 4 REVIEW Choose the letter of the answer that correctly completes each sentence. Write your answer on a separate sheet of paper.

1) For the Spanish, the former Aztec and Inca Empires became _____.
   a. New Mexico   c. India
   b. New Spain   d. China

2) The Spanish explorer _____ traveled as far west as the Mississippi River.
   a. Hernando de Soto   c. Cortés
   b. Francisco de Coronado d. Pizarro

3) _____ was a Spanish priest who tried to help Native Americans.
   a. Hernando de Soto   c. Francisco de Coronado
   b. Pizarro   d. Bartolomé de las Casas

4) Bartolomé de las Casas suggested to the Spanish king that _____ workers could take the place of Native American ones.
   a. Spanish   c. African
   b. Italian   d. Chinese

5) The Spanish used a system of forced physical labor that they called the _____.
   a. viceroy   c. encomienda
   b. plantation   d. conquistador

What do you think ?

Why did the Spanish treat Native Americans in such a cruel way?

◆**Slavery**
The owning of human beings with the belief that they are property

A slave is a person that another person owns and thinks of as property. Slaves built the Egyptian pyramids. Slaves labored in Greece and Rome. In the ancient world, people became slaves in different ways. Many were captured in wars. Others may not have been able to pay a debt, so they became property of the person they owed.

What European Country Began to Buy and Sell Slaves?

In a small way, **slavery,** or the owning of slaves, had existed in Africa for many centuries. But in Africa, slaves had rights. The owner was not allowed to overwork them. The owner had to let slaves earn money. The slaves could then buy their freedom.

In the 1440s, the Portuguese started buying slaves. They set up slave trading centers along the Gold Coast of Africa and the Gulf of Guinea. In 1518, Spain let Portugal bring African slaves to the Americas. This solved the Spanish labor problem in their American colonies.

What Was the Journey to the Americas Like for Slaves?

In Africa, slaves had rights. But the Europeans took away these rights. European slave traders and owners were cruel. The traders packed African men and women into dirty ships and locked them in chains. The chained slaves spent most of the voyage to the Americas below deck. Their food was unfit to eat, they never had enough water, and slave traders whipped them.

Why Did the Slave Trade Grow?

For over 300 years, slave traders captured and sold into slavery more than 20 million Africans. Of these 20 million, 5 million, or one-fourth, never reached the Americas. They died on ship, and the slave traders threw their bodies into the sea.

The slave trade became popular when colonization began in the Americas. For hundreds of years, African slaves were taken to the Americas. Many died on the way; those who survived had to endure harsh treatment.

Abolish
To get rid of something; to say that something is no longer legal, or lawful

Soon European colonies expanded from South and Central America to North America. As Europe settled more colonies, the slave trade grew. Slaves worked the Spanish sugar plantations in the Caribbean Islands of Cuba and Haiti. They also worked the Portuguese sugar plantations in Brazil.

The English forced slaves to work in the southern colonies of North America. (In 1713, England took control of the slave trade from Spain.) On these southern plantations, slaves worked long hours to raise rice, tobacco, and cotton for their owners. In all these places, slaves had no freedom. Cruel owners beat and killed them.

How Long Did Slavery Last in the Americas?

Slavery in the Americas lasted for almost 400 years. During that time, a number of slaves rebelled. Most of these rebellions failed, but some slaves did gain freedom.

In the 1790s, slaves on the island of Haiti led a successful rebellion. Haiti had the first government in the Americas that free Africans led. Many years passed before the United States **abolished,** or got rid of, slavery. This happened in 1865, after a civil war. In 1888, slavery ended in all of the Americas. At that time, Brazil, in South America, abolished it.

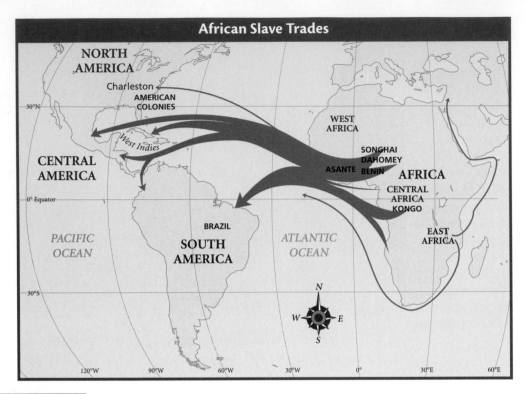

African Slave Trades

NORTH AMERICA
Charleston
AMERICAN COLONIES
30°N
West Indies
CENTRAL AMERICA
0° Equator
PACIFIC OCEAN
BRAZIL
SOUTH AMERICA
30°S

WEST AFRICA
SONGHAI
DAHOMEY
ASANTE BENIN
AFRICA
CENTRAL AFRICA
KONGO
EAST AFRICA
ATLANTIC OCEAN

N
W E
S

120°W   90°W   60°W   30°W   0°   30°E   60°E

MAP STUDY

This map shows different slave trading routes. From which area of Africa—West or Central—did the slave traders take most of the slaves? Besides the West Indies and South America, where else did traders sell slaves? What city in the North American colonies was a slave port?

SECTION 5 REVIEW On a separate sheet of paper, write *True* if the statement is true or *False* if the statement is not true. Make each false statement true by changing the underlined word.

1) The <u>Portuguese</u> were the first Europeans to begin buying and selling African slaves.

2) The slave trade made the traders <u>rich.</u>

3) Over a period of almost <u>700</u> years, traders captured 20 million African men and women.

4) England took control of the slave trade in <u>1600.</u>

5) <u>Haiti</u> was the first country in the Americas in which African slaves rebelled and won their freedom.

What do you think ❓

Why did slave traders begin to buy and sell slaves?

◆**Colonist**
A person who settles in a colony

Majority
More than half of a group of people or group of things

◆**Mayflower Compact**
The agreement made by the Pilgrims that set up a form of government for their new colony

◆**Pilgrim**
A person who came to North America for religious freedom and settled in Plymouth, Massachusetts

Spain, Portugal, the Netherlands, England, and France explored and set up colonies in the Americas. They brought change with them. Some change was good. Other change destroyed whole civilizations in the Americas. In Africa, the slave trade destroyed African life and cultures.

What Was the First English Colony in North America?

Spain was the first country to send explorers to the Americas. It also set up colonies. Then England and France did the same. In 1585, Sir Walter Raleigh established an English colony on Roanoke Island, off the coast of North Carolina. Within three years, all the **colonists**—the people who had started living there—disappeared. No one knows what happened to them.

In 1607, the English established another colony in Virginia. They named it Jamestown after King James I.

Who Helped the English Pilgrims?

In 1620, the **Pilgrims,** who wanted religious freedom, came to North America on the *Mayflower.* On board ship, they agreed to base their government on the rule of the **majority** of men settlers. A majority means that more than half of them had to agree on something to make it a law. Historians call their agreement the **Mayflower Compact.** The Pilgrims named their colony Plymouth.

Half of the Plymouth colonists died during the first winter. However, Native Americans helped them, and

The Mayflower Compact was based on the idea of rule by the majority. It was the beginning of democracy in America.

◆Settlement
A colony; a group of people who had left one place and settled in another place

the Pilgrims soon did well in their new **settlement,** or colony. In time, English settlements grew. By 1733, there were 13 English colonies on the Atlantic coast of North America.

Where Did the French Settle?

The first French colony in North America was Quebec in present-day Canada. Samuel de Champlain founded it in 1608. The French also founded settlements along the Great Lakes and the Mississippi River. (The French mostly trapped animals and traded their furs.)

In the 1680s, the French claimed Louisiana in the lower Mississippi Valley. They named this rich land after King Louis XIV. Like the Spanish, the French gave their land in North America a name—New France.

France and England tried to outdo one another in North America. Both wanted money and power. After a number of wars, France lost its lands in North America. The French and Indian War was a nine-year war between France and England. When it ended in 1763, the English dominated half of the North American continent.

How Did Plants From the Americas Help Others?

When European ships came to the Americas, they carried animals, plants, and goods. Native Americans had never seen horses, pigs, and chickens. They had never grown plants like wheat, oats, rice, apples, bananas, coffee, and sugarcane.

These same ships carried corn and potatoes back to Europe. These became an

European trade ships brought goods to and from the Americas and Europe.

◆ **Economic**
Having to do with money

Starvation
The act of dying from not having enough food to eat

important food for the whole world. Corn and potatoes were easy to grow. With more food to eat, fewer Europeans died from **starvation**—not having enough food. This led to an increase in European population.

The Native Americans grew other crops that were new to people in the rest of the world. Some of these were tomatoes; cacao—for making chocolate; lima beans; and tobacco. Native Americans were the first to use tobacco. They smoked it in pipes. At first, the Europeans used tobacco as medicine. Then they also began to smoke it.

In 1612, John Rolfe planted tobacco in Jamestown. Englishmen were willing to pay high prices for it. Tobacco became an important cash crop for colonists in Virginia and Maryland.

Who Controlled the World at the End of the 1800s?

The Europeans explored the Americas for more than two centuries. During this time, they took control of the rich lands of North America and Latin America. The Spanish, Dutch, English, and French set up colonies in North America. As the years passed, European power grew stronger throughout the world. By the late 1800s, European nations had gained political and **economic** control of India, parts of the Middle East, and most of Africa and Asia. That is, Europe controlled the government and money matters in these places.

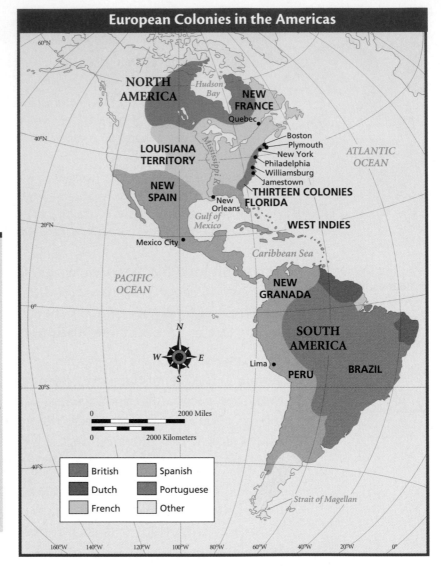

European Colonies in the Americas

NORTH AMERICA

Hudson Bay

NEW FRANCE

Quebec

Boston
Plymouth
New York
Philadelphia
Williamsburg
Jamestown

THIRTEEN COLONIES

LOUISIANA TERRITORY

Mississippi R.

NEW SPAIN

New Orleans

FLORIDA

ATLANTIC OCEAN

Gulf of Mexico

WEST INDIES

Mexico City

Caribbean Sea

PACIFIC OCEAN

NEW GRANADA

SOUTH AMERICA

Lima

PERU

BRAZIL

0   2000 Miles

0   2000 Kilometers

British   Spanish
Dutch   Portuguese
French   Other

Strait of Magellan

60°N 40°N 20°N 0° 20°S 40°S

160°W 140°W 120°W 100°W 80°W 60°W 40°W 20°W 0°

MAP STUDY

This map shows early colonies of North and South America. Which European nation controlled the area around Hudson Bay? How many nations had colonies in South America? Name three nations that had colonies in North America.

SECTION 6 REVIEW On a separate sheet of paper, write answers to these questions.

1) What two American vegetables became an important food for the world?
2) What English colony became the first to grow and remain in North America?
3) What was the Mayflower Compact?
4) Where did the French establish colonies in North America?
5) Which European nation came to dominate half of the North American continent by 1763?

What do you think ?

What do you think happened to the "Lost Colony" at Roanoke?

How the Spaniards Treated the Native Americans

Spanish settlers in the Americas treated the Native Americans cruelly. Landowners forced them to work on plantations. Others labored in mines. Thousands of Native Americans died. Many Catholic missionaries were shocked. One of them was Bartolomé de las Casas. He sailed back to Spain to ask Charles V to protect the Native Americans. Over the years, some laws were enacted in Spain to protect the Native Americans. Most, however, were not enforced in the Spanish colonies.

Las Casas lived to be more than 90 years old. He spent his long life working to defend the Native Americans. This writing is one of his letters to the pope.

That which led the Spaniards to these terrible deeds was the desire for gold, to make themselves suddenly rich, for the obtaining of dignities and honors which were no way fit for them. In a word, their greed, their ambition, gave occasion to their barbarism. For the Spaniards so little regarded the health of their souls that they allowed this great multitude to die without the least light of religion. The Indians never gave them the least cause to offer them violence until the excessive cruelties of the Spaniards, the torments and slaughters of their countrymen, moved them to take arms against the Spaniards.

Among all the notorious crimes committed by the governor, there is one not to be omitted; a certain noble Indian presenting him, perhaps more for fear than love, a present of above nine thousand crowns, the Spaniards, not content with this, tied him to a stake and stretching out his legs, put fire to them, requiring a greater sum of gold. Not able to endure the torment, he sent home for three thousand more. Notwithstanding, the Spaniards kept him so long over the fire that he died.

Sometimes it would happen that a band of Spaniards ranging abroad would light upon a mountain where the Indians were fled for protection from their cruelty. They immediately fell upon the Indians, killing the men, and taking the women captive; and when the Indians pursued them to recover their wives and children, the Spaniards immediately with the points of their swords ran the poor women and children through the bodies.

Source Reading Wrap-Up

1) Who was Bartolomé de las Casas?

2) According to las Casas, why did the Spaniards treat the Native Americans (Indians) so badly?

3) In his opinion, why did the Native Americans fight the Spaniards?

4) What story does las Casas tell about the governor to show his cruelty?

5) What general behavior toward Native Americans does las Casas describe to show Spanish cruelty?

Diseases in Human History

Cortés and his army came to Mexico in 1519. At that time, about 11 million Native Americans lived in central Mexico. By about 1650, fewer than 2 million Native Americans were left. Cruel treatment and hard work had killed some. But diseases from Europe had been the main killer.

In Europe, diseases such as measles were common. Over time, many Europeans had built up a natural immunity, or resistance, to these illnesses. To understand how immunity develops, take a look at measles. For centuries, people in Europe caught measles when they were young. There were no modern medicines. Some children died. Many survived, though. They were now immune to measles. Mothers passed on some of their immunity to their children. They might get measles, but they would recover. This happened generation after generation. Finally, fewer people died from measles.

What made smallpox, chickenpox, measles, and mumps so deadly in America? The Native Americans had never been exposed to them. They, therefore, had no immunity.

Epidemics of these diseases broke out among the Native Americans. An epidemic is a sickness that spreads quickly through a group of people. It affects most of them. The first smallpox epidemic in Mexico began in 1520. It helped the Spaniards defeat the Aztecs. Other smallpox epidemics happened later in the 1500s. Measles and flu were also serious. These diseases swept through villages, killing people of all ages. When adults died, there were fewer people to bear children. The Native American population fell each year. Whole cultures disappeared. Later, the same thing happened to Native Americans in North America.

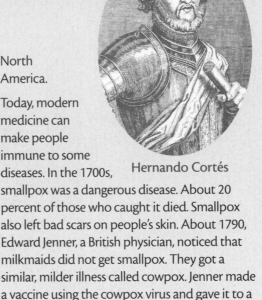

Hernando Cortés

Today, modern medicine can make people immune to some diseases. In the 1700s, smallpox was a dangerous disease. About 20 percent of those who caught it died. Smallpox also left bad scars on people's skin. About 1790, Edward Jenner, a British physician, noticed that milkmaids did not get smallpox. They got a similar, milder illness called cowpox. Jenner made a vaccine using the cowpox virus and gave it to a boy. When tested, the boy was immune to smallpox. Soon many doctors were giving vaccinations or "shots." In 1980, world health officials said that smallpox had been wiped out everywhere.

Scientists have since made vaccines against other diseases. These include measles, mumps, and polio. Most children in the United States now get these shots and others. Many developing countries do not have these health services for their children.

Spotlight Story Wrap-Up

1) Why did the Native American population in Mexico fall after 1519?

2) How do people become naturally immune to a disease?

3) What diseases did Europeans bring to the Americas?

4) What is an epidemic?

5) How did Edward Jenner help wipe out smallpox?

Chapter Summary

➥ Arab merchants and Italian city-states traded in spices and other goods from Asia. In the 1400s, other countries looked for new trade routes.

➥ Prince Henry of Portugal began a school that taught navigation. In 1487, Dias sailed around the tip of Africa, the Cape of Good Hope.

➥ Columbus believed he could reach Asia by sailing west. Queen Isabella of Spain provided money for his voyage in 1492.

➥ In 1493, the pope said that newly discovered eastern lands belonged to Portugal and western ones to Spain.

➥ Da Gama sailed around Africa to reach India in 1498. Eventually, the Portuguese, Spanish, and Dutch traded at certain ports in China.

➥ Magellan's expedition sailed west around the world in 1519–1522, exploring the Pacific Ocean. The trip proved that the world is round and that the Americas were new lands.

➥ Cortés conquered the Aztecs of Mexico in 1519. In 1532, Pizarro's men defeated the Inca Empire.

➥ Guns and horses gave the Spanish an advantage over Native Americans. European diseases also killed many Native Americans.

➥ De Soto explored Florida and reached the Mississippi River. Coronado explored the American Southwest.

➥ Aztec and Inca lands became the colony of New Spain. Under the encomienda system, Spanish land-owners used Native American workers.

➥ Spanish landowners in the Americas began to use African slaves instead of Native Americans. The slave trade was cruel and inhuman. Millions of Africans died. African slaves worked in the Caribbean, Brazil, and the English colonies in North America. Slaves in Haiti rebelled successfully in the 1790s.

➥ England and France wanted colonies in North America. The English settled Jamestown, Virginia, in 1607. In 1620, English Pilgrims settled Plymouth colony. They signed the Mayflower Compact.

➥ Champlain founded Quebec in 1608. The French had fur-trading posts around the Great Lakes. They claimed Louisiana of the lower Mississippi valley. France lost its North American lands in 1763.

➥ Europeans brought new plants and animals, such as horses, to the Americas. Exploration introduced corn, potatoes, tomatoes, chocolate, and other products to Europe.

Comprehension: Identifying Facts

On a separate sheet of paper, use the words from the Word Bank to complete each sentence.

WORD BANK
Columbus
Cortés
da Gama
Dias
Las Casas
Magellan
Montezuma
Pizarro
Prince Henry
Sir Walter Raleigh

1) _____ established a school in Portugal to help sea captains get better at navigation.

2) In 1487, _____ sailed around the tip of Africa.

3) In 1492, _____ sailed west across the Atlantic Ocean to reach Asia.

4) In 1498, _____ left Portugal with four ships and reached India.

5) In 1519, _____ began a three-year trip around the world.

6) In 1519, _____ sailed to Mexico and conquered the Aztec Empire.

7) _____ led the Aztec Empire when the Spanish landed in Mexico.

8) In 1532, _____ marched up the mountains of Peru and conquered the Inca Empire.

9) _____ was a priest who tried to help Native Americans in New Spain.

10) In 1585, _____ established an English colony that later disappeared.

Comprehension: Multiple Choice

On a separate sheet of paper, write the letter of the answer that correctly completes each sentence.

1) Europeans from _____ explored the Americas.
   a. Spain   c. France
   b. England   d. all of the above

2) The first French settlement in North America was _____.
   a. Quebec   c. Jamestown
   b. Roanoke   d. Plymouth

3) The English Pilgrims settled at _____.

   a. Roanoke   c. Plymouth

   b. Jamestown   d. Quebec

4) In 100 years, the Native American population went from 20 million to _____ million.

   a. 10   c. 6

   b. 8   d. 4

5) In 300 years, traders captured and sold into slavery more than _____ million Africans.

   a. 60   c. 20

   b. 40   d. 1

Comprehension: Understanding Main Ideas

On a separate sheet of paper, write the answers to the following questions using complete sentences, or statements.

1) Why did Portugal and Spain want to find a water route to China and India?

2) Why did so many Native Americans die under Spanish rule?

3) What new plants did the Europeans find in the Americas and how did these change European civilization?

Critical Thinking: Write Your Opinion

1) Historians give five reasons why the Spanish defeated the Aztecs and the Incas. Which of these reasons seems the most important to you and why?

2) The Spanish conquistadores said they came to the Americas for "God, Glory, and Gold." Which of these do you think was the most important to them? Explain your answer.

Test-Taking Tip	When taking a true-false test, read each statement carefully. Write *true* only when the statement is totally true. Write *false* if part or all of the statement is false.

Chapter

The Age of Reason

18

1687 to 1789

In 1687, Isaac Newton published an important scientific book. It changed the way people thought about the universe and about society. His scientific reasoning led to the Age of Reason. In this chapter, you will learn about people like Locke and Voltaire who had theories about people and government. You will spend time with enlightened rulers like Maria Theresa of Austria. You will experience the wonder of the music of Mozart—a musical genius. They will all help you understand the belief that order and balance rule the universe.

Goals for Learning

▶ To explain how Isaac Newton's work influenced the Age of Reason

▶ To explain why historians calls this historical period the Age of Reason

▶ To compare the views of Thomas Hobbes and John Locke

▶ To explain the views of Jean Jacques Rousseau concerning the general will

▶ To describe the importance of Denis Diderot's encyclopedia

▶ To name enlightened thinkers, rulers, musicians, and writers

| **1651** Hobbes publishes book on absolute power | **1690** Locke publishes book on human rights | **1748** Montesquieu publishes book on three types of government | **1774** Empress Maria Theresa establishes school for children |

1650   1700   1750   18

| **1687** Newton publishes book about the Universal Law of Gravitation | **1726** Swift publishes *Gulliver's Travels* | **1762** Rousseau publishes book on the general will | **1786** Mozart composes *The Marriage of Figaro* |

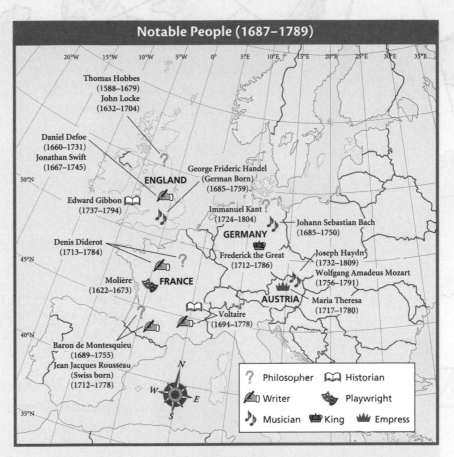

Notable People (1687–1789)

Thomas Hobbes (1588–1679)
John Locke (1632–1704)
Daniel Defoe (1660–1731)
Jonathan Swift (1667–1745)
George Frideric Handel (German Born) (1685–1759)
ENGLAND
Edward Gibbon (1737–1794)
Immanuel Kant (1724–1804)
Johann Sebastian Bach (1685–1750)
GERMANY
Denis Diderot (1713–1784)
Frederick the Great (1712–1786)
Joseph Haydn (1732–1809)
Wolfgang Amadeus Mozart (1756–1791)
Molière (1622–1673)
FRANCE
AUSTRIA
Maria Theresa (1717–1780)
Voltaire (1694–1778)
Baron de Montesquieu (1689–1755)
Jean Jacques Rousseau (Swiss born) (1712–1778)

Legend:
- ? Philosopher
- 📖 Historian
- ✍ Writer
- 🎭 Playwright
- ♪ Musician
- 👑 King
- 👑 Empress

Geography Skills

During the Age of Reason—1687 to 1789—many famous people tried to think reasonably about government, the arts, and society. They made important contributions to history, philosophy, and culture. We remember some of them for their novels and plays. We remember others for the music they wrote. We remember many of them for the way they changed people's ways of thinking.

Study the map and answer the following questions:

1) In what country did Bach write his music?

2) In what year did the philosopher John Locke die?

3) In what year was Maria Theresa of Austria born?

4) For what is Molière famous?

5) What country did the historian Edward Gibbon live in?

Behavior
The way a human being or animal acts

Predictable
Tending to act in a certain orderly way

Reason
Thinking in a logical way

In Chapter 15, you learned about Isaac Newton and his Universal Law of Gravitation. In 1687, he published his law in a book. In it, he showed how this law applied to the universe. He also showed how to use mathematics to describe the law.

What Did Newton's Law Show?

With his law, Newton showed two things. First, with good information, people can correctly predict the movement of any falling object on Earth. Second, they can also correctly predict the movement of the moon and the planets.

How did Newton discover these things? By using **reason,** or thinking in a logical way. He did not experiment. Instead, by reason alone, he discovered a mathematical law that controls the movement of planets and others objects in space.

Isaac Newton influenced people to start using scientific reasoning to solve problems of society, beginning the Age of Reason.

How Did Newton's Reasoning Influence People?

After reading Newton's book, people began to think of the universe as a kind of huge clock. A clock ticks off the minutes of the day in a **predictable,** orderly way. They believed that the universe works this way, too. It is predictable. That is, people can discover what will happen in the universe.

Newton influenced many scientists. They decided to use careful, scientific reasoning to find the truth about how nature worked. He influenced nonscientists, too. They now knew that nature followed natural laws. Perhaps other natural laws controlled the **behavior,** or actions, of human beings. If so, then

Health ✚
History in Your Life

Fake Science and Miracle Cures

Even in the Age of Reason, people could be fooled. They bought "miracle cures" from "quacks." Quacks were individuals who offered fake cures for illnesses. The name quack came from their loud sales talk. Quacks often used scientific-sounding explanations and names for their cures.

One quack treated patients with tools called "Metallic Tractors." He said the tractor could draw a sickness out of someone. This idea fooled even great thinkers such as Benjamin Franklin.

The German Franz Mesmer used a mysterious force called "animal magnetism." In this treatment, patients sat around a tub of water and held hands. Animal magnetism was then supposed to flow through them. Mesmer also used a kind of hypnotism, which put people into a trance-like state. Later, doctors used this technique.

In England, many people were convinced that a woman named Mary Tofts could give birth to rabbits! She became so popular, the king of England was willing to support her. However, it was found out that she was a fake. She was secretly buying rabbits at a local market. She and many others had fooled everyone during a time when science and careful thinking were popular.

scientific reasoning was a tool. They could use this tool to solve the problems of society.

What Was an Enlightened Thinker?

People who believed in scientific reasoning called themselves **enlightened** thinkers. They had found the light! No longer did they walk in the darkness of **ignorance,** or lack of knowledge. Enlightened thinkers asked difficult questions. They searched for the truth about how nature and human societies really work.

What Is the Age of Reason?

Newton began the Age of Reason. During this age, many enlightened thinkers had three goals:

1. They wanted to improve how people live.
2. They wanted to think clearly and logically, without letting their feelings guide them.
3. They wanted to use scientific reasoning to examine every part of society—education, religion, economics, law, and government.

◆**Enlightened**
Having a belief in reasoning; moving away from ignorance

Ignorance
The state of not knowing much

SECTION 1 REVIEW On a separate sheet of paper, write *True* if the statement is true or *False* if the statement is not true. Make each false statement true by changing the underlined word.

1) Isaac Newton discovered the Universal Law of Gravitation by using <u>experiments.</u>

2) Because of his discovery, people began to think of the universe as a giant <u>clock.</u>

3) <u>Enlightened</u> thinkers believed in scientific reasoning.

4) Enlightened thinkers used scientific reasoning to study human <u>behavior</u> and societies.

5) Because scientific reasoning was so important during this period, historians call it the Age of <u>Science.</u>

What do you think

Are there natural laws that can help us predict how people will act? Explain your answer.

The enlightened thinkers of the Age of Reason asked questions about government. What was the best form of government? Are there natural laws that people should follow in setting up a government? These thinkers used logic and reason to find answers.

Contract
A legal agreement

What Did Thomas Hobbes Say About Government?

In 1651, English philosopher Thomas Hobbes published a book on government. According to Hobbes, at one time people lived without any government. Their lives were short and unhappy. At some point, people agreed to give up their freedom to a ruler to gain order and safety.

Hobbes thought that an agreement existed between the ruler and the ruled. Under this agreement, people agreed to obey the rulers even if they ruled poorly. Hobbes said that monarchs needed absolute power to keep people from fighting among themselves. For Hobbes, order was more important than freedom.

What Rights Did Locke Believe People Were Born With?

In 1690, Englishman John Locke published another book on government. Like Hobbes, Locke thought that government should keep order in a society. He also thought that government was a **contract,** or agreement, between the ruler and those who are ruled. But the two men had different ideas, too. For example, Locke believed that people were reasonable. Given the chance, they would act in an orderly manner.

John Locke said every person has the right to life, property, and liberty. He thought government should protect these rights.

In France, Baron de Montesquieu believed that the government must have separate branches to divide the power.

Unlike Hobbes, Locke believed that people had rights. In fact, they were born with three rights: the right to life; property; and **liberty,** or freedom. The job of government was to protect these rights. Locke said that people kept these rights even when they agreed to be governed. He said that people had a right to rebel when the ruler or government did not protect their rights.

What Did Montesquieu Say About Government?

Across the English Channel in France, two enlightened thinkers also published books about government. One of them was Baron de Montesquieu. He studied the government of ancient Rome and governments in his own time. Then, in 1748, he published a book about his studies.

◆**Liberty**
Freedom

Virtue
Goodness to one another

Montesquieu thought that a spirit held together every type of government. Fear kept the dictator in office. Honor, or keeping their promises, kept monarchs ruling. Montesquieu thought that the best monarchs used their wealth and power for the good of everyone. **Virtue,** or goodness, held a republic together. Montesquieu said that people in a republic needed to elect people who would serve the good of the community.

What Are Separate Powers?

Montesquieu admired the English government of the 1700s. It divided power into three branches.

1. Parliament made the laws.
2. The king enforced the laws.
3. The courts interpreted the laws.

French thinker and writer Jean Jacques Rousseau believed that all people are equal. He also thought that people are born good, but society makes them do bad things.

Montesquieu said that separating these powers kept each of the three branches from becoming too powerful. Each branch checked and balanced the powers of the two other branches.

How Did Rousseau Differ From Hobbes?

The other French thinker and writer of this time was Jean Jacques Rousseau. Rousseau said that people had once done only good things. Why did they begin to do bad things? Because civilizations developed.

This was just the opposite of what Hobbes had said. The English philosopher believed that people were born greedy and selfish. Civilization made them responsible and orderly.

Rousseau turned Hobbes's idea upside down. He said that people were born good and that civilization

An Enlightened Government

Montesquieu thought that a government should have three parts. If political power were split, no one group would have too much power. Each branch would balance the other. This idea has become a driving force for many governments today.

These ideas were put to practice in England first, then they spread to America. Americans such as Thomas Jefferson and James Madison had studied Locke and Montesquieu. In 1787, Americans who believed in these ideas designed a government based on "separation of powers." It had three branches. The legislative branch to make laws, the executive branch to carry them out, and the judicial branch to decide what the laws mean. The United States government and other governments still use this system. (You will learn exactly how the United States government came to be in Chapter 20.)

Then and Now

Privilege
A special right given to a person or to a group of people

Value
A belief or an idea that people think is important

made them do bad things. "Man is born free," he wrote, "but everywhere he is in chains."

Rousseau strongly believed that peasants were just as good as kings and nobles. He said that no one was better than anyone else, so no one should have any special **privileges,** or rights. All were equal.

What Did Rousseau Mean by "General Will"?

In 1762, Rousseau published his book on government. In it, he disagreed with Hobbes and Locke and their idea of a contract between the ruler and the ruled. Rousseau said that in order to get along, people made a contract with each other, not with a ruler. He thought that shared customs, traditions, and **values** held together a community of people. A value is a belief or an idea that people think is important.

Rousseau called these shared customs, traditions, and values the "general will." According to Rousseau, a community expressed what it wanted through its general will. Because of this, Rousseau favored rule by the majority.

SECTION 2 REVIEW On a separate sheet of paper, write answers to these questions.

1) According to Thomas Hobbes, who should rule a government?

2) What did John Locke believe about rights?

3) Why did Montesquieu believe that powers should be separated into several branches of government?

4) What did Rousseau say about people that was different from what Hobbes said?

5) What does Rousseau's term "general will" mean?

What do you think

Why might Locke's theory of rights appeal to people today?

◆**Enlightenment**
A time in European history when thinkers and writers tried to solve the problems of society by using reason

◆**Salon**
A meeting of artists, writers, and thinkers in a Paris home during the Enlightenment

Enlightened thinkers wanted to improve government. But they also wanted to change or reform unreasonable customs and traditions. They asked society to allow people to have political, economic, and religious freedom. In fact, they thought that more liberty could improve the lives of everyone.

What Is the Enlightenment?

During the middle 1700s, many French writers and artists criticized their society. They wanted to use reason to solve society's problems. Their writings began a movement that historians call the **Enlightenment.** Enlightened thinkers lived all over Europe. But Paris became the center of the Enlightenment.

What Was a Salon?

Enlightened people met to talk about new ideas. In Paris, wealthy women invited writers, artists, and educated nobles to gather in their homes. They called these meetings **salons.** During the evening, a guest might read a poem aloud. Another guest might play some music. The guests talked about new books, plays, and the latest scientific ideas. They loved to talk and share their opinions.

Marie Therese Geoffrin had the most famous salon in Paris. Every Monday and Wednesday, she gave dinner parties for the most important people of the Enlightenment. (Jean Jacques Rousseau came to her salon.) In fact, Catherine the Great paid someone to attend Madame Geoffrin's dinners. She did this so she would know what enlightened people were talking about.

People used salons during the Enlightenment to share new ideas, poetry, and music.

What Rights Did Voltaire Think People Had?

Voltaire was an enlightened French thinker who influenced many people. He wrote histories, poetry, and over 50 plays. In these, he criticized the wealth and privileges of French kings and nobles. Twice, King Louis XV put Voltaire in jail to keep him from criticizing the French monarchy.

Voltaire defended a person's right to think and to say anything. He is reported to have said, "I do not agree with a word you say, but I will defend to the death your right to say it." Voltaire also supported freedom of religion. Free speech, free press, and religious freedom seemed to him to be rights that belonged to every person. According to Voltaire, governments had to respect these rights.

Free speech, free press, and religious freedom are important human rights, according to Voltaire.

Why Did Diderot Publish an Encyclopedia?

During the Age of Reason, scientists and other people discovered many new things. Frenchman Denis Diderot decided to publish a set of books containing all this new knowledge. He wanted to put together all this knowledge so that everyone could learn it.

Beginning in the 1740s, Diderot spent 30 years working on his encyclopedia. More than 200 important thinkers—such as Rousseau and Voltaire—wrote articles for the encyclopedia. Madame Geoffrin, famous for her salon, helped finance Diderot's work.

How Long Did Diderot Work on His Encyclopedia?

Diderot's encyclopedia was a collection of articles that explored new learning. It also questioned people in authority in every field of learning. Diderot published the first volume of his encyclopedia in 1751. For 21 years, he worked to complete his encyclopedia. Finally, in 1772, he published the final book. Publishers sold thousands of this 28-volume set in France and other countries in Europe. The work of Diderot helped spread the ideas of the Enlightenment.

What Enlightened Things Did Frederick the Great Do?

The Enlightenment influenced several monarchs in Europe. These enlightened monarchs accepted reason as important in governing. Two of these monarchs were Frederick the Great and Empress Maria Theresa of Austria.

Frederick the Great rejected the divine right of a king to rule. He thought that the idea was unreasonable. The Prussian ruler said that he was king because he was the person most able to lead. Frederick wanted to fight the ignorance and the **prejudices** in Prussia. A prejudice is an unfair and unreasonable opinion. People who are prejudiced form an opinion without having all the facts.

Frederick the Great wanted to enlighten his people and reform his country. He made the court system more just. During this time, governments often used torture to get people to confess to a crime. Frederick **banned,** or got rid of, torture, except for the crimes of murder and treason.

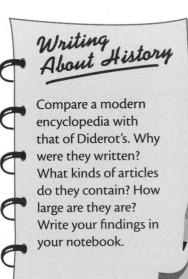

Writing About History

Compare a modern encyclopedia with that of Diderot's. Why were they written? What kinds of articles do they contain? How large are they are? Write your findings in your notebook.

Frederick asked people to be more tolerant of different Christian religions. He improved the lives of German farmers by giving them seed and rebuilding homes and barns. Frederick so impressed Voltaire that the French thinker called him "Frederick the Great." Voltaire was the first person to give the Prussian ruler that name.

What Enlightened Thing Did Empress Maria Theresa Do?

The Enlightenment also influenced other European rulers. Many of them tried to change old customs and traditions. They tried to

MARIA THERESA: 1717–1780

Empress Maria Theresa had to fight for her throne because she was a woman. Her father was the Holy Roman Emperor. When he died, other rulers denied her right to become empress. In the following war, she lost one province to Frederick the Great. Her husband, however, did become Holy Roman Emperor. As his wife, she had 16 children. Her daughter, Marie Antoinette, became queen of France.

Maria Theresa was a wise ruler who followed Enlightenment ideas. She established public education in Austria. Its goal was a better-educated workforce. Maria Theresa also made the lives of Hungarian serfs better.

improve the lives of their people. In 1774, Empress Maria Theresa of Austria used government money for an enlightened cause. She established schools for all children between the ages of 6 and 13.

SECTION 3 REVIEW On a separate sheet of paper, write the word from the Word Bank that completes each sentence.

WORD BANK
Diderot
Frederick
Geoffrin
Paris
Voltaire

1) The center of the Enlightenment was the city of _____.

2) Madame _____ held famous parties, or salons, for enlightened thinkers.

3) _____ was an enlightened thinker who favored free speech, free press, and religious freedom.

4) The encyclopedia by _____ spread the learning of the Enlightenment.

5) The enlightened ruler _____ the Great urged his people to be more tolerant of different Christian religions.

What do you think

Are free speech, free press, and religious freedom important? Explain your answer.

◆Baroque
The type of complex music developed in the late 1600s

Composer
A person who makes up music

Fugue
A type of baroque music in which the melody is repeated

Melody
A tune

As you know, Enlightenment ideas influenced scientists, philosophers, reformers, and rulers. But the idea of an orderly universe governed by natural laws also influenced musicians, writers, and painters.

What Is Baroque Music?

The Age of Reason produced important new musical forms. At the end of the 1600s and during the early 1700s, **baroque** music became popular. (This French word means *strange.*) Renaissance music had sounded simple; baroque music sounded more complex.

During this time, **composers**—people who make up music for musicians to play—wrote **fugues.** In a fugue, the composer uses different musical instruments to repeat a **melody,** or tune. Perhaps the composer has the flute play the melody first. Then the composer changes the melody a

Dancing during the Age of Reason followed a precise pattern of movement. The minuet was a popular dance. It involved slow movements, bowing, and toe pointing.

little and repeats it on a trumpet. Sometimes, the composer uses two or three melodies in one fugue. Johann Sebastian Bach and George Frederick Handel were great baroque composers.

What Is Classical Music?

By the mid-1700s, another type of music appeared. Following the ideas of the Enlightenment, this new music was orderly and balanced. Musicians called it **classical** music. Historians used the word *classical* to describe the order and balance of ancient Greek art. The musicians of the Age of Reason used the same word to describe their music.

The classical period of European music lasted from 1750 to 1820. Classical musicians developed forms of music that are still popular today. One of the most important of these new forms was the **symphony.** It is a long musical work played by a group of musicians using many different instruments.

Why Is Haydn the "Father of the Symphony"?

Joseph Haydn and Wolfgang Amadeus Mozart were two of the most important classical composers. Historians call Haydn the "father of the symphony." He was the first European to compose a complete symphony using string

Joseph Haydn wrote over a hundred symphonies in his life. He has been called the "father of the symphony." This picture shows a symphony orchestra.

and **woodwind** musical instruments. A woodwind instrument is one that a musician plays by blowing into it. During this time, artisans made these instruments out of wood.

One of the most famous composers of classical music was Wolfgang Amadeus Mozart of Austria. As a young boy, he shocked people with his musical talent. Unfortunately, he died young and poor. However, he left behind some of the world's most beautiful music.

How Did Mozart Show He Was a Musical Genius?

Amadeus Mozart was a musical genius. Haydn's student, Mozart began to compose music at age 5 and played the piano for European nobles at age 8. By age 13, he had written his first opera. He wrote more than 600 musical works before he died at age 35. However, he died a poor man. Today, his music is more popular than when he was alive. Singers and musicians perform his operas *The Magic Flute* and *The Marriage of Figaro* around the world.

Which Writers Examined Human Nature?

During the Age of Reason, writers carefully observed what was going on around them. They often wrote books about the foolish actions they had seen. In 1726, Englishman Jonathan Swift published *Gulliver's Travels.* In this book, Swift made his readers laugh at the foolish things people do. Writers observed foolish actions in France, too. It was there that Molière wrote plays. His plays made fun of the behavior of French nobles and middle-class people.

Woodwind
An instrument a musician plays by blowing into it

Other books were written based on real events. In the novel *Robinson Crusoe,* English author Daniel Defoe told the story of a shipwrecked man named Robinson Crusoe. Living on a deserted island, Crusoe had to find a way to continue his life without civilization.

What Kind of History Did People Study?

The study of history also became popular during the Age of Reason. Historians studied the civilization of ancient Greece and Rome. Edward Gibbon wrote an important book called *The Decline and Fall of the Roman Empire.*

SECTION 4 REVIEW Choose the letter of the answer that correctly completes each sentence. Write your answer on a separate sheet of paper.

1) During the Enlightenment, baroque musicians developed the _____, a new form of music.

    a. classical   c. fugue

    b. symphony   d. melody

2) Classical musicians developed the _____, a new form of music.

    a. fugue   c. baroque

    b   symphony   d. flute

3) _____ was a great baroque musician.

    a. Bach   c. Haydn

    b. Mozart   d. Defoe

4) _____was a great classical musician.

    a. Bach   c. Molière

    b. Defoe   d. Mozart

5) _____ wrote plays during the Enlightenment.

    a. Mozart   c. Molière

    b. Haydn   d. Bach

What do you think

How might the Enlightenment have influenced painters? Hint: Think about order and balance!

What Is the Enlightenment?

Immanuel Kant was a German philosopher (1724–1804). He believed in using reason to solve human problems. People who did so were called "enlightened." This excerpt is from an essay Kant wrote in 1784. In it, he explains the term "enlightenment."

Immanuel Kant

Enlightenment is man's leaving his self-caused immaturity. Immaturity is the incapacity to use one's intelligence without the guidance of another. Such immaturity is self-caused if it is not caused by lack of intelligence, but by lack of determination and courage to use one's own intelligence without being guided by another. . . . Have the courage to use your own intelligence! is therefore the motto of the enlightenment.

Through laziness and cowardice a large part of mankind . . . gladly remain immature. It is because of laziness and cowardice that it is so easy for others to usurp the role of guardians. It is so comfortable to be a minor! If I have a book which provides meaning for me, a pastor who has conscience for me, a doctor who will judge my diet for me and so on, then I do not need to exert myself. I do not have any need to think; if I can pay, others will take over the tedious job for me. The guardians who have kindly undertaken the supervision will see to it that by far the largest part of mankind, including the entire "beautiful sex," should consider the step into maturity, not only as difficult but as very dangerous. . . .

But it is more nearly possible for a public to enlighten itself: this is even inescapable if only the public is given its freedom. . . .

All that is required for this enlightenment is *freedom;* and particularly the least harmful of all that may be called freedom, namely, the freedom for man to make *public use* of his reason in all matters. . . .

The question may now be put: Do we live at present in an enlightened age? The answer is: No, but in an age of enlightenment. Much still prevents men from being placed in a position . . . to use their own minds securely and well in matters of religion. But we do have very definite indications that this field of endeavor is being opened up for men to work freely and reduce gradually the hindrances preventing a general enlightenment and an escape from self-caused immaturity. In this sense, this age is the age of enlightenment. . . .

Source Reading Wrap-Up

1) How does Kant define immaturity?

2) For Kant, what is the motto of the enlightenment?

3) According to Kant, how do people avoid becoming mature?

4) What does the public need to become enlightened?

5) Did Kant think that he lived in an enlightened age? Why or why not?

In Defense of Women's Rights

Enlightenment thinkers often wrote about the rights of men. Nearly all ignored the rights of women. Mary Wollstonecraft tried to change that attitude. In the 1700s, women had few rights. They could not own property. If they worked, their pay went to their fathers or husbands. A husband could divorce his wife and take the children. A woman could not do the same.

Mary Wollstonecraft was born in London in 1759. As was typical, her brother Edward was sent away to a good school. Mary went to a day school where she learned French and composition. Years later, she and her sisters started a school for small children. From this experience, she wrote her first book. It was called *Thoughts on the Education of Daughters.* It contained ideas that she would develop in the future.

To earn a living, she took a job as a child's governess. Afterward, she described the experience. "I entered the great gates [of the house] with the same kind of feeling I should have if I was going to the Bastille." (The Bastille was a prison in Paris.)

Finally, her luck changed. She began working for a publisher. In 1792, she went to France where the French Revolution was underway. There she wrote two more books. One was a collection of original stories for children. The other book defended the ideals of the French Revolution.

French political ideas led to Mary's most important book. Published in 1792, it was called *A Vindication of the Rights of Women. Vindication* means "defense." She wrote, "I wish to see women as neither heroines nor brutes; but reasonable creatures." Women, she argued,

Mary Wollstonecraft

should have the same rights as men. They should be entitled to a good education to develop their minds. Her book is still important in the history of women's rights.

Her book became popular. Mary became famous throughout Europe. She met other people who held similar ideas. One was William Godwin, a free-thinking political writer, whom she married. In August 1797, their daughter was born. Mary died a few days later at the age of 38.

Her daughter, Mary Godwin, also became a writer. She married the poet Percy Bysshe Shelley. In 1818, Mary Wollstonecraft Shelley wrote a book that is still famous. It tells about a scientist who created a monster. The scientist's name is the title of the book: *Frankenstein!*

Spotlight Story Wrap-Up

1) In the 1700s, men had many rights that women did not. What were some of them?

2) What was Mary Wollstonecraft's most important book?

3) What were her views about education?

4) Who was William Godwin?

5) Why is Mary Wollstonecraft's daughter famous today?

➡ The Age of Reason changed the way people thought about the universe. Ideas of order and balance influenced ideas about government.

➡ Newton's scientific discoveries introduced the ideas of natural, universal laws that could predict natural events. People began to look for natural laws in human behavior and society. Believers in reason were enlightened thinkers. They wanted to use reason to improve people's lives and all parts of society. This movement is called the Enlightenment.

➡ Thomas Hobbes, an English philosopher, believed strong rulers were needed to keep peace in society. John Locke thought that people and their government made a contract, or agreement. He wrote that people had rights to life, liberty, and property. Government was to protect those rights.

➡ Montesquieu and Rousseau were enlightened French thinkers. Montesquieu thought that government powers should be divided among separate branches. Rousseau believed that people were naturally good, but that civilization made them evil. He wrote that people made a contract with each other. Their shared values, the general will, created a community.

➡ During the Enlightenment, people met to discuss ideas. In Paris, these meetings were known as salons.

➡ Voltaire was a French philosopher and writer. He defended people's right to free speech, a free press, and religious freedom.

➡ Denis Diderot in France wrote a many-volume encyclopedia including the knowledge of the Age of Reason.

➡ Some European monarchs adopted Enlightenment ideas. Frederick the Great of Prussia rejected the idea of the "divine right" of kings. He believed in religious tolerance and made the court system more just. Maria Theresa of Austria set up schools for children.

➡ Enlightenment ideas influenced artists as well as scientists and rulers. In baroque music, composers such as Bach and Handel wrote complex pieces such as fugues.

➡ Classical music was balanced and orderly. Joseph Haydn developed the symphony form. Wolfgang Amadeus Mozart, his student, wrote hundreds of works in his short lifetime.

➡ Enlightenment writers used reason to examine society and history. These writers included Swift, Defoe, and Gibbon in England, and Molière in France.

Chapter 18   Review

Comprehension: Identifying Facts

On a separate sheet of paper, use the words from the Word Bank to complete each sentence.

WORD BANK

Handel
Diderot
Geoffrin
Hobbes
Locke
Maria Theresa
Montesquieu
Newton
Rousseau
Voltaire

1) _____ discovered a law that made Europeans begin to use scientific reasoning.

2) _____ believed that rulers should have absolute power.

3) _____ believed that people had the right to life, liberty, and property.

4) _____ believed in separation of powers in government.

5) _____ said that all people were born good.

6) Madame _____ held the most famous salon in Paris.

7) _____ criticized the French government and the king put him in jail.

8) _____ published the first encyclopedia.

9) Empress _____ of Austria was an enlightened ruler.

10) _____ was a famous baroque composer.

Comprehension: Multiple Choice

On a separate sheet of paper, write the letter of the answer that correctly completes each sentence.

1) Enlightened thinkers believed that _____ could lead them to truth.

   a. feeling   c. experiments

   b. reason   d. government

2) According to Montesquieu, the spirit of a republic is _____.

   a. virtue   c. honor

   b. fear   d. rebellion

3) Hobbes thought that order was more important than _____ in a society.

   a. government   c. freedom

   b. writing   d. virtue

4) _____ composed music during the Age of Reason.

   a. Handel   c. Bach

   b. Mozart   d. all of the above

5) Many enlightened thinkers thought that reason could solve the problems of _____.

   a. society   c. woodwind

   b. fugue   d. privilege

Comprehension: Understanding Main Ideas

On a separate sheet of paper, write the answers to the following questions using complete sentences, or statements.

1) Why do historians call the years 1687 to 1789 the Age of Reason?

2) Why do historians also call these years the Enlightenment?

3) What did Hobbes and Locke agree and disagree about with regard to government?

Critical Thinking: Write Your Opinion

1) The enlightened thinkers during the Age of Reason believed that they could make societies and people better by using reason. Do you agree with this belief?

2) According to Rousseau, people are born good. Society creates people who do bad things. What do you think of this theory? If possible, give examples to explain your answer.

| Test-Taking Tip | When taking a true-false test, look for words such as *many, some, sometimes, usually,* and *may.* These words mean that the statement can have exceptions. |

Reference materials are sources for finding different kinds of information. Here are some examples of reference materials and the kinds of information you can find in them.

General information almanac: Book of recent and historical facts and figures about many subjects

Atlas: Book of maps of countries, states, and some cities

Encyclopedia: One book or a set of books with summaries and histories of many different subjects

Gazetteer: Dictionary of geographic place names and information

Newspaper: Daily or weekly publication with national, local, sports, and business news and regular features

Periodical index: Listing of magazine articles by subject and the publication in which they appear

Internet: Worldwide computer network with information on a variety of subjects; includes on-line encyclopedias, newspapers, and periodicals

Here is a list of research questions. You could probably find the answers to all of them somewhere on the Internet. Name at least one other listed source that you could use to answer each question.

1) Where could you find a short biography of Queen Isabella of Spain?

2) What kind of government does Austria have today?

3) You remember seeing a magazine article about foods and dishes brought from Africa by slaves. Where can you find the date and name of the publication in which it appeared?

4) Where could you find a map of Spain with an inset of Madrid?

5) Where could you find information about the Andes Mountains?

6) Where could you find information about instruments used for navigation in modern submarines?

7) Where could you look for results of a vote taken in Congress yesterday?

8) What are the names of some compositions by Joseph Haydn?

9) In what part of England is Plymouth located?

10) Who is the present king of Spain?

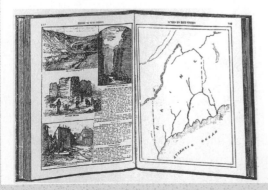

➡ As European nations developed, feelings of nationalism grew.

➡ Moorish kingdoms in Spain were centers of learning. The Catholic rulers Ferdinand and Isabella united Spain against them. By 1492, the last Moorish kingdom fell. In the 1500s, Spain was Europe's strongest nation. Its king was also the Holy Roman Emperor Charles V.

➡ Philip II of Spain sent the Spanish Armada to invade England and make it Catholic again. Fast English ships and a storm defeated the Armada.

➡ James I and Charles I of England believed in the "divine right" of kings. Civil war broke out between the king's supporters and Puritans who supported Parliament. The Puritans won and executed Charles I for treason. Cromwell led a strict military government. In 1661, Parliament restored the English monarchy. After the Glorious Revolution of 1688, William and Mary ruled England.

➡ Louis XIV of France centralized its government. He was Europe's most powerful ruler.

➡ Peter the Great and Catherine the Great were absolute rulers in Russia. Peter wanted to modernize Russia. Frederick the Great of Prussia went to war against Maria Theresa of Austria. Prussia became strong.

➡ Arab traders controlled the Asian spice trade. Other countries looked for new trade routes to Asia. Prince Henry of Portugal set up a school for sea captains. Portuguese ships sailed around the tip of Africa to India.

➡ In 1492, Columbus sailed west to reach Asia. In 1519–1522, Magellan's expedition sailed around the world and across the Pacific Ocean.

➡ Spaniards went to the Americas for "God, Gold, and Glory." They conquered the Aztecs of Mexico and the Incas in Peru.

➡ Landowners in New Spain began to bring slaves from Africa. Millions of Africans died in the slave trade.

➡ England and France started colonies in North America. France lost its North American colonies to England in 1763.

➡ Newton's discovery of natural, universal laws introduced the Age of Reason.

➡ Enlightenment thinkers wanted to use reason to improve society. Hobbes, Locke, Montesquieu, Rousseau, and Voltaire wrote about government. Locke said people had natural rights to life, liberty, and property.

➡ Handel and Bach were baroque composers. Haydn and Mozart were classical composers. The Age of Reason influenced writers such as Swift and Molière.

Comprehension: Identifying Facts

On a separate sheet of paper, use the words from the Word Bank to complete each sentence.

<table>
<tr><td>WORD BANK</td></tr>
<tr><td>absolute</td></tr>
<tr><td>conquistador</td></tr>
<tr><td>divine right</td></tr>
<tr><td>encomienda</td></tr>
<tr><td>monarch</td></tr>
<tr><td>nationalism</td></tr>
<tr><td>navigation</td></tr>
<tr><td>predictable</td></tr>
<tr><td>reason</td></tr>
<tr><td>salon</td></tr>
</table>

1) The English philosopher Hobbes said that rulers should have _____, or unlimited, power.

2) King James I of England believed that he ruled by _____.

3) When feudalism ended, _____ developed as people became loyal to their country or nation.

4) Another name for a king or a queen is _____.

5) A _____ was a Spanish conqueror who looked for gold and glory in the Americas.

6) The _____ was the Spanish system of forcing Native Americans to do physical work on plantations and in silver mines.

7) Prince Henry of Portugal established a school to teach sea captains _____.

8) Enlightened thinkers used _____ to figure out how to deal with the problems in society.

9) Newton had helped people see that _____ laws governed nature.

10) During the Enlightenment in Paris, people gathered at a _____ to discuss ideas.

Comprehension: Multiple Choice

On a separate sheet of paper, write the letter of the answer that correctly completes each sentence.

1) During the English Civil War, _____ led the Roundheads.

    a. Charles V   c. Locke

    b. Magellan   d. Cromwell

2) _____ led the expedition of ships that finally sailed around the world for the first time.

a. Montesquieu   c. Columbus

b. Magellan   d. Pizarro

3) _____ of Spain financed the voyages of Columbus.

a. Maria Theresa   c. Isabella

b. Elizabeth I   d. Catherine the Great

4) _____ began the Age of Reason.

a. Newton   c. Montesquieu

b. Hobbes   d. Locke

5) _____ wrote books during the Age of Reason.

a. Swift   c. Haydn

b. Louis XIV   d. Elizabeth

Comprehension: Understanding Main Ideas

On a separate sheet of paper, write the answers to the following questions using complete sentences, or statements.

1) What is an absolute monarch?

2) What did the Spanish want from the Americas?

3) How did the Age of Reason affect some rulers, philosophers, musicians, and writers?

Critical Thinking: Write Your Opinion

1) In Chapters 16 through 18, you experienced the age of kings, the age of exploration, and the age of reason. Which of these did you like best and why?

2) Pick a king or queen, an explorer, or an enlightened thinker that you like. What do you like best about this person? What questions would you like to ask this person?

| Test-Taking Tip | When a test item asks you to write a paragraph, make a plan first. Jot down the main idea of your paragraph. List the supporting details you can include. Then write the paragraph. |

"You cannot hope to build a better world without improving the individuals. To that end each of us must work for his own improvement, and at the same time share a general responsibility for all humanity, our particular duty being to aid those to whom we think we can be most useful."

—Marie Curie, from her *Autobiographical Notes*, 1891

Revolution, Reforms, and Empires

1750 to 1914

During the last part of the eighteenth century, two great revolutions occurred. One—the American Revolution—led to the United States of America. The other—the French Revolution—led to great change in Europe. Soon, revolution swept through Latin America, too.

But another revolution was also taking place at this time—an industrial one. Partly because of this, imperialism swept across the world. In the nineteenth century, European nations established colonies in Africa and Asia.

In this unit, you will learn about factories. You will march with revolutionaries in search of freedom. You will meet nationalism and imperialism face to face. You will watch native peoples in Asia and Africa lose control of their government and their lives. All this happens in less than 200 years, and you get to be a part of it. And along the way, you meet many important people—dreamers, fighters, and inventors.

Unit

7

Chapter 19

The Industrial Revolution

1750 to 1850

Beginning in the 1750s, workers left farms and moved to cities. There, they labored in factories instead of at home. In this chapter, you will learn more about these factories. You will meet inventors who changed the way people worked and lived. You will discover inventions such as the flying shuttle, the steam locomotive, the light bulb, and the telephone. These inventions and other great changes were all part of the Industrial Revolution.

Goals for Learning

▶ To name the economic conditions needed for industrialization to take place

▶ To explain what was revolutionary about the economic changes that took place in England during the Industrial Revolution

▶ To describe the benefits and problems of industrialization

▶ To identify important inventions that helped industrialization

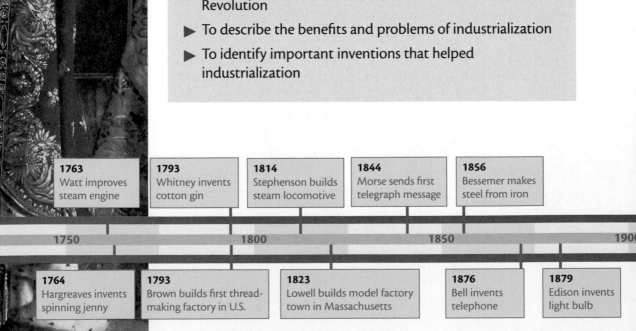

1763 Watt improves steam engine	1793 Whitney invents cotton gin	1814 Stephenson builds steam locomotive	1844 Morse sends first telegraph message	1856 Bessemer makes steel from iron

1750 — 1800 — 1850 — 1900

1764 Hargreaves invents spinning jenny	1793 Brown builds first thread-making factory in U.S.	1823 Lowell builds model factory town in Massachusetts	1876 Bell invents telephone	1879 Edison invents light bulb

The British Isles

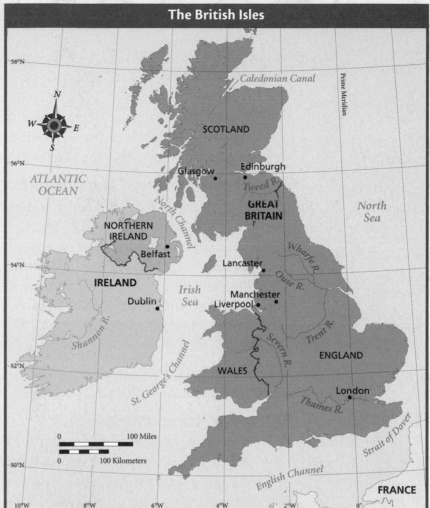

The British Isles consists of two large islands and many smaller ones. Scotland, Wales, and England are on the larger island that we call Great Britain. Between 1750 and 1850, Great Britain became the center of the Industrial Revolution. Industry changed the way people worked and where they lived.

Study the map and answer the following questions:

1) What channels separate Ireland from Great Britain?

2) What are the names of three cities in England?

3) What is the major river of Ireland?

4) In what area of Great Britain is the Caledonian Canal located?

5) What sea is to the east of Great Britain?

Geography Skills

Beginning in the 1750s, quick economic change came to England. Before then, workers made things by hand in their homes. Now they began to work in factories and use machines to produce goods. Before this time, people had used their own strength or the strength of animals to provide power. Now they used the steam engine.

◆**Capital**
Money used to make more money; money used to start a business

◆**Industrial Revolution**
The important changes that took place in the way work was done during the eighteenth and nineteenth century

◆**Natural resources**
Things—such as coal, ore, and water—that come from nature and help humans

Ore
A rock that contains metals

What Is an Industrial Revolution?

We call all these changes the **Industrial Revolution.** What does this term mean? *Industrial* means to work or labor. *Revolution* means an important change in the way something is done. So the term *Industrial Revolution* means an important change in the way people work. During the Industrial Revolution, people stopped making goods by hand. They began to use machines to produce goods.

In the mid-1700s, England had three things that helped it industrialize: **natural resources,** plenty of workers, and **capital** to build factories and machines.

What Are Natural Resources?

Factory owners need power to run machines. In the 1750s, England could industrialize because it had a source of power. In fact, it had three. Coal, iron **ore,** and rivers. The heat from burning coal turned water into steam power. The iron ore in rocks was made into iron tools and machines. Fast-moving rivers provided power for machines. Nature supplied the coal, the ore, and the rivers. We call these things natural resources. They come from nature, so they are natural. They help us, so they are resources.

Why Did England Have So Many Workers?

Factory owners need workers to run their machines. In the 1850s, England had a large group of workers. Between 1750 and 1800, the population of England increased by 50 percent because there was a new food source from the Americas—the potato.

At the same time, the English government forced farmworkers off the land. How did they do this? The government passed

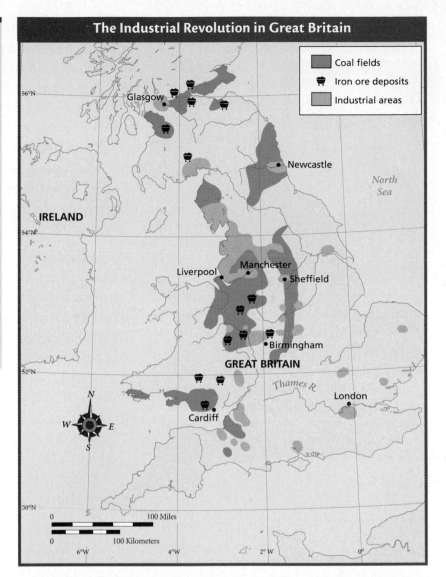

The Industrial Revolution in Great Britain

a law that allowed rich landowners to fence in open fields. For hundreds of years, poor families had farmed these unfenced lands. Now they had no land to farm. So factory owners now had two work sources—an increased population and farmers who had no land to farm.

What Is Capital?

Factory owners need power to run machines and people to work these machines. But where do the machines and the factories come from? The factory owners must buy and build them. Owners do this with capital, or money that they use to make more money.

In 1776, Adam Smith published one of the most important books on economics. It was called *An Inquiry Into the Nature of the Wealth of Nations.* Smith thought that people should be free to produce and sell products at a profit. Government should not interfere in this process. Competition would produce the best goods at the lowest prices.

Smith's ideas are called "capitalism." Capital is money that is used to produce more money. In a capitalist system, individuals and private businesses own and control most of the capital. Today, the United States is the most powerful capitalist nation in the world.

Did the Industrial Revolution Spread Beyond England?

This change in the way people worked began in England, but it soon spread to other countries. By 1860, Germany was industrialized. By the 1870s, the United States became a powerful industrial nation. Today, the process of industrialization, or getting machines to do work, is still going on.

Economists, or people who study money, often divide the people of the world into two groups. One group lives in industrialized nations that have factories to produce goods. The second group lives in developing nations that do not have an industrial economy. Nations need these things to industrialize: capital to buy machines and start up factories, a source of power to make machines work, and workers to run the machines.

◆Economist
A person who studies the way people make and use money and goods

What do you think

What are some new sources of power that factory owners use today as they industrialize?

SECTION 1 REVIEW On a separate sheet of paper, write *True* if the statement is true or *False* if the statement is not true. Make each false statement true by changing the underlined word.

1) Important economic changes beginning in the 1750s took place mainly in <u>Spain</u>.

2) By the <u>1820s</u>, the United States became an industrial nation.

3) England had <u>three</u> sources of power to run its machines.

4) England had many workers because its population increased <u>50</u> percent between 1750 and 1800.

5) Some English people had <u>capital</u> to buy machines and open factories.

Spindle
The part of a spinning wheel that twists fiber into yarn

◆ **Textile**
Cloth that workers weave from cotton, silk, or wool

For industry, people had to invent new machines and discover new sources of power. In the 1700s, English inventors made several new machines for the **textile** industry. A textile is a cloth that workers weave from cotton, silk, or wool.

What Inventions Helped the Textile Industry?

In 1733, an English weaver named John Kay invented a "flying shuttle." A shuttle is the part of a weaving machine that carries the thread from one side to the other. The flying shuttle did this more quickly than the human hand could. Because of the flying shuttle, workers could weave twice as much cloth.

To weave more cloth, workers needed more yarn. At that time, people working at home used a spinning wheel to spin yarn. Each spinning wheel had only one **spindle.** (A spindle twists thread into yarn.) But all the spinning wheels in England could not produce all the yarn the weavers needed.

Manufacturers built large textile mills like this one in Lancashire, England. These mills could produce large amounts of textiles quickly.

Then in 1764, James Hargreaves invented a machine to spin wool or cotton yarn. He called his machine the "spinning jenny." It was a spinning wheel with eight spindles instead of one. In the same year, Richard Arkwright invented a large machine that produced tighter cotton yarn than the spinning jenny.

In 1778, Samuel Crompton combined the spinning jenny and Arkwright's invention into the "spinning mule." This machine could spin a thread 150 miles long from a single pound of cotton!

Why Did Manufacturers Build Factories?

Before this time, people spun yarn at home and wove it into cloth. Textile **manufacturers** brought wool, cotton, and silk to the workers' homes. But hand work at home was slow and costly, and manufacturers wanted to save time and money. They built factories, and workers then left their homes and came to the factory to work. The factory system brought workers, machines, and a source of power together to produce a product.

This system changed the way people worked. The worker now had to work when and where the manufacturer said. The worker had to work the hours the manufacturer wanted. And, the worker had to do the amount of work the manufacturer demanded.

What Problem Did Cotton Growers Have?

Textile workers in factories now needed more cotton to spin into yarn and to weave into cloth. But getting cotton

The cotton gin allowed workers to separate seeds from cotton faster than doing it by hand. It made cotton, which is used to make cloth, a much more valuable material.

◆Export
To send a product out of one country and into another to sell; a product that is sent from one country to another

Fiber
A thread of cotton, silk, wool, or other material

from the field to the factory was hard work. Natural cotton contains sticky, tightly-held seeds. In the 1700s, people had to remove these seeds by hand. This took a lot of time.

Then, in 1793, Eli Whitney invented a machine that solved the problem. While fixing other machines in Georgia, Whitney invented the cotton gin. His invention was a wooden box with a wire brush and grille, or screen. Workers placed cotton on one side of the grille. Then the revolving brush grabbed the cotton and pushed it through the grille. The seeds were too large to pass through the screen, so the machine separated the seeds from the cotton **fiber,** or thread.

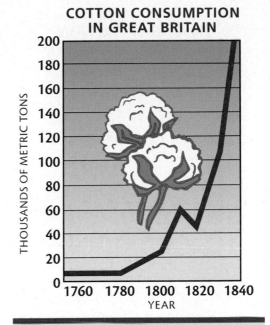

COTTON CONSUMPTION IN GREAT BRITAIN

THOUSANDS OF METRIC TONS

YEAR

GRAPH STUDY

What does this graph show? During which years did cotton consumption increase the most in Great Britain?

With the cotton gin, workers could clean cotton 50 times faster than by hand. Within 20 years, cotton became the most important **export** from the southern United States. (An export is a product that someone sends to another country to sell.) Cotton farmers exported most of this cotton to the textile factories in Great Britain.

What Is Mass Production?

Whitney made little money from his invention of the cotton gin. But he became wealthy as a gun manufacturer. Before Whitney, workers made guns one at a time. Each part of a gun was a little different from the same part on

COAL OUTPUT IN GREAT BRITAIN

MILLIONS OF TONS

40
36
32
28
24
20
16
12
8
4
0

1760 1780 1800 1820 1840

YEAR

GRAPH STUDY What does this graph show? During which years did coal output increase the most in Great Britain?

Assemble
To put the parts of something together

Coke
Purified coal

Identical
Exactly alike

Impurity
Something that makes a material not pure

◆Mass production
A way of making large amounts of the same thing in a factory

another gun. Whitney had workers make gun parts that were **identical.** That is, they were all the same.

Then the workers **assembled,** or put together, these identical parts to make identical guns. The guns were alike in every way. We call this **mass production.** It greatly cuts the time workers need to make something, so they can produce more.

What Takes Impurities Out of Iron?

Manufacturers built their new industrial machines from iron. In 1709, Englishman Abraham Darby found a way of making iron with **coke,** or purified coal. Coal became a valuable natural resource. However, making iron was still a problem because iron ore had **impurities,** or things in it that made iron products break easily. In the late 1700s, someone discovered that stirring hot iron helped burn off the impurities.

Who Found a Way to Make Steel?

In 1856, Englishman Henry Bessemer found a way to get rid of more impurities in iron. He discovered that air forced into melted iron burned away these impurities. His process produced a new product—steel. It was stronger than iron and did not break as easily. Soon, steel manufacturing became an important industry in many industrial countries. Those countries that had large amounts of coal and iron ore built steel mills.

The English built their steel mills in the north. In Germany. the Ruhr Valley became a great steel center. In the United States, Pittsburgh, Pennsylvania, became an important steel-producing city.

Henry Bessemer developed a low-cost way to make steel. Steel became an important building material after it was invented. This picture shows a steel mill.

SECTION 2 REVIEW Choose the letter of the answer that correctly completes each sentence. Write your answers on a separate sheet of paper.

1) The _____ industry became more profitable with the invention of the flying shuttle, spinning jenny, and spinning mule.

    a. steel   c. cotton

    b. iron   d. textile

2) The factory system brought together _____ to produce a product.

    a. workers   c. a source of power

    b machines   d. all of the above

3) _____ invented the cotton gin.

    a. Whitney   c. Hargreaves

    b. Kay   d. Bessemer

4) The term _____ means producing identical products in great number.

    a. spinning jenny   c. textile

    b. mass production   d. industry

5) _____ discovered a way to make steel from iron.

    a. Whitney   c. Bessemer

    b. Kay   d. Hargreaves

What do you think

What is good and what is bad about the factory system?

Locomotive
A self-propelled vehicle that runs on rails

◆Transportation
The movement of people, natural resources, and finished products from one place to another

Improved **transportation** also helped industrialization. Transportation is the movement of people and things from one place to another. Industry needs good transportation.

The problem with transportation in the early 1700s was that people had to travel on dirt roads. When rain fell, the dirt turned into thick mud that horses and carriages sunk into. In 1770, two Scotsmen—Thomas Telford and John McAdam—developed better road-building methods. Telford built roads in two layers, so water quickly ran off. McAdam built roads of crushed stone.

How Did Canals Help Industry?

For many years, manufacturers used roads to move products that did not weigh so much. Then, in the 1760s, workers dug the first modern canal in England. (The United States built its first canal in 1825.) The seven-mile-long canal stretched from Manchester to a coal mining area nearby. Now, manufacturers could easily move large amounts of coal from mines to cities, so coal became cheaper.

On a canal, manufacturers could ship heavy products like coal. But canals cost a lot of money to dig, and they needed a source of water. Good roads were a faster means of transportation for moving light products from place to place. But no one could travel fast on them in rainy weather.

English manufacturers had a problem. They needed to quickly move large amounts of products—light or heavy—to different places in any type of weather. But roads got muddy and canals needed water. What could these manufacturers do?

How Did the Steam Engine Change the Textile Industry?

The answer to the manufacturers' transportation problem was a steam **locomotive.** This is a self-propelled vehicle that runs on rails. But before learning about that, you need to know about steam engines. In 1705, the simple steam

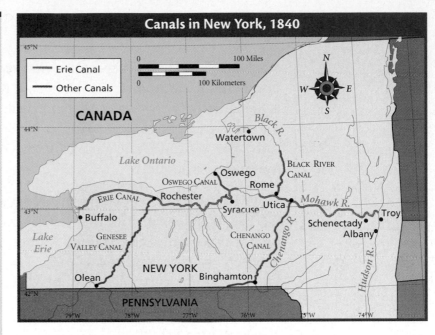

Canals in New York, 1840

Efficient
Working well with little loss of time or energy

engine was invented. Workers used it to pump water out of coal mines.

In 1763, James Watt began to look for a way to improve the steam engine and make it more **efficient,** or so it would waste little time or energy. In 1773, Watt developed a steam engine that turned wheels. Textile machines had wheels, so this new engine could operate those machines.

Up to that time, swiftly falling water produced the power to run textile machines. Manufacturers had to build textile factories next to fast-moving streams. Now manufacturers could power their textile machines with steam engines. They could build their factories anywhere. By 1800, more than 500 steam engines were powering machinery in British factories.

Who Is the Founder of Railroads?

Early in the 1800s, workers used a little steam engine on wheels to pull small carts of coal out of mines. This steam engine did the work of one or two horses. Then, in 1814, George Stephenson—a mining engineer—built a steam locomotive. It moved along iron rails, or bars, on the ground. These rails went on and on and became a kind of road, so the locomotive traveled on a road of rails, or a railroad.

Stephenson called his locomotive *Blucher*. He had discovered a way to increase the heat in the **boiler.** (A boiler is the tank that heats water.) By increasing the heat, Stephenson produced steam under higher **pressure,** or force. *Blucher* could pull almost 30 tons of coal at a speed of four miles per hour.

How Fast Could Stephenson's Next Locomotive Go?

In 1829, Stephenson built the *Rocket*—a faster locomotive. At that time, some businessmen wanted to build a railroad between Liverpool and Manchester. They had a contest to find a locomotive to quickly go this distance. Stephenson entered the contest and won.

Stephenson's *Rocket* pulled a train of cars for more than 30 miles. It reached a speed of 30 miles per hour. This meant that the *Rocket* was more powerful than 80 horses pulling together. Stephenson went on to design railroad bridges, tunnels, and the roadbed for the Liverpool and Manchester Railway. Today, historians call him the "founder of the railways."

Why Did Railroads Become Important?

Railroads became the most important form of transportation in the nineteenth century. During the 1840s and 1850s, they crossed back and forth across England. They greatly helped factory owners. How? By providing them with a fast and inexpensive way to move **raw materials** and finished products. (Raw materials are the materials such as cotton, wood, iron, and oil that workers use to make things.)

George Stephenson's *Rocket* could reach a top speed of 30 miles per hour.

Railroads

Stephenson's invention of the steam locomotive started a race. Who could develop the fastest, more efficient transportation for people and goods? After the steam locomotive came the diesel, and then the even faster electric locomotive. The first trains traveled about four miles per hour. Today, Japan and France have high-speed trains that travel up to 160 miles per hour.

Countries also began to build miles and miles of tracks. The world's longest railroad line is the Trans-Siberian Railroad. It runs 5,500 miles—from Moscow to Vladivostock.

The United States has over 150,000 miles of rail in use today. About 40 percent of goods are still shipped by rail. But less than 1 percent of city passenger transportation is by rail.

Railroads needed metal rails, cars, and locomotives. The iron and steel industry grew quickly. Railroad owners hired thousands of workers to clear land and lay railroad tracks. Other European countries also built railroad lines. In 1869, the United States completed the transcontinental railroad. It linked the two coasts together.

SECTION 3 REVIEW On a separate sheet of paper, write answers to these questions.

1) Why is good transportation needed for the growth of industry?

2) What was one big problem with transportation in the 1770s?

3) Why were canals not the best type of transportation for industry?

4) Who found a way of making the steam engine more efficient?

5) Why is George Stephenson important in the history of transportation?

What do you think

How would cheap coal help industry grow?

Industry greatly changed many cities. This picture shows the crowded living conditions and soot-filled air of Manchester, England, in 1876.

Before the 1750s, most people worked as farmers in small villages. Each family grew its own food and made its own clothing. Many people never traveled more than ten miles from where they were born.

Industrialization changed all this. People in Great Britain first experienced its changes. But in the 1800s, industrialization also changed Europe and the United States. However, British textile factories still made more than half of the world's cotton cloth. In fact, British factories produced so many goods that people called Great Britain the "workshop of the world."

What Laws Stopped the Spread of Industrialization?

For many years, Great Britain tried to keep other countries from learning the lessons of industrialization. In fact, Britain passed laws so that merchants could not sell new machines to other countries. Up until the 1840s, Britain also refused to let skilled workers leave the country. People feared that these workers could design or make tools and machinery that would help other countries industrialize.

How Did A British Worker Help the United States?

In 1789, Samuel Slater—a British factory worker—memorized how to build a spinning machine. Then he dressed himself as a simple farmer and got on a ship sailing to the United

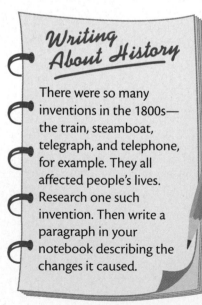

Writing About History

There were so many inventions in the 1800s—the train, steamboat, telegraph, and telephone, for example. They all affected people's lives. Research one such invention. Then write a paragraph in your notebook describing the changes it caused.

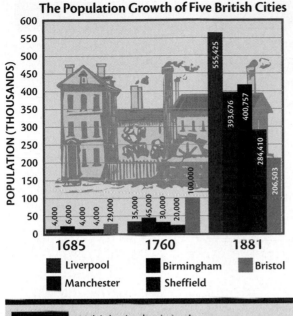

The Population Growth of Five British Cities

POPULATION (THOUSANDS)

1685: Liverpool 4,000; Manchester 6,000; Birmingham 4,000; Sheffield 4,000; Bristol 29,000

1760: 35,000; 45,000; 30,000; 20,000; 100,000

1881: 555,425; 393,676; 400,757; 284,410; 206,503

■ Liverpool ■ Birmingham ■ Bristol
■ Manchester ■ Sheffield

GRAPH STUDY Which city had the largest population in 1685? Which city had the largest population in 1881? How many people did it have?

States. (British officials would have stopped him if they had known he could build a spinning machine.) Once in the United States, Slater met Moses Brown—a Rhode Island businessman. In 1793, Brown built the first thread-making factory in the United States. He used spinning machines that Slater built.

What Did Lowell Do for His Factory Workers?

In 1823, Francis Lowell built a factory town named after himself at Lowell, Massachusetts. He hired young farm women to work in his factory. First, he taught them how to work the textile machines. Then he set up a school to teach them how to read and write. Finally, he gave them a clean place to live. Soon, textile mills spread throughout the New England states. However, few factory owners followed Lowell's ideas.

What Did Industrialization Do to Cities?

Industrialization changed the way people worked. It also changed where they lived. Before the Industrial Revolution, most people lived on farms, not in cities. Then

---

Child Labor Laws

As industry increased, factory owners began to hire children. They could pay them much lower wages than men. Children might work as many as 14 hours a day. Their working conditions were often dangerous as well. Some British orphans were treated almost like slaves.

Reformers began to force governments to stop the evils of the factory system. Reformers wanted to protect children and give them a chance to go to school. Early laws failed to correct these evils. Later laws carried more power. Today, Europe, North America, Australia, and New Zealand enforce child labor laws. In the United States, the minimum age for employment is 14. The work must be done outside of school hours, and it cannot be in manufacturing.

Careers
History in Your Life

In less developed countries, however, millions of children still work. Some as young as seven years old work in quarries, mines, and factories.

1750 to 1850   *The Industrial Revolution*   Chapter 19   **495**

Telegraph Provides Instant Communication

Samuel Morse, an artist and inventor, invented the telegraph in the United States in the 1830s. Two British men, Charles Wheatstone and William Cooke, also made a telegraph machine.

The telegraph freed communication from the problems of long distance transportation. In the United States, the Pony Express service was discontinued in 1861. The telegraph was much faster.

The telegraph also solved a traffic control problem for railroads. Using the telegraph, railroad workers could keep track of trains. This helped them avoid accidents. Railroads also used the telegraph to check on schedules, passengers, and freight shipments.

Injure
To hurt someone or to hurt oneself

◆**Labor union**
An organized group of workers who try to improve their working conditions in a factory and the amount of money they earn

manufacturers began to build factories near cities. People from the country then moved to the cities to get work.

Industrialization caused city populations to grow quickly. For example, in 1750, the English town of Manchester had less than 16,000 people. By 1850, it had become a major textile center with a population of almost 400,000. From 1800 to 1850, the number of European cities with a population of more than 100,000 doubled to nearly 50.

But bigger cities created problems. People lived in unhealthy conditions. Garbage filled the streets. Bad water and sanitation caused disease. Still, people moved to the cities to find jobs. In fact, by 1900, almost 75 percent of the people of Great Britain lived in cities.

What Problems Did Factory Workers Have?

As you know, during the Industrial Revolution, unskilled workers came to cities for work. Whole families labored in factories. Children as young as six years old worked eight to fourteen hours a day. They worked among dangerous machines. But factory owners refused to pay for doctors to help workers **injured,** or hurt, by these machines. Also, owners refused to pay workers if they were hurt or sick and could not work for a while.

Workers wanted safer factories, more pay, and shorter hours. But they could not get what they wanted, because the law did not let them form **labor unions.** A labor union

Alexander Graham Bell demonstrates how to use his telephone, which he invented in 1876.

Thomas Edison poses with perhaps his greatest invention, the light bulb. He invented it in 1879.

is an organized group of workers who try to improve things.

The workers could not change the law because they had no political power. In England, only people who owned property could vote. But most factory workers owned no property, so they could not vote. Without a vote, they could not could change the laws that kept them from forming unions.

What Two New Sources of Power Changed the World?

As you know, coal and steam provided power for the Industrial Revolution. But in the late nineteenth century, inventors discovered two new sources of power—electricity and oil.

The use of electricity began in the 1840s when Samuel F. B. Morse invented the telegraph. With this machine, he could send messages over long distances by making and breaking an electric current. In 1844, Morse sent his first message from Washington, D.C., to Baltimore, Maryland. For the message, he used a code he had created. In this code, a long or short electrical signal represented each letter of the alphabet. This was called Morse code.

In 1866, workers laid a cable on the floor of the Atlantic Ocean to carry electrical messages between the United States and Europe. Before this, messages took days to deliver; now they took minutes.

In 1876, Alexander Graham Bell invented the telephone. For the first time, a human being could hear another person's voice over an electrical wire. In 1879, Thomas Edison invented the light bulb. It provided safe light

The Wright brothers successfully flew an airplane in 1903 at Kitty Hawk, North Carolina. They went on to build planes for the U.S. Army.

to homes, businesses, and factories.

Why Was the Discovery of Gasoline Important?

Oil was another important new source of power. Before the 1860s, people mostly used oil to grease wheels. Now, they began to use it to provide heat and to power machinery.

People learned that they could make gasoline from oil. Gasoline ran the **internal combustion engine** that Gottlieb Daimler invented in 1885. The internal combustion engine made the automobile possible. In 1903, Wilbur and Orville Wright—two American men who liked to work with machines—were the first to successfully fly an airplane. They used a gasoline engine.

Internal combustion engine
An engine that burns gasoline to produce power

SECTION 4 REVIEW On a separate sheet of paper, write the word from the Word Bank that completes each sentence.

WORD BANK

Bell

Daimler

Lowell

Morse

Slater

1) In 1789, Samuel _____ left England and came to the United States to build spinning machines.

2) In 1823, Francis _____ built a model factory town in Massachusetts.

3) In 1844, Samuel _____ sent the first telegraph message.

4) In 1876, Alexander _____ invented the telephone.

5) In 1885, Gottlieb _____ built the internal combustion engine.

What do you think

Do you think industrialized nations should let workers form labor unions? Explain your answer.

A Manchester Housewife's Weekly Budget in 1833

Living and working conditions were terrible in manufacturing areas during the early 1800s in England. As a result, Parliament formed committees in the 1830s to see how factory workers were doing. Parliament wanted to know if they earned enough to feed, clothe, and house themselves. This report discusses the weekly budget of a housewife in Manchester, a manufacturing city.

A word about English money: the "s" after a number stands for shilling. A "d" means pence. One shilling contains 12 pence. Twenty shillings at this time were equal to five dollars.

Mrs. B., Manchester. This witness was accidentally met with, 13th May, 1833. She was waiting for Dr. Hawkins, to consult him about her niece's health. I took her into a room, and examined her about the customs and comforts of operative families. . . .

Her husband is a fine spinner, at Mr. M's, where he has been from 1816, has five children. Her eldest daughter, now going on 14, has been her father's helper for three years. At present her husband's earnings and her daughter's together amount to about 25s a week.

Breakfast is generally porridge, bread, and milk, lined with flour or oatmeal. On Sunday, a cup of tea and bread and butter. Dinner, on weekdays, potatoes and bacon, and bread, which is generally white. On a Sunday, a little fresh meat, no butter, egg, or pudding. Tea time every day, tea, and bread and butter; nothing extra on Sunday at tea. Supper, oatmeal porridge and milk; sometimes potatoes and milk. Sunday, sometimes a little bread and cheese for supper; never have this on a weekday. Now and then buys eggs when they are as low as a halfpenny apiece, and fries them with bacon.

They never taste any other vegetable than potatoes; never use any beer or spirits; now and then may take a gill of beer when ill, which costs a penny. . . .

The house consists of four rooms, two on each floor; the furniture consists of two beds in the same room, one for themselves and the other for the children; have four chairs, one table in the house, boxes to put clothes in, no chest of drawers, two pans and a tea kettle for boiling, a gridiron and frying pan, half a dozen large and small plates, four pair of knives and forks, several pewter spoons.

Source Reading Wrap-Up

1) What kind of work does the husband in this family do?
2) How much money does the family make in a week?
3) How many people are in this family?
4) Do you think this family's diet is a healthy one? Why or why not?
5) Do you think that the family's housing is adequate? Why or why not?

Hard Times and Charles Dickens

"Now what I want is, Facts. Teach these boys and girls nothing but Facts. Facts alone are wanted in life. Plant nothing else, and root out everything else. . . . This is the principle on which I bring up my own children, and this is the principle on which I bring up these children. Stick to the Facts, Sir!"

Charles Dickens

So wrote Charles Dickens in *Hard Times*, one of his many novels. *Hard Times* is a story about the difficult lives of textile workers. Through Dickens's novels, a reader can relive the world of nineteenth century England. He was the greatest observer of his times. And, like the schoolmaster in *Hard Times*, Dickens gathered the facts of his world. He used actual people, places, and social groups in England in his writings. But unlike the schoolmaster, Dickens's mind took "a fanciful photograph" of a person or place. He turned facts into unforgettable stories. The schoolroom and master in *Hard Times* are only examples of this ability. Dickens had a gift for describing places and creating memorable characters. As a result, he is called "the greatest master of English character since Shakespeare."

Dickens's novels captured the sights and sounds of a world that no longer exists. Today, there are no debtors' prisons. But Dickens helps the reader picture these terrible places. There are no more stagecoaches, but he makes you feel their bumpy ride. There are no more workhouses for poor orphaned children. But Dickens shows you the children. You see the poverty, hopelessness, and hard work that ages them beyond their years.

When he was a young man in the 1830s, Dickens found work as a journalist. In 1836, he published his first novel *The Pickwick Papers*. Then he wrote *Oliver Twist*. Oliver is a boy caught in a world of crime and workhouses for the poor. The novel appeared in parts in a monthly magazine. *A Christmas Carol* came next. It is the story of Ebenezer Scrooge, a greedy man with a heart of stone. In the end, Scrooge comes to a new understanding about life. He learns that joy can come from kindness to others.

Dickens's stories are a time machine to the past. Through them, we travel through time and experience a different world.

Spotlight Story Wrap-Up

1) Who was Charles Dickens?

2) Dickens said that he would take a "fanciful photograph" of a person or place. What did he mean?

3) What kind of work did Dickens do when he was young?

4) How did readers first experience the story of *Oliver Twist*?

5) Why are Dickens's novels valuable for historical purposes?

Chapter Summary

➡ The Industrial Revolution began in England in the 1750s. England could industrialize because it had coal, iron ore, and rivers as natural resources. A growing population and farmers looking for work increased the workforce. There was capital to build factories and buy machinery.

➡ By 1860, Germany was industrialized. By the 1870s, so was the United States. The world became divided into industrialized and developing nations.

➡ The English invented new machines, making textile manufacturing possible. Kay invented the flying shuttle to make weaving faster. Hargreaves developed the spinning jenny to spin yarn faster. Crompton invented the spinning mule to spin thread faster.

➡ Manufacturers built factories to save time and money. The factory system brought workers, machines, and power together to make a product.

➡ Whitney's cotton gin cleaned cotton faster. He also developed mass production to speed up the assembly of goods.

➡ Darby developed an improved way of making iron with coke. In 1856, Bessemer discovered how to make steel.

➡ Manufacturers could use roads for light-weight loads, but not when they were muddy. In the 1760s, manufacturers started using canals for heavy loads, but canals needed water.

➡ Watt improved the steam engine, so it could power factories. Stephenson built the first steam locomotive. Railroads were the most important means of transportation in the nineteenth century. They were a fast and cheap way to move raw materials and finished goods.

➡ England kept information about industrialization secret. However, in 1789, Slater built the first spinning machine in the United States.

➡ Industrialization caused the growth of cities. Workers moved to cities for jobs in factories.

➡ Workers wanted better working conditions and wages. Laws kept them from forming unions. Most workers could not vote because they did not own land.

➡ In the late nineteenth century, electricity and oil were new sources of power. Morse invented the telegraph. Bell developed the telephone. Edison invented the electric light. Daimler invented the internal combustion engine. The Wright Brothers made the first successful airplane flight.

Comprehension: Identifying Facts

On a separate sheet of paper, use the words from the Word Bank to complete each sentence.

WORD BANK
Bessemer
Daimler
Hargreaves
Kay
McAdam
Morse
Slater
Stephenson
Watt
Whitney

1) In 1733, the English weaver John _____ invented the flying shuttle.

2) In 1764, James _____ invented a machine that increased the amount of yarn that one person could spin.

3) In 1770, John _____ built roads of crushed rock and improved transportation.

4) In 1773, James _____ developed a way to make the steam engine turn wheels.

5) In 1793, Eli _____ invented a simple machine that separated the seeds from cotton.

6) In 1814, George _____ built a steam locomotive called *Blucher*.

7) In 1789, Samuel _____ brought plans for a spinning machine to the United States.

8) In 1844, Samuel _____ sent the first telegraph message.

9) In 1856, Henry _____ invented a way to remove impurities from iron to make steel.

10) In 1885, Gottlieb _____ invented the internal combustion engine.

Comprehension: Multiple Choice

On a separate sheet of paper, write the letter of the answer that correctly completes each sentence.

1) Something from nature that people use is called a _____.

   a. mass production   c. capital

   b. industrial revolution   d. natural resource

2) New machinery first helped the _____ industry.

   a. steel   c. gasoline

   b. textile   d. electric

3) The automobile was made possible by the _____ engine.

   a. internal combustion   c. iron

   b. steel   d. steam

4) A _____ is a person who hires people to work with machines to make something to sell.

   a. economist   c. manufacturer

   b. capital   d. labor union

5) _____ is a way of making large amounts of the same, or identical, thing in a factory.

   a. Mass production   c. Natural resource

   b. Raw material   d. Capital

Comprehension: Understanding Main Ideas

On a separate sheet of paper, write the answers to the following questions using complete sentences, or statements.

1) Why do historians use the word *revolution* to describe the industrial changes that took place in England during the 1700s?

2) What three conditions are necessary for an industrial revolution to take place in a country?

3) Why is a good transportation system needed for the growth of industry?

Critical Thinking: Write Your Opinion

1) Which invention from the Industrial Revolution was the most important and why?

2) During this period, would you have moved from the farm to the city to work in a factory? Explain your answer.

Test-Taking Tip | When you read true-false questions, the statement must be absolutely correct. Words like *always* and *never* tell you the question is probably false.

An Age of Revolution

1775 to 1815

Economic and political revolutions bring change. In this chapter, you will become part of the American Revolution. This change brought about a new nation—the United States. Across the ocean, the French watched this revolution and learned from it. You will see how they too revolted. Then you will meet Napoleon, a military leader. With him, you will march into a Russian winter and end up on a rocky island in the Atlantic. This chapter will help you understand how revolution changed Europe and America.

Goals for Learning

▶ To list the causes of the American Revolution

▶ To explain how the American Revolution changed the world

▶ To describe the causes of the French Revolution

▶ To describe the Reign of Terror

▶ To list the accomplishments and failures of Napoleon

1774
American colonial representatives meet in protest

1776
Declaration of Independence signed

1789
French Revolution begins

1804
Napoleon becomes emperor of France

1750   1770   1790   1810

1775
Battle of Lexington and Concord is fought

1781
American Revolutionary War ends

1793
French execute Louis XVI

1815
Wellington defeats Napoleon at Waterloo

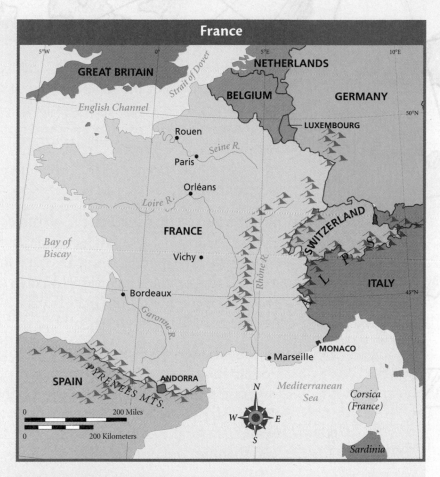

France

During this time, revolution started in America, then spread to France. Great changes took place in this European country. The common people revolted and took power away from the nobles and the king. Their cry was "Liberty, equality, and fraternity!" They wanted everyone to be part of a brotherhood in which all were free and equal.

Study the map and answer the following questions:

1) What city in France is near the Mediterranean?

2) What island in the Mediterranean did France hold?

3) What are the names of four rivers in France?

4) What mountains separate France from Spain?

5) What mountains form the boundary between Italy and France?

Geography Skills

Between 1607 and 1733, England established 13 colonies in North America. For the people living in America, the **colonists,** life was different from life in England. Land was cheap. People could earn money and not be poor anymore. For more than 150 years, England pretty much left the colonists alone. Then, in 1763, England changed the way it treated the colonies.

◆Colonist
A person who settles in a new place

◆Quarter
To provide soldiers with a place to live and food

Violate
To break a law, rule, or promise

What Law Took Away the Colonists' Rights?

From 1754 to 1763, the English and the French fought to control North America. The war cost a lot of money. After it ended, England left British soldiers in the colonies to protect the colonists. But Great Britain needed money to pay these soldiers and to pay off the war.

To raise money, the British government tried for the first time to make the colonists obey the Navigation Acts. These laws said that the colonists had to ship their trading goods on British ships. The money England got from the colonists would pay for the cost of protecting them. The colonists said that they did not need British protection.

Then, in 1765, the British government passed the Quartering Act. This law said that the colonists had to let British soldiers **quarter,** or live, in their homes. The colonists also had to feed these soldiers. The colonists said that this law **violated,** or went against, their rights.

Why Did the Colonists Dislike the Stamp Act?

In 1765, the English Parliament also passed the Stamp Act to raise money. This law put a tax on colonial newspapers, playing cards, and legal documents. In England, this type of tax was common.

Before the Stamp Act, the price of everything included a British tax. But most colonists did not know this, so they thought that the Stamp Act was new. They thought that it was the first direct tax England had placed on them.

The colonists did not like the Quartering Act. They also did not like the Stamp Act, even though it was a small tax. They said that Great Britain had not asked them if they wanted this tax. The colonists believed that England had no right to tax them unless they agreed to taxation. They refused to pay the tax, and in 1766, the British Parliament **repealed,** or did away with it.

What Did Angry Colonists Do in Boston?

In 1767, the British Parliament passed a new group of laws called the Townshend Acts. These laws placed a tax on common products, such as paper, paint, glass, and tea. Once again, the colonists said that England could not tax them without their **consent,** or agreement.

The bad feelings between Great Britain and the colonists got worse. Then, in 1770, British soldiers in Boston fired into a crowd that had tossed sticks and snowballs at them. Historians call this event the Boston Massacre.

In 1773, some colonists in Boston dressed up as Native Americans. Then they climbed on board a British merchant

The Boston Tea Party was a protest against Britain's unfair control of the tea trade. Colonists dumped over 300 chests of tea into Boston Harbor.

ABIGAIL ADAMS: 1774–1818

Abigail Smith Adams was the wife of one American president (John Adams) and the mother of another (John Quincy Adams). She was very active in her husband's career. Abigail was also one of the most influential women of her day. She supported equal education for women. She often spoke out against slavery.

We know a great deal about Abigail from her letters. She wrote to her husband while he was attending Congress during the American Revolution. There are also letters from when he was a diplomat in Europe. Still more letters present a clear picture of Washington, D.C. after 1800.

ship that was carrying tea. The colonists threw the tea into the harbor. Historians call this event the Boston Tea Party.

Why did the colonists do this? Before this, British companies had sold tea to merchants in the colonies. Then these merchants had sold tea to the colonists. In that way, the colonial merchants ran a business and made money. But Parliament had now given a British company the right to sell tea directly to colonists. This cut out colonial merchants. Clearly, the colonists and the British were not getting along.

SECTION 1 REVIEW On a separate sheet of paper, write *True* if the statement is true or *False* if the statement is not true. Make each false statement true by changing the underlined word.

1) England established <u>13</u> colonies in North America.

2) The Navigation Acts made colonists ship goods on <u>French</u> ships.

3) The colonists said that Parliament could not pass <u>laws</u> for the colonies unless the colonists agreed with them.

4) The <u>Quartering Act</u> put a tax on common items such as paper and glass.

5) In 1773, some colonists threw British <u>tea</u> into Boston harbor.

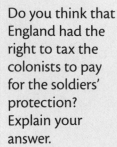

What do you think ?

Do you think that England had the right to tax the colonists to pay for the soldiers' protection? Explain your answer.

◆Boycott
To refuse to buy something; to refuse to deal with a person, business, or country

◆Minutemen
Colonial soldiers in the Revolutionary War who were ready to fight at any time

Because of the Boston Tea Party, Parliament closed the port of Boston. It also forced the colony of Massachusetts to accept military rule. This upset the colonists. In 1774, representatives from 12 colonies met in Philadelphia. They agreed to **boycott**—or refuse to buy—any British goods; to send a protest to King George III in England; and to meet again.

What Was the "Shot Heard 'Round the World"?

Before the representatives could meet again, something happened. In April 1775, British soldiers marched to Concord, Massachusetts, to seize colonial weapons. At Lexington, some soldiers called **minutemen** met the British soldiers. Someone fired a gun. This started a small battle. An American poet later wrote that this was a "shot heard 'round the world."

The British soldiers began to march back toward Boston. But their bright red uniforms were easy to see, so as they retreated, the minutemen fired on them from behind trees and rocks. By the time the British "redcoats" reached Boston, the colonists had killed a third of them.

The first shots of the American Revolutionary War came from Lexington and Concord in 1775.

◆American
Revolution
*The American
struggle against
Great Britain for
independence*

Complaint
*A statement about
something that
that tells why a
person is unhappy*

◆Declaration of
Independence
*A document the
American colonists
signed in which
they declared their
freedom from
Great Britain*

Who Wrote the Declaration of Independence?

In May 1775, the colonial representatives met again. They agreed to pay for an army that George Washington would command. On July 4, 1776, they signed the **Declaration of Independence.** In this document, they declared that the colonies were free states. They were no longer part of the British Empire. The Declaration of Independence also listed more than 20 **complaints** against King George III.

Thomas Jefferson wrote most of the document. He accepted the political ideas of John Locke. Jefferson wrote that people could change their government if that government did not protect their rights of life and liberty. Jefferson also said that people had the right to try to find happiness.

Who Helped the Colonists Fight the War?

The struggle against Great Britain—the **American Revolution**—lasted for many years. The many battles

George Washington commanded the colonial forces in the Revolutionary War.

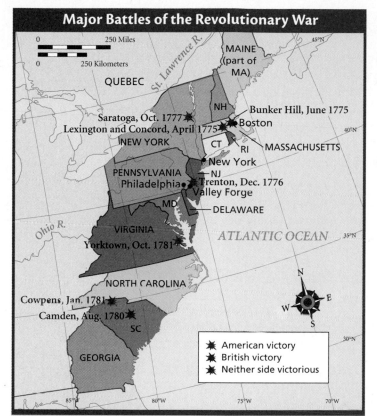

Major Battles of the Revolutionary War

American victory
British victory
Neither side victorious

MAP STUDY

This map shows the 13 colonies and the most important battles of the Revolutionary War. Name four battles that the Americans won. Name two battles that the British won. Look at the dates and find the final battle of the war. Who won it?

◆Revolutionary War
The war the American colonists fought with Great Britain

fought during this **Revolutionary War** did not go well for the colonists at first. George Washington's soldiers had little training and lacked supplies, but they managed to win some battles.

In 1777, the colonists won an important victory at Saratoga. Because of this, France sent soldiers to help the colonists defeat Great Britain. In 1778, Spain declared war on Great Britain. In 1780, the Netherlands joined the American fight. Great Britain was now at war with the colonies and with France, Spain, and the Netherlands.

What Brought an End to the War?

Finally, in 1781, the colonial army rushed southward to Yorktown, Virginia. Here, the British army, led by General Cornwallis, was trapped. In front, it faced the colonial army. At its back was the French fleet.

Because of these French ships, the British navy could not rescue Cornwallis and his soldiers. The British surrendered, and the Revolutionary War was over. Two years later, the colonists and England signed a peace treaty in Paris, France. Great Britain accepted the independence of the 13 American colonies. The American Revolution had ended.

How Did the American Revolution Affect Europe?

The British soldiers marched out of Yorktown in 1781. As they did so, their band played the song "The World Turned Upside Down." And the world had turned upside down.

Independence Day

The Fourth of July is the anniversary of American independence. It celebrates the signing of the Declaration of Independence. This national holiday first took place in Philadelphia on July 8, 1776. The Declaration was read aloud, city bells rang, and bands played. Independence is now celebrated with parades, picnics, and fireworks. In 1976, the United States was 200 years old. During the whole year, cities and towns held special events to remember independence.

Other countries also have independence days. Mexico marks its independence from Spain on September 16. Ghana celebrates independence from Great Britain on March 6.

The American Revolution brought change for Americans and for Europeans.

The Declaration of Independence said that "all men are created equal." The declaration also said that people had a right to choose their own form of government. In 1789, the people of France followed the lead of the Americans. The French also turned their world upside down.

SECTION 2 REVIEW On a separate sheet of paper, write answers to these questions.

1) Who were the minutemen?

2) In what place did the American Revolutionary War begin?

3) When did the colonial representatives sign the Declaration of Independence?

4) What European countries helped the colonists win the war?

5) Where and when did the fighting in the American Revolution end?

What do you think

What do you think life would be like in America today if the American Revolution had been a failure?

Estate
A class of people in France

Wealth
A large amount of money, property, or costly things

In the early 1770s, France probably had more money than any other nation in Europe. Throughout Europe, most educated people spoke French. Many of the most important ideas of the Enlightenment came from French thinkers. However, France had two big problems. First, French society was still like the feudal societies of the Middle Ages. Second, the king—an absolute monarch—was a weak ruler.

What Were the Three Estates?

French society was divided into three **estates,** or classes. The clergy—1 percent of the population—made up the First Estate. These religious leaders owned 10 percent of the land. The nobles—5 percent of the population—made up the Second Estate. They held all the important jobs in the government. They also controlled most of the **wealth,** or money, in their country. The Third Estate included three different groups of common people. At the top were doctors, teachers, bankers, business people, and lawyers. In the middle were city workers. At the bottom were farmers, who made up more than 80 percent of the population.

Who Paid Taxes in France?

The clergy and the nobility paid no taxes to the government. But the three groups of the Third Estate had to pay taxes on the money they made and on their land. They also had to pay taxes when they bought salt, tobacco, and soap.

How much tax money did the farmers pay? About half of what they made. They also had to work once a year on government projects without pay. The members of the Third Estate paid a lot of taxes, but they had little or no political power.

Why Did the French Government Need Money in 1789?

In 1789, the French treasury was empty. France had spent money helping the American colonies revolt against Great Britain. To raise money, the government decided to find a way to tax the nobles. They did not like this and demanded

◆**Estates-General**
The French governmental body made up of representatives from the three estates

Mob
A large group of people

that the king call a meeting of the **Estates-General.** This was a government body made up of the representatives from the three estates. The last time the Estates-General had met was in 1614.

Louis XVI agreed. The Estates-General met at Versailles on May 1, 1789. At this meeting, the representatives would decide if the nobles had to pay taxes. But each of the three estates had only one vote. So, the First and Second Estates—the clergy and the nobles—could defeat the Third Estate, which was already paying all the taxes.

What Did the Third Estate Do in 1789?

The 610 representatives of the Third Estate wanted everyone at the meeting to have a vote. They could then outvote the 591 representatives of the other two estates. But the king said that the meeting would follow the old rule of three votes.

What did the representatives of the Third Estate do? They declared that they were a National Assembly that represented the French people. The king locked them out of the meeting hall. But they simply marched outside and decided to write a constitution and call for an end to absolute monarchy. Under pressure, Louis XVI ended the meeting of the Estates General. He told the clergy and the nobles to join the National Assembly.

What Did Mobs Do in Paris in 1789?

In the 1780s, many poor people lived in Paris. Mostly, they ate bread. If the price of bread increased, they starved. Sometimes, **mobs**—large groups of people—seized carts of grain and bread because of their hunger.

The storming of the Bastille, a prison in France, became a symbol of the French Revolution.

◆Bastille
A prison in Paris

◆French Revolution
The war that the common people of France fought against the king, nobles, and one another to achieve freedom

In 1788, the grain harvest in France was poor, so bread doubled in price. In the spring of 1789, the starving people in Paris got mad. Angry mobs rioted in the streets. On July 14, 1789, these mobs attacked a city prison called the **Bastille.** The government kept a few political prisoners there as well as gunpowder. When the French soldiers joined the mob, the Bastille fell!

A noble woke Louis XVI from his sleep and told him what had happened. The angry king said, "Why, this is a revolt!" "No," the noble said. "It is a revolution." Today, the French people celebrate Bastille Day on July 14. It was the beginning of the **French Revolution.**

SECTION 3 REVIEW Choose the letter of the answer that correctly completes each sentence. Write your answer on a separate sheet of paper.

1) In the early 1770s, France probably had more _____ than any other nation in Europe.

   a. bread   c. money

   b. grain   d. population

2) The Third Estate was made up of _____.

   a. clergy   c. nobles

   b. kings   d. common people

3) Members of the Third Estate wanted an end to France's _____.

   a. clergy   c. grain harvest

   b. absolute monarchy d. Bastille

4) The Bastille in Paris is a _____.

   a. prison   c. castle

   b. palace   d. navy yard

5) The French Revolution began in _____.

   a. 1775   c. 1789

   b. 1780   d. 1791

What do you think

Why do you think the French people attacked the Bastille?

◆**Convention**
A group of people who meet to get something done

Enforce
To make sure that people follow the laws and rules

Equality
The same rights for everyone

The National Assembly quickly started to reform French government. On August 4, 1789, it ended the feudal privileges of the clergy and the nobles. It also adopted a document that gave citizens three rights—free speech, freedom of religion, and **equality** under the law. Equality means that everyone shares the same rights.

Why Did the King Leave Versailles?

In October 1789, thousands of women rioted over the cost of bread. They marched on Versailles, which was ten miles from Paris. When they got to Versailles, the women broke into the palace and killed several guards. Then they demanded that the king and queen move to Paris. Frightened, they agreed to do so. In June 1790, Louis XVI and his family tried to escape from France. But someone recognized the king. He and his family had to return to Paris.

What Type of Government Did the Assembly Form?

The National Assembly continued to make changes. By 1791, it had created a new form of government. Members of the assembly wrote a constitution that limited the king's power. This new government was a constitutional monarchy.

According to the constitution, the new Legislative Assembly had the power to make laws. The king had the power to **enforce** the laws, or put them into action. The new constitution said that all men were equal before the law. However, only property owners—less than 1 percent of the population—could be elected to the government.

What Was the Next Government of France?

The new constitutional government lasted only 11 months. In September 1792, the French abolished it. Then they elected a National Constitutional **Convention.** A convention is a group of people who meet to get something done. The Constitutional Convention met to form a new, more democratic government for France—a republic.

The new government took away all of Louis XVI's power. It gave all French men the right to vote and to hold political office. The government also decided to fight to bring freedom to all the common people in Europe.

Which Nations Tried to Stop the French Revolution?

Many French nobles, called **émigrés,** had fled France. They asked Leopold II of Austria to overthrow the new French government. In August 1791, Leopold and the king of Prussia said that all kings had the duty to "restore order to France." The armies of Great Britain, Austria, Prussia, and Spain joined together to try and defeat the French and end the French Revolution.

What Happened to Louis XVI?

The French no longer thought of Louis XVI as king. He was just a common citizen. In June 1790, he had written a letter condemning the revolution. In December 1792, the government put him on trial for treason. On January 21, 1793, they executed him. During that same year, France raised a citizen army of 300,000 men. Many French women went to war with the men.

The French created a ghastly way to put people to death: the guillotine. A heavy blade cut off the person's head. This picture shows Louis XVI before his execution by the guillotine.

Queen of France Marie Antoinette was one of the first to be sent to the guillotine in France.

◆Jacobin
A radical leader during the French Revolution

◆Moderate
One who has a slight opinion on an issue

◆Radical
One who has a strong opinion on one side or another of an issue

Who Were the Jacobins?

After the king was executed, the French peasants rebelled. Then, **moderate** and **radical** leaders in the government began to fight one another for power. A moderate leader has a slight opinion on an issue; a radical leader has a strong opinion on one side or another of an issue.

In Paris, a mob rushed into the Convention and arrested all the moderate leaders. Then the radicals—called **Jacobins**—controlled the government. The Convention formed a Committee of Public Safety. Maximilien Robespierre led the committee. He wanted to kill anyone who opposed the revolution.

What Was the Reign of Terror?

Between July 1793 and July 1794, the Jacobins executed thousands of people by chopping off their heads.

Executive
Having to do with the branch of government that puts laws into action

Guillotine
The machine the French used to execute people by chopping off their head

Legislature
The group of people in a government who make laws

Reign of Terror
The one-year period in French history when radical leaders put many people to death

Historians call this the **Reign of Terror.** One of the first people to lose her head was the woman who had been queen—Marie Antoinette. The radicals executed many nobles, but mostly they put common people to death.

For one year, Robespierre was a dictator. But the Reign of Terror ended on July 28, 1794, when the radicals sent Robespierre himself to the **guillotine.** (This was the machine the French used to execute someone.)

What Was the Directory?

During the next five years, the National Convention drew up another new constitution. (This was the third one since 1789.) They divided the **legislature,** or lawmaking body, into two houses. They established an **executive** branch—the Directory—made up of five people. (The executive branch enforced the laws.)

For a time, the Directory brought order to France. Then, in November 1799, it also fell from power. Three men took control of the government. One of them was a 30-year-old military officer named Napoleon Bonaparte.

SECTION 4 REVIEW On a separate sheet of paper, write the word from the Word Bank that completes each sentence.

1) In 1789, women marched on _____ and demanded that their rulers return to Paris.

2) The king of France at this time was _____.

3) The queen of France was _____.

4) _____ led the Reign of Terror for a year.

5) _____ of Austria called all kings to bring order to France.

WORD BANK

Leopold

Louis XVI

Marie Antoinette

Robespierre

Versailles

What do you think

Why do you think the kings of other nations opposed the French Revolution?

Tactic
A plan that helps someone win a game or a battle

Napoleon Bonaparte was born in 1769 on the small island of Corsica. As a boy, he went to a military school in France. When he was 16, he joined the king's army. The French Revolution began in 1789. At that time, Napoleon was a little-known, low-level military officer. But he developed a new military **tactic,** or plan. He moved his soldiers quickly, then put most of them at the weakest point of the enemy line.

Soldiers liked to fight for Napoleon. He was a natural leader and helped them win battles against stronger armies.

Napoleon Bonaparte saw himself as a conqueror like Alexander the Great. He became emperor of France in 1804.

Within four years, he became a general. (He was only 24.) Six years later, Napoleon took control of the disorganized government of France. Later, he said, "I found the crown of France lying on the ground, and I picked it up with a sword."

For the next 15 years, Napoleon ruled France as a military dictator. As time passed, he conquered most of Europe. His actions dominated European history from 1800 to 1815. Historians call those years the Age of Napoleon.

When Did Napoleon Become First Consul?

Napoleon dreamed of making France into a mighty empire like that of ancient Rome. He saw himself as a modern-day Alexander the Great. When Napoleon first came to power, he pretended that he was the elected leader of a democratic republic.

Then, in 1800, he asked the people of France to approve a new constitution. It gave him the title of First Consul. (Consuls led the ancient Roman republic.) As First Consul, Napoleon had more power than any other French official.

Who Crowned Napoleon As the Emperor?

In 1802, the French people voted to make Napoleon their First Consul for life. More than 3 million people voted, and only 9,000 of them voted against Napoleon. Then, on December 2, 1804, Pope Pius VII came to Paris. He waited at the Cathedral of Notre Dame to crown Napoleon emperor of France. Napoleon, dressed in purple, came into the cathedral. He walked up to the pope, took the crown from him, and placed it on his own head! Through his own military skill, he had risen to power. Now, by his own hand, he made himself Emperor Napoleon I.

A Song for the Revolution

In 1792, more than five hundred soldiers marched from Marseilles in southern France to Paris. They were all volunteers, caught up in the spirit of the Revolution. On the way, they sang a rousing song, "The War Song of the Rhine Army." This emotional song of liberty had captured the feeling of hope and revolutionary change. It was written by Claude-Joseph Rouget de L'isle, a young French army captain.

> Arise, ye sons of France!
> Your day of glory has arrived!
> Oh army of citizens!
> Form your battalions.
> March on, march on!
> All hearts dedicated
> to liberty or death!

Fine Arts

History in Your Life

The song was renamed "The Marseillaise." In 1795, it became the national anthem of France. When France became an empire, Napoleon banned "The Marseillaise." He feared that the song would continue to rouse the French to revolution. Nevertheless, in 1875 France, once again, adopted "The Marseillaise" as its national anthem.

What Was the Confederation of the Rhine?

In 1805, Britain, Austria, and Russia formed a military alliance against France. Napoleon quickly defeated the armies of Austria and Russia. From 1806 to 1812, his power increased in Europe. He took control of Italy and made himself king there. Then he ended the Holy Roman Empire. (This empire had lasted for many centuries.) In its place, he created a loose alliance of German states. He called this alliance the Confederation of the Rhine.

Napoleon let his brothers rule some of this conquered land. Louis Bonaparte became king of Holland. Jerome Bonaparte ruled over the Kingdom of Westphalia in Germany. Joseph Bonaparte ruled over the Kingdom of Naples and Sicily and later became the king of Spain.

What Mistakes Did Napoleon Make?

Only Great Britain stood against the spreading French power. In 1805, England destroyed the French fleet off the coast of Spain. In 1806, Napoleon decided to ruin the British economy by ordering other European countries to stop trading with Great Britain. He called his plan the Continental System.

But Napoleon misjudged the power of the British navy. It prevented trading ships from entering French and other European ports. The successful actions of the British navy hurt the economy of France and these other countries.

Because of their lost trade, the **neutral** European nations quickly turned against France. (A neutral country is one that does not choose either side in a war.) Napoleon's mistake had weakened French power. In 1812, he made a second mistake—a bigger one. He invaded Russia.

Why Did Napoleon Invade Russia?

In 1807, Czar Alexander I of Russia had agreed to support the Continental System. But lack of trade hurt the Russian economy. In 1812, Alexander began to trade with Britain once again. His decision made Napoleon angry.

Napoleon was a natural military leader. This painting shows him at the Battle of Eylau in 1807. Perhaps his greatest mistake was invading Russia in 1812, however.

To punish Russia, Napoleon organized the largest army in history up to that time. His Grand Army of 500,000 was made up of soldiers from all parts of the French Empire. In May 1812, this army set out to invade Russia.

How Did the Russian Army Fight?

Napoleon thought that he could defeat Russia in a few months. But the Russian army did not want to fight one big battle. Instead, it kept retreating. As the French army followed, the Russian soldiers retreated eastward, deeper and deeper into Russia. As they pulled back, the soldiers destroyed anything that could help Napoleon's invading army. The Russians left behind only burned fields and houses.

Near Moscow, the French and Russian armies finally met. The French won the battle. But when the soldiers entered the capital, they found only a burnt-out and deserted city. Once again the Russians had destroyed food and shelter that Napoleon's army needed.

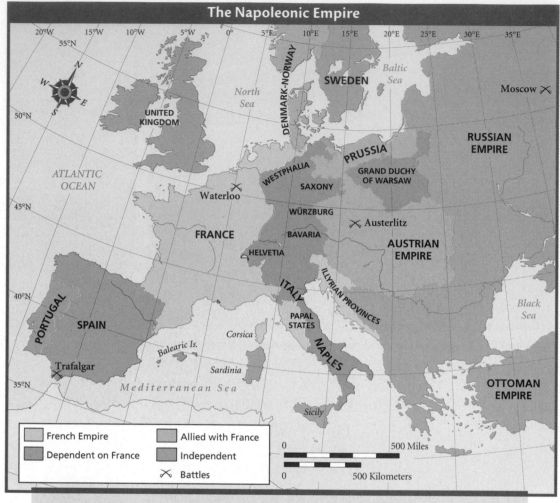

The Napoleonic Empire

Legend:
- French Empire
- Dependent on France
- Allied with France
- Independent
- ✕ Battles

0   500 Miles

0   500 Kilometers

MAP STUDY This map shows Napoleon's empire. It also shows several places he fought battles. Which empire had an alliance with Napoleon? What battles were fought in Russia?

What Happened When Napoleon Left Russia?

Napoleon sent several messages of peace. However, he heard nothing from the Russians. In October 1812—after five weeks of waiting—Napoleon ordered his army to return to France. The Grand Army had already lost thousands of soldiers. Many had died of disease. Now the soldiers faced a cold Russian winter without food and warm clothing.

◆Exile
To send someone away from his or her own country and to order this person not to come back

◆Troops
An organized group of soldiers

The Russian winter was a hard enemy. As the French army moved slowly westward, thousands of soldiers died of starvation. Many froze to death. Over 500,000 soldiers had marched boldly into Russia. Only 40,000—tired and beaten—returned to France. And only 10,000 of them were still able to fight. Napoleon's retreat from Russia was a military disaster.

Who Defeated Napoleon the First Time?

Seeing the weakened French army, Napoleon's enemies attacked. In March 1814, the British, Russian, Prussian, and Austrian armies captured Paris. The leaders removed Napoleon from power and sent him to Elba, an island off the coast of Italy. Then they restored the monarchy to France. (The brother of the executed Louis XVI became king.)

In February 1815, Napoleon escaped from Elba and returned to France. First, he declared himself emperor. Then he began to raise an army. The French king quickly sent his soldiers to stop Napoleon. When Napoleon met the king's soldiers, he asked if any one of them wished "to kill his emperor." They all cried, "Long live the emperor!"

Who Defeated Napoleon the Second Time?

For the next three months, Napoleon was once again the hero of France. During that time, he organized an army of 125,000 men. On June 18, 1815, his new army met the combined armies of Britain and Prussia at Waterloo in present-day Belgium.

The Duke of Wellington led the British and Prussian **troops,** or organized groups of soldiers. On the battlefield at Waterloo, these troops finally defeated Napoleon. Once again, he was **exiled,** or sent away, to a lonely island, this time in the South Atlantic.

Writing About History

In your notebook, write an epitaph, or writing on a tombstone, for Napoleon. What were his dreams? his accomplishments? Why did he capture the French imagination? Why did Napoleon fall from power?

In 1821, six years after the Battle of Waterloo, Napoleon Bonaparte died at the age of 52 on the rocky island of St. Helena. For a few years, his dream of a French empire came true. No one could stop his army. Then he met a Russian winter and Waterloo.

How Did Napoleon Affect History?

Napoleon's leadership had many important effects. In France, he achieved one important goal of the French Revolution—he made every man equal before the law. He did this with a new code of laws called the **Code of Napoleon.**

Napoleon's success as a military conqueror changed the political boundaries of Europe. The leaders of the French Revolution had wanted liberty and equality. Napoleon's success spread these ideas throughout Europe.

These ideas changed people. Napoleon had conquered many people. Many of them now wanted their own nation. This rising spirit of nationalism helped to shape European history throughout the nineteenth century.

SECTION 5 REVIEW On a separate sheet of paper, write answers to these questions.

1) What years in French history do historians call the Age of Napoleon?

2) What did Napoleon do before he came to power in France?

3) When did Napoleon become the emperor of France?

4) How successful was Napoleon's invasion of Russia?

5) At which battle did Napoleon meet his final defeat?

What do you think

Why do you think the Russians did not answer Napoleon's messages of peace near Moscow?

Why the French Accepted Napoleon As Emperor

The French fought a bloody revolution to get rid of a king and the nobility. Yet in a few years, the French accepted Napoleon as an emperor. Madame de Remusat was the wife of one of Napoleon's secretaries. This excerpt is her opinion why Napoleon was allowed to have such great powers.

Napoleon being crowned as emperor.

I can understand how it was that men, worn out by the Revolution and afraid of that liberty which had been so long associated with death, looked for peace under an able ruler. I can see that they regarded Napoleon's rise as an order of destiny. I know that those persons believed quite sincerely that Napoleon would use his authority to save us from anarchy.

None dared to utter the word Republic, so deeply had the Terror stained that name. And the government of the Directory had fallen into the contempt with which its chiefs were regarded. The return of the descendants of Louis XVI would never have been acceptable. And the slightest disturbance terrified the French people, in whom enthusiasm of every kind seemed to be dead.

The belief, or rather the error, that only the iron rule of a strong individual could keep order in France was very widespread. Napoleon had some grounds for his belief that he was necessary; France believed it too. And he even succeeded in persuading foreign kings that he formed a wall against republican influences, which but for him might spread widely. At the moment when Napoleon placed the crown upon his head, there was not a king in Europe who did not believe that he wore his own crown more securely because of that event. Had the new emperor added to that decisive act the gift of a liberal constitution, the peace of nations and of kings might have come about.

Well-meaning, honest folk asked nothing of him but peace. They did not trouble themselves about the form under which it was to be given. And then, he knew well that the secret weakness of the French nation was vanity, and he saw a means of gratifying it easily by the showiness that goes along with monarchial power.

Source Reading Wrap-Up

1) According to the writer, why did the French let Napoleon become their emperor?

2) Madame de Remusat mentioned the terror under the republic. What was she referring to?

3) The writer said that Napoleon convinced other kings he was "a wall against republican influences." What did she mean by this phrase?

4) Napoleon became emperor of France. Why might European kings think that this act made them safer on their thrones?

5) According to the writer, what is the secret weakness of the French? How did Napoleon take advantage of this weakness?

Another Kind of Hero

During the French Revolution and the Age of Napoleon, many people were heroes. However, not all heroes are political or military leaders. There is another kind of hero. In spite of great problems, this person reaches for worthy goals. One such hero was a musician named Ludwig van Beethoven.

He was born in Bonn, Germany, in 1770. He was trained in classical music. When he was 12, he became the assistant organist to the royal court in Bonn. Then at age 22, Beethoven went to Vienna to study with Joseph Haydn. He was Europe's greatest classical composer.

Near the end of the 1700s, Beethoven began to compose a new style of music. It was based on his own feelings.

Then a terrible thing happened to him. He started losing his hearing. In 1802, Beethoven wrote, "I was soon compelled to withdraw myself, to live life alone. If at times I try to forget all this . . . I am flung back by the doubly sad experience of my bad hearing. Yet, it is impossible for me to say to people, 'Speak louder, shout, for I am deaf.'" Fate had played a horrible trick on him. He was a great composer. But he was less and less able to hear the beautiful sounds that he created.

Beethoven did not give up. In 1808, he wrote his *Fifth Symphony*. It opens with Fate knocking on the door: *Dah-Dah-Dah Daaaaaaah!* In the end, Music wins the battle with Fate.

Beethoven was going deaf, but his deafness did not stop him from creating music.

In 1824, Beethoven conducted his *Ninth Symphony*, his last work for a large orchestra. In the last movement, a chorus sings the "Ode to

Ludwig van Beethoven

Joy." It calls for brotherhood among people throughout the world. It also states that the human struggle against Fate can end in peace and joy. When the *Ninth Symphony* ended, Beethoven stood staring at the orchestra. He could not hear the audience's thunderous applause! A musician made Beethoven turn around and face them. Then he saw what he could not hear.

Beethoven died on March 26, 1827. More than 20,000 people attended his funeral in Vienna. What did Beethoven think about his talent as a composer? In a letter years before, Beethoven had written a possible answer to that question. "There will always be thousands of princes, but there is only one Beethoven." And so there was.

Spotlight Story Wrap-Up

1) Where was Beethoven born?

2) How was Beethoven's music different from composers before him?

3) What terrible thing happened to Beethoven?

4) What feeling did Beethoven try to express in his *Ninth Symphony*?

5) Do you think that Beethoven was a hero? Explain your answer.

➡ After 1763, Britain wanted its North American colonies to pay for the war against France. Britain used the Navigation Acts, the Quartering Act, the Stamp Act, and the Townshend Acts to raise money. The colonists protested. The Boston Massacre and the Boston Tea Party followed. Representatives of the twelve colonies met in Philadelphia in 1775. They agreed to boycott British goods. Then minutemen fought British soldiers at Lexington and Concord.

➡ Jefferson wrote most of the Declaration of Independence. It stated people could change their government if it did not protect their rights. Colonial representatives signed it on July 4, 1776.

➡ The American victory at Saratoga earned French help. The Revolutionary War ended in 1781. An American army and French ships forced the British under Cornwallis to surrender.

➡ France in the 1770s consisted of three estates—the clergy, the nobles, and the common people. The Third Estate paid all the taxes. This group wanted each representative in the Estates General to have a vote. The other estates and Louis XVI refused. The Third Estate established a constitutional monarchy. It gave everyone freedom of speech and religion and equality under the law. Mobs stormed the Bastille and the French Revolution began.

➡ During the Revolution, there were several governments. In 1792, the National Constitutional Convention created a republic. It wanted to spread the revolution to other countries. Other European countries united to stop France.

➡ After an attempted escape, the king was executed and peasants rebelled. Moderates and radicals fought to control the government. The Jacobins under Robespierre came to power and began the Reign of Terror. Then came the Directory and the Consulate. Napoleon became First Consul and then First Consul for life. In 1804 he crowned himself emperor.

➡ Napoleon's victories increased French power, but he made two mistakes. The Continental System turned countries against France instead of ruining the British economy. His Russian invasion destroyed his army. Britain, Prussia, Russia, and Austria defeated Napoleon in 1814 and exiled him. He returned and was defeated at Waterloo.

➡ In France, the Code of Napoleon made every man equal under the law. Napoleon's conquests spread the ideas of the French Revolution.

Comprehension: Identifying Facts

On a separate sheet of paper, use the words from the Word Bank to complete each sentence.

WORD BANK

Alexander I
Antoinette
Bonaparte
Cornwallis
George III
Jefferson
Locke
Louis XVI
Washington
Wellington

1) _____ was the British king when the colonists rebelled.

2) Thomas _____ was the main writer of the Declaration of Independence.

3) The Declaration of Independence is based on many of the ideas of John _____.

4) George _____ commanded the colonial army.

5) General _____ surrendered the British army at Yorktown.

6) During the reign of _____, the French Revolution began.

7) The French executed Marie _____, the queen of France.

8) Napoleon _____ became the emperor of France.

9) Czar _____ of Russia decided to trade with England, so Napoleon invaded Russia.

10) The Duke of _____ defeated Napoleon at Waterloo.

Comprehension: Multiple Choice

On a separate sheet of paper, write the letter of the answer that correctly completes each sentence.

1) England enforced the _____ that said that colonists had to ship their trading goods on British ships.

  a. Stamp Act   c. Navigation Acts

  b. Townshend Acts   d. Quartering Act

2) _____ helped the colonists win the Revolutionary War.

  a. France   c. The Netherlands

  b. Spain   d. all of the above

3) At this time, French society was divided into _____ classes, or estates.

    a. three   c. nine

    b. six   d. nineteen

4) The French wanted liberty and _____ for all people.

    a. constitutions   c. equality

    b. consuls   d. boycotts

5) The leader of the French Reign of Terror was _____.

    a. Marie Antoinette   c. Cornwallis

    b. Robespierre   d. Wellington

Comprehension: Understanding Main Ideas

On a separate sheet of paper, write the answers to the following questions using complete sentences, or statements.

1) What were the colonists rebelling against during the American Revolution?

2) What were the French rebelling against during the French Revolution?

3) What is one way in which the American Revolution changed Europe and one way in which the French Revolution changed Europe?

Critical Thinking: Write Your Opinion

1) Which revolution—the American or the French—would you like to have been part of and why?

2) Pretend that Napoleon's army is marching across Russia and that you are advising the czar. What would you tell him to do?

Test-Taking Tip	When studying for a test, write your own test problems with a partner. Then complete each other's test. Double-check your answers.

Reaction, Reforms, and Revolution

1814 to 1850

The French Revolution changed Europe. The leaders of Austria, Britain, Prussia, and Russia did not like change. They feared nationalism, so they met in Vienna to stop it. In this chapter, you will see how they divided the map of Europe. Then you will find out how people rebelled—first in Greece, then in the Spanish colonies of Latin America. You will also see how Simón Bolívar and José San Martín liberated South America. Then you will sail to Europe and learn about socialist reform. There you will learn about two opposites—Metternich and Marx, and you will witness 1848, the year during which nearly 50 different rebellions broke out in Europe.

Goals for Learning

▶ To state the purpose and outcome of the Congress of Vienna

▶ To explain the difference between radicals, conservatives, and liberals

▶ To describe the wars of national liberation that occurred in the nineteenth century

▶ To explain the ideas of the socialists

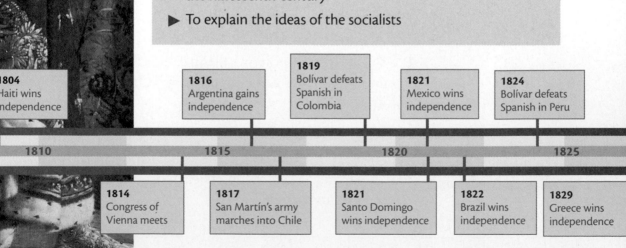

1804
Haiti wins independence

1816
Argentina gains independence

1819
Bolívar defeats Spanish in Colombia

1821
Mexico wins independence

1824
Bolívar defeats Spanish in Peru

1810   1815   1820   1825

1814
Congress of Vienna meets

1817
San Martín's army marches into Chile

1821
Santo Domingo wins independence

1822
Brazil wins independence

1829
Greece wins independence

South America

CENTRAL AMERICA

Caribbean Sea

Orinoco R.

Negro R.

Amazon R.

Amazon R.

Tapajós R.

Xingu R.

Tocantins R.

São Francisco R.

SOUTH AMERICA

Lima •

Brasilia •

ANDES

Paraguay R.

Paraná R.

Rio de Janeiro •

ATACAMA DESERT

Uruguay R.

PACIFIC OCEAN

MOUNTAINS

Santiago •

ATLANTIC OCEAN

Negro R.

10°N

0°

10°S

20°S

30°S

40°S

50°S

0   1000 Miles

0   1000 Kilometers

Falkland Islands (U.K.)

Strait of Magellan

100°W   90°W   80°W   70°W   60°W   50°W   40°W   30°W

Geography Skills

This is a modern map of South America. Portugal and Spain once controlled all this land of high mountains, dry deserts, and steamy tropical rain forests. The largest river system in the world flows through South America.

Study the map and answer the following questions:

1) What are the names of four cities in South America?

2) What are the names of five rivers in South America?

3) On which coast of South America do the Andes Mountains stand?

4) What sea is on the north coast of South America?

5) What two oceans touch the shores of South America?

◆Congress of
Vienna
*An important
meeting in
1814–1815 in
which leaders
restructured
Europe*

◆Foreign minister
*A person who
handles one
country's dealings
with other countries*

Influential
*Having the power
to change things or
to affect what
happens*

The French Revolution, which began in 1789, changed France. Ten years later, Napoleon Bonaparte seized power. The wars he fought changed Europe because he conquered other countries and gathered them into his empire.

In 1814, four European countries—Austria, Prussia, Great Britain, and Russia—defeated Napoleon and sent him into exile. Then the leaders of these countries met in Vienna, Austria. Historians call this meeting the **Congress of Vienna.**

Who Influenced the Meeting?

Many powerful leaders attended the meeting. Two were kings—William III of Prussia and Czar Alexander of Russia. The Duke of Wellington and Lord Castlereagh represented Great Britain. Charles Talleyrand came for France. But Prince Metternich of Austria was the most **influential.** He had the power to affect what happened.

After the defeat of Napoleon, the Congress of Vienna met to redraw the map of Europe.

Prince Metternich was Austria's **foreign minister.** That is, he handled his country's dealings with other nations. He hated the democratic goals of the French Revolution. In fact, he thought that they had made Europe weak. The Congress of Vienna had to cure Europe of this disease called revolution.

What Plan Did Metternich Offer?

Metternich had a plan to make Europe what it had been before the French Revolution. His plan had three main parts. First, Metternich wanted to make sure that France could not threaten

◆Balance of power
The condition that exists when all countries or all sections of government share powers or have the same amount of power

Relative
A family member

other nations again. Second, he wanted a **balance of power** in Europe. That is, he wanted the major nations to have equal strength so as to keep peace. Third, Metternich wanted to return royal families to power.

The Congress decided to restore all the kings whom Napoleon had driven from power. But what if some of them had died? Then **relatives,** or family members, would take their place on the throne. The Congress placed kings on the thrones of France, Spain, Portugal, and Sardinia in Italy.

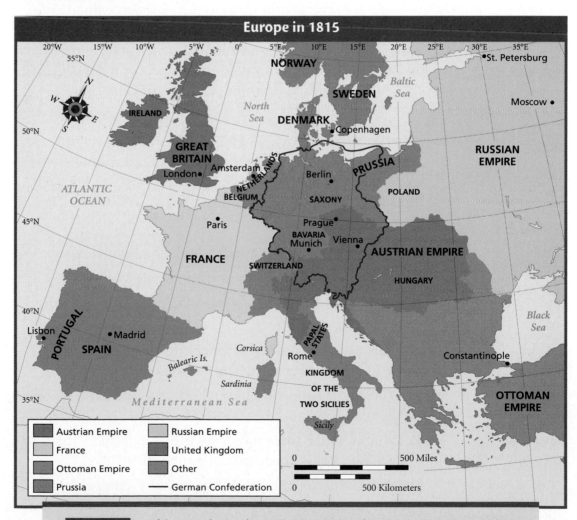

Europe in 1815

This map shows the major empires and countries in Europe in 1815. Name one city in Great Britain, in Russia, in Prussia, and in Austria. Name three other European countries.

MAP STUDY

Who Redrew the Map of Europe?

During Napoleon's reign, several nations had lost land to France. (This land became part of his empire.) The Congress gave land to the nations that had lost land to France and that had fought against Napoleon.

The Congress gave Finland and most of Poland to Russia. It gave part of northern Italy to Austria. Great Britain got the island of Ceylon, some of South Africa, and Malta in the Mediterranean Sea. Sweden gained control of Norway. Then the Congress organized the many German states into a German **Confederation.** A confederation is a group, or union, of states or countries. Austria would lead this group.

◆Confederation
A union, or group, of states or nations

What about the people in Finland, Ceylon, South Africa, and other places? What they wanted did not matter to the leaders of the Congress of Vienna. The Congress felt that this nationalism was part of the "disease" of the French Revolution.

SECTION 1 REVIEW On a separate sheet of paper, write answers to these questions.

1) Which four large nations were against the goals of the French Revolution?

2) What was the name of the meeting that these four nations held after the defeat of Napoleon?

3) Who was the most influential leader at the Congress of Vienna?

4) What were the three major parts of Metternich's plan to cure Europe of the disease of nationalism?

5) What is one way that the Congress of Vienna changed the map of Europe?

What do you think

Why would a balance of power among the major nations help to keep peace?

◆Nationality
A group of people who share the same language, culture, and history

Through all of history, people have organized themselves into groups. In the nineteenth century, nationalism became an important way to organize. People who shared the same history, traditions, customs, and language wanted to unite under one government. They wanted to become a nation. They would then be loyal to this huge family.

Why Did Metternich Fear Nationalism?

The French Revolution and the Age of Napoleon helped nationalism develop. Before the French Revolution, European armies fought for money or for kings. But the army of revolutionary France fought for the nation of France. This citizen army was loyal to, and willing to die for, their homeland.

Metternich feared nationalism. He believed that it would lead to war. He also thought that nationalism threatened the Austrian Empire. People of different **nationalities** made up the empire. (A nationality is a group of people who share the same language, culture, and history.)

Allowing each nationality to have its own nations would end the Austrian Empire. So the leaders of the Congress of Vienna tried to stop nationalism. But nationalists continued to meet in secret. They published books and planned revolutions to set up national governments.

How Did Greece Gain Its Independence?

The first successful national revolution in Europe began in Greece in 1821. For several centuries, Greece had been part of the Ottoman Empire. But now the Greeks wanted independence. They fought long and hard for it. But Greek nationalists needed help to break away from the Ottoman Empire. They got that help in 1827 when France, Britain, and Russia entered the war. These three nations sent a fleet of ships to defeat the Ottoman navy. Finally, after eight years of fighting, Greece became an independent nation.

Literature

Romanticism

Romanticism became important during the first half of the nineteenth century. It affected all the arts—literature, art, and music. Romanticism contained four basic ideas. First, feeling was as important as thinking. Second, it stressed the importance of the individual. It was especially interested in heroes. Third, it viewed nature as powerful and mysterious. Fourth, it focused on the past.

Romanticists wrote many novels and poems that people still read today. *The Three Musketeers* by Alexander Dumas is about seventeenth century France. Victor Hugo wrote *The Hunchback of Notre Dame*. Sir Walter Scott's *Ivanhoe* tells about the adventures of a knight during the Middle Ages.

Volunteer
To offer to do a job without pay; a person who offers to do a job without pay

Who Wanted Greece to Be Independent?

Even though some leaders feared nationalism, many educated people throughout Europe favored Greek nationalism. They respected the Greeks for their ancient civilization. In fact, the art, literature, and philosophy of classical Greece had become an important part of western civilization. Soldiers from other nations came to Greece and **volunteered** to fight for independence. A volunteer is a person who offers to do a job without pay.

The most famous volunteer was Lord Byron, an English poet who loved Greece. But Byron did not live to see Greece win its independence. In 1824, he died there during the revolution. Five years later, Greece won its independence.

SECTION 2 REVIEW On a separate sheet of paper, write *True* if the statement is true or *False* if the statement is not true. Make each false statement true by changing the underlined word.

1) Being <u>loyal</u> to a nation is an important part of nationalism.

2) The French Revolution gave birth to <u>nationalism.</u>

3) Many different nationalities made up the <u>Austrian Empire.</u>

4) The major European countries tried to <u>help</u> the spread of nationalism.

5) The first successful national revolution began in <u>Austria.</u>

What do you think **?**

Why would people of different nationalities want to form different countries?

Nationalism led Greece to independence. It also became a force in Latin America. This geographic region includes Mexico, Central America, the islands of the Caribbean Sea, and the continent of South America. In the early nineteenth century, Spain, France, and Portugal ruled this large area.

Which Latin American Colony Revolted First?

The first successful revolt in Latin America took place on the island of Hispaniola in the Caribbean Sea. France controlled the western half of the island. Spain controlled the eastern half. African slaves worked the island's sugar plantations. In 1794, a formerly enslaved African named Toussaint L'Ouverture led a revolt of free blacks and slaves. They forced the French to leave the island. L'Ouverture became the first governor of the western half of the island.

Toussaint L'Ouverture led a revolt of free blacks and slaves against the French in Hispaniola in 1794.

In 1802, the French put L'Ouverture in prison, where he died. Then Napoleon tried to retake the island, but he failed. In 1804, black rebels established the independent country of Haiti on the western half of the island. It was the first independent country in Latin America. Santo Domingo—the eastern half of the island—gained its independence from Spain in 1821.

Who Rejected Spanish Rule in South America?

Napoleon conquered Spain in 1808. To keep control of Spain, Napoleon made his brother king. That meant a Frenchman ruled Spain and the Spanish colonies. Some people in the colonies did not want a French ruler.

◆Creole
A wealthy landowner who had been born in a Spanish colony in the Americas but whose ancestors came from Spain

◆Peninsular
A person who came to South America from Spain and held an important office in the colonial government

Two groups of people dominated the Spanish colonies in South America. The most important group was the **peninsulars.** They had been born in Spain, and they held the most important offices in the colonial government. The second group was the **creoles.** These wealthy landowners had been born in South America, but their ancestors had come from Spain. When Napoleon's French brother became king of Spain, many peninsulars became loyal to him. But many creoles did not.

Two creole leaders rejected Spanish rule. One was Simón Bolívar in New Granada, the northern area of South America. The other was José San Martín in the southern area. Together they freed much of South America from Spanish rule.

Simón Bolívar came from a wealthy creole family. His army defeated the Spanish in Colombia in 1819.

When Did Bolívar Free New Granada?

Simón Bolívar was born into a wealthy family in Venezuela. In 1810, he led a revolution to free this colony from Spanish control. At first, he had little success. Then in 1819, his army defeated the Spanish in Colombia.

Bolívar became president of the new nation of Great Colombia. He dreamed of uniting all the colonies of South America into one great nation. But his dream did not come true. Great Colombia became the nations of Colombia, Ecuador, and Venezuela.

What Colonies Did San Martín Free?

José San Martín's native land was Argentina in the southern part of South America. Argentina had gained its independence in 1816, and San Martín wanted it to remain free.

But San Martín feared that Argentina would lose its freedom. Spain still controlled Chile and Peru in the southern part of South America. So San Martín organized an army. It crossed the Andes Mountains and captured Santiago, Chile, in 1817.

In 1821, San Martín moved his army by sea to Lima, Peru. The Spanish forces retreated into the mountains. San Martín now needed a larger army to force the Spanish out of the mountains, so he met with Simón Bolívar.

No one knows what the two men said to each other during their historic meeting. But after the meeting, Bolívar took command of San Martín's army. San Martín left South America and sailed to Europe. He never returned, and died there in 1850.

Bolívar led his army and San Martín's up into the Andes Mountains. In December 1824, they defeated the Spanish army. Spain no longer controlled colonial lands in South America.

Who Led Mexico to Independence?

In 1821, Mexico freed itself from Spanish control after an 11-year struggle. Native Americans played an important role in the revolution. It began when Miguel Hidalgo, a poor Mexican priest, challenged the Native American peasants to rebel against their Spanish landowners. Quickly, they formed an army.

Hidalgo's army began a 200-mile march to Mexico City. By the time it got there, the army had 60,000 men. In 1811, at

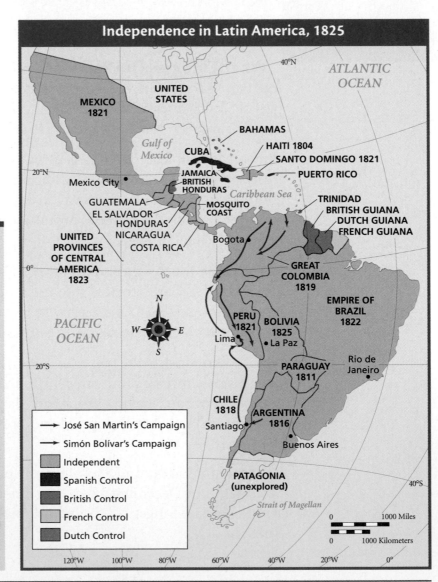

Independence in Latin America, 1825

MAP STUDY

This map shows independent Latin American countries in 1825. It also shows European-controlled colonies at that time. What colony became independent in 1811? When did the United Provinces of Central America become independent? When did Bolivia become independent?

Mexico City, this army met the main force of the Spanish army. The Spanish captured and executed Hidalgo.

José Morelos, another priest, took Hidalgo's place. Morelos and his peasant army of rebels were successful. By 1813, they controlled most Mexican land outside of the major cities. Representatives of the peasants met and declared Mexico an independent republic.

What Did Mexican Creoles Fear?

The Native Americans in Mexico wanted independence from Spain. But wealthy Mexican creoles wanted it, too. However, they feared that a new government would give their land to the landless peasants. So in 1815, creole soldiers captured and executed Morelos. Six years later, in 1821, creole leaders successfully revolted against Spain and achieved independence. Brazil, the largest colony in South America, won its independence from Portugal peacefully in 1822.

SECTION 3 REVIEW On a separate sheet of paper, write the word from the Word Bank that completes each sentence.

WORD BANK
Bolívar
Hidalgo
Morelos
L'Ouverture
San Martín

1) Toussaint _____ led slaves on the island of Hispaniola to independence.

2) Simón _____ led the people of New Granada, in the northern part of South America, to independence.

3) The armies of José _____ freed Chile and Peru.

4) Miguel _____, a priest, began a revolution in Mexico.

5) José _____, another priest, also led the Mexican peasants in their revolt.

What do you think

What might San Martín and Simón Bolívar have said to one another at their famous meeting?

◆Conservative
A person who likes the old political order and resists revolution or change

◆Liberal
A person who wants change; a person who wants to limit the absolute power of kings and nobles and give power to the middle class

Violence
Great physical force; actions that hurt others

The French Revolution gave birth to the ideas of nationalism, liberty, and equality. These ideas and the events of the French Revolution brought into being three political groups—conservatives, liberals, and radicals.

What Is a Conservative?

Conservatives were mainly rich landowners and nobles. They formed the upper class of most societies. As a group, they liked the old political order. In fact, conservatives thought that revolution was dangerous. They thought that it brought only disorder and pain. Because of this, they supported the absolute power of kings.

What Is a Liberal?

Usually, **liberals** were wealthy businessmen and merchants. As such, they belonged to the upper middle class. But many people in the middle class had no political power. The liberals wanted to limit the absolute power of kings and nobles and give power to the middle class. How did they plan on doing this? With a written constitution and an elected parliament.

Most liberals wanted only some people to have the right to vote. They feared democracy, because they did not trust that the uneducated working class and the poor would vote reasonably.

What Is a Radical?

You read about radical leaders in Chapter 20. The word *radical* means "root." Radicals wanted to change society down to its very roots. They wanted monarchies to become democracies in which every man had the right to vote.

Many radicals were willing to use **violence,** or great physical force, to bring about change in society. The French Reign of Terror had frightened conservatives and liberals. It did not frighten radicals. They saw it as necessary to make France into a true democracy.

The condition of the poor in Paris in 1831 was a reminder why radicals were calling for reforms.

Who Ruled France From 1814 to 1824?

In 1793, the French had executed Louis XVI for treason. The monarchy ended. Then, after Napoleon's defeat in 1814, the monarchy was restored to France. The king's brother became King Louis XVIII. He ruled from 1814 to 1824.

Louis XVIII tried to please both the conservatives and the liberals. Conservatives wanted him to support the right of nobles to rule. Liberals wanted him to give more people in the middle class the right to vote. The king could not please both groups, so neither group was happy with him.

What Kind of Power Did Charles X Want?

When Louis XVIII died in 1824, his brother became king as Charles X. He wanted to be an absolute monarch. So he asked the French legislature to pass laws that limited the rights of many people. When the legislature refused to do this, Charles X closed it down.

Next, the king called for an election to get representatives for a new legislature. He thought it would be a conservative one. However, the election results surprised Charles X. The French people voted for liberals.

How Did Charles X Bring About a Rebellion?

Charles wanted to end the power of this new liberal legislature. In July 1830, he issued new laws. These laws abolished the legislature, limited voting rights, and ended freedom of the press. Historians call these laws the July **Ordinances.** An ordinance is a law set forth by someone in government. French newspapers encouraged their readers to ignore the king's laws.

On July 28, 1830, middle-class liberals, workers, and students took to the streets of Paris in protest. They built barriers in the streets. The king then sent his soldiers to break up the riots. But many soldiers refused to shoot the rioters. In fact, some troops joined the protest movement. When Charles X saw this, he fled to England. Once again, the French had forced a king from his throne.

Who Became the "Citizen King"?

Many of the working-class rebels thought that the July Revolution, as it was called, would make France a republic. They wanted this to happen because in a republic, every man could vote. But middle-class leaders wanted a constitutional monarchy instead of a republican form of government.

With middle-class support, Louis Philippe (the cousin of Charles X) became king. Historians call him the "citizen king" because he dressed like a middle-class businessman. He often walked through Paris and spoke to the people he met there.

What Other European Nationalists Rebelled?

Between 1830 and 1848, France influenced rebels in other countries. People in Belgium rebelled against the Netherlands in 1830 and freed

Louis Philippe was known as the "citizen king" because he sided with the middle class.

Photography

Did you know that you probably see more than 1,000 camera images a day? Yet the photograph was unknown before 1827!

French inventor Joseph Niepce made the first photograph from nature that year. It showed the courtyard of his house. In 1844, the first book of photographs was published in Paris. It contained photos of the Egyptian countryside.

Photographs have become popular for several reasons. They tell the truth. Photographs of the United States Civil War first showed what war is really like. Scientists use photos to record information about whatever they are studying—humans, animals, space. People have used them to win support for causes, such as helping the poor. Photographs also record important personal events. Museums even consider photography an art form.

themselves. Polish people also tried to rebel and win their independence from Russia. But the Russian army defeated them. Nationalists in Italy and Germany also rebelled. Austrian troops put down the revolt in Italy. The Confederation of German States used force to end the rebellion in Germany.

SECTION 4 REVIEW On a separate sheet of paper, write answers to these questions.

1) What three political groups came out of the French Revolution?

2) Who followed Louis XVIII as king of France?

3) In what year did the July Revolution in France take place?

4) Who was known as the "citizen king"?

5) When did Belgium free itself from rule by the Netherlands?

What do you think

Why would Charles X want a conservative legislature?

◆Socialist
A person who wants to end the private ownership of land and factories

In 1848, revolutions swept through Europe. Once again, the French rebelled against their government. This time, French radicals demanded that workers be given the right to vote. Louis Philippe, the citizen king said, "There will be no reform. I do not wish it."

In February 1848, the people of Paris took to the streets in a protest against their government. The king sent troops to restore order. Then a mob marched on the king's palace. After he fled to England, revolutionary leaders set up a Second French Republic to govern the nation. (The French established the First Republic during the French Revolution of 1789.)

What Did Socialists Want?

The new republican government had trouble because the radical leaders were divided into two groups. One group wanted to reform only the French political system. The second group wanted both political and economic reform.

Louis Blanc—a **socialist**—led the second group. Socialists wanted to end the private ownership of land and factories.

Revolutions swept through Europe in 1848.

Louis Blanc, a French socialist, set up workshops to give jobs to people who had none.

In Chapter 19, you read about the Industrial Revolution. In that chapter, you learned that a nation needs three things to industrialize—natural resources, plenty of workers, and capital. In France, as in most countries, only a few people owned land and had the capital to build factories and machines.

How Did Socialists Frighten the Middle Class?

The socialists believed that private ownership caused the poor economic conditions of the working class. They wanted the state to control the land and the factories. This radical idea frightened the middle class.

Blanc demanded that the government establish workshops to give jobs to people who had none. For a time, the government did this, but then it closed the workshops. This angered the workers, so they rioted.

Before the riots ended, government soldiers had killed thousands of workers. This violence upset the French people. They blamed the radical socialists for these riots and disorder. The French then wrote a new constitution. It called for the election of a parliament and a powerful president.

Who Brought Peace to France?

In December 1848, the French voters elected Louis Napoleon Bonaparte (Napoleon III) as their new president. (Napoleon Bonaparte was his uncle.) Louis Napoleon brought order to France. Soon after his election, he set aside the republican form of government.

In 1851, Louis Napoleon declared that he was the only ruler of France. Many French people liked this change. In an election, more than 90 percent of the voters supported Napoleon III as a single powerful leader. So France achieved peace, but lost democracy. Napoleon III ruled France for nearly 20 years.

What Did Utopian Socialists Think?

Not all socialists agreed on the best way to improve the lives of the working class. One group—the **utopian** socialists— thought that they could reform society peacefully. The word *utopian* comes from a book Thomas More, an Englishman, wrote in 1516. It was about a future society where everyone worked together for the good of all. Utopia was a perfect society. No one was poor, no one committed any crimes, and no one fought. Utopian socialists believed that people could live and work together peacefully if they had the chance to do so.

What Did Marx Think About Factory Owners?

A German named Karl Marx thought that the utopian socialists were dreamers. Marx said that all societies were made up of the "haves" and the "have-nots." The "haves" have power and wealth. The "have-nots" have nothing. They have no money and no power.

Marx said that powerful leaders would never willingly give up their power. He thought workers would always fight with factory and land owners. Marx believed that all of history was a class struggle between the rich (the "haves") and the poor (the "have-nots"). He thought that factory owners used workers. That is, the owners grew rich from the labor of the workers. Factory owners paid workers low wages and kept the profit from the business for themselves.

◆Utopia
A type of society in which everyone works peacefully together for the good of all

What Kind of Society Did Marx See in the Future?

Marx believed that workers could improve their lives and gain power only by violent revolution. In his book *The Communist Manifesto*, Marx wrote, "Workers of the world, unite!" He believed that workers had ". . . nothing to lose . . . but their chains." Marx called these industrial workers the **proletariat**.

In the future, Marx saw a society that had no need for government. Each member of this society would be equal. There would be no rich or poor. The ideas of Karl Marx influenced the last years of the nineteenth century and the first years of the twentieth.

Karl Marx believed that only violent revolution could improve workers' lives.

◆Proletariat
The working class according to Marx

What Ended the Old Ways of Government?

Throughout 1848, violent revolutions occurred in the Italian states, in Prussia, and in the Austrian Empire. Nearly 50 rebellions broke out in different areas of Europe. Some revolutionaries wanted national independence. Others wanted more say in who governed them. Some rebellions combined both goals. In the end, all these revolutions failed.

But the rebellions ended the system that the Congress of Vienna established in 1814. When a revolt broke out in Austria, Prince Metternich fled to England. The old ruling order was finished. Nationalism had become the most important organizing force for societies.

As time passed, noble families lost their power and privilege. Like all members of the royal class, Czar Nicholas of Russia was nervous. He said, "What remains standing in Europe?"

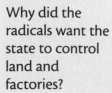

Reading With Fingertips

The Frenchman Louis Braille was a blind teacher of blind children and teenagers. In 1824, he invented a reading system that enables blind people to read. He based it on Charles Barbier's night reading principle. Barbier developed it so that the military could read messages at night. His system was made up of dots pressed into paper.

Braille's system uses six raised dots arranged in cells, or letter spaces. Each cell contains three rows and two columns. Each letter, number, and punctuation mark has its own layout of larger and smaller dots. Braille taught people how to read these dots with their fingertips.

Braille was first printed by hand. A sharp, pointed tool raised small dots on heavy paper. In 1892, the stereotyping machine made it possible to transfer dots to printing plates. For today's books, computer programs translate print into Braille. The blind can also write Braille. They use a Braillewriter, which resembles a typewriter.

SECTION 5 REVIEW Choose the letter of the answer that correctly completes each sentence. Write your answer on a separate sheet of paper.

1) The "Year of Revolutions" is _____.
   - a. 1776
   - b. 1789
   - c. 1815
   - d. 1848

2) A _____ wants to end the private ownership of land and factories.
   - a. absolute monarch
   - b. socialist
   - c. conservative
   - d. liberal

3) The _____ socialists believed that they could peacefully bring about a perfect society.
   - a. utopian
   - b. communist
   - c. conservative
   - d. radical

4) _____ called industrial workers the proletariat.
   - a. Louis Philippe
   - b. Louis Napoleon Bonaparte
   - c. Karl Marx
   - d. Prince Metternich

5) The author of *The Communist Manifesto* said that society is made up of _____.
   - a. the "have"
   - b. the "have-nots"
   - c. class struggle
   - d. all of the above

What do you think **?**

Why did the radicals want the state to control land and factories?

The Communist Manifesto

Karl Marx and Friedrich Engels were the leaders of a new social movement. They thought it would change history. They believed that a workers' revolution would take place in England. They were wrong, however. Then in 1848, the two men published a pamphlet.

Karl Marx and Friedrich Engels

This Communist Manifesto *stated their beliefs. Marx and Engels argued that workers (proletariat) would overthrow the owners of business (bourgeoisie). Marx and Engels called themselves Communists. Their revolutionary ideas would become an important force in the twentieth century.*

In the earlier times of history, we find almost everywhere a complicated arrangement of society into various orders of social rank. In ancient Rome, we have patricians, knights, plebeians, slaves; in the Middle Ages, feudal lords, vassals, guild-masters, journeymen, apprentices, serfs.

The modern bourgeois society [middle class factory owners] that has sprouted from the ruins of feudal society . . . has but established new classes, new conditions of oppression, new forms of struggle in place of the old ones. . . .

The modern labourer . . . instead of rising with the progress of industry, sinks deeper and deeper below the conditions of existence of his own class. He becomes a pauper [poor person] . . . . And here it becomes evident that the bourgeoisie is unfit any longer to be the ruling class in society. . . . What the bourgeoisie therefore produces, above all, are its own grave diggers. Its fall and the victory of the proletariat are equally inevitable. . . .

The Communists turn their attention chiefly to Germany, because that country is on the eve of a bourgeois revolution that is bound to be carried out under more advanced conditions of European civilization and with a much more developed proletariat than that of England in the seventeenth, and of France in the eighteenth century, and because the bourgeois revolution in Germany will be but the prelude to an immediately following proletarian revolution. . . .

The Communists openly declare that their ends can be attained only by the forcible overthrow of all existing social conditions. Let the ruling classes tremble at a communist revolution. The proletarians have nothing to lose but their chains. They have a world to win.

Working men of all countries, unite!

Source Reading Wrap-Up

1) According to this writing, what two classes made up society in his day?
2) Who were the bourgeoisie?
3) The authors said that workers were sinking "deeper and deeper below the conditions of existence." What did they mean?
4) Why might non-Communists fear the Communists?
5) Why did the authors believe that workers should rebel?

Dressing for Success

Throughout history, clothes have been a symbol of success, social status, and wealth. Fashions change for many reasons. For example, during the Middle Ages in Europe, both men and women wore long gowns. They only had buckles to hold their clothing together. Clothing, therefore, had to be large enough to pull over the head. Then in the 1200s, the crusaders returned from the Middle East, bringing back buttons. Buttons could make clothes fit closer to the body.

In the 1400s, women still dressed mostly in floor-length gowns. Men began to wear tight-fitting jackets though. They also wore hose to show off the shape of their legs. Over the years, the dress of upper class men became more fancy and colorful. This trend continued for the next three centuries.

Benjamin Franklin's arrival at the French court in 1779 showed how men's clothing would change. Franklin decided not to wear the fancy, colorful clothes in style at the time. He wore a simple black coat and matching knee breeches. Franklin's dress caused a new fashion trend. His clothes were thought to be the perfect symbol of the "natural man" of the middle class.

In 1789, the French Estates General met. Members of the Third Estate, or common people, could not wear colors or decorated ornaments. After the French Revolution swept the upper class from power, their fashion-setting days ended. Instead, the clothing of the middle class became the acceptable style of dress. Men dressed in dark-colored jackets and trousers. Men's fashion kept this same basic suit well into the twentieth century.

People wore fancy, elaborate clothing in Europe during the 1700s.

Here is an interesting fact from the history of clothing styles. The upper classes often passed clothing styles down to the working class. In the 1700s, the upper class wore powdered wigs, colorful jackets, and knee breeches. In the 1800s, household servants dressed this way. To get dressed up, gentlemen of the nineteenth century wore a tuxedo. In the twentieth century, waiters in fancy restaurants sport tuxedos.

Spotlight Story Wrap-Up

1) Besides modesty and warmth, why do people dress as they do?
2) How did the button change men's clothing in Europe?
3) Why was Benjamin Franklin's clothing the talk of the French court?
4) What impact did the French Revolution have on clothing styles?
5) In your opinion, how are fashion styles set today?

➥ Britain, Prussia, Austria, and Russia defeated and exiled Napoleon in 1814. They met at the Congress of Vienna to decide France's fate.

➥ Metternich had three goals. France should never threaten other nations again. Major European nations should have equal strength. This balance of power would keep the peace. Royal families should return to power and end nationalism.

➥ The congress divided the French empire among European countries and established a German Confederation. It also put royal families back on their thrones.

➥ The ancient Greeks contributed much to western civilization. Many Europeans supported Greek independence from the Ottoman Empire because of this.

➥ Nationalism spread to Latin America. Led by L'Ouverture, Haiti gained its independence from France. Later Santo Domingo won independence from Spain.

➥ In northern South America, Bolívar freed Colombia, Ecuador, and Venezuela. San Martín freed Chile and Peru. Later Brazil got its freedom from Portugal peacefully.

➥ Fathers Hidalgo and Morelos led Mexican peasants successfully against the Spanish. But Mexican creoles wanted power for themselves. This struggle delayed Mexican independence until 1821.

➥ Conservatives were mainly rich landowners and nobles. They supported absolute royal power. Liberals were usually wealthy businessmen and merchants. They wanted a say in the government. They supported a constitutional monarchy and an elected parliament. Radicals wanted to change monarchies to democracies and were willing to use force.

➥ A series of kings ruled France. Charles X's desire to be an absolute ruler caused the Revolution of 1830. Between 1830 and 1848 other people revolted: Belgians, Poles, Italians, and Germans.

➥ Europe was torn by revolutions in 1848, but they all failed. In France, revolution founded a republic. The revolutionaries, however, were divided. Liberals wanted to reform the political system. Socialists wanted to end the private ownership of land and factories. Louis Napoleon was elected president and declared himself Napoleon III.

➥ Karl Marx wrote *The Communist Manifesto*. He believed only violent revolution could improve workers' lives.

Comprehension: Identifying Facts

On a separate sheet of paper, use the words from the Word Bank to complete each sentence.

WORD BANK
Alexander
Blanc
Bolívar
Byron
Hidalgo
Marx
Metternich
L'Ouverture
Philippe
San Martín

1) Prince _____ of Austria was the most influential leader at the Congress of Vienna.

2) Czar _____ of Russia represented his nation at the Congress of Vienna.

3) Lord _____, an English poet, supported the Greek war for independence.

4) Toussaint _____ led the slave revolt against the French in Haiti.

5) Simón _____ liberated New Granada from Spain.

6) José _____ led an army into Chile to free it from Spanish control.

7) The Mexican priest Miguel _____ challenged the Indian peasants to rebel against the Spanish.

8) Louis _____ became the "citizen king" of France in 1830.

9) Louis _____ led one group of French socialists.

10) Karl _____ wrote *The Communist Manifesto*.

Comprehension: Multiple Choice

On a separate sheet of paper, write the letter of the answer that correctly completes each sentence.

1) The French Revolution gave birth to _____.
   a. nationalism
   b. liberty
   c. equality
   d. all of the above

2) _____ led revolts against the Spanish in Latin America.
   a. Byron
   b. Blanc
   c. Metternich
   d. San Martín

3) At the Congress of Vienna, _____ said that nationalism was a disease and that he had the cure for it.

   a. Metternich   c. Louis Philippe

   b. Marx   d. Byron

4) A _____ is a person who likes the old order of things.

   a liberal   c. conservative

   b. radical   d. socialist

5) A _____ is a person who wants to end the private ownership of land and factories.

   a. conservative   c. monarch

   b. socialist   d. peninsular

Comprehension: Understanding Main Ideas

On a separate sheet of paper, write the answers to the following questions using complete sentences, or statements.

1) What is nationalism?

2) Why did the leaders at the Congress of Vienna fear nationalism?

3) How did events in France in the nineteenth century influence other European and colonial revolutionaries?

Critical Thinking: Write Your Opinion

1) Prince Metternich believed nationalism was like a disease. He said, "When France sneezes, Europe catches cold." What did Metternich mean? If possible, use an example of a "sneeze" and a "cold" in your answer.

2) The political group called the conservatives thought that revolution was a danger to society. Do you agree with them? Why or why not?

Test-Taking Tip	When a teacher announces a test, listen carefully. Write down the topics that will be included. Write down the names of any specific readings the teacher says to review.

Chapter

Nationalism and Imperialism

22

1840 to 1914

As you know, nationalism is the loyalty people have for their country. This became a powerful force for change in the world. In this chapter, you will learn about three Italian nationalists who united Italy. Then you will see how Germany was brought together as one nation. Finally, you will learn about imperialism, where European powers took control of Asia and Africa.

Goals for Learning

▶ To explain nationalism and imperialism

▶ To list some characteristics of nationalism

▶ To identify the leaders of Italian unification

▶ To explain how Germany became a unified nation

▶ To explain the reasons behind imperialism

▶ To describe the effects of imperialism on Asia and Africa

1842
Europeans divide China into spheres of influence

1858
British government begins to rule India

1859
Workers begin to build the Suez Canal

1871
Prussia defeats France; Germany becomes one country

1909
South Africa becomes a British colony

1845   1865   1885   1905

1848
Mazzini leads unsuccessful revolt in Italy

1860
Garibaldi unites most of Italy

1867
Japanese revolution returns power to Emperor Meiji

1904
Japan defeats Russia and gains Korea

1912
Italy controls Tripoli

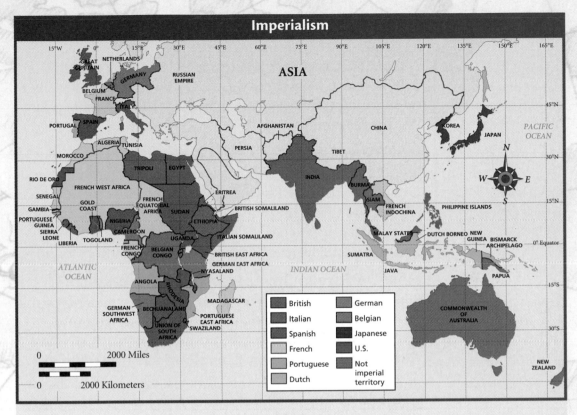

Imperialism

ASIA

British	German
Italian	Belgian
Spanish	Japanese
French	U.S.
Portuguese	Not imperial territory
Dutch	

0   2000 Miles

0   2000 Kilometers

Geography Skills

Between 1850 and 1900, the world went through great change. By 1900, a few powerful nations dominated the map. Many countries in Europe had huge empires in Africa and Asia. The European powers divided nearly all of Africa among themselves. Outsiders also controlled much of Asia. This map shows European and American imperialism in Africa, Europe, and Asia.

Study the map and answer the following questions:

1) Which European power controlled the largest empire?

2) What country controlled the island of Madagascar?

3) What are the names of three African colonies that Portugal controlled?

4) What were the major Dutch colonies in Asia?

5) What country controlled Australia?

Foreign
From another country; having to do with another country

Multilingual
A society in which a number of languages are spoken

Nationalism swept across Europe in the 1800s and early 1900s. As you have already learned, nationalism is loyalty to one's country. But there are many other things that make up nationalism.

How Does Language Affect Nationalism?

A common language is an important part of nationalism. Usually the people of one country speak the same language. This unites them. In some countries, however, people speak more than one language. This kind of country is **multilingual.** However, they are still loyal to their country.

How Do Foreign Invaders Affect Nationalism?

Sometimes people lose their land. **Foreign** invaders (people from other countries) might take it over. For example, powerful neighbors have taken over Poland over the years. Also, for many years, non-Chinese leaders ruled China.

But nationalism can remain even if people lose their land or government. In fact, being invaded often makes people have more nationalism. For example, today many Palestinians are scattered throughout the Middle East. They are now fighting for a land of their own.

How Do Government and History Affect Nationalism?

Having only one government is another part of nationalism. For example, people who live in the 50 states of the United States follow the laws in the Constitution. They also follow the laws made by the government in Washington, D.C.

A common history is another part of nationalism. In American schools, students study the history of the United States. They feel pride in their shared history. The flag, the symbol of Uncle Sam, and the "Star-Spangled Banner" mean something special to all Americans.

Students in other countries also study their history so they will love their country, be loyal to it, and value

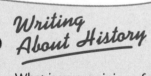

Writing About History

What is your opinion of nationalism? Use examples to explain your opinion. Are there events in the current news that influence what you think? How about the recent past? Write your opinion in your notebook.

MARIE CURIE: 1867–1934

Marie Curie was a Polish-born French chemist. She and her husband, Pierre, studied radioactivity, which is the energy in atoms. Marie received the Nobel Prize in physics in 1903 and in chemistry in 1911.

The Curies wanted everyone benefit from their studies. During World War I, Marie helped equip ambulances with x-ray equipment to help wounded soldiers. She even drove ambulances to the front lines. She also taught others how to use the equipment.

Her work meant that she was often near radioactive materials. Its dangers were not known at the time. Radiation gave her cancer. In a twist of fate, today we use controlled radiation to treat cancer.

their **heritage.** Heritage is made up of all the traditions our ancestors have passed down to us.

Heritage
The traditions ancestors have passed down to their descendants

How Does Culture Affect Nationalism?

A common culture is another part of nationalism. The people of a nation often share the same beliefs, customs, religion, music, and way of life. A belief in freedom, democracy, and equality unites Americans. A common religion unites people in nations such as Israel or Iran. Both Japan and China have a culture that is different from other countries. In any country, the citizens may be different from one another. But they all love their country and feel loyal to it. That is nationalism.

SECTION 1 REVIEW On a separate sheet of paper, write *True* if the statement is true or *False* if the statement is not true. Make each false statement true by changing the underlined word.

1) Some countries are <u>multilingual</u> because the people speak more than one language.
2) When people lose their land to foreign invaders, they sometimes gain more <u>nationalism.</u>
3) Nationalism makes people feel <u>disloyal</u> to their country.
4) People in a nation share a common culture that may include customs, <u>religion,</u> and music.
5) Nationalism is the <u>hate</u> people have toward their country.

What do you think ?

What do you think is the most important symbol of your country? Why?

◆Prime minister
The leader in some democratic government systems

The Napoleonic Wars gave birth to nationalism in Italy. In Chapter 21, you read about the Congress of Vienna, which met in 1814 after Napoleon's defeat. The leaders of this meeting divided Italy into about 30 states and provinces. Austria, France, and Spain controlled these provinces.

What Did Giuseppe Mazzini Do?

Many people in Italy had strong nationalist feelings. In 1848, revolts broke out in many states. Giuseppe Mazzini led the rebellion. Historians call him the "soul" of Italian unity because he stood for its spirit of freedom. But Mazzini's rebellion failed. Thousands of soldiers from Austria and France marched into Italy and put down the revolt. For the next 20 years, French troops controlled Rome.

What Did Camillo di Cavour Do?

Count Camillo di Cavour then stepped forward to lead the fight for unity. He was the **prime minister** of the Kingdom

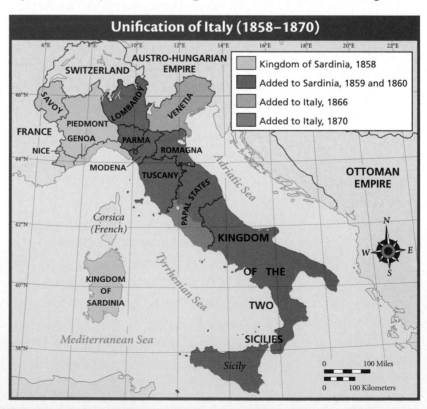

Unification of Italy (1858–1870)

Legend:
- Kingdom of Sardinia, 1858
- Added to Sardinia, 1859 and 1860
- Added to Italy, 1866
- Added to Italy, 1870

MAP STUDY

This map shows how Italy became unified as one country by adding territory between 1858 and 1870. What states became part of the Kingdom of Sardinia in 1859 and 1860? What state was added to Italy in 1866?

of Sardinia. A prime minister is the leader in some democratic government systems.

Sardinia was the only Italian state that an Italian dynasty ruled. (Remember that France, Austria, and Spain ruled all the other Italian states.) In 1848, Sardinia declared war on Austria. This action won the respect of people in all the states of Italy.

Cavour was a skilled politician, and he figured out a way to free the Italian states from outside rule. First, he made a secret agreement with France. Together, they declared war against Austria in 1859. The combined French-Sardinian army defeated Austria.

Next, nationalist revolts broke out in the northern provinces that Austria controlled. By 1860, all these provinces had become part of the Kingdom of Sardinia. Cavour planned how to get two major powers to fight one another and leave Italy alone. Historians call him the "brain" of Italian unity.

Giuseppe Garibaldi, the "sword" of Italian unity, united almost all of Italy.

What Did Giuseppe Garibaldi Do?

Cavour united the northern states of Italy. At the same time, he secretly helped nationalists in the southern states. In May 1860, a small army of Italian nationalists invaded the island of Sicily. Giuseppe Garibaldi led them.

Garibaldi always wore a red shirt in battle. His supporters imitated him, and the red shirt became their uniform. The "Red Shirts" swept through Sicily and marched northward toward Rome. There, Garibaldi's army met up with Sardinian troops. Together, they had united almost all of Italy. Because of his great military feats, historians call Garibaldi the "sword" of the revolution.

Who Became Italy's First King?

In March 1861, a parliament representing almost all of the Italian states met and chose a ruler. King Victor Emmanuel II of Sardinia became the first

Vatican City

From 756 to 1870, the pope ruled much of central Italy. However, with the unification of Italy, the pope's rule was reduced to one city-state, Vatican City. Established in 1929, Vatican City is the world's smallest independent country. Located in northwestern Rome, it has an area of 110 acres.

Medieval and Renaissance walls surround the city. The most important building is Saint Peter's Church. The Vatican, the pope's palace, is also within these walls. The Sistine Chapel is part of this palace. Michelangelo painted its ceiling. The government offices of the Roman Catholic Church are also found here.

Vatican City has its own currency, postal system, and telephone and telegraph services. It also has a railroad station and a radio station. Its population is less than 1,000.

king of a unified Italy. In 1870, the last independent state became part of Italy. Rome became the capital of Italy. But the parliament set aside part of Rome for the pope's use. Vatican City is still the home of the pope and the center of the Roman Catholic Church.

SECTION 2 REVIEW Choose the letter of the answer that correctly completes each sentence. Write your answer on a separate sheet of paper.

1) After 1814, _____ controlled most of the 30 states in Italy.
   a. Austria   c. Spain
   b. France   d. all of the above

2) The "soul" of Italian unity was _____.
   a. Mazzini   c. Cavour
   b. Garibaldi   d. Victor Emmanuel II

3) The "brain" of Italian unity was _____.
   a. Mazzini   c. Cavour
   b. Garibaldi   d. Victor Emmanuel II

4) The "sword" of Italian unity was _____.
   a. Mazzini   c. Cavour
   b. Garibaldi   d. Victor Emmanuel II

5) The first king of Italy was _____.
   a. Mazzini   c. Cavour
   b. Garibaldi   d. Victor Emmanuel II

What do you think ?

Red is an easy color to shoot at. So why would Garibaldi wear red in battle?

The Napoleonic Wars gave birth to nationalism in Germany, too. Like Italy, Germany had many independent states. From 1814 to 1815, the Congress of Vienna organized the German Confederation. It included 38 German states and their rulers. But the confederation was weak.

Soon, the idea of unifying Germany became popular. The people in all the German states spoke German. They also had the same culture and shared the same land.

Why Did the 1848 German Revolution Fail?

The revolts that swept over Europe in 1848 affected Germany. In April 1849, representatives of the German states met in a parliament and issued a constitution. The parliament asked the Prussian king, Frederick Wilhelm IV, to become king of all the German states. (Prussia was the largest German state.)

The king refused the offer and said, "I do not accept a crown offered from the gutter." He meant that the people of Germany, and not the princes of all the states, had offered him the crown. He wanted the nobles, not the common people, to choose him.

Soon, fighting broke out between the liberals and the conservatives. The liberals wanted gradual change and a democratic government; the conservatives wanted none of this. Then King Wilhelm sent his Prussian army to break up the parliament. When the liberal leaders fled, the conservatives once again controlled the German states.

How Did Bismarck Plan to Unite the German States?

After the 1848 revolution failed, most German nationalists thought that only Prussia could unite Germany. Prussia was the strongest German state and had the best army. In 1862, Otto von Bismarck became prime minister of Prussia. Bismarck, a member of the rich landlord class, was loyal to the Prussian king. He wanted to unite all the German states under Prussia's leadership.

In 1862, Otto von Bismarck became Prussia's prime minister. He helped unite Germany.

Bismarck, who was a conservative, did not believe in democratic rule. In his first speech as prime minister, he told the Prussian parliament that the only way to solve problems was "by blood and iron." For him, "blood" meant war and "iron" meant a king with absolute power.

What Is Militarism?

Bismarck wanted to make Prussia into a great military power. He forced the Prussian parliament to give him money to build a strong army. He believed that war would unite the German states. Historians have a name for this belief: **militarism.** For such a country, nothing is more important than the military.

Who Won the Austro-Prussian War?

In 1864, Bismarck's army defeated Germany's northern neighbor, Denmark. Then, in 1866, his army defeated Austria in seven weeks. To do this, Bismarck used Prussia's new railroads and better weapons. After Austria's defeat, Bismarck forced its neighbor to give up some of its German land. Austria gave Hungary its independence.

Austria and Hungary each had its own parliament and officials. However, the Austrian emperor was still the king of Hungary. Also, the two countries had one **policy**, or plan, toward other countries. They also shared one army. Historians call this new empire Austria-Hungary.

◆Militarism
A nation's warlike policy or practice

◆Policy
A plan that helps a person or a country make a decision

How Did Bismarck Start the Franco-Prussian War?

Next, Bismarck and Prussia went to war with France. It started when the French **ambassador,** a representative of the French government, came to Prussia. He wanted to talk to the king about who should become the next king of Spain.

Bismarck then lied to the newspapers about what the two men said to one another. His lie made the French think that the Prussian king had said something rude to their ambassador. It made the Germans think that the French ambassador had threatened them. Nationalists in both countries felt that they had to go to war. Only then could they defend their national honor.

Who Won the Franco-Prussian War?

The well-trained Prussian army moved quickly. In 1870, German soldiers poured into northern France. At the Battle of Sedan, the Prussian army defeated the French and

The Prussians defeated the French in 1871 to end the Franco-Prussian War. After this war, all of the German states unified.

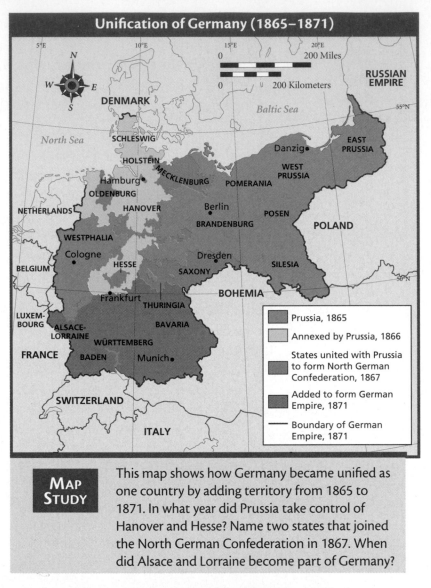

Unification of Germany (1865–1871)

MAP STUDY

This map shows how Germany became unified as one country by adding territory from 1865 to 1871. In what year did Prussia take control of Hanover and Hesse? Name two states that joined the North German Confederation in 1867. When did Alsace and Lorraine become part of Germany?

◆Siege
The act of surrounding a city or fort with an army and cutting off its supplies to make the people on the inside surrender

captured about 100,000 French soldiers. Included among them was the French ruler, Napoleon III.

The Prussian army surrounded Paris and cut off its supplies. After this four-month **siege,** Paris surrendered. Bismarck forced the French to sign a treaty called the Treaty of Frankfurt. According to the treaty, France had to pay Prussia a huge sum of money. It also had to give up two important territories, Alsace and Lorraine. These provinces, which lay on the border with Germany, contained France's richest coal and iron fields.

What Was the Second Reich?

The Franco-Prussian War brought all the German states together. After the Austro-Prussian War, Prussia took control of northern Germany. Then it formed the North German Confederation. After the Franco-Prussian War, the people in the four southern states joined the rest of Germany.

William I agreed to become the first **kaiser,** or emperor, of Germany. He was crowned in January 1871 at the French palace of Versailles. Historians call this new German empire the Second **Reich.** The German word *reich* means empire or nation. The Holy Roman Empire was the First Reich in that part of Europe.

SECTION 3 REVIEW On a separate sheet of paper, write answers to these questions.

1) Why did many Germans look to Prussia for leadership in unifying Germany?

2) Why did Bismarck build up a great army?

3) How did Bismarck's actions lead to the Franco-Prussian war?

4) What were the results of the Franco-Prussian war?

5) Who became the first kaiser of a united Germany?

◆Kaiser
The emperor of Germany

◆Reich
The German word for empire

What do you think

Why do you think the Treaty of Frankfurt probably made the French feel ashamed?

Colonialism
The controlling of colonies; another name for imperialism

Imperialism
Control or influence a powerful nation has over a weaker colony

Market
A place to sell goods

Mother country
A nation that controls a colony

Imperialism occurs when a powerful nation controls a weaker country. During the 1500s, many European countries set up colonies in the Americas. Spain controlled most of Latin America and England controlled most of North America. **Colonialism,** or the controlling of colonies, is another name for imperialism.

By the beginning of the 1800s, however, wars like the American Revolutionary War had changed Europe's opinion about colonialism. Colonies seemed to cause more trouble than they were worth. However, by 1900, the industrialized countries of Europe, Japan, and the United States controlled nearly the whole world. How did this happen? There are many reasons.

How Did Industrialism Help Imperialism?

The Industrial Revolution was one reason why imperialism spread. Factory owners in industrialized nations needed the natural resources and raw materials of other countries. To keep their factories running, they needed coal, iron ore, gold, silver, tin, and copper. They could get these from colonies.

Queen Victoria of England rides on top of an elephant in Delhi, India, in this picture.

These same nations needed places to sell their manufactured goods. That is, they needed **markets.** By taking over colonies, they could control markets. Each major nation let its colonies buy only those goods manufactured in the **mother country**—the nation that controls a colony.

How Did Nationalism Help Imperialism?

Some countries thought that an empire would make them look important in the eyes of the world. Italy, Germany, Japan, and the United States thought colonies would make them as powerful as England and France. Many countries agreed with the statement that "there has never been a great power without great colonies."

How Did Militarism Help Imperialism?

In the late 1800s, many countries built up their military power. Sea power was especially important, because it helped nations control trade routes. Mother countries could use their colonies as military bases. Ships from these mother countries could stop at colonial ports to get supplies for the military.

How Did Attitudes Help Imperialism?

Many people in Europe and the United States thought that they were better than people from the East. They thought that these people—especially Africans and Asians—were ignorant and uncivilized. Westerners believed that they should bring Christianity and western civilization to these countries.

SECTION 4 REVIEW On a separate sheet of paper, write answers to these questions.

1) What is imperialism?

2) Why did many countries lose interest in imperialism at the beginning of the 1800s?

3) What is the connection between the Industrial Revolution and imperialism?

4) What is the connection between nationalism and imperialism?

5) Why do you think Europeans and Americans thought of themselves as better than people from Africa and Asia?

What do you think ?

Was imperialism a good thing? Explain your answer.

By the 1600s, Britain was the greatest sea power in the world. It was also the most industrialized country and the country that did the most trading. Because of all this, Britain wanted colonies in Asia. Soon, the British would brag that "the sun never sets on the British empire."

Why Was India Important to Britain?

The Moghul Empire ruled most of India in the 1500s and 1600s, but it collapsed in 1707. India was then divided into many weak, independent states. By the mid-1700s, France and Britain were fighting each other for control of India. Britain won. At first, the British ruled India through a privately owned company—the British East India Company. However, in 1858, the British government took over direct rule of India.

India won its independence in 1947. But for nearly 100 years, India was very important to Britain. It provided Britain with natural resources and raw materials for industry. Its large population also provided an important market for British goods.

This picture shows the Prince of Wales being welcomed to India.

THE LAST OF THE REDCOATS

During the American Revolution, British soldiers wore white pants, a shiny black hat, and a bright red coat. Because of these bright coats, people called them "redcoats" or "lobster backs." Their uniforms looked great in a parade, but an enemy could easily see these red coats.

Years later, while fighting in India, the British soldiers decided to make the enemy's job harder. They covered their uniforms with brown dirt in the dry season and with mud in the wet season. In time, the British adopted the dull yellowish-brown color of Indian dirt for their battle uniforms. Today, we call this "khaki." It comes from the Indian word for dust.

♦Sphere of influence
An area in which only one foreign country can trade

Because India was important to Britain, the British did everything they could to protect India from other imperialistic countries. In the late 1800s, Russia threatened India on its northwest boundaries. To protect India, Britain took over neighboring Afghanistan.

Why Was Southeast Asia Important to Europe?

France also threatened British interests in India. France took over much of Southeast Asia, an area that became known as French Indochina. (Today, this area includes the countries of Vietnam, Laos, and Cambodia.) The British took over Burma to keep the French from expanding westward. (India lies to the west of Burma.) Soon Ceylon, Malaya, and Singapore also fell under British control.

When Did Europe Insist on More Trade With China?

China lies east of India. For years Chinese rulers had allowed only limited trade with other countries. By the late 1800s, however, this limited trade no longer satisfied the Europeans. They forced China to give them special trade rights.

After 1842, Great Britain, France, Germany, and Russia took over Chinese land and important sea ports. These nations divided China up into four different trading areas. Each European power controlled the trade in one of these areas. Historians call this a **sphere of influence.** The Europeans said that China was still an independent country. However, its rulers had no say in the European-controlled trade.

What Happened in Japan in 1867?

For a while, people thought that Japan, too, might fall to Europe's imperialism. However, a revolution in 1867 ended

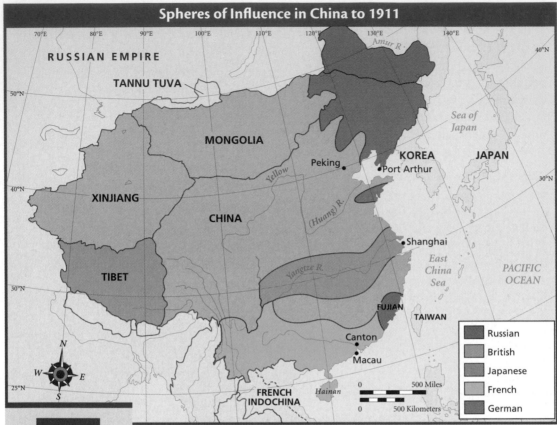

Spheres of Influence in China to 1911

RUSSIAN EMPIRE

TANNU TUVA

MONGOLIA

XINJIANG

CHINA

TIBET

Peking

Port Arthur

KOREA

JAPAN

Sea of Japan

Shanghai

East China Sea

PACIFIC OCEAN

FUJIAN

TAIWAN

Canton

Macau

FRENCH INDOCHINA

Hainan

Yellow (Huang) R.

Yangtze R.

Amur R.

Legend	
	Russian
	British
	Japanese
	French
	German

0 — 500 Miles
0 — 500 Kilometers

MAP STUDY

This map shows the spheres of influences, or trading areas, in China that existed until 1911. Which European power had a sphere of influence along the Yangtze River? Which country had a sphere of influence in Korea? In what lands did the French have a sphere of influence?

the rule of the shogun and returned political power to Emperor Meiji. This revolution brought great change to Japan.

After 1867, new leaders governed Japan in the emperor's name. They introduced many reforms, and Japan set out to become a modern, industrialized nation. It adopted western ideas in transportation and education. It abolished feudalism. Then the Japanese leaders wrote a constitution based on the German system Bismarck had developed.

How Did Japan Become Imperialistic?

Next, Japan began to develop a western-style army. In 1876, its leaders passed a law that ordered all young men to serve in the army. Soon Japan had a modern army and navy. Japan used its new military power to become imperialistic. From 1894 to 1895, it went to war with China. China lost and had to give Japan some of its territory.

China was a victim of European imperialism. This cartoon from 1900 shows the Russian bear, the British lion, the German eagle, and other European nations preparing to divide the Chinese dragon.

In 1904, Japan went to war with Russia and won again. It took over Korea and gained important trading rights in Russian-controlled lands in China. Like many European countries, Japan was now an imperialistic world power.

SECTION 5 REVIEW On a separate sheet of paper, write the word from the Word Bank that completes each sentence.

WORD BANK
Afghanistan
France
Great Britain
Japan
Russia

1) In 1858, _____ took over direct rule of India.

2) In the late 1800s, Great Britain took over _____.

3) In the late 1800s, _____ took over much of Southeast Asia.

4) _____ became a military power after its revolution in 1867.

5) Japan became a world power after it defeated China in 1895 and _____ in 1904.

What do you think

China was once the most powerful and richest country in the world. But in the 1800s, Europeans began to control its trade. Why did that happen?

◆Protectorate
An independent country whose foreign policy is controlled by a major power

As you know, Europeans wanted colonies in Asia. They wanted them in Africa, too. In the 1870s, Europeans raced one another for colonies there.

What Colonies Did Britain Control in Africa?

By the end of the 1800s, Great Britain controlled what are now the nations of Sudan, Nigeria, Ghana, Kenya, and Uganda. In 1900, it took over Nigeria. South Africa became a British colony in 1909.

In 1859, workers began to build the Suez Canal. When it was finished over ten years later, it connected the Mediterranean and Red Seas. The canal made the trip from Europe to India and the Far East much shorter. In 1875, Britain took control of the canal.

A few years later, Egypt became a British **protectorate.** As a protectorate, Egypt stayed independent, but Britain controlled its foreign policy. In return, Britain protected Egypt from attacks by other countries.

The Suez Canal was finished in 1869. It links the Mediterranean Sea and the Red Sea. This image shows the opening ceremony of this important waterway.

How Big Was the French Empire in Africa?

By 1847, France had gained control of Algeria. Soon, France established the largest European empire in Africa. This empire stretched 2,500 miles from the Atlantic Ocean eastward to Sudan. France's holdings in Africa were large, but not rich. Still, other countries respected France for having such a large empire.

The Suez Canal

The Suez Canal is a human-made waterway. The canal is 121 miles long, and ocean-going vessels can use it. Most of the canal is limited to single lane traffic. Several bays, however, allow ships to pass each other.

Ferdinand de Lesseps, a French diplomat and engineer, developed the plans for the canal. He then got Egyptian and French support to build it. Work finally began in 1859. It took over ten years to complete the canal. Because of this success, de Lesseps later headed the Panama Canal project.

The Suez Canal was originally built as a shortcut to the European empires in Asia. Today, the canal is an important link to oil. Giant tankers pass through it, carrying oil from the Persian Gulf to Europe and America.

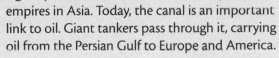

Industrial Technology

History in Your Life

How Big Was the German Empire in Africa?

Germany united as a nation in 1871. It entered the race for African colonies late. Even so, by 1900, only France and Britain had larger empires in Africa. Germany's colonies were far apart and not rich. However, its military strength worried other European countries. When Germany asked these countries to come to a meeting in Berlin, they came. There they talked about African boundaries. However, no one asked any Africans to come to the meeting.

What Other European Countries Controlled Africa?

Many other nations had colonies in Africa. Spain and Portugal had the oldest colonies. Belgium had a large empire in central Africa. Italy, which came late to Africa, had little success there. It tried to take over Ethiopia, but was defeated. In 1912, Italy did take control of Tripoli in what is now the nation of Libya. Tripoli was large, but poor.

Many European nations scrambled for empires, but some nations got little or nothing of value. They felt angry at those who got wealth from their colonies. This led to fighting.

Was Imperialism Good or Bad?

Europeans said that imperialism was good. It brought great improvements in health, transportation, and education to Africa and Asia. It introduced the ideas of constitutional government. It also brought jobs and industry to the colonies.

However, much of the colonial people thought that imperialism was bad. They felt that Europeans got more out of imperialism than they did. Factories in Africa and Asia supplied cheap goods to Europe. But these factories—owned by Europeans—destroyed native industry and many people lost their jobs.

Also, the colonial people had no control over their government or their country's natural resources. Europeans took the best land and the richest sources of gold, iron, silver, copper, or other valuable natural resources found in the ground.

How Did Europeans Treat Native People?

Europeans thought they were better than the native people of Africa and Asia. They tried to change the religion, the language, and the way of life of these colonized people. This showed that they had little respect for native culture and customs. In time, this led to a wave of nationalism among the people of Africa and Asia.

SECTION 6 REVIEW On a separate sheet of paper, write answers to these questions.

1) What colonies did Britain have in Africa?

2) What did France gain from its African empire?

3) What other European countries besides Britain, France, and Germany had colonies in Africa?

4) In what ways did imperialism help the colonized people in Africa?

5) Why did colonized people in Africa dislike imperialism?

What do you think

Why would Europeans want Africans to give up their language, religion, and customs?

"That Was No Brother"

The first meeting between white explorers and Africans must have been terrifying to both groups. The Africans had never seen white-skinned people before. The whites were far from home and few in number compared to the Africans. Misunderstandings were likely to occur. This excerpt describes such a meeting from an African's viewpoint.

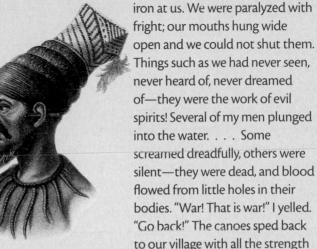

When we heard that the man with the white flesh was journeying down the [river] we were open-mouthed with astonishment. We stood still. All night long the drums announced the strange news—a man with white flesh! That man, we said to ourselves, has a white skin. He will be one of our brothers who were drowned in the river. All life comes from the water, and in the water he has found life. Now he is coming back to us, he is coming home. . . .

We will prepare a feast, I ordered. We will go to meet our brother and escort him into the village with rejoicing! We donned our ceremonial garb. We assembled the great canoes. We listened for the gong which would announce our brother's presence . . . Presently the cry was heard: He is approaching. . . . Now he enters the river! Halloh! We swept forward, my canoe leading, the others following, with songs of joy and with dancing, to meet the first white man our eyes had beheld, and to do him honor.

But as we drew near his canoes there were loud reports, bang! bang! and fire staves spat bits of iron at us. We were paralyzed with fright; our mouths hung wide open and we could not shut them. Things such as we had never seen, never heard of, never dreamed of—they were the work of evil spirits! Several of my men plunged into the water. . . . Some screamed dreadfully, others were silent—they were dead, and blood flowed from little holes in their bodies. "War! That is war!" I yelled. "Go back!" The canoes sped back to our village with all the strength our spirits could impart to our arms.

That was no brother! That was the worst enemy our country had ever seen. . . .

Now tell me: has the white man dealt fairly by us? Oh, do not speak to me of him! You call us wicked men, but you white men are much more wicked! You think because you have guns you can take away our land and our possessions. You have sickness in your heads, for that is not justice.

Source Reading Wrap-Up

1) Who did the Africans think the white man was?
2) How did the Africans prepare to greet the white man?
3) How did the white man greet the Africans?
4) Why does the writer call white men wicked?
5) After reading the article, what is your opinion of what the white man did?

"Dr. Livingstone, I Presume?"

For many years, Africa was called the unexplored continent. The African desert made it hard to travel there by land. Africa's rivers had many waterfalls and rapids that made travel difficult.

In the nineteenth century, religious explorers set out for Africa. They wanted to bring Christianity and education to the Africans. One of the most famous was David Livingstone. Livingstone went to Africa to spread Christianity. He also hated slavery and wanted to end the slave trade. In time, he became well known and was loved by many Africans.

Between 1841 and 1873, Livingstone made three long trips to Africa. In 1849, he crossed the vast Kalahari Desert. On this trip he explored the Zambezi River. Six years later, he followed that river eastward to the coast. On that trip, he explored a giant waterfall. He named it Victoria Falls after the English queen, Queen Victoria.

In 1865, he set out to find the source of the Nile River. He began at Cape Town on the southern tip of Africa and went north. For many years nothing was heard from him. Many people thought he had died or become lost.

An American newspaper, the *New York Herald*, sent a reporter to find Livingstone. The reporter, Henry Stanley, traveled for 126 days in search of Livingstone. He sent back daily accounts of what he was seeing and learning in Africa. Some African guides took him to Ujiji on Lake Tanganyika. In his newspaper account, Stanley described what happened next. "The expedition at last comes to a halt. . . . I alone have a few more steps to make. . . . As I come nearer I see

Henry Stanley met up with David Livingstone near Lake Tanganyika in Africa.

the white face of an old man. . . . We raise our hats and I say, Dr. Livingstone, I presume?"

The two men became friends and explored together. By the end of the trip, Africa fascinated Stanley. In 1873, Dr. Livingstone died. Stanley continued to explore.

Explorers like Livingstone and Stanley were very important in the scramble for African territory. Their writings and speeches made people more interested in Africa. They also convinced some people that slavery was evil and should be stopped.

Spotlight Story Wrap-Up

1) Why did African geography discourage its exploration?

2) Why did the missionary explorers go to Africa?

3) What river and waterfall did Livingstone explore on his expeditions?

4) On his first trip to Africa, whom did Henry Stanley work for? What did he do?

5) How did Livingstone and Stanley contribute to the scramble for Africa?

➡ Nationalism means that a group of people have one language and a common history. They share the same customs, music, way of life, and religion.

➡ Mazzini was the soul of Italian independence. He led a failed revolt in 1848. Cavour was the brain of Italian unity. He got French support for Sardinia's war against Austria. The war won independence for several Italian provinces. Garibaldi was the sword of Italian independence. He and his Red Shirts freed Sicily. They joined Sardinian troops near Rome and united Italy. Victor Emmanuel II became Italy's first king. The pope only kept control of a small area in Rome.

➡ The German Revolution of 1848 failed. The Prussian ruler refused the German parliament's crown and broke it up. German nationalists believed only Prussia, the strongest German state, could unite Germany. In 1862, Bismarck became its prime minister.

➡ Bismarck used militarism to conquer the German states. He defeated Austria, which resulted in the formation of Austria-Hungary.

➡ In the Franco-Prussian War of 1870, Prussia defeated France and won French territory. The remaining independent German states joined Prussia to become Germany. William I became its first kaiser in 1871.

➡ In imperialism or colonialism, a stronger nation controls weaker ones for its own benefit. The Industrial Revolution contributed to this policy. Factory owners needed raw materials from colonies and used them as markets for their goods.

➡ Countries believed that having colonies made them important world powers. Since sea power was especially important, colonies were used as military bases.

➡ In Asia, Britain took control of India, Burma, Ceylon, Malaya, and Singapore. France took Indochina.

➡ After 1842, Britain, France, Germany, and Russia divided China into trading areas. They were called spheres of influence.

➡ After 1867, Japan modernized and went to war against China and then Russia. It won Korea and trading rights in China.

➡ European powers divided Africa into colonies. Britain controlled Egypt and the Suez Canal, South Africa, and several other colonies. French colonies were mainly in West Africa. Germany, Portugal, Spain, and Belgium also had colonies.

Comprehension: Identifying Facts

On a separate sheet of paper, use the words from the Word Bank to complete each sentence.

WORD BANK

Bismarck
Cavour
Garibaldi
Great Britain
Japan
Mazzini
Meiji
Napoleon III
Prussia
William I

1) _____ was an Italian nationalist and the "soul" of Italian unity.

2) _____ was a skilled politician and the "brain" of Italian unity.

3) _____ was a fine soldier and the "sword" of Italian unity.

4) _____ was the Prussian prime minister who wanted to unite all the German states under Prussia's leadership.

5) The strongest German state was _____.

6) In the Battle of Sedan, Prussian soldiers captured _____ and 100,000 other prisoners.

7) The first kaiser of a united Germany was _____.

8) Emperor _____ began to make Japan a modern and powerful nation.

9) _____ controlled the colony of India.

10) _____ defeated Russia in 1904 and won control of Korea.

Comprehension: Multiple Choice

On a separate sheet of paper, write the letter of the answer that correctly completes each sentence.

1) A nation's warlike policy or practice is called _____.
   a. imperialism   c. nationalism
   b. colonialism   d. militarism

2) The love people have for their country is _____.
   a. nationalism   c. colonialism
   b. militarism   d. protectorate

3) Another name for a German emperor is _____.

    a. conservative   c. kaiser

    b. liberal   d. protectorate

4) The control by a powerful nation of a weaker one is _____.

    a. militarism   c. nationalism

    b. imperialism   d. kaiser

5) Bismarck believed in _____ for Germany.

    a. imperialism   c. militarism

    b. nationalism   d. all of the above

Comprehension: Understanding Main Ideas

On a separate sheet of paper, write the answers to the following questions using complete sentences, or statements.

1) What is imperialism?

2) Which countries became imperial powers during the nineteenth century?

Critical Thinking: Write Your Opinion

1) Do you agree or disagree with Bismarck that leaders must decide problems with "blood and iron"? Explain your answer.

2) Do you believe imperialism was more a force for good or a force for evil? Explain your answer.

3) Why do you think Europeans gained control over Africa so easily?

Test-Taking Tip   When taking a short-answer test, first answer the questions you know. Then go back to spend time on the questions you are less sure of.

Comparing and contrasting reveals how things are alike and how they are different. People, ideas, and events are sometimes compared and contrasted in writing. Look for words that signal comparing and contrasting when you read.

> To compare, ask: "How are these things alike?"
>
> To contrast, ask: "How are these things different?"

- To decide if things are being compared, look for words, such as:

> also   both   like   similar
>
> Cavour, like Garibaldi, was a leader in the unification of Italy.

- To decide if things are being contrasted, look for words, such as:

> but   however   instead
> not   only   while
>
> Cavour was called the "brain" of the revolution while Garibaldi was called the "sword."

Decide whether each of these sentences compares or contrasts.

1) Mazzini's revolt was unsuccessful; however, Cavour's gained Sardinia's freedom.

2) Cavour worked to unite the northern Italian states while Garibaldi fought in the south.

3) Both Cavour and Garibaldi were Italian heroes.

4) Germany, like Italy, had many independent states.

5) Ironically, it was not a German, but Napoleon, who began German unification.

Compare and contrast the effects of imperialism. Focus on what happened between imperialistic European nations and the named areas. In your notebook, write one sentence about each item. Be sure to use words that compare and contrast.

6) India

7) Southeast Asia

8) China

9) Japan

10) Egypt

The Industrial Revolution began in England in the 1750s. England could industrialize because it had natural resources, workers, and capital.

The English invented new machinery. The factory system brought workers, machines, and power together. The making of iron was improved, and steel was invented. Canals and the locomotive improved transportation. New inventions included the telegraph, telephone, electric light, internal combustion engine, and the airplane.

After 1763, Britain wanted its North American colonies to pay for the war against France. The colonists protested. Then colonial representatives signed the Declaration of Independence. The French helped Americans win a revolution against Britain.

France in the 1770s consisted of three estates—the clergy, the nobles, and the common people. The Third Estate paid all the taxes. This group established a constitutional monarchy in 1789. In 1792, the National Constitutional Convention created a republic. The Jacobins under Robespierre began the Reign of Terror. Then came the Directory and the Consulate. In 1804, Napoleon crowned himself emperor.

Napoleon's victories increased French power, but he made two mistakes. The Continental System turned countries against France. His Russian invasion destroyed his army. The allies defeated Napoleon in 1814 and again at Waterloo. In France, the Code of Napoleon made every man equal under the law. Napoleon's conquests spread the ideas of the French Revolution.

Under Metternich's lead, the Congress of Vienna reorganized Europe. It promoted the balance of powers.

Nationalism was a major force. Bolívar and San Martín freed South American countries from Spain. Father Hidalgo began the Mexican fight for independence.

Conservatives supported absolute royal power. Liberals favored a constitutional monarchy. Radicals wanted to change monarchies to democracies. In 1848, there were revolutions throughout Europe. None succeeded. In France, Napoleon III became emperor. Marx believed only violent revolution could improve workers' lives.

Mazzini, Cavour, and Garibaldi won Italian independence. By 1870, Bismarck had united Germany.

The Industrial Revolution made colonies into sources of raw materials and markets. Imperialism made Asia and Africa into European colonies.

Comprehension: Identifying Facts

On a separate sheet of paper, use the words from the Word Bank to complete each sentence.

WORD BANK

boycott

capital

conservative

equality

imperialism

liberal

nationalism

militarism

natural resources

raw materials

1) Things such as coal, ore, and water that come from nature and help humans are _____.

2) Workers use _____ to make a finished product.

3) People use _____ to make more money or to start a business.

4) Before the American Revolution started, the colonists decided to _____, or not buy, tea from Britain.

5) The French people wanted _____, or the same rights for all people.

6) A _____ is a person who likes the old political order and fears revolution or change.

7) A _____ is a person who wants to limit absolute power and give power to more people.

8) People who love their country are practicing _____.

9) When a powerful nation controls weaker countries, the larger nation is practicing _____.

10) Having a warlike policy or practice is _____.

Comprehension: Multiple Choice

On a separate sheet of paper, write the letter of the answer that correctly completes each sentence.

1) James _____ helped to create the Industrial Revolution by inventing a machine that produced more yarn.

    a. Edison   c. Morse

    b. Whitney   d. Hargreaves

2) Thomas _____ wrote the Declaration of Independence that gave reasons for the American Revolution.

    a. Jefferson   c. Wellington

    b. Washington   d. Locke

3) At the Congress of Vienna, Prince _____ of Austria tried to return Europe to the old forms of government.

   a. Wellington   c. Metternich

   b. L'Ouverture   d. Marx

4) _____ led revolts against the Spanish in Latin America.

   a. Bolívar   c. L'Ouverture

   b. San Martín   d. all of the above

5) Emperor _____ began to turn Japan into an imperial power.

   a. Meiji   c. Louis XVI

   b. Alexander I   d. none of the above

Comprehension: Understanding Main Ideas

On a separate sheet of paper, write the answers to the following questions using complete sentences, or statements.

1) What is one connection between the Industrial Revolution and imperialism, or colonialism?

2) What is one connection between the American Revolution and imperialism, or colonialism?

3) What is one connection between nationalism and war?

Critical Thinking: Write Your Opinion

1) In this unit, you learned about many revolutions. Which of these revolutions interested you the most and why?

2) In this unit, you learned about many people. Which of these people seemed the most interesting? Which would you like to know more about and why?

| Test-Taking Tip | After you have completed a test, reread each question and answer. Ask yourself: Have I answered the question that was asked? Have I answered it completely? |

"Human beings come in all sizes and shapes and in a variety of colors. This rich diversity is matched by an equal diversity in regard to religious beliefs and political ideologies. We are thrown together on this planet and we have to live together. That is why the Charter imposes the imperative on all human beings to . . . live together in peace with one another as good neighbors."

—U Thant, Secretary-General of the United Nations (1962–1971), speaking in 1964

Conflict and Challenges

1914 to 1955

Wars unlike history had ever seen before filled the first half of the twentieth century. World War I and World War II were large and devastating. Millions of people were killed or injured.

You will learn how World War I began in 1914 and lasted four long years. During this time, a revolution started in Russia. You will see how and why it started. After World War I, you will see how World War II started in 1939. After World War II, you will see how the United Nations formed. You will also learn how this organization got involved in a war in Korea in 1950 to try to contain communism.

World War I

1914 to 1919

Y ou learned about imperialism, nationalism, and militarism in earlier chapters. Now you will see how these caused World War I. This war was unlike any before it. It featured modern weapons, terrible fighting conditions, and enormous loss of life. In this chapter, you will learn how it started, how it was fought, how it ended, and what it meant for those involved.

Goals for Learning

▶ To explain how imperialism, nationalism, and militarism caused war

▶ To describe how the alliance system helped cause, rather than prevent, World War I

▶ To identify the major countries of the Central Powers and the Allies in World War I

▶ To describe the role the United States played in World War I

▶ To describe the different goals the Big Four powers had at the peace conference

▶ To explain the chief parts of the Treaty of Versailles

▶ To describe the social, economic, and political effects of World War I

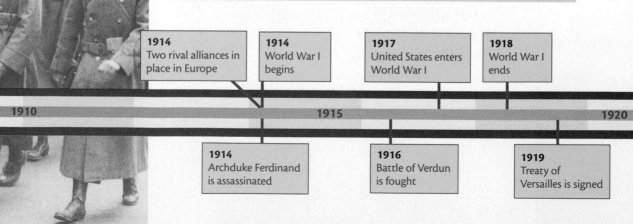

1914
Two rival alliances in place in Europe

1914
World War I begins

1917
United States enters World War I

1918
World War I ends

1910

1915

1920

1914
Archduke Ferdinand is assassinated

1916
Battle of Verdun is fought

1919
Treaty of Versailles is signed

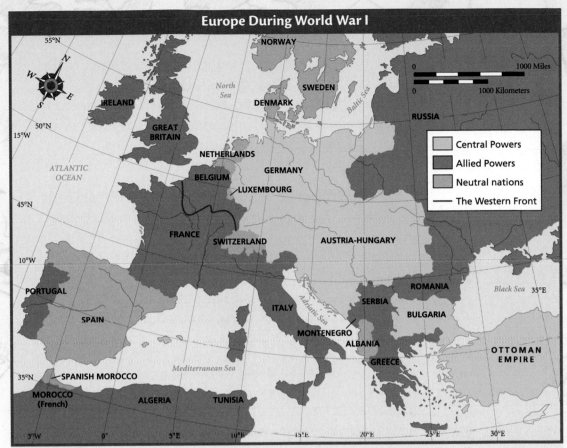

Europe During World War I

Central Powers
Allied Powers
Neutral nations
The Western Front

Geography Skills

During World War I, Europe was divided into two alliances. Germany and Austria-Hungary were the major Central Powers. France, Russia, and Great Britain were the main Allied Powers. Some countries were neutral. That is, they took neither side. This map shows the central, allied, and neutral powers during World War I. It also shows the western front.

Study the map and answer the following questions:

1) To what alliance did Italy belong?

2) To what alliance did Bulgaria belong?

3) Where was the western front?

4) What are the names of three neutral countries shown on this map?

5) German U-boats were an important weapon against British naval power. In what sea would they have been most effective?

Rival
One who tries to do better than another; to try to outdo another country or person

In Chapter 22, you read about the powerful imperialistic nations of France, Great Britain, Germany, Austria-Hungary, Italy, and Russia. These imperialistic powers did not have equal shares of land and riches, so they became **rivals.** That is, they tried to outdo one another. At first, this led to jealousy. Then it led to mistrust. Finally, it led to war.

Why Did Imperial Nations Become Militarized?

As they became more mistrustful of one another, these imperial nations built bigger armies and navies. For example, William II, Germany's kaiser, wanted his navy to be equal to Britain's. Britain then had to build an even larger navy. All these industrialized nations also built bigger, more deadly weapons. Countries were becoming more militarized.

What Was the Alliance System?

At first, the countries of Europe tried to prevent war. They formed alliances and agreed to aid one another if attacked. After all, one country would surely not attack another if that meant fighting with several countries instead of one.

By 1914, two rival alliances were in place. Germany, Austria-Hungary, and Italy made up the Triple Alliance. Great Britain, France, and Russia made up the Triple Entente.

What Event Started World War I?

Nationalism had helped nations like Italy and Germany to unite. But by the 1900s, the spirit of nationalism had become a problem for some nations.

Serbs living in Austria-Hungary wanted to be part of Serbia, a

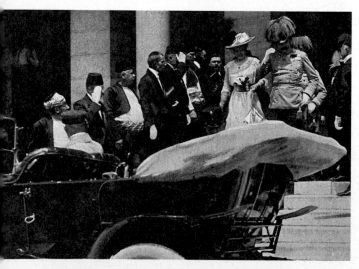

The assassination of Archduke Franz Ferdinand and his wife, Sophie, was the spark that caused World War I. This photo shows Ferdinand and Sophie just before they were killed.

MATA HARI: 1876–1917

Mata Hari was a famous spy during World War I. The real Mata Hari began life as Margaretha Zelle. At 21, she moved to the Dutch East Indies with her husband. The unhappy marriage soon ended. She then went to Paris and called herself "Mata Hari," or "eye of day." There she became a popular dancer. Mata Hari knew many men, most of them French, British, and Russian military officers. She was also close to German officials. In 1916, she went to Germany to learn how to be a spy. For years she spied for the Germans during the war. In 1917, the French arrested her for selling military information to Germany. She was then found guilty and shot.

neighboring country. Many Serbs lived in Sarajevo, which was a city in Austria-Hungary. To try to improve relations with the Serbs, the Austrian emperor sent his nephew Franz Ferdinand to Sarajevo. On Sunday, June 28, 1914, Ferdinand and Sophie, his wife, were killed as they rode through the streets of Sarajevo.

Austria-Hungary blamed the Serbians. On July 28, 1914, Austria declared war on Serbia. Next, Russia said it would protect Serbia. A few days later, Germany declared war on Russia. France then came into the war in support of Serbia. Next, Great Britain honored its alliance with France. What started out as a small revolt exploded into a big war.

SECTION 1 REVIEW On a separate sheet of paper, write answers to these questions.

1) How did imperialism cause World War I?

2) How did militarism cause World War I?

3) How did the alliance system cause World War I?

4) How did nationalism cause World War I?

5) What event in Sarajevo led to World War I?

What do you think

What could have kept World War I from happening?

◆**Allied Powers**
Allied nations of Great Britain, France, Russia, Italy, and eventually, the United States and Japan

◆**Central Powers**
Allied nations of Germany, Austria-Hungary, Turkey, and Bulgaria

When fighting started in August 1914, millions of soldiers marched eagerly to battle. They thought they would be home by Christmas. But Christmas came and went and still they fought. In fact, they fought for four long years.

On one side of the war were Austria-Hungary, Germany, Bulgaria, and the Ottoman Empire of Turkey. Historians call them the **Central Powers** because they were countries in central Europe.

Historians call the other side the **Allied Powers,** or the Allies. The Allies included France, Russia, Great Britain, Italy, and several smaller countries. Later, Japan and the United States joined the Allies.

Where Was the Western Front of the War?

The Central Powers and the Allies fought World War I all over the world. But during the earliest months of the war, most fighting took place in Belgium and northern France. We call this the western front. Germany wanted a quick victory over France. It could then turn east and defeat Russia on the eastern front.

Soldiers spent much of World War I fighting in trenches. Many new weapons made World War I the first modern war.

Many submarines, or "U-boats," were used to sink enemy ships in World War I.

The fastest way to Paris, the capital of France, was through Belgium, which was a neutral nation. That is, it took neither side in the war. Nevertheless, Germany attacked Belgium and moved quickly to within 15 miles of Paris. But the Allies stopped the Germans at the Marne River. This ended Germany's hope for a quick victory over France on the western front.

What Was Trench Warfare?

For the next two years, both sides fought a bitter war on the western front. Soldiers dug **trenches,** or long, narrow ditches, where they ate, slept, and watched the enemy. **Barbed wire** protected these trenches. This type of wire has sharp metal spikes on it. Between the two series of trenches was an area the soldiers called "no man's land."

Many soldiers died fighting in the trenches, but neither side won much territory. For example, in the Battle of Verdun in 1916, each side lost more than 300,000 men. However, the German army advanced only four miles.

How Were Airplanes and Submarines Used?

During World War I, nations fought in the air for the first time. However, the use of airplanes in World War I was limited. But both sides used submarines on a large scale. Germany called its submarines **U-boats.** They sank many Allied and neutral ships carrying food and supplies. To

This cartoon shows the Allies fighting the Central Powers, represented here as a dragon.

◆Convoy
A group of ships that travel together for protection

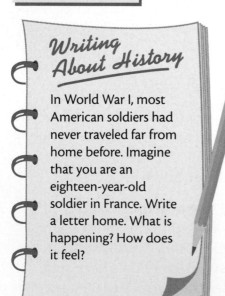

Writing About History

In World War I, most American soldiers had never traveled far from home before. Imagine that you are an eighteen-year-old soldier in France. Write a letter home. What is happening? How does it feel?

protect their supplies against the U-boats, the Allies organized **convoys.** In these convoys, warships traveled all along the outer edge of a group of supply ships.

What Were Three New Weapons in World War I?

During World War I, both sides developed new weapons. The machine gun changed war forever. This type of gun fires bullets rapidly without reloading. A well-placed machine gun could wipe out thousands of soldiers. It fired so fast that the only way an army could protect itself was to take cover in trenches.

Early in 1915, the Germans introduced poison gas. The Allies quickly followed the German example. This deadly gas settled in the trenches and blinded and choked the soldiers there. But gas was risky. If the wind suddenly shifted, the gas could kill your own troops.

The tank was another new weapon. The British introduced it in 1916 to smash through the barbed wire that protected the trenches. By the end of the war, both sides were using tanks.

Who Fought on the Eastern Front?

Along the eastern front, Russians and Serbs fought Austrians, Germans, and Turks. The Allied soldiers were poorly prepared and sometimes went to battle without weapons. The Central Powers forced the Russians to retreat. But the Russian army kept thousands of German troops fighting for over three years.

◆ Unrestricted
  warfare
  *War that is not
  restricted to a
  certain area or
  boundary*

In 1916, a million Russian soldiers died in an attack on Austria. Short on food, guns, and supplies, the Russians grew tired of war. They blamed their problems on the czar.

In 1918, after a revolution in Russia, Russia and Germany signed the Treaty of Brest Litovsk. It ended the war for Russia. Because of the treaty, Russia had to give Finland, Estonia, Latvia, Lithuania, the Ukraine, and part of Poland to Germany.

When Did the United States Enter the War?

In 1917, Germany announced that it would begin **unrestricted warfare** in waters around Britain. That is, German U-boats would sink any ship—even ones from neutral countries—that sailed into the waters surrounding the British Isles.

Germany knew that this plan would lead to war with the United States, which had been a neutral country. Its leaders thought that they could force Britain to surrender before American troops and supplies arrived in Europe. But on April 6, 1917, the U.S. Congress declared war on Germany. Soon more than a million American soldiers landed in Europe.

The World War I "Doughboy"

In the early 1900s, most Americans believed in citizen soldiers. Men became soldiers for the length of a war and then returned to civilian life. When America entered World War I, therefore, the army was very small. A draft law was passed in 1917, calling up all men between 21 and 30. The ages later became 18 to 45. Draftees received combat training. They learned how to be part of a bayonet charge and use a gas mask. Their rifles fired one shot at a time.

Today, the United States has a professional volunteer army. Volunteers sign up for a set number of years. They can then choose whether or not to re-enlist. Besides combat training, the army trains people in medicine, languages, computers, and other fields. It has changed in other ways, too. The military was segregated in World War I. African Americans served in separate army units. In 1918, there were no black marines and few women in the military. Today, these groups make up almost 25 percent of the army.

◆**Armistice**
An agreement to stop fighting

When Did World War I End?

By 1918, after four long years of war, both the Central Powers and the Allies were tired. Germany no longer had trained troops to replace those killed in battle. The fresh American troops tipped the balance in favor of the Allies. On November 11, 1918, Germany agreed to an **armistice,** or an end to fighting. On the eleventh day at the eleventh hour of the eleventh month, the great war ended.

SECTION 2 REVIEW Choose the letter of the answer that correctly completes each sentence. Write your answers on a separate sheet of paper.

1) _____ fought on the Allied side in World War I.
   - a. Turkey
   - b. Bulgaria
   - c. Austria
   - d. Great Britain

2) On the western front, soldiers lived in _____ and faced one another across a "no man's land."
   - a. tanks
   - b. airplanes
   - c. trenches
   - d. U-boats

3) World War I lasted for _____ years.
   - a. two
   - b. four
   - c. six
   - d. seven

4) The United States entered the war in _____.
   - a. 1914
   - b. 1915
   - c. 1916
   - d. 1917

5) World War I ended in _____.
   - a. 1917
   - b. 1918
   - c. 1919
   - d. 1920

What do you think

Germany decided to attack any ship in the waters around Britain. Why did this lead to war with the United States?

Reparation
Payment for war damage

World War I ended in November 1918, and the Allies won. The next year, the Allied leaders met at Versailles in France to create a peace treaty. The "Big Four"—Britain, France, Italy, and the United States—made most of the big decisions. Each of them wanted something different from the peace meeting.

What Did the United States Want?

President Woodrow Wilson represented the United States at the peace meeting. He wanted the Big Four to keep peace by treating the defeated nations fairly. He asked the Allies to do the following:

1. End secret treaties between nations.
2. Permit every nation to sail in all the seas and oceans of the world.
3. Reduce the size of armies and navies in each nation.
4. Change the boundaries of nations so people of the same nationality could live together.
5. Organize a league of nations that would settle future problems between countries without going to war.

The peace conference was held at the Hall of Mirrors at Versailles. The United States, France, Britain, and Italy made most of the big decisions.

What Did France Want?

Premier George Clemenceau represented France at the peace meeting. Because the war had been fought mostly on the western front, France had suffered greatly. Clemenceau wanted to punish Germany and keep it weak. He wanted Germany to make **reparations** for the war. That is, Clemenceau wanted Germany to pay for the cost of the war. France also demanded that Germany

The four Allied leaders at the peace conference were (from left): Vittorio Orlando (Italy), Lloyd George (Great Britain), George Clemenceau (France), and Woodrow Wilson (United States).

return Alsace and Lorraine. (France had lost these two territories to Germany in the Franco-Prussian War.)

What Did Britain Want?

Prime Minister Lloyd George represented Great Britain at the peace meeting. Like the French, the British wanted to punish Germany and make it give its African colonies to Britain. Also, the English did not want the French to become too powerful.

What Did Italy Want?

Prime Minister Vittorio Orlando represented Italy at the meeting. In 1915, the Allies had signed a secret treaty with Italy. They promised to give Italy more land if it entered the war on the Allied side. Orlando wanted the Allies to honor this treaty.

◆Treaty of Versailles
The treaty that ended World War I

What Happened to Germany?

The leaders at Versailles finally agreed on a treaty. The **Treaty of Versailles** forced Germany to do the following:

1. Return Alsace and Lorraine to France.
2. Divide its African colonies between France and Great Britain.
3. Give its colonies in the Pacific to Japan.
4. Accept full responsibility for causing the war.
5. Repay the Allies for most of the cost of the war.

These terms were so harsh that Germany at first refused to sign the treaty. Finally, however, the German leaders signed it in 1919. They represented an angry people who felt that the Allies had treated them unfairly.

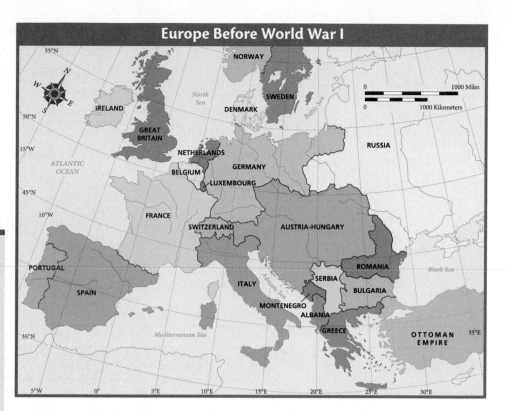

Europe Before World War I

55°N NORWAY

North Sea SWEDEN

IRELAND DENMARK Baltic Sea

50°N

15°W GREAT BRITAIN

RUSSIA

NETHERLANDS GERMANY

45°N BELGIUM

LUXEMBOURG

10°W

ATLANTIC OCEAN

FRANCE SWITZERLAND AUSTRIA-HUNGARY

PORTUGAL ROMANIA Black Sea

SERBIA

SPAIN ITALY Adriatic Sea BULGARIA

MONTENEGRO

35°N ALBANIA

Mediterranean Sea GREECE OTTOMAN EMPIRE 35°E

5°W 0° 5°E 10°E 15°E 20°E 25°E 30°E

0 1000 Miles
0 1000 Kilometers

Europe After World War I

55°N NORWAY FINLAND

ESTONIA

North Sea SWEDEN LATVIA

IRELAND DENMARK Baltic Sea LITHUANIA

50°N RUSSIA

15°W GREAT BRITAIN EAST PRUSSIA (Germany)

NETHERLANDS GERMANY POLAND

BELGIUM

45°N LUXEMBOURG CZECHOSLOVAKIA

Versailles •

10°W ALSACE-LORRAINE

ATLANTIC OCEAN FRANCE SWITZERLAND AUSTRIA

HUNGARY ROMANIA

PORTUGAL YUGOSLAVIA Black Sea

SPAIN ITALY Adriatic Sea

BULGARIA

35°N ALBANIA

Mediterranean Sea GREECE TURKEY 35°E

5°W 0° 5°E 10°E 15°E 20°E 25°E 30°E

0 1000 Miles
0 1000 Kilometers

MAP STUDY

The top map shows what Europe looked like just before World War I. The bottom map shows Europe after the war. Were there more countries in Europe before or after the war? What happened to Austria-Hungary after the war?

◆League of Nations
A group of leaders from many nations who met to solve problems between countries

What Happened to the Austro-Hungarian Empire?

The Treaty of Versailles broke up the Austro-Hungarian Empire. Austria and Hungary became two countries. The treaty also created two new countries—Yugoslavia and Czechoslovakia. Some Austro-Hungarian land went to Poland, Italy, and Romania. The treaty carved Finland, Estonia, Latvia, and Lithuania out of the western part of the old Russian Empire.

What Was the League of Nations?

The Treaty of Versailles created the **League of Nations.** It was a group of leaders from the nations of the world. They wanted to keep peace. These leaders began to meet at Geneva, Switzerland, to talk over their problems.

However, the league was weak because some countries did not join. Also, the league could not force countries to obey its rulings. These weaknesses became clear in the 1930s. At that time, the league could not prevent the outbreak of World War II.

SECTION 3 REVIEW On a separate sheet of paper, write *True* if the statement is true or *False* if the statement is not true. Make each false statement true by changing the underlined word.

1) After World War I, the Allies met at Versailles in <u>Italy.</u>

2) President <u>Woodrow Wilson</u> represented the United States at the meeting.

3) France and Great Britain both wanted to make <u>Africa</u> pay for its part in the war.

4) <u>Italy</u> wanted more land.

5) The Treaty of Versailles set up a weak <u>League of Nations.</u>

What do you think

The Treaty of Versailles treated Germany and the other Central Powers poorly. What are two things that could happen because of this?

Bankrupt
Unable to pay one's debts

Generation
All the people born about the same time

◆**Total war**
A war in which a country uses all its resources to win

World War I was the first **total war.** A total war is more than two armies fighting on a battlefield. Cities, farms, factories, and people living at home become part of it.

What Were the Social Effects of the War?

As a result of World War I, Russia, Germany, Austria-Hungary, and France lost a whole **generation.** A generation is all the people born about the same time. In fact, France lost one out of every five men between the ages of 20 and 44. In the war, both soldiers and civilians suffered and died.

What Were the Economic Effects of the War?

Historians do not know what the war cost. One guess is about $350 billion. Many governments raised taxes and borrowed large sums of money to pay for the war. The United States lent $10 billion to its allies.

By the end of the war, every major European country was **bankrupt.** They could not pay off their debts because they had no money. Cities and farms—especially in France and Belgium—lay in ruin. Many people had no jobs.

Before World War I, Europe controlled most of the world's power and wealth. The war changed all this. The Central Powers had destroyed 40 percent of Britain's trading ships during the war. Other trading nations like the United States and Japan took over the European markets.

Many soldiers were wounded in the war.

What Were the Political Effects of the War?

Democracy spread because of the war. In Germany, Austria-Hungary, and Russia, governments elected by the people replaced monarchies. However, in Russia, a dictatorship soon replaced the new democratic government.

The Treaty of Versailles created new countries. But some of these had large numbers of foreign people. For example, Poland and Czechoslovakia had large groups of German-speaking people. This caused problems in the future.

How Did the War Affect the United States?

As a result of World War I, the United States became a world power. Its economy was healthier than that of other countries. It became the world's banker. Yet many Americans wanted the United States to stay out of **world affairs**, or events happening around the world. This, too, created problems in the future.

SECTION 4 REVIEW On a separate sheet of paper, write the word from the Word Bank that completes each sentence.

WORD BANK

banker

bankrupt

dictator

generation

total war

1) World War I was a _____ because it included armies, cities, factories, farms, and people living at home.

2) At the end of the war, many European nations were _____ and had no money to pay their war debts.

3) As a result of the war, Russia, Germany, France, and Austria-Hungry lost a whole _____ of men.

4) Because of the war, Russia became democratic, and then a _____ took over the government.

5) Because of the war, the United States became the world's _____.

What do you think

How do you think the death of so many people in World War I made soldiers feel about the people they fought against?

The Next War

This picture, titled "Shadows," shows the bleakness of World War I.

In August 1914, European nations plunged into the Great War. World War I ended four years later. It had destroyed millions of lives. It had also ended many old ways of life. Many soldiers had gone to war with grand ideas of honor and glory. The reality was different. War was wet trenches, poison gas, and artillery fire. Soldiers saw lives being wasted. Their views quickly changed. This change is clear in the poetry written during the war. Early poems are often about heroism. Later poems show shock and anger.

Britain had many fine soldier-poets. One was Siegfried Sassoon. He wrote bitterly, "when it was all said and done, the war was mainly a matter of holes and ditches." The poem that follows is by Wilfred Owen, a young British officer. He was killed a week before the war ended.

War's a joke for me and you,
While we know such dreams are true.
Out there, we've walked quite friendly up to
    Death;
Sat down and eaten with him, cool and bland,
Pardoned his spilling mess-tins in our hand.
We've sniffed the green thick odour of his
    breath,

Our eyes wept, but our courage didn't writhe.
He's spat at us with bullets and he's coughed
Shrapnel. We chorused when he sang aloft;
We whistled while he shaved us with his scythe.
Oh, Death was never enemy of ours!
We laughed at him, we leagued with him, old
    chum.
No soldier's paid to kick against his powers.
We laughed, knowing that better men would
    come,
And greater wars; when each proud fighter brags
He wars on Death for lives; not men for flags.

Source Reading Wrap-Up

1) How have the soldiers in this poem become friendly with Death?

2) What weapons has Death used against the soldiers?

3) Death is often pictured with a scythe, a long blade used for cutting grass. How does Owen use that image?

4) Many soldiers could not talk about the war. Would civilians think of death like Owen did in this poem?

5) Owen says that a proud fighter, "Wars on Death for lives; not men for flags." What does he mean?

Death at Sarajevo

June 28, 1914, was a hot Sunday in Sarajevo. Despite the heat, crowds of people filled the streets. They were waiting for Archduke Franz Ferdinand and his wife, Sophie. People were curious to see the archduke. He would be the next emperor of Austria-Hungary. His visit was supposed to improve Austria's image.

Sarajevo was the capital of Bosnia, a small Balkan state. Bosnia's people were Slavs. They had become independent of the Ottoman Empire less than 40 years earlier. Then the Austro-Hungarian Empire had taken control of the area. Many Bosnians hated Austrian rule. They wanted to be part of nearby Serbia, a Slav state. Some joined a secret society known as the Black Hand. Its slogan was "Union or Death."

That June morning, the archduke and duchess rode to the town hall in an open car. With them was the military governor of Bosnia. No one realized that several Black Hand members were waiting along the route. Suddenly a man stepped forward and threw a bomb. It exploded in the street and wounded officers in the next car. The official party went on with the scheduled program. At its end, the archduke decided to visit a wounded officer in the hospital. The duke had his driver stop while he gave him new directions.

Standing only a few feet away was 19-year-old Gavrilo Princip. He was one of the Black Hand members in the plot. Princip pulled out a small gun and fired twice. The first shot struck the Duchess Sophie. She died instantly. The second bullet struck Franz Ferdinand near the heart. He uttered a few last words, then his head fell back. He died a few minutes later.

Police seized Princip, kicking and beating him. They took him to jail. Next, the Austrians arrested every known revolutionary in Sarajevo. Because he was young, Princip was sentenced to only 20 years in jail. That was the maximum sentence.

The sudden, brutal murders shocked the world. Austrian officials blamed Serbia. They were determined to punish Serbia. Austria called on its ally, Germany, for help. Then Austria declared war on Serbia. Serbia asked its ally, Russia, to come to its aid. Within a few days, Russia and Germany had declared war. Soon most of the continent was involved. Members of both European alliances immediately got ready for war. The shots in Sarajevo triggered World War I.

Spotlight Story Wrap-Up

1) Who was Franz Ferdinand?
2) Why did many people in Sarajevo dislike Austrian rule?
3) What was the Black Hand?
4) Who killed the archduke and duchess? How was he punished?
5) What were the effects of the shootings at Sarajevo?

➡ In the late 1800s, powerful European nations competed for both land and military power. They formed alliances to aid each other in case of war.

➡ Germany, Austria-Hungary, and Italy made up the Triple Alliance. Great Britain, France, and Russia were the Triple Entente.

➡ A Serbian nationalist killed Austrian Archduke Franz Ferdinand and his wife in June 1914. This act triggered World War I. The alliance system brought the major European nations into the war.

➡ The nations in World War I divided into the Central Powers and the Allied Powers. The Central Powers were Austria-Hungary, Germany, Bulgaria, and Turkey (the Ottoman Empire). The Allies included France, Russia, Britain, Italy, and smaller nations. Japan and the United States later joined the Allies.

➡ Early fighting was mainly along the western front in Belgium and France. On the eastern front, Russians and Serbs fought Germans, Austrians, and Turks. After its revolution, Russia signed the Treaty of Brest Litovsk. Russia dropped out of the war in 1918.

➡ World War I relied on trench warfare. New weapons were also used: airplanes, submarines, machine guns, poison gas, and tanks.

➡ The United States was neutral until April 1917. It entered the war because Germany declared unrestricted war on shipping. The United States joined the Allies. In November 1918, Germany agreed to an armistice.

➡ The "Big Four"—Britain, France, Italy, and the United States—shaped the peace treaty. Each nation had different goals. Britain and France wanted repayments and land from Germany. American President Woodrow Wilson wanted to end secret treaties and cut back militarism. Wilson also wanted to start a league of nations. It was supposed to solve problems between nations without going to war.

➡ The Treaty of Versailles gave Germany's colonies to France, Britain, and Japan. Germany had to give land back to France and pay the costs of war. The treaty broke up the Austro-Hungarian Empire. It created many new nations.

➡ World War I was a total war that involved civilians. The war was costly in money and lives. Several European countries lost millions of men of fighting age. Trade and industries were also ruined.

➡ New democratic governments began in several countries. The United States became a world power with a strong economy.

Comprehension: Identifying Facts

On a separate sheet of paper, use the words from the Word Bank to complete each sentence.

WORD BANK
alliance
armistice
bankrupt
civilians
convoy
neutral
reparations
rivals
trenches
U-boat

1) Imperialism led to countries becoming _____ and trying to outdo one another.

2) Before the war, many countries made an _____ with one another and agreed to help one another.

3) Belgium was a _____ country during the war because it chose neither side.

4) During the war, the Allies used the _____ to protect its ships at sea.

5) The Germans used the _____, a type of submarine, to destroy Allied ships.

6) World War I soldiers lived in _____, or long narrow ditches, that protected them from enemy fire.

7) The war killed both soldiers and _____, or people not in the military.

8) On November 11, 1918, Germany agreed to an _____, or an end to the fighting.

9) As a result of the war, all the major European countries were _____ and had no money to pay their debts.

10) At Versailles, France demanded that Germany make _____, or payments for war debts

Comprehension: Multiple Choice

On a separate sheet of paper, write the letter of the answer that correctly completes each sentence.

1) _____ fought as part of the Central Powers in World War I.

  a. Japan   c. The United States

  b. France   d. Germany

2) During World War I, the industrial nations developed _____.

  a. tanks   c. machine guns

  b. poison gas   d. all of the above

3) _____ represented France at the Versailles peace meeting.

   a. Clemenceau   c. George

   b. Wilson   d. Ferdinand

4) _____ represented Britain at the peace meeting.

   a. Orlando   c. Wilson

   b. George   d. Clemenceau

5) Some historians guess that World War I cost _____.

   a. $700 trillion   c. $350 billion

   b. $850 billion   d. $700 million

Comprehension: Understanding Main Ideas

On a separate sheet of paper, write the answers to the following questions using complete sentences, or statements.

1) What were the causes of World War I?

2) What were three terms of the Treaty of Versailles?

3) What were three economic effects of World War I?

Critical Thinking: Write Your Opinion

1) If you had been a German in 1919, how would you have felt about the Treaty of Versailles?

2) Do you think having a large and powerful military causes or prevents war? Explain your answer.

Test-Taking Tip   If you are asked to compare and contrast things on a test, be sure to tell how they are alike and how they are different.

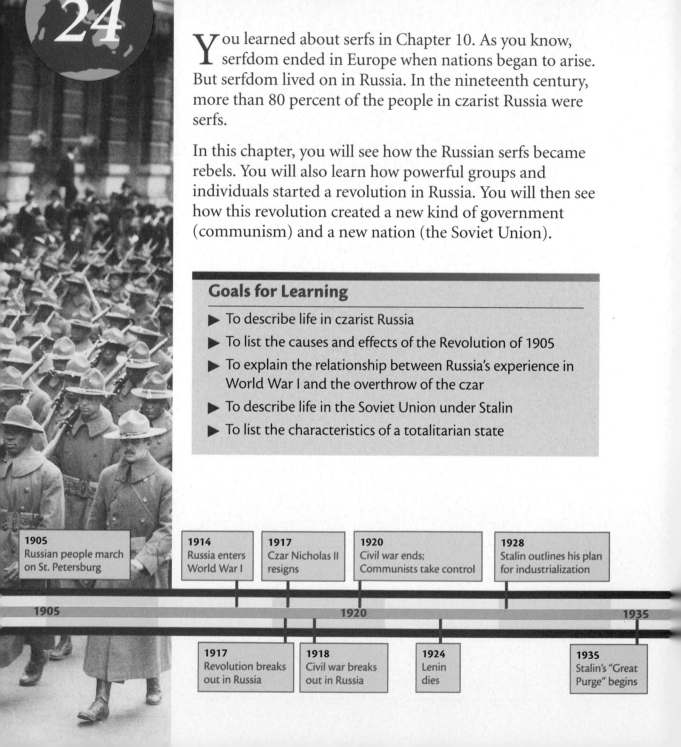

Chapter 24

The Russian Revolution and the Communist State

1905 to 1939

You learned about serfs in Chapter 10. As you know, serfdom ended in Europe when nations began to arise. But serfdom lived on in Russia. In the nineteenth century, more than 80 percent of the people in czarist Russia were serfs.

In this chapter, you will see how the Russian serfs became rebels. You will also learn how powerful groups and individuals started a revolution in Russia. You will then see how this revolution created a new kind of government (communism) and a new nation (the Soviet Union).

Goals for Learning

▶ To describe life in czarist Russia

▶ To list the causes and effects of the Revolution of 1905

▶ To explain the relationship between Russia's experience in World War I and the overthrow of the czar

▶ To describe life in the Soviet Union under Stalin

▶ To list the characteristics of a totalitarian state

1905
Russian people march on St. Petersburg

1914
Russia enters World War I

1917
Czar Nicholas II resigns

1920
Civil war ends; Communists take control

1928
Stalin outlines his plan for industrialization

1905   1920   1935

1917
Revolution breaks out in Russia

1918
Civil war breaks out in Russia

1924
Lenin dies

1935
Stalin's "Great Purge" begins

The Development of the Soviet Union

Map labels include: ARCTIC OCEAN, East Siberian Sea, Laptev Sea, Kara Sea, PACIFIC OCEAN, Sea of Okhotsk, LITHUANIA, FINLAND, ESTONIA, LATVIA, POLAND, Leningrad, Kiev, Moscow, ROMANIA, BULGARIA, Black Sea, TURKEY, Volga R., Yekaterinburg, Stalingrad, Aral Sea, Caspian Sea, IRAN, AFGHANISTAN, CHINA, Ob R., Irtysh R., Yenisey R., Lena R., Irkutsk, MONGOLIA, Vladivostok, UNION OF SOVIET SOCIALIST REPUBLICS

0 — 1000 Miles
0 — 1000 Kilometers

Union of Soviet Socialist Republics in 1939
Controlled by Bolsheviks in 1919

This chapter is about revolution and change in Russia. A group called the Bolsheviks led the revolution. This map shows the area that the Bolsheviks controlled in 1919. The map also shows the border of the Soviet Union in 1939. This was the new nation that formed as a result of this revolution.

Study the map carefully and answer the following questions:

Geography Skills

1) What cities did the Bolsheviks control in 1919?

2) What seas are shown on this map?

3) What rivers are shown on this map?

4) What countries bordered the Soviet Union to the south?

5) What does this map tell you about the size of the Soviet Union in 1939?

◆Autocracy
A government in which one person has unlimited power

One important result of World War I was the Russian Revolution of 1917. In less than a week, rebels overthrew the czar. But people before them had planted the seeds of the revolution.

What Was the Autocracy of Russia?

In the 1800s, Russia was an **autocracy**—a government in which one person rules with unlimited power. In Russia, that person was the czar. He controlled the lives of his people and expected them to obey him without question.

In the late 1800s, more than 80 percent of the Russian people were serfs. As you know, serfs could not leave the land on which they worked. The nobles, who owned the land, completely controlled the serfs. The nobles could beat, buy, and sell any serf. (Serfdom had ended in the rest of Europe by 1850.)

Who Gave More Rights to the Russians?

In 1855, Alexander II became czar. In 1861, he ended serfdom and freed millions of serfs and their families. He sold them land and gave them 49 years to pay for it. The czar also introduced the jury system, gave Russians more rights, and let more people go to school.

This was a time of great promise for Russia. But it was also a time of trouble. Russians had their first taste of freedom, so now they wanted more because they still had few rights. When the nobles, the university students, and the peasants demanded more freedom, Alexander II refused.

Czar Alexander II freed the serfs and their families in 1861, ending serfdom in Russia.

One cause of the Russian Revolution was the widespread suffering of peasants. The czar used soldiers called "cossacks" (as shown on the horse) to control the peasants by force.

What Did Russian Revolutionaries Do to Alexander II?

When the czar refused to give them more rights, many Russians began thinking of revolting. Twice, revolutionaries tried unsuccessfully to kill Alexander. To win back the people's support, the czar's advisers asked him to establish a legislature. But on the day Alexander agreed to this, a young revolutionary killed him.

Who Took Away Russian Rights?

The next czar, Alexander III, went back to the old ways. Perhaps he believed that the changes his father started had led to his death. Alexander III and later czars took no interest in reform. Their actions fed the flames of revolution.

When Did the Industrial Revolution Come to Russia?

You read about the Industrial Revolution in Chapter 19. It began in England in the eighteenth century and quickly spread to other countries. But Russia's industry did not begin to grow until a century later in the late 1800s. From 1866 to 1876, Russia built 10,000 miles of railroads.

Railroads led to a growth in industry. When industry develops in cities, many farmers leave the land and go to the cities to work. This happened in England and throughout Europe. It happened in Russia, too.

The Russian cities of St. Petersburg, Moscow, and Baky became centers of industry. By 1900, over two million Russians were working in cities. There, the **standard of living** improved. A standard of living is a way to judge how well a person or a family is living. The Russian standard of living was still far behind the rest of Europe.

> **Standard of living**
> *A way to judge how well a person or a family is living*

Why Did the Czar Declare War on Japan?

In 1894, Nicholas II became czar. He faced many problems. The nobles still owned most of the land. The poor paid heavy taxes, while the nobles paid no taxes at all. Factory workers worked long hours for little pay. Many educated Russians wanted a more **democratic** government in which all people had equal rights.

To get people to think about something besides change, Nicholas II declared war on Japan in 1904. (Japan and Russia both had interests in Korea and China.) This was called the Russo-Japanese War. When Russia lost the war, people demanded more change.

What Happened on Bloody Sunday?

On January 22, 1905, thousands of workers, women, and children marched to the czar's palace in St. Petersburg. They wanted better working conditions, more freedom, and an elected national assembly. They came in peace, but Nicholas ordered his soldiers to fire on the crowd. The soldiers killed hundreds of workers. Russians call this day Bloody Sunday.

Hundreds were killed when soldiers fired on crowds in 1905. The massacre became known as Bloody Sunday.

GRIGORI RASPUTIN: c. 1872–1916

Rasputin was a Siberian peasant who became a monk and healer. Later, he moved to St. Petersburg. Although Rasputin lived an immoral life, he had an interesting personality.

The royal heir, Alexei, had hemophilia. With this disease, even minor bumps can cause severe bleeding. At that time, the bleeding could not be controlled. Rasputin was somehow able to help Alexei. Czar Nicholas II and Czarina Alexandra then began taking Rasputin's advice about officials and policies. However, Rasputin's advice was not very good, and it caused many problems. To end Rasputin's influence, some nobles assassinated him. First, they poisoned him, but he survived. Then they shot him several times and drowned him.

◆**Duma**
The Russian parliament

After Bloody Sunday, Russia exploded. Workers refused to work. Riots broke out. Groups of peasants attacked the nobles and burned their estates. The czar promised to give the people more freedom if they would stop the violence. He even agreed to the election of a Russian parliament, or **Duma.** However, after three months, Czar Nicholas dismissed the Duma. He believed that he alone had the right to govern.

SECTION 1 REVIEW On a separate sheet of paper, write answers to these questions.

1) What reforms did Czar Alexander II make?

2) Why did Czar Alexander III undo his father's changes?

3) How did the Industrial Revolution change Russia?

4) Why was the Russo-Japanese war of 1904 a mistake for Czar Nicholas II?

5) What did Nicholas II do after the Revolution of 1905?

What do you think

Why would both Russian serfs and Russian nobles want reform?

♦Socialism
An economic and political theory in which the government owns and controls the major means of production

After the Revolution of 1905, the spirit of rebellion continued to grow in Russia. But the revolutionaries could not agree on how change should happen. Some wanted to limit the czar's power and create a constitutional monarchy like Great Britain's. Others thought a completely new form of government was needed.

What Do Socialists Want?

Many Russians thought **socialism** would solve Russia's problems. Socialism is an economic and political theory. Under socialism, the government controls the economy of a nation. Representing the people, the government owns all the land, industries, and transportation.

Socialists want the government to make sure that every citizen has a job and earns a good living. In a socialistic society, no one owns property and no one makes a profit by buying or selling. The most influential of all the early socialists was a German named Karl Marx.

Women marched on St. Petersburg in 1917 demanding bread. This forced Czar Nicholas II to step down as ruler of Russia.

The Russian Orthodox Church

Byzantine missionaries took Christianity to Russia in the 900s. By the 1400s, the Russian Orthodox Church was self-governing. The patriarch, the head of the church, lived in Moscow. For centuries, Orthodox priests and monks had great influence. The church was central in the lives of many ordinary Russians. They kept icons in their homes. Some czars used the church to support their absolute rule.

The Russian Revolution was a disaster for the church. It lost power and property. Still, millions of people remained faithful. After the Soviet Union collapsed in 1991, Russia had a great religious revival. Some Russians have joined other churches. The Russian Orthodox Church, however, remains the most important.

♦ **Abdicate**
To give up power as a ruler

Provisional
For a short time; not final

How Did World War I Affect Russia?

World War I was probably the single most important cause of the Russian Revolution of 1917. Russia went to war against Austria and Hungary in 1914. Quickly, millions of men volunteered to fight. But the war went badly for Russia. Millions of Russians were killed, wounded, or taken prisoner.

Then things in Russia got even worse. Factories could not produce enough guns and bullets. The people had to live with little food, fuel, and other needed supplies.

Why Did Czar Nicholas II Abdicate?

On the morning of February 24, 1917, news came that stores in St. Petersburg had no bread. Women became angry. "We want bread! We want bread!" they shouted. Soon a crowd formed. They carried banners, shouted, and sang. Some of their signs said "End the War" and "Down with the Czar."

Police and soldiers fought the crowds. Then some soldiers joined the workers and their wives. The troops of Czar Nicholas II refused to obey him. He had to **abdicate** as ruler. That is, he gave up his power.

What Did the Provisional Government Do?

After the czar abdicated, no one was sure who would govern Russia. Members of the Duma chose several leaders to act as a **provisional** government. (A provisional government rules for only a short time.) Meanwhile, workers and soldiers in the cities formed **soviets,** or councils. These soviets soon took over city government.

Soon the provisional government made a bad mistake. It chose to continue the war against Germany. But the Russians were tired of war. Many soldiers left the Russian army. Back at home, groups of peasants attacked the estates of nobles and took over their land.

SECTION 2 REVIEW Choose the letter of the answer that correctly completes each sentence. Write your answers on a separate sheet of paper.

1) Under _____, a government owns all the land, the industries, and the means of transportation.

    a. democracy   c. socialism

    b. monarchy   d. constitutional monarchy

2) _____ was a German who influenced the Russian Revolution.

    a. Nicholas II   c. Alexander II

    b. Karl Marx   d. Rasputin

3) Probably the single most important cause of the Russian Revolution was _____.

    a. World War I   c. a provisional government

    b. Bloody Sunday   d. the Duma

4) During World War I, conditions in Russia got worse because _____.

    a. factories could not produce bullets and guns

    b. food was scarce

    c. millions of soldiers died or were wounded

    d. all of the above

5) In 1917, the Russians forced _____ to abdicate.

    a. Alexander II   c. Nicholas II

    b. Alexander III   d. Karl Marx

What do you think ?

Why do you think the czar's soldiers joined the workers who were rebelling on February 25, 1917?

◆**Bolshevik**
A revolutionary socialist group in Russia

◆**Communism**
An economic system in which there is no private property and the government produces goods

◆**Militia**
A group of people who can be called to military service when something dangerous happens suddenly

The **Bolsheviks** were a revolutionary socialist group. For many years, they plotted against the czar. Their party was small, but it was well organized and got things done.

A man who called himself Lenin led the Bolsheviks. He became a revolutionary when the czar's soldiers killed his brother. Many Russians liked his promise of "Peace, Land, and Bread." But the Russian government arrested him and then exiled him. Lenin stayed away from Russia for 17 years.

What Was the Red Guard?

In the fall of 1917, the Bolsheviks took over the Russian government. They formed a **militia**—a group of people who can be called to military service very quickly when needed. This militia, called the Red Guard, seized the government by force on November 6 and 7. The Red Guard then arrested the leaders of the provisional government.

This change in government was almost bloodless. The Bolsheviks moved quickly to establish control. They gave their party a new name—the Communist Party. Lenin became its leader. This party believed in **communism.** Like socialism, communism is an economic system in which there is no private property and the government produces goods.

The Communist Party gave Russia a new name. It became the Union of Soviet Socialist Republics (U.S.S.R.), or the Soviet Union.

Lenin was the leader of the Communist Party, which took over the Russian government in 1917.

What Did the Communist Government Do?

Many Russians did not support the Communists. In the first free elections to choose an assembly, they were outvoted two to one. The Communists simply closed the assembly after only one day. Lenin then kept his promise to the Russian people and pulled Russia out of World War I. The Communists signed a peace treaty with Germany in March 1918. Russia had to give up about a third of its European territory.

Who Were the Whites and the Reds?

Some Russians opposed Lenin and the Communists. In the summer of 1918, these non-Bolsheviks formed a "White" army. A number of national **minorities** in Russia supported the Whites. (A minority is a small group of like people within a larger group.) The Ukrainians, Poles, and Finns saw this as a way to break away from Russian rule. Countries like Great Britain, France, Japan, and the United States sent troops to fight the "Reds"—the Bolshevik army.

This photo shows the Richelieu Steps in Russia. This is where the czar's soldiers fired on the crowd on Bloody Sunday, which started revolution and conflict in Russia.

What Happened During the Russian Civil War?

The Whites and the Reds fought a civil war that lasted until 1920. During the war, 15 million Russians died, many from starvation. Disease—especially the flu—killed many people. Among those who died was Czar Nicholas II and his family. The Bolsheviks shot them because they did not want the White army to rescue the royal family.

The Reds finally defeated the Whites because the Communist army had better leaders and was more unified. The Reds also won the support of the peasants and the workers. But the civil war left Russia with many problems. Factories had closed

Many people starved during the Russian civil war. This picture shows barefoot and starving children during the war.

and there was nothing to trade. The millions who had died included the brightest and most skilled people in Russia.

What Did Lenin Do After His Victory?

After seizing power, Lenin and the Communist government did the following:

1. They took control of all major industries. Workers' councils managed the factories.

2. They divided the land among the peasants. The government taxed surplus, or extra, grain. However, it allowed the peasants to sell their goods to make extra money.

3. They swept away the old class system of Russia. No longer was anyone called a noble.

4. They took away any land the Orthodox Church owned. They also asked people to give up religion.

5. They created a powerful dictatorship. The Communist Party completely controlled the government and the economy.

6. They established a secret police force that used terror against all enemies of the revolution.

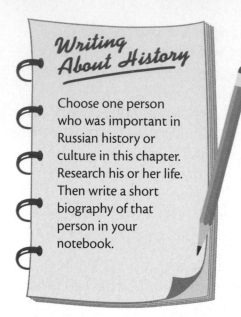

Writing About History

Choose one person who was important in Russian history or culture in this chapter. Research his or her life. Then write a short biography of that person in your notebook.

Successor
One who follows another in a position

What Happened After Lenin Died?

In 1922, Lenin became sick. Two Communist leaders began fighting to become his **successor**—the one who would take over the government.

Most people expected Leon Trotsky to become the new party leader. He had founded the Red Guard and had beaten the Whites in the civil war, so he was a well-known, popular leader. He was also an excellent writer and speaker.

Trotsky's rival was Joseph Stalin. He was a quiet man and not well known, but he had a high-ranking position in the Communist Party. Stalin had used his power to appoint his followers to key positions in the government.

In 1924, Lenin died. By 1927, Stalin had won the support of most party members. He expelled Trotsky from the Communist Party and forced him to leave the Soviet Union. Trotsky settled in Mexico. Soviet spies murdered him there in 1940.

SECTION 3 REVIEW On a separate sheet of paper, write the word from the Word Bank that completes each sentence.

WORD BANK
Lenin
Reds
Stalin
Trotsky
Whites

1) The formerly exiled leader of the Bolsheviks was _____.

2) The Bolsheviks came to be called the _____.

3) The people who opposed the Bolsheviks became known as the _____.

4) The founder of the Red Guard was _____.

5) _____ became leader of the Soviet Union after Lenin's death.

What do you think

Why was Lenin smart to promise "Peace, Land, and Bread" to the Russian people?

◆**Collective farm**
A large farm owned by many peasants and run by the government

Consumer goods
Products that people buy

Heavy industry
The manufacturing of products, such as machines and raw materials, for use in other industries

Quota
A fixed amount that is the goal to be reached

The name Stalin means "man of steel." Like steel, Stalin was cold and strong. He wanted the Soviet Union to be strong too so other countries would not attack it. Stalin said, "We are 50 to 100 years behind the advanced countries. We must make up this gap . . . or they will crush us."

How Did Stalin Plan to Industrialize Russia?

In 1928, Stalin began to industrialize Russia by building **heavy industry.** Heavy industries like steel mills and power stations make products that other industries use. The government poured lots of money into heavy industry. However, it put only a little money into industry that produced **consumer goods.** Goods like clothing and shoes became scarce in Russia.

Why Did the Government Set Up Collective Farms?

The Communist government controlled the Russian economy. It told factories what to produce. It set **quotas,** or fixed amounts, for how much each factory should produce. It told workers where to work and for how long.

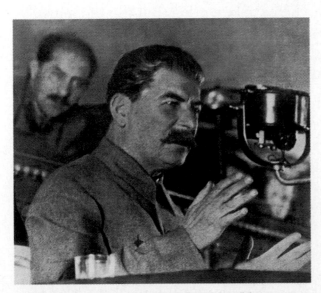

Joseph Stalin ruled the Soviet Union harshly. He turned his country into an industrialized nation, but he used cruel methods to do it.

In 1928, the government abolished privately owned farms and replaced them with **collective farms.** Stalin believed that fewer workers could produce more food on collective farms.

According to Stalin, the peasants owned the collective farms. However, his government ran them. The workers on these collective farms had to sell their grains, vegetables, and fruits to the government at fixed prices. The government paid the peasants according to the amount of work they had done.

Why Did Stalin Send People to Siberia?

Most peasants hated these collective farms. They did not want to give up the land they had just won in the revolution. Some burned their grain and killed their farm animals rather than turn them over to the government. Stalin answered back by shipping some of these peasants to Siberia. Many died there of starvation. He ordered the death of thousands of farmers and their families. Historians believe that between 5 and 10 million peasants died.

What Is a Totalitarian State?

Stalin made the Soviet Union an industrial power, but he also made it a **totalitarian state.** A totalitarian state is a dictatorship in which a small group of people controls every part of the lives of a country's citizens. People have no rights. The government expects citizens to obey without question.

Stalin kept total control over newspapers and radio by **censorship.** That is, he checked all written material to make sure it supported the government. He expected writers and artists to praise him and the Soviet Union.

Stalin had once studied to be a priest. But this did not stop him from attacking religion. He closed many churches and made them into storehouses. He ordered schools to teach children that religion had kept Russia from moving ahead.

What Was Life Like in Russia Under Stalin?

Under Stalin, everyone in the Soviet Union lived in fear. His government arrested people who received letters or packages from foreign countries. People who spoke out against the government were sometimes never seen again. When managers of farms and factories did not meet their quotas, the government exiled them to Siberia.

In many ways, Stalin, with his unlimited power, was like the czars. He crushed anyone who he thought was disloyal. He encouraged children to report their parents if they did or said anything disloyal. His secret police watched everyone.

What Happened During the Great Purge?

Stalin's "Great Purge" caused great suffering among the Russian people. Historians believe millions died from Stalin's plan to rid his enemies.

Even members of the Communist Party were not safe from Stalin. During the 1930s, he **purged,** or removed from office, thousands of members of the Communist Party.

During the Great Purge of 1935–1939, Stalin arrested millions of men and women. Among them were government workers and army officials. He even accused Lenin's original supporters—the old Bolsheviks—of being disloyal.

◆Purge
To remove from office; to clean by getting rid of unwanted things

Stalin held public trials. At these trials, he forced accused persons to confess that they were guilty of crimes. He did not need any proof of guilt to sentence these people to death. Historians believe that millions of people died in this purge.

How Did Stalin Change Russia?

Stalin died in 1953. As ruler, he had changed the Soviet Union—both for the good and the bad. What was good about his rule? The Soviet Union had been a country that was behind the times. By 1953, it was a powerful industrialized nation. It provided health care for its citizens and better education. Stalin also gave women more opportunities to do things. People's standard of living improved, too.

But the living conditions for Russians remained poor compared to other industrialized nations. Also, the government controlled their lives more than the czar had done. Under Stalin, millions of Russians had suffered and died.

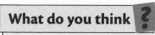

The World's Largest Country

Russia is the largest country in the world. It sprawls across northern Europe and Asia. Russia has about 6,600,000 square miles of land. It is almost twice as large as China or the United States. The Volga is the longest river in Europe. It flows near Moscow into the Caspian Sea.

Steppes, or grasslands, cover much of western and central Russia. They run from Ukraine across Russia into Kazakhstan. Summers are short and hot. Winters are long and snowy. Grains and sugar beets grow in the fertile *chernozem*, or "black earth," of Ukraine. A low mountain range, the Urals, separates the steppes from Siberia.

Siberia is the Asian part of Russia. It stretches east to the Pacific Ocean. Northern Siberia has a subarctic climate—the ground is partly frozen all year. Huge, thick forests cover other areas. Siberia has about three-quarters of Russia's mineral wealth.

SECTION 4 REVIEW On a separate sheet of paper, write *True* if the statement is true or *False* if the statement is not true. Make each false statement true by changing the underlined word.

1) <u>Stalin</u> thought Russia was not as advanced as other countries.

2) Stalin planned to industrialize Russia by pouring money into <u>heavy industry.</u>

3) Stalin forced farmers to work on <u>privately owned</u> farms.

4) Under Stalin, Russia became a <u>totalitarian state</u> that controlled the lives of all its citizens.

5) During his time as ruler, Stalin sent many people into exile in <u>Antarctica.</u>

What do you think ?

How might the Russian people have felt when their factories produced only a few consumer goods?

The Poetry of Alexander Pushkin

Russian artists and writers of the 1800s produced many great works. Many were very nationalistic. They often used folk songs and stories as the basis of their works.

Russian composers such as Tchaikovsky and Rimsky-Korsakov wrote beautiful music. The artist Ilya Repin painted powerful historical pictures. It was in literature, however, that Russians did their best work. For example, several Russian writers produced classic novels. Count Leo Tolstoy's Anna Karenina *is the story of a woman who sacrifices everything for love. His* War and Peace *recounts the Russians' heroic fight to save their country from Napoleon. Fyodor Dostoevsky's* Crime and Punishment *is a chilling psychological murder mystery. Anton Chekhov wrote short stories and plays about a Russian society facing change.*

Alexander Pushkin (1799–1837) was part African. His great-grandfather had come to Russia as a servant of Peter the Great. Pushkin was a great Russian poet—perhaps the greatest. He introduced Romantic poetry into Russia. He died at age 38 from wounds received in a duel. Even today, Russians love Pushkin's poetry and can quote from it. In 1999, they celebrated his 200th birthday. This excerpt is from one of his poems.

> Rulers! Your crown and throne were given you
> By law—and not by nature;
> You stand above the people,
> But eternally higher than you is the law.
> And learn this, O rulers:
> Neither punishment nor reward,
> Neither bloody dungeon nor altar
> Will provide you with secure
> protection.

Alexander Pushkin (1799–1837)

> First place yourselves
> Under the protection of trustworthy laws;
> And freedom and peace will
> Forever stand guard
> Over throne and people.

Source Reading Wrap-Up

1) What does Pushkin mean when he says, "Rulers! Your crown and throne were given you by law—and not by nature"?

2) Does Pushkin think a ruler can keep power by force or bribery? Quote from the poem to explain your answer.

3) Many poems have a theme, an idea to which everything else is related. What is the theme of Pushkin's poem?

4) What does Pushkin hope the ruler will do?

5) Do you think the last czars followed Pushkin's advice? Give evidence from the chapter to back up your opinion.

Marx Was Wrong

In the nineteenth century, Russia was mainly an undeveloped nation of farmers. Yet the first Communist revolution took place there. This fact would have surprised Karl Marx, the father of communism.

Marx was born in Germany in 1818. He saw the changes brought by the Industrial Revolution. People left their farms to find work in factories. Workers put in long hours for very little money. Often the machinery was noisy and dangerous. Even women and young children worked more than 12 hours a day for low pay. Factory owners, however, became rich.

Marx traveled to other industrial countries in Europe. He concluded that the economic system had to change. He became a writer. In 1848, Marx and Friedrich Engels published their ideas in *The Communist Manifesto*. It stated that the Industrial Revolution was making the rich richer and the poor poorer. Marx predicted that industrial workers would start a revolution.

But the revolutions Marx expected did not happen. Conditions in the industrialized countries improved. Standards of living got better. More factory-made goods were available. Even poor workers could afford to buy them. Workers formed unions to win more rights, and working conditions improved. Instead of rebelling, some workers moved to America.

Revolution broke out in Russia because most Russians were poor farmers, not industrial workers. They worked long and hard. Only the landowners became rich. The czars' government did not seem to care. A small group of revolutionaries, the Bolsheviks, thought that Marx's ideas could solve Russia's problems. Communism would allow everyone to share in the nation's wealth.

Did things work out as Marx predicted? He had said that in time the workers would take over the government. Eventually, a classless society would form. Government would no longer be needed. There would be a pure state of communism.

These changes did not happen in the Soviet Union. Rather, it became a powerful totalitarian state. Instead of having an autocratic czar, the Communist Party ran an all-powerful government. It still had total control over people's lives. Finally in the 1990s, the Communist system failed. Today, the people of the former Soviet Union are moving toward another kind of government. What that will be is not clear. Nor is it certain what their new economic system will be.

Spotlight Story Wrap-Up

1) What bad effects of the Industrial Revolution did Karl Marx observe?

2) In what book did Marx predict a workers' revolution?

3) Why was it surprising that the first Communist revolution occurred in Russia?

4) What is meant by a "classless society"?

5) How did the Soviet Union differ from what Marx had predicted about life under communism?

CHAPTER SUMMARY

➡ In the 1800s, Russia was an autocracy. The czar was an absolute ruler. More than 80 percent of Russians were serfs.

➡ In the mid-1800s, Czar Alexander II freed the serfs, reformed education, and gave people more rights. Revolutionaries who wanted more reforms killed him. His son Alexander III ignored calls for reform.

➡ The Industrial Revolution reached Russia in the late 1800s. Russia built railroads and factories. The standard of living for factory workers improved, but most people remained poor.

➡ In 1894, Nicholas II became czar. Many Russians wanted change, but Nicholas ignored them. Instead, he declared war on Japan in 1904, but Russia lost.

➡ In 1905, workers and others held a peaceful march in St. Petersburg. Soldiers killed hundreds on that "Bloody Sunday." When revolts continued, the czar promised more rights and an elected assembly, the Duma.

➡ Many Russians wanted socialism, a system in which the government runs a nation's economy. They followed the ideas of Karl Marx.

➡ World War I made things worse for the Russians. In 1917, a revolution forced Nicholas II to resign. Leaders of the Duma formed a government. Councils called soviets ran city governments.

➡ The Bolsheviks were revolutionary socialists led by Lenin. They took over the Russian government in 1917 and became the Communist Party. They called Russia "the Soviet Union." It then dropped out of World War I.

➡ Non-Bolsheviks formed a "White" army to fight the Bolshevik "Red" army. Civil war continued until 1920. The Bolsheviks killed the czar and his family.

➡ With the support of peasants and workers, the Red army won. Lenin's new government took over industry, gave land to peasants, and set up a dictatorship. They took power away from nobles and the Orthodox Church.

➡ After Lenin died, Joseph Stalin defeated his rival, Leon Trotsky, and became the new leader of Russia. Stalin wanted to develop Russian heavy industry quickly. The government also took peasant land for collective farms. When peasants objected, Stalin had them killed or sent to Siberia.

➡ Russia became a totalitarian state. A small group used fear to control people's lives. In the 1930s, Stalin held purges. Millions were arrested, and then they were sentenced to death or sent to labor camps. Russia became a powerful industrialized nation, but its people had few freedoms.

Comprehension: Identifying Facts

On a separate sheet of paper, use the words from the Word Bank to complete each sentence.

WORD BANK

Alexander II

Japan

Lenin

Nicholas II

Serfdom

Socialist

Stalin

Totalitarian

White

World War I

1) _____ ended in Russia much later than it did in the rest of Europe.

2) Czar _____ introduced change into Russia and gave his people some freedom.

3) "Bloody Sunday" took place during the rule of Czar _____.

4) When Russia lost its war with _____, people began to demand more change.

5) _____ societies have no private ownership of property.

6) _____ was probably the single most important cause of the Russian Revolution of 1917.

7) The leader of the Bolsheviks was _____.

8) In the Russian civil war, several foreign countries helped the _____ army.

9) _____ had a plan to industrialize Russia.

10) _____ states are governments in which a small group totally controls the lives of all the citizens.

Comprehension: Multiple Choice

On a separate sheet of paper, write the letter of the answer that correctly completes each sentence.

1) Under the czars, Russia was a(n) _____.
   a. democracy   c. autocracy
   b. constitutional monarchy   d. totalitarian state

2) A _____ government is set up for only a short time.
   a. provisional   c. Communist
   b. socialist   d. democratic

3) The _____ was a revolutionary socialist group.

    a. Whites   c. Collective Farmers

    b. Duma   d. Bolsheviks

4) After Lenin and his followers came to power, he _____.

    a. took control of all industry

    b. gave land to the peasants

    c. swept away the class system

    d. all of the above

5) Stalin conducted a _____ in which the government killed millions of workers that he thought were disloyal.

    a. minority   c. militia

    b. purge   d. provisional

Comprehension: Understanding Main Ideas

On a separate sheet of paper, write the answers to the following questions using complete sentences, or statements.

1) Why did the Russians revolt against Czar Nicholas II?

2) What is one way in which life improved for the common person under Stalin?

3) What is one way in which life got worse for the common person under Stalin?

Critical Thinking: Write Your Opinion

1) Stalin wanted to change Russia into a modern industrial power. What was wrong with the way he did it? Explain your answer.

2) Karl Marx, one of the fathers of communism, believed that being rich or poor affects the way a person thinks. Do you agree or disagree? Explain your answer.

Test-Taking Tip   When studying for a test, review any tests or quizzes you took earlier that cover the same information.

Chapter

25

Revolutions and the Rise of Dictators

1911 to 1938

You have studied a lot about nationalism. In the early 1900s, nationalism and hard economic times led to dictators in Europe. These dictators gained total control of their people. Powerful military leaders also took control of Japan. You will see how these changes affected Europe and Asia. You will also learn how the events in this chapter set the stage for another terrible war, World War II.

Goals for Learning

▶ To explain why dictators come to power

▶ To explain the common things fascist governments share

▶ To explain how the Nazis gained power in Germany

▶ To describe how the Chinese began to build a modern nation after the overthrow of the government in 1911

▶ To explain how military leaders took over the government of Japan

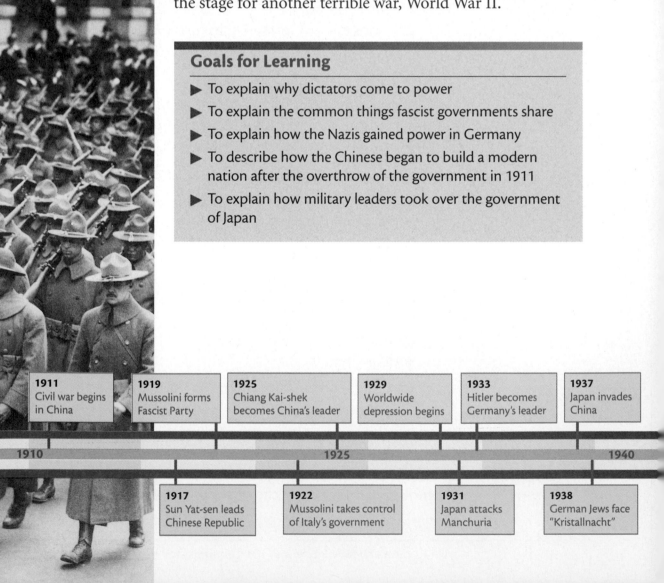

1911 Civil war begins in China	1919 Mussolini forms Fascist Party	1925 Chiang Kai-shek becomes China's leader	1929 Worldwide depression begins	1933 Hitler becomes Germany's leader	1937 Japan invades China

1910   1925   1940

1917 Sun Yat-sen leads Chinese Republic	1922 Mussolini takes control of Italy's government	1931 Japan attacks Manchuria	1938 German Jews face "Kristallnacht"

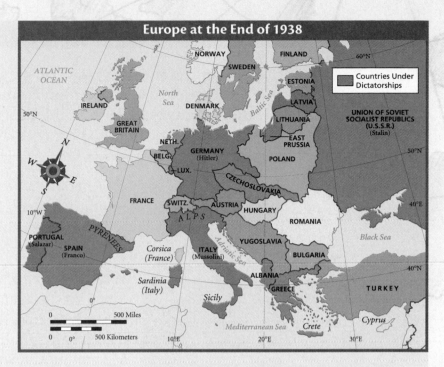

Europe at the End of 1938

By the end of 1938, fascist dictators controlled much of Europe. These powerful men threatened Europe's smaller, weaker countries. A year later, these dictators plunged the world into war. This map shows what Europe looked like at the end of 1938. It also shows the countries under the control of a dictator.

Study the map and answer the following questions:

Geography Skills

1) What are the names of five European countries that dictators controlled in 1938?

2) What were the names of five European dictators?

3) Which dictator controlled the most land?

4) Why did countries like Belgium, the Netherlands, and Denmark fear the rise of a German dictator?

5) In case of war, why would Britain be more difficult to conquer than France?

◆**Veteran**
A person who has served in the military, especially during a war

During World War I, Italy fought on the side of the Allies. The Italians wanted to win territory from Germany and Austria-Hungary. After the war, the Treaty of Versailles disappointed them. They wanted more land than the treaty gave them.

World War I also brought economic and political problems to Italy. The war left the country in debt. Many people lost their jobs. Many political parties arose, and the government was weak.

Mussolini became dictator of Italy in 1922. He was known as "Il Duce," which means "the leader."

Who Were the "Black Shirts"?

Many Italians blamed the democratic government for all of their nation's problems. Some feared a Communist revolution in Italy like the one in Russia. Benito Mussolini used this deep fear of communism and revolution to win power. Most of his followers were **veterans.** That is, they had fought for Italy in World War I. They became known as "Black Shirts."

In 1919, Mussolini formed the Fascist Party. It opposed both communism and democracy. As Italy's problems grew, the industrialists, the members of the aristocracy, and the middle class began to support Mussolini's party. He promised to make Italy as great as the ancient Roman Empire.

How Did Mussolini Gain Power?

In 1922, the Black Shirts marched on Rome. Then the king of Italy gave Mussolini the power to govern. Soon he became a dictator. His followers called him "Il Duce," or "the leader."

Mussolini told the people in Italy that they must "believe, fight, obey." He did not even allow workers to strike. Everyone had to be loyal to the state and to its leader—Mussolini. His secret police arrested, beat up, and sometimes killed anyone who spoke out against the government.

What Is Fascism?

Fascism developed during the twentieth century. This government system is a little different in each country, but they share the following:

1. They have only one party and one leader. **Fascists**—the people who believe in fascism—ban all other political parties.

2. They demand total obedience to the state and to its leader.

3. They take away individual rights and freedom. That is, the state takes away freedoms that belong to each and every person. The government censors all books and newspapers.

4. They preach **extreme** nationalism. (Extreme nationalists go the farthest they can go in preaching and spreading nationalism.)

5. They build up military power. Fascists believe that military force wins land for their country and makes it great.

Whom Did Mussolini Influence?

Fascists from other countries admired Italy's fascist dictatorship and borrowed ideas from it. In Spain, a fascist named Francisco Franco set himself up as dictator. In Germany, Adolf Hitler carefully watched Mussolini. In a few years, Hitler would become the most feared fascist leader in the world.

Extreme
The farthest something can go

◆**Fascism**
A form of government in which a dictator and the dictator's party totally control a government

◆**Fascist**
A person who believes in fascism

THE LEAGUE OF NATIONS FAILS

When World War I ended, world leaders met to discuss peace. U.S. President Woodrow Wilson wanted to create an organization to which every nation belonged. He thought this organization could prevent war. That is, it could keep wars from happening.

The Treaty of Versailles formed this organization—the League of Nations. The nations of the league promised to defend the territory and independence of all its members.

A test of the league's strength came in October 1935 when Italy attacked Ethiopia. Ethiopian Emperor Haile Selassie asked the league for help. It voted to force Italy to withdraw through economic means. That is, member nations refused to buy goods from Italy or to sell it war materials.

However, Great Britain and France did not want to upset Italy. They wanted Italy's support against Germany. Great Britain failed to close the Suez Canal, and Italy used the Suez to get war supplies. Italy was then able to defeat Ethiopia.

In 1935, the league failed to stop Italy. It tried to make everyone happy. Instead, it made everyone mad. Ethiopia lost its independence and the league lost its best chance of preventing war through nations working together.

SECTION 1 REVIEW On a separate sheet of paper, write answers to these questions.

1) What problems led to the rise of Mussolini in Italy?

2) Who supported the Fascist Party in Italy?

3) Who were the "Black Shirts"?

4) What are five ways in which most fascist governments are alike?

5) What are the names of two other fascist leaders besides Mussolini, and what countries did they lead?

What do you think

Dictators often do mean and ugly things. Why do you think people allow dictators to rule them?

◆Inflation
A quick increase in prices

◆Nazi
The Nationalist Socialist German Workers' Party led by Hitler

◆Swastika
The Nazi symbol of a cross with its arms bent

◆Weimar Republic
The post-World War I democratic government in Germany

When German soldiers returned home after World War I, they found little work. Because the war had destroyed many factories, people had few goods to sell at home or to foreign markets. Prices went up quickly. This is called **inflation.**

What Was the Weimar Republic?

At the end of the war, the Allies forced Kaiser William II of Germany to step down. Then the German people set up a democratic government and wrote a constitution. They called their new government the **Weimar Republic** because they wrote their constitution in the city of Weimar.

The Weimar Republic had problems. Some Germans blamed it for accepting the mean terms of the Treaty of Versailles. Army officers said that socialists and liberals in the government had been disloyal during the war. Both the Communists and other political groups opposed the new democratic government, too. However, none of them had a majority.

The dictator in Germany was Adolf Hitler. He took control of the German government in 1933.

Who Were the Nazis?

A man named Adolf Hitler joined one of these parties—the Nationalist Socialist German Workers' Party. It was called **Nazi** for short. The Nazis adopted a red flag with a black **swastika** as its symbol. A swastika is a cross with its arms bent. Soon Hitler, who had loved fighting in the war, became the Nazi leader.

People called one group of Hitler's followers the "Brown Shirts" or "Storm Troopers." Carrying weapons and wearing brown shirts, they broke up meetings of other political parties. Some Germans feared Hitler's followers, but others admired them.

Geography History in Your Life

Hitler and *Lebensraum*

Hitler wanted to rebuild Germany into a great power. To do this, Hitler said that Germany needed more living space, or *Lebensraum*. This idea was a basic part of his policy. In theory, Hitler meant empty lands where Germans could settle. But in reality, any land that Germany would take already belonged to other people. Germany was no more crowded than most of Europe.

Many historians think that *Lebensraum* was just an excuse. It justified Hitler's plans to conquer his neighbors. He found other reasons to claim their land, too. For example, many ethnic Germans lived in Czechoslovakia. Nearby Austria was another German-speaking country. Also, the Treaty of Versailles, which ended World War I, had deeply wounded German pride. France had gotten land from Germany. So had Poland. Beyond Poland were the rich farmlands of the Ukraine in the Soviet Union. Taking more land would bring Hitler more power.

◆**Depression**
A time of economic collapse when businesses lose money and people become poor

Inferior
Not as good as someone or something else

◆**Reichstag**
The national assembly of the Weimar Republic

Superior
Better than someone or something else

What Did Hitler Say in His Book?

In 1923, Hitler tried to take control of the German government by force, but he failed. Then the leaders of the Weimar Republic arrested and jailed him. During his jail term, he wrote *Mein Kampf,* which means "My Struggle."

In his book, Hitler said that the German people were **superior,** or better than, other people. He also said that everyone else was **inferior,** or less important than, the German people. Hitler came up with a plan to make Germany a powerful nation once again.

How Did the Depression Help the Nazis?

In 1929, a long drop in business activity—a **depression**—took place all over the world. By 1932, nearly 40 percent of the factory workers in Germany had no jobs. Many turned to communism. But the middle class and the wealthy were tired of inflation; they feared the Communists. Many of them turned to Hitler because he opposed communism. Soon the Nazis became the largest political party in Germany.

What Did Hitler Do As Dictator?

In 1933, Hitler became head of the German government. Then he called for an election. (The Nazi Party still did not have a majority in the German assembly, or **Reichstag.**

The Gestapo was Hitler's secret police force.

Hitler needed a majority to become really powerful.)

Just before the election, someone set the Reichstag building on fire. No one knows who started the fire—maybe the Nazis. Hitler blamed the Communists. In the election, many German people, fearing revolution, voted for the Nazis. The Nazis did not win the election, but Hitler later took control of the Reichstag.

Next, Hitler made himself dictator. He called himself the **Fuehrer,** which means "leader." As dictator, Hitler did the following:

1. Banned all other political parties and all labor unions.
2. Made all army officers promise to obey his orders.
3. Censored all books, magazines, newspapers, radio programs, and movies.
4. Burnt all books that contained ideas opposed to Nazism.
5. Established a secret police force called the **Gestapo.** It made sure that no one said anything against Hitler or the Nazis.
6. Rebuilt the German army into a powerful war machine.

◆**Fuehrer**
The name given to Adolph Hitler meaning "leader"

◆**Gestapo**
Hitler's secret police force

How Did Hitler Feel About the Jewish People?

Many Germans had suffered during World War I. But Hitler thought that the Jewish people had made money on the war. He blamed them for all the problems in Germany.

Of course, this was silly. Many German Jews had served with honor in World War I. In fact, only about 1 percent of all Germans were Jews, and many of them had contributed greatly to German culture. Yet, Hitler called them disloyal and inferior.

What Was Kristallnacht?

Hitler decided to rid Germany of all Jews. First, he took away their German citizenship. Then he ordered that Jews

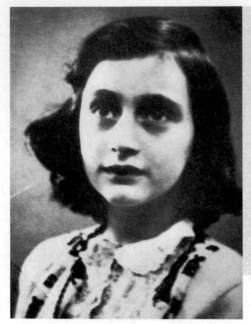

◆Kristallnacht
The period of terror toward the Jewish people in Germany in November, 1938, meaning "Night of Broken Glass"

Synagogue
The building where Jews worship

could not marry non-Jews or play the music of non-Jewish composers. Next, Hitler said that Jews could not work for non-Jews. Jews could not teach or work in hospitals or banks. Finally, he ordered all Jews to wear a yellow star on their clothes.

The Nazis encouraged violence against the Jews. On November 9, 1938, non-Jewish Germans broke into and destroyed many businesses Jews owned and many **synagogues** where they worshipped. Historians call this **Kristallnacht,** or "Night of Broken Glass."

SECTION 2 REVIEW On a separate sheet of paper, write *True* if the statement is true or *False* if the statement is not true. Make each false statement true by changing the underlined word.

1) After World War I, Germany wrote a constitution for a monarchy.
2) The name of Germany's new government was the Versailles Republic.
3) The leader of the Nazis was Hitler.
4) The Nazis took control of the Reichstag.
5) The German word Kristallnacht means "Night of Broken Glass."

What do you think ?

Why do you think Hitler ordered Jews to wear yellow stars?

During the Age of Imperialism, Europe and Japan carved out spheres of influence in China. European powers controlled Chinese mines, railroads, and some factories. But Chinese nationalists hated imperialism. They wanted to free China from foreign influence.

What Did Sun Yat-sen Want for China?

Sun Yat-sen led the Chinese nationalists. He wrote a book called *Three Principles of the People,* which greatly influenced his country. In his book, he wrote that he wanted three things for China:

1. A strong national government free of foreign control.
2. A democratic government that the Chinese people controlled.
3. Better living conditions for all the Chinese people.

Why Did the Soviet Union Help Sun Yat-sen?

In 1911, Sun Yat-sen and the Chinese revolutionaries overthrew the government and formed a republic.

However, for the next five years, civil war tore China apart. In 1917, Sun Yat-sen became leader of the republic. But military leaders who wanted power for themselves still controlled much of China.

Sun Yat-sen asked the European nations for help. They would not help, because Sun Yat-sen had criticized them for being imperialists. Sun Yat-sen then turned to the Soviet Union. Lenin, the Russian leader at the time, agreed to send money and military supplies to China. He thought that his country and China faced the same enemies. Lenin also wanted to introduce communism to China.

What Started a Civil War in China?

In 1925, Sun Yat-sen died. Then Chiang Kai-shek, an army general, became China's leader. Chiang did not trust the Soviet Union or the Communists. Soon after taking power, he ordered the Soviet advisers out of China and nearly wiped

Sun Yat-sen was the leader of the Chinese nationalists. He wanted to free China from foreign influence.

out the Chinese Communist Party. Only a few Communists managed to escape.

Mao Zedong was one of the Communists who fled to the Chinese countryside. With his supporters, he fought a long civil war against Chiang. Several times during this war, Chiang almost destroyed the Communists.

What United the Chinese People?

In this war, bankers and business people in the cities along China's coast supported Chiang. The peasants supported Mao Zedong because the Communists took land from the rich and divided it among the landless peasants.

China's civil war stopped for a while in 1937 when Japan invaded China. The Japanese killed many Chinese people and destroyed cities, farms, and factories. Then all the Chinese people united to fight their common enemy.

SECTION 3 REVIEW Choose the letter of the answer that correctly completes each sentence. Write your answer on a separate sheet of paper.

1) Chinese _____ hated foreign influence in China.

    a. industrialists   c. imperialists
    b. nationalists   d. Communists

2) Sun Yat-sen wanted _____ for the Chinese people.

    a. a strong national government
    b. a democratic government
    c. better living conditions
    d. all of the above

3) After Sun Yat-sen died, _____ led China.

    a. Chiang Kai-shek   c. Hitler
    b. Lenin   d. Mao Zedong

4) The leader of the Chinese Communists was _____.

    a. Chiang Kai-shek   c. Mao Zedong
    b. Sun Yat-sen   d. Lenin

5) In 1937, _____ invaded China and the Chinese people stopped their civil war.

    a. Japan   b. Germany   c. Italy   d. Russia

What do you think ?

Why do you think some Chinese people hated imperialism?

◆**Great Depression**
The worldwide depression that began in the United States in 1929

The **Great Depression** started in the United States in 1929 and spread all over the world. It was hard on Japan, because people no longer had money to buy Japanese silk. Some Japanese companies that had exported goods to other countries went out of business. Many workers had no jobs. The Japanese people blamed its government for their problems.

Who Became the Real Leaders of Japan?

In the 1920s, the Japanese government had become more democratic. Before then, it had not allowed many people to vote. Now they had this right. When the depression hit in the 1930s, some people blamed democracy. Military officers did so because they wanted more power.

In the fascist countries of Italy and Germany, one military man ruled all the people. This was not true in Japan. In the 1930s, a small group of military men gained power in the government. They said that the emperor ruled. But in fact, the military ruled in his name. General Hideki Tojo—the minister of war—was the chief speaker for the military.

However, Japan's government had at least four things in common with the fascist governments of Germany and Italy.

1. It arrested anyone who spoke out against it.

2. It controlled the press and censored newspapers and radio.

3. It ordered schools to teach children that they must always obey.

4. Its secret police made people afraid to say or do anything against the government.

General Hideki Tojo led a group of military leaders in Japan. He would lead a government takeover in 1941.

Why Did Japan Attack Manchuria?

In September 1931, Japan attacked Manchuria. (This Chinese province bordered on Japanese-controlled Korea.) Japan quickly overran Manchuria. The Japanese said that they had freed the province from China. But Japan completely controlled this new state, which it renamed Manchukuo.

Dictators

Throughout history, powerful leaders have taken power by force. They have absolute power and do not allow opposition. Their word is law. In the early 1800s, Napoleon Bonaparte conquered much of Europe. Napoleon began as an enemy of monarchy, but then he became a dictator. Also in the 1800s, most of Latin America won its independence from Spain. Since then, dictators called *"caudillos"* have often ruled these countries.

In the 1930s, Franco won the civil war in Spain and became its dictator. Two other dictators—Mussolini in Italy and Hitler in Germany—took the world to war.

In recent years, people have overthrown dictators in the Philippines and Indonesia. Yet dictators keep coming to power. Unfortunately, dictators still rule smaller nations around the world today.

Why had Japan attacked Manchuria? For two reasons. First, Japan's military leaders wanted Manchuria's coal and iron for industry. Second, Japan had too many people. But Manchuria had few people. The Japanese leaders wanted people from Japan to move to Manchuria and settle there.

What Alliance Developed?

During the 1930s, Germany and Italy had developed close ties. In 1936, Germany and Japan agreed to join together to fight the spread of communism. In 1937, Italy agreed to this, too. The three nations would later agree to help each other if one of them went to war. That war—World War II—was coming closer and closer.

SECTION 4 REVIEW On a separate sheet of paper, write the word from the Word Bank that completes each sentence.

WORD BANK
Germany
Great Depression
Italy
Manchuria
Tojo

1) Because of the _____, many Japanese companies went out of business after 1929.
2) General _____ ruled Japan in the 1930s.
3) Japan attacked _____ in 1931.
4) In 1936, _____ and Japan joined together to fight the spread of communism.
5) Japan, Germany, and _____ formed an alliance.

What do you think

In Chapter 12, you read about Japanese feudalism and the samurai. How might this tradition have prepared the Japanese people for military leadership?

The Terror of Kristallnacht

The night of November 9, 1938, was a nightmare for German Jews. That night, Nazis and their supporters destroyed Jewish homes and shops. They burned synagogues. The event is known as "Kristallnacht," or "night of broken glass." More than 90 Jews were killed and hundreds were hurt. About 30,000 Jewish men were arrested. In a small town in western Germany, a young Jewish worker watched a crowd attack his synagogue. This excerpt describes what happened.

This photo shows broken windows of a Jewish shop after Kristallnacht, the "night of broken glass."

The crowd tore the Holy Ark wide open; and three men who had smashed the Ark, threw the Scrolls of the Law of Moses out. He threw them—these Scrolls, which had stood in their quiet dignity, draped in blue or wine-red velvet, with their little crowns of silver covering the tops of the shafts by which the Scroll was held during the service—to the screaming and shouting mass of people which had filled the little synagogue. The people caught the Scrolls as if they were amusing themselves with a ballgame—tossing them up into the air again, while other people flung them further back until they reached the street outside. Women tore away the red and blue velvet and everybody tried to snatch some of the silver adorning the Scrolls. . . .

Naked and open, the Scrolls lay in the muddy autumn lane; children stepped on them and others tore pieces from the fine parchment on which the Law was written—the same Law which the people who tore it apart had, in vain, tried to absorb for over a thousand years. . . .

When the first rays of a cold and pale November sun penetrated the heavy dark clouds, the little synagogue was but a heap of stone, broken glass, and smashed-up woodwork.

Where the two well-cared-for flower beds had flanked both sides of the gravel path leading to the door of the synagogue, the children had lit a bonfire and the parchment Scrolls gave enough food for the flames to eat up the smashed-up benches and doors, and the wood, which on the day before had been the Holy Ark for the Scrolls of the Law of Moses.

Source Reading Wrap-Up

1) What was kept in the Holy Ark of the synagogue?

2) What did the Scrolls usually look like?

3) What did the crowd do with the Scrolls?

4) How did the synagogue look the morning after it was attacked?

5) How did this attack reflect Nazi beliefs?

Adolf Hitler inspects his troops.

Hitler's Rise To Power

In 1919, Germany was defeated and in ruins. The Treaty of Versailles took away its military strength. The treaty also ordered Germany to pay $33 billion in war damages to the Allies. Germans were angry and bitter. Things got worse in the next few years. Inflation soared. By late 1923, German money was worth almost nothing. Many people were out of work and hungry. The Weimar government was too weak to do anything. The times were ripe for revolution.

Playing on these feelings, many nationalist groups formed. One was the National Socialist German Workers' Party. The name was soon shortened to "Nazis." A former soldier named Adolf Hitler became its leader. In fiery speeches, Hitler blamed Germany's troubles on the Versailles Treaty. He attacked the Weimar government. He denounced capitalists and the Jews. Hitler organized a private army of 15,000 "brown shirts." Their emblem was the swastika.

In 1923, the Nazis staged a putsch—an attempt to overthrow the state government of Bavaria. About 3,000 people, including government leaders, were holding a rally at a Munich beer hall. Hitler's "brown shirts" surrounded the hall. They set up a machine gun in the entrance. Hitler jumped up on a table and fired his gun into the air. He shouted, "The national revolution has begun!" He then led his men toward the center of the city, but police stopped them. They arrested Hitler and most of the top Nazi leaders.

Hitler and other top Nazi leaders were sent to prison for treason. There he wrote *Mein Kampf* (*My Struggle*). The book stated his political ideas and plans. It stressed nationalism and racism. *Mein Kampf* would become the guidebook of nazism. It also made Hitler famous in Germany.

From 1924 to 1929, Germany began to recover. Many Nazis lost interest and drifted away. Then the worldwide depression hit Germany. Once again workers were unemployed and hungry. Slowly, Hitler began to rebuild the Nazi Party. This time, however, he worked to get political power.

By late 1932, the Nazi Party was the strongest in Germany. Hitler was getting valuable help from people who preferred nazism to communism. The Nazis did not yet have a majority in the Reichstag, however. Still, no political party could rule without their help. In 1933, another government crisis occurred. Hitler promised to support the government if he were made leader. On January 30, 1933, he took office as chancellor. Six months later, he was dictator of Germany.

Spotlight Story Wrap-Up

1) What conditions set the stage for the rise of nationalism in Germany?
2) Who did Hitler blame for Germany's hard times?
3) What happened in the Beer Hall putsch?
4) What was *Mein Kampf*?
5) How did Hitler eventually become leader of Germany?

➥ Italians felt that the Allies had cheated them in the Treaty of Versailles.

➥ In 1919, Mussolini formed the Fascist Party. It opposed both democracy and communism. Army veterans known as "Black Shirts" joined the party.

➥ The king of Italy turned power over to Mussolini or "Il Duce." He became a dictator. Industrialists, aristocrats, and the middle class supported him.

➥ Fascism demands total obedience to one party and leader. The state censors books and newspapers and denies free speech. Fascists believe in nationalism and military power.

➥ In Germany, the Weimar Republic was the democratic government after World War I. Many small political groups opposed it.

➥ Adolf Hitler led a fascist party known as the Nazis. His followers, the "Brown Shirts," attacked other parties.

➥ In 1923, Nazi leaders were jailed for trying to take over the government. While there, Hitler wrote *Mein Kampf*. It said Germany was superior to other nations. It also described Hitler's plan to make Germany strong again.

➥ A depression and fear of communism helped Hitler gain power. By 1933, he was head of the government. As dictator, or Fuehrer, he censored all media and banned other political parties. He made the army powerful and set up a secret police, the Gestapo. He began to persecute German Jews.

➥ In China, Sun Yat-sen led a nationalist movement. He wanted China to have a strong, democratic government without foreign control. A revolution in 1911 overthrew the monarchy but led to civil war. Only the Soviet Union sent Sun Yat-sen help.

➥ After Sun Yat-sen died, Chiang Kai-shek led the Nationalists. Bankers and business people supported him. He conducted a long civil war against Mao Zedong's Chinese Communists. Many peasants supported Mao. The Chinese united to fight a Japanese invasion in 1937.

➥ Japan's government became more democratic after World War I. However, the depression hurt the economy. Military leaders used this problem to gain power. General Tojo was their spokesman. They demanded strict obedience, censored the media, and used secret police.

➥ In 1931, Japan invaded Manchuria, a Chinese province rich in iron and coal. Later Japan became allies with Germany and Italy against communism.

Comprehension: Identifying Facts

On a separate sheet of paper, use the words from the Word Bank to complete each sentence.

WORD BANK

Chiang Kai-shek

Fascism

Fuehrer

Hitler

Il Duce

Mao Zedong

Mussolini

Nazi

Sun Yat-sen

Tojo

1) _____ wrote a book that gave three goals for China.

2) _____ led the Chinese Communists.

3) _____ fought a civil war against the Chinese Communists.

4) Benito _____ became Italy's dictator.

5) Italians called their dictator _____, which means "leader."

6) Adolf _____ led the Nationalist Socialist German Workers' Party.

7) _____ is another name for the Nationalist Socialist German Workers' Party.

8) Germans called their dictator _____, which also means "leader."

9) General _____ led a small group of military leaders who held power in Japan in the 1930s.

10) _____ is a government of one party and one leader.

Comprehension: Multiple Choice

On a separate sheet of paper, write the letter of the answer that correctly completes each sentence.

1) A person who has served in the military, especially during a war, is a _____.

   a. veteran   c. synagogue

   b. Gestapo   d. swastika

2) To be _____ is to be better than something or someone else.

   a. inflation   c. individual

   b. inferior   d. superior

3) The Nazi Party chose a special cross, the _____ , as a symbol.

  a. Reichstag   c. swastika

  b. Gestapo   d. Nazi

4) The name of Germany's government after World War I was the _____.

  a. Fascist Party   c. Nationalist Party

  b. Weimar Republic   d. Communist Party

5) Hitler wrote _____ while in jail.

  a. *Mein Kampf*   c. *The Communist Manifesto*

  b. *The Iliad*   d. *Three Principles of the People*

Comprehension: Understanding Main Ideas

On a separate sheet of paper, write the answers to the following questions using complete sentences, or statements.

1) Why did Italy and Germany choose fascism and dictators after World War I?

2) What are six things Hitler did when he became the dictator of Germany?

3) What are four things that Japan's government had in common with Nazi Germany and fascist Italy during the 1930s?

Critical Thinking: Write Your Opinion

1) Mussolini wrote that fascism "was born of the need for action." What do you think he meant?

2) Imagine that you are a Jewish veteran of World War I living in Germany. Describe how you feel about Hitler's attacks on the Jews.

| Test-Taking Tip | When studying for a test, learn the most important points. Practice writing or saying the material out loud. Have a partner listen to check if you are right. |

Chapter

26

World War II

1939 to 1945

You have read a lot about nationalism, imperialism, and militarism. They caused World War I. These ideas caused another war in Europe, Asia, and the Pacific: World War II.

In this chapter, you will watch Hitler ignore the Treaty of Versailles. You will see how people rush into subways to avoid the bombs during the Battle of Britain. You will witness how an invading German army faces a cold winter in the Soviet Union, much like Napoleon's army did 130 years earlier. You will see the destruction caused by Japanese bombs at Pearl Harbor. Then you will see how an atomic bomb destroys cities in Japan and ends World War II. These events and more make up World War II, the most destructive war ever fought.

Goals for Learning

▶ To explain the major causes of World War II

▶ To list the countries that fascist dictators and nations invaded

▶ To explain why the policy of appeasement failed

▶ To list the successes of the Axis Powers

▶ To list the successes of the Allies

▶ To explain what brought an end to World War II

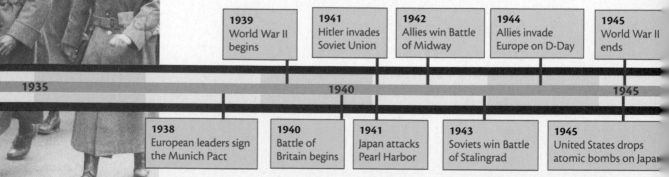

| 1939 World War II begins | 1941 Hitler invades Soviet Union | 1942 Allies win Battle of Midway | 1944 Allies invade Europe on D-Day | 1945 World War II ends |

1935   1940   1945

| 1938 European leaders sign the Munich Pact | 1940 Battle of Britain begins | 1941 Japan attacks Pearl Harbor | 1943 Soviets win Battle of Stalingrad | 1945 United States drops atomic bombs on Japan |

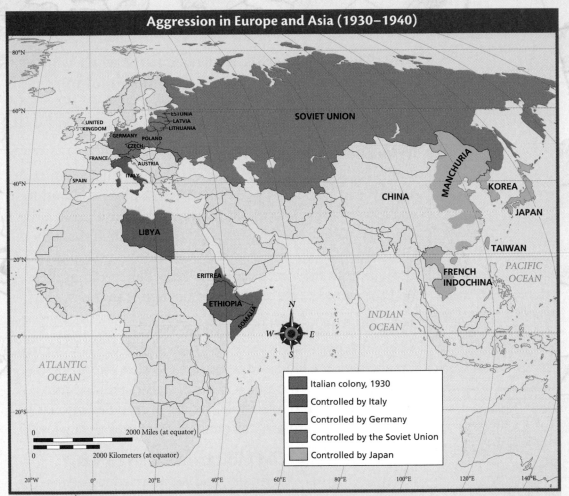

Aggression in Europe and Asia (1930–1940)

Italian colony, 1930
Controlled by Italy
Controlled by Germany
Controlled by the Soviet Union
Controlled by Japan

Geography Skills

In the 1930s, Japan, Germany, Italy, and the Soviet Union took over the land and resources of neighboring countries. Because they were strong, they believed they had the right to rule other nations. This map shows aggression in Europe and Asia from 1930 to 1940.

Study the map carefully and answer the following questions:

1) What area of China did the Japanese conquer?

2) What French territory in Asia did the Japanese capture?

3) What countries did Germany conquer?

4) What African colonies did Italy control?

5) Which country—Germany, Italy, Japan, or the Soviet Union—controlled the most land?

Axis
A make-believe line that goes through the middle of an object that spins around it

◆**Axis Powers**
The alliance of Germany, Italy, and Japan during World War II

Crisis
A time of danger; a turning point in events

Glorify
To praise someone or something

The 1930s brought **crisis,** or danger, to the whole world. Once again, the countries of Europe stood ready to fight. In Chapter 23, you learned that nationalism, imperialism, and militarism caused World War I. They also led to World War II.

Why Did Nationalism Lead to War?

Italy's Mussolini and Germany's Hitler were nationalists. So were the military leaders of Japan. Mussolini promised to make Italy as great as the Roman Empire. Hitler called the German people the "master race." He preached that all other people were inferior. Italy, Germany, and Japan thought that they were superior. They believed that they had the right to rule all the inferior people in the world.

Why Did Imperialism Lead to War?

These three countries were also imperialistic. They wanted to take over the land and resources of other countries. Japan tried to create a new empire. Italy expanded into Africa and tried to make the Mediterranean Sea into an "Italian lake." Germany annexed Austria and Czechoslovakia.

Why Did Militarism Lead to War?

Italy, Germany, and Japan tried to form a military **axis** around which the world would turn. An axis is a make-believe line that goes through the middle of an object. The object spins on the axis. For this reason, historians called the three nations the **Axis Powers.**

The three Axis nations spent great sums of money on the military. They developed new weapons and built large armies. They **glorified** war. That is, they welcomed it. They said that dying for their country was the highest honor a person could ever have.

Writing About History

Pretend that you represent a world organization that tries to prevent wars around the world. In your notebook, write ten things that your organization would do to try to prevent a world war.

What Are Four Other Causes of World War II?

Nationalism, imperialism, and militarism led to World War II. But four other things did, too.

First, the Treaty of Versailles, which ended World War I, punished Germany severely. Hitler and the German people began to hate. They wanted to make the Allies pay for what Germany had suffered.

Second, the breakdown of the world economy after 1929 helped nations turn to war. During the Great Depression, many businesses failed. World trade almost stopped. The money of some countries became almost worthless. The Treaty of Versailles made Germany and Austria pay for World War I damages. This destroyed the economies of these two countries. These hard times encouraged the rise of dictators. People were willing to follow leaders who promised a better way of life.

Third, the three Axis countries were totalitarian dictatorships. They did not believe in personal freedom or in free elections. They did not believe in freedom of speech or equality. They wanted to destroy democracy.

Fourth, the failure of the League of Nations was a cause of World War II. The league was never strong. Its more powerful members refused to cooperate. It had little power to use against countries that broke its rules. The United States never joined the league. Germany and Japan dropped out in 1933; Italy left it in 1936. The league expelled Russia in 1939.

All of these set the stage for World War II. It would be even more destructive than the first.

The Great Depression ruined the world economy. In the United States, people had to wait in line for food and jobs.

The Great Depression

Prices go up and down. Unemployment rises and falls. Even rich countries like the United States have economic slowdowns. The most serious are called "depressions."

In 1929, the American stock market crashed. That event started the Great Depression in the United States. Factories and banks closed throughout the country. Unemployment soared to about 13 million—one-fourth of all workers.

When the American economy crashed, the economies in other nations suffered. Inflation soared. Money became almost worthless. In Germany, people piled paper money into wheelbarrows just to buy bread.

Economics

History in Your Life

To lessen the Great Depression, the government provided jobs and relief. To avoid another depression, the government started programs that would help a slipping economy. It also passed laws to make banks safer and to watch the stock market. Today, the economy suffers from shorter, less serious slowdowns. They usually affect parts of the country or particular industries.

SECTION 1 REVIEW Choose the letter of the answer that correctly completes each sentence. Write your answer on a separate sheet of paper.

1) _____ was one cause of World War II.

   a. Communism   c. Revolution

   b. Monarchy   d. Nationalism

2) Germany, Japan, and Italy formed the _____ Powers.

   a. Allied   c. European

   b. Axis   d. democratic

3) All three countries felt _____ to other people.

   a. superior   c. weaker

   b. inferior   d. less powerful

4) The _____ was a cause of World War II.

   a. failure of the League of Nations   c. Treaty of Versailles

   b. Great Depression   d. all of the above

5) The _____ never joined the League of Nations.

   a. Russians   c. Americans

   b. Germans   d. Italians

What do you think ?

What do you think was the most important cause of World War II?

As you know, Japan invaded Manchuria in 1931. The League of Nations ordered Japan to remove its troops. Instead, Japan dropped out of the league. You also know that in 1935, Italy invaded Ethiopia and the league did nothing. Italy then made Ethiopia a colony. Then, in 1939, Italy invaded Albania, a nation between Italy and Greece. Five days later, it became part of the Italian Empire.

What Did Hitler Want?

You know a lot about the Treaty of Versailles. It limited the size of Germany's army and the number of weapons it could have. However, Hitler ignored the treaty. He ordered all young German men to serve in the army. Then he ordered Germany's factories to produce guns, tanks, airplanes, and other weapons. Hitler said, "Today, Germany; tomorrow, the world!"

How Did Hitler Break the Treaty of Versailles?

The Treaty of Versailles barred German troops from the Rhineland, an area of Germany that bordered France. But in March 1936, Hitler sent troops there. Great Britain and France protested, but did nothing because they feared war.

The Treaty of Versailles also said that Germany and Austria—who were allies in World War I—could not unite again. But in 1938, Hitler said that all German-speaking people should be one. He ignored the treaty again by invading and annexing Austria. (However, he did not ask the Austrians what they wanted.) Once again, Britain and France took no military action.

Why Did Hitler Want the Sudetenland?

Hitler had invaded the Rhineland and Austria and no one did anything. He then turned to Czechoslovakia. (It was one of the new countries that the Treaty of Versailles created after World War I.) About three million Germans lived in the area of northwestern Czechoslovakia that bordered Germany. (People called this area the Sudetenland.) Hitler demanded control over it.

Hitler (right) met with European leaders in Munich, Germany, in 1938. There they signed the Munich Pact, which gave Hitler control of the Sudetenland. Pictured to the left is Britain's Prime Minister Neville Chamberlain.

What Did the Munich Pact Give Hitler?

The British and the French had promised to protect Czechoslovakia against its enemies. On September 29, 1938, British Prime Minister Neville Chamberlain met with Hitler in Munich, Germany. Chamberlain invited French and Italian leaders to participate in the **conference,** or meeting. However, he did not invite leaders from the Soviet Union or from Czechoslovakia.

At the conference, the leaders signed the **Munich Pact.** It gave Hitler control of the Sudetenland. In return, he promised not to attack the rest of Czechoslovakia. When Chamberlain returned to England, cheering crowds greeted him. He said that now they would have "peace in our time." However, six months later, Hitler took over the rest of Czechoslovakia.

Why Did Appeasement Fail?

Great Britain and France did not help Ethiopia, Austria, or Czechoslovakia. They hoped to avoid war. They followed a policy of **appeasement.** That is, they gave in to the fascist dictators. Britain and France hoped that the dictators would be happy with what they had and would not attack other countries. This policy failed. It did not satisfy the dictators' desire for new lands. Instead, it made them demand more because they thought Britain and France were weak and inferior.

Why Did Germany and Russia Sign a Treaty?

Soon, Germany and Russia signed a treaty. They agreed not to make war against each other. No one could understand why Hitler and Stalin signed this treaty. After all, Hitler hated Communism, and Stalin hated Fascism.

But both countries gained something from their treaty. The Soviets got two things. First, the treaty allowed them to

◆Appeasement
A policy of making others happy or content; giving in so that others will be happy and will not cause a war

Conference
A meeting to discuss ideas and plans

◆Munich Pact
A 1938 agreement between Great Britain and Germany to appease Hitler

◆Front
The place where armies fight; the battle line

avoid war—for the time being. It gave them time to strengthen their military forces. Second, the treaty gave them control of Latvia, Estonia, and Lithuania.

Germany also gained two things from the treaty. First, it protected Germany against fighting a two-**front** war. (A front is the place where armies are fighting. So a two front-war would be one in which an army has to fight in two different places at the same time.) Second, the treaty left Germany free to invade Poland.

What Sparked World War II?

On September 1, 1939, Hitler (believing that Great Britain and France would do nothing) invaded Poland from the west. At the same time, the Soviet Union attacked from the east.

Now the British and French leaders gave up their policy of appeasement. They had proof that the policy did not work. It only made dictators hungry for more. On September 3, 1939, Britain and France declared war on Germany. World War II had begun.

Who Fought World War II?

Historians call the two sides in the war the Axis and the Allies. The three major Axis powers were Germany, Italy, and Japan. A few other nations supported them. When war broke out, the Allies included only France and Britain. Later, the Soviet Union, the United States, and 48 other nations joined the Allies.

SECTION 2 REVIEW On a separate sheet of paper, write answers to these questions.

1) What countries did Italy and Germany invade during the 1930s?
2) What are three ways in which Germany ignored the Treaty of Versailles?
3) Why did France and Great Britain do nothing to stop Hitler's annexation of Austria and Czechoslovakia?
4) What did the Soviet Union get from its treaty with Germany?
5) What happened in September 1939 that sparked the beginning of World War II?

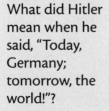

What do you think ❓

What did Hitler mean when he said, "Today, Germany; tomorrow, the world!"?

Blitzkrieg
The quick and forceful method of attack that Germany used in World War II; "lightning war"

Maginot line
A line of concrete forts built by France along its border with Germany

World War II began on September 3, 1939. But for seven months, no fighting took place. Then, in April 1940, German troops began to attack. Quickly, they conquered Denmark, Norway, the Netherlands, Luxembourg, and Belgium.

To do this, Germany invented the **blitzkrieg,** or "lightning war." Using the fastest new machines—airplanes, tanks, trucks, and motorcycles—the Germans rushed deep into enemy territory. They defeated an enemy country before it could defend itself.

What Was the Maginot Line?

After World War I, the French built a line of defense along its border with Germany to protect itself. France's defense was the **Maginot line**—a line of concrete forts.

But by conquering Belgium, Hitler got around the Maginot line. On June 16, 1940, German troops marched into Paris. Six days later, the French surrendered to Germany. Hitler now controlled almost all of Western Europe.

How Was World War II a Total War?

Now Great Britain stood alone. It prepared for a German invasion. The new British Prime Minister Winston Churchill said, "We shall defend our island, whatever the cost may be. . . . We shall never surrender."

The Axis tried to force England's surrender by waging "total war." As you know from Chapter 23, in a total war, both soldiers and civilians suffer from bombing, sickness, and lack of food. A country uses all its resources to destroy all the resources of another country.

Where Did the Battle of Britain Take Place?

The battle between Hitler's air force and the British air force began in August 1940 and lasted for over a year. It took place in the skies over Britain. Day and night, German planes bombed London, Britain's capital. To escape the

bombs, thousands of Londoners slept in underground
railroad stations.

◆Arsenal
*A place where a
country stores or
makes weapons*

◆Destroyer
*A small, fast
warship that uses
guns and other
weapons to protect
ships from
submarines*

◆Lend-Lease
program
*A program
developed by
Franklin Roosevelt
that allowed
Britain to borrow
war supplies from
the United States
during World War II*

bombs, thousands of Londoners slept in underground
railroad stations.

In the Battle of Britain, as it was called, Germany lost 2,300
planes, while England lost only 900. In October 1941,
Hitler stopped the air war. This was his first defeat. Now he
decided to starve the English into surrendering. German
submarines began sinking merchant ships headed for
Britain. As British supplies got low, Churchill asked the
United States for help.

How Did the United States Help Britain?

When war broke out in Europe, the United States declared
itself neutral. However, President Roosevelt asked the
United States to become an "**arsenal** of democracy." (An
arsenal is a place where someone stores or makes weapons.)

Roosevelt sent 50 old **destroyers** to Britain. These small,
fast warships used guns and other weapons to protect
merchant ships from submarines. In return, the United
States received the use of eight British naval bases along the
Atlantic Coast. Roosevelt also developed the **Lend-Lease
program.** Through this program, Britain borrowed
supplies from the United States.

Why Did Hitler Invade the Soviet Union?

After the failure of the Battle of Britain, Hitler decided to
attack his ally—the Soviet Union. He ignored their treaty
because he wanted the Soviet oil fields, grain, and other
resources.

At first, the Germans won one battle after another. By
December 1941, they had almost reached Moscow and
Leningrad—the two most important Soviet cities. But then
the Russians stopped retreating.

Who Won the Battle of Stalingrad?

Soon a terribly cold winter caught the Germans
unprepared. Many soldiers in both armies died. Historians
call the six-month Battle of Stalingrad a turning point in
the war. Before Stalingrad, the Soviets retreated. After
Stalingrad, the Germans did.

Tanks were very important weapons in World War II.

Like Napoleon in 1812, Hitler did not understand how bad and how long a Soviet winter is. As you know from Chapter 20, the Russian army destroyed anything that might help Napoleon in his 1812 retreat. Now, 130 years later, the Soviets destroyed anything that might help Hitler. The Soviets burned crops and blew up houses, dams, and bridges. By February 2, 1943, they had defeated Hitler.

Where Else Did the Axis Fight?

In 1940 and 1941, the Axis invaded Greece and Yugoslavia. Then they attacked British possessions in North Africa. Next, they threatened the Suez Canal, which was the British lifeline to India. But in May 1943, the Axis forces in North Africa surrendered. Historians consider the Battle of El Alamein in Egypt another important turning point in the war. As Churchill said: "Up to Alamein we survived; after Alamein we conquered."

Communication in History

Breaking the Enemy's Code

Even in peacetime, governments send messages in code. In wartime, breaking codes can help win the war. During World War II, the Allies broke several top-secret German and Japanese codes. Much of the information about these codes is still secret, however.

In 1939, Polish spies got a German coding machine. It was called "Enigma." British mathematicians and code-breakers worked for months to solve Enigma's system. When they did, it was called the "Ultra secret." Ultra let the British decode messages between Hitler and his generals. Sometimes the British knew battle plans before the German generals did.

By August 1939, American code-breakers had cracked Japan's diplomatic code. The Japanese used it in messages between Tokyo and its embassies. The code-breakers named it "Magic." They then faced two problems until war broke out in 1941. First, they were a small team, but they received a huge volume of messages. Second, the decoded messages were in Japanese. Few Americans could read it.

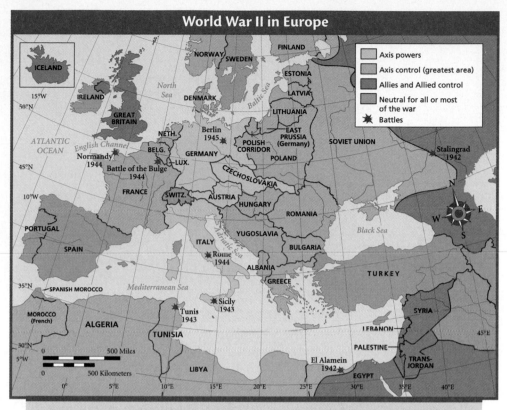

World War II in Europe

Legend:
- Axis powers
- Axis control (greatest area)
- Allies and Allied control
- Neutral for all or most of the war
- ✴ Battles

MAP STUDY This map shows lands under control of the Axis and the Allies during World War II. It also shows several key battles. What countries did the Axis powers control? What countries did the Allies control? Name three important World War II battles.

Why Did Japan Attack Pearl Harbor?

Between 1939 and 1941, Japan tried to gain more power. It depended on the United States for gasoline and old iron to help it wage war and gain power. Then the United States stopped selling the Japanese these materials. Japan prepared for war with the United States. Japanese leaders decided to cripple the U.S. Pacific Fleet, which was stationed in Pearl Harbor, Hawaii.

On Sunday, December 7, 1941, Japanese planes attacked Pearl Harbor. In this surprise raid, the Japanese killed over 2,500 Americans; sank or badly damaged 18 American ships; and destroyed 188 American planes. The next day, the United States declared war on Japan.

This photo shows the destruction caused by Japanese planes at Pearl Harbor. The attack forced the United States into the war.

But within months, Japan conquered northern and central China, the Philippines, and most of Southeast Asia, including the Dutch East Indies and French Indochina.

SECTION 3 REVIEW On a separate sheet of paper, write the word from the Word Bank that completes each sentence.

WORD BANK
Blitzkrieg
Britain
El Alamein
Pearl Harbor
Stalingrad

1) _____ war was different from fighting during World War I because it was a quick attack.

2) During the Battle of _____, Germany fought an air and bombing war and lost.

3) During the Battle of _____, Germany fought a bitter winter and lost.

4) The Allies won a major victory at _____ in Egypt.

5) On December 7, 1941, the Japanese attacked _____, killed many Americans, and destroyed many ships and planes.

What do you think ?

Americans were faced with a difficult problem when the Japanese bombed Pearl Harbor. What would have been your reaction to the problem?

Defensive
Protecting oneself rather than attacking others

◆**Guerilla warfare**
A type of fighting that involves small attacks against an enemy or the things it needs and uses

◆**Occupied country**
A country that the Axis powers took over and stayed in

From September 1939 to the summer of 1942, the Axis Powers had things pretty much their own way. Then the tide turned; the Allies began to win in the Pacific and in Europe.

In June 1942, the Allies won a great naval victory at Midway Island. Historians call this battle a turning point in the Pacific. The Allies forced Japan to retreat and go on the **defensive.** (To be on the defensive is to defend oneself rather than to attack others.) When the Allies captured Guadalcanal in 1943, Japan went into full retreat.

In 1943, the Soviets defeated Hitler at Stalingrad. At about the same time, Allied troops swept enemy troops out of North Africa.

What Did Civilians Do in the War?

During the war, Germany occupied, or took over, many European countries. In these **occupied countries,** even in Germany itself, civilians secretly fought against the Nazis. People with great courage secretly organized and fought for their freedom. They were members of "The Resistance." That is, they resisted, or opposed, the Germans occupying their country. They used **guerilla warfare** to get at the enemy. In this kind of fighting, Resistance fighters blew up

TOKYO ROSE: 1916–

"Tokyo Rose" was actually many women. Americans in the Pacific gave that name to several female Japanese radio announcers. They played popular American music mixed with messages that tried to affect homesick soldiers. Later, reporters identified Iva Toguri d'Aquino as the "real Tokyo Rose." Toguri was Japanese-American. She was visiting Japan when the war broke out. Unable to get home, she took a job at the Japan Broadcasting Corporation. After the war, the press played up her guilt. In 1948, she was tried for treason in San Francisco, but many felt her trial was unfair. She spent six years in jail.

bridges, railroads, and factories. Hitler had to send thousands of troops into these occupied countries to guard important transportation and supply centers.

How Long Did the Allies Fight in Italy?

On July 10, 1943, the Allies invaded Italy and opened up a new front. They quickly overran the island of Sicily. This forced Mussolini to resign. A new government was formed.

This new government signed an armistice with the Allies. But thousands of German troops remained in Italy. It was not until June 4, 1944, that Allied troops freed Rome from German control. However, parts of Italy stayed under German control until the spring of 1945.

What Was D-Day?

In the early morning hours of June 6, 1944, a large Allied army invaded France. Historians call this **D-Day.** By the end of August, Paris was free for the first time since 1940. The Allies had driven out the Germans who occupied Paris. Now they prepared to attack Germany.

D-Day brought an Allied attack from the west. At the same time, Soviet forces attacked Germany from the east. During 1944, the Soviets successfully pushed the Germans back. By

Aircraft carriers such as these were used during the war in the Pacific.

General Dwight D. Eisenhower was the Allied commander in Europe.
He became President of the United States in 1953.

◆Kamikaze
A Japanese pilot who crashed his plane into an enemy ship and destroyed it and himself

◆V-E Day
The day the allies completed their victory in Europe: May 8, 1945; stands for "Victory in Europe Day"

October 1944, almost all of eastern and central Europe was under Soviet control.

What Was the Allied Battle Plan in the Pacific?

In the Pacific, the Allies used a plan called "island hopping." That is, they fought their way north to Japan by leapfrogging from one island to another. They attacked some Japanese-controlled islands but ignored, or leapfrogged, others. The Allies then cut off supplies to the islands they ignored.

Things were going badly for Japan. It called on its young pilots to die for their country with honor. These pilots were called **kamikazes.** They crashed their planes, loaded with bombs, into Allied ships.

What Ended World War II in Europe?

In March 1945, the Allies crossed the Rhine River on Germany's western border. Soviet forces marched toward Berlin from the east. In April, the Allied forces met at the Elbe River and Russian troops captured Berlin. On April 30, 1945, Hitler killed himself. Seven days later, on May 7, Germany surrendered. Historians call the next day, May 8, **V-E Day**—Victory in Europe Day.

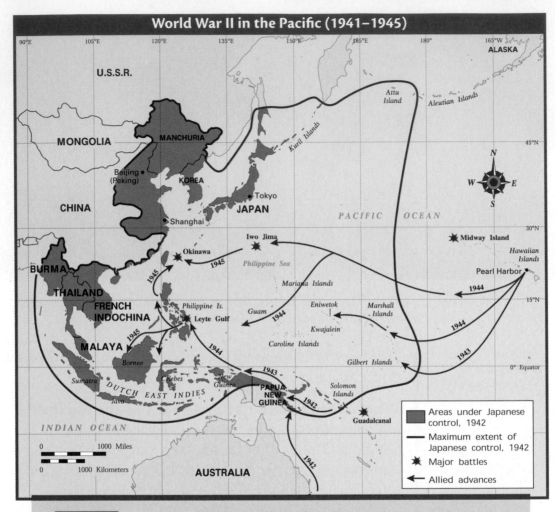

World War II in the Pacific (1941–1945)

U.S.S.R.

MONGOLIA

MANCHURIA

Beijing (Peking)

KOREA

CHINA

Shanghai

Tokyo

JAPAN

PACIFIC OCEAN

ALASKA

Attu Island

Aleutian Islands

Kuril Islands

45°N

30°N

BURMA

THAILAND

FRENCH INDOCHINA

MALAYA

Sumatra

Java

Borneo

Celebes

DUTCH EAST INDIES

INDIAN OCEAN

Okinawa

1945

1945

Iwo Jima

Philippine Sea

Mariana Islands

Philippine Is.

Leyte Gulf

Guam

1944

New Guinea

PAPUA NEW GUINEA

1943

1944

Eniwetok

Kwajalein

Caroline Islands

Marshall Islands

Gilbert Islands

Solomon Islands

Guadalcanal

1943

1942

Midway Island

Hawaiian Islands

Pearl Harbor

1944

1944

1943

15°N

0° Equator

1942

AUSTRALIA

0   1000 Miles

0   1000 Kilometers

| | Areas under Japanese control, 1942 |
| Maximum extent of Japanese control, 1942 |
| Major battles |
| Allied advances |

MAP STUDY

This map shows major battles in the Pacific, Japanese-controlled lands and waters, and Allied advances during World War II. Name three major battles in the Pacific. Name four areas in Asia that Japan controlled in 1942.

◆Atomic bomb
A bomb that uses nuclear energy and has much destructive power

Nuclear
Having to do with atoms or energy from atoms

What Ended World War II in the Pacific?

Now the Allies turned their full attention to Japan. Day and night, American planes bombed Japanese cities. President Harry Truman, who became president after Roosevelt died in 1945, did not want to invade Japan. He knew that many American soldiers would be killed.

On August 6, 1945, Truman approved the use of the world's first **atomic bomb.** This type of bomb was **nuclear.** It used energy from atoms, which gave it much destructive

"A BLINDING FLASH CUT SHARPLY ACROSS THE SKY"

In May 1941, President Roosevelt set up a secret program—the Manhattan Project—to build a special bomb. On August 6, 1945, three American planes flew over Hiroshima, Japan. At exactly 8:15 A.M., a B-29 bomber called the *Enola Gay* dropped this ten-foot atomic bomb.

The bomb weighed about 8,000 pounds. It carried about two pounds of uranium, which gave it enormous energy. In fact, the bomb had the explosive power of 20,000 tons—or 40 million pounds—of TNT.

A Japanese man who was about three miles from the blast center described the scene. He said, "A blinding flash cut sharply across the sky. . . . At the same moment as the flash, the skin over my body felt a burning heat . . . and then a . . . huge 'boom.'" He saw a large mushroom-shaped cloud rise nearly 27,000 feet over Hiroshima.

The temperature at the center of the blast was at least about 10,800° Fahrenheit. Fires broke out everywhere. Then rain began to fall. It was made up of large, black drops. This black rain was radioactive. It caused blood cancer, loss of hair, high fever, and death.

No one knows how many people died in the attack on Hiroshima. Perhaps as many as 140,000 to 150,000 persons died immediately from burns. However, during the months that followed, more than 200,000 people died from the aftermath of the bomb.

In a park in downtown Hiroshima, the Japanese have built a monument to those who died. On it, they wrote "Rest in peace; For we shall not repeat the evil." Let's hope the world never does.

The atomic bomb that was dropped on Hiroshima destroyed almost everything it touched. Hundreds of thousands of Japanese people were killed.

The Nuclear Age

The Nuclear Age began in August 1945. Atomic fireballs burned Hiroshima and Nagasaki to the ground. Many people were grateful that the war had ended, but they were also horrified. They feared this immense new energy source. Soon several other countries developed this bomb. For years, nations competed in a nuclear arms race. Finally, many countries agreed to limit nuclear tests and weapons. Some have refused to follow these rules, however.

Nuclear energy has peaceful uses, too. Some people believe it is a clean, safe source of energy. France, the Soviet Union, and other countries depend on nuclear power plants. But many people in the United States doubt its safety. Nuclear medicine is another peaceful use. Tiny amounts of radioactive materials find and treat disease.

◆V-J Day
The day the Allies completed their victory in Japan: September 2, 1945; stands for "Victory in Japan Day"

power. The United States dropped it on the Japanese city of Hiroshima. But Japan did not surrender. Three days later, the United States dropped a second atomic bomb on the city of Nagasaki. On August 14, 1945, Japan agreed to end the war. On September 2, Japan officially surrendered. Historians call this **V-J Day**—Victory in Japan Day. World War II was over.

SECTION 4 REVIEW On a separate sheet of paper, write *True* if the statement is true or *False* if the statement is not true. Make each false statement true by changing the underlined word.

1) Historians consider the Battle of <u>Midway</u> a turning point in the war in the Pacific.

2) Many European <u>civilians</u> fought the war as members of the Resistance.

3) The <u>Axis</u> invaded Italy in 1943.

4) D-Day is the name for the Allied invasion of <u>Japan.</u>

5) President <u>Truman</u> gave the command to drop an atomic bomb on Japan to end the war.

What do you think

Do you think the United States did the right thing by dropping atomic bombs on Japan? Explain your answer.

The Atlantic Charter

In August 1941, President Roosevelt and Prime Minister Churchill met secretly on a ship off Newfoundland's coast. They discussed their goals for a free, democratic postwar world: the Atlantic Charter. This excerpt contains parts of the Atlantic Charter.

First, their countries seek no aggrandizement, territorial or other;

Second, they desire to see no territorial changes that do not accord with the freely expressed wishes of the people concerned;

Third, they respect the right of all peoples to choose the form of government under which they will live; and they wish to see sovereign rights and self-government restored to those who have been forcibly deprived of them;

Fourth, they will endeavor, with due respect for their existing obligations, to further the enjoyment by all States, great and small, victor or vanquished, of access, on equal terms, to the trade and to the raw materials of the world which are needed for their economic prosperity;

Fifth, they desire to bring about the fullest collaboration between all nations in the economic field with the object of securing, for all, improved labor standards, economic advancement, and social security;

Sixth, after the final destruction of the Nazi tyranny, they hope to see established a peace which will afford to all nations the means of dwelling within their own boundaries, and which will afford assurance that all men in all the lands may live out their lives in freedom from fear and want;

Seventh, such a peace should enable all men to traverse the high seas and oceans without hindrance;

Franklin Roosevelt (left) and Winston Churchill (right).

Eighth, they believe that all of the nations of the world, for realistic as well as spiritual reasons, must come to the abandonment of the use of force. Since no future peace can be maintained if land, sea, or air armaments continue to be employed by nations which threaten, or may threaten, aggression outside of their frontiers, they believe, pending the establishment of a wider and permanent system of general security, that the disarmament of such nations is essential. They will likewise aid and encourage all other practicable measures which will lighten for peace-loving peoples the crushing burden of armaments.

Source Reading Wrap-Up

1) Imperialism was a cause of World War II. Summarize the items of the Charter that relate to imperialism.

2) Britain and the United States wanted to encourage democracy. Briefly state what the Charter says about these goals.

3) What does the Charter say about world economies?

4) Which World War II Axis Power is named?

5) Militarism was another cause of World War II. How does the Charter propose to lessen militarism?

Operation Overlord—The Story of D-Day

The largest invasion in history began on June 6, 1944. History remembers it as "D-Day." General Dwight D. Eisenhower was the supreme Allied commander in Europe. He gave the signal to begin Operation Overlord, the long-awaited invasion of France. It involved more than 170,000 soldiers, thousands of planes and ships, and tons of equipment. The target was the Normandy coast of France.

The weather was terrible. A bad storm raged at sea. Rain was falling. Eisenhower had already postponed the invasion by one day. He could not wait any longer. Despite the weather, he grinned and said "OK, we'll go."

Bad luck and mistakes marked the first hours of D-Day. The first Allied soldiers in Normandy were the "pathfinders." They parachuted into France. Their job was to mark landing zones for paratroopers. They would place marker lights and radar beacons. More paratroopers would follow them.

But the pathfinders' planes met heavy firing from the ground below. Only about a third landed near their targets. Few markers were in place when the first paratroopers jumped. As a result, many paratroopers did not land at their assigned locations. Some of the 13,000 paratroopers landed safely. The Germans shot others before they reached the ground.

D-Day involved a huge Allied fleet. It included over 6,000 battleships, cruisers, destroyers, and landing crafts of all types. On signal, the battleship guns began firing their 14-inch shells. Overhead, planes bombed coastal areas.

Each landing craft carried hundreds of men. They were mostly British, American, Canadian, and free French soldiers. Many became seasick from the choppy water.

American soldiers land on the coast of France during D-Day.

The Americans had two beaches as their goals. They were code-named "Omaha" and "Utah." The Germans had fortified Omaha beach. Concrete and steel posts jutted from the sand. They exploded if a landing craft hit them. Barbed wire was strung between posts. The beach defenses were deadly. Troops remembered the landing as "Bloody Omaha."

The men who landed at Utah beach were luckier. They landed about a mile south of their target. This point was only lightly defended. Tanks, trucks, and supplies went ashore almost unopposed. While 3,000 men died at Omaha beach, fewer than 200 died at Utah beach.

By nightfall, D-Day was over. History's largest invasion was a success. There were 155,000 Allied soldiers in Normandy. They had freed 80 miles of French territory. In the months to come, Allied forces would sweep toward Germany.

Spotlight Story Wrap-Up

1) Who was Dwight D. Eisenhower?
2) What was the role of the "pathfinders"?
3) Which countries had soldiers at the Normandy invasion?
4) How were the battles at Omaha beach and Utah beach different?
5) Explain why most historians consider D-Day a success.

CHAPTER SUMMARY

➡ Italy, Germany, and Japan—the Axis Powers—were strongly nationalistic and imperialistic in the 1930s. They built strong military forces and glorified war.

➡ German anger at the Treaty of Versailles and worldwide economic problems caused World War II. Other causes were the Axis dictatorships and the failure of the League of Nations.

➡ In the 1930s, Italy took over Ethiopia and Albania.

➡ Hitler broke many provisions of the Treaty of Versailles. He enlarged the army and built weapons. He invaded the Rhineland and Austria. In 1938, he demanded the Sudetenland section of Czechoslovakia.

➡ To avoid war, France and Britain followed a policy of appeasement. They did not act against Italy or Germany. The Munich Pact gave Hitler the Sudetenland.

➡ Germany and the Soviet Union signed a treaty not to attack one another. In September 1939, the two countries invaded Poland. Then Britain and France declared war on them.

➡ In 1940, Germany launched the "blitzkrieg" and quickly conquered most of Western Europe. The Maginot Line of defense failed, and France surrendered.

➡ The Axis then waged total war against Great Britain. German planes bombed England in the Battle of Britain. Although a neutral country, the United States aided Britain through the Lend-Lease program.

➡ Germany invaded the Soviet Union for its oil and grain. The Russian winter stopped the Germans, however. After the battle of Stalingrad, the Germans retreated.

➡ The British fought the Axis in North Africa. The British victory at El Alamein, Egypt, was a turning point.

➡ In December 1941, Japanese forces attacked the American fleet at Pearl Harbor, Hawaii. The United States declared war on the Axis Powers. Japan quickly conquered much of China and Southeast Asia. The Allied victory at Midway in 1942 was a turning point in the Pacific war.

➡ After an Allied invasion, a new Italian government signed an armistice. Allied forces invaded France on D-Day in June 1944. The Soviet army attacked German armies from the east. In 1945, the two armies met. Germany surrendered in May.

➡ To avoid invading Japan, President Harry Truman decided to use an atomic bomb. Bombs were dropped on Hiroshima and Nagasaki in August 1945, and Japan surrendered.

Comprehension: Identifying Facts

On a separate sheet of paper, use the words from the Word Bank to complete each sentence.

1) Hitler said that the _____ people were the "master race" and were superior to everyone else.

2) The _____ could not prevent World War II, because it was weak and its most powerful members would not cooperate.

3) In 1931, Japan invaded _____.

4) Hitler ignored the Treaty of Versailles when he sent German troops into the _____.

5) _____ is the name of the policy Britain and France followed when they let Germany take over the Sudetenland.

6) Roosevelt's Lend-Lease program made the _____ an "arsenal for democracy."

7) Civilians in Nazi-controlled countries organized to fight for their freedom and became the _____.

8) _____ is the name of the Allied invasion of France.

9) The United States dropped an atomic bomb on _____ on August 6, 1945.

10) World War II ended when _____ agreed to end the fighting on August 14, 1945.

Comprehension: Multiple Choice

On a separate sheet of paper, write the letter of the answer that correctly completes each sentence.

1) Japan, Germany, and Italy were the three _____ Powers in World War II.

    a. Allied   c. Pacific

    b. Axis   d. Western

2) Great Britain, France, the United States, the Soviet Union, and 48 other nations were the _____ in World War II.

    a. Allies   c. League of Nations

    b. Axis   d. Eastern Powers

3) The _____ was a turning point in World War II.

 a. Battle of Stalingrad   c. Battle of Midway

 b. Battle of El Alamein   d. all of the above

4) Japan tried to cripple the U.S. Navy with a surprise attack on _____.

 a. Midway   c. Pearl Harbor

 b. Guadalcanal   d. San Francisco

5) _____ pilots gave their lives to destroy U.S. ships.

 a. Kamikaze   c. Maginot line

 b. Blitzkrieg   d. Resistance

Comprehension: Understanding Main Ideas

On a separate sheet of paper, write the answers to the following questions using complete sentences, or statements.

1) What are seven causes of World War II?

2) What caused the United States to stop being neutral and to enter World War II?

Critical Thinking: Write Your Opinion

1) Why do you suppose appeasement was popular at first? What happened in World War I that might explain appeasement? Why did it fail?

2) Could Germany have won the war if it had not attacked the Soviet Union? Explain your answer.

3) Why did the Axis have nearly everything its own way in the first half of the war, but not in the second half?

| Test-Taking Tip | When studying for a test, use the titles and subtitles in the chapter to help you recall the information. |

The Aftermath of World War II

1945 to 1955

As you know, the Treaty of Versailles after World War I left many people hating others. Dictators took over. This led to World War II. In this total war, millions of troops and civilians died.

In this chapter, you will see the results of that total world war, which ended in 1945. You will see the horrors of Nazi concentration camps. Then you will witness how the United Nations started and how Europe was rebuilt after the war. You will also see how two superpowers became rivals and began a new kind of war: a cold war.

Goals for Learning

▶ To describe the social, economic, and political results of World War II

▶ To describe the makeup of the United Nations

▶ To explain how the cold war began

▶ To describe America's role in rebuilding war-torn Europe

▶ To describe one time when the cold war threatened to become a real war

▶ To list the causes and results of the Korean War

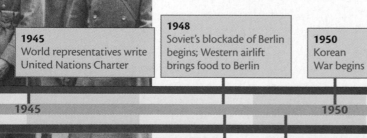

1945
World representatives write United Nations Charter

1948
Soviet's blockade of Berlin begins; Western airlift brings food to Berlin

1950
Korean War begins

1955
Soviet Union and its satellites form Warsaw Pact

1945   1950   1955

1948
U.S. begins Marshall Plan to rebuild Europe

1949
Twelve European countries form NATO

1953
Korean War ends with a truce

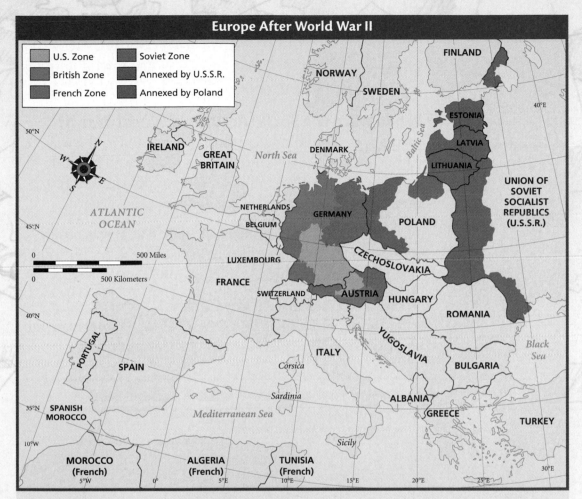

Europe After World War II

Legend:
- U.S. Zone
- British Zone
- French Zone
- Soviet Zone
- Annexed by U.S.S.R.
- Annexed by Poland

Map labels: FINLAND, NORWAY, SWEDEN, IRELAND, GREAT BRITAIN, DENMARK, ESTONIA, LATVIA, LITHUANIA, UNION OF SOVIET SOCIALIST REPUBLICS (U.S.S.R.), NETHERLANDS, BELGIUM, GERMANY, POLAND, LUXEMBOURG, CZECHOSLOVAKIA, FRANCE, SWITZERLAND, AUSTRIA, HUNGARY, ROMANIA, PORTUGAL, SPAIN, ITALY, YUGOSLAVIA, BULGARIA, SPANISH MOROCCO, ALBANIA, GREECE, TURKEY, MOROCCO (French), ALGERIA (French), TUNISIA (French)

Water labels: ATLANTIC OCEAN, North Sea, Baltic Sea, Mediterranean Sea, Black Sea, Corsica, Sardinia, Sicily

Scale: 500 Miles / 500 Kilometers

Geography Skills

After World War II, France, Great Britain, the Soviet Union, and the United States divided up Germany into four zones. Each country controlled one zone.

But the Soviet Union continued to fear the West. It created a buffer zone between itself and Western Europe by setting up Communist governments in Eastern Europe. Then, to protect themselves against the Soviet Union, the countries of Western Europe formed the North Atlantic Treaty Organization (NATO).

This map shows the division of Germany and the countries that the Soviet Union took over in Eastern Europe after World War II.

Study the map carefully and answer the following questions:

1) What part of Germany was under Soviet control?
2) What part of Germany was under U.S., French, and British control?
3) What part of Germany became part of Poland?
4) What three countries along its border did the Soviet Union annex and make communistic?
5) Why might some Eastern European countries fear a reunited Germany?

◆Concentration
camp
*A large prison
death camp*

World War II ended in 1945. However, we still live with its social, economic, and political results.

What Were the Social Results of World War II?

As many as 60 million people may have died in the war. China and the Soviet Union lost as many as 22 million people each. Nearly 8 million Germans died and nearly 2 million Japanese. About 300,000 Americans died.

The number of people killed in World War II was nearly four times the number killed in World War I. In this total war, many civilians died.

What Are Concentration Camps?

After the war, the Allies discovered German **concentration camps.** These were places where the Germans kept

World War II Casualties

Country	Number of Soldiers	War deaths	Wounded
Australia	1,000,000	26,976	180,864
Austria	800,000	280,000	350,117
Belgium	625,000	8,460	55,513
Brazil	40,334	943	4,222
Bulgaria	339,760	6,671	21,878
Canada	1,086,343	42,042	53,145
China	17,250,521	1,324,516	1,762,006
Czechoslovakia	—	6,683	8,017
Denmark	—	4,339	—
Finland	500,000	79,047	50,000
France	—	201,568	400,000
Germany	20,000,000	3,250,000	7,250,000
Greece	—	17,024	47,290
Hungary	—	147,435	89,313
India	2,393,891	32,121	64,354
Italy	3,100,000	149,496	66,716
Japan	9,700,000	1,270,000	140,000
Netherlands	280,000	6,500	2,860
New Zealand	194,000	11,625	17,000
Norway	75,000	2,000	—
Poland	—	664,000	530,000
Romania	650,000	350,000	—
South Africa	410,056	2,473	—
U.S.S.R.	—	6,115,000	14,012,000
United Kingdom	5,896,000	357,116	369,267
United States	16,112,566	291,557	670,846
Yugoslavia	3,741,000	305,000	425,000

everyone they did not like. In these death camps, the Nazis carried out a program of **genocide** against the Jews. That is, Hitler tried to wipe out all the Jews of Europe. His Nazis murdered six million Jews in the death camps. Historians call Hitler's plan to kill all the Jews the **Holocaust.**

The Nazis also killed many Slavic peoples—Poles, Ukrainians, and Russians—in these camps. They killed political prisoners who thought differently from them; Gypsies; and the **mentally ill,** who had a sickness of the mind.

What Were the Economic Results of World War II?

Before the war, Europe had led the world's economy. Large empires had made Britain and France rich and powerful. Now they no longer controlled many of their colonies. Their economies had fallen apart.

Some historians have guessed that the war may have cost four trillion dollars. It wrecked the economy of most countries—except the United States. Most countries had borrowed money to pay for weapons. If they had goods to export after the war, they could pay back this money. But they had nothing to sell because the war had destroyed their factories.

Why Did Refugees Flee Their Countries?

The war also destroyed homes, farms, highways, bridges, and railroads. People had no food. Because of this, millions of **refugees** fled their countries. They went to other countries to find a new and better life.

These refugees fled from cities that lay in ruins. Only three major cities in Germany and England escaped bombing. The war damaged the capitals of Germany, Poland, Austria, the Netherlands, and Hungary.

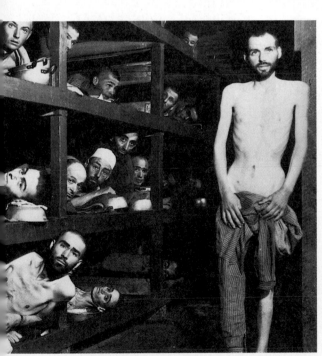

Those in concentration camps suffered through terrible treatment, including cramped living conditions. This photo shows prisoners at Dachau in Germany.

Invisible
Unseen; cannot be seen

◆**Iron Curtain**
The invisible boundary between Western Europe and Eastern Europe after World War II

◆**Satellite**
A nation that another nation tightly controls

◆**Superpower**
A nation that has more power and money than other countries

What Were the Political Results of World War II?

Because of the war, the political power of the world shifted. Two countries—the United States and the Soviet Union—became much more powerful than any others. For this reason, historians called them **superpowers.**

The United States and the Soviet Union had been allies in World War II. But after the war, they grew apart. Before long, an **invisible,** or unseen, boundary separated democratic Western Europe from Communist-controlled Eastern Europe. Winston Churchill called this invisible boundary the **Iron Curtain.**

What Political Changes Took Place in Italy and Germany?

After the war, the Italians voted to set up a republic. But the Allies divided Germany into four zones. Britain, France, the Soviet Union, and the United States each controlled one zone. In 1949, the western zones united under a new democratic government called the Federal Republic of Germany, or West Germany. The Soviets set up a Communist government in their zone called the German Democratic Republic, or East Germany.

What Political Changes Took Place in Eastern Europe?

The Communists took control of Eastern Europe. Poland, Yugoslavia, Czechoslovakia, Romania, Bulgaria, Albania, and Hungary set up Communist governments. They became **satellites** of the Soviet Union. A satellite nation is tightly controlled by another nation.

What Political Changes Took Place in Japan?

After the war ended, the United States placed Japan under the control of General Douglas MacArthur. (He had been a leader in the war in the Pacific.) He introduced the Japanese to democracy. They wrote a new constitution that protected individual rights. They gave up militarism. The Allies said that the Japanese could have only a small military force for self-defense. The emperor remained as head of state, but the people no longer viewed him as a god.

Rosie the Riveter

"Rosie the Riveter" was an American heroine of a World War II song. When Rosie's boyfriend was drafted, she went to work in a defense plant. Rosie became the symbol for female war workers. They made bombs and tanks. They welded battleships. Until then, most women had worked in traditional fields, such as teaching or nursing. The war opened up new kinds of work to women.

When the war ended, returning soldiers wanted their jobs back. Society and the media encouraged women to quit their jobs. The 1950s ideal for women centered on home and family.

American women never really left the workforce, however. In 1995, almost 59 percent of adult women had jobs. They were 46 percent of the workforce.

SECTION 1 REVIEW Choose the letter of the answer that correctly completes each sentence. Write your answer on a separate sheet of paper.

1) World War II killed _____ million people in China.
   a. 10   c. 20
   b. 12   d. 22

2) The Nazis killed _____ million Jews in concentration camps.
   a. 2   c. 6
   b. 4   d. 8

3) The Nazis also killed _____ in concentration camps.
   a. Americans   c. Chinese
   b. Japanese   d. Slavic people

4) Bombs and troops destroyed _____ and left Europe in ruins.
   a. factories   c. homes
   b. railroads   d. all of the above

5) After the war, the Allies divided Germany into _____ zones.
   a. 4   c. 2
   b. 3   d. 5

What do you think ?

Why do you think refugees wanted to leave their countries and go to other European countries after the war?

Charter
A constitution; a set of statements that explains a group's purpose

Organization
A group of people joined together for a common purpose

Permanent
Lasting

Security
Safety

United Nations (UN)
The international organization that works to settle disagreements, improve the way people live, and keep peace around the world

In August 1941, President Roosevelt and Prime Minister Churchill began to work together to establish **security,** or safety, in the world. They wanted all countries to unite to protect everyone from war.

In April 1945, representatives of many nations met in San Francisco, California. They met to establish an **organization,** or group, to replace the League of Nations. It was called the **United Nations (UN).** Its representatives wrote a **charter,** or constitution, for this new organization. It has six major parts. Each has a special job.

Who Belongs to the General Assembly?

The first branch of the UN is the General Assembly. All member nations belong to it. Each nation—no matter how large or how small—has only one vote. The assembly debates world problems. If it votes for UN action on an issue, the matter goes to the Security Council.

What Does the Security Council Do?

The Security Council listens to arguments between nations and tries to settle them peacefully. It has 15 members. Britain, China, France, the United States, and the Soviet Union became the **permanent** members of the council. (That is, they were always to be members.) Ten other nations are elected to it. They serve two-year terms. The five permanent members of the council have veto power. Any one of them can stop the council from taking any action. The council members have used this veto many times.

The United Nations Charter was signed in 1945.

Writing About History

The founders of the United Nations listed its goals. In your opinion, what should be the goals of such an international organization? List your choices in your notebook. Include supporting reasons.

Agency
A group that provides a service

◆**Trust territory**
A territory that the Allies took from the countries that lost World War I and World War II

Who Heads the Secretariat?

The Secretariat handles the day-to-day work of the UN. The Secretary-General of the UN heads the Secretariat. A large group of people from many countries help. They work in the UN building in New York.

What Does the International Court of Justice Do?

The International Court of Justice handles questions of law that arise between member nations. It listens to arguments between countries and decides what can be done. However, it has no power to carry out the actions of its rulings.

What Does the Economic and Social Council Do?

The Economic and Social Council tries to stop wars by improving the way people live. It does this through its **agencies,** or groups that provide special services.

• The United Nations Educational, Scientific, and Cultural Organization (UNESCO) gives advice to needy countries in Africa, Asia, and Latin America.

• The United Nations International Children's Emergency Fund (UNICEF) cares for sick, starving, and homeless children in dozens of countries.

• The Food and Agricultural Organization (FAO) helps farmers grow more food.

• The World Health Organization (WHO) improves people's health.

• The International Labor Organization (ILO) improves working conditions and living standards around the world.

What Does the Trusteeship Council Do?

This council takes care of all **trust territories.** The Allies took these territories from the countries that lost World War I and World War II. The council prepares these territories to rule themselves. Most of these territories are now independent countries.

GOLDA MEIR: 1898–1978

Golda Meir was born in Russia. Her family moved to Milwaukee in 1906. She later taught school there and worked with the Labor Zionist Party.

In 1921, Golda and her husband moved to Palestine. There she worked for the Zionist movement. After Israel became a nation, Meir was elected to the Knesset, the Israeli parliament. She was labor minister and then foreign minister. Later, she helped organize the Labor Party. As prime minister (1969–1974), Meir tried to bring peace to the Middle East.

How Successful Has the UN Been?

The UN can be proud of what it has done since 1945. Over 150 nations are now members. It provides a place where nations can present their views to the world. It has helped colonial people gain independence. It has helped keep peace in many places in the world. It has wiped out smallpox and protected millions of people from other diseases.

However, the UN has failed to stop some wars. (This was especially true for the conflict between Arab countries and Israel, the new nation formed after World War II. You'll read about this nation in Chapter 28.) It has not been able to get nations to give up their weapons. It still does not have its own military force. Instead, it depends on its members to volunteer soldiers. Some nations refuse to obey UN orders. Some nations refuse to pay their share of the UN's costs.

SECTION 2 REVIEW On a separate sheet of paper, write answers to these questions.

What do you think ?

Why did the representatives who wrote the UN charter give five powerful nations on the Security Council veto power?

1) What are the six major branches of the United Nations?

2) Which five countries became the permanent members of the Security Council?

3) What are three agencies of the Economic and Social Council?

4) Why is the Trusteeship Council almost out of business?

5) What is one success and one failure of the UN?

Buffer zone
A neutral area that separates two warring countries

Cold war
The war of propaganda between the United States and the Soviet Union after World War II

Propaganda
One-sided information meant to change people's thinking

Truman Doctrine
President Truman's plan to stop the spread of communism

Both the United States and the Soviet Union came out of World War II as strong economic and military powers. The United States lost 300,000 men and women in battle, but the Axis bombed no American cities. However, 22 million Soviets lost their lives. The Soviet Union fought much of the war on its own soil.

Why Did the Soviet Union Expand Into Eastern Europe?

In both world wars, the enemy had attacked the Soviet Union from the west. Soviet leaders wanted a **buffer zone,** or neutral area, between them and Western Europe. To get this zone, Stalin set up Communist governments in most Eastern European states. He wanted this buffer zone to keep Western Europe from invading the Soviet Union.

What Was the Cold War?

Soon, the United States and the Soviet Union began a **cold war.** That is, they became rivals who used words and ideas as weapons instead of bullets. They fought the cold war with **propaganda,** or one-sided information. They used this propaganda to change people's way of thinking.

Which Countries Did the Truman Doctrine Help?

At the end of the war, the Communists threatened to take control of Greece and Turkey. But American President Harry Truman wanted to prevent the spread of communism.

In 1947, Truman announced the **Truman Doctrine.** This plan gave economic and military help to nations threatened by an outside power. The Truman Doctrine helped Greece and Turkey defeat the Communists. But it also showed the world that the United States would do everything short of war to contain communism.

Whom Did the Marshall Plan Help?

Both communism and economic collapse threatened Europe. In 1948, the U.S. Congress approved the

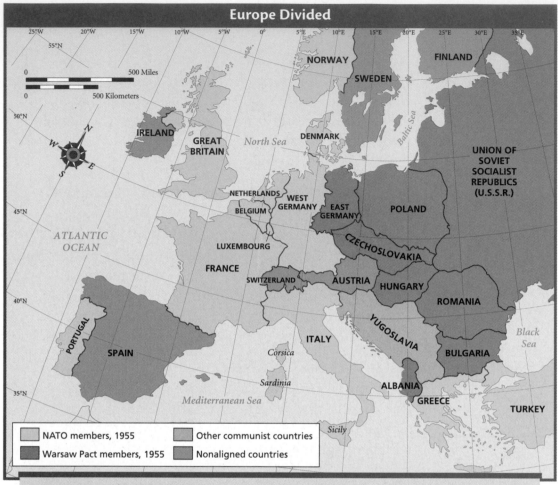

Europe Divided

NORWAY
SWEDEN
FINLAND
IRELAND
GREAT BRITAIN
North Sea
DENMARK
Baltic Sea
UNION OF SOVIET SOCIALIST REPUBLICS (U.S.S.R.)
NETHERLANDS
WEST GERMANY
EAST GERMANY
POLAND
BELGIUM
ATLANTIC OCEAN
LUXEMBOURG
CZECHOSLOVAKIA
FRANCE
SWITZERLAND
AUSTRIA
HUNGARY
ROMANIA
PORTUGAL
SPAIN
Corsica
ITALY
YUGOSLAVIA
BULGARIA
Black Sea
Sardinia
Mediterranean Sea
ALBANIA
GREECE
TURKEY
Sicily

500 Miles
500 Kilometers

- NATO members, 1955
- Warsaw Pact members, 1955
- Other communist countries
- Nonaligned countries

MAP STUDY This map shows how Europe was divided by two alliances—NATO and the Warsaw Pact. Which alliance did most countries of Western Europe join? Which country in the Warsaw Pact was probably the most powerful? Which Communist country was not a member of either alliance?

♦**Marshall Plan**
The American plan to rebuild Europe after World War II

Marshall Plan, or European Recovery Program. It helped European nations get back on their feet after the war. The United States gave $12 billion in food, fuel, machines, and other goods to 16 different countries. (The Soviet Union and its satellites refused help.)

The Marshall Plan was a big success. By 1950, Britain, France, and West Germany were producing 25 percent more goods than they had before the war. Instead of being rivals, some European countries began to work together for economic growth.

The Marshall Plan helped European nations rebuild after World War II.

What Two Military Alliances Brought Countries Together?

In 1948, the Communists took complete control of Czechoslovakia. They forced Finland to sign a treaty with them and tried to take over Berlin. The West was afraid. It thought that the cold war might suddenly become hot.

Several nations formed the **North Atlantic Treaty Organization (NATO).** They said that an attack on any one of them would be an attack on all of them. Today, NATO has 19 members. It has taken part in many missions to keep world peace.

♦North Atlantic Treaty Organization (NATO)
A group of 19 nations committed to protecting one another from attack and keeping world peace

♦Warsaw Pact
A treaty that set up a military alliance between the Soviet Union and its satellite nations

In 1955, the Soviet Union established the **Warsaw Pact.** This treaty set up a military alliance between the Soviet Union and its satellites in Eastern Europe.

SECTION 3 REVIEW On a separate sheet of paper, write *True* if the statement is true or *False* if the statement is not true. Make each false statement true by changing the underlined word.

1) The <u>United States</u> lost more than 22 million people in World War II and fought much of the war on its own soil.

2) President <u>Truman</u> wanted to contain communism.

3) The cold war was a war of <u>propaganda.</u>

4) The <u>Marshall Plan</u> helped rebuild Europe after World War II.

5) NATO was an alliance among 19 countries of <u>Eastern</u> Europe.

What do you think

In Chapter 23, you learned that alliances led to World War I. Why do you think nations once again formed alliances?

◆Berlin Airlift
The Western method of getting around the 1948 Soviet blockade by flying supplies into Berlin

In 1948, the cold war of propaganda threatened to become a real war in Berlin. (Berlin had been the capital of Nazi Germany.) After World War II, Berlin was located completely within the Soviet zone. Britain, France, the United States, and the Soviet Union agreed that each would control a part of Berlin. The Soviet Union said that the Western powers could enter Berlin through the zones they controlled.

Why Did the Soviets Set Up a Blockade?

In June 1948, the Soviets tried to take over all of Berlin by starving the people living there. To do this, they used a blockade. That is, they "blocked" all roads, waterways, and railroads into the city. The people of Berlin had no food, fuel, or other necessary supplies. The Soviets thought that the United States, France, and Britain would abandon Berlin. Then the Soviets would control all of it.

How Did the West Get Around the Blockade?

President Truman said,"The United States is going to stay. Period." Almost immediately the West began to use planes to fly in supplies. For more than a year, American and British planes brought tons of food and fuel to the people of Berlin. Planes took off and landed around the clock at the rate of one every three minutes. During the blockade, the pilots flew over 277,000 flights. They brought the people of Berlin more than two million tons of supplies.

Why Did the Soviets Stop the Blockade?

Historians call this the **Berlin Airlift** because the West "lifted" supplies into the air and took them to Berlin. With this airlift, the Western powers showed one big thing—they would not let the Communists control any more European land. The West was going to contain communism.

All this made the Soviets mad, but they did not shoot down any Western planes. They did not want to start a war. In May 1949, the Soviets stopped blockading Berlin.

The Berlin Airlift brought tons of food and supplies to the people of Berlin in 1948.

What Started the Korean War?

Korea lies between China and Japan. In 1919, Japan made Korea part of its empire. When World War II ended, Soviet forces took over the northern half of Korea. American forces occupied the south. North Korea became the People's Democratic Republic. South Korea became the Republic of Korea. The 38th parallel of latitude became the border that divided the two republics. On June 25, 1950, Communist troops crossed this border into South Korea.

How Did the UN Help South Korea?

South Korea asked the United Nations to stop the North Koreans. The UN Security Council voted to send aid to South Korea. (The Soviet Union was not attending the UN meetings at that time. If it had been, the Soviets probably would have vetoed any UN action.)

The UN asked its members to organize an army to help South Korea. Seventeen nations

About 34,000 American soldiers were killed in battle during the Korean War, which was fought from 1950–1953.

◆Truce
An agreement to stop a war for a time

volunteered soldiers to fight under the UN flag. American General Douglas MacArthur led the army.

How Did the UN Troops Push Back the Communists?

By September 1950, the Communists controlled most of Korea. However, the UN forces got behind the North Korean lines. Then they made a surprise attack that cut the Communist forces in two and forced them to retreat.

By November, UN forces had pushed the Communists back to the Yalu River, the border between China and North Korea. It looked as if the war was over. The UN hoped that Korea would become one country again.

What Happened When China Entered the War?

As the UN army neared the Yalu River, Communist China suddenly joined the war on the side of North Korea. Over 300,000 Chinese soldiers pushed the UN troops south.

By January 1951, all UN forces had retreated from North Korea. For the next six months, the two sides fought. Finally, the front settled in the area just north of the 38th parallel.

Why Did President Truman Fire General MacArthur?

To end the war, General MacArthur wanted to drop the atomic bomb on China. Chinese cities supplied war materials to the North Korean and Chinese soldiers. But President Truman said that the United States wanted only one thing—to protect the independence of South Korea. It did not want to win an all-out victory against the Communists. Truman fired MacArthur because of their differences.

General Douglas MacArthur (right) led the UN forces during the Korean War.

What Ended the Korean War?

In July 1951, truce talks began. A **truce** is an agreement to stop a war for a time. The talks dragged on for two years. Finally, the two

Map Study

This map shows the Korean War. What parallel of latitude divided North and South Korea? Near what small city did Communist forces push UN troops in September 1950? What river did the Chinese cross when they entered the war?

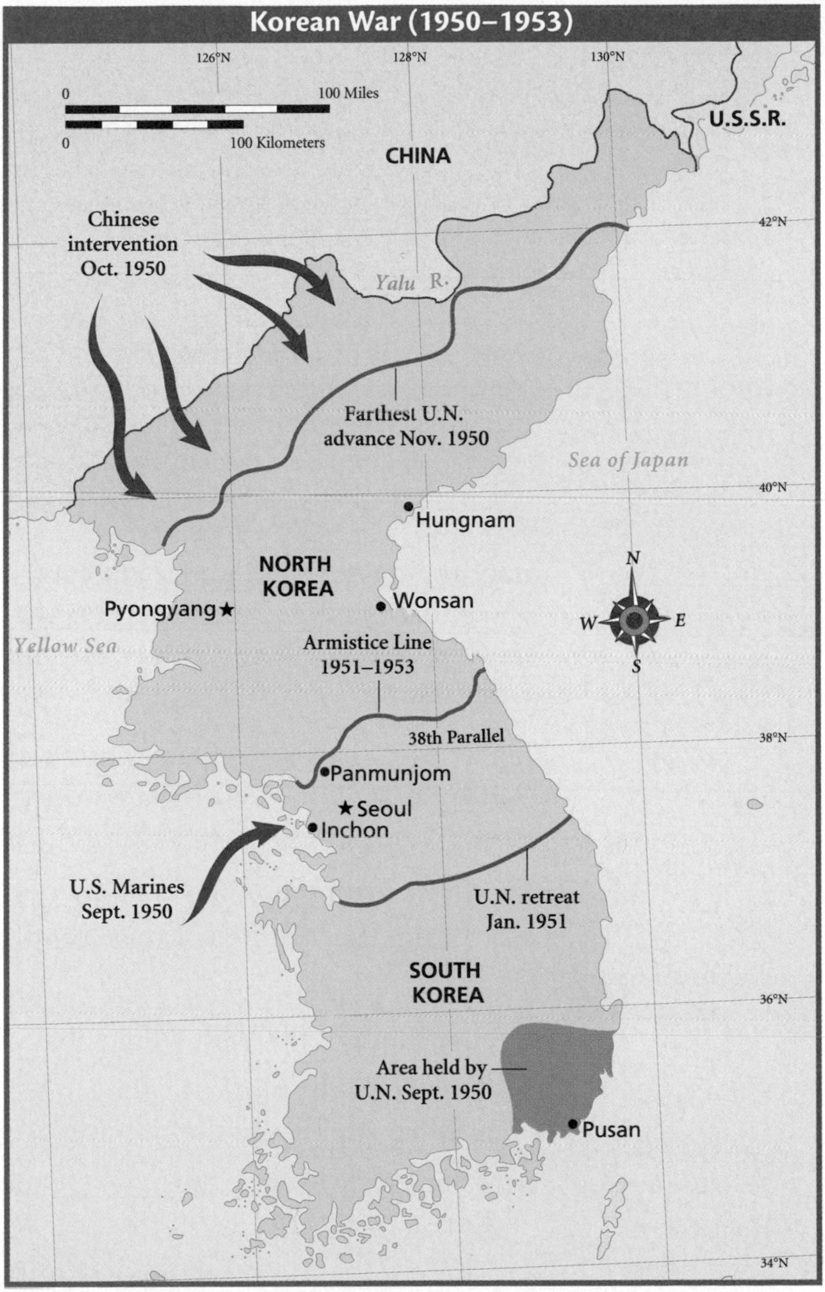
Korean War (1950–1953)
126°N
128°N
130°N
0
100 Miles
0
100 Kilometers
CHINA
U.S.S.R.
42°N
40°N
38°N
36°N
34°N
Chinese intervention Oct. 1950
Yalu R.
Farthest U.N. advance Nov. 1950
Sea of Japan
Hungnam
NORTH KOREA
Wonsan
Pyongyang
Yellow Sea
Armistice Line 1951–1953
38th Parallel
Panmunjom
Seoul
Inchon
U.S. Marines Sept. 1950
U.N. retreat Jan. 1951
SOUTH KOREA
Area held by U.N. Sept. 1950
Pusan
N
S
E
W

sides signed an armistice. It left Korea divided. The border between the two Koreas was almost what it had been before the war.

Why Was the Korean War Important?

The Korean War was important for three reasons. First, it showed that the UN could stop an attack on a member

The Jet Age

New technology often comes out of war. In 1939, Germany made the first successful flight of a plane powered by jet engines. By 1944, German Messerschmitt fighters were flying combat missions. They flew at nearly 550 miles an hour. The first American jet was built in 1942. After the war, the United States and the Soviet Union worked to build faster warplanes. By the Korean War in the 1950s, they had succeeded. The Americans had the F-86 Sabre jet. The Soviets had the MiG-15.

Technology
History in Your Life

Jet planes soon changed passenger travel. Trips were faster, and there were fewer stops to refuel. Britain built the first large passenger jet in 1952. American companies soon followed. In 1958, a Boeing 707 carried passengers across the Atlantic. The first "jumbo jet" was the Boeing 747 in 1970. It could carry more than 400 people. In 1976, the Concorde took passenger jets past the speed of sound.

nation. Second, it showed that China could hold its own in a war that did not use atomic weapons. Third, it showed that the cold war between the two superpowers would continue.

Since 1953, the United States has continued to support South Korea. It has become an industrial powerhouse in Asia. North Korea remains Communist.

SECTION 4 REVIEW On a separate sheet of paper, write the word from the Word Bank that completes each sentence.

WORD BANK
Berlin
Great Britain
Soviet Union
United Nations
United States

1) In June 1948, the Soviets blockaded _____ because they thought the West would abandon it.

2) To get past the blockade, the United States and _____ airlifted supplies to the starving people.

3) After World War II, the _____ took control of North Korea.

4) The _____ occupied South Korea.

5) When North Korean troops invaded their country, the South Koreans asked the _____ for help.

What do you think

Since neither the Communists nor the UN troops won the Korean War, was it worth fighting?

The United Nations Charter

One of the most important results of World War II was the creation of the United Nations (UN). It replaced the League of Nations. The League had been started after World War I. The United States, however, had refused to join the League, which weakened it. The League could not keep the peace. Allied leaders wanted to change this situation.

During World War II, Allied leaders had met often to plan strategy. They made plans for future cooperation. In January 1942, 26 Allied nations held a meeting. They first used the name "United Nations" to describe their group. In April 1945, before the war ended, representatives of about 50 nations met in San Francisco. They drew up a charter, or constitution, for the new organization. The United States was a leading supporter of the group. The United States quickly voted to approve the UN Charter. It begins:

We the people of the United Nations are determined to save future generations from the scourge of war, which twice in our lifetime has brought untold sorrow to mankind. We are determined to reaffirm our faith in fundamental human rights, in the dignity and worth of the human person, and in the equal rights of men and women and of nations large and small. We are determined to establish conditions under which justice and respect for the duties arising from treaties and other parts of international law can be maintained. We are determined to promote social progress and better standards of life in greater freedom. To achieve these goals, we will practice tolerance and will live together in peace with one another as good neighbors. We are also determined to unite our strength to maintain

This shows the first session of the UN Security Council in 1946.

international peace and security, and to insure that armed force shall not be used except in the interests of all. And, finally, we are determined to use international means to promote the economic and social advancement of all peoples. To accomplish these aims we have resolved to combine our efforts. And so our Governments, through representatives assembled in the city of San Francisco, have agreed to present this Charter of the United Nations. And they do hereby establish an international organization to be known as the United Nations.

Source Reading Wrap-Up

1) What two wars is the Charter referring to in its opening sentence?
2) What rights does the Charter reaffirm?
3) What are two other goals of the United Nations according to the Charter?
4) How will member nations achieve those goals?
5) Does the Charter expect possible threats to international peace in the future? If yes, how will the United Nations deal with them?

The Dachau Concentration Camp

Dachau was the first Nazi concentration camp in Germany. It became a model for camps built later. Dachau opened in March 1933. It was on the grounds of a former ammunition factory near Munich. Prisoners included political opponents, Jews, and people who were not considered normal. Some were religious leaders who spoke out against the Nazis.

It is hard to know how many people were held at Dachau. The camp originally held 5,000 persons. It was expanded in 1937. Between 1938 and 1945, the camp registered more than 200,000 people. Thousands more passed through on their way to other camps. Others died before their names were recorded.

The prisoners lived in 32 "blocks," or barracks. Each block was built for 180 persons. Later, more than 800 people lived in that same space. Each morning and evening the prisoners had to answer a roll call. To prevent escapes, the camp was fenced with electric barbed wire and a wall. On one side was a water-filled ditch. Watch towers stood at key points. Guards with machine guns kept watch. If one prisoner escaped, all the others were punished.

The camp crematorium and gas chamber stood outside the walls. A crematorium is a building in which bodies of the dead are burned. New arrivals at Dachau were told to undress and shower. But the "showers" contained poison gas, not water. Thousands of people were gassed and then burned. The smell of burning bodies often filled the air. Perhaps about 70,000 people died at Dachau.

Over the camp gate hung the sign reading "Arbeit Macht Frei." That means, "Work makes

A prisoner of Dachau shows an American soldier the crematorium.

you free." This was a lie. Prisoners worked in the gravel pits. They broke up large rocks and moved them. They worked from sunrise to sunset. If workers stopped, Nazi guards kicked or hit them with rifles.

Prisoners never had enough food. On April 29, 1945, American troops freed Dachau. The camp had nearly 30,000 prisoners. Many looked like walking skeletons. Some were so ill and weak that they soon died. The soldiers were horrified by what they found. General Dwight D. Eisenhower wrote, ". . . I have never at any other time experienced an equal sense of shock."

Some years later, the acting mayor of Berlin said, "Every German . . . must feel responsible . . . for the sins committed . . . in the name of Germany." Today there are chapels and a museum at Dachau.

Spotlight Story Wrap-Up

1) What and where was Dachau?
2) Who were sent to Dachau?
3) How did the Nazis try to prevent prisoners from escaping?
4) What happened in the "showers" and crematorium?
5) What did American soldiers find when they freed Dachau?

World War II killed about 60 million people, both soldiers and civilians. Millions of Jews and others were killed in Nazi concentration camps. This genocide is called the Holocaust.

World War II hurt the economies of most nations except the United States. Major nations lost their colonial empires. Refugees moved to other countries.

The United States and the Soviet Union became superpowers. The Soviet Union had fought on its own land, suffering heavy losses. As a protective "buffer zone," Stalin set up Communist governments in neighboring Eastern Europe countries.

An invisible "Iron Curtain" separated Soviet-dominated Eastern Europe from democratic Western Europe. Germany was divided into democratic West Germany and Communist East Germany.

During American occupation, Japan built a democratic government. Its only army is for self-defense.

The United Nations (UN) was formed in 1945 to prevent future wars. All member nations belong to the General Assembly, which debates problems. Representatives from 15 nations make up the Security Council, which decides UN actions. Five permanent members (Britain, France, China, the United States, the Soviet Union) have veto power.

The Secretary-General heads the Secretariat, which handles day-to-day business. The International Court of Justice settles questions of international law. Agencies of the Economic and Social Council, such as UNICEF, work to improve people's lives. The UN Trusteeship Council oversees territories taken from countries defeated in World Wars I and II. Most territories have become independent.

The United Nations has both succeeded and failed. It provides a meeting place and has helped keep peace. Soldiers from member nations serve as peacekeepers. The UN depends on members for funding.

Rivalry between the United States and the Soviet Union became the Cold War. Under the Truman Doctrine, the United States helped Greece and Turkey resist Communist takeovers. The Marshall Plan helped Western Europe rebuild.

In 1948, the United States and its European allies formed the North Atlantic Treaty Organization (NATO), a military alliance. In 1955, the Soviet Union set up the Warsaw Pact with its satellite countries.

There were many conflicts between the superpowers, including the Berlin Airlift in Germany and the Korean War.

Comprehension: Identifying Facts

On a separate sheet of paper, use the words from the Word Bank to complete each sentence.

1) Every member nation in the United Nations is represented in the _____.

2) Britain, China, France, the United, States, and the Soviet Union became the five permanent members of the UN _____.

3) The _____ handles the day-to-day operations of the UN.

4) The _____ helped Europe recover from World War II.

5) _____ is a military alliance that binds together 19 nations of the world.

6) The _____ was a military alliance between the Soviet Union and its satellites in Eastern Europe.

7) The _____ was an attempt to contain communism.

8) In 1948, the Soviets tried to blockade _____.

9) In June 1950, the Communists tried to expand into _____.

10) Communist soldiers from _____ crossed into North Korea to join the fighting there.

WORD BANK
Berlin
China
General Assembly
Marshall Plan
NATO
Security Council
Secretariat
South Korea
Truman Doctrine
Warsaw Pact

Comprehension: Multiple Choice

On a separate sheet of paper, write the letter of the answer that correctly completes each sentence.

1) As many as _____ million people died in World War II.

a. 22   c. 60

b. 47   d. 85

2) The Nazis killed six million Jews in the _____.

a. Holocaust   c. Buffer Zone

b. General Assembly   d. Trust Territory

3) The Soviet Union set up a _____ to protect it from attacks from the West.

    a. concentration camp c. propaganda

    b. buffer zone   d. 38th parallel

4) The United States and the Soviet Union used _____ against one another in their cold war.

    a. genocide   c. propaganda

    b. refugees   d. concentration camps

5) _____ won the Korean War.

    a. China   c. North Korea

    b. The United States d. none of the above

Comprehension: Understanding Main Ideas

On a separate sheet of paper, write the answers to the following questions using complete sentences, or statements.

1) What is one social, one economic, and one political outcome of World War II?

2) What are the six major branches of the United Nations and what do they do?

3) How did the Marshall Plan help Europe?

Critical Thinking: Write Your Opinion

1) The United States and Great Britain used an airlift to help the people in Berlin during the Soviet blockade. If they had not done this, what might have happened?

2) During the Korean War, General MacArthur wanted to drop the atomic bomb on China. President Truman wanted to limit the war. Who was right? Explain your answer.

Test-Taking Tip When taking a test where you must write your answer, read the question twice to make sure you understand what is being asked.

Political cartoons are drawings about political events. Some are intended to make people laugh. They may poke fun at a political figure. However, the main point of a political cartoon is to encourage people to think about current issues. Political cartoons express a viewpoint about a political issue or topic. Cartoonists reveal various opinions in a drawing. They can persuade others to support their opinion through the cartoon.

Cartoons often use symbols, or objects that stand for something else. In the cartoon on this page, the bomb-shaped object stands not just for the atomic bomb but also for the climate of fear around it. Notice that a house and family are perched on the bomb. What do you think they stand for?

Peace Today

Cartoonists use labels or captions to help readers interpret their drawing. This cartoon has three labels. One is "atomic bomb." The others are "world control" and "world destruction." The bomb is balanced on the cliff labeled "world control." It is teetering over a deep canyon called "world destruction." The cartoonist, Ruben Goldberg, has added a caption, too: "Peace Today." The cartoon was published in 1948, only three years after the first atomic bombs were dropped on Japan.

Study the cartoon. Then answer these questions.

1) What do the house and family stand for?
2) Why is the bomb balanced between "world control" and "world destruction"?
3) What does the cartoon show about people's feelings in 1948?
4) What does the caption "Peace Today" add to the cartoon?
5) Find a current political cartoon in your newspaper. Write what you think it means.

➡ Military alliances and nationalism led to World War I (1914–1918). The Allies were France, Russia, Britain, Italy, Japan, and the United States. They defeated the Central Powers (Austria-Hungary, Germany, Bulgaria, and Turkey).

➡ World War I was a total war. Armies used trench warfare and many new weapons.

➡ The Treaty of Versailles blamed Germany for the war and broke up the Austro-Hungarian Empire. It created new democratic nations.

➡ Russia had begun to industrialize in the 1800s, but most people were poor. In 1905, workers rebelled and Nicholas II briefly gave in to some demands. A revolution in 1917 overthrew him.

➡ Lenin's Bolsheviks (later called Communists), took over the Russian government. Russia became the Soviet Union.

➡ Stalin made the Soviet Union a totalitarian state. The government developed heavy industry and collective farms. Stalin had opponents killed or sent to Siberia.

➡ Fascism opposed both democracy and communism. It demanded total obedience to the state. Mussolini gained power in Italy. Adolf Hitler led the Nazis in Germany.

➡ In China, Sun Yat-sen led a nationalist revolution in 1911. Later Chiang Kai-shek led a civil war against Mao Zedong's Chinese Communists. Military leaders took power in Japan in the 1930s.

➡ The Axis Powers (Italy, Germany, and Japan) were nationalistic. They seized territory in the 1930s, but France and Britain did not stop them. In 1939, Germany and the Soviet Union invaded Poland. France and Britain then declared war.

➡ Hitler conquered Western Europe. Japan conquered Southeast Asia and much of China. The United States entered the war in 1941.

➡ The battles of Stalingrad (Russia), El Alamein (North Africa), and Midway (Pacific) were turning points in the war. Allied forces invaded France in June 1944. Germany surrendered in May 1945. The United States used atomic bombs against Japan, which surrendered in August 1945.

➡ The United States and the Soviet Union became superpowers after the war. They formed opposing military alliances. Russian and American rivalry caused conflicts in Berlin and Korea.

➡ The United Nations (UN) was formed in 1945 to avoid future wars.

Comprehension: Identifying Facts

On a separate sheet of paper, use the words from the Word Bank to complete each sentence.

WORD BANK
abdicate
armistice
blitzkrieg
civilians
genocide
kamikaze
satellite
superior
trenches
veterans

1) During World War I, the soldiers in Western Europe lived in _____.

2) Both World War I and World War II were total wars, because the warring sides bombed cities and killed many _____.

3) On November 11, 1918, Germany agreed to an _____, or an end to World War I.

4) Russian rebels made Czar Nicholas II _____, or give up his throne.

5) Some _____ who had fought in World War I became followers of Mussolini in Italy.

6) Hitler told the German people that they were _____, or better than other people.

7) Germany began World War II with a _____, or lightning war.

8) Toward the end of World War II, the Japanese used _____ pilots to destroy Allied ships.

9) In World War II, Germany followed a policy of _____ in an attempt to kill all Jews in Europe.

10) After World War II, the Soviet Union controlled many _____ nations to its west.

Comprehension: Multiple Choice

On a separate sheet of paper, write the letter of the answer that correctly completes each sentence.

1) _____ fought as part of the Central Powers in World War I.

    a. England   c. The United States

    b. France   d. Germany

2) Germany, Italy, and Japan formed the _____ Powers in World War II.

    a. Allied   c. Veteran

    b. Axis   d. Western

3) The _____ were a socialist group in Russia.

    a. Bolsheviks   c. Allies

    b. czars   d. Axis

4) _____ was a leader of the Chinese Communists.

    a. Sun Yat-sen   c. Mao Zedong

    b. Tojo   d. Chiang Kai-shek

5) Many countries came together after World War II and started the _____.

    a. League of Nations   c. Iron Curtain

    b. United Nations   b. Berlin Airlift

Comprehension: Understanding Main Ideas

On a separate sheet of paper, write the answers to the following questions using complete sentences, or statements.

1) What is one cause and one result of World War I?

2) What is one cause and one result of World War II?

3) What is one thing the United Nations has done successfully?

Critical Thinking: Write Your Opinion

1) If you had to fight in a war, which war—World War I, World War II, the Korean War—would you choose to fight in and why?

2) If you could be someone from this unit, who would you be and why?

Test-Taking Tip   When you read over your written answer, imagine that you are someone reading it for the first time. Ask yourself if the ideas and information make sense. Revise and rewrite to make the answer as clear as you can.

Africa ONLINE

ZIMBABWE

Africa | Côte d'Ivoire | Ghana | Kenya | Tanzani

Poetry Reading

NEWS & INFORMATION

BUSINESS & FINANCE

COMPUTING

TRAVEL

SPORTS

EDUCATION

HEALTH

MUSIC

WOMEN

KIDS

OUR SERVICES

CONTACT US

Excerpt from "Song of Ocol"
by Okot p'Bitek
(Heinemann African Writers
Series)

Are you thinki
"It's time to g
on the Interne

Please click below
women's fo

Enter
Chatroc

You woman from Kikuyuland
Let that burden slide,
Fall from your back
You are no mere
Donkey cart;
Cut that *mukwa* cord
Cutting a valley in your head,
Burn the *kyondo* sacks
That bow you down

"I have fought against white domination, and I have fought against black domination. I have cherished the idea of a democratic and free society in which all persons live together in harmony and with equal opportunities. It is an ideal which I hope to live for and to achieve. But if needs be, it is an ideal for which I am prepared to die."

—Nelson Mandela, South African political leader and president; he said this at his trial in 1964 and repeated it on his release from prison in 1990

© 1997 Africa Online Inc.
All rights reserved.

Shut up you
Bush poet from Kiambu

Header Photo Credit:

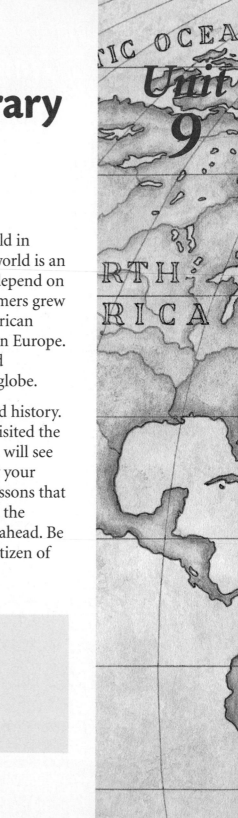

The Contemporary World

1946 to the Present

The contemporary world is the world in which you are living today. This world is an interdependent one. That is, you depend on people around the world. You eat food farmers grew in Asia and Africa. You listen to Latin American music. Your family may drive a car made in Europe. These products, mass communication, and technology link you to people around the globe.

With this unit, you end your study of world history. What an adventure it has been! You have visited the past. Now you will look at the present. You will see new nations develop. You will also see how your global village changes. You will learn the lessons that prepare you to greet the future. Where will the twenty-first century take you? Changes lie ahead. Be ready to meet it and to grow into a good citizen of this global village we call Earth.

New Nations Emerge

28

1946 to 1999

A s you know, before World War II, European nations controlled many colonies in Africa, Asia, and the Middle East. After the war, people in these colonies wanted to be free to make their own economic and political decisions.

In this chapter, you will watch colony after colony in Africa become independent. You will also learn about apartheid. Then you will journey to the Middle East where the Israelis and the Palestinians fight for many years. Next, you will cross overland to India and learn about Gandhi. His leadership brought freedom to India. Then you will travel to China and Vietnam where fierce wars were fought.

Goals for Learning

▶ To explain how the countries of Africa gained their independence

▶ To describe apartheid

▶ To explain the problems that exist between the Israelis and the Palestinians

▶ To explain the two problems that faced Gandhi in unifying India

▶ To describe the two groups that fought for control of China and to detail the outcome of this struggle

▶ To detail the events of the Vietnam War

1948
Gandhi is assassinated

1946
Nationalists and Communists begin to fight a civil war in China

1948
Union of South Africa adopts policy of apartheid

1960
Vietnam War begins

1975
North Vietnamese take control of Saigon

1994
Nelson Mandela is elected president of South Africa

1945   1970   1995

1947
British India is divided into the free nations of India and Pakistan

1948
Israel becomes a nation; fighting begins with Arabs

1964
Nelson Mandela is jailed in South Africa

1976
North and South Vietnam unite

1995
Israeli Prime Minister Yitzhak Rabin is assassinated

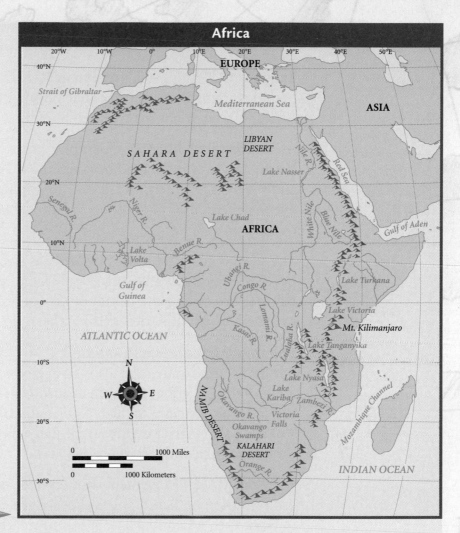

Africa

20°W 10°W 0° 10°E 20°E 30°E 40°E 50°E

EUROPE

Strait of Gibraltar

Mediterranean Sea

ASIA

SAHARA DESERT

LIBYAN DESERT

Nile R.

Red Sea

Lake Nasser

Senegal R.

Niger R.

Lake Chad

AFRICA

White Nile

Blue Nile

Gulf of Aden

Lake Volta

Benue R.

Ubangi R.

Congo R.

Lake Turkana

Gulf of Guinea

Kasai R.

Lomami R.

Lualaba R.

Lake Victoria

Mt. Kilimanjaro

ATLANTIC OCEAN

Lake Tanganyika

Lake Nyasa

Lake Kariba

Zambezi R.

NAMIB DESERT

Okavango R.

Victoria Falls

Okavango Swamps

Mozambique Channel

KALAHARI DESERT

Orange R.

INDIAN OCEAN

40°N 30°N 20°N 10°N 0° 10°S 20°S 30°S

N W E S

0 _____ 1000 Miles

0 _____ 1000 Kilometers

Geography Skills

This is a topographic map of current-day Africa. That is, it shows Africa's mountains, deserts, lakes, swamps, and rivers. Study the map carefully and answer the following questions:

1) Which African coast—the east or the west—has the most mountains?

2) What are the names of three deserts in Africa?

3) What are the names of three lakes in Africa?

4) What are the names of three rivers in Africa?

5) What ocean lies to the east of Africa?

Between 1945 and 1990, more than 50 African countries became independent nations. The number is large because Africa is large. It has many different cultures.

Africa has three different geographic areas. The first is North Africa. It is the land between the Mediterranean Sea and the Sahara Desert. Muslim Arabs and Muslim Berbers live there. But they have different cultural and religious roots.

The second geographic area in Africa is the sub-Sahara. It lies below the Sahara Desert. People from many different cultures live on the land south of the Sahara. The third geographic area in Africa is its southern tip.

What Is African Nationalism?

For many years, native Africans struggled to gain economic and political freedom from their European colonial rulers. We call their struggle **African Nationalism.** Beginning in 1900, the **Pan-African Movement** met several times to plan for the political independence of Africa.

The Pan-African Movement wanted Africans to achieve economic strength and political peace. To do this, they had to work with what they had in common. The movement helped native Africans and their descendants in every part of the world. The group trained people who became political leaders of several new African nations.

What African Nations Were Independent After World War II?

When World War II ended, North Africa had only three independent nations—Egypt, Ethiopia, and Liberia. At the southern tip of the continent lay South Africa, which also had self-rule. Between North Africa and South Africa lay all the other land of this huge continent. Britain, France, Belgium, and Portugal controlled most of this in-between land.

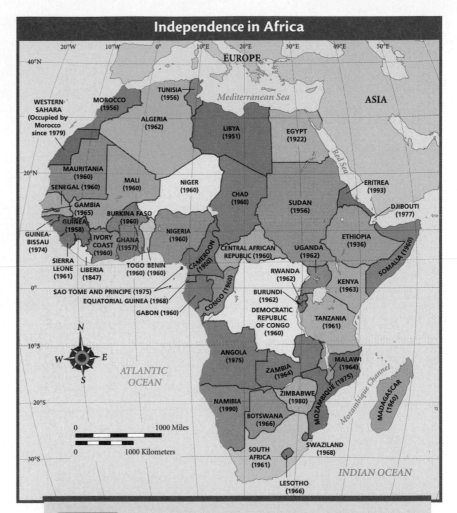

Independence in Africa

EUROPE

ASIA

Mediterranean Sea

Red Sea

TUNISIA (1956)

MOROCCO (1956)

WESTERN SAHARA (Occupied by Morocco since 1979)

ALGERIA (1962)

LIBYA (1951)

EGYPT (1922)

MAURITANIA (1960)

SENEGAL (1960)

MALI (1960)

NIGER (1960)

CHAD (1960)

SUDAN (1956)

ERITREA (1993)

DJIBOUTI (1977)

GAMBIA (1965)

GUINEA (1958)

BURKINA FASO (1960)

GUINEA-BISSAU (1974)

IVORY COAST (1960)

GHANA (1957)

NIGERIA (1960)

CAMEROON (1960)

CENTRAL AFRICAN REPUBLIC (1960)

UGANDA (1962)

ETHIOPIA (1936)

SOMALIA (1960)

SIERRA LEONE (1961)

LIBERIA (1847)

TOGO (1960)

BENIN (1960)

SAO TOME AND PRINCIPE (1975)

EQUATORIAL GUINEA (1968)

GABON (1960)

CONGO (1960)

RWANDA (1962)

BURUNDI (1962)

DEMOCRATIC REPUBLIC OF CONGO (1960)

KENYA (1963)

TANZANIA (1961)

ANGOLA (1975)

ZAMBIA (1964)

MALAWI (1964)

Mozambique Channel

MADAGASCAR (1960)

NAMIBIA (1990)

ZIMBABWE (1980)

MOZAMBIQUE (1975)

ATLANTIC OCEAN

BOTSWANA (1966)

SWAZILAND (1968)

SOUTH AFRICA (1961)

LESOTHO (1966)

INDIAN OCEAN

0   1000 Miles

0   1000 Kilometers

MAP STUDY This map shows the political boundaries of each African nation and the year it became independent. Name two nations that became independent in the 1950s. In what year did Niger become an independent nation? What was the last country in Africa to become independent? What year did it become independent? How long has South Africa been an independent nation?

How Did World War II Affect African Nationalism?

World War II weakened the political position of all the European colonial powers. During World War II, more than 200,000 Africans fought on the side of their British and French colonial rulers. After the war, these people felt they had earned the right to rule themselves.

Kwame Nkrumah (center) became the leader of Ghana after it gained its independence in 1957.

What French Colonies Became Independent?

The European colonial powers denied self-rule and independence. France in particular did not want to lose its colonies in North Africa. However, Morocco and Tunisia—both French colonies—gained their independence.

But France wanted to hold on to the colony of Algeria. The French went to war with the Arab and Berber people living there. This war lasted from 1954 to 1961. But in 1962, Algeria, the last French colony in North Africa, finally won its independence.

What Was the First Independent Nation in Sub-Sahara Africa?

African Nationalism also spread to the European colonies in sub-Sahara Africa. The first new nation in this area was Ghana. Its people gained their independence in 1957.

Great Britain had ruled this area—called the Gold Coast—for 113 years. The people living there named their new nation after an ancient African empire. Kwame Nkrumah was the new African leader of Ghana. He said, "There is a new Africa in the world."

What Other Nations Became Independent?

Over the next 20 years, the "new Africa" continued to grow. In 1960 alone, 17 African nations gained their independence. Because of this, historians call 1960 "the year of Africa."

By the 1980s, more than 50 African countries had become independent nations. These new nations included Kenya, Mali, Nigeria, Senegal, Zaire, and Zimbabwe. Eritrea—the last area to gain its independence—became a nation in 1993.

What Is Apartheid?

Until the 1960s, the Union of South Africa was the only self-governing nation in the southern part of the continent. It belonged to the **British Commonwealth of Nations**—a group of nations that is loyal to the British monarch.

South Africa was different from the rest of Africa because whites controlled it. In 1948, the white-controlled government in South Africa made **apartheid** its official

JOMO KENYATTA: c. 1890–1978

Jomo Kenyatta spent his life working for black rule in Kenya. As a boy, he attended a Scottish mission school. There he was called Johnstone Kamau.

As an adult, Kenyatta joined a political group. It was trying to change British colonial rule. Local government officials would not listen, however. In 1931, Kenyatta went to England to work there for the desired changes. In England, he took the name *Jomo*, or "burning spear."

Kenyatta returned to Kenya in 1946 and worked for independence. Then he was jailed for his beliefs and actions. After Kenyan independence in 1963, he became its first president.

Nelson Mandela (center) was sent to prison for 26 years for his actions against the white minority government in South Africa. However, when he was released from prison, he helped end apartheid and became the president of South Africa.

policy. This policy set blacks and other nonwhite South Africans apart from whites. White South Africans refused to give black and other nonwhite people any political, economic, or social rights. Whites did not allow nonwhites to vote. Whites decided where nonwhites could live.

Great Britain and other nations protested this apartheid policy. South Africa then withdrew from the British Commonwealth. In 1961, South Africa became a republic.

How Did Black South Africans Fight Apartheid?

In 1976, a protest against apartheid turned into a riot. More than 500 people—mostly blacks—were killed. In 1983, a car bomb near a military base killed or injured more than 100 people. **The African National Congress (ANC),** a black nationalist group, said it had done the bombing.

As black South Africans struggled for equal rights, some used violence. Others did not. Bishop Desmond Tutu led nonviolent protests against apartheid. For his efforts to free South Africa from apartheid, Tutu was awarded the Nobel Peace Prize in 1984.

In 1986, the South African government said that blacks could no longer **demonstrate** against apartheid. That is, they could not join together with other blacks to protest and march against apartheid. But blacks continued to protest. The South African government put many black political leaders in jail.

Why Was Nelson Mandela Jailed for 26 Years?

On the first day that young Rolihlahla Mandela went to school in South Africa, his teacher gave him an English name—Nelson. In his native language, Rolihlahla means "he who pulls the branch of a tree." The English translate this word as "trouble maker." As an adult, Nelson Mandela did make trouble for those who wanted apartheid. He changed the history of his country.

In June 1964, a South African court sentenced Mandela to life in prison. The court said that Mandela had tried to overthrow the white minority government. The government wanted to silence Mandela because he worked to gain political, economic, and social rights for black South Africans. For 26 years, he remained in prison.

Who Released Mandela From Prison?

The South African government locked Mandela behind prison walls. But he still became a hero for black South Africans. In 1989, F. W. de Klerk became president of the Republic of South Africa.

By this time, the black protest to end apartheid was growing stronger. President de Klerk **legalized** the African National Congress. (That is, he said that people could join it without breaking the law.) In 1990, de Klerk released Mandela from prison.

How Did Mandela Help South Africans?

The ANC declared that Mandela was its leader. Right away, Mandela called for an end to white privileges. For four years, Mandela and de Klerk negotiated over black political, economic, and social rights.

Multiracial
Having to do with people of different races

Finally, the two leaders agreed to a plan. It provided for South Africa's first **multiracial** election. Multiracial means all the people and all races. A multiracial election means everyone can vote. Because of their work together, de Klerk and Mandela were awarded the 1993 Nobel Peace Prize.

In 1994, the people of South Africa elected Mandela to be their president. He served one term. Then, in 1999, at the age of 80, he retired from public office. People around the world honored him. He had broken down apartheid and united a divided nation.

SECTION 1 REVIEW On a separate sheet of paper, write answers to these questions.

1) Into how many geographic areas is Africa divided?

2) What is African Nationalism?

3) What is the name of the first nation created south of the Sahara Desert?

4) How was the nation of South Africa different from other African nations?

5) Why do many South Africans and other people think that Nelson Mandela is a hero?

What do you think

Why do you think the small white minority in South Africa adopted a policy of apartheid?

Persecute
To be mean or unfair to someone because of that person's ideas or political beliefs

More than 2,000 years ago, Palestine was the home of the Jewish people. But because of wars and troubles, many Jews moved to countries in Europe. However, in these places, some people **persecuted** them. That is, people were mean and unfair to the Jews. For centuries, they dreamed of a Jewish homeland. There they would be safe; they could follow their own traditions.

What Homeland Did the Jewish People Choose?

In the nineteenth century, Jewish leaders began to discuss the idea of creating a Jewish nation in Palestine. By 1900, Jews were moving into the dry, desert land of Palestine. However, for many generations, Palestine had been the home of Palestinian Arabs.

How Did World War II Affect the Jewish People?

When World War I ended, Britain gained control of Palestine. In the 1930s, many Jews moved there to escape the Nazis in Germany. As you know, during World War II, the Nazis murdered over six million Jews. After the war, Jewish people wanted a homeland more than ever. They believed that only there would they be safe.

How Did Israel Become a Nation?

After World War II, thousands of Jews left Europe to create their own nation in Palestine. The British could not stop them from settling there. Finally, Britain decided to leave Palestine. The United Nations was left to control it.

In 1947, the United Nations voted to divide Palestine into Jewish and Arab states. In May 1948, Jewish leader David Ben-Gurion said that the new nation of Israel existed. The neighboring Arab nations opposed the creation of a Jewish nation.

Dr. Chaim Weizmann took the oath as the first president of Israel in 1948.

Displace
*To move people
from their home or
land; to force
people to leave
their home or land*

What Was the Outcome of the 1948 Arab-Israeli War?

These Arab countries—Egypt, Iraq, Jordan, Lebanon, and Syria—attacked Israel. Nearly 400,000 Arabs in Palestine fled the area because of the fighting. These Palestinian refugees settled in Lebanon, Jordan, and Syria.

The Israeli army quickly defeated the invading Arab armies. As a result, Israel gained most of the land in Palestine. Egypt and Jordan took the remaining land.

In the next 30 years, Israel fought four more wars against the Arab nations that surrounded it. Each time, Israel defeated their armies. However, the defeated Arab nations still refused to admit that Israel was a nation. Arab leaders even refused to meet with Israeli officials to discuss peace.

What Did the PLO Want?

These wars **displaced** many Palestinian Arabs. They ended up in refugee camps. They had no land that was theirs to

◆Palestinian
Liberation
Organization
(PLO)
*The group of
Palestinians
dedicated to
regaining from
Israel their
homeland in
Palestine*

◆Terrorist
*A person who uses
violence to frighten
people and to get
them to obey*

live on. These displaced people demanded that they be given their own nation within Palestine.

Some Palestinian Arabs formed the **Palestinian Liberation Organization (PLO)**. By the 1970s, many members of the PLO had become **terrorists.** They used violence to frighten Israeli citizens and to force them to leave Palestine. The PLO staged raids on Israel from neighboring Arab nations, such as Lebanon. In the early 1980s, Israel invaded Lebanon to rid it of the PLO.

When Did Children Get Involved in the Fight?

In 1987, violence spread to areas that lay south of Lebanon called the West Bank and the Golan Heights. Young Palestinian children and women put up barriers in the streets. Then they threw rocks at Israeli soldiers. They killed a few soldiers and injured others. But the soldiers also killed and injured some Arab women and children.

MAP STUDY

This map shows what Israel looked like before and after the Arab-Israeli War in 1967. Beirut is a city in what Arab country? What river forms the eastern border of Israel? What land did Israel occupy in 1967? What Arab country lies to the east of the Golan Heights? What Arab country lies to the east of the West Bank?

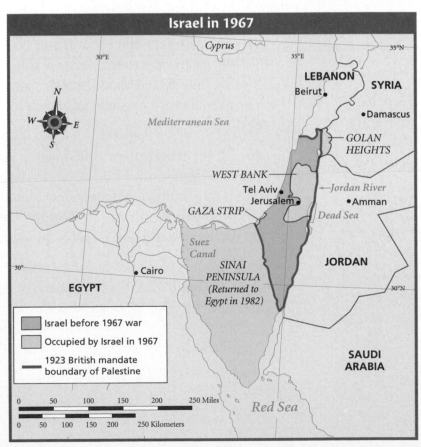

Israel in 1967

- Israel before 1967 war
- Occupied by Israel in 1967
- 1923 British mandate boundary of Palestine

After this, the Israeli soldiers arrested hundreds of Palestinians. Israel believed that controlling the West Bank was necessary for its security. In fact, hundreds of Israeli families had already built homes in the West Bank.

How Did the Israelis and the Palestinians Work Together?

During the 1990s, the Palestinian Arabs began to work with the Israelis to obtain Palestinian self-rule. In 1994, the Israelis allowed the Palestinians to take control of much of the Gaza Strip and the West Bank. (A few hundred thousand Jewish settlers and more than two million Palestinians live in the West Bank and the Gaza Strip.)

In 1995, Palestinian self-rule was expanded to more towns in the West Bank. But many Israelis living in these towns protested. Then, in 1995, an Israeli citizen assassinated Yitzhak Rabin, the prime minister of Israel. He had opposed the government's peace policy.

Why Do the Israelis Not Want to Give Up Land?

In 1998, Israel celebrated because it had been a nation for 50 years. The Israelis had fought again and again to keep their homeland. However, the Palestinians did not celebrate.

Instead, the Palestinians called, once again, for the creation of their own nation. They began to argue and fight with the Israelis over land. The Palestinians want Israel to give up land in return for peace. The government of Israel thinks that giving up land will weaken its security.

World leaders want the Israelis and Palestinians to negotiate again and to create peace in the Middle East. Both sides now search for the right solution.

Jerusalem

Jerusalem is one of the world's oldest cities. People have lived there for about 4,000 years. It was the center of ancient Jewish culture. Jewish kings ruled from there. King Solomon built the Temple on the Temple Mount. One of its walls still stands. It is called the Western Wall. Jews go there to pray.

Today the city is the capital of modern Israel. That country took control of East Jerusalem in the 1967 war. Palestinians also claim Jerusalem as their capital.

Jerusalem is holy to Christians and Muslims, too. Jesus taught in Jerusalem. The Last Supper and the Crucifixion both took place there. For Muslims, the Dome of the Rock is a holy shrine. They believe Muhammad rose to heaven from there.

SECTION 2 REVIEW On a separate sheet of paper, write *True* if the statement is true or *False* if the statement is not true. Make each false statement true by changing the underlined word.

1) <u>Arabs</u> occupied Palestine when some Jewish people returned to it in 1900.

2) Israel became a nation in <u>1918.</u>

3) Israel <u>lost</u> its 1948 war with five Arab countries.

4) The <u>PLO</u> is an organization that wants the Arab Palestinians to have their own nation.

5) In 1995, an <u>Israeli</u> citizen assassinated the prime minister of Israel.

What do you think

Do you think the Arab Palestinians should have their own nation? Explain your answer.

◆Passive resistance
A nonviolent way of protesting for political and social change

As you know from Chapters 2 and 12, India is located on the huge continent of Asia. For much of its history, many different people speaking many different languages lived in India. This happened partly because many different groups of people have invaded India.

What European Countries Took Control of India?

Since the 1500s, Europeans traded with India. By the 1700s, France controlled much of southern India. In addition, the British East Indian Trading Company sold Indian silks and other products throughout the world.

In 1763, Great Britain took control of large areas of India. As time passed, Britain drove the French from their trading posts in India. In 1858, Britain made all of India into a colony.

Why Did Indians Want Self-Rule?

Many Indians did not want their country to be a British colony. They wanted independence. They felt that the British treated them as second-class citizens in their own country. New industries and transportation served British needs, not the needs of the Indian people. The best jobs in India went to the British.

How Did Gandhi Bring Independence to India?

In 1885, a group of Indian leaders founded the Indian National Congress. Soon, it developed into the Congress Party. Its purpose was to gain political power for Indians.

In 1920, India's most important nationalist leader began to help India achieve independence. Mohandas Gandhi and his followers used **passive resistance** to fight British rule. This is a nonviolent way to get political and social change. For nearly 30 years, Gandhi led boycotts, protests, and work stoppages against the British. Finally, in 1947, Britain gave India its independence.

Gandhi wanted to make India a united nation. But he faced two major problems. The first problem was the caste system. The second problem was religious differences.

Why Was the Caste System a Problem for India?

In Chapter 2, you learned about the four main castes, or classes, of people in India. You probably remember that these castes divided according to work, money, skin color, and religious beliefs.

The members of each caste remained in the caste for life and followed its rules. For example, a person could marry only within the same caste. Another rule was that all the people in a caste did the same kind of work.

Gandhi knew that India could never be a true democracy as long as the caste system existed, so India's new constitution ended it. This constitution gave every Indian the right to vote. It opened schools that would educate all Indian children. It taught all these students Hindi, the national language. In time, India became the world's largest democracy.

Mohandas Gandhi helped India gain its independence from Britain in 1947.

Why Were Religious Differences a Problem for India?

The second problem that stood in the way of uniting India was religious differences. The majority of people in India were Hindus. They followed the Hindu religion. However, millions of Indians were Muslims. This Muslim minority wanted its own nation.

In August 1947, two new nations were created: India and Pakistan. Muslim Pakistan was further divided into East and West Pakistan. These two areas were more than 1,000 miles apart.

Religious differences between Hindus and Muslims led to violence. More than 500,000 people died in this struggle. Gandhi wanted to stop the violence. So, as a protest, he did not eat food for many days. But on January 30, 1948, a Hindu assassinated him. This man believed that Gandhi no longer supported the Hindus.

SECTION 3 REVIEW On a separate sheet of paper, write the word from the Word Bank that completes each sentence.

WORD BANK

Gandhi

Great Britain

Hindus

Muslims

Pakistan

1) In 1858, _____ took control of India and made it a colony.

2) In 1920, _____ began to lead the Indian people in passive resistance.

3) The majority of people in India were _____.

4) The minority of people in India were _____.

5) In 1947, part of India became the nation of _____.

What do you think

Why would the caste system have kept India from becoming a true democracy?

As you know from Chapter 22, European nations had colonies both in Africa and in Asia. China was not a colony. But Europe still had economic control over it. After World War II, China wanted to be independent from European nations.

What Two Groups Fought to Control China?

In Chapter 25, you read about the struggle between the Communists and the non-Communists for control of China. This struggle began in 1927. Mao Zedong led the Communist forces. Chiang Kai-shek led the Nationalists. For ten years their two armies fought each other. This civil war left China weak and divided.

What Happened When Japan Invaded China?

In 1937, Japan invaded China. Chiang Kai-shek and Mao Zedong stopped fighting each other; they united to fight the Japanese. But neither side trusted the other.

Mao Zedong led Communist forces in China. He set up a Communist government there in 1949.

Each side fought the Japanese in a different way. The Communists used guerrilla warfare against the Japanese. The Communists worked closely with the Chinese peasants. The Nationalists, however, fought the Japanese in the usual way. They stayed mostly in the cities of southwest China.

How Did the Two Groups Differ After World War II?

When World War II ended in 1945, the fighting between the Communists and the Nationalists started again. Their civil war lasted from 1946 to 1949.

Chiang Kai-shek's Nationalists had a large army. The United States sent them billions of dollars for weapons and training. But Chiang's government was both greedy and inefficient. His military officers argued with each other.

However, Mao Zedong's Communist forces were united in their cause. Many of the Chinese people supported them. The Soviet Union—the first Communist nation—sent them weapons and supplies.

Which Group Won Control of China?

By 1948, the Communists had the upper hand in China. One city after another fell to them. As this happened, thousands of soldiers deserted Chiang's army and joined Mao's forces. By the fall of 1949, Chiang Kai-shek and his government had lost control of China.

Chiang and his followers fled the mainland of China and crossed over to the small island of Taiwan. After 22 years of struggle, the Communists set up a new government in China. They called it the People's Republic of China.

Why Did Mao Zedong and the United States Not Trust One Another?

Mao Zedong did not trust the United States for two reasons. First, the United States had helped Chiang Kai-shek. Second, the United States had supported imperialism around the world.

"Made in Asia"

Where were your shoes made? Your CD player? Many products like these come from Japan, China, or Korea. Since 1945, Asian economies have grown quickly. Postwar Japan had the fastest-growing economy in the world. Other countries like South Korea, Taiwan, Singapore, and Hong Kong also grew. China, India, and Indonesia have developed more recently.

Asian nations differ greatly. Still, they share some attitudes. People will work hard for long hours. They want to learn new things. For example, the Japanese studied other countries' methods. They became efficient at making quality products. In addition, most governments help industries develop.

Consumer Science

History in Your Life

At first, Asian countries depended on selling their goods to Europe and America. Things have changed in Asian societies, however. A middle class has grown up in these nations. People can buy cars, color TVs, and pagers. They travel and use credit cards. Asian consumers have become the fastest-growing market for Asian goods.

But the United States did not trust Mao either. The U.S. government thought that the Chinese Communists threatened freedom in Asia. The United States refused to recognize the Communist government as the legal government of China. Instead, the United States supported the Nationalist government on the island of Taiwan.

But in 1972, the United States changed its policy toward the People's Republic of China. For the first time, the United States recognized it as the legal government of the Chinese people.

SECTION 4 REVIEW Choose the letter of the answer that correctly completes each sentence. Write your answer on a separate sheet of paper.

1) The leader of the Chinese Nationalists was _____.

    a. Mao Zedong   c. Lenin
    b. Chiang Kai-shek   d. Gandhi

2) The leader of the Chinese Communists was _____.

    a. Mao Zedong   c. Tojo
    b. Chiang Kai-shek   d. Mandela

3) The Chinese Nationalists and Communists united to fight against the _____ in World War II.

    a. Americans   c. Japanese
    b. British   d. French

4) After the war, the two groups fought one another again and the _____ won.

    a. Nationalists   c. Nazis
    b. Republicans   d. Communists

5) In 1972, the United States recognized that the legal government of China was the _____.

    a. People's Republic of China
    b. Nazis
    c. Nationalists
    d. Chiang Kai-shek Party

What do you think ❓

Why did Mao Zedong and his followers win the civil war in China?

◆**Election**
An act by which people choose someone or something by voting

After World War II, nationalist independence movements spread across Southeast Asia. In 1946, the United States gave the Philippine Islands their independence. South of the Philippines, the Netherlands gave freedom to Indonesia. However, France refused to free its colonial lands in Indochina.

What Did Ho Chi Minh Want for Vietnam?

Japan had conquered Indochina during World War II. The Vietnamese, under the leadership of Ho Chi Minh, fought against the Japanese. After the war, Ho Chi Minh wanted Vietnam to be an independent nation, not a French colony.

Between 1946 and 1954, Ho Chi Minh and his Communist followers fought a fierce guerrilla war against the French. The United States sent aid to the French. The United States did not want another Communist government in Asia. However, in 1954, the Vietnamese Communist forces captured a French fort. Because of this, the French government decided that it could not win the war

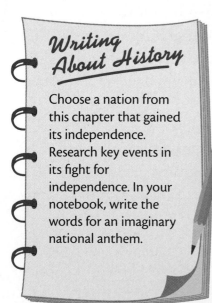

Writing About History

Choose a nation from this chapter that gained its independence. Research key events in its fight for independence. In your notebook, write the words for an imaginary national anthem.

What Happened After the Communists Defeated France?

Ho Chi Minh and the French agreed to divide Vietnam into two areas. The Communist area became known as North Vietnam. The non-Communist area became South Vietnam. Two other areas in Indochina became independent: Cambodia and Laos.

The division of Vietnam was not meant to be permanent. The government of South Vietnam was supposed to hold an **election**. In an election, people choose someone or something by voting. In this election, the Vietnamese people would choose how to unite their country.

Despite sending 500,000 American troops to fight in Vietnam, the United States could not win the war. The U.S. began pulling out its troops in 1969.

But this election never took place. North Vietnam began a guerrilla war to unite Vietnam into one Communist nation. Communists in South Vietnam joined this struggle.

What Did the United States Do About the Guerrilla War?

In the early 1960s, the United States began to send military advisers to South Vietnam. Their job was simply to help the South Vietnamese government. But by 1968, nearly 500,000 American troops were fighting a war in South Vietnam. However, many Americans protested this war.

The Vietnam War lasted from 1960 to 1975. In 1969, the United States government started to gradually withdraw its forces from South Vietnam. The American plan was to turn the fighting of the war entirely over to the South Vietnamese army. The United States called this plan **Vietnamization.**

◆Vietnamization
The U.S. plan to turn the fighting of the Vietnam War over to the South Vietnamese army

What United North and South Vietnam?

After the United States pulled its soldiers out of Vietnam, the South Vietnamese government collapsed. In April 1975, the North Vietnamese took control of South Vietnam's capital city, Saigon.

The next year, North and South Vietnam united into one Communist country, the Socialist Republic of Vietnam. The government gave a new name to Saigon. It became Ho Chi Minh City. Today, after many years of struggle, the United States and the Socialist Republic of Vietnam are slowly finding ways to work together.

This is a current map of Southeast Asia. What large country lies on the northern border of Vietnam? Is Ho Chi Minh City (Saigon) in the northern or southern part of Vietnam? Which nation lies to the northeast of Thailand? Which nation lies to the southeast of Thailand?

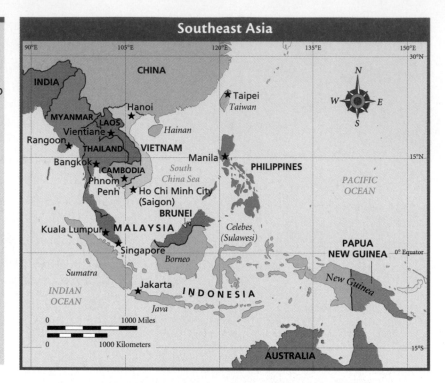

Southeast Asia

SECTION 5 REVIEW On a separate sheet of paper, write *True* if the statement is true or *False* if the statement is not true. Make each false statement true by changing the underlined word.

1) <u>France</u> controlled Vietnam until 1954.

2) The Communists, led by <u>Mao Zedong,</u> fought for an independent Vietnam.

3) Vietnam was divided into North Vietnam, South Vietnam, Cambodia, and <u>Laos.</u>

4) The United States supported the <u>North</u> Vietnamese army in the Vietnam War.

5) In 1975, the North Vietnamese took control of <u>Saigon,</u> which was the South Vietnamese capital.

What do you think ?

Should the United States have fought in the Vietnam War? Explain your answer.

African "Familyhood"

Tanganyika was a British colony. Julius Nyerere led its independence movement. When independence came, he became president. In 1964, Tanganyika and Zanzibar united as Tanzania. Nyerere was the first president of the new nation. He also led in the formation of the Organization of African Unity. It works for cooperation among African nations. The following is from Nyerere's writing titled "Education for Self-Reliance."

Julius Nyerere led Tanganyika to independence.

Our first step, therefore, must be to re-educate ourselves. . . . In our traditional African society we were individuals within a community. We took care of community, and the community took care of us. We neither needed nor wished to exploit our fellow men. . . .

The Government must go back to the traditional African custom of landholding. That is to say, a member of society will be entitled to a piece of land on condition that he uses it.

. . . Tanganyika today is a poor country. The standard of living of the masses of our people is shamefully low. But if every man and woman in the country takes up the challenge and works to the limit of his or her ability for the good of the whole society, Tanganyika will prosper; and that prosperity will be shared by all her people. . . .

The foundation, and the objective, of African socialism is the extended family. The true African socialist does not look on one class of men as his brethren and another as his natural enemies. . . . He rather regards all men as his brethren—as members of his ever extending family. . . .

"Ujamaa," then, or "familyhood," describes our socialism. It is opposed to capitalism, which seeks to build a happy society on the basis of the exploitation of man by man; and it is equally opposed to doctrinaire socialism, which seeks to build its happy society on a philosophy of inevitable conflict between man and man.

We, in Africa, have no more need of being "converted" to socialism than we have of being "taught" democracy. Both are rooted in our own past—in the traditional society which produced us. Modern African socialism can draw from its traditional heritage the recognition of "society" as an extension of the basic family unit. But it can no longer confine the idea of the social family within the limits of the tribe, nor, indeed, of the nation. . . .

Our recognition of the family to which we all belong must be extended yet farther—beyond the tribe, the community, the nation, or even the continent—to embrace the whole society of mankind. . . .

Source Reading Wrap-Up

1) How was land divided in traditional Africa?
2) According to Nyerere, how can Tanganyika become prosperous?
3) What does *Ujamaa* mean?
4) How were family and society related in traditional Africa?
5) How does Nyerere think the idea of "family" must be expanded?

The Spinning Wheel and Salt—Weapons of the Indian Revolution

Mahatma Gandhi was the father of Indian independence. He was a man of ideas, trained as a lawyer. Gandhi believed in nonviolence. He thought that passive resistance was his people's best weapon. This is a form of nonviolent protest. It is used against laws seen as unfair. Gandhi believed that the force of truth could defeat British military force. Violence would not work.

In 1919, British colonial laws changed. Some Indian leaders organized strikes and riots against the laws. That led to a tragedy in the town of Amritsar. About 10,000 Indians were at a protest meeting. British soldiers fired on the unarmed crowd. Hundreds of Indians were killed or injured. Amritsar was a turning point. Gandhi decided to work for independence. In 1920, he became head of the Indian National Congress. The Congress Party became India's largest political party.

Indian leaders wanted both political and economic freedom. Great Britain sold India a lot of cotton cloth. That made the colony a valuable market for British industry. Gandhi urged Indians not to buy British cotton goods. He encouraged them to spin cotton thread and weave their own cloth. He hoped that this would make India less valuable to Britain. The simple spinning wheel became a powerful symbol. Gandhi himself wore only homespun cloth. He was often seen beside a spinning wheel.

Gandhi told his followers to disobey unfair British laws. One of those laws was the Salt Act. The law made it a crime to make salt from sea water. Indians had to buy expensive salt from the

Gandhi (center) used passive resistance to gain India's independence.

government. In 1930, Gandhi started a "salt march" to the sea in protest. He began the 200-mile march with 78 followers. Every day more and more people joined the march.

The march lasted 24 days. When it reached the sea, there were hundreds of people. They began to make salt the traditional way. They boiled sea water to get the salt out of it. More Indians joined Gandhi and his followers. Thousands of people—including Gandhi—were arrested.

Under constant pressure, the British changed many laws. In 1935, India won some self-government. Full independence finally came in 1947. When the country was divided, violence did occur. Still, India had won independence with two simple weapons—salt and the spinning wheel.

Spotlight Story Wrap-Up

1) What is passive resistance?
2) Describe what happened in Amritsar in 1919.
3) What political party did Gandhi lead?
4) Why did the spinning wheel become a symbol of Indian independence?
5) What was the salt march?

➡ In 1900, European nations controlled most of Africa. The Pan-African Movement led the struggle for African independence.

➡ African nationalism grew after World War II. France lost a war to keep its colony of Algeria. Ghana, a British colony, became the first independent nation in sub-Saharan Africa in 1957.

➡ A minority of white settlers controlled South Africa. The policy of apartheid strictly separated nonwhite and white South Africans.

➡ The African National Congress was one nationalist group. Its leader Nelson Mandela spent 26 years in prison for protesting apartheid. In 1994, he was elected president in South Africa's first multiracial election.

➡ After World War II, many Jews moved to Palestine, but Arabs already lived there. In 1947, the United Nations divided Palestine into Jewish and Arab states. Jewish leaders declared the new nation of Israel.

➡ Israel won several wars against neighboring Arab countries. Because of these wars, many Palestinians became refugees. Some formed the Palestinian Liberation Organization (PLO), which led terrorist attacks on Israel. In the 1990s, some Arab and Israeli leaders worked toward peace and Palestinian self-rule.

➡ India was a British colony. Many Indians wanted independence. The Congress Party under Mohandas Gandhi fought the British, using passive resistance.

➡ India became an independent democracy in 1947. People in every caste had political rights. Religious differences led to the creation of Pakistan as a Muslim state.

➡ Beginning in 1927, Chinese Nationalists and Communists fought a civil war. They united to fight the Japanese in World War II.

➡ The Chinese civil war began again after World War II. The Communists won in 1949. Mao Zedong set up a Communist government—the People's Republic of China. In 1972, the United States accepted the People's Republic as a legal government.

➡ Southeast Asia was a French colony, Indochina. Ho Chi Minh, a Communist, led the Vietnamese fight for independence. After a French defeat, Indochina was divided into North and South Vietnam, Cambodia, and Laos.

➡ North Vietnam began a guerrilla war to unite Vietnam under Communist rule. The United States helped South Vietnam. After the United States left in 1975, all Vietnam became one Communist nation.

Comprehension: Identifying Facts

On a separate sheet of paper, use the words from the Word Bank to complete each sentence.

WORD BANK

Ben-Gurion

Chiang

Ethiopia

France

Gandhi

Great Britain

Mao

Mandela

Tutu

Vietnam

1) After World War II, _____ was one of only three independent nations in Africa.

2) Bishop Desmond _____, who worked to get rid of apartheid, was awarded the Nobel Peace Prize in 1984.

3) The white minority in South Africa put Nelson _____ in jail for 26 years.

4) In 1948, David _____ announced a new nation: Israel.

5) _____ controlled India from 1858 to 1947.

6) Mohandas _____ used passive resistance to gain freedom for India.

7) The nationalist leader in China in 1927 was _____ Kai-shek.

8) The Communist leader in China in 1927 was _____ Zedong.

9) The Communist leader in _____ in 1946 was Ho Chi Minh.

10) _____ had colonies in Indochina after World War II.

Comprehension: Multiple Choice

On a separate sheet of paper, write the letter of the answer that correctly completes each sentence.

1) The South African policy of not letting blacks vote or choose where to live is _____.

   a. Vietnamization   c. apartheid

   b. African Nationalism d. Pan-African Movement

2) In _____ soldiers hide, make surprise attacks, and set traps for the enemy.

   a. guerilla warfare   c. persecution

   b. multiracial   d. apartheid

3) _____ have fought the Israelis for land to set up a nation.

    a. Arab Palestinians   c. Chinese Communists

    b. Vietnamese Communists d. Japanese

4) The United States used a plan called _____ to get out of a guerilla war in Southeast Asia.

    a. African Nationalism   c. Pan-African Movement

    b. Vietnamization   d. British Commonwealth

5) _____, the president of the Republic of South Africa, was awarded the Nobel Prize in 1993.

    a. de Klerk   c. Ho Chi Minh

    b. Tutu   d. Yitzhak Rabin

Comprehension: Understanding Main Ideas

On a separate sheet of paper, write the answers to the following questions using complete sentences, or statements.

1) Why did India divide into two countries?

2) What two Chinese groups fought over control of China? Which side won? Why?

3) Why did the United States fight a war in Vietnam?

Critical Thinking: Write Your Opinion

1) How would you solve the problems in the Middle East between the Palestinians and the Israelis?

2) Do you think Gandhi's passive resistance would have worked to end apartheid in South Africa? Explain your answer.

Test-Taking Tip	Review your corrected tests. You can learn from previous mistakes.

A Changing World

29

1950 to the Present

In this chapter, you will see how people around the world continue to make history. In Africa, you will see how people have begun to flock to the cities. In the Middle East, you will see how problems continue to develop. In Russia, you will say good-bye to communism. You will also learn how other former Communist countries have gained their freedom. Finally, in Latin America, you will learn about the campesinos who demanded land reform. This chapter will show you how the world continues to change even in recent times.

Goals for Learning

▶ To explain the problems Africa faces today

▶ To describe why conflicts still exist in the Middle East

▶ To explain the changes in Asian countries

▶ To explain why communism failed in the Soviet Union and Eastern Europe

▶ To describe the changes in European countries

▶ To list the problems Latin America faces

1991
Soviet Union comes to an end

1953
Khrushchev becomes Soviet leader and works for reform

1978
Israeli and Egyptian leaders meet in United States

1980
Iraq invades Iran

1989
Chinese students protest in Tiananmen Square

1990
East and West Germany unite

1999
War over Kosovo begir

1960   1980   2000

1964
Brezhnev becomes Soviet leader and stops reform

1979
Iranians hold 52 Americans hostage

1985
Gorbachev becomes Soviet leader and introduces glasnost and perestroika

1991
Persian Gulf War begins and en

1990
Iraq invades Kuwait

Russia and the Commonwealth of Independent States

During the 1980s, the republics of the Soviet Union started to seek their independence. Then, in December 1991, the Soviet Union came to an end. At the same time, three republics—Russia, Ukraine, and Belarus—formed the Commonwealth of Independent States (CIS). Soon other republics joined them. This map shows the members of the CIS.

Geography Skills

Study the map and answer these questions:

1) How many nations of the Commonwealth are shown on this map?

2) Which of these nations is the largest in land area?

3) Which seems to be the smallest in land area?

4) Which of these is the farthest east?

5) Which of these is the farthest south?

Conflict
Fighting; not being able to agree on something

Migrant
A person who has left one place and moved to another

Slum
An area of a city with too many people, poor housing, and low-income families

◆**Urbanization**
Becoming more like a city

Africa is a continent in change. As you know from Chapter 22, the countries of Africa became European colonies in the nineteenth century. Chapter 28 explained how these colonies became independent nations after World War II ended in 1945.

Today, many African economies are growing at an average rate of over 5 percent. These nations have made real progress toward democratic rule. Their people live with less violent **conflict** than they did ten years ago. (Conflict happens when people fight and do not agree.) Trade is growing, and Africa is reconnecting with the world economy.

How Has Rapid Urbanization Affected Africa?

But Africa is a continent in crisis. One of its biggest problems is rapid **urbanization.** That is, Africa's cities are growing too quickly. Many people are leaving the countryside to find a better life in these cities. Often they have no skills or education, so they cannot find jobs.

Lack of food and water causes many problems in a number of African countries.

This large number of **migrants**—people who have left one place and moved to another—puts a strain on city services. Often the city cannot provide good transportation and sanitation. Many people live in **slums** with no electricity, running water, or sewers. A slum is an area of a city with too many people, poor housing, and low-income families. People face health problems and only a few get enough to eat.

Why Does Africa Have a Lack of Food?

Famine is a big problem for Africa. Since the 1970s, many African people have starved to death. They do not have enough food to eat. Five things explain this lack of food.

1. Africa's population growth is greater than that of any other continent.

2. Since the 1970s, Africa has experienced several **droughts.** A drought is a long period without much rain.

3. Africa is growing less food because its farmers have little **fertilizer, pesticides,** and fuel. Fertilizer makes the soil grow crops; pesticides kill the bugs that eat the crops.

4. Many African countries pay more attention to industry than to farming.

5. In many parts of Africa, civil wars have damaged farming.

The nations of Africa and more powerful countries will have to work together to solve these many problems.

SECTION 1 REVIEW On a separate sheet of paper, write *True* if the statement is true or *False* if the statement is not true. Make each false statement true by changing the underlined word.

1) During the nineteenth century, <u>South America</u> made colonies out of many African countries.

2) These colonies became independent nations in the years after <u>World War II.</u>

3) One of the biggest problems for Africa is <u>slow</u> urbanization.

4) Another problem for Africa is <u>famine.</u>

5) Since the 1970s, Africa has experienced several <u>droughts.</u>

Drought
A long period of time without much rain

Fertilizer
A substance that makes the soil grow crops

Pesticide
A substance that kills the bugs that eat the crops

What do you think ❓

How would a civil war damage farming?

◆Ayatollah
A religious leader of Iran

◆Shah
An Iranian ruler

The major countries in the Middle East do not seem to trust one another. Their main problem is the Palestinian issue. You read about it in Chapter 28.

What Were the Results of Middle East Peace Talks?

The United States has encouraged Israel and its neighbors to settle their problems. In 1978, President Jimmy Carter brought together leaders from Egypt and Israel at Camp David, Maryland. Their agreement formed the basis for an Arab-Israeli peace treaty. Prime Minister of Israel Yitzhak Rabin agreed to trade land for peace.

Israel has also reached out to its other Arab neighbors, Jordan and Syria. In 1994, Jordan signed a peace treaty with Israel. However, Syria and Israel could not agree. This is partly because some Arabs oppose the peace process. Instead, they support terrorist groups like Hamas. On the other side, some Israelis fear that a self-ruling Palestine will threaten the security of their country.

In October 1998, leaders of the Middle East met with U.S. President Bill Clinton for nine days. Israel agreed to withdraw from more Palestinian land. The Palestinians agreed to get rid of terrorism. The United States agreed to guarantee security.

How Did the Shah of Iran Help His Country?

Until 1979, the **Shah**—Iran's ruler—tried to make his country into a modern nation. He began new industry. He built schools, highways, and factories. He gave women more freedom.

But many peasants still had no land of their own. Many people had no jobs. Also, the **ayatollahs**—the religious leaders of Iran—thought that the Shah was destroying traditional values. The Shah had his secret police arrest anyone who did not like what he was doing. He became a cruel dictator. Many Iranians opposed him.

Why Did the Shah of Iran Flee His Country?

In the late 1970s, many people began to support Ayatollah Khomeini. He wanted religious leaders to rule Iran. In January 1979, these people forced the Shah to flee Iran. Then Khomeini's new government took over Iran.

Much of the anger against the Shah was directed toward the United States. The U.S. gave aid to the Jewish people in Israel. The Iranians said that the United States was the enemy of all Muslims. In 1979, the problem got worse. To show their hatred of the United States, some Iranians captured 52 Americans and made them **hostages** for almost 15 months. The Iranians held these people against their will. Eventually, the hostages were released.

Ayatollah Khomeini took control of Iran in 1979.

What Caused a War Between Iran and Iraq?

Iran and Iraq are neighbors. Iranians are mainly Shiite Muslims; Iraqis are Sunni Muslims. Iranians are Persians; Iraqis are Arabs. Because of these differences, the two neighbors have a long history of conflict.

◆Hostage
Someone held against his or her will until certain demands are met

After 1979, Iran tried to influence the large Shiite community in Iraq. This alarmed the Sunni Muslims, who led the Iraqi government. In September 1980, Iraqi troops invaded Iran. The war between the two countries lasted eight years. It killed more than a million people. It also damaged the oil industry of both countries.

The Iraqis had better weapons, and they used poison gas. The Iranians, however, had a larger army and better airplanes. Both sides attacked international shipping. Because of this, the United States sent ships to the area. They protected the shipping lanes through which ships transported much of the world's oil. In 1988, the United Nations helped to end the war.

Why Did Iraq Invade Kuwait?

The war with Iran left Iraq with a weakened economy and big debts. Iraq owed money to its neighbor, Kuwait. On August 2, 1990, Iraqi troops invaded Kuwait. They wanted to take over its rich oil fields. Saudi Arabia feared that Iraq might attack it, too. If Iraq took over both Kuwait and Saudi Arabia, it would control nearly 40 percent of the world's oil. Because of this, it would have great influence in the world.

What Caused the Persian Gulf War?

The UN Security Council ordered Iraq to withdraw from Kuwait, but Iraq refused to leave. In January 1991, an international force began an air war against Iraq. Iraq responded by firing missiles on Saudi Arabia and Israel. Iraqi soldiers did horrible things to people in Kuwait. They also took $1.6 billion from Kuwait.

The Persian Gulf War in 1991 lasted only about 100 hours. UN forces defeated the Iraqis and freed Kuwait.

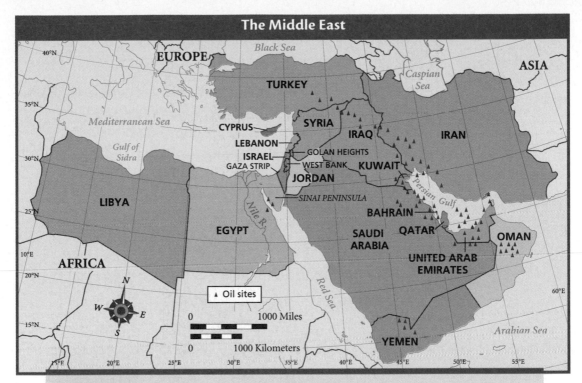

The Middle East

This map of the Middle East shows the various countries and oil sites. Which country is bigger—Iraq or Iran? In what direction does Kuwait lie from Iraq? Where in the Middle East is the most oil? What body of water lies between Iran and Kuwait?

Iraq would not leave Kuwait without force. Soldiers from the United States, Great Britain, and France invaded. Troops from Arab countries also joined the fight. After about 100 hours of fighting, the allies defeated the Iraqis. Kuwait was free. Historians call this conflict the Persian Gulf War.

After the war, Iraqi leader Saddam Hussein remained in power. Two Iraqi groups—the Shiite Muslims and the Kurds—had opposed him in the war. He began to make war on them and removed nearly 1.5 million Iraqi Kurds from their villages. Many died.

What Problems Still Remain in the Middle East?

Some good things have happened for people of the Middle East. For example, oil and industry have created new wealth. More people can now go to school and their health is better. But the distance between the rich and the poor seems to be growing. Families seem to be breaking down.

Some people have become Islamic **fundamentalists.** They have returned to traditional religious values and have rejected much of modern life. In the United States, Christian fundamentalism is also growing. India has Hindu fundamentalists. Israel has Jewish fundamentalists who sometimes challenge the government's authority.

SECTION 2 REVIEW Choose the letter of the answer that correctly completes each sentence.

1) The prime minister of Israel in the 1990s was _____.

    a. Hamas   c. Clinton

    b. Rabin   d. Hussein

2) In 1979, Ayatollah _____ took over the Iranian government.

    a. Shah   c. Khomeini

    b. Hussein   d. Hamas

3) In 1980, _____ invaded Iran.

    a. Iraq   c. Kuwait

    b. Saudi Arabia   d. the United States

4) In 1990, Iraq invaded _____.

    a. Iran   c. Kuwait

    b. Libya   d. Israel

5) _____ fought against Shiite Muslims and Kurds in his own country.

    a. Rabin   c. Shah

    b. Khomeini   d. Hussein

What do you think ?

Why is oil such an important resource for the Middle East?

◆Human rights
The right to life, liberty, and pursuit of happiness

Invest
To give money to a company with the hope of making more money

In Chapters 25 and 28, you read about Mao Zedong and the Communist control of China. After Mao died in 1976, China began to change.

What Was Deng's Plan for Economic Reform in China?

China's new leader, Deng Xiaoping, called for changes in farming, industry, science, and the military. He let people own businesses and property again. He invited foreign countries to **invest** in China's businesses. To invest is to give money to a company with the hope of making more money.

These new economic reforms changed China's standard of living. Many families could buy such things as televisions, radios, and fans. But the reforms had a bad side, too. A gap developed between the rich and the poor. Crime increased. Food prices went up. The government closed down inefficient factories, so some people lost their jobs.

What Happened in Tiananmen Square?

In May 1989, more than 3,000 students went on a hunger strike in Tiananmen Square in Beijing—China's capital city. They wanted a democratic, not a Communist, government. Soon, more than a million people went out on the streets and called for change.

Through television, the whole world learned about the protest. But on June 4, 1989, soldiers marched into Tiananmen Square and killed hundreds of protesters. The government put many student leaders in jail and tortured or executed them.

After that, President Clinton called for more **human rights** in China. That is, he said that people everywhere had the right to life, liberty, and the pursuit of happiness.

Why Has Japan Become an Economic Power?

Japan is among the world's top producers of goods and services. It has the second largest economy in the world.

(Only the economy of the United States is stronger.) People who study its economy give three reasons for its success.

1. The government works with large companies to plan industrial growth.

2. These companies get their money from banks. Many Japanese people save their money in banks, so the banks have lots of money to loan the companies.

3. Japanese people like to work together. They are hard workers who produce products quickly and at a low cost. They are well educated and highly skilled.

What Is Happening to China's Economy?

China's economy is growing, too. It is now the world's third largest economy. People expect it to pass Japan in the next ten years and become second to the United States. China's population of 1.2 billion people provides a cheap supply of labor. Also, all these people are becoming **consumers.** That is, they want to buy things such as telephones, radios, televisions, and cars.

China's capital city is Beijing. Many people ride bicycles rather than motorized vehicles.

What Other Asian Countries Have Better Economies?

South Korea, Taiwan, Singapore, Hong Kong, and Thailand have also experienced economic growth. South Korea builds ships and automobiles. Taiwan produces everything from toys to electronics. Singapore and Hong Kong are big in manufacturing and banking. Thailand's economy has grown because foreign business owners can make money there. The people of Thailand make very little money.

Since 1988, Aung San Suu Kyi has led the fight for democracy in Myanmar (Burma). Leadership is a family trait. Her father, Aung San, is called the father of independent Burma.

In 1988, Myanmans protested against military rule. As a result, troops shot or arrested thousands. Aung San spoke out for human rights. She helped the National League for Democracy win 80 percent of the seats in parliament. The rulers ignored the results and kept her under house arrest for six years. In 1991, she won the Nobel Peace Prize. The generals still limit her freedom to speak and travel, however.

What Economic Problems Does Asia Have?

In June 1997, the money supply of Thailand collapsed. Soon, this crisis spread to Indonesia, Malaysia, the Philippines, and South Korea. It bankrupt many Asian banks and businesses. This happened for two reasons.

First, in the 1980s, many Asian businesses borrowed money from banks. Then, factories began producing more than they could sell and prices went down. These businesses could not repay what they had borrowed. Soon, both the banks and the businesses had no money.

Second, foreign investors got worried. They pulled their money out of Asia. Then they invested it in other countries.

SECTION 3 REVIEW On a separate sheet of paper, write answers to these questions.

1) How did Deng's economic plan change China?

2) Who protested against China's Communist government in 1989?

3) What is one reason why Japan became the most important economy of Asia?

4) Why is China's economy growing?

5) What is one thing that led to the economic crisis in Asia?

What do you think ?

Why have foreign countries invested in Asian businesses?

Throughout its history, the Soviet Union has had serious economic problems. However, it became a major industrial nation by the late 1930s. But the Soviet people did not have many consumer goods. Soviet leader Joseph Stalin did not allow anyone to protest this lack of goods. In fact, he sent protesters to prison or executed them.

Why Did Khrushchev's Reform Efforts Fail?

Stalin died in 1953. Nikita Khrushchev became the Soviet leader. He ended the government's cruel treatment of the Soviet people. Then he reformed the economy. First, he told factory managers to produce more consumer goods. Then he allowed artists and writers some freedom to create what they wanted.

But in 1964, all this changed. Leonid Brezhnev, who opposed reform, replaced Khrushchev. Brezhnev punished anyone who spoke out against the government.

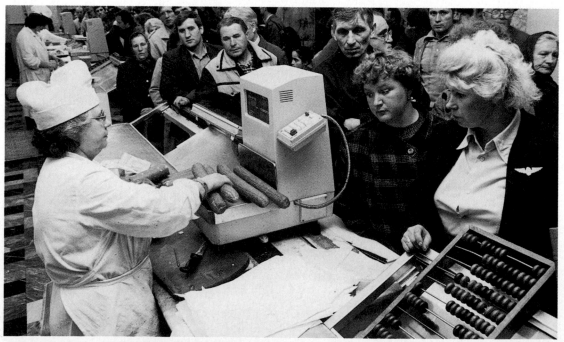

In the 1980s and 1990s, Russian citizens had to wait in long lines to buy things they needed because goods were scarce. Prices were very high and wages were low.

Soviet leader Mikhail Gorbachev (right) meets with U.S. President Ronald Reagan (left).

What Was the Soviet Economy Like in 1985?

In 1985, Mikhail Gorbachev became the Soviet leader. He was a younger man with new ideas. But he faced big problems. For example, the Soviet economy was falling apart. People spent hours a day standing in lines to buy food and clothing. Prices were high and wages were low. (A pair of winter boots cost most people a month's wages!)

◆Glasnost
A Russian word that means openness; under Gorbachev it meant openness in government

◆Perestroika
An economic policy used by Gorbachev to encourage factories to produce the goods people wanted

How Did Gorbachev Reform the Soviet Union?

Gorbachev introduced a policy of **glasnost,** or openness, in government. He allowed a freer press. He also allowed people to speak out against the government. To help rebuild the economy, Gorbachev introduced **perestroika.** That is, he let factories produce all the goods people wanted.

Then Gorbachev moved his country toward a more democratic government by creating a parliament. The Russian people elected representatives to this parliament from the Communist Party and other parties. In May 1989, the Soviet parliament met for the first time. Gorbachev allowed its representatives to speak freely.

What People Wanted Independence?

At that time, the Soviet Union was made up of 92 different groups of people who spoke 112 different languages. Some of these people began to demand independent nations of their own. Between 1988 and 1990, people in Azerbaijan, Estonia, Latvia, Lithuania, Moldavia, Soviet Georgia, and Uzbekistan demanded independence.

What Caused the Soviet Union to Collapse?

This worried the Soviet army and the secret police. If the Soviet Union broke up, their power and influence would end. They tried to overthrow Gorbachev. But a leader named Boris Yeltsin led thousands of Russians against the army and police. Their government takeover, or **coup,** failed. Yeltsin became a hero.

On December 1, 1991, the Ukraine voted for independence from the Soviet Union. Within days, other Soviet republics declared their independence, too. Gorbachev tried to stop the breakup, but he could not. He stepped down from office. On December 25, 1991, the Soviet flag was lowered from the Kremlin for the last time. The Soviet Union no longer existed.

What Problems Does Russia Still Have?

The Russian republic elected Yeltsin to be its president. Russia was the largest republic of the former Soviet Union. Yeltsin tried to keep some of the former Soviet Union together by forming the Commonwealth of Independent

Boris Yeltsin (waving) became the president of Russia after the collapse of the Soviet Union. Though many Russians disagreed with how he ran the country, he was re-elected in 1996.

◆**Free-market capitalism**
The system that allows for private ownership of business

States (CIS). This is a group of 12 of the former Soviet republics. However, it has very little power.

Yeltsin also pushed for **free-market capitalism.** This is a system that allows for private ownership of business. Yeltsin also wanted to increase the power of the presidency. Some thought that this was an attempt to become a dictator. Others thought Russia needed a strong president to face the many changes necessary to become a free market.

Reform in Russia has not been easy. Some new businesses and a new middle class have developed. But crime and dishonesty have also increased. Health care is poor. Also, factory workers are not producing as many goods. The government is unable to collect most taxes. It does not have money to take care of the old and poor. In 1998, the government could not even pay its bills.

Yeltsin was once again elected president in 1996. However, many Russians do not agree with his leadership. Many foreign investors have pulled their money out of Russia. Today, this once powerful nation is only a shadow of what it once was.

SECTION 4 REVIEW On a separate sheet of paper, write the word from the Word Bank that completes each sentence.

WORD BANK

Brezhnev

Glasnost

Gorbachev

Khrushchev

Yeltsin

1) _____ became the Soviet leader in 1953 and made the government less cruel.

2) In 1964, the Soviet leader _____ punished anyone who spoke out against the government.

3) _____ introduced a policy of perestroika, which changed the Soviet economy.

4) _____ became a hero by putting down a police and army coup.

5) _____ helped to bring about openness in the Soviet Union.

What do you think ❓

What should the Russian government do to make its new country successful?

◆**Solidarity**
The name of the Polish shipbuilder's union that went out on strike in 1980

Strike
The act of refusing to work until certain demands are met

Eastern Europe revolted against Communist rule many times: Hungary in 1956; Czechoslovakia in 1968; and Poland in 1956, 1979, and 1981. All these rebellions failed. Then, in 1989, the people of Eastern Europe rose up against their Communist leaders and forced them out.

How Did Hungary Cut a Hole in the Iron Curtain?

Since Gorbachev had encouraged a policy of glasnost, the Hungarian government began to allow its citizens more freedom of speech and assembly. Then, on May 2, 1989, Hungarian soldiers cut down the barbed-wire fence between Austria and Hungary.

This 150-mile fence and its minefield had been built in 1969. On one side of the fence was the Communist nation of Hungary. On the other was the democratic nation of Austria.

With the fence gone, people could travel freely to Austria. Soon thousands of people from East Germany, Poland, and Czechoslovakia moved through Hungary to freedom in the West.

In October 1989, communism came to an end in Hungary. One reformer said, "Communism does not work. We must start again at zero." Hungarian leaders tried to create a democracy with a constitution.

How Did Communists in Poland Give Up Power?

In 1980, a group of workers in a shipyard in Gdansk, Poland, went on **strike.** That is, they refused to work in an attempt to improve their working conditions. (Striking was not legal in Poland.) The workers formed a non-Communist union. These workers wanted Poland's Communist government to recognize their union as legal. They called their group "**Solidarity**," or unity.

For eight years, Solidarity struggled to bring about reform. Then, in 1989, the Communist Polish government agreed to share power. In free elections, the citizens of Poland elected representatives. Solidarity won a huge victory.

When Did the Government of East Germany Fall?

In 1989, East Germans took to the streets demanding reform. Soon, all the members of the East German government **resigned,** or gave up their jobs. Then, the new government said that its citizens could travel anywhere!

Thousands of Germans rushed to the **Berlin Wall.** (Since 1961, this wall had divided the people of East and West Berlin.) People hammered down the wall. They danced, cried, and cheered. Then, on October 3, 1990, East and West Germany unified under the West German government. For 45 years, they had been divided; now they were united again.

Who Led the Serbs Into Ethnic Cleansing?

Like the Soviet Union, Yugoslavia was made up of many different ethnic groups. In 1990, Slobodan Milosevic began to lead the Serbian republic of Yugoslavia into war with the other republics. He began a policy of **ethnic cleansing.**

German citizens hammered down the Berlin Wall in 1989.

◆Tariff
*A tax that
countries put on
goods they import
or export*

That is, his Christian Serbian soldiers killed nearly 250,000 Bosnian Muslims because they were not Serbs. Finally, a treaty was signed that divided Bosnia into two parts.

Milosevic next began a war in Kosovo. Nearly 90 percent of its people are ethnic Albanians. Because they were not Serbs, Milosevic tried to force them to leave the country. Hundreds of thousands of refugees fled Kosovo.

On March 24, 1999, NATO began air strikes against Yugoslavia. NATO hoped that air strikes would force Milosevic to let Kosovo govern itself. The air strikes stopped after a few weeks. But the whole area in and around Yugoslavia remains a hot spot in world affairs.

What Steps Has Europe Taken Toward Union?

After World War II, people in Europe wanted to get rid of trade barriers and **tariffs** among its many countries. A tariff is a tax that countries put on goods they import or export. In 1952, six European nations agreed to create a tariff-free

Secretary of State Madeleine Albright visits American troops in Kosovo in 1999.

Former Soviet Occupied Countries

Currency
The form of money a country uses

market for European coal and steel products. They succeeded. They met again in 1992 and agreed to reduce trade barriers even more and to create one form of **currency** (money) for Europe.

For many years, the French have called their money the franc. The Germans have called theirs the mark. Now, 11 European countries share the euro. On January 1, 1999, it became the new currency for Austria, Belgium, Finland, France, Germany, Ireland, Italy, Luxembourg, the Netherlands, Portugal, and Spain.

This is a big step toward creating a united Europe. As time passes, the euro will replace the currency of each European country. This will unite Europe because everyone will use one currency—just as people do in the United States.

Why Did NATO Expand?

After World War II ended, 12 countries formed NATO. These countries agreed to support each other in case the Soviet Union attacked them. Soon, other countries joined the alliance.

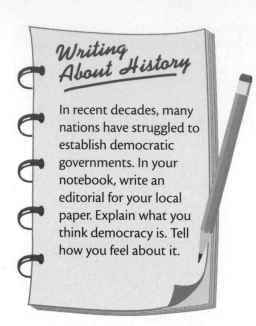

Then in 1991, the Soviet Union collapsed. Many people then wanted to get rid of NATO. Others wanted to expand it. Its supporters thought that NATO could bring democracy to all of Europe. Since that time, NATO has expanded. Poland, Hungary, and the Czech Republic—all of which used to be under Soviet control—joined NATO in 1999.

But as more countries join NATO, Russia, which is not a NATO member, has become an outsider. NATO has said that it will keep **nuclear weapons** out of Eastern Europe. (The atomic bomb and missiles are examples of nuclear weapons.) NATO has also promised to share its plans and policies with Russia.

◆Nuclear weapon
A powerful weapon, such as an atomic bomb or missile

SECTION 5 REVIEW On a separate sheet of paper, write answers to these questions.

1) Why was cutting the barbed-wire fence in Hungary important for the people behind the Iron Curtain?

2) What was Solidarity in Poland?

3) To what did the tearing down of the Berlin Wall lead?

4) What is one way in which the European countries are uniting?

5) What can NATO do for the European countries that used to be controlled by Russia?

What do you think

Would it be a good idea for Russia to become a member of NATO? Why or why not?

◆Campesino
A poor peasant who works the land, but does not own it

◆Western Hemisphere
The western half of Earth

Latin America exports its oil, tin, copper, and iron ore. But when the price drops on an export, governments must borrow money. Then they use all the money they earn from their exports to pay back what they borrowed. Depending on just a few exports causes problems for Latin America.

Why Are the Campesinos Demanding Land Reform?

Another problem in Latin America is the distance between the rich and the poor. Nearly 600 million people live in Latin America. But the majority of them are poor peasants, landless farmworkers, and factory workers. A small, rich group controls most of the money. This group includes the landowners, factory owners, and military leaders.

In Paraguay, a few rich landowners control 80 percent of the farmland. This is true in most of the rest of Latin America, too. Many poor people, called **campesinos,** work this land, but they do not own it.

In many countries, these campesinos are demanding land reform. They want the government to break up the large farms and divide the land among the poor. Land reform has been most successful in Cuba, Mexico, Nicaragua, and Peru.

What Has the United States Taken From Latin America?

In Chapter 21, you read about the struggle for freedom in Latin America. During that time, the United States encouraged wars of independence in Latin America. In 1823, President James Monroe warned European nations to stay out of the **Western Hemisphere**—the western half of Earth.

Then, in 1846, Mexico and the United States went to war. At the end of the war, Mexico had to give California and all the land between Texas and California to the United States. After a war in 1898, the United States seized Puerto Rico.

Next, the United States encouraged the people of Panama to revolt. In that way, the United States could build a canal there. The United States wanted this canal so it could sail its warships from the Atlantic to the Pacific Ocean.

Women buying and selling food in Guatemala, Central America.

Baseball Around the World

Do you love *béisbol*? Do you play *besoboru*? These are the words for baseball in Spanish and Japanese. Baseball has been popular in countries around the world for more than a hundred years. Players from countries such as Cuba and Japan now play for American major league teams.

How did baseball spread outside the United States? American missionaries took it to Japan in the 1870s. During the Spanish-American War (1898), American soldiers brought the game to the Philippines.

The Japanese saw baseball as a new kind of martial art. By the early 1900s, it was the country's most popular sport. American major league players toured Japan in the 1920s and 1930s. Baseball then spread to Korea and Taiwan.

Baseball is played in Mexico, the Caribbean, and Central America, too. Tours and spring training also helped introduce it there. Each year, national teams from these areas play in the Caribbean Series.

◆North American Free Trade Agreement (NAFTA)
An agreement that links the economies of Canada, Mexico, and the United States

How Has the United States Helped Latin America?

But the United States has also helped Latin America by giving it large sums of money in foreign aid. Now, some nations of the Western Hemisphere are joining together to get rid of trade barriers like tariffs. The first of their agreements was the **North American Free Trade Agreement (NAFTA).** It links together the economies of Canada, Mexico, and the United States.

SECTION 6 REVIEW On a separate sheet of paper, write *True* if the statement is true or *False* if the statement is not true. Make each false statement true by changing the underlined word.

1) Landowners, factory <u>workers,</u> and military leaders control most of the money in Latin America.

2) Latin America <u>imports</u> only a few natural resources like oil and iron ore.

3) Land reform has been most successful in Cuba, <u>Mexico,</u> Nicaragua, and Peru.

4) In 1823, President <u>Monroe</u> warned European countries to stay out of Latin America.

5) The North American Free Trade Agreement links together the economies of <u>Canada,</u> Mexico, and the United States.

What do you think

What should the United States do to improve the life of the poor in Latin America?

Extraordinary Times

In 1989, the Czech people began peaceful protests against the Communist government. These actions brought about the "velvet revolution," a revolution without violence.

Vaclav Havel, a well-known Czech playwright, was a leader in this struggle. He was jailed several times because he supported democracy and

Vaclav Havel

human rights. In December 1989, he was elected president of the new democratic Czechoslovakia. (It would later split into two new countries: the Czech Republic and Slovakia.) In February 1990, Havel spoke before the U.S. Congress. This excerpt is part of his speech.

When they arrested me on October 27, I was living in a country ruled by the most conservative Communist government in Europe. . . . Today, less than four months later, I am speaking to you as the representative of a country that has set out on the road to democracy, a country where there is complete freedom of speech, which is getting ready for free elections, and which wants to create a prosperous market economy and its own foreign policy. . . .

We are living in very extraordinary times. The human face of the world is changing so rapidly that none of the familiar political speedometers are adequate.

We playwrights, who have to cram a whole human life or an entire historical era in a 2-hour play, can scarcely understand this rapidity ourselves. And if it gives us trouble, think of the trouble it must give to political scientists, who spend their whole lives studying the realm of the

probable. And have even less experience with the realm of the improbable than us, the playwrights. . . .

As long as people are people, democracy in the full sense of the word will always be no more than an ideal; one may approach it as one would a horizon, in ways that may be better or worse, but it can never be fully attained. In this sense you are merely approaching democracy. . . . But you have one great advantage. You have been approaching democracy uninterruptedly for more than 200 years, and your journey . . . has never been disrupted by a totalitarian system. Czechs and Slovaks . . . have approached democracy for a mere 20 years, between the two world wars, and now for the $3^1/_2$ months since the 17th of November last year.

. . . I will end where I began; history has accelerated. I believe that once again it will be the human mind that will notice this acceleration, give it a name, and transform those words into deeds.

Source Reading Wrap-Up

1) What recent changes in Czechoslovakia does Havel list?
2) Why does he say these are "extraordinary times"?
3) What comparison does Havel make between playwrights and political scientists?
4) According to Havel, what keeps people from reaching complete democracy?
5) How is Czechoslovakia's experience with democracy different from that of the U.S.?

Fall of an Empire

Some historians call the Soviet Union the world's last empire. In 1917, the Russian Revolution ended the empire of the czars. The Soviet Union, though, took over its territory. Officially, the country's name was the Union of Soviet Socialist Republics. It had 13 republics, based somewhat on ethnic groupings. The Russians made up the largest and most powerful group.

Shortly before World War II, the Soviet leader Joseph Stalin made a deal with Nazi Germany. In return for Russian neutrality, the Soviet Union got Latvia, Lithuania, and Estonia. After World War II, most of Eastern Europe also came under Soviet control.

In 1985, Mikhail Gorbachev became the Soviet leader. He believed that the Soviet system would have to change to survive. Gorbachev offered a program of economic "restructuring," or perestroika. He called for political openness, or glasnost. As this policy developed, it gave the republics more independence. Western leaders welcomed these reforms. Hard-line Communist Party leaders were furious.

Gorbachev's reforms changed Eastern Europe first. Events were quick and dramatic. In 1989, Poland and Czechoslovakia held democratic elections. The Berlin Wall between East and West Berlin fell. Then Germany was reunited in late 1990. Later, other Iron Curtain countries formed democratic governments.

Inside the Soviet Union, events also moved quickly. In 1990, Latvia, Lithuania, and Estonia declared their independence. That same year, reform parties were also set up. A reformer named Boris Yeltsin also quit the Communist Party. In 1991, the Russian Republic held its first free election. The people elected Yeltsin president.

A modern Russian family.

In August 1991, some hard-line Communists plotted to get rid of Gorbachev. He and his family were on vacation near the Black Sea. Armed men surrounded his country house. In Moscow, security troops tried to take control. Tanks blocked the streets. They surrounded the parliament building. But thousands of Russians who wanted democracy protested. Yeltsin climbed on a tank and encouraged them. The crisis soon ended, but the Soviet Union was crumbling. In late August, the Soviet legislature took away the Communist Party's power. Then even more republics broke away from the Soviet Union.

In December 1991, Russia, the Ukraine, and Belarus formed a new alliance. It was called the Commonwealth of Independent States (CIS). Russia took over running most of the Soviet central government. Then on December 25, Gorbachev resigned. The huge red Soviet flag over the Kremlin came down. The Soviet Union, formed in 1922, was over.

Spotlight Story Wrap-Up

1) What was the structure of the former Soviet Union?
2) How did Lithuania become a Soviet republic?
3) What reforms did Gorbachev introduce?
4) How did Gorbachev's reforms affect Eastern Europe?
5) How did Boris Yeltsin become president of Russia?

➡ Economies in African nations are growing quickly. Starvation occurs and people in cities face poor living conditions.

➡ Israel made peace with Egypt (1978) and Jordan (1994). Conflicts continued in the Middle East. Palestinian self-rule was a major issue.

➡ The Shah of Iran tried to modernize the country but used harsh methods. A religious leader, Ayatollah Khomeini, led a revolution against him in 1979.

➡ Iranians and Iraqis follow different branches of Islam and belong to different ethnic groups. Iraq invaded Iran in 1980, starting an eight-year war. The war threatened world oil supplies.

➡ In 1990, Iraqi leader Saddam Hussein invaded Kuwait to take control of its oil fields. In the Persian Gulf War, an international military force defeated Iraq.

➡ After Mao Zedong's death, Chinese leader Deng Xiaoping made economic changes. He encouraged private business and foreign investment. In 1989 in Tiananmen Square, soldiers attacked students. They were marching for democracy and human rights.

➡ Japan has the world's second largest economy. The economies of other Asian nations, such as South Korea and Singapore, have also grown. An economic crisis hit Asian nations in 1997. Many banks and businesses failed.

➡ Mikhail Gorbachev became the Soviet leader in 1985. He allowed more freedom (glasnost), reformed the economy (perestroika), and moved toward democracy.

➡ In 1991, the Soviet Union broke into independent republics. Boris Yeltsin was elected president of Russia. He has tried to continue economic reforms, but crime and poverty have hurt many Russians.

➡ Changes in the Soviet Union affected Eastern Europe. In 1989, people in Hungary, Poland, and East Germany overthrew Communist governments. The Berlin Wall came down, and Germany was reunited.

➡ The breakup of Yugoslavia brought conflicts. Serbian leader Slobodan Milosevic went to war against other ethnic groups in Bosnia and Kosovo.

➡ Western European nations worked toward economic unity. They adopted a new currency, the euro.

➡ Land reform is an issue in many Latin American nations. Most people are poor. Mexico, Canada, and the United States signed the North American Free Trade Agreement (NAFTA) to encourage trade.

Comprehension: Identifying Facts

On a separate sheet of paper, use the words from the Word Bank to complete each sentence.

WORD BANK

ayatollah

campesinos

currency

ethnic cleansing

fundamentalist

glasnost

nuclear

perestroika

tariff

urbanization

1) Because many people are flocking to the cities, Africa faces rapid _____.

2) The name for a religious leader in Iran is _____.

3) A _____ likes traditional religious values and rejects much of modern life.

4) Gorbachev introduced _____, or openness, to the Soviet Union.

5) Gorbachev also introduced _____, which was a looser economic policy.

6) Milosevic introduced _____ in Bosnia.

7) NATO has agreed not to put _____ weapons in Eastern Europe.

8) Several European countries have gotten rid of the _____, or tax, on certain imports and exports.

9) Several European countries have also agreed to use one _____, or form of money.

10) The _____ in Latin America are demanding land reform.

Comprehension: Multiple Choice

On a separate sheet of paper, write the letter of the answer that correctly completes each sentence.

1) Some Iranians took 52 Americans hostage in _____.

    a. 1978   c. 1989

    b. 1979   d. 1999

2) The United States, Britain, and France fought the Persian Gulf War in _____.

    a. 1990   c. 1995

    b. 1991   d. 1999

3) Chinese students protested in Tiananmen Square in
_____.

    a. 1985   c. 1992

    b. 1989   d. 1998

4) The Soviet Union came to an end in _____.

    a. 1980   c. 1990

    b. 1986   d. 1991

5) NATO began air strikes against Yugoslavia and Slobodan
Milosevic in _____.

    a. 1990   c. 1997

    b. 1993   d. 1999

Comprehension: Understanding Main Ideas

On a separate sheet of paper, write the answers to the
following questions using complete sentences, or statements.

1) What is one problem that Africans face today?

2) What is one problem that people in the Middle East face
today?

3) What is one problem that people in Asia face today?

Critical Thinking: Write Your Opinion

1) In Chapter 24, you read about the Russian Revolution of
1917. Which is more important—that revolution or the
Russian Revolution of 1991? Explain your answer.

2) A small minority of people have most of the money in
Latin America. What would you do to change that?

Test-Taking Tip   Make sure you have the same number of answers on
your paper as there are items on the test.

A New Century Begins

1990 to the Present

This is the last chapter of your world history book. In this text, you have traveled through time from ancient India, China, and Sumeria to modern nations. Now, in this final chapter, you will discover the global village that is Earth. You will see how the Internet and mass communication link the nations of our global village. Then you will learn how modern technology can be harmful. You will also learn about the joining together of the world economies. Finally, you will see what farming and industry have done to the environment. This chapter shows you what life is like today.

Goals for Learning

▶ To define the terms *global village* and *mass communication*
▶ To explain how technology and energy help build a global village
▶ To explain why some people worry about new technology
▶ To describe the economic interdependence of modern industrial nations and developing countries
▶ To explain why global trade is important
▶ To explain some environmental problems the world faces

1990s
Internet expands the use of computers

1997
Recession begins in Thailand and spreads worldwide

1990   1995   2000

1992
International leaders meet to discuss environmental problems

1997
International leaders meet once again to discuss environmental problems

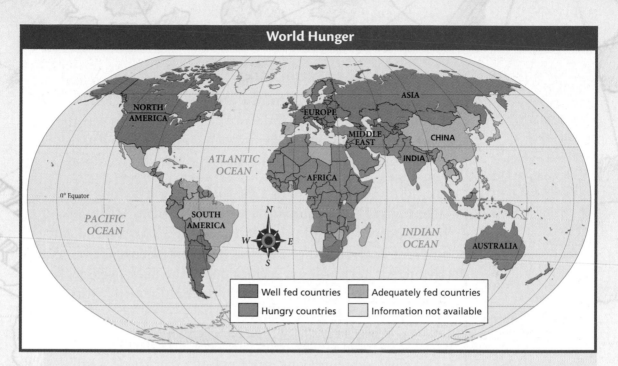

World Hunger

NORTH AMERICA · ASIA · EUROPE · MIDDLE EAST · CHINA · INDIA · ATLANTIC OCEAN · AFRICA · 0° Equator · PACIFIC OCEAN · SOUTH AMERICA · INDIAN OCEAN · AUSTRALIA

N W E S

Well fed countries   **Adequately fed countries**
Hungry countries   **Information not available**

Geography Skills

Many countries of the world have enough food to feed their people. But some countries do not. The climate is much hotter and drier near the equator than it is farther away, so that is where growing food is difficult. Many of these hungry nations have deserts in their land. This world map shows world hunger.

Study the map and answer the questions:

1) Which continent has the most serious problem with hunger?

2) What are three places where people are well fed?

3) On which coast of South America is there a hunger problem?

4) Do people in China have more or less food than people in Australia?

5) Do people in India have more or less food than people in North America?

Employ
To hire someone to work; to use something

◆**Global village**
The term used to describe the sharing of ideas, cultures, and traditions throughout the world

◆**Multinational corporation**
A company that hires people and has business interests around the world

Technology
The use of science to do practical things

Today, Earth seems smaller than it used to be. Its physical size is the same as it was for the ancient Romans. The distance between Spain and Cuba is the same as it was for Christopher Columbus. The miles from France to Russia are still the same as they were for Napoleon. So what has changed?

What Has Made the World Into a Global Village?

Today, people around the world share ideas, art, music, and different ways of living. This has happened because of advances in **technology.** Technology is the use of science to do practical things. Because of this technology, the world is changing into a **global village.**

What is a global village? The word *global* comes from the word *globe,* which means our Earth. As you know, a village is a place where a few hundred people live and work together. People who live in a village know most, if not all, their neighbors. Villagers share ideas and traditions. They share their lives. A global village, then, is a term used to describe the sharing of ideas, cultures, and traditions around the world.

We all live in Earth's global village. This picture shows Tokyo, Japan.

Today, for the first time in history, modern technology—motion pictures, computers, video cameras, CD players, television—allows people from around the world to share their lives. Technology also enables businesses to **employ,** or hire, workers all over the world. We call these companies **multinational corporations.**

Technology links the whole world together. Technology makes the globe we live on into one village—a global village. We have begun to share our cultures around the globe.

How Has Mass Communication Created Our Global Village?

Mass communication is one of the major reasons that the world is becoming a global village. **Mass communication** is messages directed at many people. Businesses and private or governmental groups prepare these messages.

Newspaper and magazine **advertising** provides mass communication in print. Advertising is the selling or the announcing of something. Motion pictures, television, radio, and musical recordings provide mass communication **electronically.** That is, people produce them by using inventions that run on electricity.

Today, electronic communications connect people everywhere. Since the end of World War II, American television, movies, music, fast food, and clothing styles have helped to shape this new global culture. Around the world, many business people and government officials speak English.

But the global culture has also changed the United States. Music from Asia, Africa, and Latin America influence American popular music. Americans eat foods from around the world.

Communication in History

Your Phone Is Ringing

You hear them ringing everywhere. Cell phones ring in pockets and purses. People talk on the street and in their cars. Regular telephone messages move through wires and cables. Cell phones, however, send messages through the air. They travel much like radio waves. A World War II invention inspired the cell phone. It was the "walkie-talkie" used by soldiers in combat. After the war, inventors worked to adapt this technology. The first commercial cell phone clicked on in 1983.

Cellular phone technology spread quickly. Wireless networks put a low-power transmission tower in each area, or "cell." As the phone user travels, the call moves from cell to cell. Over longer distances, global networks use satellites to relay messages.

Cell phones are more than a convenience. People in a dangerous situation can call for help. In some places around the world, telephone wires did not reach distant towns. Cell phones have brought phone service there.

How Has the Internet Linked Our World?

The computer started a technological revolution as important as the Industrial Revolution. People use computers in businesses, schools, and homes. They are used to store information, figure math problems, and write things.

In the 1990s, the **Internet** expanded the use of computers. The Internet is an **international** computer network. (That is, the information on it goes around the world. It involves different nations.) This computer network connects millions of computer users all over the world. However, for some time, only universities and governmental agencies used the Internet.

All this changed with the development of the **World Wide Web.** It made the Internet easier to use and opened it to businesses and individuals. Because of the Internet, the whole world is linked electronically for the first time in history. E-mail lets us write messages to people anywhere in the world almost instantly.

How Does Space Exploration Create Our Global Village?

The Soviet Union placed *Sputnik,* the first space satellite, into orbit around Earth in October 1957. Today, dozens of communication satellites send and receive radio, television, and telephone signals. Because of this, people around the globe can see television shows produced thousands of miles away. They can talk on the telephone to friends who live half way around the globe.

On July 20, 1969, nearly a billion people watched on television as Neil Armstrong stepped from his spaceship. As his foot touched the moon's surface, Armstrong said, "That's one small step for a man, but a giant leap for mankind." An American was the first person to land on the moon, but Americans do not own it. The nations of the world have agreed that the moon and all of outer space are international areas.

◆**International**
Among nations; around the world; involving different nations

◆**Internet**
An international computer network

◆**World Wide Web**
A network of information on the Internet open to businesses and individuals

---

THE POPULATION EXPLOSION

At the time of the Roman Empire, the population of the world was 200 million. Around the year 1800, the population reached a billion. In 1920, it reached 2 billion. In 1960, it reached 3 billion. In 1975, it reached 4 billion. In 1988, it reached 5 billion. In 1999, it reached 6 billion.

Do you notice how the population is growing faster? The time between a billion and two billion was 120 years. The time between five billion and six billion was only 11 years. Scientists have calculated that by 2025, the population of the world will be 9 billion. By the year 2200, it will be 138 billion! This will leave only one square foot of land for each human being to live on. The earth will not support such a huge population.

In the past, increases in the food supply and control of disease allowed people to live longer. Today, however, the food supply is not growing as fast as the population is. The world's food supply is increasing at about 1 percent a year. The world's population, however, has been increasing at the rate of 1.5 percent a year.

In 1965, President Lyndon Johnson said that the most important thing we had to do was to work for peace on earth. But the next most important challenge to the human family was the "race between the food supply and the population increase." President Johnson said that the race was being lost.

Since the 1960s, scientists have been looking for ways to increase the food supply. Some have worked to make plants disease-free. Others want to "farm" the oceans for animal and plant life that will feed the world. As time moves on, our growing population will continue to be a major problem for the governments of the world.

Russia and the United States are now working together to build a permanent International Space Station. For more than 30 years, the two countries raced against one another into space. But now these countries and 14 others are building a space station. When completed, it will be twice the size of a football field and cost $60 billion.

This is the biggest project in the history of science and technology. The crew of the International Space Station will become an international community. They will live and work miles above planet Earth.

"Space: the Final Frontier . . ."

In the 1500s, explorers needed courage and imagination. They sailed to new parts of the world. They had few maps to guide them. New technology helped, however. Better instruments measured speed and location. Shipbuilders designed sturdy ocean-going ships.

Nearly 500 years later, explorers traveled to new worlds in outer space. Courage and technology were still important. In April 1961, a Soviet cosmonaut became the first person in space. The first American space flight came a month later. From there, space exploration has reached greater and greater successes with many new types of spacecraft. Several unmanned ships have been sent deep into outer space. In 1996, *Pathfinder* landed on Mars and took many amazing photos of its surface. Some day, people may even live on the moon or in space stations.

SECTION 1 REVIEW Choose the letter of the answer that correctly completes each sentence. Write your answer on a separate sheet of paper.

1) Mass _____ is messages sent to many people.
- a. global
- b. multinational
- c. international
- d. communication

2) Companies that employ workers all over the world are _____.
- a. multinational
- b. technology
- c. mass communication
- d. global village

3) American _____ help shape the global culture.
- a. movies
- b. fast-food
- c. clothing
- d. all of the above

4) The _____ is an international computer network.
- a. technology
- b. Internet
- c. culture
- d. global village

5) A new International Space Station is being built by _____ nations.
- a. 2
- b. 14
- c. 16
- d. 25

What do you think ?

What is your favorite form of mass communication and why?

Energy
Power that comes from wood, coal, electricity, oil, the sun, water, and wind; makes machines work; and produces heat

Environment
The land, sea, and air of our world

Photoelectric cell
An invention that can produce electricity from light

Pollution
The act of making the air, water, or land unclean and unhealthy

Progress in technology depends on **energy.** Energy is power that comes from things such as oil, wood, coal, electricity, the sun, water, and wind. Energy makes machines work. It produces heat. Without energy, no work can be done.

What Have Coal and Oil Done to Our Global Village?

As you know from Chapter 19, coal was a source of energy in the nineteenth century. It produced energy for factories, homes, and steam locomotives. Oil has been the major source of energy in the twentieth century. It runs our factories, heats our homes, and powers our cars, trucks, trains, and planes.

But the burning of coal and oil has also created serious problems for our world. Air and water **pollution** creates health problems for humans. Pollution occurs when air, water, or land become unclean and unhealthy. Pollution threatens the life of many plants and animals. It threatens our **environment**—the land, sea, and air of our world.

What Is Wrong With Using Nuclear Energy?

During the first part of the twenty-first century, scientists must look for a clean source of energy. They must find one that will not hurt our environment. Scientists once thought that nuclear power was a clean source of energy. But it produces deadly waste products.

Also, people have died from accidents at nuclear power plants in the United States, Russia, and India. Even so, nuclear power plants produce about 20 percent of the electricity in the United States, Japan, and Great Britain. In France, 70 percent of the nation's electricity comes from nuclear power.

Some scientists look to wind and water as clean sources of energy. Technology can use both of them to produce electricity. The **photoelectric cell** is an invention that can produce electricity from light. Today, many businesses and

Is nuclear energy the answer to the world's energy needs? Although it is used in many countries, it can be dangerous. This photo shows a destroyed nuclear power plant in Chernobyl, Ukraine. It exploded in 1986, killing 31 people.

homes use photoelectric cells to create electricity. Engineers have designed cars that run on electricity produced by photoelectric cells.

How Has Technology Changed Medicine?

Doctors now remove a person's heart and fix it. They replace livers and hips. They sew fingers, arms, and legs onto a person who has lost them in an accident. Technology makes all this possible.

Engineers have invented new machines to help doctors figure out what diseases people have.

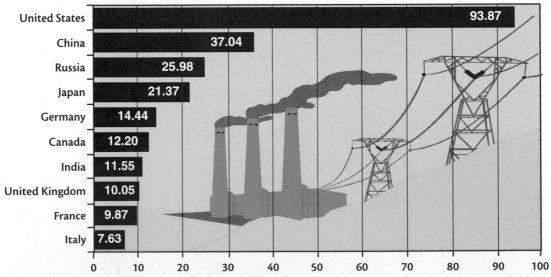

The World's Major Consumers of Energy
Numbers indicate quadrillion British thermal units (Btu).

Country	Btu
United States	93.87
China	37.04
Russia	25.98
Japan	21.37
Germany	14.44
Canada	12.20
India	11.55
United Kingdom	10.05
France	9.87
Italy	7.63

GRAPH STUDY This graph shows the countries that use the most energy. Which country uses the most energy? Why do you think this is true?

One machine helps doctors see the inside of the body. Doctors use **lasers** to cut and seal wounds. A laser is a tool that produces high-energy beams of light.

What Is the Electronic Superhighway?

The **electronic superhighway** sends information from telephones, television, and computers. This information is now reaching many areas of the world. As this happens, cultures around the world influence one another. Today, some electronic programs translate one language into another. People can communicate even though they do not speak or write the same language. This "electronic culture" is going to change our global village.

Can New Technology Harm Our Global Village?

In the early part of the twentieth century, people predicted that technology would solve many of the world's problems. Electricity would provide the energy for many labor-saving machines. People would work only a few hours a week. Everyone would have an automobile. Airplanes would fill the sky.

At the time, people did not see how the military would use technology to fight World War I and II. They did not see what technology would do to our environment. Today, some people think that we are losing our freedom. People can find out too much information about us. Every time we use a credit card, a computer files the information away. Computers also contain information about medicines we take. The government collects information about us and stores it on computers.

Electronic superhighway
A communication network that sends data from telephones, televisions, and computers

Laser
A tool that produces high-energy beams of light

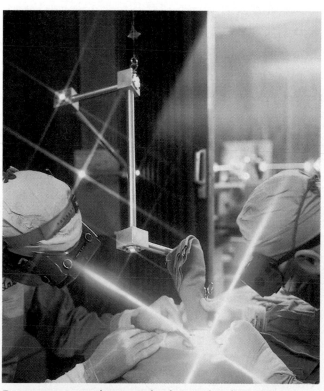

Doctors now use lasers and other technology to treat people. Medicine is one area that technology has influenced greatly.

If you've ever heard of a black hole, you know something about Stephen Hawking. This physicist has made major discoveries about the universe. A black hole, for instance, is a region in space with intense gravity. The collapse of a huge star would have caused it. Not even light can escape a black hole. Hawking's main field is quantum physics, the study of units that make up the atom.

Hawking is a professor of mathematics at Cambridge University in England. Because of a disease of the nervous system, he uses a wheelchair. He speaks with the help of a computer.

But who will decide how to use all this information? How can we control what people know about us? Does having this information give some people control over us? If technology can cause harm, should we limit its development? Who will decide what that limit is? These important questions have no easy answers.

SECTION 2 REVIEW On a separate sheet of paper, write answers to these questions using complete sentences.

1) What has been the primary source of energy in the twentieth century?

2) What is one example of a clean source of energy?

3) What is one improvement that technology has brought to medicine?

4) How does the electronic superhighway affect our global village?

5) What is one thing that worries people today about new technology?

What do you think

Are you worried about new technology? Explain your answer.

◆Developing
country
*A nation that is
slowly developing
its industry and
economy*

◆Free-market
economy
*An economy in
which
manufacturers try
to satisfy
consumers' wants
and needs*

Interdependent
*Depending on one
another*

◆Northern
Hemisphere
*The northern half
of Earth*

◆Southern
Hemisphere
*The southern half
of Earth*

◆Subsistence
farming
*A type of farming
in which people
grow crops mostly
for their own use,
not to sell*

The global village is **interdependent.** What happens in one nation affects every other nation. For example, when the price of oil from the Middle East goes up, manufacturers in the United States have to spend more to produce goods. Consumers then pay more when they buy these goods.

What Is a Free-Market Economy?

Most rich countries have a **free-market economy.** In such an economy, manufacturers satisfy the wants and needs of consumers. The government lets factories produce what they like.

The **Northern Hemisphere** contains most of the successful free-market countries. Among these are the United States, Canada, Germany, France, and Great Britain. Asia's strongest economy is in Japan. These countries have well-organized farming and industrial systems and make use of technology.

What Problems Do Developing Countries Have?

Economists call many nations in the **Southern Hemisphere** the **developing countries.** That is, they are slowly developing their industries and economies. In these poor nations, most people do **subsistence farming.** This means that they grow crops mostly for their own use. They do not sell what they grow.

These developing nations face many problems. First, they are overpopulated. This leads to hunger, pollution, and political unrest. It has also led to the destruction of the Amazon rain forest and the overuse of croplands in Asia. Second, in many developing countries, students attend school for only two or three years. Only about half the people in these countries can read and write. Third, industrialization requires money. Most poor developing countries have only raw materials to sell. (The industrialized countries set the cost for these raw materials.) They have no consumer goods to trade to other countries. But poor

countries want consumer goods, so they buy more than they sell. Money flows out of these countries.

What Is a Recession?

◆**Recession**
An economic slowdown

In Chapter 29, you learned that in June 1997 the money supply of Thailand collapsed. As you recall, the crisis spread to South Korea, Indonesia, Malaysia, and Russia. Soon, banks and businesses went bankrupt. People lost their jobs and had no money to buy things. Because no one was buying consumer goods, even more businesses closed down. Economists call this a **recession,** or an economic slowdown.

How Did the Recession Affect Japan and the United States?

Many people in Japan lost their jobs because of the recession. This is important because Japan is the economic engine for Asia. It keeps things moving there.

The recession also affected the United States. People in other countries had no money to buy goods from the United States. U.S. companies lost money and some workers lost jobs. However, one good thing also happened as a result of the recession. The bankrupted Asian companies no longer had a need for oil to supply energy to their factories. The

Major World Economic Groups

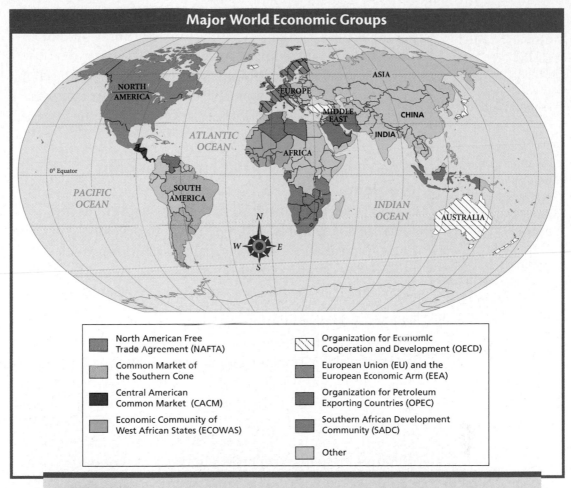

Legend:

- North American Free Trade Agreement (NAFTA)
- Common Market of the Southern Cone
- Central American Common Market (CACM)
- Economic Community of West African States (ECOWAS)
- Organization for Economic Cooperation and Development (OECD)
- European Union (EU) and the European Economic Arm (EEA)
- Organization for Petroleum Exporting Countries (OPEC)
- Southern African Development Community (SADC)
- Other

MAP STUDY This map shows eight major economic groups in today's world. The North American Free Trade Agreement (NAFTA) relates to countries on which continent? In what areas of the world are the Organization for Petroleum Exporting Countries (OPEC) located?

Compete
To try to do better than someone else

Middle East lowered its oil price. This meant that the United States had to pay less for oil, so gasoline prices in the United States went down.

Who Is to Blame for the Recession?

Some people blame multinational corporations for the recession. These companies manufacture and sell goods in many countries. They control a growing share of world trade. They **compete,** or work against, businesses in developing countries.

◆International
Monetary Fund
(IMF)
*An organization
that has a supply of
money to give to
needy members*
◆World Bank
*An international
group that directs
money from the
industrialized
nations to the
developing
countries*

Businesses in developing countries cannot win when they are up against a foreign multinational corporation. For example, a business might make a product that a multinational makes, too. But the multinational can sell its product cheaper. Multinationals can move their factories from one developing country to another to get the lowest cost for labor and materials.

Who Helps Nations That Have Economic Problems?

For 50 years, industrialized nations have given money, food, medicine, tools, and machinery to developing nations. Each year, the 21 most industrialized nations provide billions of dollars to roughly 182 nations. In one third of these countries, people live on less than two dollars a day.

The industrialized nations send their money through two international organizations: the **World Bank** and the **International Monetary Fund (IMF).** The World Bank directs money from industrialized nations to developing ones. It helps build dams, mines, roads, and bridges. It also helps to improve education, health, and the environment. The IMF is an organization of 182 nations. It has a supply of money to help its members in times of economic crisis.

SECTION 3 REVIEW On a separate sheet of paper, write the word from the Word Bank that completes each sentence.

WORD BANK

free-market

interdependent

overpopulation

recession

subsistence

1) The world's richest countries generally have a _____ economy.

2) People of less developed countries are often _____ farmers.

3) Economists call an economic slowdown a _____.

4) Nations of the world are _____, because what happens in one affects all the others.

5) Many developing countries face the problem of _____, which has led to hunger and pollution.

What do you think ?

Would Earth be in better shape if countries did not depend on one another? Explain your answer.

◆Fossil fuel
Fuel made from coal, oil, or natural gas

◆Global warming
The heating up of Earth from the burning of wood, coal, oil, and gasoline

In the 1960s, astronauts went into space. They took pictures that showed Earth as a beautiful, blue planet. But today, satellite pictures show polluted air and water.

What Pollutes Our Air and Water?

Air pollution affects our health, and it may change our climate. The burning of coal, oil, and natural gas causes most air pollution. These kinds of fuels are called **fossil fuels.** We also have water pollution. Farming and industry have poisoned lakes and rivers.

Farmers around the world now use fertilizers to make crops grow and pesticides to kill bugs. Rain makes these chemicals run off into rivers, lakes, and oceans. Then they end up in the bodies of fish and other animals. People who eat these animals or drink the water get sick. The problem is most serious in developing countries where many people cannot get clean water.

We all have to work to keep our environment clean. Farming, industry, and carelessness cause water pollution.

What Is Global Warming?

Since the 1980s, scientists have warned us about **global warming.** They believe that gases from cars and factories are heating up the earth. Burning wood, coal, oil, or natural gas releases carbon dioxide. Trees remove this gas from the air and release oxygen into the air for us to breathe. But overpopulated countries are now cutting down forests and jungles to provide farmland and firewood.

Many people fear that this will increase the carbon dioxide in the air and raise Earth's temperature. This might change rainfall patterns around

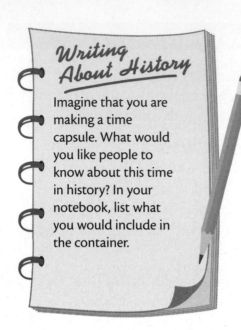

Writing About History

Imagine that you are making a time capsule. What would you like people to know about this time in history? In your notebook, list what you would include in the container.

the world. Too much rain would cause floods; too little rain would cause droughts and famine. Scientists also believe that the polar ice caps are melting. This will raise the sea levels and flood cities like New York, which are on the coast. If this happens, two billion people around the world would have to move inland.

What Nations Have Environmental Problems?

Many American cities suffer from industrial air pollution. Russia and Eastern Europe suffer from it, too. When the Communists controlled them, they kept producing goods, no matter what happened to the environment.

Many developing African countries made the same mistake. They wanted to develop their economies quickly, but they ignored the environment. Now many Africans are starving to death. Farmers have killed their animals for food. Some ate the seeds they needed for next year's crop.

Asia depends on coal and oil for fuel. Its cars and factories are giving off high levels of carbon monoxide. The worst problems are in the cities. Asia has 8 of the world's 15 largest cities. All have major problems with air and water pollution.

The developing countries of Latin America have problems, too. Just breathing the air in Mexico City is equal to smoking two packs of cigarettes a day. The city's pollution may cause 100,000 deaths a year.

How Are Nations Attacking Environmental Problems?

People all over the world care about the environment. In 1992, representatives from 178 countries met to talk about it. They agreed to reduce air pollution and to save forests.

Polluting the land harms wildlife and takes away the natural beauty of an area. Volunteering to help clean up your community is one way to stop pollution.

In June 1997, world leaders met again. But many thought that the nations of the world had not made much progress since 1992. What is good for one nation may be bad for another. For example, many developing countries depend on the production and export of wood, coal, and oil. But what happens if the industrial countries cut back on the use of these fuels? The environment may improve, but the economies of the developing countries go downhill.

The truth is that the global environment is less healthy than it once was. Air pollution is growing. Also, people are using up resources like water, forests, topsoil, and fish faster than they can be replaced.

However, some good things are happening. The growth in world population is slowing. Farmers are growing more food. The majority of people around the world are now living longer and healthier lives.

How Can We Help Save the Environment?

We can do at least three things to help the environment. We can reduce the kinds of packages manufacturers sell things in. We can reuse things. We can recycle things that we no longer use. All of us depend on the same earth to supply us with our needs. We must work to improve the quality of life for all people without destroying the earth's environment.

SOME LESSONS OF HISTORY

Human history has been going on for thousands of year. What does it teach us? One thing we learn is that people from many different cultures faced hard problems in the past. We know the following about these people and their problems:

- Some met challenges with courage, good sense, and good will. They improved our world, and we owe them our thanks. We can learn from them.

- Others acted badly. They created terrible problems and caused many people to suffer. But even their terrible actions can teach us something— what not to do!

- Some ignored the past. We can do this, too, but then we will make the same mistakes others have made. The past shapes the present. It influences the future.

- No one has ever been able to predict for sure what the future will bring. But we can say one sure thing—the future belongs to all of us.

SECTION 4 REVIEW On a separate sheet of paper, write *True* if the statement is true or *False* if the statement is not true. Make each false statement true by changing the underlined word.

1) All around Earth, people face the problem of air and water <u>pollution.</u>

2) Since the <u>1890s</u>, scientists have been warning us about global warming.

3) Burning wood, coal, and oil puts <u>oxygen</u> in the air.

4) Scientists believe that too much <u>carbon dioxide</u> in the air will change Earth's temperature.

5) In <u>1992</u> and 1997, people from around the world met to talk about environmental problems.

What do you think ❓

What do you fear about pollution?

What Is Childhood?

In 1995, Craig Kielburger was a 12-year-old student in Toronto, Canada. One morning he read a newspaper article that changed his life. It told about the murder of Iqbal Masih, a young Pakistani. Iqbal had worked to end child slave labor. Craig took up this fight. He began a human rights group, Free the Children. This reading is from his book.

What is a good and normal childhood in the world today? In my travels I have found two extremes. In many developing countries, children are often asked to work long hours at hazardous jobs with no opportunity to play or to go to school. They are not allowed to develop physically, intellectually, and emotionally as they should. They support entire families. They fight in wars. They are given too much responsibility at too young an age.

On the other hand, in many industrialized countries everything is done for children. They are segregated most of their lives with members of their own age group and are given little opportunity to assume responsibility, or to develop a social conscience, or to learn through interaction with adults. Through media they learn to be consumers, to gain their self-image through the electronic toys they own and the labels they wear. They, too, are exploited. They see violence and suffering on the news every day but are told that they are too young to do anything about it. They are conditioned to become passive bystanders. This is the other extreme. . . .

We want to help free children from both extremes.

Children are not simply empty vessels to be filled. They are people with ideas, talents, opinions, and dreams. Children believe they can fly, that there is

Craig Kielburger (left) began his own human rights group.

nothing to stop their dreams from coming true. Some may call that wishful thinking, or simply being naive. Some call young people idealists, as if it were a stage they need to outgrow. But I feel the world could do with more idealists, that there are never too many dreamers.

It was the dreamers of the world who thought that one day the Berlin Wall would fall, that apartheid in South Africa would end, and that a human would walk on the moon. Because we are young, full of ideals, and full of dreams, we are not afraid of taking an idea that to some seems impossible and striving to make it a reality. . . .

Source Reading Wrap-Up

1) What is childhood like in developing countries?
2) What keeps children in richer countries from developing a social conscience?
3) What do children learn from the media?
4) How does Kielburger picture young people?
5) Some would say young people have nothing to offer the real world. Do you agree or disagree? Why or why not?

Themes in History

An old saying goes, "History repeats itself." Look back over the thousands of years you have studied. Probably you can see many continuing themes. Certain types of events seem to happen again and again.

One theme in history is the rise and fall of empires. In every time and place, leaders have wanted power. They have conquered and ruled other lands and people. The earliest empires began in Mesopotamia more than 4,000 years ago. Ancient history, in fact, sometimes looks like the history of empires. Babylon, Egypt, and Persia each ruled huge territories. Alexander the Great built the largest empire of all. Eventually, all those empires disappeared. In China, dynasties ruled for a time, then lost power. In modern times, Spain, Britain, France, Japan, and Russia have all had empires.

Empires fall for different reasons. Some, like Alexander's, depended on one strong leader. After the leader's death, the empire fell apart. Other empires grew weak before they were defeated. The Roman Empire declined for centuries. Finally, Germanic invaders brought it to an end. Sometimes empires were defeated by new technology. North Africans with guns defeated Songhai. Spaniards with guns and horses conquered the Incas.

The search for freedom is another major theme. Throughout history, individuals have rebelled against power. In the 1790s, the people of France began a bloody revolution. It ended the monarchy. In the 1800s, Latin American colonies won independence from Spain. After World War II, colonies around the world struggled to become independent. Some went to war. In India, Gandhi used a new way to win independence from

Britain. He urged nonviolent methods like strikes.

Today there is a new emphasis on human rights. This issue combines justice with freedom. Human rights supporters want fair treatment for all people. They work particularly on behalf of people without power. Human rights is not a new issue. Gandhi wanted fair treatment for India's "untouchables." Today, activists work for the rights of children, the poor, and others.

Technology is another theme in human history. The earliest men and women made tools. Technology helped build civilizations. It has also changed history. Iron tools changed warfare and farming. The Chinese learned to make silk and porcelain. That encouraged trade ties between Asia and Europe. With better ships and navigation, explorers could make long sea voyages. Printing helped spread learning. Today, cell phones and the Internet link the whole world.

Spotlight Story Wrap-Up

1) Name some empires from ancient times.
2) What are some causes for the fall of empires?
3) How have people shown their desire for freedom?
4) Name one advance in technology that changed history. What did it change?
5) Identify a theme in history that you have noticed. Include an example.

Chapter Summary

➡ Modern technology has made the world a "global village." People around the world share ideas and cultures. Technology helps businesses become multinational corporations that have workers in many countries.

➡ Mass communication includes advertising and electronic communication. American culture influences other parts of the world.

➡ Computers have many uses. The Internet is an international computer network. The World Wide Web links people through electronics. These media are part of the "electronic superhighway."

➡ The Soviet satellite *Sputnik* began the age of space exploration in 1957. An American astronaut made the first moon landing in 1969. Nations of the world consider space an international area.

➡ The United States and the Soviet Union competed in space for many years. Today they are working with other countries to build a permanent International Space Station.

➡ Modern technology depends on energy from various sources. However, burning coal and oil pollutes the environment. Nuclear power plants produce deadly waste; accidents are a danger.

➡ Modern technology has also changed medicine with new equipment, such as lasers.

➡ Rapid changes in technology raise questions about individual privacy.

➡ Most rich countries have a free-market economy and well-developed industries and technology. Most of these nations are in the Northern Hemisphere.

➡ Developing nations are building their industries and economies. Many people in these nations live by subsistence farming. Overpopulation and education are problems. Developing nations also lack money. Most industrialized nations supply aid to poorer countries. Aid comes through the World Bank and International Monetary Fund.

➡ A recession in 1997 hurt the economies of Asian nations. This crisis affected the entire world economy. Some people blamed it on multinational corporations.

➡ Land, air, and water pollution are global problems.

➡ Developing nations have pollution problems because of fast, uncontrolled growth.

➡ World leaders have discussed environmental problems. Their problem is to balance the needs of industrial nations and developing countries.

Comprehension: Identifying Facts

On a separate sheet of paper, use the words from the Word Bank to complete each sentence.

WORD BANK
developing
energy
environment
free-market
global warming
interdependent
international
mass communication
photoelectric cell
technology

1) The Internet is an _____ computer network that goes around the world and among many nations.

2) Television, advertising, and movies are examples of _____, which is messages directed at many people.

3) The global village is partly the result of advances in _____, which is the use of science to do practical things.

4) Progress in technology depends on _____, which makes machines work and produces heat.

5) The _____ is an invention that can produce electricity from light.

6) The burning of coal and oil threatens our _____, which is the land, sea, and air of Earth.

7) The Southern Hemisphere has many _____ countries, which are just beginning to grow their economies.

8) The nations of the world have become _____. They depend on one another.

9) Most industrial countries have a _____ economy in which manufacturers meet the needs and wants of consumers.

10) Many scientists are worried about _____, which could change Earth's temperature.

Comprehension: Multiple Choice

On a separate sheet of paper, write the letter of the answer that correctly completes each sentence.

1) A _____ is a tool that produces high-energy beams of light.

   a. laser   c. recession

   b. technology   d. subsistence

2) The _____ directs money from industrialized nations to developing countries.

a. International Monetary Fund   c. World Wide Web

b. Internet   d. World Bank

3) The _____ has 182 members whom it helps in times of economic crisis.

a. World Bank   c. International Monetary Fund

b. World Wide Web   d. Internet

4) The _____ is a network of information on the Internet open to businesses and individuals.

a. World Bank   c. International Monetary Fund

b. World Wide Web   d. free market

5) A _____ corporation hires people from around the world and does business around the world.

a. multinational   c. advertising

b. electronic   d. mass communication

Comprehension: Understanding Main Ideas

On a separate sheet of paper, write the answers to the following questions using complete sentences, or statements.

1) What is one way that mass communication has helped create a global village?

2) What is one source of energy that may be safe and may not pollute our environment?

3) What is one problem that developing countries have?

Critical Thinking: Write Your Opinion

1) Should the countries with the greatest wealth do more to help the less developed countries? Explain your answer.

2) What is one way you can reduce, reuse, or recycle to help the environment?

Test-Taking Tip Learn from your mistakes. Review corrected homework and identify your errors.

As American citizens, we vote to elect leaders and decide certain issues. As voters, we can do many things to find out about different candidates and issues. We can read newspapers. We can listen to political debates on radio and TV. Or we can attend political rallies and hear candidates speak in person. We can read articles about candidates in news magazines. We can get information from the political party of our choice. We can study the voting record of a candidate already in office. These actions show his or her position on issues.

Voter Registration Application
For U.S. Citizens

Many people around the world vote for their political leaders. Each country has its own voting process. Here is how it works in the United States. To vote, qualified persons 18 and older must first register at a city or county clerk's office. In some places, they can register by mail or at the polls on election day. Polling places are usually open from 7 A.M. to 8 P.M. Each voter must vote at the assigned polling place in his or her district. Local newspapers usually list polling places and hours. Voters also can get this information from local government offices. Voters who will be out of town on election day may request an absentee ballot in person or by mail. They may then mark and send in the absentee ballot ahead of the election.

At the polls, voters fill out a ballot. If necessary, election judges can show voters how to mark a ballot. Different districts use various machines and methods. Voters may have to pull a lever on a machine or punch holes. On paper, they may mark Xs with a pen. To ensure privacy, voters make their choices in a private booth.

After the polls close, election judges at each polling place count the votes. They deliver the count to the city or county clerk's office. When all the votes are counted, a winner is declared. Television, radio, and newspapers then give election results.

Find out the answers to these questions. Then you'll be ready to vote when the time comes.

1) How long must you live in your state and district before you can vote?

2) Where do you register to vote?

3) How do you register to vote?

4) Where do you vote?

5) How can you get an absentee ballot?

6) How do you fill out the ballot?

7) How are the votes counted?

8) In what day, month, and year can you vote in a national election for the first time?

As a future voter, explain how you would answer these questions.

9) How can you decide which candidates to vote for?

10) Why do you think it is important to vote in elections?

➥ In 1945, European nations controlled most of Africa. By the 1980s, there were 50 new African countries. African economies are growing quickly, but famine and overcrowded cities are problems.

➥ Apartheid hurt the black majority in South Africa. Nationalist leader Nelson Mandela helped end apartheid and became its president in 1994.

➥ The new Jewish state of Israel fought several wars with Arab countries. Some displaced Palestinians became terrorists. By the 1990s, Arab and Israeli leaders were working toward peace. Palestinian self-rule was a major issue.

➥ Indian nationalists used passive resistance to gain independence from Britain in 1947. Pakistan was established as a separate Muslim state.

➥ In China, a Communist victory in the civil war established the People's Republic in 1949.

➥ The French colony of Indochina was divided into North and South Vietnam, Cambodia, and Laos. When Communist North Vietnam waged war against South Vietnam, the United States helped it. Many Americans opposed the war. A Communist government united Vietnam in 1975.

➥ Oil and religion caused conflict in the Persian Gulf region. A religious revolution in Iran overthrew the Shah. Iraq and Iran fought a long war. Iraqi leader Saddam Hussein invaded Kuwait but was stopped by an international force.

➥ Asian economies, especially those of Japan and China, have prospered. An economic crisis in 1997 hurt many Asian nations. The Chinese Communist government violently stopped pro-democracy demonstrators at Tiananmen Square in 1989.

➥ Following Gorbachev's reforms, the Soviet Union broke up in 1991. People in Eastern Europe overthrew Communist governments in 1989. Ethnic wars broke out in the former Yugoslavia. Western European nations moved toward economic union, with a new currency, the euro.

➥ Land reform is a major problem in Latin America.

➥ Modern technology made the world a "global village." Mass communication lets people share ideas and culture.

➥ Beginning in 1957, the United States and Soviet Union competed in space. Today Russia and the United States cooperate with other nations on space projects.

➥ Technology depends on energy. Many energy sources cause pollution or other hazards. World leaders try to balance the needs of rich and poor nations while protecting the environment.

Unit 9 Review

Comprehension: Identifying Facts

On a separate sheet of paper, use the words from the Word Bank to complete each sentence.

1) Neil _____ stepped on the moon in 1969.

2) The _____ has 182 members that can depend on getting money from it in times of economic problems.

3) The _____ gives money from industrialized nations to developing countries.

4) Slobodan _____ led the Serbian people in ethnic cleansing during the 1990s.

5) Israel and _____ disagree on who should live on what land in the Middle East.

6) The Ayatollah _____ wanted religious leaders to rule Iran.

7) The Communist soldiers from North Vietnam used _____ in the Vietnam War by making surprise attacks and setting traps.

8) A _____ is a medical tool that produces high-energy beams of light.

9) Many _____ corporations do business around the world.

10) The _____ is a network of information on the Internet.

Comprehension: Multiple Choice

On a separate sheet of paper, write the letter of the answer that correctly completes each sentence.

1) Mohandas _____ used passive resistance to gain freedom for India.
   a. Mao
   b. Tutu
   c. Chiang
   d. Gandhi

2) Today, Africa faces the problem of _____.
   a. rapid urbanization
   b. famine
   c. drought
   d. all of the above

3) _____ led the Soviet Union during the 1980s and 1990s.

   a. Stalin
   c. Mao Zedong
   b. Khrushchev
   d. Gorbachev

4) The main source of energy in the twentieth century has been _____.

   a. wood
   c. oil
   b. water
   d. wind

5) Both the air and the water of our global village have been _____.

   a. polluted
   c. energized
   b. thinned
   d. left alone

Comprehension: Understanding Main Ideas

On a separate sheet of paper, write the answers to the following questions using complete sentences, or statements.

1) What is one problem that Israelis and Palestinians face?

2) What is one problem that Latin America faces today?

3) What is one way that technology draws people closer together?

Critical Thinking: Write Your Opinion

1) Some people think that industrialized nations should be feeding the hungry around the world instead of spending money for space exploration. What do you think and why?

2) What lessons have you learned from your study of world history?

Test-Taking Tip After you have taken a test, go back and reread the questions and your answers. Ask yourself, "Do my answers show that I understood the question?"

ARCTIC OCEAN

NORWAY
SWEDEN
FINLAND
ESTONIA
LATVIA
LITHUANIA
GERMANY
POLAND
BELARUS
CZECH
AUSTRIA
HUNGARY
MOLDOVA
ITALY
BOSNIA
ROMANIA
YUGOSLAVIA
BULGARIA
ALBANIA
GREECE
TURKEY
AZERBAIJAN
GEORGIA
ARMENIA
EUROPE
UKRAINE

RUSSIA

ASIA

KAZAKHSTAN

MONGOLIA

Sea of
Okhotsk

Caspian
Sea

UZBEKISTAN
KYRGYZSTAN
TURKMENISTAN
TAJIKISTAN

CHINA

NORTH
KOREA
SOUTH
KOREA

Sea of
Japan

JAPAN

TUNISIA
Mediterranean
Sea
ISRAEL
JORDAN
SYRIA
IRAQ
KUWAIT
UNITED
ARAB EMIRATES
SAUDI ARABIA
LIBYA
EGYPT

IRAN
AFGHANISTAN

PAKISTAN

NEPAL
BHUTAN
INDIA

East
China
Sea

TAIWAN

40°N

NORTH
PACIFIC
OCEAN

AFRICA

NIGER
CHAD
SUDAN
ERITREA
YEMEN
Red
Sea
OMAN
Arabian Sea

Gulf of Aden

INDIA
BANGLADESH
MYANMAR
LAOS

Bay
of Bengal

THAILAND

South
China
Sea

Philippine
Sea

PHILIPPINES

20°N

NIGERIA
CAMEROON
CENTRAL AFRICAN
REPUBLIC
DEM. REP.
OF CONGO
(ZAIRE)
UGANDA
ETHIOPIA
SOMALIA
GABON
ONGO
RWANDA
BURUNDI
KENYA

SRI LANKA

CAMBODIA
VIETNAM
BRUNEI
MALAYSIA
SINGAPORE

TANZANIA

INDIAN
OCEAN

Java Sea

INDONESIA

PAPUA
NEW GUINEA

Arafura Sea

0° Equator

ANGOLA
ZAMBIA
MALAWI

ZIMBABWE
MADAGASCAR

Timor Sea

Coral Sea

NAMIBIA
BOTSWANA

MOZAMBIQUE
SWAZILAND
SOUTH
AFRICA
LESOTHO

FIJI

NEW CALEDONIA

20°S

AUSTRALIA

Great Australian
Bight

Tasman Sea

NEW ZEALAND

40°S

20°E   40°E   60°E   80°E   100°E   120°E   140°E   160°E

60°S

80°S

ANTARCTICA

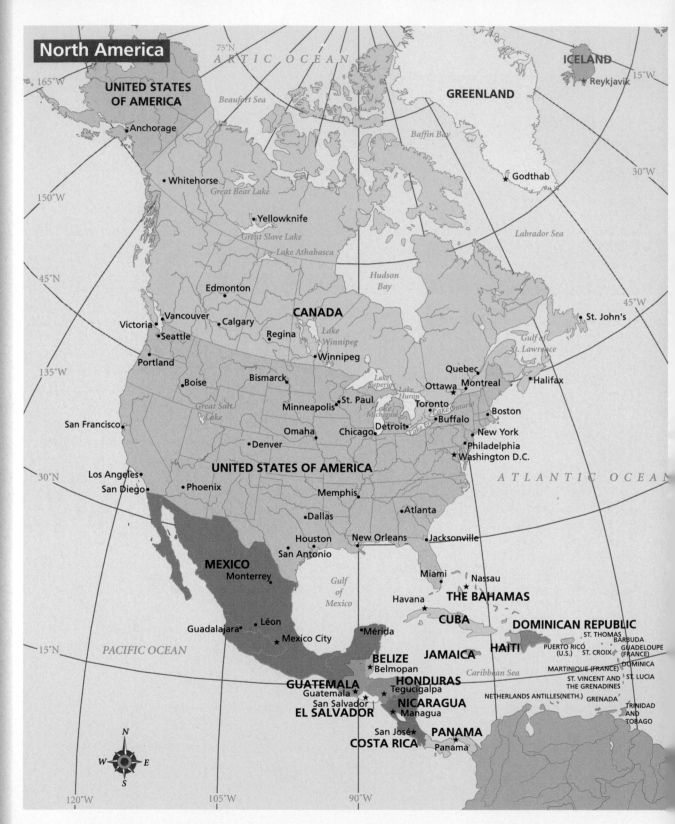

North America

ARTIC OCEAN

UNITED STATES OF AMERICA

• Anchorage

• Whitehorse

Beaufort Sea

Great Bear Lake

• Yellowknife

Great Slave Lake

• Lake Athabasca

Baffin Bay

GREENLAND

ICELAND

★ Reykjavik

★ Godthab

Labrador Sea

CANADA

• Edmonton

• Vancouver   • Calgary

Victoria •   • Regina

• Seattle

Portland •

Hudson Bay

Lake Winnipeg

• Winnipeg

Quebec •

★ Ottawa • Montreal

• St. John's

• Halifax

Gulf of St. Lawrence

• Boise

• Bismarck

Great Salt Lake

• Minneapolis

• St. Paul

Lake Superior

Lake Huron

Lake Michigan

Toronto •

Lake Ontario

• Boston

Lake Erie

• Buffalo

San Francisco •

• Omaha

• Chicago

• Detroit

• New York

UNITED STATES OF AMERICA

• Denver

• Philadelphia

★ Washington D.C.

Los Angeles •

• Phoenix

ATLANTIC OCEAN

San Diego •

• Memphis

• Dallas

• Atlanta

Houston •

• San Antonio

• New Orleans

• Jacksonville

MEXICO

• Monterrey

Gulf of Mexico

• Miami

★ Nassau

Havana ★

THE BAHAMAS

Guadalajara •

• Léon

★ Mexico City

• Mérida

CUBA

DOMINICAN REPUBLIC

ST. THOMAS

BARBUDA

PUERTO RICO (U.S.)

ST. CROIX

GUADELOUPE (FRANCE)

HAITI

JAMAICA

MARTINIQUE (FRANCE)

DOMINICA

ST. VINCENT AND THE GRENADINES

ST. LUCIA

BELIZE

★ Belmopan

HONDURAS

Caribbean Sea

GUATEMALA

Guatemala ★

★ Tegucigalpa

NETHERLANDS ANTILLES(NETH.)

GRENADA

TRINIDAD AND TOBAGO

San Salvador ★

NICARAGUA

EL SALVADOR

★ Managua

PACIFIC OCEAN

San José ★

COSTA RICA

PANAMA

• Panama

Caribbean Sea

ST. LUCIA

GRENADA

South America

Managua ●

San José ●

Panama ●

Barranquilla ●

Caracas ●

Valencia ●

Cúcuta ●

Medellín ●

Bogotá ★

Puerto Ayacucho ●

VENEZUELA

Georgetown ●

Paramaribo ●

GUYANA

SURINAME ★ Cayenne

FRENCH
GUIANA

COLOMBIA

Mitú ●

Macapá ●

Belém ●

ECUADOR ★ Quito

Galápagos
Islands

Guayaquil ●

Santarém ●

Fortaleza ●

Teresina ●

Talara ●

PERU

Recife ●

Trujillo ●

Porto Velho ●

BRAZIL

Maceió ●

Aracaju ●

Huánuco ●

Barreiras ●

Salvador ●

LIMA ★

Ica ●

Cuzco ●

BOLIVIA

La Paz ●

Santa Cruz ●

★ Brásilia

Goiânia ●

★ **Sucre**

Iquique ●

Antofagasta ●

PARAGUAY

Rio de Janeiro ●

São Paulo ●

PACIFIC OCEAN

CHILE

★ **Asunción**

Córdoba ●

Rosario ●

URUGUAY

★ Santiago

Buenos Aires ★

★ Montevideo

Concepción ●

ARGENTINA

ATLANTIC OCEAN

Valdivia ●

Puerto Montt ●

N
W E
S

Comodoro Rivadavia ●

FALKLAND ISLANDS
(U.K.)

SOUTH GEORGIA ISLAND
(U.K.)

10°N

0°

10°S

20°S

30°S

40°S

50°S

90°W   80°W   70°W   60°W   50°W   40°W

Europe

Reykjavik ★ ICELAND

Norwegian Sea

NORTH ATLANTIC OCEAN

Faroe Islands

SWEDEN

FINLAND

NORWAY

RUSSIA

Gulf of Bothnia

Helsinki ★

Oslo ★

★ Tallinn

Stockholm ★

ESTONIA

Baltic Sea

LATVIA

North Sea

Riga ★

Moscow ★

DENMARK

LITHUANIA

Vilnius ★

Belfast ★

★ Copenhagen

★ Minsk

IRELAND

Dublin ★

BELARUS

NETHERLANDS

U. K.

Amsterdam ★

Berlin ★

Warsaw ★

★ Kiev

London ★

GERMANY

POLAND

UKRAINE

English Channel

Brussels ★

BELGIUM

LUX.

Prague ★

★ Paris

CZECH REP.

Ostrava ★

Vienna ★

SLOVAKIA

★ Bratislava

MOLDOVA

FRANCE

Bern ★

AUSTRIA

★ Budapest

Chisinau ★

SWITZERLAND

HUNGARY

ROMANIA

Bay of Biscay

SLOVENIA

Monte Carlo ★

★ Zagreb

Belgrade ★

Bucharest ★

Black Sea

MONACO

BOSNIA AND HERZEGOVINA

ITALY

CROATIA

YUGOSLAVIA

BULGARIA

★ Varna

Adriatic Sea

Sarajevo ★

PORTUGAL

ANDORRA

★ Madrid

Corsica

★ Rome

MACEDONIA

★ Skopje

Sofia ★

Ankar

Lisbon ★

SPAIN

Tiranë ★

ALBANIA

Sardinia

Balearic Islands

Tyrrhenian Sea

Aegean Sea

GREECE

Gibraltar ★

Algiers ★

Ionian Sea

★ Athens

Rabat ★

Tunis ★

★ Valletta

MALTA

N

W E

S

Mediterranean Sea

Tripoli ★

Alexandria

Asia and Australia

RUSSIA

•Moscow

•Novosibirsk

East Siberian Sea

Bering Sea

Sea of Okhotsk

Karaganda

KAZAKHSTAN

Ulaanbaatar•

MONGOLIA

AZERBAIJAN

GEORGIA

TURKMENISTAN

UZBEKISTAN

Black Sea

ARMENIA

Tashkent•

KYRGYZSTAN

TURKEY

TAJIKISTAN

SYRIA

•Tehran

AFGHANISTAN

Beijing•

CHINA

NORTH KOREA

Pyongyang•

Seoul•

SOUTH KOREA

JAPAN

•Tokyo

Baghdad

IRAQ

IRAN

ISRAEL

JORDAN

KUWAIT

QATAR

PAKISTAN

New Delhi

BHUTAN

NEPAL

Chengdu•

East China Sea

PACIFIC OCEAN

U.A.E.

SAUDI ARABIA

INDIA

Dhaka

MYANMAR

TAIWAN

OMAN

Red Sea

BANGLADESH

Calcutta•

Hanoi•

Hong Kong

•Sanaa

YEMEN

Bombay•

Rangoon

LAOS

Vientiane•

•Manila

THAILAND

KAMPUCHEA

Bangkok•

VIETNAM

Colombo•

Phnom Penh

BRUNEI

PHILIPPINES

•Davao

SRI LANKA

MALAYSIA

Kuala Lumpur•

INDIAN OCEAN

Jakarta•

Java Sea

I N D O N E S I A

PAPUA NEW GUINEA

Port Moresby•

Timor Sea

Arafura Sea

Coral Sea

FIJI

NEW CALEDONIA

AUSTRALIA

Perth•

Great Australian Bight

Adelaide•

•Canberra

Tasman Sea

Auckland•

Wellington•

NEW ZEALAND

N

W E

S

30°E 60°E 90°E 120°E 150°E 180°E

75°N

60°N

45°N

30°N

15°N

0°

30°S

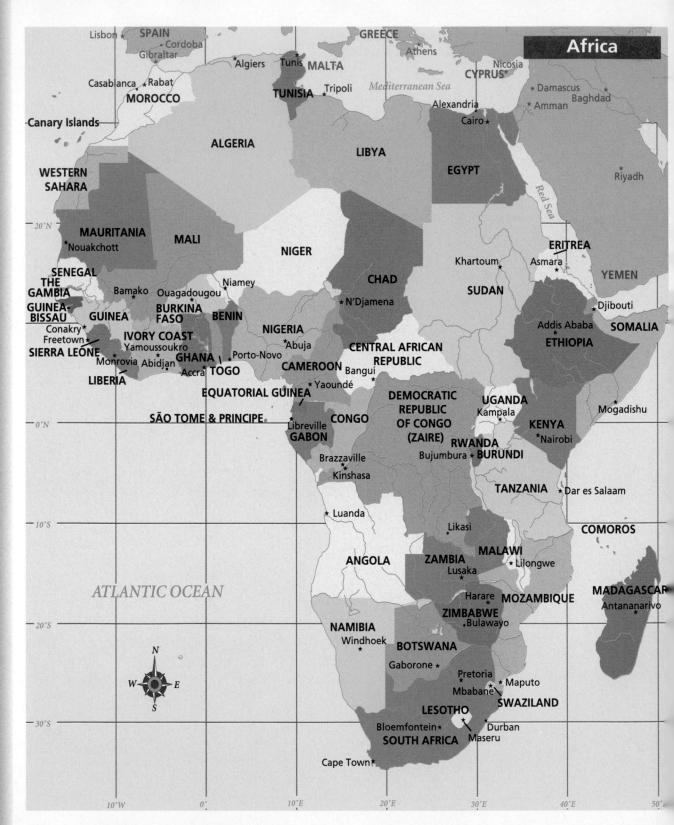

Africa

Lisbon
SPAIN
• Cordoba
Gibraltar
Algiers ★
Tunis
MALTA
GREECE
Athens •
Nicosia
CYPRUS ★
• Damascus
Casablanca
• Rabat
Baghdad ★
MOROCCO
TUNISIA
Tripoli
Mediterranean Sea
Alexandria
Amman ★

Canary Islands

ALGERIA
LIBYA
EGYPT
Cairo ★
Riyadh ★

20°N

WESTERN
SAHARA

MAURITANIA
• Nouakchott
MALI
NIGER
Khartoum •
ERITREA
Asmara
★
YEMEN

SENEGAL
THE
GAMBIA
Bamako •
Niamey •
CHAD
N'Djamena ★
SUDAN
Addis Ababa •
Djibouti
SOMALIA

GUINEA-
BISSAU
Ouagadougou
BURKINA
FASO
BENIN
NIGERIA
• Abuja
CENTRAL AFRICAN
REPUBLIC
ETHIOPIA

Conakry
Freetown
GUINEA
IVORY COAST
GHANA
Porto-Novo
CAMEROON
Bangui •

SIERRA LEONE
Yamoussoukro
Accra
TOGO
Yaoundé ★

Monrovia
Abidjan

LIBERIA
EQUATORIAL GUINEA
DEMOCRATIC
REPUBLIC
OF CONGO
(ZAIRE)
UGANDA
Kampala •
KENYA

SÃO TOME & PRINCIPE
Libreville
CONGO
• Nairobi
Mogadishu •

0°N
GABON
RWANDA
Brazzaville
Bujumbura ★ BURUNDI
Kinshasa

Luanda •
TANZANIA
Dar es Salaam

10°S
Likasi •
COMOROS

MALAWI
ANGOLA
ZAMBIA
Lilongwe
Lusaka •
MADAGASCAR
Antananarivo
★

ATLANTIC OCEAN
Harare
MOZAMBIQUE
ZIMBABWE
• Bulawayo

20°S
NAMIBIA
BOTSWANA
Windhoek ★

N
Gaborone ★
Pretoria •
Maputo
W E
Mbabane
SWAZILAND

S
LESOTHO
Durban •
30°S
Bloemfontein •
Maseru
SOUTH AFRICA

Cape Town ★

10°W
0°
10°E
20°E
30°E
40°E
50°E

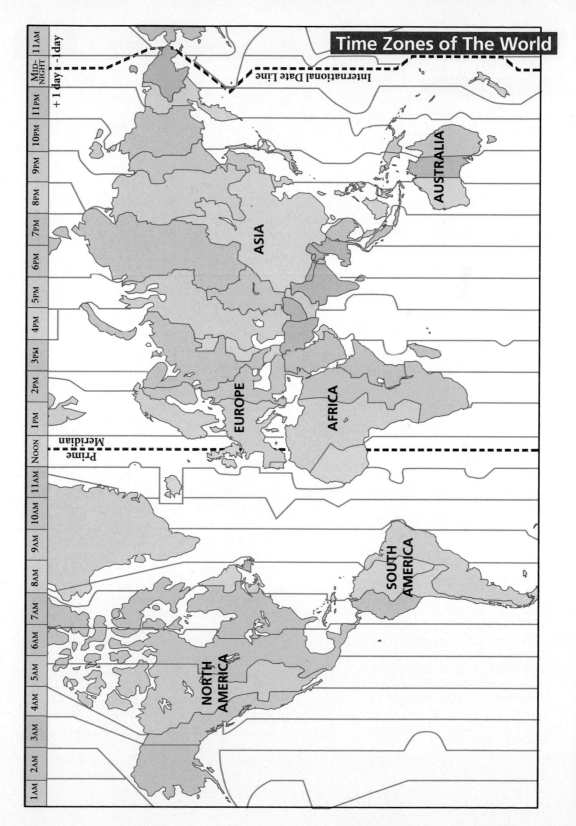

Time Zones of The World

International Date Line

+ 1 day | - 1 day

11AM | MID-NIGHT | 11PM | 10PM | 9PM | 8PM | 7PM | 6PM | 5PM | 4PM | 3PM | 2PM | 1PM | NOON | 11AM | 10AM | 9AM | 8AM | 7AM | 6AM | 5AM | 4AM | 3AM | 2AM | 1AM

Prime Meridian

ASIA

AUSTRALIA

EUROPE

AFRICA

NORTH AMERICA

SOUTH AMERICA

Glossary

A

Abacus (ab´ ə kəs) A tool that helps people add and do other things with numbers (p. 299)

Abandon (ə ban´ dən) To leave behind; to give up (p. 278)

Abdicate (ab´ də kāt) To give up power as a ruler (p. 617)

Abolish (ə bol´ ish) To get rid of something; to say that something is no longer legal, or lawful (p. 441)

Absolute monarch (ab´ sə lüt mon´ ərk) A monarch whose power is unlimited (p. 399)

Absorb (ab sôrb´) To soak up (p. 378)

Accurate (ak´ yər it) Correct (p. 183)

Acropolis (ə krop´ ə lis) A hill on which the people in a Greek city built their main temple (p. 147)

Adapt (ə dapt´) To change something to make it fit a different purpose (p. 303)

Adopt (ə dopt´) To begin to use (p. 124)

Advanced (ad vanst´) Beyond the beginning stage (p. 172)

Advertising (ad´ vər tiz ing) The selling or the announcing of something (p. 761)

Advice (ad vīs´) Ideas about how to do something (p 256)

Adviser (ad vī´ zər) A person who gives advice (p. 413)

African National Congress (ANC) (af´ rə kən nash´ ə nəl kong´ gris) A black nationalist group in Africa (p. 708)

African Nationalism (af´ rə kən nash´ ə nə liz´ əm) The struggle by native African people to gain their economic and political freedom from European colonial rulers (p. 704)

Agency (ā´ jən sē) A group that provides a service (p. 681)

Alabaster (al´ ə bas´ tər) A stone through which light can shine (p. 60)

Alliance (ə lī´ əns) An agreement to work together to help one another (p. 101)

Allied Powers (al´ īd pou´ ərs) Allied nations of Great Britain, France, Russia, Italy, and eventually, the United States and Japan during World War I (p. 594)

Ally (al´ ī) A friend; a country or person who helps another (p. 179)

Alms (ämz) The money or care that one gives to the poor and needy (p. 266)

Ambassador (am bas´ ə dər) A person sent to represent his or her government in another country (p. 567)

Amber (am´ bər) The hard, yellowish remains of a liquid that comes out of trees (p. 382)

American Revolution (ə mar´ ə kən rev ə lü´ shən) The American struggle against Great Britain for independence (p. 510)

Anatomy (ə nat´ ə mē) The structure of a human or animal body (p. 381)

Anglican Church (ang´ glə kən chėrch) The church established by Henry VIII (p. 356)

Annex (ə neks´) To take over; to add a piece of land to one's country (p. 125)

Announcement (ə nouns´ mənt) The statement of something that is to happen or that has happened (p. 266)

Annul (ə nul´) To announce that a marriage never existed between two people (p. 355)

Anthropologist (an thrə pol´ ə jist) A person who studies the beginnings and the behavior of people (p. 37)

Apartheid (ə pärt´ hīt) The official policy of the Union of South Africa that refused to give black and other nonwhite people any political, economic, or social rights (p. 707)

Appeasement (ə pēz´ mənt) A policy of making others happy or content; giving in so that others will be happy and will not cause a war (p. 656)

Aqueduct (ak´ wə dukt) A bridge that carries flowing water (p. 192)

Arch (ärch) A curved opening that supports something (p. 83)

Archaeologist (är´ kē ol´ ə jist) A person who finds and studies the things humans left behind in the past (p. 37)

Archbishop (ärch´ bish´ əp) The top religious leader in a church province (p. 356)

Archer (är´ chər) A soldier who fights with a bow and arrows (p. 98)

Architect (är´ kə tekt) A person who draws plans for buildings (p. 330)

Architecture (är´ kə tek chər) The art of building (p. 152)

Aristocrat (ə ris´ tə krat) A member of the powerful ruling class (p. 147)

Armada (är mä´ də) A large fleet of warships (p. 404)

Armistice (är´ mə stis) An agreement to stop fighting (p. 598)

Armor (är′ mər) A metal covering that protects the body in battle (p. 124)

Arsenal (är′ sə nəl) A place where a country stores or makes weapons (p. 659)

Artifact (är′ tə fakt) An object made by a person (p. 37)

Artisan (är′ tə zən) A person who makes useful, and often beautiful, objects for everyday use (p. 69); a person who works with his or her hands to create something (p. 98)

Assassinate (ə sas′ n āt) To kill someone who is important or in government (p. 183)

Assemble (ə sem′ bəl) To put the parts of something together (p. 488)

Assembly (ə sem′ blē) A meeting; a group of people who meet to pass laws (p. 149)

Astronomer (ə stron′ ə mər) A person who keeps track of the stars, the sun, and the planets (p. 104)

Astronomy (ə stron′ ə mē) The study of the stars (p. 160)

Atomic bomb (ə tom′ ik bom) A bomb that uses nuclear energy and has much destructive power (p. 666)

Attract (ə trakt′) To pull something toward oneself (p. 378)

Authority (ə thôr′ ə tē) Power; the right to tell someone what to do (p. 348)

Autocracy (ȯ tok′ rə sē) A government in which one person has unlimited power (p. 612)

Axis (ak′ sis) A make-believe line that goes through the middle of an object that spins around it (p. 652)

Axis Powers (ak′ is pou′ ərs) The alliance of Germany, Italy, and Japan during World War II (p. 652)

Ayatollah (ä′ yä tō′ lə) An Iranian ruler (p. 734)

B

Balance of power (bal′ əns ov pou′ ər) The condition that exists when all countries or all sections of government share powers or have the same amount of power (p. 535)

Ban (ban) To get rid of; to make something not legal (p. 463)

Bankrupt (bang′ krupt) Unable to pay one's debts (p. 603)

Baptism (bap′ tiz əm) A ritual by which a person becomes a Christian (p. 354)

Barbarian (bär bâr′ ē ən) An uncivilized person (p. 302)

Barbaric (bär bar′ ik) Not civilized; not having good government and the things that make life easier (p. 223)

Barbed wire (bärbd wīr) Wire that has sharp metal spikes on it (p. 595)

Baroque (bə rōk′) The type of music developed in the late 1600s (p. 465)

Barrier (bar′ ē ər) Something that blocks the way; a wall (p. 177)

Barter (bär′ tər) To trade by exchanging things without using money (p. 106)

Basin (ba′ sn) A bowl-like area for storing water (p. 123)

Basis (bā′ sis) The idea or reason behind something (p. 206)

Bastille (ba stēl′) A prison in Paris (p. 515)

Battle ax (bat′ l aks′) A broad ax used in battle (p. 248)

Behavior (bi hā′ vyər) The way a human being or animal acts (p. 454)

Berlin Airlift (bər lin′ âr′ lift) The Western method of getting around the 1948 Soviet blockade by flying supplies into Berlin (p. 686)

Berlin Wall (bər lin′ wȯl) The wall that divided the people of East and West Berlin (p. 747)

Betray (bi trā′) To stop being loyal to someone; to do something to hurt someone (p. 200)

Bible (bī′ bəl) Hebrew and Christian book that is thought to be holy (p. 88)

Biology (bī ol′ ə jē) The study of living things (p. 160)

Bishop (bish′ əp) A priest who is in charge of other priests and a number of churches (p. 253)

Bison (bī′ sn) Another name for buffalo (p. 42)

Blacksmith (blak′ smith) A person who works with iron and makes tools and weapons (p. 249)

Blitzkrieg (blits′ krēg) The quick and forceful method of attack that Germany used in World War II; "lightning war" (p. 658)

Blood vessel (blud ves′ al) A tube in the body through which blood passes (p. 381)

Boar (bôr) A wild pig-like animal (p. 42)

Boiler (boi′ lar) A tank that heats water (p. 492)

Bolshevik (bōl′ shə vik) A revolutionary socialist group in Russia (p. 619)

Border (bôr′ dər) The dividing line between two countries (p. 196)

a	hat	e	let	ī	ice	ȯ	order	u̇	put	sh	she		a	in about
ā	age	ē	equal	o	hot	oi	oil	ü	rule	th	thin	ə	e	in taken
ä	far	ėr	term	ō	open	ou	out	ch	child	ᴛʜ	then		i	in pencil
â	care	i	it	ȯ	saw	u	cup	ng	long	zh	measure		o	in lemon
													u	in circus

Boundary (boun´ dər ē) The dividing line between one country and another (p. 398)

Boyar (bō yär´) A Russian noble who owned land (p. 228)

Boycott (boi´ kot) To refuse to buy something; to refuse to deal with a person, business, or country (p. 509)

Bribe (brīb) To pay someone to do something a certain way (p. 150)

British Commonwealth of Nations (brit´ ish kom´ ən welth ov nā´ shəns) A group of nations around the world that is loyal to the British monarch (p. 707)

Bronze (bronz) A hard metal made of a blend of copper and tin (p. 43)

Buddha (bü´ də) A name meaning the "Enlightened One;" the name given to Siddhartha Gautama, the founder of Buddhism (p. 290)

Buffer zone (buf´ ər zōn)A neutral area that separates two warring countries (p. 683)

Burden (bėrd´ n) A heavy load (p. 414)

Bushido (bü´ shē dō) The warrior code of honor in Japan (p. 307)

Buttress (but´ ris) A structure that holds up or gives support to something; to hold up (p. 254)

C

Calculate (kal´ kyə lāt) To figure something out (p. 38)

Calligraphy (kə lig´ rə fē) The art of beautiful handwriting (p. 306)

Calvinism (kal´ və niz əm) The Protestant religion founded by John Calvin (p. 358)

Campesino (käm pā sē´ nō) A poor peasant who works the land, but does not own it (p. 751)

Canal (kə nal´) A waterway made by humans (p. 67)

Capital (kap´ ə təl) The city from which a ruler, or emperor, rules (p. 100); money used to make more money; money used to start a business (p. 482)

Caravan (kar´ ə van) A group of traders traveling together, usually through deserts (p. 118)

Cardinal (kärd´ n əl) A high official of the Roman Catholic Church (p. 413)

Caste (kast) A class of people in India (p. 64)

Cathedral (kə thē´ drəl) The church where the bishop is the main priest (p. 253)

Causeway (kóz´ wā) A paved road over water that connects two pieces of land (p. 279)

Cavalier (kav ə lir´) A person who fought for the king in the English Civil War (p. 409)

Cavalry (kav´ əl rē) Soldiers on horseback (p. 98)

Censor (sen´ sər) To prevent someone from reading or viewing something (p. 361)

Censorship (sen´ sər ship) The banning of all material that those in power do not want people to see (p. 624)

Central (sen´ trəl) The main part or middle of something (p. 414)

Central Powers (sen´ trəl pou´ ərs) Allied nations of Germany, Austria-Hungary, Turkey, and Bulgaria in World War I (p. 594)

Century (sen´ chər ē) A period of a hundred years (p. 144)

Ceremony (ser´ ə mō nē) The actions and words of a special event (p. 226)

Challenge (chal´ ənj) To question if something is right or wrong; to invite someone to fight (p. 181)

Chapel (chap´ əl) A small church (p. 338)

Character (kar´ ik tər) In language, a symbol that means something (p. 70)

Chariot (char´ ē ət) A two-wheeled, horse-drawn carriage (p. 98)

Charter (chär´ tər) A constitution; a set of statements that explains a group's purpose (p. 680)

Chemistry (kem´ ə strē) The science in which people study the makeup of substances and how one substance changes when another is added (p. 270)

Chorus (kôr´ əs) A group of actors who stand on stage and talk about what is happening in a Greek play (p. 158)

Christianity (kris chē an´ ə tē) The religion based on the teachings of Jesus Christ and the Bible (p. 199)

Circulate (sėr´ kyə lāt) To move in a pattern from one place to another (p. 382)

City-state (sit´ ē - stāt) A city surrounded by villages on the surrounding land (p. 80)

Civilian (sə vil´ yən) A person who is not in the military (p. 295)

Civilization (siv ə lə zā´ shən) A people who have cities and government; a large group of people with a high level of development as a group (p. 44)

Civilized (siv´ ə līzd) Having more of the things that make life easier (p. 193)

Civil service (siv´ əl sėr´ vis) A system of government run by civilians (p. 295)

Civil War (siv´ əl wôr) Fighting between people within their own country (p. 121)

Classical (klas´ ə kəl) A type of music from the 1700s and 1800s that is orderly and balanced; in the style of ancient Greece or Rome (p. 466)

Clergy (klėr´ jē) The people who lead a religion (p. 324)

Code (kōd) A group of laws (p. 85)

Code of Napoleon (kōd ov nə pō´lē ən) A code of law Napoleon passed that made all men equal in France (p. 526)

Coemperor (kō em´ pər ər) A person who rules only part of an empire while another emperor rules another part (p. 204)

Coke (kōk) Purified coal (p. 488)

Cold war (kōld wôr) The war of propaganda between the United States and the Soviet Union after World War II (p. 683)

Collapse (kə laps´) To fall apart (p. 71)

Collective farm (kə lek´ tiv färm) A large farm owned by many peasants and run by the government (p. 623)

Colonialism (kə lō´ nē ə liz əm) The controlling of colonies; another name for imperialism (p. 570)

Colonist (kol´ ə nist) A person who settles in a colony (p. 443); a person who settles in a new place (p. 506)

Column (kol´ əm) A tall, solid structure used to support a building; a pillar (p. 157)

Combine (kəm bīn´) To put together into one (p. 126)

Comedy (kom´ ə dē) A type of Greek play in which the writer makes fun of important people (p. 158)

Comic (kom´ ik) Funny; causing laughter (p. 334)

Commandment (kə mand´ mənt) A rule, or way to act (p. 89)

Communion (kə myü´ nyən) A ritual by which people grow in their faith and give thanks to God for Jesus Christ (p. 354)

Communism (kom´ yə niz əm) An economic system in which there is no private property and the government produces goods (p. 619)

Community (kə myü´ nə tē) A group of people with something in common, such as a topic of study, a belief, or an area in which to live (p. 381)

Compass (kum´ pəs) A tool for finding direction by using a magnet (p. 298)

Compete (kəm pēt´) To try to do better than someone else (p. 771)

Complaint (kəm plānt´) A statement about something that tells why a person is unhappy (p. 510)

Composer (kəm pō´ zər) A person who makes up music (p. 465)

Compromise (kom´ prə mīz) An agreement in which both sides give up something so as to stop arguing (p. 357)

Concentration camp (kon sən trā´ shən kamp) A large prison death camp (p. 676)

Conclude (kən klüd´) To look at facts and arrive at a belief or decision (p. 373)

Conclusion (kən klü´ zhən) An answer; a decision reached through step-by-step thinking (p. 370)

Concrete (kon krēt´) A mixture of sand, water, and other materials that hardens to become rocklike (p. 207)

Condemn (kən dem´) To say that someone must suffer or die; to say that something is wrong (p. 195)

Confederation (kən fed ə rā´ shən) A union, or group, of states or nations (p. 536)

Conference (kon´ fər əns) A meeting to discuss ideas and plans (p. 656)

Conflict (kon´ flikt) Fighting; not being able to agree on something (p. 732)

Congress of Vienna (kong´ gris ov vē en´ ə) An important meeting in 1814–1815 in which leaders restructured Europe (p. 534)

Conquer (kong´ kər) To defeat (p. 105)

Conquistador (kon kē´ stə dôr) A Spanish conqueror; a person seeking gold and glory (p. 433)

Consent (kən sent´) To agree to something (p. 507)

Conservative (kən sėr´ və tiv) A person who likes the old political order and resists revolution or change (p. 544)

Constellation (kon stə lā´ shən) A picture made by a group of stars (p. 104)

Constitution (kon stə tü´ shən) A body of laws that states the rights of the people and the power of the government (p. 417)

Constitutional monarchy (kon stə tü´ shə nəl mon´ ər kē) A form of government in which a king and queen rule, but there are laws of a democracy (p. 412)

Consul (kon səl´) A Roman leader who served a one-year term (p. 174)

Consumer (kən sü´ mər) Someone who buys and uses things (p. 740)

Consumer goods (kən sü´ mər gùds) Products that people buy (p. 623)

Contagious (kən tā´ jəs) Able to spread from one person to another (p. 269)

Contract (kon´ trakt) A legal agreement (p. 457)

Contradict (kon trə dikt´) To go against; to say the opposite of what has been said (p. 377)

a	hat	e	let	ī	ice	ô	order	ù	put	sh	she	ə	a in about
ā	age	ē	equal	o	hot	oi	oil	ü	rule	th	thin		e in taken
ä	far	ėr	term	ō	open	ou	out	ch	child	ᴛʜ	then		i in pencil
â	care	i	it	ò	saw	u	cup	ng	long	zh	measure		o in lemon
													u in circus

Convent (kon´ vent) A place where nuns live and work together (p. 242)

Convention (kən ven´ shən) A group of people who meet to get something done (p. 516)

Convert (kən vėrt´) To change one's religion to another religion or another belief (p. 433)

Convoy (kon´ voi) A group of ships that travel together for protection (p. 596)

Core (kôr) The center of something (p. 382)

Counter (koun´ tər) To speak out or fight back against something or someone (p. 361)

Counter-Reformation (koun´ tər-ref ər mā´ shən) The Catholic Church's reforms that attempted to fight the Protestant Reformation (p. 361)

Coup (kü) An overthrow of the government (p. 744)

Courtyard (kôrt´ yärd) A yard where a noble could hold court (p. 251)

Covenant (kuv´ ə nənt) An agreement (p. 89)

Create (krē āt´) To make something (p. 64)

Creation (krē ā´ shən) The act of making something; the making of the world (p. 338)

Creative (krē ā´ tiv) To use one's imagination to create things (p. 325)

Creole (krē´ ōl) A wealthy landowner who had been born in a Spanish colony in the Americas but whose ancestors came from Spain (p. 540)

Crisis (krī´ sis) A time of danger; a turning point in events (p. 652)

Criticize (krit´ ə sīz) To say that someone has done wrong; to find wrong in something (p. 332)

Crowbar (krō´ bär) An iron or steel bar that a person can use as a lever (p. 281)

Crucify (krü´ sə fī) To hang someone on a cross so that the person dies (p. 200)

Crusade (krü sād´) Any of the military journeys taken by Christians to win the Holy Land from the Muslims (p. 243)

Crusader (krü sā´ dər) A person who goes on a crusade (p. 243)

Cubit (kyü´ bit) A measurement that is the length of an arm from the end of the middle finger to the elbow (p. 130)

Culture (kul´ chər) The values, attitudes, and customs of a group (p. 34)

Cuneiform (kyü nē´ ə fôrm) Sumerian writing (p. 82)

Currency (kėr´ ən sē) The form of money a country uses (p. 749)

Cycle (sī´ kəl) Events that keep happening, one after another (p. 64)

Cyrillic alphabet (si ril´ ik al´ fə bet) The alphabet invented by Cyril and Methodius and used to translate the Bible into Slavic languages (p. 226)

Czar (zär) The ruler of Russia; a Russian title that means "caesar" (p. 229)

D

Dagger (dag´ ər) A sharp-pointed knife used for stabbing (p. 248)

Daimyo (dī´ myo) A great landowner in feudal Japan (p. 306)

D-Day (dē-dā) The Allied invasion of France in 1944 (p. 664)

Debate (di bāt´) To talk about something; to have two or more sides talk about something (p. 194)

Decay (di kā´) To rot away or spoil (p. 40)

Declaration of Independence (dek lə rā´ shən ov in di pen´ dəns) A document signed by the American colonists in which they declared their freedom from Great Britain (p. 510)

Decline (di klīn´) To lose power; to turn downward (p. 196)

Defensive (di fen´ siv) Protecting oneself rather than attacking others (p. 663)

Delta (del´ tə) An area of fertile land at the mouth of a river (p. 116)

Democracy (di mok´ rə sē) Rule by the people (p. 148)

Democratic (dem ə krat´ ik) Having to do with a government in which all people have equal rights (p. 614)

Demonstrate (dem´ ən strāt) To join together with other people to protest and march against something (p. 709)

Depression (di presh´ ən) A time of economic collapse when businesses lose money and people become poor (p. 638)

Descendant (di sen´ dənt) A person who comes from a specific group of people (p. 437)

Desire (di zīr´) To wish for something; a wish for something (p. 291)

Destroyer (di stroi´ ər) A small, fast warship that uses guns and other weapons to protect ships from submarines (p. 659)

Detect (di tekt´) To discover or find out (p. 299)

Developing country (di vel´ ə ping kun´ trē) A nation that is slowly developing its industry and economy (p. 769)

Development (di vel´ əp mənt) Growth of something (p. 63)

Diary (dī´ ər ē) A daily record of what happens to a person (p. 34)

Dictator (dik´ tā tər) A person who rules a country with force and makes all the laws (p. 174)

Dike (dīk) A bank of earth that keeps out water (p. 80)

Direct democracy (də rekt´ di mok´ rə sē) A type of government in which each citizen votes on everything (p. 149)

Disaster (də zas´ tər) Something that causes harm or problems (p. 116)

Disciple (də sī´ pəl) A follower of someone (p. 201)

Disobey (dis ə bā´) To go against an order or rule (p. 399)

Displace (dis plās´) To move people from their home or land; to force people to leave their home or land (p. 712)

Dissect (di sekt´) To cut open something that was once alive to study it (p. 336)

District (dis´ trikt) A certain area of a place (p. 60)

Divine (də vīn´) Having something to do with the gods or with God (p. 199)

Divine right (də vīn´ rīt) The belief that God chooses the ruler of a nation (p. 406)

Divorce (də vôrs´) To end a marriage (p. 355)

Document (dôk´ yə mənt) An important paper (p. 407)

Dominate (dom´ ə nāt) To control (p. 98)

Drain (drān) To draw off water from a swampy or wet place (p. 123)

Drama (drä´ mə) A play to act out on a stage (p. 333)

Drawbridge (drȯ´ brij) A bridge that can be raised or lowered over a moat (p. 250)

Drought (drout) A long period of time without much rain (p. 733)

Duma (dü´ mə) The Russian parliament (p. 615)

Dynasty (dī´ nə stē) A family that rules a country over a long period of time (p. 69)

E

Eclipse (i klips´) The hiding of the sun by the moon (p. 43)

Economic (ek ə nom´ ik) Having to do with money (p. 445)

Economist (i kon´ ə mist) A person who studies the way people make and use money and goods (p. 484)

Economy (i kon´ ə mē) The system of making and trading things (p. 121)

Efficient (ə fish´ ənt) Working well with little loss of time or energy (p. 491)

Elder (el´ dər) An experienced, older person (p. 358)

Elect (i lekt´) To choose by voting (p. 175); a Calvinistic term for those whom God has chosen to save (p. 358)

Election (i lek´ shən) An act by which people choose someone or something by voting (p. 722)

Electronic (i lek tron´ ik) Powered by electricity (p. 761)

Electronic superhighway (i lek tron´ ik sü´ pər hī wā) A communication network that sends data from telephones, televisions, and computers (p. 767)

Ellipse (i lips´) The shape of an egg; an oval with both ends alike (p. 373)

Embers (em´ bərz) The glowing remains of a fire (p. 40)

Émigré (em´ ə grā) A French noble who fled France during the French Revolution (p. 517)

Emperor (em´ pər ər) A person who rules an empire; a king (p. 184)

Empire (em´ pīr) A nation in which someone rules a large area of land (p. 98)

Employ (em ploi´) To hire someone to work; to use something (p. 760)

Employer (em ploi´ ər) A person who hires someone else to work for him or her (p. 324)

Encomienda (en kōmē´ endə) The Spanish system of forcing Native Americans to do physical work on plantations (p. 437)

Energy (en´ ər jē) Power that comes from wood, coal, electricity, oil, the sun, water, and wind; makes machines work; and produces heat (p. 765)

Enforce (en fôrs´) To make sure that people follow the laws and rules (p. 516)

Enlightened (en līt´ nd) The state of knowing the truth (p. 290); having a belief in reasoning; moving away from ignorance (p. 455)

Enlightenment (en līt´ n mənt) A time in European history when thinkers and writers tried to solve the problems of society by using reason (p. 461)

Enslave (en slāv´) To force people to become slaves (p. 151)

Entertainment (en tər tān´ mənt) Plays and other things that amuse people (p. 195)

Environment (en vī´ rən mənt) The land, sea, and air of our world (p. 765)

Equality (i kwol´ ə tē) The same rights for everyone (p. 516)

Establish (e stab´ lish) To set up (p. 295)

a	hat	e	let	ī	ice	ȯ	order	u̇	put	sh	she	ə	a	in about
ā	age	ē	equal	o	hot	oi	oil	ü	rule	th	thin		e	in taken
ä	far	ėr	term	ō	open	ou	out	ch	child	ᴛʜ	then		i	in pencil
â	care	i	it	ȯ	saw	u	cup	ng	long	zh	measure		o	in lemon
													u	in circus

Estate (e stāt´) A large piece of land with a house on it (p. 306); a class of people in France (p. 513)

Estates-General (e stāts´-jen´ ər əl) The French governmental body made up of representatives from the three estates (p. 514)

Eternal (i tėr´ nl) Lasting forever (p. 192)

Ethics (eth´ iks) The study of what is good and bad (p. 160)

Ethnic cleansing (eth´ nik klenz´ ing) The act of getting rid of a group of people because their religion or race is different from the majority group (p. 747)

Evidence (ev´ ə dəns) Facts and information (p. 256)

Exaggerate (eg zaj´ ə rāt) To make better, larger, or more important than in real life (p. 309)

Excommunicate (ek skə myü´ nə kāt) To say that someone can no longer be a member of a church (p. 353)

Execute (ek´ sə kyüt) To kill someone for a crime (p. 332)

Executive (eg zek´ yə tiv) Having to do with the branch of government that puts laws into action (p. 519)

Exile (eg´ zīl) To send someone away from his or her own country and to order this person not to come back (p. 525)

Expand (ek spand´) To grow; to stretch (p. 102)

Expedition (ek spə dish´ ən) A long journey of discovery (p. 431)

Expel (ek spel´) To throw out of something (p. 65)

Experimental science (ek sper ə men´ tl sī´ əns) Science that begins with and depends on careful experiments and measurements (p. 377)

Exploration (ek splə rā´ shən) The act of looking around some unknown place (p. 429)

Export (ek spôrt´) To send a product out of one country and into another to sell; a product that is sent from one country to another (p. 487)

Extreme (ek strēm´) The farthest something can go (p. 635)

F

Faith (fāth) To believe in God; a religion (p. 255)

Famine (fam´ ən) A time when crops do not grow and there is no food (p. 89)

Fascism (fash´ iz əm) A form of government in which a dictator and the dictator's party totally control a government (p. 635)

Fascist (fash´ ist) A person who believes in fascism (p. 635)

Fast (fast) To give up eating food for a while (p. 264)

Fertile (fėr´ tl) Able to grow crops (p. 58)

Fertile Crescent (fėr´ tl kres´ nt) An area of land in the Middle East shaped like a quarter moon (p. 87)

Fertilizer (fėr´ tl ī zər) A substance that makes the soil grow crops (p. 733)

Feudalism (fyü´ dl iz əm) A political and military system based on the holding of land (p. 246)

Fever (fē´ vər) A high body temperature (p. 129)

Fiber (fī´ bər) A thread of cotton, silk, wool, or other material (p. 487)

Fief (fēf) Land, and everything on it, which a lord gave to a vassal (p. 246)

Finance (fī´ nans) To provide the money for something (p. 428)

Fleet (flēt) A group of ships (p. 153)

Foreign (fôr´ ən) From another country; having to do with another country (p. 560)

Foreigner (fôr´ ə nər) A person from another country (p. 124)

Foreign minister (fôr´ ən min´ ə stər) A person who handles one country's dealings with other countries (p. 534)

Formation (fôr mā´ shən) A shape or pattern (p. 404)

Fossil fuel (fos´ əl fyü´ əl) Fuel made from coal, oil, or natural gas (p. 773)

Founded (found´ əd) To have begun a country or city; to have built a city (p. 172)

Free-market capitalism (frē-mär´ kit kap´ ə tə liz əm) The system that allows for private ownership of business (p. 745)

Free-market economy (frē-mär´ kit i kon´ ə mē) An economy in which manufacturers try to satisfy consumers' wants and needs (p. 769)

French Revolution (french rev ə lü´ shən) The war that the common people of France fought against the king, nobles, and one another to achieve freedom (p. 515)

Fresco (fres´ kō) A painting done in wet plaster on a wall (p. 336)

Front (frunt) The place where armies fight; the battle line (p. 657)

Fuehrer (fyùr´ ər) The name given to Adolph Hitler meaning "leader" (p. 639)

Fugue (fyüg) A type of baroque music in which the melody is repeated (p. 465)

Fundamentalist (fun də mən´ tl ist) A person who likes traditional religious values and rejects much of modern life (p. 738)

G

Gamble (gam´ bəl) To bet money on the outcome of something (p. 358)

Generation (jen ə rā´ shən) All the people born about the same time (p. 603)

Genius (jē´ nyəs) A person born with special skills that make him or her different from ordinary people (p. 333)

Genocide (jen´ ə sīd) Mass murder of a group of people (p. 677)

Gentile (jen´ tīl) A non-Jew (p. 201)

Geography (jē og´ rə fē) The science that deals with land, weather, bodies of water, and plant and animal life (p. 58)

Geometry (jē om´ ə trē) The study of the measurement of flat and round things (p. 164)

Gestapo (gə stä´ pō) Hitler's secret police force (p. 639)

Glasnost (glas´ nost) A Russian word that means openness; under Gorbachev it meant openness in government (p. 743)

Glaze (glāz) A coat of shiny polish (p. 103)

Global (glō´ bəl) Having to do with the whole world (p. 36)

Global village (glō´ bəl vil´ ij) The term used to describe the sharing of ideas, cultures, and traditions throughout the world (p. 760)

Global warming (glō´ bəl wôrm ing) The heating up of Earth from the burning of wood, coal, oil, and gasoline (p. 773)

Glorify (glôr´ ə fī) To praise someone or something (p. 652)

Glorius Revolution (glôr´ ē əs rev ə lü´ shən) The period in England that involved the overthrow of James II and the crowning of William and Mary (p. 411)

Goddess (god´ is) A woman god (p. 157)

Goods (gůdz) Things that have been grown or made for sale or trade (p. 223)

Gospel (gos´ pəl) One of four books of the New Testament part of the Bible; a word that means "good news" (p. 199)

Gothic (goth´ ik) A style of architecture with thin walls, pointed arches, many windows, and flying buttresses (p. 254)

Govern (guv´ ərn) To rule (p. 101)

Governor (guv´ ər nər) A ruler of a province or state (p. 101)

Gravity (grav´ ə tē) The force that pulls things to Earth and keeps them from floating into space (p. 294); the force that pulls objects toward the center of Earth and gives objects weight (p. 377)

Great Depression (grāt di presh´ ən) The worldwide depression that began in the United States in 1929 (p. 643)

Guarantee (gar ən tē´) A promise that something will happen (p. 350)

Guerilla warfare (gə ril´ ə wôr´ fär) A type of fighting that involves small attacks against an enemy or the things it needs and uses (p. 663)

Guillotine (gil´ ə tēn) The machine the French used to execute people by chopping off their head (p. 519)

H

Habeas Corpus (hā´ bē as kôr´ pəs) A law that says that the government has to charge someone with a crime before putting the person in prison (p. 411)

Haiku (hī´ kü) A three-line poem with 17 syllables (p. 305)

Hajj (haj) The pilgrimage to Mecca that is a religious duty of all Muslims (p. 266)

Hari-kari (har´ ē-kar´ ē) To kill oneself with a knife (p. 307)

Heavy industry (hev´ ē in´ də strē) The manufacturing of products, such as machines and raw materials, for use in other industries (p. 623)

Hegira (hi jī´ rə) Muhammad's flight from danger in Mecca to safety in Medina (p. 264)

Hellenism (hel´ ə niz əm) The blend of western and eastern cultures made possible by Alexander the Great (p. 163)

Hellenistic Age (hel ə nis´ tik āj) The time between 323 B.C. and 31 B.C. when Greek culture influenced the world (p. 164)

Helot (hel´ ət) A slave in Sparta (p. 151)

Heresy (her´ ə sē) A teaching or a belief that a religious authority thinks is false (p. 376)

Heretic (her´ ə tik) A person who teaches a belief that a religious authority thinks is false (p. 349)

Heritage (her´ ə tij) The traditions ancestors have passed down to their descendants (p. 561)

Heroic (hi rō´ ik) Brave and bold (p. 144)

Hieroglyphics (hī ər ə glif´ iks) A kind of picture writing in Egypt (p. 126)

a	hat	e	let	ī	ice	ȯ	order	ů	put	sh	she	ə	{	a	in about
ā	age	ē	equal	o	hot	oi	oil	ü	rule	th	thin			e	in taken
ä	far	ėr	term	ō	open	ou	out	ch	child	ᴛʜ	then			i	in pencil
à	care	i	it	ȯ	saw	u	cup	ng	long	zh	measure			o	in lemon
														u	in circus

Hinduism (hin´ dü iz əm) The main religion of India that stresses the belief in the Vedas (p. 63)

Historian (hi stôr´ ē ən) One who is an expert of history (p. 34)

History (his´ tər ē) The record of past events and the story of what happened to people in the past (p. 34)

Holocaust (hol´ ə kȯst) Hitler's plan to kill all the Jews in Europe (p. 677)

Holy (hō´ lē) Following God's ways (p. 222)

Holy Land (hō´ lē land) Palestine; the area where Jesus of Nazareth lived (p. 243)

Homeland (hōm´ land) The land that belongs to a people; the country people call their home (p. 199)

Hostage (hos´ tij) Someone held against his or her will until certain demands are met (p. 735)

Household (hous´ hōld) All the people who live and work inside a house (p. 250)

Huguenot (hyü´ gə not) A French Calvinist (p. 359)

Human rights (hyü´ mən rīts) The right to life, liberty, and pursuit of happiness (p. 739)

Humanism (hyü´ mə niz əm) A belief that human actions, ideas, and works are important (p. 326)

Humanist (hyü´ mə nist) A person who believes in humanism (p. 326)

Humanity (hyü man´ ə tē) The human race (p. 34)

Hymn (him) A song of praise (p. 64)

Hypothesis (hī poth´ ə sis) An educated guess about an answer to a problem (p. 370)

I

Icon (ī´ kon) A small picture of a saint or Jesus (p. 224)

Identical (ī den´ tə kəl) Exactly alike (p. 488)

Idol (ī´ dl) A statue of a god that people worship (p. 265)

Ignorance (ig´ nər əns) The state of not knowing much (p. 455)

Ignorant (ig´ nər ənt) To have little knowledge or education (p. 326)

Ikebana (i kä bä´ nə) The Japanese art of arranging flowers (p. 309)

Immunity (i myü´ nə tē) A natural protection against a disease (p. 435)

Imperfection (im pər fek´ shən) Something that makes a thing or person not perfect (p. 207)

Imperialism (im pir´ ē ə liz əm) Control or influence a powerful nation has over a weaker country (p. 570)

Import (im pôrt´) To bring into a country something or someone from another place (p. 438)

Impurity (im pyür´ ə tē) Something that makes a material not pure (p. 488)

Independence (in di pen´ dəns) Being free; being able to govern one's self (p. 155)

Independent (in di pen´ dənt) Self-governing, separate, free (p. 147)

Indulgence (in dul´ jəns) A church paper that says that a person will not be punished after death for sinning during life (p. 351)

Industrial Revolution (in dus´ trē əl rev ə lü´ shən) The important changes that took place in the way work was done during the eighteenth and nineteenth century (p. 482)

Inferior (in fir´ ē ər) Not as good as someone or something else (p. 638)

Infidel (in´ fə dəl) One who does not believe in the religion another person believes (p. 273)

Inflation (in flā´ shən) A quick increase in prices (p. 637)

Influence (in´ flü əns) An effect; to affect someone or something (p. 108)

Influential (in flü en´ shəl) Having the power to change things or to affect what happens (p. 534)

Inherit (in her´ it) To receive money, land, or a title from someone who has died (p. 402)

Injure (in jər´) To hurt someone or to hurt oneself (p. 496)

Inoculate (in ok´ yə lāt) To put a small part of a disease in a person to keep the person from getting the disease; to give a person a shot (p. 294)

Insane (in sān´) To be ill in one's mind (p. 194)

Inspector (in spek´ tər) Someone who looks at how things are being done (p. 106)

Interdependent (in tər di pen´ dənt) Depending on one another (p. 769)

Internal combustion engine (in tėr´ nl kəm bus´ chən en´ jən) An engine that burns gasoline to produce power (p. 498)

International (in tər nash´ ə nəl) Among nations; around the world; involving different nations (p. 762)

International Monetary Fund (IMF) (in tər nash´ ə nəl mon´ ə ter ē fund) An organization that has a supply of money to give to needy members (p. 772)

Internet (in´ tər net) An international computer network (p. 762)

Interpret (in tėr´ prit) To explain something (p. 35)

Interpretation (in tėr prə tā´ shən) An explanation of the meaning of something (p. 35)

Invade (in vād´) To attack or march into another country (p. 67)

Invest (in vest´) To give money to a company with the hope of making more money (p. 739)

Invisible (in viz´ ə bəl) Unseen; cannot be seen (p. 678)

Iron Curtain (i´ ərn kȇrt´ n) The invisible boundary between Western Europe and Eastern Europe after World War II (p. 678)

Irrigate (ir´ ə gāt) To bring water to fields and crops (p. 61)

Isolate (ī´ sə lāt) To keep apart or away from others (p. 66)

Ivory (ī´ vər ē) The name for the tusks, or teeth, of animals like the elephant and the walrus (p. 69)

J

Jacobin (jak´ ə bən) A radical leader during the French Revolution (p. 518)

Jade (jād) A precious stone that is usually green (p. 69)

Jesuit (jesh´ ü it) A member of the Catholic religious order known as the Society of Jesus (p. 361)

Jihad (ji häd´) A struggle to follow God's will and to spread Islam (p. 268)

Joust (joust) A contest between two knights carrying lances and riding horses (p. 252)

Judaism (jü´ dē iz əm) The religion developed by the Hebrews that Jews practice today (p. 89)

Jury (jür´ ē) A group who listens to court cases and decides what is right (p. 150)

K

Kabuki (kä bü´ kē) A Japanese play with exaggerated actions (p. 309)

Kaiser (kī´ zər) The emperor of Germany (p. 569)

Kami (ka´ mi) Spirits of the Shinto religion (p. 303)

Kamikaze (kä mi kä´ zē) A Japanese pilot who crashed his plane into an enemy ship and destroyed it and himself (p. 665)

Knight (nīt) A soldier who fought for a lord (p. 246)

Knighted (nīt´ əd) To be made a knight (p. 248)

Koran (kô rän´) The holy book of Islam (p. 265)

Kremlin (krem´ lən) The center of the Russian church and the Russian government (p. 229)

Kristallnacht (krē´ stäl näkt) The period of terror toward the Jewish people in Germany in November, 1938, meaning "Night of Broken Glass" (p. 640)

L

Labor union (lā´ bər yü´ nyən) An organized group of workers who try to improve the working conditions in a factory and the amount of money they earn (p. 496)

Laborer (lā´ bər ər) A person who does hard work with his or her hands (p. 175)

Lance (lans) A steel-tipped spear (p. 248)

Laser (lā´ zər) A tool that produces high-energy beams of light (p. 767)

League of Nations (lēg ov nā´ shəns) A group of leaders from many nations who met to solve problems between countries (p. 602)

Legal (lē´ gəl) Lawful; based on the law of the government (p. 80)

Legalize (lē´ gə līz) To make lawful (p. 709)

Legislature (lej´ ə slā chər) The group of people in a government who make laws (p. 519)

Lend-Lease program (lend-lēs prō´ gram) A program developed by Franklin Roosevelt that allowed Britain to borrow war supplies from the United States during World War II (p. 659)

Liberal (lib´ ər əl) A person who wants change; a person who wants to limit the absolute power of kings and nobles and give power to the middle class (p. 544)

Liberty (lib´ ər tē) Freedom (p. 458)

Literature (lit´ ər ə chür) Written works that have lasting influence (p. 231)

Litter (lit´ ər) A stretcher for carrying people (p. 107)

Locomotive (lō´ kə mō´ tiv) A self-propelled vehicle that runs on rails (p. 490)

Logic (loj´ ik) The study of how to think (p. 160)

Logical (loj´ ə kəl) Clear, reasonable, step-by-step thinking (p. 373)

Loot (lüt) To rob or steal; the treasure that those who have won a war take away with them (p. 99)

Lord (lôrd) A king or a noble who gave land to someone else (p. 246)

Lottery (lot´ ər ē) A system of picking names from a container so that each person has an equal chance of being chosen (p. 149)

Loyal (loi´ əl) Faithful (p. 126)

Lutheran Church (lü´ thər ən chȇrch) The church established by Martin Luther (p. 353)

Lyre (līr) A small musical instrument with strings (p. 195)

a	hat	e	let	ī	ice	ô	order	ù	put	sh	she	ə	a	in about
ā	age	ē	equal	o	hot	oi	oil	ü	rule	th	thin		e	in taken
ä	far	ėr	term	ō	open	ou	out	ch	child	ᵺ	then		i	in pencil
â	care	i	it	ȯ	saw	u	cup	ng	long	zh	measure		o	in lemon
													u	in circus

Maginot line (mazh´ ə nō līn) A line of concrete forts built by France along its border with Germany (p. 658)

Magnify (mag´ nə fī) To make something appear larger than it is (p. 383)

Maize (māz) A corn-like plant (p. 277)

Majority (mə jôr´ ə tē) More than half of a group of people or group of things (p. 443)

Maneuver (mə nü´ vər) To move around (p. 155)

Manor (man´ ər) The part of a fief that peasants farm for the lord (p. 249)

Manufacturer (man yə fak´ chər ər) A person who hires people to work with machines to make something to sell (p. 486)

Market (mär´ kit) A place to sell goods (p. 570)

Marshall Plan (mär´ shəl plan) The American plan to rebuild Europe after World War II (p. 684)

Martial art (mär´ shəl ärt) A way of fighting and defending oneself (p. 306)

Mass communication (mas kə myü nə kā´ shən) Messages directed at many people (p. 761)

Mass production (mas prə duk´ shən) A way of making large amounts of the same thing in a factory (p. 488)

Massacre (mas´ ə kər) The act of killing many people who are often defenseless (p. 359)

Masterpiece (mas´ tər pēs´) A piece of art that seems almost perfect (p. 299)

Mayflower Compact (mā´ flou ər kom´ pakt) The agreement made by the Pilgrims that set up a form of government for their new colony (p. 443)

Melody (mel´ ə dē) A tune (p. 465)

Mentally ill (men´ tl ē il) Having a sickness of the mind (p. 677)

Merchant (mėr´ chənt) One who buys and sells; one who trades (p. 85)

Messiah (mə sī´ ə) A king sent by God who will save people from something (p. 199)

Method (meth´ əd) A way of doing something (p. 370)

Mighty (mī´ tē) Powerful (p. 177)

Migrant (mī´ grənt) A person who has left one place and moved to another (p. 732)

Migrate (mī´ grāt) To move from one place to another (p. 151)

Militarism (mil´ ə tə riz əm) A nation's warlike policy or practice (p. 566)

Military (mil´ ə ter ē) Having to do with the army or other people who fight wars (p. 80)

Military state (mil´ ə ter ē stāt) A place in which a ruler keeps power through the military (p. 417)

Militia (mə lish´ ə) A group of people who can be called to military service when something dangerous happens suddenly (p. 619)

Millet (mil´ it) A type of grain (p. 69)

Minister (min´ ə stər) A person who can lead a religious ceremony in a Protestant church (p. 353)

Minority (mə nôr´ ə tē) A small group of like people within a larger group (p. 620)

Minutemen (min´ it men) Colonial fighters in the Revolutionary War who were ready to fight at any time (p. 509)

Miracle (mir´ ə kəl) An amazing or wonderful event that no one can explain (p. 200)

Missionary (mish´ ə ner ē) A person who travels to another country or place to preach a religion (p. 304)

Moat (mōt) A dug-out area filled with water that circles a castle (p. 250)

Mob (mob) A large group of people (p. 514)

Moderate (mod´ ər it) One who has a slight opinion on an issue (p. 518)

Monarch (mon´ ərk) A king or a queen (p. 398)

Monastery (mon´ ə ster ē) A place where monks live and work together (p. 242)

Monk (mungk) A member of a religious order (p. 226)

Monsoon (mon sün´) Seasonal winds (p. 58)

Monument (mon´ yə mənt) An object or building that stands in place and is usually made of some kind of stone (p. 42)

Mood (müd) The feeling of something or someone (p. 299)

Morality (mə ral´ ə tē) A way of behaving toward others (p. 90)

Mosque (mosk) A Muslim place of worship (p. 270)

Mother country (muᴛʜ´ ər kun´ trē) A nation that controls a colony (p. 570)

Multilingual (mul ti ling´ gwəl) A society in which a number of languages are spoken (p. 560)

Multinational corporation (mul ti nash´ ə nəl kôr pə rā shən) A company that hires people and has business interests around the world (p. 760)

Multiracial (mul ti rā´ shəl) Having to do with people of different races (p. 710)

Mummify (mum´ ə fī) To wrap a dead body in strips of cloth so as to keep the body from decaying (p. 124)

Munich Pact (myü´ nik pakt) A 1938 agreement between Great Britain and Germany to appease Hitler (p. 656)

Muslim (muz´ ləm) A follower of the religion that Muhammad founded in Arabia in the seventh century (p. 243)

Nationalism (nash´ ə nə liz əm) Loyalty to one's country or nation (p. 398)

Nationality (nash ə nal´ ə tē) A group of people who share the same language, culture, and history (p. 537)

Native (nā´ tiv) Someone born in a particular place (p. 431)

Natural resources (nach´ ər əl ri sôrs´ əs) Things—such as coal, ore, and water—that come from nature and help humans (p. 482)

Navigate (nav´ ə gāt) To steer or sail a boat or ship (p. 87)

Navigation (nav ə gā´ shən) The science of planning and directing the route of a ship (p. 426)

Nazi (nä´ tsē) The Nationalist Socialist German Workers' Party led by Hitler (p. 637)

Negotiate (ni gō´ shē āt) To talk together, make bargains, and agree on something (p. 434)

Neutral (nü´ trəl) Not taking any side in a war or argument (p. 520)

Nirvana (nir vä´ nə) A condition of complete emptiness in which a person's soul finds perfect peace (p. 291)

Noble (nō´ bəl) A person of high birth (p. 69)

Noh drama (nō´ drä´ mə) A Japanese play with only two actors (p. 309)

Nomad (nō´ mad) A person who moves from place to place (p. 40)

North American Free Trade Agreement (NAFTA) (nôrth ə mer´ ə kən frē trād ə grē´ mənt (naf´ tə)) An agreement that links the economies of Canada, Mexico, and the United States (p. 752)

North Atlantic Treaty Organization (NATO) (nôrth at lan´ tik trē´ tē ôr gə nə zā´ shən (nā´ tō)) A group of 19 nations committed to protecting one another from attack and keeping world peace (p. 685)

Northern Hemisphere (nôr´ ᴛʜərn hem´ ə sfir) The northern half of Earth (p. 769)

Nuclear (nü´ klē ər) Having to do with atoms or energy from atoms (p. 666)

Nuclear weapon (nü´ klē ər wep´ ən) A powerful weapon, such as an atomic bomb or missile (p. 750)

Nun (nun) A woman who leaves her home and enters a convent (p. 242)

Obelisk (ob´ ə lisk) A tall, pointed stone pillar (p. 126)

Observe (əb zėrv´) To view; to see and look at (p. 104)

Obsidian (ob sid´ ē ən) A volcanic glass (p. 40)

Occupied country (ok´ yə pīd kun´ trē) A country that the Axis powers took over and stayed in (p. 663)

Offering (ó´ fər ing) A gift made to a god (p. 127)

Opera (op´ ər ə) A play in which people sing all the words (p. 301)

Oppose (ə pōz´) To be against something (p. 413)

Ordinance (ôrd´ n əns) A law set forth by someone in government (p. 546)

Ore (ôr) A rock that contains metals (p. 482)

Organization (ôr gə nə zā´ shən) A group of people joined together for a common purpose (p. 680)

Organize (ôr´ gə nīz) To set up; to get a series or number of things in order (p. 125)

Outnumber (out num´ bər) To have more soldiers, ships, or war machines than someone else has (p. 153)

Page (pāj) A young noble who learned certain behaviors to become a knight (p. 246)

Palestinian Liberation Organization (PLO) (pal ə stin´ ē ən lib´ ə rā shən ôr gə nə zā shən) The group of Palestinians dedicated to regaining from Israel their homeland in Palestine (p. 713)

Pan-African Movement (pan-af´ rə kən müv´ mənt) A group that planned ways in which Africans could achieve economic strength and political peace (p. 704)

Papyrus (pə pī´ rəs) A reed from the Nile River used to make paper (p. 129)

Parliament (pär´ lə mənt) The English council or lawmaking assembly (p. 256)

Pass (pas) An open place in a mountain (p. 58)

Passive resistance (pas´ iv ri zis´ təns) A nonviolent way of protesting for political and social change (p. 716)

Patio (pat´ ē ō) An inner room open to the sky (p. 60)

Patriarch (pā´ trē ärk) A leader of the church (p. 224)

Patrician (pə trish´ ən) In Rome, a person who owned land and helped a ruler govern (p. 172)

a	hat	e	let	ī	ice	ô	order	ù	put	sh	she		ə	a	in about
ā	age	ē	equal	o	hot	oi	oil	ü	rule	th	thin			e	in taken
ä	far	ėr	term	ō	open	ou	out	ch	child	ᴛʜ	then			i	in pencil
â	care	i	it	ò	saw	u	cup	ng	long	zh	measure			o	in lemon
														u	in circus

Patriotic (pā trē ot´ ik) Loyal toward one's country; love for one's country (p. 152)

Patron (pā´ trən) A person who supports an artist with money (p. 336)

Pax Romana (paks rō mä´ nə) The Roman peace that began during the reign of Augustus Caesar (p. 193)

Peasant (pez´ nt) A poor farmer or farmworker (p. 246)

Peninsula (pə nin´ sə lə) Land surrounded by water on three sides (p. 58)

Peninsular (pə nin´ sə lər) A person who came to South America from Spain and held an important office in the colonial government (p. 540)

Perestroika (per ə stoi´ kə) An economic policy used by Gorbachev to encourage factories to produce the goods people wanted (p. 743)

Permanent (pėr´ mə nənt) Lasting (p. 680)

Persecute (pėr´ sə kyüt) To be mean or unfair to someone because of that person's ideas or political beliefs (p. 711)

Pesticide (pes´ tə sīd) A substance that kills the bugs that eat the crops (p. 733)

Petition of Right (pə tish´ ən ov rīt) An English document that brought about more democracy (p. 407)

Pharaoh (fâr´ ō) A king, or ruler, of Egypt (p. 119)

Philosopher (fə los´ ə fər) A person who seeks answers to what is true and what is good (p. 159)

Photoelectric cell (fō tō i lek´ trik sel) An invention that can produce electricity from light (p. 765)

Physics (fiz´ iks) The study of matter (p. 160)

Pictogram (pik´ tə gram) A picture symbol, or figure; a type of early writing (p. 61)

Pilgrim (pil´ grəm) A person who travels to visit a holy place (p. 243); a person who came to North America for religious freedom and settled in Plymouth, Massachusetts (p. 443)

Pilgrimage (pil´ grə mij) The journey pilgrims take (p. 243)

Plague (plāg) A disease that spreads from person to person and kills many people (p. 197)

Plank (plangk) A long, wide, flat piece of wood (p. 177)

Plantation (plan tā´ shən) A large area of farmland (p. 437)

Plaster (plas´ tər) A mixture of sand, water, and lime that gives a smooth finish to a wall (p. 336)

Plateau (pla tō´) A flat area that rises above the land close by (p. 66)

Plebeian (pli bē´ ən) A common person in Rome who was not wealthy (p. 175)

Policy (pol´ ə sē) A plan that helps a person or a country make a decision (p. 566)

Polis (pō´ ləs) The Greek name for a city-state (p. 147)

Political (pə lit´ ə kəl) Having to do with governing (p. 176)

Politician (pol ə tish´ ən) A government leader; someone who runs for office (p. 182)

Politics (pol´ ə tiks) The study of government (p. 160)

Pollution (pə lü´ shən) The act of making the air, water, or land unclean and unhealthy (p. 765)

Pope (pōp) The head of the Roman Catholic Church (p. 232)

Population (pop yə lā´ shən) All the people of a town, or country, or of the world (p. 175)

Porcelain (pôr´ sə lin) A hard, shiny pottery made from a baked white clay (p. 300)

Portrait (pôr´ trāt) A drawing of a person (p. 336)

Powerful (pou´ ər fəl) Having great power (p. 121)

Practical (prak´ tə kəl) Useful; having to do with the use of the thing (p. 206)

Preach (prēch) To talk about the gods or how to live (p. 108)

Predict (pri dikt´) To tell the future (p. 104)

Predictable (pri dikt´ ə bəl) Tending to act in a certain orderly way (p. 454)

Prehistory (prē his´ tər ē) The time before humans left written records (p. 40)

Prejudice (prej´ ə dis) An unfair opinion; an opinion formed without collecting all the facts (p. 463)

Pressure (presh´ ər) A force produced by pressing on something (p. 492)

Priest (prēst) A religious leader (p. 81)

Primary source (prī´ mer ē sôrs) A first-hand account of a historical event (p. 34)

Prime minister (prīm min´ ə stər) The leader in some democratic government systems (p. 562)

Principle (prin´ sə pəl) A main idea (p. 223)

Prism (priz´ əm) A three-sided object that can be seen through (p. 378)

Privilege (priv´ ə lij) A special right given to a person or to a group of people (p. 460)

Profit (prof´ it) The amount of money left over after paying for the cost of doing business (p. 430)

Project (proj´ ekt) A plan of work; a series of jobs (p. 118)

Proletariat (prō lə târ´ ē ət) The working class according to Marx (p. 551)

Propaganda (prop ə gan´ də) One-sided information meant to change people's thinking (p. 683)

Prophet (prof´ it) A person who speaks for God (p. 199)

Protectorate (prə tek´ tər it) An independent country whose foreign policy is controlled by a major power (p. 576)

Protestant (prot´ ə stənt) A reformer who protested against the Catholic Church; a Christian who does not belong to the Roman Catholic Church (p. 354)

Province (prov´ əns) An area, such as a state, that is part of a larger country (p. 101)

Provisional (prə vish´ ə nəl) For a short time; not final (p. 617)

Public (pub´ lik) Having to do with government; having to do with the people (p. 149)

Pulley (pul´ ē) A wheel for a rope to pass over (p. 164)

Purgatory (pėr´ gə tôr ē) A place of suffering after death (p. 351)

Purge (pėrj) To remove from office; to clean by getting rid of unwanted things (p. 625)

Purify (pyür´ ə fī) To make clean and simple (p. 357)

Puritan (pyür´ ə tən) An English Protestant who wanted to purify the Anglican Church (p. 357)

Q

Quarter (kwör´ tər) To provide soldiers with a place to live and food (p. 506)

Quota (kwō´ tə) A fixed amount that is the goal to be reached (p. 623)

R

Radical (rad´ ə kəl) One who has a strong opinion on one side or another of an issue (p. 518)

Radiocarbon dating (rā dē ō kär´ bən dāt ing) A way of measuring the radioactivity of historic artifacts to determine how old they are (p. 38)

Raid (rād) To attack suddenly; a surprise attack (p. 144)

Ramp (ramp) A smooth stairway (p. 83)

Raw materials (rȯ mə tir´ ē əls) Materials that are used to make things (p. 492)

Reason (rē´ zn) To think in a logical way (p. 454)

Reasonable (rē´ zn ə bəl) To make sense; fair (p. 206)

Rebel (ri bel´) To disobey or fight against (p. 101)

Rebellion (ri bel´ yən) A fight by people against a government; a struggle for change (p. 324)

Recession (ri sesh´ ən) An economic slowdown (p. 770)

Reflect (ri flekt´) To bounce off an object or to show an image of something (p. 378)

Reform (ri fôrm´) To make something better through change (p. 180)

Reformation (ref ər mā´ shən) A mass movement that challenged and changed the Catholic religion in Europe (p. 350)

Reformer (ri fôr´ mər) A person who tries to change a system (p. 348)

Refugee (ref yə jē´) A person who is forced to flee from his or her country (p. 677)

Reich (rīk) The German word for empire (p. 569)

Reichstag (rīk´ stag) The national assembly of the Weimar Republic (p. 638)

Reign (rān) To rule; the period of time a king or queen rules (p. 85)

Reign of Terror (rān ov ter´ ər) The one-year period in French history when radical leaders put many people to death (p. 519)

Reincarnation (rē in kär nā´ shən) The rebirth of the soul into a new body (p. 64)

Reject (ri jekt´) To refuse to accept something or someone (p. 375)

Related (ri lāt´ tid) Connected in some way to another person, idea, or thing; born into the same family (p. 303)

Relative (rel´ ə tiv) A family member (p. 535)

Relay (rē´ lā) To pass along from one to another (p. 106)

Relic (rel´ ik) An object from the past that has something to do with God or with a holy person who follows God's ways (p. 222)

Religious (ri lij´ əs) Having to do with a belief in a higher being (p. 63)

Religious order (ri lij´ əs ôr´ dər) A group of monks who live and work together (p. 226)

Renaissance (ren´ ə säns) Rebirth; a period in European history that focused on being an individual and expanding on creative thoughts and ideas (p. 325)

Reparation (rep ə rā´ shən) Payment for war damages (p. 599)

Repeal (ri pēl´) To do away with a law (p. 507)

Representative (rep ri zen´ tə tiv) A person who speaks and governs for another (p. 174)

Republic (ri pub´ lik) A type of government with no king in which a few people represent, or speak for, the many (p. 174)

a	hat	e	let	ī	ice	ô	order	ù	put	sh	she		ə {	a	in about
ā	age	ē	equal	o	hot	oi	oil	ü	rule	th	thin			e	in taken
ä	far	ėr	term	ō	open	ou	out	ch	child	ŦH	then			i	in pencil
â	care	i	it	ȯ	saw	u	cup	ng	long	zh	measure			o	in lemon
														u	in circus

Resign (ri zīn´) To give up a job (p. 747)

Resolution (rez ə lü´ shən) A formal statement that a governmental body writes (p. 407)

Restoration (res tə rā´ shən) The period that saw monarchy return to England in 1660 (p. 410)

Restore (ri stôr´) To bring something back (p. 410)

Retire (ri tīr´) To give up one's job (p. 183)

Revolutionary War (rev ə lü´ shə ner ē wôr) The war the colonists fought with Great Britain (p. 511)

Revolve (ri volv´) To move around something (p. 372)

Riot (rī´ ət) A noisy and sometimes deadly uprising (p. 180)

Ritual (rich´ ü əl) A ceremony (p. 353)

Rival (rī´ vəl) One who tries to do better than another; to try to outdo another country or person (p. 592)

Romanesque (rō mə nesk´) A style of building that was like what the Romans built with thick walls and arches (p. 254)

Roman Inquisition (rō´ mən in kwə zish´ ən) A Catholic court that inquired into the beliefs of people to see if they were heretics (p. 361)

Roundhead (round´ hed) A Puritan who fought for Parliament in the English Civil War (p. 410)

S

Sacrifice (sak´ rə fīs) To offer a gift to a god by killing or burning something (p. 82)

Saint (sānt) A person who follows God's ways (p. 222)

Salon (sə lon´) A meeting of artists, writers, and thinkers in a Paris home during the Enlightenment (p. 461)

Salvation (sal vā´ shən) Eternal happiness for one's soul (p. 350)

Samurai (sam´ ü rī) A Japanese warrior who received land from a lord and fought for him (p. 306)

Sanitation (san ə tā´ shən) The act of making something free from disease, or healthy and clean (p. 208)

Satellite (sat´ l īt) A nation that another nation tightly controls (p. 678)

Scholar (skol´ ər) A well-educated person who has a great deal of knowledge about something (p. 42)

Scientific law (sī ən tif´ ik lò) A pattern in nature that someone can predict (p. 379)

Scientific method (sī ən tif´ ik meth´ əd) A set of steps to follow to reach a true end (p. 370)

Scribe (skrīb) In ancient times, a person who could read and write (p. 70)

Scroll (skrōl) A roll of papyrus (p. 129)

Sculptor (skulp´ tər) A person who carves statues (p. 330)

Sculpture (skulp´ chər) A carving from stone or other hard material (p. 103)

Secondary source (sek´ ən der ē sôrs) A second-hand account of a historical event; an account written by a person who was not there (p. 34)

Security (si kyùr´ ə tē) Safety (p. 680)

Self-discipline (self-dis´ ə plin) The power to control one's feelings and actions (p. 307)

Self-sufficient (self-sə fish´ ənt) Being able to take care of one's needs without help (p. 249)

Senate (sen´ it) A governing body (p. 172)

Senator (sen´ ə tər) A person who is the member of a senate (p. 180)

Serf (sèrf) A peasant who was bound to the land and whose life was controlled by the lord of the manor (p. 249)

Settlement (set´ l mənt) A colony; a group of people who had left one place and settled in another place (p. 444)

Sewer (sü´ ər) An underground pipe that carries away dirty water and human waste (p. 208)

Shah (shä) An Iranian ruler (p. 734)

Shinto (shin´ tō) The Japanese religion that involves a love of nature and worship of spirits (p. 303)

Shogun (shō´ gun) A Japanese word that means "great general;" a military dictator (p. 305)

Siege (sēj) The act of surrounding a city or fort with an army and cutting off its supplies to make the people on the inside surrender (p. 568)

Silt (silt) A rich layer of soil left behind after a flood (p. 60)

Sinful (sin´ fəl) Going against religious rules (p. 358)

Slave (slāv) A person who someone owns and is treated like property (p. 277)

Slavery (slā´ vər ē) The owning of human beings with the belief that they are property (p. 440)

Slum (slum) An area of a city with too many people, poor housing, and low-income families (p. 732)

Smelt (smelt) To quickly cool hot iron that has been hammered to remove any unwanted materials (p. 98)

Socialism (sō´ shə liz əm) An economic and political theory in which the government owns and controls the major means of production (p. 616)

Socialist (sō´ shə list) A person who wants to end the private ownership of land and factories (p. 548)

Society (sə sī´ ə tē) A group of people whose members live together for the good of all (p. 71)

Solidarity (sol ə dar´ ə tē) The name of the Polish shipbuilder's union that went out on strike in 1980 (p. 746)

Sonnet (son´ it) A 14-line poem about one idea (p. 333)

Soul (sōl) A person's spirit (p. 291)

Southern Hemisphere (suŦH´ ərn hem ə sfir) The southern half of Earth (p. 769)

Soviet (sō´ vē et) A Russian council (p. 618)

Sphere of influence (sfir ov in´ flü əns) An area in which only one foreign country can trade (p. 573)

Spice (spīs) A part of a plant that gives flavor when added to food (p. 244)

Spindle (spin´ dl) The part of a spinning wheel that twists fiber into yarn (p. 485)

Squire (skwīr) A young noble who learned how to ride a horse and use weapons so as to become a knight (p. 246)

Standard of living (stan´ dərd ov liv´ ing) A way to judge how well a person or a family is living (p. 613)

Starvation (stär vā´ shən) The act of dying from not having enough food to eat (p. 445)

Static electricity (stat´ ik i lek tris´ ə tē) The electricity that builds up in something and is produced when one object rubs up against another (p. 382)

Strait (strāt) A narrow strip of water that connects two bigger bodies of water (p. 431)

Strike (strīk) The act of refusing to work until certain demands are met (p. 746)

Structure (struk´ chər) Something, like a building, that has been built (p. 339)

Stupa (stü´ pə) A large building in which a holy monk is buried (p. 293)

Stylus (stī´ ləs) A sharp, pointed writing tool (p. 82)

Subcontinent (sub kon´ tə nənt) A large piece of land that is somewhat smaller than a continent (p. 58)

Submarine (sub´ mə rēn) A ship that travels beneath the surface of water (p. 337)

Subsistence farming (səb sis´ təns färm ing) A type of farming in which people grow crops mostly for their own use, not to sell (p. 769)

Successor (sək ses´ ər) One who follows another in a position (p. 622)

Superior (sə pir´ ē ər) Better than someone or something else (p. 638)

Superpower (sü´ pər pou ər) A nation that has more power and money than other countries (p. 678)

Surgery (sėr´ jər ē) The cutting open of a person's body to repair it (p. 294)

Surplus (sėr´ pləs) Extra of anything; more than a person needs (p. 269)

Survey (sər vā´) To measure land (p. 130)

Survive (sər vīv´) To continue to be; to stay alive (p. 205)

Swastika (swäs´ tə kə) The Nazi symbol of a cross with its arms bent (p. 637)

Symbol (sim´ bəl) Something that stands for something else (p. 70)

Symphony (sim´ fə nē) A long musical work played by a group of musicians using many different instruments (p. 466)

Synagogue (sin´ ə gòg) The building where Jews worship (p. 640)

System (sis´ təm) A way of doing something; a plan for doing something (p. 84)

T

Tablet (tab´ lit) A flat writing pad (p. 61)

Tactic (tak´ tik) A plan that helps someone win a game or a battle (p. 520)

Tanka (täng´ kə) A five-line poem with 31 syllables (p. 305)

Tariff (tar´ if) A tax that countries put on goods they import or export (p. 748)

Tax (taks) Money that people pay to support the government (p. 180)

Technology (tek nol´ ə jē) The use of science to do practical things (p. 760)

Temple (tem´ pəl) A place in which to honor gods (p. 81)

Term (tėrm) A period of time a person serves in a government office (p. 174)

Terraced (ter´ ist) Going upward like steps (p. 104)

Territory (ter´ ə tôr ē) A large area of land (p. 180)

Terrorist (ter´ ər ist) A person who uses violence to frighten people and to get them to obey (p. 713)

Textile (tek´ stīl) Cloth that workers weave from cotton, silk, or wool (p. 485)

Theater (trē´ ə tər) A place where people present plays (p. 147)

Theory (thir´ ē) A statement that explains why or how something happens (p. 372)

Thesis (thē´ sis) A statement or an idea that people argue about or try to prove (p. 352)

Title (tī´ tl) A name that shows what a person does (p. 229)

a	hat	e	let	ī	ice	ò	order	ù	put	sh	she		ə	{	a	in about
ā	age	ē	equal	o	hot	oi	oil	ü	rule	th	thin				e	in taken
ä	far	ėr	term	ō	open	ou	out	ch	child	ŦH	then				i	in pencil
â	care	i	it	ò	saw	u	cup	ng	long	zh	measure				o	in lemon
															u	in circus

Tolerant (tol´ ər ənt) To respect the beliefs of others (p. 410)

Tomb (tüm) A place to bury a dead body (p. 119)

Tory (tôr´ ē) A person who supported a strong monarchy in England (p. 411)

Total war (tō´ tl wôr) A war in which a country uses all its resources to win (p. 603)

Totalitarian state (tō tal ə ter´ ē ən stāt) A government in which a small group totally controls the lives of its country's citizens (p. 624)

Tournament (tèr´ nə mənt) In the Middle Ages, a contest between knights on horseback (p. 252)

Tradition (trə dish´ ən) A custom, idea, or belief handed down from one person to the next (p. 398)

Tragedy (traj´ ə dē) A type of Greek play in which the hero has too much pride and is defeated in the end (p. 158)

Translate (tran slāt´) To change the words of one language into those of another (p. 84)

Transport (tran spôrt´) To move from one place to another (p. 60)

Transportation (tran spər tā´ shən) The movement of people, natural resources, and finished products from one place to another (p. 490)

Treason (trē´ zn) The act of turning against the laws and people of your own land; helping the enemy (p. 407)

Treasury (trezh´ ər ē) The money collected by the government and used to pay for things (p. 196)

Treaty of Versailles (trē´ tē ov ver sī´) The treaty that ended World War I (p. 600)

Trench (trench) A long narrow ditch (p. 595)

Trial (trī´ əl) A court case in which a jury examines evidence and decides if an accused person has done wrong (p. 256)

Tribune (trib´ yün) A person who protected the rights of the common people (p. 175)

Tribute (trib´ yüt) Taxes paid to a stronger ruler or nation (p. 99)

Triumvirate (trī um´ vər it) Rule by three people (p. 182)

Troops (trüps) An organized group of soldiers (p. 525)

Truce (trüs) An agreement to stop a war for a time (p. 688)

Truman Doctrine (trü´ mən dok´ trən) President Truman's plan to stop the spread of communism (p. 683)

Trust territory (trust ter´ ə tôr ē) A territory that the Allies took from the countries that lost World War I and World War II (p. 681)

Tutor (tü´ tər) A teacher who teaches one person at a time (p. 327)

Tyrant (tī rənt´) A leader who rules by force and not by law (p. 148)

U

U-boat (yü´-bōt) A German submarine (p. 595)

Unify (yü´ nə fī) To connect; to bring together as one (p. 106)

Unique (yü nēk´) The only one of its kind (p. 293)

Unite (yü nīt´) To bring together as one (p. 118)

United Nations (UN) (yü nī´ tid nā´ shəns) The international organization that works to settle disagreements, improve the way people live, and keep peace around the world (p. 680)

Universe (yü´ nə vèrs) All the planets and stars that exist in space (p. 372)

University (yü nə vèr´ sə tē) A school where students study many subjects of higher learning (p. 253)

Unrestricted warfare (un ri strik´ tid wôr´ fâr) War that is not restricted to a certain area or boundary (p. 597)

Urbanization (èr bə nə zā´ shən) Becoming more like a city (p. 732)

Utopian (yü tō´ pē ən) A type of society in which everyone works peacefully together for the good of all (p. 550)

V

Value (val´ yü) A belief or an idea that people think is important (p. 460)

Vassal (vas´ əl) A person who received land from a king or noble and gave loyalty in return (p. 246)

Vatican (vat´ ə kən) The home of the pope (p. 338)

Vaulted (vȯl´ təd) A ceiling that is high, arched, and covers a large space (p. 207)

Veche (ve´ shē) The Russian assembly that represented all free, adult male citizens (p. 228)

V-E Day (vē´-ē´ dā) The day the allies completed their victory in Europe: May 8, 1945; stands for "Victory in Europe Day" (p. 665)

Veteran (vet´ ər ən) A person who has served in the military, especially during a war (p. 634)

Veto (vē´ tō) To say no to a ruling or law (p. 174)

Viceroy (vīs´ roi) An official who governs land for the king or queen (p. 437)

Vietnamization (vē et nə miz ā´ shən) The U.S. plan to turn the fighting of the Vietnam War over to the South Vietnamese army (p. 723)

Violate (vī′ ə lāt) To break a law, rule, or promise (p. 506)

Violence (vī′ ə ləns) Great physical force; actions that hurt others (p. 544)

Virtue (vėr′ chü) Goodness to one another (p. 458)

Vision (vizh′ ən) A visit from God or from one of God's angels (p. 264)

V-J Day (vē′-jā′ dā) The day the Allies completed their victory in Japan: September 2, 1945; stands for "Victory in Japan Day" (p. 668)

Volunteer (vol ən tir′) To offer to do a job without pay; a person who offers to do a job without pay (p. 538)

Vote (vōt) To choose leaders and pass laws (p. 149)

Vow (vou) To promise something; a promise (p. 350)

W

Warsaw Pact (wôr′ sȯ pakt) A treaty that set up a military alliance between the Soviet Union and its satellite nations (p. 685)

Wealth (welth) A large amount of money, property, or costly things (p. 513)

Wealthy (wel′ thē) Rich, having wealth (p. 125)

Weimar Republic (vī′ mər ri pub′ lik) The post-World War I democratic government in Germany (p. 637)

Western Hemisphere (wes′ tərn hem′ ə sfir) The western half of Earth (p. 751)

Whig (wig) A person who supported the English Parliament (p. 411)

Woodwind (wud′ wind) An instrument a musician plays by blowing into it (p. 467)

World affair (wėrld ə fâr′) An event, or happening, that takes place in the world and affects many countries (p. 604)

World Bank (wėrld bangk) An international group that directs money from the industrialized nations to the developing countries (p. 772)

Worldly (wėrld lē) To have nothing to do with religion (p. 331)

World Wide Web (wėrld wīd web) A network of information on the Internet open to businesses and individuals (p. 762)

Worship (wėr′ ship) To honor and praise a god (p. 81)

Z

Ziggurat (zig′ u̇ rat) A building like a pyramid with a base and four sides and a top smaller than the bottom (p. 81)

Zodiac (zō′ dē ak) The 12 constellations named by the Chaldean priests (p. 104)

a	hat	e	let	ī	ice	ȯ	order	u̇	put	sh	she	ə	a in about
ā	age	ē	equal	o	hot	oi	oil	ü	rule	th	thin		e in taken
ä	far	ėr	term	ō	open	ou	out	ch	child	ᴛʜ	then		i in pencil
â	care	i	it	ȯ	saw	u	cup	ng	long	zh	measure		o in lemon
													u in circus

Index

Bubonic Plague, 325
Buddha, 288, 290-91, 313
Buddhism, 288, 291-93, 304, 310, 313, 317
Buffer zone, 683
Bulgaria, 226, 594, 678
Burma, 291, 573, 581, 741
Bushido, 307, 313
Buttress, 254
Byron, 538
Byzantine Empire, 204, 210-11, 220, 222-27, 229, 236-37, 268, 317

C

Caesar, Julius, 170, 182-84, 187, 203, 215. *See also* Augustus
Cairo, 118-19
Calendars, 37-38, 47, 51, 127, 183, 203, 264, 277-78, 285
Caligula, 190, 194, 211
Calvinism, 346, 358-60, 365, 391
Calvin, John, 346, 358-60, 363, 365, 391
Cambodia, 722
Campesinos, 751
Canaan, 87, 89-90, 93, 102, 137
Canada, 233, 424, 444, 752, 769, 777
Canals, 490, 501, 585, 751
Canton, 430
Canute, 220, 233
Capital, 100, 482-84, 585
Capitalism, 484
Caracalla, 210
Cardinals, 413
Caribbean Islands, 441, 449
Carter, Howard, 131
Carter, Jimmy, 734
Carthage, 87, 93, 177-79, 187, 215
Cartoons, political, 696
Castes, 64-65, 75, 291, 293, 313, 717, 727
Castiglione, Baldassare, 341
Castile, 401
Castlereagh, 534
Castles, 250-52, 259
Catherine of Aragon, 355, 365
Catherine the Great, 396, 416-17, 421, 461
Catholics, 357, 359-60, 362, 365, 391, 401-2, 404, 409-11, 421, 433, 438
Cavaliers, 409-10, 421
Cavendish, Margaret, 384

Cavour, Camillo di, 562-63, 581, 585
Celsius, Anders, 383
Censorship, 624
Central America, 262, 277, 285, 317, 433, 441, 539
Central Powers, 591, 594, 596, 598, 603, 607
Cervantes, Miguel de, 322, 334, 343, 391
Ceylon, 536, 573, 581
Chaldean Empire, 96, 105
Chaldeans, 96, 101-2, 104, 106, 110-111, 137
Chamberlain, Neville, 656, 671
Champlain, Samuel de, 424, 444, 449
Champollion, Jean François, 122
Channa, 290
Charlemagne, Charles the Great, 220-21, 232, 255, 237, 317
Charles I of England and Scotland, 406-10, 421
Charles I of Spain, 396, 402, 421, 431
Charles II of England and Scotland, 410-11, 421
Charles V, 354-55, 396, 402-3, 421, 434, 438, 447
Charles VII, 415
Charles X, 545-46, 555
Chaucer, Geoffrey, 333
Chess, 251
Chiang Kai-shek, 632, 641-42, 647, 719-20, 727
Child labor, 495-96, 777
Chile, 532, 541, 555
China, 56-57, 66-72, 74-75, 268-69, 288-89, 291, 297-304, 311, 313, 425-28, 430, 449, 560, 573-75, 581, 641-43, 647, 662, 676, 680, 690, 693, 719-21, 739-40
Christianity, 37, 45-46, 108, 111, 190, 199, 201-3, 211, 222-26, 236-37, 240-45, 254-55, 259, 265, 269, 285, 309, 313, 339, 348-50, 401, 463, 571, 580, 617, 715, 738
Churches, 253-55
Churchill, Winston, 658-60, 669, 678, 680, 693
City-states, 80, 84-87, 93, 96, 137, 143, 148, 151-55, 167, 172, 180, 187, 215, 329, 343, 391, 426
Civilizations, 44, 47, 51, 56-61, 75, 78-80, 93, 114-15, 133, 137, 142, 144, 215
Civil service, 295
Civil wars, 121, 196, 225, 232, 237, 275, 298, 408-9, 421, 434-35, 441, 547, 610, 621, 629, 632, 641-42, 647, 702, 719, 727
Classical music, 466-67, 471, 528
Claudius, 195, 197, 211
Clemenceau, George, 599
Clement V, 348
Clement VII, 355

H

Henry VIII, 346, 355-56, 365, 391

Henry the Navigator, 426, 449

Heretic, 349

Herodotus, 156

Hidalgo, Miguel, 541-43, 555, 585

Hideki Tojo, 643

Hieroglyphics, 122, 126, 277-78

Hinduism, 63-65, 73, 75, 137, 290-91, 293-94, 313, 717-18, 738, 755

Hindu Kush, 58

Hiroshima, 667-68, 671

Hispaniola, 539

Hippodrome, 222

Historians, 34, 37, 39, 47, 51, 243, 264, 325, 348, 468, 603

Histories or Tales of Times Passed With Morals, 380

History, 34-37, 47, 51, 468, 560, 778

History in Your Life, 38, 68, 82, 123, 158, 182, 203, 230, 254, 273, 300, 325, 351, 380, 405, 430, 455, 495, 521, 538, 577, 626, 638, 654, 690, 720, 752, 770

Hitler, Adolf, 632, 635, 637-40, 644-47, 650, 652-60, 663-64, 666, 671, 677, 693

Hittites, 92, 98

Hobbes, Thomas, 398, 452, 457-60, 471

Ho Chi Minh, 722-23, 727

Holland, 240, 250, 400, 522

Holocaust, 677, 693

Holy Land, 240-41, 243-44, 259, 272

Holy Roman Empire, 353, 355, 365, 402-3, 421, 464, 522

Homeland, 199

Homer, 142, 144-45, 167

Honduras, 277

Hong Kong, 740

Horseshoes, 250, 259

Huguenots, 346, 359-60, 365

Humanism, 326

Human origins, 46

Human rights, 452, 458, 470, 739

Hundred Years' War, 342

Hungary, 566, 581, 602, 617, 629, 677-78, 746, 750

Hunger, 733, 759

Huns, 190, 204, 211, 294

Hussein, Saddam, 737, 755

Huss, John, 346, 349-50, 365, 391

Huygens, Christian, 383, 386

Hyksos, 114, 124, 133, 137

I

Iceland, 233, 237

Ignatius of Loyola, 361, 365

Igor, 228

Ikebana, 309

Ikhnaton, 114, 127, 133

Illiad, 142, 144, 167, 215

Immunity, 448

Imperialism, 558-59, 570-78, 581, 585, 590, 592, 607, 652-53, 720

Imports, 438

Incas, 262, 279-81, 285, 317, 424, 434-37, 449

Independence, 155

Independence Day, 512

India, 37, 56-64, 73, 75, 106, 111, 268-70, 288-96, 301, 313, 325, 425-31, 445, 449, 572-73, 581, 660, 716-18, 726, 738, 755, 765

Indian National Congress, 716, 726-27

Indian Ocean, 427, 431

Indochina, 573, 662, 722

Indonesia, 644, 722, 741, 770

Indus River Valley, 56, 58, 60-63, 69, 75, 106, 137, 162

Industrialization, 484, 494-96, 501, 549, 610, 613, 623, 629

Industrialized nations, 484, 501, 570, 574, 592, 625, 772, 775, 777, 779

Industrial Revolution, 480-501, 570, 581, 585, 628, 762

Inflation, 637

Inquiry Into the Nature of the Wealth of Nations, An, 484

Institutes of the Christian Religion, 346, 358, 363

International Court of Justice, 681, 693

International Labor Organization (ILO) , 681

International Monetary Fund (IMF), 772

International Space Station, 763, 779

Internet, 758, 762, 779

Iran, 85, 734-36, 755

Iraq, 712, 735-37, 755

Ireland, 749

Iron, 92, 98, 111, 133, 247, 249, 273, 480, 488, 493, 501, 644

Iron Curtain, 678, 754

Iron ore, 482-83, 501

Irrigation, 116, 118

Isabella of Castile, 401-2, 421

Isabella of Spain, 428, 449

Iscariot, Judas, 200

Islam, 262, 264-66, 268-69, 274, 285, 317, 401
Island hopping, 665
Israel, 45, 89-90, 93, 702, 711-15, 727, 734-36, 755
Istanbul, 220, 225, 237
Italy, 170-87, 190-211, 222-23, 231, 237, 326-31,
    336, 340, 343, 355, 362, 402-3, 421, 426, 522,
    525, 535-36, 547, 551, 562-64, 571, 577, 581,
    592, 594, 599-600, 602, 607, 634-36, 643-44,
    647, 651-52, 655, 657, 664, 671, 678, 693, 749
Ivan the Great, 220, 229-30, 237, 317
Ivan the Terrible, 220, 229, 237
Ivory, 426

J

Jabir, 270
Jacobins, 517, 529, 585
James I of England and Scotland, 406, 420-21,
    443
James II of England and Scotland, 411, 421
Jamestown, 424, 443, 445, 449
Japan, 288, 291, 303-10, 313, 400, 428, 430, 570-
    71, 573-75, 581, 594, 600, 603, 614, 641-44,
    647, 651-53, 655, 657, 661-67, 676, 678, 687-88,
    693, 719, 722, 739-40, 755, 769, 770
Jefferson, Thomas, 459, 510, 529
Jenne, 276
Jenner, Edward, 448
Jerome Bonaparte, 522
Jerusalem, 96, 102, 110, 245, 715
Jesuits, 361-62, 391, 433
Jesus, 37, 45, 47, 190, 199-202, 211, 215, 224, 241,
    243, 265, 336, 339, 353, 715
Jets, 690
Jewelry, 69, 71, 281
Jews, 38, 45, 89, 102, 110-111, 199-201, 211, 215,
    222, 236, 244, 259, 265, 269, 285, 421, 632, 639-
    40, 645, 647, 677, 692-93, 711, 714-15, 727,
    735, 738, 755. *See also* Hebrews
Jihad, 268
Jimmu, 303
Joan of Arc, 415
John, 258
John II of Portugal, 427
Johnson, Lyndon, 763
Jordan, 712, 734
Joseph Bonaparte, 522
Judah, 90, 93
Judaism, 89, 108, 111, 137, 265

Judges, 255-56
Julius II, 338, 340
Jupiter, 375, 387
Jury, 150, 255-56, 259, 612
Justinian, 206, 210-11, 220, 222-25, 237, 317
Jutes, 233, 237

K

Kaaba, 265
Kabuki, 309, 313
Kaiser, 569
Kami, 303
Kamikazes, 665, 671
Kant, Immanuel, 469
Kao-tsu, 298
Kay, John, 485, 501
Keita, Sundiata, 273
Kenya, 576, 707
Kenyatta, Jomo, 707
Kepler, Johannes, 373-74, 379, 391
Khomeini, Ayatollah, 735
Khrushchev, Nikita, 730, 742, 755
Kiev, 220, 227-28, 236-37, 317
Knights, 246-48, 252, 259, 308, 313, 317
Knossos, 144
Koran, 265-66, 274, 285, 317
Korea, 291, 297, 303-4, 313, 575, 581, 687-90, 698
Korean War, 674, 687-90, 693
Kosovo, 730, 748, 755
Kremlin, 229-30, 237, 744, 754-55
Kristallnacht, 632, 639-40, 645, 647
Kublai Khan, 288, 301, 311, 313
Kumbi, 273
Kush, 273
Kuwait, 730, 736-37, 755

L

Labor Party, 682
Labor unions, 497
L'Angely, 420
Language, 41, 45, 61, 65, 70, 75, 84, 179, 226, 254-
    55, 271, 285, 293, 333, 343, 560, 767
Las Casas, Bartolomé de, 438-39, 447
Last Supper, 336, 343
Latin, 172, 179, 187, 215, 223, 254-55, 259, 333,
    370

McAdam, John, 490

Mecca, 262, 264-66, 274, 285

Medes, 101

Medici, Lorenzo de, 322, 330-32, 338, 343, 391

Medici, Piero, 331-32

Medicine, 208, 269, 281, 285, 317, 325, 448, 766, 779

Medina, 264, 285

Mediterranean Sea, 84, 87, 90, 92-93, 116, 133, 144, 162, 167, 172, 178, 180, 187, 191-92, 329, 343, 426, 536, 576, 652

Meiji, 558, 574

Mein Kampf, 638, 646

Meir, Golda, 682

Memphis, 118, 133

Menes, 118, 133, 137

Mennonites, 356

Meroë, 273

Mesmer, Franz, 455

Mesopotamia, 78-80, 82, 85-87, 89, 93, 96, 98-99, 101, 111, 119, 137, 269, 294

Methodius, 226

Metternich, 532, 534-35, 537, 551, 555, 585

Mexico, 277, 279, 285, 433-34, 437, 448, 512, 532, 539, 542-43, 622, 751-52, 774

Michelangelo, 322, 338-40, 343, 391, 564

Microscope, 368

Middle Ages, 220-37, 240-59, 283, 288, 302, 317, 324, 326, 343, 348, 370, 420

Middle East, 78-93, 96-97, 100, 102, 110, 163, 244, 259, 285, 297, 301, 445, 560, 682, 711-15, 727, 734-38, 769, 771

Middle Kingdom, 114, 123-24, 133, 137

Midway, 650, 671

Milan, 329, 343

Militarism, 566, 571, 590, 592, 607, 652-53, 678, 693

Military state, 417

Militia, 619

Milosevic, Slobodan, 747-48

Ming emperors, 302

Minoan civilization, 144, 167

Minutemen, 509, 529

Miracle cures, 455

Mississippi River, 424, 437, 444, 449

Moderate, 517

Mohenjo-Daro, 60, 75

Moghul Empire, 288, 295-96, 313, 317, 572

Moldavia, 743

Molière, 467, 471

Mona Lisa, 322, 336, 343

Monarchy, 398-400, 406, 410-13, 457-58, 462-63, 471, 525, 544-45, 555, 604, 707

Money, 770

Mongol dynasty, 220, 230, 237, 288, 294, 301-2, 313, 317

Monroe, James, 751

Monsoons, 58-59, 61, 75

Montesquieu, Baron de, 452, 458-59, 471

Montezuma, 433-35

Moon, 762, 764, 779

Moors, 401-2, 421

Morelos, José, 543, 555

More, Thomas, 550

Morocco, 276, 706

Morse, Samuel F. B., 480, 496-97, 501

Moscow, 228-30, 237, 317, 523, 613, 617

Moses, 45, 89, 93, 137

Mosques, 270, 312

Mother country, 570

Mozart, Wolfgang Amadeus, 452, 466-67, 471

Muhammad, 243, 262, 264-66, 268, 285, 317, 401, 715

Multinational corporations, 760, 771-72, 779

Mummify, 124

Munich Pact, 650, 656, 671

Murasaki Shikibu, 307

Musa, Mansa, 274-75, 285

Muses, 158

Music, 465-67, 471, 521, 528, 761

Muslims, 38, 236, 240-41, 243-45, 259, 264-70, 273-74, 276, 283, 285, 294-96, 300, 704, 715, 717, 735, 737, 748, 755

Mussolini, Benito, 632, 634-35, 644, 647, 652, 664, 671

Mycenae, 144-46, 167, 215

Myths, 46, 82, 166

N

Nagasaki, 309, 668, 671

Napier, John, 382-83, 387

Naples, 331, 522

Napoleon Bonaparte I, 122, 504, 519-27, 529, 534-36, 539-40, 545, 555, 562, 585, 644

Napoleon Bonaparte III, Louis, 550, 555, 568, 585

Napoleonic Wars, 562, 565

National Assembly, 514, 516

National Constitutional Convention, 516-18, 529, 585

Nationalism, 396, 398, 421, 526, 532, 536-39, 544, 547, 551, 555, 558, 560-67, 571, 578, 581, 590, 592, 607, 632, 635, 641, 647, 652-53, 702, 719, 721, 727

Nationalist Socialist German Workers' Party. *See* Nazis

National League for Democracy, 741

Native Americans, 424, 433-35, 437-38, 443-45, 447-49, 507, 542

Natives, 431, 578

Natural resources, 482, 501, 578, 585

Navigation Acts, 506, 529

Nazareth, 199, 243, 336

Nazis, 637-40, 645-47, 663, 671, 674, 677, 692-93, 711, 727

Nebuchadnezzar, 96, 102-5, 110-111, 137

Nefertiti, 127

Neo-Babylonia, 102

Nero, 195, 202, 211

Netherlands, 362, 402-3, 421, 443, 511, 546, 677, 722, 749

Neutral, 522

Newcastle Circle, 384

Newfoundland, 233, 669

New Kingdom, 114, 125-26, 133

New Spain, 437, 449

Newton, Issac, 368, 373, 378-80, 383, 386-87, 391, 452, 454-55, 471

Nibelungenlied, 255

Nicaragua, 37, 751

Nicholas II, 610, 614-15, 617, 621, 629

Nicholas of Russia, 551

Niepce, Joseph, 547

Nigeria, 576, 707

Nile River, 106, 114-16, 119, 122-23, 133, 137, 162, 269, 273

Nineveh, 96, 100-2, 111, 137

Nkrumah, Kwame, 706-7

Nobles, 69, 246, 250-52, 256-59, 305-6, 313, 324-25, 364, 398, 413-20, 460, 513, 516-18, 529, 544-45, 555, 565, 585, 612, 614-15

Noble Truths, 291, 313

Noh drama, 309, 313

Nok, 273

Nomads, 40, 44, 47, 51, 67, 89, 93, 124, 264, 294, 401

Normandy, 670

Normans, 179, 220, 234

North Africa, 178, 181, 192, 223, 268, 272-73, 276, 283, 285, 421, 660, 704, 706, 727

North America, 233, 237, 357, 362, 417, 437, 441, 443-46, 449, 506, 570

North American Free Trade Agreement (NAFTA), 752

North Atlantic Treaty Organization (NATO), 674-75, 685, 693, 748-49, 755

North German Confederation, 569

North Korea, 687-90

North Star, 87, 93, 432

North Vietnam, 702, 722-23, 727

Norway, 232, 362, 536

Notre Dame, 255, 521

Novum Organum, 385

Nuclear energy, 765, 779

Nuclear power plants, 765

Nuclear weapons, 750

Nyerere, Julius, 725

O

Obelisk, 126

Occupied country, 663, 671

Oceania, 284

Octavian, 183-84, 187, 190, 215. *See also* Caesar, Augustus

Odoacer, 190, 205, 211, 215

Odyssey, 142, 144, 167, 215

Oil, 497-98, 501, 736-37, 755, 765, 771, 775, 779

Old Kingdom, 114, 118-19, 121, 123-24, 133, 137

Olga, the Grand Princess, 228, 236

Olmecs, 262, 277, 281, 285, 317

Olympic Games, 161

Omar Khayyám, 270

Opera, 467

Operation Overload, 670

Organization of African Unity, 725

Orlando, Vittorio, 600

Orléans, 415

Ottoman Empire, 225, 537, 555, 594, 606

P

Pacific Ocean, 431, 449

Pages, 246, 259

Pakistan, 702, 717, 727

Palestine, 90, 199, 201, 211, 241, 243-45, 259, 317, 560, 702, 711-14, 727, 734

Palestinian Liberation Organization (PLO), 713
Pan-African Movement, 704, 727
Panama, 751
Pantheon, 207
Paper, 114, 129, 133, 301
Paraguay, 751
Paris, 231, 237, 329, 359, 414, 461, 471, 514-17, 525, 546, 548, 568, 595, 658, 664
Parliament, 256, 259, 356, 400, 406-12, 421, 458, 499, 506-9, 544, 549, 555, 563, 743
Parthenon, 157-58
Partricians, 170, 172, 174-76, 180, 187, 215
Passive resistance, 716
Pathfinder, 764
Patriarch, 224
Patriotic, 152
Patron, 336
Paul III, 361
Pax Romana, 190, 193, 211, 215
Peace of Augsburg, 354
Pearl Harbor, 650, 661, 671
Peasants, 246, 249, 259, 317, 322, 324, 364
Peasants' War, 364
Peloponnesian peninsula, 155
Peloponnesian War, 153, 155, 160, 165, 167, 215
Peloponnesus, 151, 167
Peninsula, 58, 215
Pepper, 430
Perestroika, 730, 743, 754-55
Pericles, 165
Perrault, Charles, 380
Persia, 96, 101, 105-9, 111, 128, 133, 142, 153-55, 162, 167, 222-23, 268, 294, 297
Persian Gulf War, 730, 736-37, 755
Peru, 424, 434, 532, 541, 555, 751
Peter the Great, 396, 416, 421
Petition of Right, 407-8, 412, 421
Petrarch, 333
Pharaohs, 119-21, 123-26, 127, 130-33, 137
Phidias, 158
Philip II of Macedon, Greece, 155, 167, 215
Philip II of Spain, 357, 403-4, 421
Philip III of Spain, 399
Philip IV, 348
Philippine Islands, 431, 644, 662, 722, 741
Philistia, 90
Phoenicia, 78, 87-88, 90, 92-93, 102, 137, 177
Photography, 547
Pictograms, 61, 70, 75

Pietà, 338
Pilate, Pontius, 200
Pilgrimage, 243, 259, 274, 285
Pilgrims, 243, 245, 259, 266, 424, 443-44, 449
Pius VII, 521
Pizarro, Francisco, 424, 434-35, 437, 449
Plague, 197, 225, 324, 343, 378
Plantation, 437
Plato, 159-60, 167, 215, 330, 340
Plays, 158-59, 167, 301, 309, 313, 333-34, 343, 391
Plebeians, 170, 175-76, 180-81, 187, 215
Plow, 250, 259
Plymouth, 424, 443, 449
Poetry, 270, 297, 305, 313, 627
Poison gas, 596, 607
Poland, 226, 536, 560, 597, 602, 604, 657, 677-78, 746-47, 750, 754-55
Policy, 566
Polis, 147, 167
Political, 176
Politician, 182
Politics, 161
Pollution, 765, 773-75, 779
Polo, Marco, 311, 351
Pompeii, 198
Pompey the Great, 182-83, 187
Pope, 232, 237
Population, 175, 763, 775
Porcelain, 297, 300-1, 313, 317
Portugal, 424, 426-27, 429-30, 440, 443, 449, 535, 539, 543, 555, 577, 581, 704, 749
Portuguese, 405, 430, 440, 449
Pottery, 32, 41, 47, 51, 61, 75, 83, 172, 281
Prejudice, 463
Prehistory, 40, 44, 47, 51
Presbyterian Church, 360
Primary source, 34-35, 47, 51
Prime minister, 400, 562
Princip, Gavrilo, 606
Printing, 288, 297, 301, 317, 334-35, 343, 391
Proletariat, 551
Propaganda, 683, 686, 693
Protectorate, 576
Protestantism, 346-47, 354, 356-62, 365, 391, 403-4, 407, 411, 421
Protests, 548, 709, 714, 718, 726-27, 739
Province, 101
Prussia, 416-17, 421, 463, 471, 517, 525, 529, 534, 551, 555, 565-69, 581

Veterans, 634
Veto, 174-76, 187
Viceroy, 437
Victor Emmanuel II of Sardinia, 563-64, 581
Vienna, 532, 534
Vietnam, 722-23
Vietnam War, 702, 723, 727
Vikings, 220, 232-33, 236-37, 317
Vinci, Leonardo da, 322, 336-37, 340, 343, 370, 391
Virginia, 424, 443, 449
Visigoths, 204-5, 211, 215
V-J Day, 668
Vladimir, 227-28, 236
Voltaire, 452, 462-63, 471
Voting, 149, 174-75, 180, 497, 501, 514, 517, 521, 544-46, 710, 717, 782

W

Warsaw Pact, 674, 685, 693
Washington, George, 510-11
Waterloo, 504, 525-26, 529, 585
Waterwheel, 250, 259
Watt, James, 480, 491, 501
Weapons, 32, 40, 47, 51, 98, 111, 124, 133, 247-49, 298, 592, 596, 607, 677, 682
Weimar Republic, 637-38, 647
Wellington, 504, 525, 534
West Africa, 272, 275-76, 317
West Bank, 713-14
Western Hemisphere, 751
Western Europe, 226-27, 231-32, 237, 242, 250, 256, 259, 324, 347, 416, 678, 683
West Germany, 678, 684, 693, 730, 747, 755
Wheatstone, Charles, 496
Whigs, 411
Whitney, Eli, 480, 487, 501
William, Duke of Normandy, 234, 237, 317
William of England and Scotland, 411, 421
William I, 569, 581
William I, the Conqueror, 247, 272
William II, 592, 607, 637, 647, 676
William III of Prussia, 534
Wilson, Woodrow, 599, 636
Windmill, 240, 250, 259
Wollstonecraft, Mary, 470
Women, 210, 302, 470, 679
World Bank, 772
World Health Organization (WHO), 681
World War I, 400, 561, 590-607, 610, 612, 617, 620, 629, 634, 636, 698
World War II, 303, 602, 632, 644, 647, 650-71, 693, 698, 704, 711, 719, 727
World Wide Web, 762, 779
Wright, Wilbur and Orville, 498, 501
Writing About History, 44, 71, 85, 105, 127, 152, 175, 192, 232, 250, 280, 305, 326, 353, 377, 417, 434, 463, 494, 525, 536, 560, 596, 622, 635, 652, 681, 722, 750, 774
Wycliffe, John, 348-49, 365, 391

X

Xerxes, 154-55, 167

Y

Yalu River, 688
Yangtze River, 66-67, 75, 298, 313
Yathrib, 264
Yellow River Valley, 56, 66-69, 72, 75, 137, 298
Yellow Sea, 67
Yeltsin, Boris, 744-45, 754-55
Yuan dynasty, 301, 313
Yugoslavia, 226, 602, 660, 678, 747-48, 755

Z

Zaire, 707
Zama, 179, 187
Zanzibar, 725
Zhou, 71
Ziggurats, 81-82, 84, 93, 104
Zimbabwe, 707
Zionist Party, 682
Zoroaster, 96, 108, 111, 137

Acknowledgments

Acknowledgment is made for permission to reprint and record the following copyrighted material. In the case of any omissions, the publisher will be pleased to make suitable acknowledgments in future editions.

Page 73: From *The Bhagavad Gita* translated by Juan Mascaro (Penguin Classics, 1962) copyright © Juan Mascaro, 1962. Reproduced by permission of Penguin Books Ltd.

Page 91: From *Babylonian and Assyrian Laws, Contracts and Letters,* edited by C. H. W. Johns (New York: Charles Scribner's Sons, 1904), Simon and Schuster.

Page 109: From *Persia, The Immortal Kingdom* by Ghirshman, Roman, Vladimir Minorsky (NY: Little, Brown and Company).

Page 131: From *The Tomb of Tut-ankh-amen* by Howard Carter and A. C. Mace (New York: Dover Publications, Inc.).

Page 165: "Pericles' Funeral Oration" from *The Peloponnesian War* by Thucydides, translated by Rex Warner (Penguin Classics, 1954) copyright © Rex Warner, 1954. Reproduced by permission of Penguin Books Ltd.

Page 185: From *A History of Rome* by Moses Hadas. Copyright © 1956 by Moses Hadas. Used by permission of Doubleday, a division of Random House, Inc.

Page 209: Source: Lucius Annaeus Seneca, *Moral Essays,* translated by John W. Basore, Harvard University Press.

Page 257: From "A Crusader's Letter" from *Readings in European History, Volume 1,* edited by James Harvey Robinson (NY: Silver Burdett Ginn, 1904).

Page 283: From *Ibn Battuta in Black Africa* by Said Hamdun and Noel King, pp. 46–48, © 1975 Markus Wiener Publishers, Princeton, NJ. Reprinted with the permission of Markus Wiener Publishers.

Page 311: From *The Travels of Marco Polo* by Manuel Komroff. Copyright 1926 by Boni & Liveright, Inc., renewed 1953 by Manuel Komroff. Copyright 1930 by Horace Ligheright, Inc., renewed © 1958 by Manuel Komroff. Reprinted by permission of Liveright Publishing Corporation.

Page 363: Reproduced from *Calvin: Institutes of the Christian Religion* (Library of Christian Classics) edited by John T. McNeil. Used by permission of Westminster John Knox Press.

Page 469: From *The Philosophy of Kant.* Translated, edited with introduction by Carl J. Friedrich. Copyright © 1949 by Random House, Inc. Reprinted by permission of Random House, Inc.

Page 499: From *Readings in European History* by Bernard, © 1958. Reprinted by permission of Prentice-Hall, Inc., Upper Saddle River, NJ.

Page 605: By Wilfred Owen, from *The Collected Poems of Wilfred Owen.* Copyright © 1963 by Chatto & Windus, Ltd. Reprinted by permission of New Directions Publishing Corp.

Page 777: Excerpt from Chapter 16 "What Is Childhood?" from *Free the Children* (www.freethechildren.org) by Craig Kielburger and with Kevin Major. Copyright © 1998 by Craig Kielburger. Reprinted by permission of HarperCollins Publishers, Inc.

Images

Cover, back to front: Scala/Art Resource, NY; The Granger Collection, Ltd.; Private Collection/Bridgeman Art Library, London/Superstock; The Granger Collection, Ltd.; Erich Lessing/Art Resource, NY; Lascaux Caves, France/Superstock; Ray Manley/SuperStock; Corbis; Africa Online; background, Judy King

Unit 1
Page 30, Lascaux Caves, France/SuperStock

Chapter 1
Page 37, Woodfin Camp & Associates, Inc.; p. 38, Kenneth Garrett /NGS Image Collection; p. 39, Corbis; p. 42, Historic Buildings and Monuments Commission for England; p. 45, The Granger Collection, Ltd.; p. 46, Archaeological Museum, Athens, Greece/Spiros Tselentis/SuperStock

Unit 2
Page 54, Ray Manley/SuperStock

Chapter 2
Page 61, Kim Winship; p. 63, SuperStock; p. 66, James Stanfield/NGS Image Collection; p. 70, Giraudon/Art Resource, NY; p. 71, The Granger Collection, Ltd.; p. 73, Victoria & Albert Museum, London/Art Resource, NY; p. 74, Woodfin Camp & Associates, Inc.

Chapter 3
Page 81 (illustration), Gary King; p. 81 (photo), Dean Conger/NGS Image Collection; p. 82, Jennifer Koski; p. 84, Marcel Lewinski; p. 89, The Granger Collection, Ltd.; p. 91, Smithsonian Institute; p. 92, The Granger Collection, Ltd.

Chapter 4
Page 100, Library of Congress; p. 101, The Granger Collection, Ltd.; p. 102, Marcel Lewinski; p. 108, The Granger Collection, Ltd.; p. 109, The Granger Collection, Ltd.; p. 110, Marcel Lewinski

Chapter 5
Page 116, Kenneth Garrett/NGS Image Collection; p. 119, Woodfin Camp & Associates, Inc.; p. 120, Steve Vidler/SuperStock; p. 122, The Trustees of the British Museum; p. 125, SuperStock; p. 126, Marcel Lewinski; p. 129, Musee du Louvre, Paris/Bridgeman Art Library, London/SuperStock; p. 130, Egyptian Museum, Cairo, Egypt/Giraudon, Paris/SuperStock; p. 131, Egyptian National Museum, Cairo, Egypt/Kurt Scholz/ SuperStock; p. 132, The Granger Collection, Ltd.

Unit 3
Page 140, Scala/Art Resource, NY

Chapter 6
Page 145, Woodfin Camp & Associates, Inc.; p. 147, Greek National Tourist Organization; p. 149, Acropolis Museum, Athens, Greece/Spiros Tselentis/SuperStock; p. 151, Smithsonian Institute; p. 155, Vanni/Art Resource, NY; p. 156, Acala/Art Resource, NY; p. 157, Library of Congress; p. 159, SuperStock; p. 160, The Granger Collection, Ltd.; p. 162, p. 165, Library of Congress; p. 166, Scala/Art Resource, NY

Chapter 7
Page 174, Corbis; p. 177, SuperStock; p. 180, Library of Congress; p. 183, Scala/Art Resource, NY; p. 184, The Granger Collection, Ltd.; p. 186, Library of Congress

Chapter 8
Page 192, Library of Congress; p. 193, Richard Nowitz/NGS Image Collection; p. 194, The Granger Collection, Ltd.; p. 196, p. 200, Library of Congress; p. 201, p. 204, The Granger Collection, Ltd.; p. 206, Woodfin Camp & Associates, Inc.; p. 209, Roman Villa In Nennig/A.K.G., Berlin/SuperStock; p. 210, The Granger Collection, Ltd.

Unit 4
Page 281, The Granger Collection, Ltd.

Chapter 9
Page 223, Church of San Vitale, Ravenna, Italy/ET Archive, London/SuperStock; p. 226, Corbis; p. 228, Judy King; p. 230, Art Resource, NY; p. 231, p. 235, Corbis; p. 236, Scala/Art Resource, NY

Chapter 10
Page 242, Marcel Lewinski; p. 244, The Granger Collection, Ltd.; p. 245, Galleria Degli Uffizi, Florence, Italy/ET Archive, London/SuperStock; p. 247, Library of Congress; p. 249, p. 251, Bettman Archive, Inc.; p. 253, Corbis; p. 255, Ray Manley/SuperStock; p. 257, p. 258, The Granger Collection, Ltd.

Chapter 11
Page 264, Murat Ayranci/SuperStock; p. 265, Jack Novak/ SuperStock; p. 270, p. 274, The Granger Collection, Ltd.; p. 278, SuperStock; p. 279, The Granger Collection, Ltd.; p. 283, James Stanfield/NGS Image Collection; p. 284, SuperStock

Chapter 12
Page 290, The Granger Collection, Ltd.; p. 293, Hubertus Kanus/SuperStock; p. 298, The Granger Collection, Ltd.; p. 299, The Nelson-Atkins Museum of Art, Kansas City, Missouri (Purchase: Nelson Trust); p. 301, The Granger Collection, Ltd.; p. 303, Victoria & Albert Museum, London/ Art Resource, NY; p. 307, The Granger Collection, Ltd.; p. 309, SuperStock; p. 311, SuperStock; p. 312, SuperStock

Unit 5
Page 320, Private Collection/Bridgeman Art Library, London/SuperStock

Chapter 13
Page 324, The Granger Collection, Ltd.; p. 327, Erich Lessing/Art Resource, NY; p. 328, The Granger Collection, Ltd.; p. 329, Scala/Art Resource, NY; p. 330, The Granger Collection, Ltd.; p. 334, Culver Pictures, Inc./SuperStock; p. 335, Erich Lessing/Art Resource, NY; p. 336, Biblioteca Reale, Turin, Italy/SuperStock; p. 337, Corbis; p. 338, Library of Congress; p. 339, The Granger Collection, Ltd.; p. 340, Corbis; p. 341, p. 342, The Granger Collection, Ltd.

Chapter 14
Page 348, The Granger Collection, Ltd.; p. 350, Corbis; p. 355, p. 359, p. 362, The Granger Collection, Ltd.; p. 364, SuperStock

Chapter 15
Page 370, Bakken Library; p. 372, p. 373, Corbis; p. 374, Library of Congress; p. 376, Private Collection/ET Archive, London/SuperStock; p. 379, The Granger Collection, Ltd.; p. 381, Library of Congress; p. 383, The Granger Collection, Ltd.; p. 384, Judy King; p. 385, National Portrait Gallery, London, England /SuperStock; p. 386, The Granger Collection, Ltd.

Unit 6
Page 394, The Granger Collection, Ltd.

Chapter 16
Page 399, Musee des Beaus-Arts, Rouen/SuperStock; p. 402, p. 404, p. 406, p. 409, The Granger Collection, Ltd.; p. 410, Musee Historique, Versailles Palace/Explorer, Paris/SuperStock; p. 413, The Granger Collection, Ltd.; p. 414, Palace of Versailles, France/SuperStock; p. 415, p. 416, p. 419, The Granger Collection, Ltd.; p. 420, Christie's Images/SuperStock

Chapter 17
Page 426, Corbis; p. 428, The Granger Collection, Ltd.; p. 433, Michael Zabe/Art Resource, NY; p. 435, p. 438, p. 441, p. 443, The Granger Collection, Ltd.; p. 444, SuperStock; p. 445, A. K. G., Berlin/SuperStock; p. 447, The Granger Collection, Ltd.; p. 448, Newberry Library/SuperStock

Chapter 18
Page 454, p. 457, p. 458, The Granger Collection, Ltd.; p. 459, Library of Congress; p. 461, The Granger Collection, Ltd.; p. 462, Giraudon/Art Resource, NY; p. 464, Christie's Images/SuperStock; p. 465, p. 466, p. 467, p. 469, The Granger Collection, Ltd.; p. 470, Tate Gallery, London/Art Resource, NY

Unit 7
Page 478, Erich Lessing/Art Resource, NY

Chapter 19
Page 484, p. 485, The Granger Collection, Ltd.; p. 486, Corbis; p. 489, Library of Congress; p. 492, p. 494, The Granger Collection, Ltd.; p. 497 (top), Culver Pictures, Inc./SuperStock; p. 497 (bottom), SuperStock; p. 498, Culver Pictures, Inc./SuperStock; p. 499, The Granger Collection, Ltd.; p. 500, National Portrait Gallery, London/SuperStock

Chapter 20
Page 507, Corbis; p. 508, p. 509, p. 510, The Granger Collection, Ltd.; p. 514, Explorer, Paris/SuperStock; p. 517, The Granger Collection, Ltd.; p. 518, SuperStock; p. 520, Corbis; p. 523, Erich Lessing/Art Resource, NY; p. 527, The Granger Collection, Ltd.; p. 528, Erich Lessing/Art Resource, NY

Chapter 21
Page 534, Library of Congress; p. 539, The Granger Collection, Ltd.; p. 540, Corbis; p. 541, The Granger Collection, Ltd.; p. 545, Library of Congress; p. 546, Giraudon/Art Resource, NY; p. 548, The Granger Collection, Ltd.; p. 549, p. 551, Library of Congress; p. 553, p. 554, The Granger Collection, Ltd.

Chapter 22
Page 561, p. 563, The Granger Collection, Ltd.; p. 566, Erich Lessing/Art Resource, NY; p. 567, p. 570, p. 572, The Granger Collection, Ltd.; p. 575, Library of Congress; p. 576, The Granger Collection, Ltd.; p. 579, A. K. G., Berlin/SuperStock; p. 580, The Granger Collection, Ltd.

Unit 8
Page 588, Corbis

Chapter 23
Page 592, p. 593, The Granger Collection, Ltd.; p. 594, p. 595, Corbis; p. 596, The Granger Collection, Ltd.; p. 599, Library of Congress; p. 600, Woodfin, Camp & Associates, Inc.; p. 603, Corbis; p. 605, Library of Congress; p. 606, A. K. G., Berlin/SuperStock

Chapter 24
Page 612, The Granger Collection, Ltd.; p. 613, Library of Congress; p. 614, The Granger Collection, Ltd.; p. 615, p. 616, p. 619, Corbis; p. 620, p. 621, Library of Congress; p. 623, The Granger Collection, Ltd.; p. 625, p. 627, Corbis

Chapter 25
Page 634, Library of Congress; p. 637, p. 639, Corbis; p. 640, AP/World Wide; p. 641, Library of Congress; p. 643, p. 645, The Granger Collection, Ltd.; p. 646, Library of Congress

Chapter 26
Page 653, p. 656, Corbis; p. 660, The Granger Collection, Ltd.; p. 662, Library of Congress; p. 663, p. 664, Corbis; p. 665, Library of Congress; p. 667, Woodfin Camp & Associates, Inc.; p. 669, p. 670, The Granger Collection, Ltd.

Chapter 27
Page 677, Corbis; p. 680, Library of Congress; p. 682, Black Star; p. 685, p. 687, p. 688, p. 691, p. 692, Corbis; p. 696, Rube Goldberg™ and © of Rube Goldberg Inc., Distributed by United Media

Unit 9
Page 700, Africa Online

Chapter 28
Page 706, Corbis; p. 707, p. 708, Woodfin Camp & Associates, Inc.; p. 712, A. K. G. Berlin/SuperStock; p. 717, The Granger Collection, Ltd.; p. 719, p. 723, Woodfin Camp & Associates, Inc.; p. 725, The Granger Collection, Ltd.; p. 726, Library of Congress

Chapter 29
Page 732, Woodfin Camp & Associates, Inc.; p. 735, Corbis; p. 736, Woodfin Camp & Associates, Inc.; p. 740, AP Photo; p. 741, p. 742, Corbis; p. 743, Woodfin Camp & Associates, Inc.; p. 744, Corbis; p. 747, Woodfin Camp & Associates, Inc.; p. 748, Corbis; p. 751, Mia & Klaus Matthes/SuperStock; p. 753, AP Photo; p. 754, Corbis

Chapter 30
Page 760, George Hunter/SuperStock; p. 766, Woodfin Camp & Associates, Inc.; p. 767, Tony Linck/SuperStock; p. 768, Woodfin Camp & Associates, Inc.; p. 770, Black Star; p. 773, Super/Stock; p. 775, Woodfin Camp & Associates, Inc.; p. 777, Free the Children; p. 778, Corbis